555 Verben
ENGLISCH

Alle Formen, alle Zeiten – komplett konjugiert

von
Dr. Christiane Wirth

PONS GmbH
Stuttgart

PONS

555 Verben ENGLISCH

Alle Formen, alle Zeiten - komplett konjugiert

von
Dr. Christiane Wirth

Der Grammatikteil basiert auf ISBN 978-3-12-562832-8.

1. Auflag 2018

www.pons.de
E-Mail: info@pons.de

Redaktion: Torsten Lasse
Logoentwurf: Erwin Poell, Heidelberg
Logoüberarbeitung: Sabine Redlin, Ludwigsburg
Einbandgestaltung: Ilham Widmann, Stuttgart
Satz: Satzkasten, Stuttgart
Druck und Bindung: Publikum d.o.o, Serbien

ISBN: 978-3-12-562143-5

Inhalt

Zu diesem Buch

Dieses Buch enthält **alle wichtigen englischen Verben** auf dem Niveau A1 - B1 des Europäischen Referenzrahmens, ob regelmäßig oder unregelmäßig.

Zu jedem Verb gibt es **eine komplette Seite** mit allen Zeiten und Formen.

Bei jedem Verb finden Sie mehrere **Zusatzinformationen,** die Ihnen die Besonderheiten der Verben und ihrer Konjugation näher bringen, wie z. B. orthographische Anpassungen.

Ergänzend dazu steht Ihnen eine **Kurzgrammatik** zur Verfügung, mit der Sie sich das nötige Grundwissen zum Thema ‚Verben' sowie einen Überblick über die Bildung und den Gebrauch der Zeitformen verschaffen können.

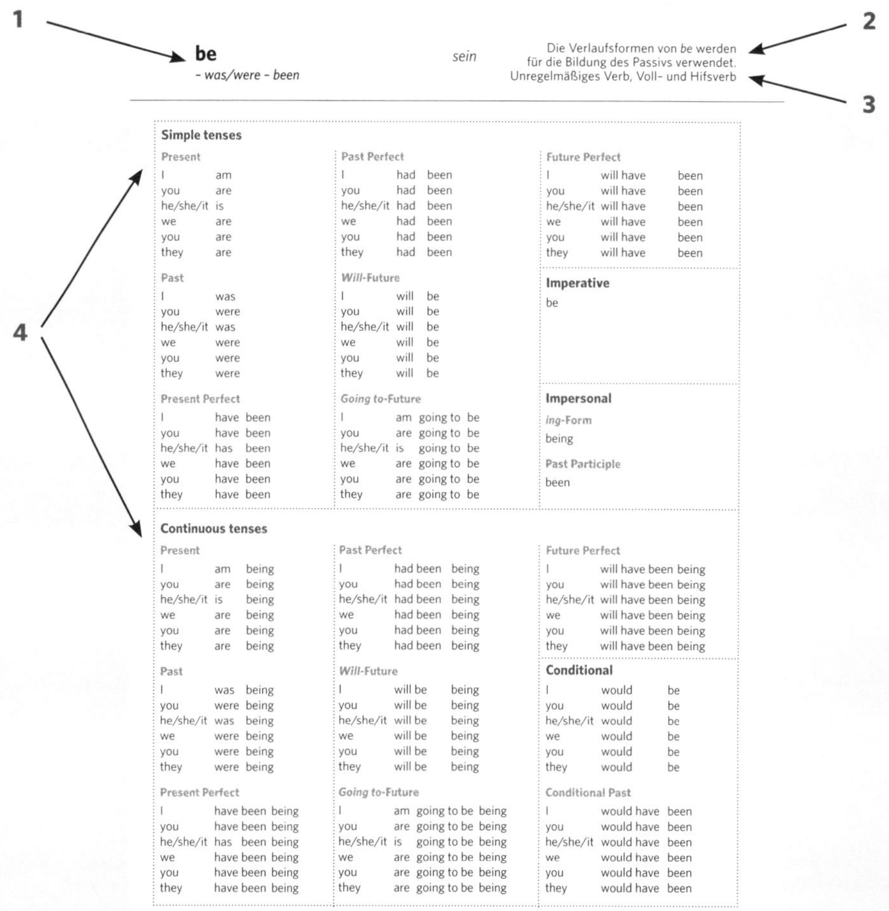

be - *was/were* - *been*   *sein*

Die Verlaufsformen von *be* werden für die Bildung des Passivs verwendet.
Unregelmäßiges Verb, Voll- und Hifsverb

Simple tenses

Present		Past Perfect			Future Perfect		
I	am	I	had	been	I	will have	been
you	are	you	had	been	you	will have	been
he/she/it	is	he/she/it	had	been	he/she/it	will have	been
we	are	we	had	been	we	will have	been
you	are	you	had	been	you	will have	been
they	are	they	had	been	they	will have	been

Past		*Will*-Future		
I	was	I	will	be
you	were	you	will	be
he/she/it	was	he/she/it	will	be
we	were	we	will	be
you	were	you	will	be
they	were	they	will	be

Imperative

be

Present Perfect			*Going to*-Future			
I	have	been	I	am	going to	be
you	have	been	you	are	going to	be
he/she/it	has	been	he/she/it	is	going to	be
we	have	been	we	are	going to	be
you	have	been	you	are	going to	be
they	have	been	they	are	going to	be

Impersonal

ing-Form

being

Past Participle

been

Continuous tenses

Present			Past Perfect			Future Perfect	
I	am	being	I	had been	being	I	will have been being
you	are	being	you	had been	being	you	will have been being
he/she/it	is	being	he/she/it	had been	being	he/she/it	will have been being
we	are	being	we	had been	being	we	will have been being
you	are	being	you	had been	being	you	will have been being
they	are	being	they	had been	being	they	will have been being

Past			*Will*-Future			Conditional		
I	was	being	I	will be	being	I	would	be
you	were	being	you	will be	being	you	would	be
he/she/it	was	being	he/she/it	will be	being	he/she/it	would	be
we	were	being	we	will be	being	we	would	be
you	were	being	you	will be	being	you	would	be
they	were	being	they	will be	being	they	would	be

Present Perfect			*Going to*-Future			Conditional Past		
I	have been	being	I	am	going to be being	I	would have	been
you	have been	being	you	are	going to be being	you	would have	been
he/she/it	has been	being	he/she/it	is	going to be being	he/she/it	would have	been
we	have been	being	we	are	going to be being	we	would have	been
you	have been	being	you	are	going to be being	you	would have	been
they	have been	being	they	are	going to be being	they	would have	been

44

1. **Verb mit Grundformen und Übersetzung.** Bei unregelmäßigen Verben finden Sie hier die drei folgenden Grundformen: Infinitiv, Past Simple und Past Participle. Die Verben sind in diesem Buch alphabetisch von A bis Z sortiert.

2. **Kurzcharakteristik:** Hinweise zu den Besonderheiten und Unregelmäßigkeiten in der Konjugation.

3. **Verbart:** Hier erfahren Sie, ob es sich um ein regelmäßiges oder unregelmäßiges Verb handelt.

4. **Verbformen:** Für jedes Verb werden alle Konjugationsformen für alle wichtigen Zeiten angegeben.

Grammatikbegriffe in der Übersicht

Englisch	Lateinischer Ursprung	Deutsch
active	Aktiv	Tätigkeitsform
antonym	Antonym	Gegenwort
auxiliary	Hilfsverb	Hilfszeitwort
conditional present	Konditional I	Bedingungsform I
conditional past	Konditional II	Bedingungsform II
conjugation	Konjugation	Beugung des Zeitworts
continuous form	progressive Form	Verlaufsform
consonant	Konsonant	Mitlaut
future	Futur I	unvollendete Zukunft
future 2 (future perfect)	Futur II	vollendete Zukunft
gerund	Gerundium	Gerundium
imperative	Imperativ	Befehlsform
infinitive	Infinitiv	Grundform des Zeitworts
intransitive verb	intransitives Verb	Zeitwort ohne direktes Objekt
irregular verb	unregelmäßiges Verb	unregelmäßiges Zeitwort
modal verb	Modalverb	Modalverb
object	Objekt	Ergänzung
participle	Partizip	Mittelwort
passive	Passiv	Leideform
past	Präteritum	Vergangenheit
past participle	Partizip Perfekt	Mittelwort der Vergangenheit
past perfect	Plusquamperfekt	Vorvergangenheit
plural	Plural	Mehrzahl
present	Präsens	Gegenwart
present perfect	Perfekt	vollendete Gegenwart
pronoun	Pronomen	Fürwort
reflexive verb	reflexives Verb	rückbezügliches Zeitwort
regular verb	regelmäßiges Verb	regelmäßiges Zeitwort
simple form	–	einfache Form
singular	Singular	Einzahl
subject	Subjekt	Satzgegenstand
synonym	Synonym	sinnverwandtes Wort
transitive verb	transitives Verb	Zeitwort mit direktem Objekt
verb	Verb	Zeitwort
vowel	Vokal	Selbstlaut

AE = amerikanisches Englisch
BE = britisches Englisch

Grammatik

I. Verbkategorien

Die Veränderung des Verbs wird Konjugation genannt. Im Folgenden sehen Sie eine Übersicht der Kategorien, nach denen sich Verben in der Konjugation verändern.

1. Person und Numerus *(person and number)*

Genauso wie im Deutschen gibt es im Englischen drei Personen, die im **Singular** (Einzahl) und im **Plural** (Mehrzahl) verwendet werden.

	Singular	Plural
1. Person	I	we
2. Person	you	you
3. Person	he, she, it	they

2. Tempus und Aspekt *(tense and aspect)*

Das **Tempus** drückt aus, wann etwas passiert. Zunächst einmal unterscheidet man dabei drei Zeitstufen: die Vergangenheit *(past)*, die Gegenwart *(present)* und die Zukunft *(future)*. Darüber hinaus versteht man unter **Aspekt** die Art und Weise, in der die Zeit vom Sprecher erfahren wird. Im Englischen unterscheidet man drei Aspekte: Verbformen können einfach *(simple)*, in ihrem Verlauf *(continuous)*[1] und als vollendet *(perfect)* erfahren werden.

Aus den beiden Kategorien **Tempus** und **Aspekt** ergeben sich im Englischen die folgenden zwölf Zeitformen:

Gegenwart	**Present Simple**	He **plays** football.
	Present Continuous	He **is playing** football.
	Present Perfect	He **has played** football.
	Present Perfect Continuous	He **has been playing** football.
Vergangenheit	**Past Simple**	He **played** football.
	Past Continuous	He **was playing** football.
	Past Perfect	He **had played** football.
	Past Perfect Continuous	He **had been playing** football.
Zukunft	**Future I**	He **will play** football.
	Future I Continuous	He **will be playing** football.
	Future II	He **will have played** football.
	Future II Continuous	He **will have been playing** football.

[1] In vielen Grammatikbüchern findet man anstatt *continuous* auch die Bezeichnung *progressive*.

Darüber hinaus gibt es noch zwei Zeitformen, die zur Bildung von irrealen **Konditionalsätzen** (Bedingungssätzen) gebraucht werden:

Gegenwart	**Conditional II**	He **would play** football.
Vergangenheit	**Conditional Past**	He **would have played** football.

Mehr zur Bildung und zum Gebrauch dieser Zeitformen erfahren Sie unter **III. Tempus** ab Seite 12.

3. Modus *(mood)*

Unter **Modus** versteht man die Art und Weise, in der der Sprecher die durch ein Verb ausgedrückte Handlung auffasst. Im Englischen gibt es drei Modi: den **Indikativ** *(indicative)*, den **Konjunktiv** *(subjunctive)* und den **Imperativ** *(imperative)*.

Indikativ	He **plays** football.
Konjunktiv	If he **played** football, he would be happier.
Imperativ	**Play** football!

Mehr zu den Modi im Englischen finden Sie unter **IV. Modus** auf Seite 20.

4. Aktiv und Passiv *(active and passive voice)*

Viele Verben können sowohl aktiv als auch passiv gebraucht werden. Im **Aktiv** steht die handelnde Person im Vordergrund, während im **Passiv** die Handlung selbst hervorgehoben wird.

Aktiv	He **plays** football.
Passiv	Football **is played** with two teams.

Mehr zur Bildung des **Passivs** im Englischen lesen Sie auf Seite 21.

II. Verbarten

Im Englischen gibt es eine Reihe von unterschiedlichen Verbarten. Die wichtigsten lernen Sie im Folgenden kennen.

1. Vollverben, Hilfsverben und Modalverben

a) Vollverben *(full verbs)*

Die meisten Verben gehören zu den **Vollverben**. Das bedeutet:
- Sie können in Aussagesätzen allein (ohne ein Hilfsverb) stehen.
- Sie können im Passiv stehen.
- Sie können in der **ing**-Form stehen.

Aussagesatz	He **plays** football.
Passiv	Football **is played** with two teams.
ing-Form	He **is playing** football.

b) Hilfsverben *(auxiliary verbs)*

Verben, die man in Verbindung mit Vollverben benutzt, um zusammengesetzte Zeitformen oder bestimmte Satztypen zu bilden, nennt man **Hilfsverben**. Im Englischen unterscheidet man drei Hilfsverben: **be**, **do** und **have**.

be

Das Hilfsverb **be** benötigt man zur Bildung von **Continuous**-Formen und beim **Passiv**:

Present Continuous	He **is** playing football.
Present Perfect Continuous	He **has been** playing football.
Past Continuous	He **was playing** football.

Past Perfect Continuous	He **had been** playing football.
Future I Continuous	He **will be** playing football.
Future II Continuous	He **will have been** playing football.

Passiv	Football **is** played with two teams.

Verneinte Aussagesätze und Fragen, in denen **be** als Hilfsverb auftritt, benötigen nicht zusätzlich das Hilfsverb **do**. Man kann die konjugierte Form von **be** direkt verneinen und auch eine Frage direkt mit der konjugierten Form von **be** beginnen:

Verneinung	He **isn't** playing football.
Frage	**Is** he playing football?

Achtung! Häufig verwendet man auch **Kurzformen** von **be**:

be		
I am	→	I'm
you are	→	you're
he / she / it is	→	he's / she's / it's
we are	→	we're
you are	→	you're
they are	→	they're

do

Das Hilfsverb **do** benutzt man in Verbindung mit Vollverben für die **Verneinung** von Aussagesätzen und bei der Bildung von **Fragen**:

Verneinung	He **doesn't** play football.
Frage	**Does** he play football?

have

Das Hilfsverb **have** wird zur Bildung von **Perfect**-Formen benötigt:

Present Perfect	He **has** played football.
Present Perfect Continuous	He **has** been playing football.
Past Perfect	He **had** played football.
Past Perfect Continuous	He **had** been playing football.
Future II	He will **have** played football.
Future II Continuous	He will **have** been playing football.
Conditional Past	He would **have** played football.

Verneinte Aussagesätze und Fragen, in denen **have** als Hilfsverb auftritt, benötigen nicht zusätzlich das Hilfsverb **do**. Man kann die konjugierte Form von **have** direkt verneinen und auch eine Frage direkt mit der konjugierten Form von **have** beginnen:

Verneinung	He **hasn't** played football.
Frage	**Has** he played football?

Achtung! Häufig benutzt man auch für **have** und **had** die folgenden **Kurzformen**:

have			**had**		
I have	→	I've	I had	→	I'd
you have	→	you've	you had	→	you'd
he / she / it has	→	he's / she's / it's	he / she / it had	→	he'd / she'd / it'd
we have	→	we've	we had	→	we'd
you have	→	you've	you had	→	you'd
they have	→	they've	they had	→	they'd

c) Modalverben *(modal verbs)*

In Verbindung mit einem Vollverb im Infinitiv gibt es im Englischen eine Reihe von **Modalverben** oder **modalen Hilfsverben** *(modal auxiliary verbs)*, die zum einen die Möglichkeit oder Wahrscheinlichkeit einer Handlung beschreiben können, zum anderen aber auch dazu dienen, Fähigkeiten, Erlaubnisse, Absichten oder Verbote auszudrücken.

Die wichtigsten Modalverben im Englischen sind **can / could**, **may / might**, **must**, **shall / should** und **will / would**.

Grammatikalische Besonderheiten

Bei Modalverben fehlt in der 3. Person Singular die Endung **-s**:

He can play football. *Er kann Fußball spielen.*

Modalverben besitzen in der Regel nur eine Form, das heißt, sie sind unveränderlich und haben keine **ing**-Form und kein **Past Participle**.
Verneinte Aussagesätze und Fragen, in denen ein Modalverb auftritt, werden ohne das Hilfsverb **do** gebildet:

Verneinung	He **can't** play football.
Frage	**May** I play football?

Nach einem Modalverb folgt immer ein Vollverb im Infinitiv ohne **to**:

He should play football. *Er soll Fußball spielen.*

Modalverben und ihre Bedeutung

can / could

Das Modalverb **can** drückt vor allem eine *Fähigkeit* aus, oder es wird dazu benutzt, um *Erlaubnis* zu bitten:

He can play football.	*Er kann Fußball spielen.*	(Fähigkeit)
Can I play football?	*Darf ich Fußball spielen?*	(Erlaubnis)

Could wird zum einen als Vergangenheitsform von **can** benutzt, um eine *Fähigkeit* zu beschreiben. Es bringt aber auch eine *höfliche Bitte* oder eine *Möglichkeit* zum Ausdruck:

He could play football.	*Er konnte Fußball spielen.*	(Fähigkeit)
Could I play football?	*Dürfte ich Fußball spielen?*	(höfliche Bitte)
We could play football.	*Wir könnten Fußball spielen.*	(Möglichkeit)

may / might

Die Modalverben **may** und **might** werden dazu benutzt, um *Erlaubnis* zu *bitten*, eine *Erlaubnis* zu *erteilen* oder eine *Möglichkeit* auszudrücken:

May / Might I play football?	*Darf ich Fußball spielen?*
You may / might play football.	*Du darfst Fußball spielen.*
He may / might play football.	*Er spielt möglicherweise Fußball.*

must

Das Modalverb **must** benutzt man, um auszudrücken, dass jemand etwas tun *muss*. Beachten Sie jedoch, dass die verneinte Form **must not** (Kurzform **mustn't**) *nicht dürfen* bedeutet:

You must play football.	*Du musst Fußball spielen.*
You mustn't play football.	*Du darfst nicht Fußball spielen.*

shall / should

Mit dem Modalverb **shall** spricht man über die *Zukunft*:

You shall play football one day.	*Du wirst eines Tages Fußball spielen.*

Should benutzt man häufig, um eine *Verpflichtung* auszudrücken:

You should play football.	*Du solltest Fußball spielen.*

will / would

Das Modalverb **will** drückt *Zukünftigkeit* aus:

You will play football.	*Du wirst Fußball spielen.*

Would benutzt man häufig in *unerfüllbaren Bedingungssätzen*:

I would play football if I were you.	*An deiner Stelle würde ich Fußball spielen.*

Achtung! Häufig benutzt man auch für **will** und **would** die folgenden **Kurzformen**:

will			**would**		
I will	→	I'll	I would	→	I'd
you will	→	you'll	you would	→	you'd
he / she / it will	→	he'll / she'll / it'll	he / she / it would	→	he'd / she'd / it'd
we will	→	we'll	we would	→	we'd
you will	→	you'll	you would	→	you'd
they will	→	they'll	they would	→	they'd

2. Transitive und intransitive Verben *(transitive and intransitive verbs)*

Eine Reihe von Verben benötigt im Satz mindestens *ein* Objekt, also eine Ergänzung. Solche Verben nennt man **transitive Verben**:

Anne likes dogs.	*Anne mag Hunde.*
Peter kissed Mary.	*Peter küsste Mary.*

Oft werden auch *zwei* Objekte benötigt:

Jeremy wrote me a letter.	*Jeremy schrieb mir einen Brief.*
Paul gave me a book.	*Paul gab mir ein Buch.*

Als **intransitive Verben** bezeichnet man dagegen Verben, die *kein* Objekt benötigen:

Anne slept.	*Anne schlief.*
The children cried.	*Die Kinder weinten.*

Manche Verben können sowohl **transitiv** als auch **intransitiv** gebraucht werden:

John is reading a book. — *John liest gerade ein Buch.*
John is reading. — *John liest gerade.*

3. Reflexive Verben und Reflexivpronomen
(reflexive verbs and reflexive pronouns)

Reflexive Verben sind Verben, die in Verbindung mit den folgenden **Reflexivpronomen** *(myself, yourself, ...)* verwendet werden:

I	enjoy	**myself**
you	enjoy	**yourself**
he	enjoys	**himself**
she	enjoys	**herself**
it	enjoys	**itself**

we	enjoy	**ourselves**
you	enjoy	**yourselves**
they	enjoy	**themselves**

Einige reflexive Verben im Deutschen sind jedoch im Englischen nicht reflexiv und benötigen daher kein Reflexivpronomen. Hier ein paar Beispiele:

I didn't shave yesterday. — *Gestern habe ich mich nicht rasiert.*
I need to wash first. — *Ich muss mich erst waschen.*
Have you dressed? — *Hast du dich schon angezogen?*

4. Verben ohne Verlaufsform *(non-progressive/stative verbs)*

Eine Reihe von Verben im Englischen kommt normalerweise nicht in der **Verlaufsform** *(continuous/progressive form)* vor. Diese lassen sich in drei Gruppen unterteilen:

Verben der Wahrnehmung
Zu diesen Verben gehören z. B. **notice, see, hear** und **feel**.

I saw / ~~was seeing~~ her at the pub. — *Ich sah sie in der Kneipe.*

Verben des Wissens, der Meinung, des Gefühls oder des Wunsches
Zu dieser Gruppe zählen unter anderem die Verben **know, believe, think, like, want** und **wish**.

She knows / ~~is knowing~~ a lot. — *Sie weiß eine Menge.*

Weitere Verben
Eine Reihe von weiteren Verben kommt ebenfalls normalerweise nicht in der Verlaufsform vor. Dazu gehören z. B. **be, have, possess, belong, seem, mean, sound** und **look**.

You look / ~~are looking~~ beautiful! — *Du siehst schön aus!*

III. Tempus
Auf den folgenden Seiten erfahren Sie mehr über den Gebrauch und die Bildung der verschiedenen Zeitformen im Englischen.

1. Present Simple
Man benutzt das **Present Simple** für Aussagen, die die Gegenwart betreffen, oder auch für Gewohnheiten und immer wiederkehrende Ereignisse. Darüber hinaus kann man im **Present Simple** auch über die Zukunft sprechen, z. B. wenn es um Abfahrts- oder Ankunftszeiten geht:

Our train <u>leaves</u> at 8 o'clock.
Unser Zug fährt um acht Uhr ab.

Das **Present Simple** wird mit der Grundform des Verbs gebildet. Nur die 3. Person Singular *(he/she/it)* wird verändert, indem ein **-s** angehängt wird.

Aussage		**Verneinung**			**Frage**		
I/We/ You/They	live.	I/We/ You/They	do not (don't)	live.	Do	I/we/ you/they	live?
He/She/It	lives.	He/She/It	does not (doesn't)	live.	Does	he/she/it	live?

* Verneinte Sätze werden durch Hinzufügen von **do not/does not** oder **don't/doesn't** gebildet. Fragen werden gebildet, indem **do/does** am Satzanfang hinzugefügt wird. Hier bleibt die Grundform des Verbs erhalten.

Achten Sie bei den folgenden Verben auf die richtige **Schreibung** der **Present Simple**-Formen in der 3. Person Singular:

Verben, die auf *-ch, -sh, -ss, -o, -x* enden	Anhängen von *-es*	watch push go	watch**es** push**es** go**es**
Verben, die auf einen Konsonanten + *-y* enden	Anhängen von *-ies* Wegfall von *-y*	study try carry	stud**ies** tr**ies** carr**ies**
Aber: Verben, die auf einen Vokal + *-y* enden	Anhängen von *-s*	play buy enjoy	play**s** buy**s** enjoy**s**

Auch die **Aussprache** des **-s** in der 3. Person Singular ist im **Present Simple** unterschiedlich, je nachdem, was für ein Laut der Endung vorausgeht. Die Endung **-s** wird gesprochen:

nach stimmlosen Konsonanten	stimmlos* (**-s**)	waits gets cuts	wie ss in „nass" z. B. [gets]
nach stimmhaften Konsonanten und Vokalen	stimmhaft* (**-z**)	runs opens allows	wie s in „Sahne" z. B. [rʌnz]
nach einem Zischlaut, bei Bildung der 3. Person Singular auf *-es*	silbisch (**-iz**)	changes watches washes	wie das erste s in „business" z. B. ['wɒʃɪz]

* Es gibt zwei Arten von Konsonanten (Mitlauten) im Englischen: Bei **stimmhaften** Konsonanten spüren Sie bei der Aussprache eine Vibration am Kehlkopf. Diese Vibration spürt man bei **stimmlosen** Konsonanten nicht.

2. Present Continuous

Mit dem **Present Continuous** drückt man in der Gegenwart Handlungen aus, deren Verlauf man betonen möchte und die gerade im Gange sind:

I <u>am washing</u> the dishes. *Ich spüle gerade das Geschirr.*

Das **Present Continuous** wird mit der passenden Form von **to be (is / am / are)** + **ing**-Form eines Vollverbs gebildet.

Aussage			Verneinung			Frage		
I	am	living.	I	am not ('m not)	living.	Am	I	living?
He / She / It	is	living.	He /She / It	is not ('s not)	living.	Is	he / she / it	living?
We / You / They	are	living.	We / You / They	are not ('re not)	living.	Are	we / you / they	living?

* Verneinte Sätze werden durch Hinzufügen von **not** (**n't**) nach dem Pronomen gebildet. Bei der Frageform steht **am** / **is** / **are** am Anfang des Satzes.

Achten Sie bei den folgenden Verben auf die richtige **Schreibung** der **ing**-Form:

Verben, die auf -e enden	Wegfall von -e Anhängen von *-ing*	have dance	hav**ing** danc**ing**
Verben, die auf -ee enden	Anhängen von *-ing*	see	see**ing**
Verben, deren Endkonsonant betont ist und einem Vokal folgt	Konsonant wird verdoppelt	stop plan get begin	stop**ping** plan**ning** get**ting** begin**ning**

AUSNAHME: Im britischen Englisch (BE) wird ein **-l** am Ende, das einem Vokal folgt, auch bei unbetonter Silbe verdoppelt: cancel cancelling (BE) canceling (AE)

3. Present Perfect

Das **Present Perfect** ist streng von der **Past Simple**-Form zu unterscheiden, da es entgegen der einfachen Vergangenheit einen Bezug zur Gegenwart hat. Das **Present Perfect** bildet eine Brücke zwischen Vergangenheit und Gegenwart und wird häufig für Handlungen in der Vergangenheit benutzt, die eine Auswirkung auf die Gegenwart haben:

Have you found your keys? *Hast du deinen Schlüssel schon gefunden?*

Man bildet das **Present Perfect** mit **have** / **has** und dem **Past Participle** eines Vollverbs. Die regelmäßigen Formen werden durch Anhängen von **-ed** gebildet. Besonderheiten zur **Schreibung** und **Aussprache** der regelmäßigen Formen des **Past Participle** finden Sie auf den Seiten 15 und 16.

Aussage			Verneinung			Frage		
I / We / You / They	have	lived.	I / We / You / They	have not (haven't)	lived.	Have	I / we / you / they	lived?
He / She / It	has	lived.	He / She / It	has not (hasn't)	lived.	Has	he / she / it	lived?

* Verneinte Sätze werden durch Hinzufügen von **not** (**n't**) vor dem **Past Participle** gebildet. Bei der Frageform steht **have** / **has** am Anfang des Satzes.

4. Present Perfect Continuous

Das **Present Perfect Continuous** wird ähnlich wie das **Present Perfect** verwendet, jedoch steht hierbei der Verlauf einer Handlung im Vordergrund:

I have been working for two hours. *Ich habe zwei Stunden lang gearbeitet.*

Man bildet das **Present Perfect Continuous** mit **have / has been** + **ing**-Form eines Vollverbs.

Aussage			**Verneinung**			**Frage**		
I / We / You / They	have	been living.	I / We / You / They	have not (haven't)	been living.	Have	I / we / you / they	been living?
He / She / It	has	been living.	He / She / It	has not (hasn't)	been living.	Has	he / she / it	been living?

* Verneinte Sätze werden durch Hinzufügen von **not** (**n't**) vor dem Vollverb gebildet. Bei der Frageform steht **have** / **has** am Anfang des Satzes.

Besonderheiten zur **Schreibung** der **ing**-Form können Sie auf Seite 14 nachlesen.

5. Past Simple

Das **Past Simple** ist eine der gebräuchlichsten Vergangenheitsformen. Mit dem **Past Simple** berichtet man über Vorgänge in der Vergangenheit, die keinen direkten Bezug zur Gegenwart haben:

I went to the cinema last night. *Gestern Abend ging ich ins Kino.*

Man bildet das **Past Simple**, indem man **-ed** an die Grundform des Verbs anhängt.

Aussage		**Verneinung**			**Frage**		
I	lived.	I	did not (didn't)	live.	Did	I	live?
He / She / It		He / She / It				he / she / it	
We / You / They		We / You / They				we / you / they	

* Die Verneinung wird mit **did not** (**didn't**) und der Grundform gebildet. Fragen werden mit dem Hilfsverb **do** gebildet. **Did** ist die Vergangenheitsform von **do** / **does** und steht am Anfang des Satzes. Das Verb steht in der Grundform.

Achten Sie bei der **Schreibung** der Endung **-ed** im **Past Simple** und **Past Participle** auf die folgenden Besonderheiten:

Verben, die auf *-e* enden	Anhängen von *-d*	arrive change	arrive**d** change**d**
Verben, die auf einen Konsonanten + *-y* enden	*-y* wird zu *-ied*	carry try study	carr**ied** tr**ied** stud**ied**
Verben, die auf einen Vokal + Konsonant enden	Konsonant wird verdoppelt	stop plan	stop**ped** plan**ned**
Verben mit zwei Silben, die auf einen Konsonanten enden	Konsonant wird nur verdoppelt, wenn die letzte Silbe betont wird	prefer *aber* visit offer	prefer**red** visit**ed** offer**ed**

AUSNAHME: Im BE wird ein **-l** am Ende auch bei unbetonter Silbe verdoppelt.
Im AE trifft dies nicht zu: travel travelled (BE)
travel traveled (AE)

Auch bei der **Aussprache** des **-ed** im **Past Simple** und **Past Participle** gibt es einige Besonderheiten. Die Endung **-ed** wird gesprochen:

nach stimmlosen Konsonanten (nach *-p*, *-f*, *-ss* usw.)	stimmlos (**-t**)	asked looked stopped	wie t in „Takt" z. B. [ɑːskt]
nach stimmhaften Konsonanten und Vokalen (nach *-b*, *-v*, *-g* usw.)	stimmhaft (**-d**)	allowed listened opened	wie d in „Ende" z. B. ['əʊpənd]
nach *-d* und *-t*	silbisch (**-id**)	needed waited wanted	wie id in „Widder" z. B. ['niːdɪd]

6. Past Continuous

Man verwendet das **Past Continuous** vor allem für Handlungen, die in der Vergangenheit zum Zeitpunkt einer neu einsetzenden Handlung bereits im Gange waren. Die neu einsetzende Handlung steht dabei im **Past Simple**:

I was listening to music when the telephone rang. — *Ich hörte gerade Musik, als das Telefon klingelte.*

Das **Past Continuous** wird mit **was / were** + **ing**-Form eines Vollverbs gebildet.

Aussage			**Verneinung**			**Frage**		
I / He / She / It	was	living.	I / He / She / It	was not	living.	Was	I / he / she / it	living?
We / You / They	were	living.	We / You / They	were not	living.	Were	we / you / they	living?

* Verneinte Sätze werden durch Hinzufügen von **not** (**n't**) nach **was** bzw. **were** gebildet. Bei der Frageform steht **was / were** am Anfang des Satzes.

Besonderheiten zur **Schreibung** der **ing**-Form können Sie auf Seite 14 nachlesen.

7. Past Perfect

Das **Past Perfect** benutzt man, um auszudrücken, dass ein Ereignis oder eine Handlung vor einem anderen Ereignis in der Vergangenheit stattgefunden hat:

When we had eaten, we went to the cinema. — *Nachdem wir gegessen hatten, gingen wir ins Kino.*

Man bildet das **Past Perfect** mit **had** und dem **Past Participle** eines Vollverbs. Die regelmäßigen Formen werden durch Anhängen von **-ed** gebildet. Besonderheiten zur **Schreibung** und **Aussprache** der regelmäßigen Formen des **Past Participle** finden Sie auf den Seiten 15 und 16.

Aussage			**Verneinung**			**Frage**		
I	had	lived.	I	had not (hadn't)	lived.	Had	I	lived?
He / She / It			He / She / It				he / she / it	
We / You / They			We / You / They				we / you / they	

* Verneinte Sätze werden durch Hinzufügen von **not** (**n't**) nach **had** gebildet. Bei der Frageform steht **had** am Anfang des Satzes.

8. Past Perfect Continuous

Das **Past Perfect Continuous** wird ähnlich wie das **Past Perfect** verwendet, jedoch steht hierbei der Verlauf einer Handlung im Vordergrund:

I had been working for two hours. *Ich hatte zwei Stunden lang gearbeitet.*

Man bildet das **Past Perfect Continuous** mit **had been** + **ing**-Form eines Vollverbs.

Aussage			Verneinung			Frage		
I He / She / It We / You / They	had	been living.	I He / She / It We / You / They	had not (hadn't)	been living.	Had	I he /she / it we / you / they	been living?

* Verneinte Sätze werden durch Hinzufügen von **not** (**n't**) zwischen **had** und **been** gebildet. Bei der Frageform steht **had** am Anfang des Satzes.

Besonderheiten zur **Schreibung** der **ing**-Form können Sie auf Seite 14 nachlesen.

9. Future I

Mit dem **Future I** spricht man über Vorhersagen für die Zukunft:

I will be in London tomorrow. *Ich werde morgen in London sein.*

Das **Future I** wird mit **will** und der Grundform eines Vollverbs gebildet.

Aussage			Verneinung			Frage		
I He / She / It We / You / They	will	live.	I He / She / It We / You / They	will not (won't)	live.	Will	I he / she / it we / you / they	live?

* Verneinte Sätze werden durch Hinzufügen von **not** nach **will** gebildet. Achtung! Kurzform: **won't**. Bei der Frageform steht **will** am Anfang des Satzes.

Beachten Sie, dass es im Englischen auch andere Möglichkeiten gibt, um über die Zukunft zu reden.

Wenn man z. B. über Abfahrts- und Ankunftszeiten in der Zukunft spricht, benutzt man oft das **Present Simple**:

Our train leaves tomorrow at eight o'clock. *Unser Zug fährt morgen um acht Uhr ab.*

Wenn man von festen Absichten für die Zukunft spricht, verwendet man anstatt **will** eine Konstruktion mit einer konjugierten Form von **be** (**am** / **are** / **is**) + **going to**:

I am going to wash the dishes tomorrow. *Ich werde das Geschirr morgen spülen.*

10. Future I Continuous

Mit dem **Future I Continuous** spricht man - ähnlich wie beim **Future I** - über Vorhersagen für die Zukunft, allerdings steht hierbei der Verlauf einer Handlung im Vordergrund:

I will be working all day tomorrow. *Ich werde morgen den ganzen Tag arbeiten.*

Das **Future I Continuous** wird mit **will be** + **ing**-Form eines Vollverbs gebildet.

Aussage			Verneinung			Frage		
I	will be	living.	I	will not (won't) be	living.	Will	I	be living?
He/She/It			He/She/It				he/she/it	
We/You/They			We/You/They				we/you/they	

* Verneinte Sätze werden durch Hinzufügen von **not** zwischen **will** und **be** gebildet. Bei der Frageform steht **will** am Anfang des Satzes.

Besonderheiten zur **Schreibung** der **ing**-Form können Sie auf Seite 14 nachlesen.

11. Future II

Das **Future II** benutzt man, um in der Zukunft über die Vergangenheit zu sprechen:

I will have finished my work tomorrow. *Morgen werde ich meine Arbeit erledigt haben.*

Man bildet das **Future II** mit **will have** und dem **Past Participle** eines Vollverbs. Die regelmäßigen Formen werden durch Anhängen von **-ed** gebildet. Besonderheiten zur **Schreibung** und **Aussprache** der regelmäßigen Formen des **Past Participle** finden Sie auf den Seiten 15 und 16.

Aussage			Verneinung			Frage		
I	will have	lived.	I	will not (won't) have	lived.	Will	I	have lived?
He/She/It			He/She/It				he/she/it	
We/You/They			We/You/They				we/you/they	

* Verneinte Sätze werden durch Hinzufügen von **not** zwischen **will** und **have** gebildet. Bei der Frageform steht **will** am Anfang des Satzes.

12. Future II Continuous

Das **Future II Continuous** benutzt man ähnlich wie das **Future II**, jedoch steht hierbei der Verlauf einer Handlung im Vordergrund:

I will have been working a lot by this time tomorrow. *Morgen um diese Zeit werde ich eine Menge gearbeitet haben.*

Man bildet das **Future II Continuous** mit **will have been** + **ing**-Form eines Vollverbs.

Aussage			Verneinung			Frage		
I	will have been	living.	I	will not (won't) have been	living.	Will	I	have been living?
He/She/It			He/She/It				he/she/it	
We/You/They			We/You/They				we/you/they	

* Verneinte Sätze werden durch Hinzufügen von **not** nach **will** gebildet. Bei der Frageform steht **will** am Anfang des Satzes.

Besonderheiten zur **Schreibung** der **ing**-Form können Sie auf Seite 14 nachlesen.

13. Conditional II

Das **Conditional II** wird mit **would** + Grundform eines Vollverbs gebildet.

Aussage			Verneinung			Frage		
I	would	live.	I	would not (wouldn't)	live.	Would	I	live?
He/She/It			He/She/It				he/she/it	
We/You/They			We/You/They				we/you/they	

* Verneinte Sätze werden durch Hinzufügen von **not** (**n't**) nach **would** gebildet. Bei der Frageform steht **would** am Anfang des Satzes.

14. Conditional Past

Das **Conditional Past** wird mit **would have** und dem **Past Participle** eines Vollverbs gebildet. Die regelmäßigen Formen bildet man durch Anhängen von **-ed**. Besonderheiten zur **Schreibung** und **Aussprache** der regelmäßigen Formen des **Past Participle** finden Sie auf den Seiten 15 und 16.

Aussage			Verneinung			Frage		
I	would have	lived.	I	would not (wouldn't) have	lived.	Would	I	have lived?
He/She/It			He/She/It				he/she/it	
We/You/They			We/You/They				we/you/they	

* Verneinte Sätze werden durch Hinzufügen von **not** (**n't**) nach **would** gebildet. Bei der Frageform steht **would** am Anfang des Satzes.

Die beiden Formen **Conditional II** und **Conditional Past** werden vor allem in **Bedingungssätzen** *(conditional clauses)* verwendet. Im Englischen unterscheidet man drei Arten von Bedingungssätzen:

erfüllbare Bedingung

Wenn eine Bedingung erfüllbar ist, benutzt man im **if**-Satz das **Present Simple** und im Hauptsatz das **Future I**:

If I feel better, I will work tomorrow. — *Wenn ich mich besser fühle, arbeite ich morgen.*

unerfüllbare Bedingung

Bei einer unerfüllbaren Bedingung benutzt man im **if**-Satz das **Past Simple** und im Hauptsatz das **Conditional II**:

If I felt better, I would work tomorrow. — *Wenn ich mich besser fühlen würde, würde ich morgen arbeiten.*

nicht mehr erfüllbare Bedingung

Bei einer nicht mehr erfüllbaren Bedingung verwendet man im **if**-Satz das **Past Perfect** und im Hauptsatz das **Conditional Past**:

If I had felt better, I would have worked. — *Wenn ich mich besser gefühlt hätte, hätte ich gearbeitet.*

IV. Modus

Im Englischen unterscheidet man drei Modi des Verbs: den **Indikativ** *(indicative)*, den **Konjunktiv** *(subjunctive)* und den **Imperativ** *(imperative)*.

1. Indikativ *(indicative)*

In Aussagesätzen stehen die meisten Verben im **Indikativ**:

He plays football.	*Er spielt Fußball.*

2. Konjunktiv *(subjunctive)*

Den **Konjunktiv** benutzt man im Englischen vor allem in *Bedingungssätzen*, für *Wünsche* oder in einer Reihe von *feststehenden Wendungen*:

Bedingungssätze

If I were you, I would call her.	*An deiner Stelle würde ich sie anrufen.*
If you had called her, she would have been happy.	*Wenn du sie angerufen hättest, wäre sie glücklich gewesen.*

Wünsche

I wish you were here.	*Ich wünschte mir, dass du hier wärst.*

feststehende Wendungen

God save the Queen!	*Gott schütze die Königin!*
So be it!	*So sei es!*

3. Imperativ *(imperative)*

Um einen *Befehl* oder eine *Aufforderung* auszudrücken, benutzt man den **Imperativ** (die Befehlsform).

Der **Imperativ** für die **2. Person Singular** und die **2. Person Plural** entspricht der Form des **Infinitivs**:

<u>Come</u> in, Peter.	*Komm / Kommen Sie herein, Peter!*
<u>Be</u> careful, you two.	*Seid vorsichtig, ihr beiden!*

Einen **verneinten Imperativ** bildet man mit **do not / don't + Infinitiv**:

<u>Don't walk</u> on the grass.	*Betreten Sie bitte nicht den Rasen!*

Den **Imperativ**, bei dem der Sprecher mit eingeschlossen ist, bildet man mit **let us / let's + Infinitiv**:

<u>Let's go</u> shopping.	*Lass(t) uns einkaufen gehen!*

V. Passiv

Bildung

Im Englischen bildet man das **Passiv** (die Leideform) mit einer konjugierten Form des Hilfsverbs **be** und dem **Past Participle** eines Vollverbs.

Gebrauch

Das **Passiv** findet man vor allem in Sach- und Fachtexten. Man beschreibt mit dem **Passiv**, was mit einer Person oder Sache gemacht wird.

Aktiv

He waters the flowers.

Passiv

The flowers are watered.

Beim **Aktiv** steht die *handelnde Person* im Mittelpunkt, beim **Passiv** der *Vorgang* selbst.

Da die Person nicht so wichtig ist, muss sie auch nicht genannt werden. Soll eine handelnde Person genannt werden, steht sie in Verbindung mit der Präposition **by**:

The flowers are watered by the gardener. *Die Blumen werden vom Gärtner gegossen.*

Beachten Sie, dass **Passivformen** unterschiedlich ins Deutsche übersetzt werden können, je nachdem, ob ein *Zustand* oder ein *Vorgang* beschrieben wird:

The door is locked.	*Die Tür ist geschlossen.*	(Zustand)
	Die Tür wird geschlossen.	(Vorgang)

accept

annehmen

Regelmäßiges Verb

Simple tenses

Present

I	accept
you	accept
he/she/it	accepts
we	accept
you	accept
they	accept

Past

I	accepted
you	accepted
he/she/it	accepted
we	accepted
you	accepted
they	accepted

Present Perfect

I	have	accepted
you	have	accepted
he/she/it	has	accepted
we	have	accepted
you	have	accepted
they	have	accepted

Past Perfect

I	had	accepted
you	had	accepted
he/she/it	had	accepted
we	had	accepted
you	had	accepted
they	had	accepted

Will-Future

I	will	accept
you	will	accept
he/she/it	will	accept
we	will	accept
you	will	accept
they	will	accept

Going to-Future

I	am	going to	accept
you	are	going to	accept
he/she/it	is	going to	accept
we	are	going to	accept
you	are	going to	accept
they	are	going to	accept

Future Perfect

I	will have	accepted
you	will have	accepted
he/she/it	will have	accepted
we	will have	accepted
you	will have	accepted
they	will have	accepted

Imperative

accept

Impersonal

ing-Form

accepting

Past Participle

accepted

Continuous tenses

Present

I	am	accepting
you	are	accepting
he/she/it	is	accepting
we	are	accepting
you	are	accepting
they	are	accepting

Past

I	was	accepting
you	were	accepting
he/she/it	was	accepting
we	were	accepting
you	were	accepting
they	were	accepting

Present Perfect

I	have been	accepting
you	have been	accepting
he/she/it	has been	accepting
we	have been	accepting
you	have been	accepting
they	have been	accepting

Past Perfect

I	had been	accepting
you	had been	accepting
he/she/it	had been	accepting
we	had been	accepting
you	had been	accepting
they	had been	accepting

Will-Future

I	will be	accepting
you	will be	accepting
he/she/it	will be	accepting
we	will be	accepting
you	will be	accepting
they	will be	accepting

Going to-Future

I	am	going to be	accepting
you	are	going to be	accepting
he/she/it	is	going to be	accepting
we	are	going to be	accepting
you	are	going to be	accepting
they	are	going to be	accepting

Future Perfect

I	will have been	accepting
you	will have been	accepting
he/she/it	will have been	accepting
we	will have been	accepting
you	will have been	accepting
they	will have been	accepting

Conditional

I	would	accept
you	would	accept
he/she/it	would	accept
we	would	accept
you	would	accept
they	would	accept

Conditional Past

I	would have	accepted
you	would have	accepted
he/she/it	would have	accepted
we	would have	accepted
you	would have	accepted
they	would have	accepted

achieve

erreichen

+ **-ing** → ~~e~~ / + **-d** nicht **-ed**
Regelmäßiges Verb

Simple tenses

Present

I	achieve
you	achieve
he/she/it	achieves
we	achieve
you	achieve
they	achieve

Past

I	achieved
you	achieved
he/she/it	achieved
we	achieved
you	achieved
they	achieved

Present Perfect

I	have	achieved
you	have	achieved
he/she/it	has	achieved
we	have	achieved
you	have	achieved
they	have	achieved

Past Perfect

I	had	achieved
you	had	achieved
he/she/it	had	achieved
we	had	achieved
you	had	achieved
they	had	achieved

Will-Future

I	will	achieve
you	will	achieve
he/she/it	will	achieve
we	will	achieve
you	will	achieve
they	will	achieve

Going to-Future

I	am	going to	achieve
you	are	going to	achieve
he/she/it	is	going to	achieve
we	are	going to	achieve
you	are	going to	achieve
they	are	going to	achieve

Future Perfect

I	will have	achieved
you	will have	achieved
he/she/it	will have	achieved
we	will have	achieved
you	will have	achieved
they	will have	achieved

Imperative

achieve

Impersonal

ing-Form

achieving

Past Participle

achieved

Continuous tenses

Present

I	am	achieving
you	are	achieving
he/she/it	is	achieving
we	are	achieving
you	are	achieving
they	are	achieving

Past

I	was	achieving
you	were	achieving
he/she/it	was	achieving
we	were	achieving
you	were	achieving
they	were	achieving

Present Perfect

I	have been	achieving
you	have been	achieving
he/she/it	has been	achieving
we	have been	achieving
you	have been	achieving
they	have been	achieving

Past Perfect

I	had been	achieving
you	had been	achieving
he/she/it	had been	achieving
we	had been	achieving
you	had been	achieving
they	had been	achieving

Will-Future

I	will be	achieving
you	will be	achieving
he/she/it	will be	achieving
we	will be	achieving
you	will be	achieving
they	will be	achieving

Going to-Future

I	am	going to be	achieving
you	are	going to be	achieving
he/she/it	is	going to be	achieving
we	are	going to be	achieving
you	are	going to be	achieving
they	are	going to be	achieving

Future Perfect

I	will have been	achieving
you	will have been	achieving
he/she/it	will have been	achieving
we	will have been	achieving
you	will have been	achieving
they	will have been	achieving

Conditional

I	would	achieve
you	would	achieve
he/she/it	would	achieve
we	would	achieve
you	would	achieve
they	would	achieve

Conditional Past

I	would have	achieved
you	would have	achieved
he/she/it	would have	achieved
we	would have	achieved
you	would have	achieved
they	would have	achieved

act

handeln

Regelmäßiges Verb

Simple tenses

Present

I	act
you	act
he/she/it	acts
we	act
you	act
they	act

Past

I	acted
you	acted
he/she/it	acted
we	acted
you	acted
they	acted

Present Perfect

I	have	acted
you	have	acted
he/she/it	has	acted
we	have	acted
you	have	acted
they	have	acted

Past Perfect

I	had	acted
you	had	acted
he/she/it	had	acted
we	had	acted
you	had	acted
they	had	acted

Will-Future

I	will	act
you	will	act
he/she/it	will	act
we	will	act
you	will	act
they	will	act

Going to-Future

I	am	going to	act
you	are	going to	act
he/she/it	is	going to	act
we	are	going to	act
you	are	going to	act
they	are	going to	act

Future Perfect

I	will have	acted
you	will have	acted
he/she/it	will have	acted
we	will have	acted
you	will have	acted
they	will have	acted

Imperative

act

Impersonal

ing-Form

acting

Past Participle

acted

Continuous tenses

Present

I	am	acting
you	are	acting
he/she/it	is	acting
we	are	acting
you	are	acting
they	are	acting

Past

I	was	acting
you	were	acting
he/she/it	was	acting
we	were	acting
you	were	acting
they	were	acting

Present Perfect

I	have been	acting
you	have been	acting
he/she/it	has been	acting
we	have been	acting
you	have been	acting
they	have been	acting

Past Perfect

I	had been	acting
you	had been	acting
he/she/it	had been	acting
we	had been	acting
you	had been	acting
they	had been	acting

Will-Future

I	will be	acting
you	will be	acting
he/she/it	will be	acting
we	will be	acting
you	will be	acting
they	will be	acting

Going to-Future

I	am	going to be	acting
you	are	going to be	acting
he/she/it	is	going to be	acting
we	are	going to be	acting
you	are	going to be	acting
they	are	going to be	acting

Future Perfect

I	will have been	acting
you	will have been	acting
he/she/it	will have been	acting
we	will have been	acting
you	will have been	acting
they	will have been	acting

Conditional

I	would	act
you	would	act
he/she/it	would	act
we	would	act
you	would	act
they	would	act

Conditional Past

I	would have	acted
you	would have	acted
he/she/it	would have	acted
we	would have	acted
you	would have	acted
they	would have	acted

Regelmäßiges Verb

Simple tenses

Present

I	add
you	add
he/she/it	adds
we	add
you	add
they	add

Past

I	added
you	added
he/she/it	added
we	added
you	added
they	added

Present Perfect

I	have	added
you	have	added
he/she/it	has	added
we	have	added
you	have	added
they	have	added

Past Perfect

I	had	added
you	had	added
he/she/it	had	added
we	had	added
you	had	added
they	had	added

Will-Future

I	will	add
you	will	add
he/she/it	will	add
we	will	add
you	will	add
they	will	add

Going to-Future

I	am	going to	add
you	are	going to	add
he/she/it	is	going to	add
we	are	going to	add
you	are	going to	add
they	are	going to	add

Future Perfect

I	will have	added
you	will have	added
he/she/it	will have	added
we	will have	added
you	will have	added
they	will have	added

Imperative

add

Impersonal

ing-Form

adding

Past Participle

added

Continuous tenses

Present

I	am	adding
you	are	adding
he/she/it	is	adding
we	are	adding
you	are	adding
they	are	adding

Past

I	was	adding
you	were	adding
he/she/it	was	adding
we	were	adding
you	were	adding
they	were	adding

Present Perfect

I	have been	adding
you	have been	adding
he/she/it	has been	adding
we	have been	adding
you	have been	adding
they	have been	adding

Past Perfect

I	had been	adding
you	had been	adding
he/she/it	had been	adding
we	had been	adding
you	had been	adding
they	had been	adding

Will-Future

I	will be	adding
you	will be	adding
he/she/it	will be	adding
we	will be	adding
you	will be	adding
they	will be	adding

Going to-Future

I	am	going to be	adding
you	are	going to be	adding
he/she/it	is	going to be	adding
we	are	going to be	adding
you	are	going to be	adding
they	are	going to be	adding

Future Perfect

I	will have been	adding
you	will have been	adding
he/she/it	will have been	adding
we	will have been	adding
you	will have been	adding
they	will have been	adding

Conditional

I	would	add
you	would	add
he/she/it	would	add
we	would	add
you	would	add
they	would	add

Conditional Past

I	would have	added
you	would have	added
he/she/it	would have	added
we	would have	added
you	would have	added
they	would have	added

admit

zugeben

Konsonantenverdopplung
Regelmäßiges Verb

Simple tenses

Present

I	admit
you	admit
he/she/it	admits
we	admit
you	admit
they	admit

Past

I	admitted
you	admitted
he/she/it	admitted
we	admitted
you	admitted
they	admitted

Present Perfect

I	have	admitted
you	have	admitted
he/she/it	has	admitted
we	have	admitted
you	have	admitted
they	have	admitted

Past Perfect

I	had	admitted
you	had	admitted
he/she/it	had	admitted
we	had	admitted
you	had	admitted
they	had	admitted

Will-Future

I	will	admit
you	will	admit
he/she/it	will	admit
we	will	admit
you	will	admit
they	will	admit

Going to-Future

I	am	going to	admit
you	are	going to	admit
he/she/it	is	going to	admit
we	are	going to	admit
you	are	going to	admit
they	are	going to	admit

Future Perfect

I	will have	admitted
you	will have	admitted
he/she/it	will have	admitted
we	will have	admitted
you	will have	admitted
they	will have	admitted

Imperative

admit

Impersonal

ing-Form

admitting

Past Participle

admitted

Continuous tenses

Present

I	am	admitting
you	are	admitting
he/she/it	is	admitting
we	are	admitting
you	are	admitting
they	are	admitting

Past

I	was	admitting
you	were	admitting
he/she/it	was	admitting
we	were	admitting
you	were	admitting
they	were	admitting

Present Perfect

I	have been	admitting
you	have been	admitting
he/she/it	has been	admitting
we	have been	admitting
you	have been	admitting
they	have been	admitting

Past Perfect

I	had been	admitting
you	had been	admitting
he/she/it	had been	admitting
we	had been	admitting
you	had been	admitting
they	had been	admitting

Will-Future

I	will be	admitting
you	will be	admitting
he/she/it	will be	admitting
we	will be	admitting
you	will be	admitting
they	will be	admitting

Going to-Future

I	am	going to be	admitting
you	are	going to be	admitting
he/she/it	is	going to be	admitting
we	are	going to be	admitting
you	are	going to be	admitting
they	are	going to be	admitting

Future Perfect

I	will have been	admitting
you	will have been	admitting
he/she/it	will have been	admitting
we	will have been	admitting
you	will have been	admitting
they	will have been	admitting

Conditional

I	would	admit
you	would	admit
he/she/it	would	admit
we	would	admit
you	would	admit
they	would	admit

Conditional Past

I	would have	admitted
you	would have	admitted
he/she/it	would have	admitted
we	would have	admitted
you	would have	admitted
they	would have	admitted

Simple tenses

Present

I	affect
you	affect
he/she/it	affects
we	affect
you	affect
they	affect

Past

I	affected
you	affected
he/she/it	affected
we	affected
you	affected
they	affected

Present Perfect

I	have	affected
you	have	affected
he/she/it	has	affected
we	have	affected
you	have	affected
they	have	affected

Past Perfect

I	had	affected
you	had	affected
he/she/it	had	affected
we	had	affected
you	had	affected
they	had	affected

Will-Future

I	will	affect
you	will	affect
he/she/it	will	affect
we	will	affect
you	will	affect
they	will	affect

Going to-Future

I	am	going to	affect
you	are	going to	affect
he/she/it	is	going to	affect
we	are	going to	affect
you	are	going to	affect
they	are	going to	affect

Future Perfect

I	will have	affected
you	will have	affected
he/she/it	will have	affected
we	will have	affected
you	will have	affected
they	will have	affected

Imperative

affect

Impersonal

ing-Form

affecting

Past Participle

affected

Continuous tenses

Present

I	am	affecting
you	are	affecting
he/she/it	is	affecting
we	are	affecting
you	are	affecting
they	are	affecting

Past

I	was	affecting
you	were	affecting
he/she/it	was	affecting
we	were	affecting
you	were	affecting
they	were	affecting

Present Perfect

I	have been	affecting
you	have been	affecting
he/she/it	has been	affecting
we	have been	affecting
you	have been	affecting
they	have been	affecting

Past Perfect

I	had been	affecting
you	had been	affecting
he/she/it	had been	affecting
we	had been	affecting
you	had been	affecting
they	had been	affecting

Will-Future

I	will be	affecting
you	will be	affecting
he/she/it	will be	affecting
we	will be	affecting
you	will be	affecting
they	will be	affecting

Going to-Future

I	am	going to be	affecting
you	are	going to be	affecting
he/she/it	is	going to be	affecting
we	are	going to be	affecting
you	are	going to be	affecting
they	are	going to be	affecting

Future Perfect

I	will have been	affecting
you	will have been	affecting
he/she/it	will have been	affecting
we	will have been	affecting
you	will have been	affecting
they	will have been	affecting

Conditional

I	would	affect
you	would	affect
he/she/it	would	affect
we	would	affect
you	would	affect
they	would	affect

Conditional Past

I	would have	affected
you	would have	affected
he/she/it	would have	affected
we	would have	affected
you	would have	affected
they	would have	affected

agree

zustimmen

+ **-d** nicht **-ed**
Regelmäßiges Verb

Simple tenses

Present

I	agree
you	agree
he/she/it	agrees
we	agree
you	agree
they	agree

Past

I	agreed
you	agreed
he/she/it	agreed
we	agreed
you	agreed
they	agreed

Present Perfect

I	have	agreed
you	have	agreed
he/she/it	has	agreed
we	have	agreed
you	have	agreed
they	have	agreed

Past Perfect

I	had	agreed
you	had	agreed
he/she/it	had	agreed
we	had	agreed
you	had	agreed
they	had	agreed

Will-Future

I	will	agree
you	will	agree
he/she/it	will	agree
we	will	agree
you	will	agree
they	will	agree

Going to-Future

I	am	going to	agree
you	are	going to	agree
he/she/it	is	going to	agree
we	are	going to	agree
you	are	going to	agree
they	are	going to	agree

Future Perfect

I	will have	agreed
you	will have	agreed
he/she/it	will have	agreed
we	will have	agreed
you	will have	agreed
they	will have	agreed

Imperative

agree

Impersonal

ing-Form

agreeing

Past Participle

agreed

Continuous tenses

Present

I	am	agreeing
you	are	agreeing
he/she/it	is	agreeing
we	are	agreeing
you	are	agreeing
they	are	agreeing

Past

I	was	agreeing
you	were	agreeing
he/she/it	was	agreeing
we	were	agreeing
you	were	agreeing
they	were	agreeing

Present Perfect

I	have been	agreeing
you	have been	agreeing
he/she/it	has been	agreeing
we	have been	agreeing
you	have been	agreeing
they	have been	agreeing

Past Perfect

I	had been	agreeing
you	had been	agreeing
he/she/it	had been	agreeing
we	had been	agreeing
you	had been	agreeing
they	had been	agreeing

Will-Future

I	will be	agreeing
you	will be	agreeing
he/she/it	will be	agreeing
we	will be	agreeing
you	will be	agreeing
they	will be	agreeing

Going to-Future

I	am	going to be	agreeing
you	are	going to be	agreeing
he/she/it	is	going to be	agreeing
we	are	going to be	agreeing
you	are	going to be	agreeing
they	are	going to be	agreeing

Future Perfect

I	will have been	agreeing
you	will have been	agreeing
he/she/it	will have been	agreeing
we	will have been	agreeing
you	will have been	agreeing
they	will have been	agreeing

Conditional

I	would	agree
you	would	agree
he/she/it	would	agree
we	would	agree
you	would	agree
they	would	agree

Conditional Past

I	would have	agreed
you	would have	agreed
he/she/it	would have	agreed
we	would have	agreed
you	would have	agreed
they	would have	agreed

Simple tenses

Present

I	allow
you	allow
he/she/it	allows
we	allow
you	allow
they	allow

Past

I	allowed
you	allowed
he/she/it	allowed
we	allowed
you	allowed
they	allowed

Present Perfect

I	have	allowed
you	have	allowed
he/she/it	has	allowed
we	have	allowed
you	have	allowed
they	have	allowed

Past Perfect

I	had	allowed
you	had	allowed
he/she/it	had	allowed
we	had	allowed
you	had	allowed
they	had	allowed

Will-Future

I	will	allow
you	will	allow
he/she/it	will	allow
we	will	allow
you	will	allow
they	will	allow

Going to-Future

I	am	going to	allow
you	are	going to	allow
he/she/it	is	going to	allow
we	are	going to	allow
you	are	going to	allow
they	are	going to	allow

Future Perfect

I	will have	allowed
you	will have	allowed
he/she/it	will have	allowed
we	will have	allowed
you	will have	allowed
they	will have	allowed

Imperative

allow

Impersonal

ing-Form

allowing

Past Participle

allowed

Continuous tenses

Present

I	am	allowing
you	are	allowing
he/she/it	is	allowing
we	are	allowing
you	are	allowing
they	are	allowing

Past

I	was	allowing
you	were	allowing
he/she/it	was	allowing
we	were	allowing
you	were	allowing
they	were	allowing

Present Perfect

I	have been	allowing
you	have been	allowing
he/she/it	has been	allowing
we	have been	allowing
you	have been	allowing
they	have been	allowing

Past Perfect

I	had been	allowing
you	had been	allowing
he/she/it	had been	allowing
we	had been	allowing
you	had been	allowing
they	had been	allowing

Will-Future

I	will be	allowing
you	will be	allowing
he/she/it	will be	allowing
we	will be	allowing
you	will be	allowing
they	will be	allowing

Going to-Future

I	am	going to be	allowing
you	are	going to be	allowing
he/she/it	is	going to be	allowing
we	are	going to be	allowing
you	are	going to be	allowing
they	are	going to be	allowing

Future Perfect

I	will have been allowing
you	will have been allowing
he/she/it	will have been allowing
we	will have been allowing
you	will have been allowing
they	will have been allowing

Conditional

I	would	allow
you	would	allow
he/she/it	would	allow
we	would	allow
you	would	allow
they	would	allow

Conditional Past

I	would have	allowed
you	would have	allowed
he/she/it	would have	allowed
we	would have	allowed
you	would have	allowed
they	would have	allowed

answer

antworten

Regelmäßiges Verb

Simple tenses

Present

I	answer
you	answer
he/she/it	answers
we	answer
you	answer
they	answer

Past

I	answered
you	answered
he/she/it	answered
we	answered
you	answered
they	answered

Present Perfect

I	have	answered
you	have	answered
he/she/it	has	answered
we	have	answered
you	have	answered
they	have	answered

Past Perfect

I	had	answered
you	had	answered
he/she/it	had	answered
we	had	answered
you	had	answered
they	had	answered

Will-Future

I	will	answer
you	will	answer
he/she/it	will	answer
we	will	answer
you	will	answer
they	will	answer

Going to-Future

I	am	going to	answer
you	are	going to	answer
he/she/it	is	going to	answer
we	are	going to	answer
you	are	going to	answer
they	are	going to	answer

Future Perfect

I	will have	answered
you	will have	answered
he/she/it	will have	answered
we	will have	answered
you	will have	answered
they	will have	answered

Imperative

answer

Impersonal

ing-Form

answering

Past Participle

answered

Continuous tenses

Present

I	am	answering
you	are	answering
he/she/it	is	answering
we	are	answering
you	are	answering
they	are	answering

Past

I	was	answering
you	were	answering
he/she/it	was	answering
we	were	answering
you	were	answering
they	were	answering

Present Perfect

I	have	been	answering
you	have	been	answering
he/she/it	has	been	answering
we	have	been	answering
you	have	been	answering
they	have	been	answering

Past Perfect

I	had been	answering
you	had been	answering
he/she/it	had been	answering
we	had been	answering
you	had been	answering
they	had been	answering

Will-Future

I	will be	answering
you	will be	answering
he/she/it	will be	answering
we	will be	answering
you	will be	answering
they	will be	answering

Going to-Future

I	am	going to be	answering
you	are	going to be	answering
he/she/it	is	going to be	answering
we	are	going to be	answering
you	are	going to be	answering
they	are	going to be	answering

Future Perfect

I	will have been	answering
you	will have been	answering
he/she/it	will have been	answering
we	will have been	answering
you	will have been	answering
they	will have been	answering

Conditional

I	would	answer
you	would	answer
he/she/it	would	answer
we	would	answer
you	would	answer
they	would	answer

Conditional Past

I	would have	answered
you	would have	answered
he/she/it	would have	answered
we	would have	answered
you	would have	answered
they	would have	answered

+ -ing → ~~e~~ / + -d nicht -ed
im BE auch **apologise**
Regelmäßiges Verb

sich entschuldigen

apologize

Simple tenses

Present

I	apologize
you	apologize
he/she/it	apologizes
we	apologize
you	apologize
they	apologize

Past

I	apologized
you	apologized
he/she/it	apologized
we	apologized
you	apologized
they	apologized

Present Perfect

I	have	apologized
you	have	apologized
he/she/it	has	apologized
we	have	apologized
you	have	apologized
they	have	apologized

Past Perfect

I	had	apologized
you	had	apologized
he/she/it	had	apologized
we	had	apologized
you	had	apologized
they	had	apologized

Will-Future

I	will	apologize
you	will	apologize
he/she/it	will	apologize
we	will	apologize
you	will	apologize
they	will	apologize

Going to-Future

I	am	going to	apologize
you	are	going to	apologize
he/she/it	is	going to	apologize
we	are	going to	apologize
you	are	going to	apologize
they	are	going to	apologize

Future Perfect

I	will have	apologized
you	will have	apologized
he/she/it	will have	apologized
we	will have	apologized
you	will have	apologized
they	will have	apologized

Imperative

apologize

Impersonal

ing-Form

apologizing

Past Participle

apologized

Continuous tenses

Present

I	am	apologizing
you	are	apologizing
he/she/it	is	apologizing
we	are	apologizing
you	are	apologizing
they	are	apologizing

Past

I	was	apologizing
you	were	apologizing
he/she/it	was	apologizing
we	were	apologizing
you	were	apologizing
they	were	apologizing

Present Perfect

I	have been	apologizing
you	have been	apologizing
he/she/it	has been	apologizing
we	have been	apologizing
you	have been	apologizing
they	have been	apologizing

Past Perfect

I	had been	apologizing
you	had been	apologizing
he/she/it	had been	apologizing
we	had been	apologizing
you	had been	apologizing
they	had been	apologizing

Will-Future

I	will be	apologizing
you	will be	apologizing
he/she/it	will be	apologizing
we	will be	apologizing
you	will be	apologizing
they	will be	apologizing

Going to-Future

I	am	going to be	apologizing
you	are	going to be	apologizing
he/she/it	is	going to be	apologizing
we	are	going to be	apologizing
you	are	going to be	apologizing
they	are	going to be	apologizing

Future Perfect

I	will have been apologizing
you	will have been apologizing
he/she/it	will have been apologizing
we	will have been apologizing
you	will have been apologizing
they	will have been apologizing

Conditional

I	would	apologize
you	would	apologize
he/she/it	would	apologize
we	would	apologize
you	would	apologize
they	would	apologize

Conditional Past

I	would have	apologized
you	would have	apologized
he/she/it	would have	apologized
we	would have	apologized
you	would have	apologized
they	would have	apologized

appear

erscheinen

Regelmäßiges Verb

Simple tenses

Present

I	appear
you	appear
he/she/it	appears
we	appear
you	appear
they	appear

Past

I	appeared
you	appeared
he/she/it	appeared
we	appeared
you	appeared
they	appeared

Present Perfect

I	have	appeared
you	have	appeared
he/she/it	has	appeared
we	have	appeared
you	have	appeared
they	have	appeared

Past Perfect

I	had	appeared
you	had	appeared
he/she/it	had	appeared
we	had	appeared
you	had	appeared
they	had	appeared

Will-Future

I	will	appear
you	will	appear
he/she/it	will	appear
we	will	appear
you	will	appear
they	will	appear

Going to-Future

I	am	going to	appear
you	are	going to	appear
he/she/it	is	going to	appear
we	are	going to	appear
you	are	going to	appear
they	are	going to	appear

Future Perfect

I	will have	appeared
you	will have	appeared
he/she/it	will have	appeared
we	will have	appeared
you	will have	appeared
they	will have	appeared

Imperative

appear

Impersonal

ing-Form

appearing

Past Participle

appeared

Continuous tenses

Present

I	am	appearing
you	are	appearing
he/she/it	is	appearing
we	are	appearing
you	are	appearing
they	are	appearing

Past

I	was	appearing
you	were	appearing
he/she/it	was	appearing
we	were	appearing
you	were	appearing
they	were	appearing

Present Perfect

I	have been	appearing
you	have been	appearing
he/she/it	has been	appearing
we	have been	appearing
you	have been	appearing
they	have been	appearing

Past Perfect

I	had been	appearing
you	had been	appearing
he/she/it	had been	appearing
we	had been	appearing
you	had been	appearing
they	had been	appearing

Will-Future

I	will be	appearing
you	will be	appearing
he/she/it	will be	appearing
we	will be	appearing
you	will be	appearing
they	will be	appearing

Going to-Future

I	am	going to be	appearing
you	are	going to be	appearing
he/she/it	is	going to be	appearing
we	are	going to be	appearing
you	are	going to be	appearing
they	are	going to be	appearing

Future Perfect

I	will have been	appearing
you	will have been	appearing
he/she/it	will have been	appearing
we	will have been	appearing
you	will have been	appearing
they	will have been	appearing

Conditional

I	would	appear
you	would	appear
he/she/it	would	appear
we	would	appear
you	would	appear
they	would	appear

Conditional Past

I	would have	appeared
you	would have	appeared
he/she/it	would have	appeared
we	would have	appeared
you	would have	appeared
they	would have	appeared

+ **-ing** → ~~e~~ / + **-d** nicht **-ed**
Regelmäßiges Verb

schätzen

appreciate

Simple tenses

Present

I	appreciate
you	appreciate
he/she/it	appreciates
we	appreciate
you	appreciate
they	appreciate

Past

I	appreciated
you	appreciated
he/she/it	appreciated
we	appreciated
you	appreciated
they	appreciated

Present Perfect

I	have	appreciated
you	have	appreciated
he/she/it	has	appreciated
we	have	appreciated
you	have	appreciated
they	have	appreciated

Past Perfect

I	had	appreciated
you	had	appreciated
he/she/it	had	appreciated
we	had	appreciated
you	had	appreciated
they	had	appreciated

Will-Future

I	will	appreciate
you	will	appreciate
he/she/it	will	appreciate
we	will	appreciate
you	will	appreciate
they	will	appreciate

Going to-Future

I	am	going to	appreciate
you	are	going to	appreciate
he/she/it	is	going to	appreciate
we	are	going to	appreciate
you	are	going to	appreciate
they	are	going to	appreciate

Future Perfect

I	will have	appreciated
you	will have	appreciated
he/she/it	will have	appreciated
we	will have	appreciated
you	will have	appreciated
they	will have	appreciated

Imperative

appreciate

Impersonal

ing-Form

appreciating

Past Participle

appreciated

Continuous tenses

Present

I	am	appreciating
you	are	appreciating
he/she/it	is	appreciating
we	are	appreciating
you	are	appreciating
they	are	appreciating

Past

I	was	appreciating
you	were	appreciating
he/she/it	was	appreciating
we	were	appreciating
you	were	appreciating
they	were	appreciating

Present Perfect

I	have been	appreciating
you	have been	appreciating
he/she/it	has been	appreciating
we	have been	appreciating
you	have been	appreciating
they	have been	appreciating

Past Perfect

I	had been	appreciating
you	had been	appreciating
he/she/it	had been	appreciating
we	had been	appreciating
you	had been	appreciating
they	had been	appreciating

Will-Future

I	will be appreciating
you	will be appreciating
he/she/it	will be appreciating
we	will be appreciating
you	will be appreciating
they	will be appreciating

Going to-Future

I	am	going to be	appreciating
you	are	going to be	appreciating
he/she/it	is	going to be	appreciating
we	are	going to be	appreciating
you	are	going to be	appreciating
they	are	going to be	appreciating

Future Perfect

I	will have been appreciating
you	will have been appreciating
he/she/it	will have been appreciating
we	will have been appreciating
you	will have been appreciating
they	will have been appreciating

Conditional

I	would	appreciate
you	would	appreciate
he/she/it	would	appreciate
we	would	appreciate
you	would	appreciate
they	would	appreciate

Conditional Past

I	would have	appreciated
you	would have	appreciated
he/she/it	would have	appreciated
we	would have	appreciated
you	would have	appreciated
they	would have	appreciated

approach

sich nähern

+ **-es** in 3. Person Singular
Regelmäßiges Verb

Simple tenses

Present

I	approach
you	approach
he/she/it	approaches
we	approach
you	approach
they	approach

Past

I	approached
you	approached
he/she/it	approached
we	approached
you	approached
they	approached

Present Perfect

I	have	approached
you	have	approached
he/she/it	has	approached
we	have	approached
you	have	approached
they	have	approached

Past Perfect

I	had	approached
you	had	approached
he/she/it	had	approached
we	had	approached
you	had	approached
they	had	approached

Will-Future

I	will	approach
you	will	approach
he/she/it	will	approach
we	will	approach
you	will	approach
they	will	approach

Going to-Future

I	am	going to	approach
you	are	going to	approach
he/she/it	is	going to	approach
we	are	going to	approach
you	are	going to	approach
they	are	going to	approach

Future Perfect

I	will have	approached
you	will have	approached
he/she/it	will have	approached
we	will have	approached
you	will have	approached
they	will have	approached

Imperative

approach

Impersonal

ing-Form

approaching

Past Participle

approached

Continuous tenses

Present

I	am	approaching
you	are	approaching
he/she/it	is	approaching
we	are	approaching
you	are	approaching
they	are	approaching

Past

I	was	approaching
you	were	approaching
he/she/it	was	approaching
we	were	approaching
you	were	approaching
they	were	approaching

Present Perfect

I	have been	approaching
you	have been	approaching
he/she/it	has been	approaching
we	have been	approaching
you	have been	approaching
they	have been	approaching

Past Perfect

I	had been	approaching
you	had been	approaching
he/she/it	had been	approaching
we	had been	approaching
you	had been	approaching
they	had been	approaching

Will-Future

I	will be	approaching
you	will be	approaching
he/she/it	will be	approaching
we	will be	approaching
you	will be	approaching
they	will be	approaching

Going to-Future

I	am	going to be	approaching
you	are	going to be	approaching
he/she/it	is	going to be	approaching
we	are	going to be	approaching
you	are	going to be	approaching
they	are	going to be	approaching

Future Perfect

I	will have been approaching
you	will have been approaching
he/she/it	will have been approaching
we	will have been approaching
you	will have been approaching
they	will have been approaching

Conditional

I	would	approach
you	would	approach
he/she/it	would	approach
we	would	approach
you	would	approach
they	would	approach

Conditional Past

I	would have	approached
you	would have	approached
he/she/it	would have	approached
we	would have	approached
you	would have	approached
they	would have	approached

+ **-ing** → ~~e~~ / + **-d** nicht **-ed**
Regelmäßiges Verb

ankommen

arrive

Simple tenses

Present

I	arrive
you	arrive
he/she/it	arrives
we	arrive
you	arrive
they	arrive

Past

I	arrived
you	arrived
he/she/it	arrived
we	arrived
you	arrived
they	arrived

Present Perfect

I	have	arrived
you	have	arrived
he/she/it	has	arrived
we	have	arrived
you	have	arrived
they	have	arrived

Past Perfect

I	had	arrived
you	had	arrived
he/she/it	had	arrived
we	had	arrived
you	had	arrived
they	had	arrived

Will-Future

I	will	arrive
you	will	arrive
he/she/it	will	arrive
we	will	arrive
you	will	arrive
they	will	arrive

Going to-Future

I	am	going to	arrive
you	are	going to	arrive
he/she/it	is	going to	arrive
we	are	going to	arrive
you	are	going to	arrive
they	are	going to	arrive

Future Perfect

I	will have	arrived
you	will have	arrived
he/she/it	will have	arrived
we	will have	arrived
you	will have	arrived
they	will have	arrived

Imperative

arrive

Impersonal

ing-Form

arriving

Past Participle

arrived

Continuous tenses

Present

I	am	arriving
you	are	arriving
he/she/it	is	arriving
we	are	arriving
you	are	arriving
they	are	arriving

Past

I	was	arriving
you	were	arriving
he/she/it	was	arriving
we	were	arriving
you	were	arriving
they	were	arriving

Present Perfect

I	have been	arriving
you	have been	arriving
he/she/it	has been	arriving
we	have been	arriving
you	have been	arriving
they	have been	arriving

Past Perfect

I	had been	arriving
you	had been	arriving
he/she/it	had been	arriving
we	had been	arriving
you	had been	arriving
they	had been	arriving

Will-Future

I	will be	arriving
you	will be	arriving
he/she/it	will be	arriving
we	will be	arriving
you	will be	arriving
they	will be	arriving

Going to-Future

I	am	going to be	arriving
you	are	going to be	arriving
he/she/it	is	going to be	arriving
we	are	going to be	arriving
you	are	going to be	arriving
they	are	going to be	arriving

Future Perfect

I	will have been	arriving
you	will have been	arriving
he/she/it	will have been	arriving
we	will have been	arriving
you	will have been	arriving
they	will have been	arriving

Conditional

I	would	arrive
you	would	arrive
he/she/it	would	arrive
we	would	arrive
you	would	arrive
they	would	arrive

Conditional Past

I	would have	arrived
you	would have	arrived
he/she/it	would have	arrived
we	would have	arrived
you	would have	arrived
they	would have	arrived

ask

fragen

Regelmäßiges Verb

Simple tenses

Present

I	ask
you	ask
he/she/it	asks
we	ask
you	ask
they	ask

Past

I	asked
you	asked
he/she/it	asked
we	asked
you	asked
they	asked

Present Perfect

I	have	asked
you	have	asked
he/she/it	has	asked
we	have	asked
you	have	asked
they	have	asked

Past Perfect

I	had	asked
you	had	asked
he/she/it	had	asked
we	had	asked
you	had	asked
they	had	asked

Will-Future

I	will	ask
you	will	ask
he/she/it	will	ask
we	will	ask
you	will	ask
they	will	ask

Going to-Future

I	am	going to	ask
you	are	going to	ask
he/she/it	is	going to	ask
we	are	going to	ask
you	are	going to	ask
they	are	going to	ask

Future Perfect

I	will have	asked
you	will have	asked
he/she/it	will have	asked
we	will have	asked
you	will have	asked
they	will have	asked

Imperative

ask

Impersonal

ing-Form

asking

Past Participle

asked

Continuous tenses

Present

I	am	asking
you	are	asking
he/she/it	is	asking
we	are	asking
you	are	asking
they	are	asking

Past

I	was	asking
you	were	asking
he/she/it	was	asking
we	were	asking
you	were	asking
they	were	asking

Present Perfect

I	have	been	asking
you	have	been	asking
he/she/it	has	been	asking
we	have	been	asking
you	have	been	asking
they	have	been	asking

Past Perfect

I	had been	asking
you	had been	asking
he/she/it	had been	asking
we	had been	asking
you	had been	asking
they	had been	asking

Will-Future

I	will be	asking
you	will be	asking
he/she/it	will be	asking
we	will be	asking
you	will be	asking
they	will be	asking

Going to-Future

I	am	going to be	asking
you	are	going to be	asking
he/she/it	is	going to be	asking
we	are	going to be	asking
you	are	going to be	asking
they	are	going to be	asking

Future Perfect

I	will have been	asking
you	will have been	asking
he/she/it	will have been	asking
we	will have been	asking
you	will have been	asking
they	will have been	asking

Conditional

I	would	ask
you	would	ask
he/she/it	would	ask
we	would	ask
you	would	ask
they	would	ask

Conditional Past

I	would have	asked
you	would have	asked
he/she/it	would have	asked
we	would have	asked
you	would have	asked
they	would have	asked

assist

helfen

Regelmäßiges Verb

Simple tenses

Present

I	assist
you	assist
he/she/it	assists
we	assist
you	assist
they	assist

Past

I	assisted
you	assisted
he/she/it	assisted
we	assisted
you	assisted
they	assisted

Present Perfect

I	have	assisted
you	have	assisted
he/she/it	has	assisted
we	have	assisted
you	have	assisted
they	have	assisted

Past Perfect

I	had	assisted
you	had	assisted
he/she/it	had	assisted
we	had	assisted
you	had	assisted
they	had	assisted

Will-Future

I	will	assist
you	will	assist
he/she/it	will	assist
we	will	assist
you	will	assist
they	will	assist

Going to-Future

I	am	going to	assist
you	are	going to	assist
he/she/it	is	going to	assist
we	are	going to	assist
you	are	going to	assist
they	are	going to	assist

Future Perfect

I	will have	assisted
you	will have	assisted
he/she/it	will have	assisted
we	will have	assisted
you	will have	assisted
they	will have	assisted

Imperative

assist

Impersonal

ing-Form

assisting

Past Participle

assisted

Continuous tenses

Present

I	am	assisting
you	are	assisting
he/she/it	is	assisting
we	are	assisting
you	are	assisting
they	are	assisting

Past

I	was	assisting
you	were	assisting
he/she/it	was	assisting
we	were	assisting
you	were	assisting
they	were	assisting

Present Perfect

I	have been	assisting
you	have been	assisting
he/she/it	has been	assisting
we	have been	assisting
you	have been	assisting
they	have been	assisting

Past Perfect

I	had been	assisting
you	had been	assisting
he/she/it	had been	assisting
we	had been	assisting
you	had been	assisting
they	had been	assisting

Will-Future

I	will be	assisting
you	will be	assisting
he/she/it	will be	assisting
we	will be	assisting
you	will be	assisting
they	will be	assisting

Going to-Future

I	am	going to be	assisting
you	are	going to be	assisting
he/she/it	is	going to be	assisting
we	are	going to be	assisting
you	are	going to be	assisting
they	are	going to be	assisting

Future Perfect

I	will have been	assisting
you	will have been	assisting
he/she/it	will have been	assisting
we	will have been	assisting
you	will have been	assisting
they	will have been	assisting

Conditional

I	would	assist
you	would	assist
he/she/it	would	assist
we	would	assist
you	would	assist
they	would	assist

Conditional Past

I	would have	assisted
you	would have	assisted
he/she/it	would have	assisted
we	would have	assisted
you	would have	assisted
they	would have	assisted

assume

annehmen

\+ **-ing** → ~~e~~ / + **-d** nicht **-ed**
Regelmäßiges Verb

Simple tenses

Present

I	assume
you	assume
he/she/it	assumes
we	assume
you	assume
they	assume

Past

I	assumed
you	assumed
he/she/it	assumed
we	assumed
you	assumed
they	assumed

Present Perfect

I	have	assumed
you	have	assumed
he/she/it	has	assumed
we	have	assumed
you	have	assumed
they	have	assumed

Past Perfect

I	had	assumed
you	had	assumed
he/she/it	had	assumed
we	had	assumed
you	had	assumed
they	had	assumed

Will-Future

I	will	assume
you	will	assume
he/she/it	will	assume
we	will	assume
you	will	assume
they	will	assume

Going to-Future

I	am	going to	assume
you	are	going to	assume
he/she/it	is	going to	assume
we	are	going to	assume
you	are	going to	assume
they	are	going to	assume

Future Perfect

I	will have	assumed
you	will have	assumed
he/she/it	will have	assumed
we	will have	assumed
you	will have	assumed
they	will have	assumed

Imperative

assume

Impersonal

ing-Form

assuming

Past Participle

assumed

Continuous tenses

Present

I	am	assuming
you	are	assuming
he/she/it	is	assuming
we	are	assuming
you	are	assuming
they	are	assuming

Past

I	was	assuming
you	were	assuming
he/she/it	was	assuming
we	were	assuming
you	were	assuming
they	were	assuming

Present Perfect

I	have been	assuming
you	have been	assuming
he/she/it	has been	assuming
we	have been	assuming
you	have been	assuming
they	have been	assuming

Past Perfect

I	had been	assuming
you	had been	assuming
he/she/it	had been	assuming
we	had been	assuming
you	had been	assuming
they	had been	assuming

Will-Future

I	will be	assuming
you	will be	assuming
he/she/it	will be	assuming
we	will be	assuming
you	will be	assuming
they	will be	assuming

Going to-Future

I	am	going to be	assuming
you	are	going to be	assuming
he/she/it	is	going to be	assuming
we	are	going to be	assuming
you	are	going to be	assuming
they	are	going to be	assuming

Future Perfect

I	will have been	assuming
you	will have been	assuming
he/she/it	will have been	assuming
we	will have been	assuming
you	will have been	assuming
they	will have been	assuming

Conditional

I	would	assume
you	would	assume
he/she/it	would	assume
we	would	assume
you	would	assume
they	would	assume

Conditional Past

I	would have	assumed
you	would have	assumed
he/she/it	would have	assumed
we	would have	assumed
you	would have	assumed
they	would have	assumed

attack

Regelmäßiges Verb

Simple tenses

Present

I	attack
you	attack
he/she/it	attacks
we	attack
you	attack
they	attack

Past

I	attacked
you	attacked
he/she/it	attacked
we	attacked
you	attacked
they	attacked

Present Perfect

I	have	attacked
you	have	attacked
he/she/it	has	attacked
we	have	attacked
you	have	attacked
they	have	attacked

Past Perfect

I	had	attacked
you	had	attacked
he/she/it	had	attacked
we	had	attacked
you	had	attacked
they	had	attacked

Will-Future

I	will	attack
you	will	attack
he/she/it	will	attack
we	will	attack
you	will	attack
they	will	attack

Going to-Future

I	am	going to	attack
you	are	going to	attack
he/she/it	is	going to	attack
we	are	going to	attack
you	are	going to	attack
they	are	going to	attack

Future Perfect

I	will have	attacked
you	will have	attacked
he/she/it	will have	attacked
we	will have	attacked
you	will have	attacked
they	will have	attacked

Imperative

attack

Impersonal

ing-Form

attacking

Past Participle

attacked

Continuous tenses

Present

I	am	attacking
you	are	attacking
he/she/it	is	attacking
we	are	attacking
you	are	attacking
they	are	attacking

Past

I	was	attacking
you	were	attacking
he/she/it	was	attacking
we	were	attacking
you	were	attacking
they	were	attacking

Present Perfect

I	have been	attacking
you	have been	attacking
he/she/it	has been	attacking
we	have been	attacking
you	have been	attacking
they	have been	attacking

Past Perfect

I	had been	attacking
you	had been	attacking
he/she/it	had been	attacking
we	had been	attacking
you	had been	attacking
they	had been	attacking

Will-Future

I	will be	attacking
you	will be	attacking
he/she/it	will be	attacking
we	will be	attacking
you	will be	attacking
they	will be	attacking

Going to-Future

I	am	going to be	attacking
you	are	going to be	attacking
he/she/it	is	going to be	attacking
we	are	going to be	attacking
you	are	going to be	attacking
they	are	going to be	attacking

Future Perfect

I	will have been	attacking
you	will have been	attacking
he/she/it	will have been	attacking
we	will have been	attacking
you	will have been	attacking
they	will have been	attacking

Conditional

I	would	attack
you	would	attack
he/she/it	would	attack
we	would	attack
you	would	attack
they	would	attack

Conditional Past

I	would have	attacked
you	would have	attacked
he/she/it	would have	attacked
we	would have	attacked
you	would have	attacked
they	would have	attacked

attempt

versuchen

Regelmäßiges Verb

Simple tenses

Present

I	attempt
you	attempt
he/she/it	attempts
we	attempt
you	attempt
they	attempt

Past

I	attempted
you	attempted
he/she/it	attempted
we	attempted
you	attempted
they	attempted

Present Perfect

I	have	attempted
you	have	attempted
he/she/it	has	attempted
we	have	attempted
you	have	attempted
they	have	attempted

Past Perfect

I	had	attempted
you	had	attempted
he/she/it	had	attempted
we	had	attempted
you	had	attempted
they	had	attempted

Will-Future

I	will	attempt
you	will	attempt
he/she/it	will	attempt
we	will	attempt
you	will	attempt
they	will	attempt

Going to-Future

I	am	going to	attempt
you	are	going to	attempt
he/she/it	is	going to	attempt
we	are	going to	attempt
you	are	going to	attempt
they	are	going to	attempt

Future Perfect

I	will have	attempted
you	will have	attempted
he/she/it	will have	attempted
we	will have	attempted
you	will have	attempted
they	will have	attempted

Imperative

attempt

Impersonal

ing-Form

attempting

Past Participle

attempted

Continuous tenses

Present

I	am	attempting
you	are	attempting
he/she/it	is	attempting
we	are	attempting
you	are	attempting
they	are	attempting

Past

I	was	attempting
you	were	attempting
he/she/it	was	attempting
we	were	attempting
you	were	attempting
they	were	attempting

Present Perfect

I	have been	attempting
you	have been	attempting
he/she/it	has been	attempting
we	have been	attempting
you	have been	attempting
they	have been	attempting

Past Perfect

I	had been	attempting
you	had been	attempting
he/she/it	had been	attempting
we	had been	attempting
you	had been	attempting
they	had been	attempting

Will-Future

I	will be	attempting
you	will be	attempting
he/she/it	will be	attempting
we	will be	attempting
you	will be	attempting
they	will be	attempting

Going to-Future

I	am	going to be	attempting
you	are	going to be	attempting
he/she/it	is	going to be	attempting
we	are	going to be	attempting
you	are	going to be	attempting
they	are	going to be	attempting

Future Perfect

I	will have been attempting
you	will have been attempting
he/she/it	will have been attempting
we	will have been attempting
you	will have been attempting
they	will have been attempting

Conditional

I	would	attempt
you	would	attempt
he/she/it	would	attempt
we	would	attempt
you	would	attempt
they	would	attempt

Conditional Past

I	would have	attempted
you	would have	attempted
he/she/it	would have	attempted
we	would have	attempted
you	would have	attempted
they	would have	attempted

Simple tenses

Present

I	attract
you	attract
he/she/it	attracts
we	attract
you	attract
they	attract

Past

I	attracted
you	attracted
he/she/it	attracted
we	attracted
you	attracted
they	attracted

Present Perfect

I	have	attracted
you	have	attracted
he/she/it	has	attracted
we	have	attracted
you	have	attracted
they	have	attracted

Past Perfect

I	had	attracted
you	had	attracted
he/she/it	had	attracted
we	had	attracted
you	had	attracted
they	had	attracted

Will-Future

I	will	attract
you	will	attract
he/she/it	will	attract
we	will	attract
you	will	attract
they	will	attract

Going to-Future

I	am	going to	attract
you	are	going to	attract
he/she/it	is	going to	attract
we	are	going to	attract
you	are	going to	attract
they	are	going to	attract

Future Perfect

I	will have	attracted
you	will have	attracted
he/she/it	will have	attracted
we	will have	attracted
you	will have	attracted
they	will have	attracted

Imperative

attract

Impersonal

ing-Form

attracting

Past Participle

attracted

Continuous tenses

Present

I	am	attracting
you	are	attracting
he/she/it	is	attracting
we	are	attracting
you	are	attracting
they	are	attracting

Past

I	was	attracting
you	were	attracting
he/she/it	was	attracting
we	were	attracting
you	were	attracting
they	were	attracting

Present Perfect

I	have been	attracting
you	have been	attracting
he/she/it	has been	attracting
we	have been	attracting
you	have been	attracting
they	have been	attracting

Past Perfect

I	had been	attracting
you	had been	attracting
he/she/it	had been	attracting
we	had been	attracting
you	had been	attracting
they	had been	attracting

Will-Future

I	will be	attracting
you	will be	attracting
he/she/it	will be	attracting
we	will be	attracting
you	will be	attracting
they	will be	attracting

Going to-Future

I	am	going to be	attracting
you	are	going to be	attracting
he/she/it	is	going to be	attracting
we	are	going to be	attracting
you	are	going to be	attracting
they	are	going to be	attracting

Future Perfect

I	will have been	attracting
you	will have been	attracting
he/she/it	will have been	attracting
we	will have been	attracting
you	will have been	attracting
they	will have been	attracting

Conditional

I	would	attract
you	would	attract
he/she/it	would	attract
we	would	attract
you	would	attract
they	would	attract

Conditional Past

I	would have	attracted
you	would have	attracted
he/she/it	would have	attracted
we	would have	attracted
you	would have	attracted
they	would have	attracted

avoid

verhindern

Regelmäßiges Verb

Simple tenses

Present

I	avoid
you	avoid
he/she/it	avoids
we	avoid
you	avoid
they	avoid

Past

I	avoided
you	avoided
he/she/it	avoided
we	avoided
you	avoided
they	avoided

Present Perfect

I	have	avoided
you	have	avoided
he/she/it	has	avoided
we	have	avoided
you	have	avoided
they	have	avoided

Past Perfect

I	had	avoided
you	had	avoided
he/she/it	had	avoided
we	had	avoided
you	had	avoided
they	had	avoided

Will-Future

I	will	avoid
you	will	avoid
he/she/it	will	avoid
we	will	avoid
you	will	avoid
they	will	avoid

Going to-Future

I	am	going to	avoid
you	are	going to	avoid
he/she/it	is	going to	avoid
we	are	going to	avoid
you	are	going to	avoid
they	are	going to	avoid

Future Perfect

I	will have	avoided
you	will have	avoided
he/she/it	will have	avoided
we	will have	avoided
you	will have	avoided
they	will have	avoided

Imperative

avoid

Impersonal

ing-Form

avoiding

Past Participle

avoided

Continuous tenses

Present

I	am	avoiding
you	are	avoiding
he/she/it	is	avoiding
we	are	avoiding
you	are	avoiding
they	are	avoiding

Past

I	was	avoiding
you	were	avoiding
he/she/it	was	avoiding
we	were	avoiding
you	were	avoiding
they	were	avoiding

Present Perfect

I	have been	avoiding
you	have been	avoiding
he/she/it	has been	avoiding
we	have been	avoiding
you	have been	avoiding
they	have been	avoiding

Past Perfect

I	had been	avoiding
you	had been	avoiding
he/she/it	had been	avoiding
we	had been	avoiding
you	had been	avoiding
they	had been	avoiding

Will-Future

I	will be	avoiding
you	will be	avoiding
he/she/it	will be	avoiding
we	will be	avoiding
you	will be	avoiding
they	will be	avoiding

Going to-Future

I	am	going to be	avoiding
you	are	going to be	avoiding
he/she/it	is	going to be	avoiding
we	are	going to be	avoiding
you	are	going to be	avoiding
they	are	going to be	avoiding

Future Perfect

I	will have been	avoiding
you	will have been	avoiding
he/she/it	will have been	avoiding
we	will have been	avoiding
you	will have been	avoiding
they	will have been	avoiding

Conditional

I	would	avoid
you	would	avoid
he/she/it	would	avoid
we	would	avoid
you	would	avoid
they	would	avoid

Conditional Past

I	would have	avoided
you	would have	avoided
he/she/it	would have	avoided
we	would have	avoided
you	would have	avoided
they	would have	avoided

+ -ing → ~~e~~ / + -d nicht -ed
Regelmäßiges Verb

backen

bake

Simple tenses

Present

I	bake
you	bake
he/she/it	bakes
we	bake
you	bake
they	bake

Past

I	baked
you	baked
he/she/it	baked
we	baked
you	baked
they	baked

Present Perfect

I	have	baked
you	have	baked
he/she/it	has	baked
we	have	baked
you	have	baked
they	have	baked

Past Perfect

I	had	baked
you	had	baked
he/she/it	had	baked
we	had	baked
you	had	baked
they	had	baked

Will-Future

I	will	bake
you	will	bake
he/she/it	will	bake
we	will	bake
you	will	bake
they	will	bake

Going to-Future

I	am	going to	bake
you	are	going to	bake
he/she/it	is	going to	bake
we	are	going to	bake
you	are	going to	bake
they	are	going to	bake

Future Perfect

I	will have	baked
you	will have	baked
he/she/it	will have	baked
we	will have	baked
you	will have	baked
they	will have	baked

Imperative

bake

Impersonal

ing-Form

baking

Past Participle

baked

Continuous tenses

Present

I	am	baking
you	are	baking
he/she/it	is	baking
we	are	baking
you	are	baking
they	are	baking

Past

I	was	baking
you	were	baking
he/she/it	was	baking
we	were	baking
you	were	baking
they	were	baking

Present Perfect

I	have been	baking
you	have been	baking
he/she/it	has been	baking
we	have been	baking
you	have been	baking
they	have been	baking

Past Perfect

I	had been	baking
you	had been	baking
he/she/it	had been	baking
we	had been	baking
you	had been	baking
they	had been	baking

Will-Future

I	will be	baking
you	will be	baking
he/she/it	will be	baking
we	will be	baking
you	will be	baking
they	will be	baking

Going to-Future

I	am	going to be	baking
you	are	going to be	baking
he/she/it	is	going to be	baking
we	are	going to be	baking
you	are	going to be	baking
they	are	going to be	baking

Future Perfect

I	will have been	baking
you	will have been	baking
he/she/it	will have been	baking
we	will have been	baking
you	will have been	baking
they	will have been	baking

Conditional

I	would	bake
you	would	bake
he/she/it	would	bake
we	would	bake
you	would	bake
they	would	bake

Conditional Past

I	would have	baked
you	would have	baked
he/she/it	would have	baked
we	would have	baked
you	would have	baked
they	would have	baked

be

- was/were - been

sein

Die Verlaufsformen von *be* werden für die Bildung des Passivs verwendet. Unregelmäßiges Verb, Voll- und Hifsverb

Simple tenses

Present

I	am
you	are
he/she/it	is
we	are
you	are
they	are

Past

I	was
you	were
he/she/it	was
we	were
you	were
they	were

Present Perfect

I	have	been
you	have	been
he/she/it	has	been
we	have	been
you	have	been
they	have	been

Past Perfect

I	had	been
you	had	been
he/she/it	had	been
we	had	been
you	had	been
they	had	been

Will-Future

I	will	be
you	will	be
he/she/it	will	be
we	will	be
you	will	be
they	will	be

Going to-Future

I	am	going to	be
you	are	going to	be
he/she/it	is	going to	be
we	are	going to	be
you	are	going to	be
they	are	going to	be

Future Perfect

I	will have	been
you	will have	been
he/she/it	will have	been
we	will have	been
you	will have	been
they	will have	been

Imperative

be

Impersonal

ing-Form

being

Past Participle

been

Continuous tenses

Present

I	am	being
you	are	being
he/she/it	is	being
we	are	being
you	are	being
they	are	being

Past

I	was	being
you	were	being
he/she/it	was	being
we	were	being
you	were	being
they	were	being

Present Perfect

I	have been	being
you	have been	being
he/she/it	has been	being
we	have been	being
you	have been	being
they	have been	being

Past Perfect

I	had been	being
you	had been	being
he/she/it	had been	being
we	had been	being
you	had been	being
they	had been	being

Will-Future

I	will be	being
you	will be	being
he/she/it	will be	being
we	will be	being
you	will be	being
they	will be	being

Going to-Future

I	am	going to be	being
you	are	going to be	being
he/she/it	is	going to be	being
we	are	going to be	being
you	are	going to be	being
they	are	going to be	being

Future Perfect

I	will have been	being
you	will have been	being
he/she/it	will have been	being
we	will have been	being
you	will have been	being
they	will have been	being

Conditional

I	would	be
you	would	be
he/she/it	would	be
we	would	be
you	would	be
they	would	be

Conditional Past

I	would have	been
you	would have	been
he/she/it	would have	been
we	would have	been
you	would have	been
they	would have	been

Simple tenses

Present

I	become
you	become
he/she/it	becomes
we	become
you	become
they	become

Past

I	became
you	became
he/she/it	became
we	became
you	became
they	became

Present Perfect

I	have	become
you	have	become
he/she/it	has	become
we	have	become
you	have	become
they	have	become

Past Perfect

I	had	become
you	had	become
he/she/it	had	become
we	had	become
you	had	become
they	had	become

***Will*-Future**

I	will	become
you	will	become
he/she/it	will	become
we	will	become
you	will	become
they	will	become

***Going to*-Future**

I	am	going to	become
you	are	going to	become
he/she/it	is	going to	become
we	are	going to	become
you	are	going to	become
they	are	going to	become

Future Perfect

I	will have	become
you	will have	become
he/she/it	will have	become
we	will have	become
you	will have	become
they	will have	become

Imperative

become

Impersonal

***ing*-Form**

becoming

Past Participle

become

Continuous tenses

Present

I	am	becoming
you	are	becoming
he/she/it	is	becoming
we	are	becoming
you	are	becoming
they	are	becoming

Past

I	was	becoming
you	were	becoming
he/she/it	was	becoming
we	were	becoming
you	were	becoming
they	were	becoming

Present Perfect

I	have been	becoming
you	have been	becoming
he/she/it	has been	becoming
we	have been	becoming
you	have been	becoming
they	have been	becoming

Past Perfect

I	had been	becoming
you	had been	becoming
he/she/it	had been	becoming
we	had been	becoming
you	had been	becoming
they	had been	becoming

***Will*-Future**

I	will be	becoming
you	will be	becoming
he/she/it	will be	becoming
we	will be	becoming
you	will be	becoming
they	will be	becoming

***Going to*-Future**

I	am	going to be	becoming
you	are	going to be	becoming
he/she/it	is	going to be	becoming
we	are	going to be	becoming
you	are	going to be	becoming
they	are	going to be	becoming

Future Perfect

I	will have been becoming
you	will have been becoming
he/she/it	will have been becoming
we	will have been becoming
you	will have been becoming
they	will have been becoming

Conditional

I	would	become
you	would	become
he/she/it	would	become
we	would	become
you	would	become
they	would	become

Conditional Past

I	would have	become
you	would have	become
he/she/it	would have	become
we	would have	become
you	would have	become
they	would have	become

begin
- began - begun

beginnen

Konsonantenverdopplung
Unregelmäßiges Verb

Simple tenses

Present

I	begin
you	begin
he/she/it	begins
we	begin
you	begin
they	begin

Past

I	began
you	began
he/she/it	began
we	began
you	began
they	began

Present Perfect

I	have	begun
you	have	begun
he/she/it	has	begun
we	have	begun
you	have	begun
they	have	begun

Past Perfect

I	had	begun
you	had	begun
he/she/it	had	begun
we	had	begun
you	had	begun
they	had	begun

Will-Future

I	will	begin
you	will	begin
he/she/it	will	begin
we	will	begin
you	will	begin
they	will	begin

Going to-Future

I	am	going to	begin
you	are	going to	begin
he/she/it	is	going to	begin
we	are	going to	begin
you	are	going to	begin
they	are	going to	begin

Future Perfect

I	will have	begun
you	will have	begun
he/she/it	will have	begun
we	will have	begun
you	will have	begun
they	will have	begun

Imperative

begin

Impersonal

ing-Form

beginning

Past Participle

begun

Continuous tenses

Present

I	am	beginning
you	are	beginning
he/she/it	is	beginning
we	are	beginning
you	are	beginning
they	are	beginning

Past

I	was	beginning
you	were	beginning
he/she/it	was	beginning
we	were	beginning
you	were	beginning
they	were	beginning

Present Perfect

I	have been	beginning
you	have been	beginning
he/she/it	has been	beginning
we	have been	beginning
you	have been	beginning
they	have been	beginning

Past Perfect

I	had been	beginning
you	had been	beginning
he/she/it	had been	beginning
we	had been	beginning
you	had been	beginning
they	had been	beginning

Will-Future

I	will be	beginning
you	will be	beginning
he/she/it	will be	beginning
we	will be	beginning
you	will be	beginning
they	will be	beginning

Going to-Future

I	am	going to be	beginning
you	are	going to be	beginning
he/she/it	is	going to be	beginning
we	are	going to be	beginning
you	are	going to be	beginning
they	are	going to be	beginning

Future Perfect

I	will have been	beginning
you	will have been	beginning
he/she/it	will have been	beginning
we	will have been	beginning
you	will have been	beginning
they	will have been	beginning

Conditional

I	would	begin
you	would	begin
he/she/it	would	begin
we	would	begin
you	would	begin
they	would	begin

Conditional Past

I	would have	begun
you	would have	begun
he/she/it	would have	begun
we	would have	begun
you	would have	begun
they	would have	begun

+ **-ing** → ~~e~~ / + **-d** nicht **-ed**
Regelmäßiges Verb

sich verhalten

behave

Simple tenses

Present

I	behave
you	behave
he/she/it	behaves
we	behave
you	behave
they	behave

Past

I	behaved
you	behaved
he/she/it	behaved
we	behaved
you	behaved
they	behaved

Present Perfect

I	have	behaved
you	have	behaved
he/she/it	has	behaved
we	have	behaved
you	have	behaved
they	have	behaved

Past Perfect

I	had	behaved
you	had	behaved
he/she/it	had	behaved
we	had	behaved
you	had	behaved
they	had	behaved

Will-Future

I	will	behave
you	will	behave
he/she/it	will	behave
we	will	behave
you	will	behave
they	will	behave

Going to-Future

I	am	going to	behave
you	are	going to	behave
he/she/it	is	going to	behave
we	are	going to	behave
you	are	going to	behave
they	are	going to	behave

Future Perfect

I	will have	behaved
you	will have	behaved
he/she/it	will have	behaved
we	will have	behaved
you	will have	behaved
they	will have	behaved

Imperative

behave

Impersonal

ing-Form

behaving

Past Participle

behaved

Continuous tenses

Present

I	am	behaving
you	are	behaving
he/she/it	is	behaving
we	are	behaving
you	are	behaving
they	are	behaving

Past

I	was	behaving
you	were	behaving
he/she/it	was	behaving
we	were	behaving
you	were	behaving
they	were	behaving

Present Perfect

I	have been	behaving
you	have been	behaving
he/she/it	has been	behaving
we	have been	behaving
you	have been	behaving
they	have been	behaving

Past Perfect

I	had been	behaving
you	had been	behaving
he/she/it	had been	behaving
we	had been	behaving
you	had been	behaving
they	had been	behaving

Will-Future

I	will be	behaving
you	will be	behaving
he/she/it	will be	behaving
we	will be	behaving
you	will be	behaving
they	will be	behaving

Going to-Future

I	am	going to be	behaving
you	are	going to be	behaving
he/she/it	is	going to be	behaving
we	are	going to be	behaving
you	are	going to be	behaving
they	are	going to be	behaving

Future Perfect

I	will have been	behaving
you	will have been	behaving
he/she/it	will have been	behaving
we	will have been	behaving
you	will have been	behaving
they	will have been	behaving

Conditional

I	would	behave
you	would	behave
he/she/it	would	behave
we	would	behave
you	would	behave
they	would	behave

Conditional Past

I	would have	behaved
you	would have	behaved
he/she/it	would have	behaved
we	would have	behaved
you	would have	behaved
they	would have	behaved

believe

glauben

+ **-ing** → ~~**e**~~ / + **-d** nicht **-ed**
Regelmäßiges Verb

Simple tenses

Present

I	believe
you	believe
he/she/it	believes
we	believe
you	believe
they	believe

Past

I	believed
you	believed
he/she/it	believed
we	believed
you	believed
they	believed

Present Perfect

I	have	believed
you	have	believed
he/she/it	has	believed
we	have	believed
you	have	believed
they	have	believed

Past Perfect

I	had	believed
you	had	believed
he/she/it	had	believed
we	had	believed
you	had	believed
they	had	believed

Will-Future

I	will	believe
you	will	believe
he/she/it	will	believe
we	will	believe
you	will	believe
they	will	believe

Going to-Future

I	am	going to	believe
you	are	going to	believe
he/she/it	is	going to	believe
we	are	going to	believe
you	are	going to	believe
they	are	going to	believe

Future Perfect

I	will have	believed
you	will have	believed
he/she/it	will have	believed
we	will have	believed
you	will have	believed
they	will have	believed

Imperative

believe

Impersonal

ing-Form

believing

Past Participle

believed

Continuous tenses

Present

I	am	believing
you	are	believing
he/she/it	is	believing
we	are	believing
you	are	believing
they	are	believing

Past

I	was	believing
you	were	believing
he/she/it	was	believing
we	were	believing
you	were	believing
they	were	believing

Present Perfect

I	have	been	believing
you	have	been	believing
he/she/it	has	been	believing
we	have	been	believing
you	have	been	believing
they	have	been	believing

Past Perfect

I	had been	believing
you	had been	believing
he/she/it	had been	believing
we	had been	believing
you	had been	believing
they	had been	believing

Will-Future

I	will be	believing
you	will be	believing
he/she/it	will be	believing
we	will be	believing
you	will be	believing
they	will be	believing

Going to-Future

I	am	going to be	believing
you	are	going to be	believing
he/she/it	is	going to be	believing
we	are	going to be	believing
you	are	going to be	believing
they	are	going to be	believing

Future Perfect

I	will have been	believing
you	will have been	believing
he/she/it	will have been	believing
we	will have been	believing
you	will have been	believing
they	will have been	believing

Conditional

I	would	believe
you	would	believe
he/she/it	would	believe
we	would	believe
you	would	believe
they	would	believe

Conditional Past

I	would have	believed
you	would have	believed
he/she/it	would have	believed
we	would have	believed
you	would have	believed
they	would have	believed

Unregelmäßiges Verb

(ver)biegen

bend

- bent - bent

Simple tenses

Present

I	bend
you	bend
he/she/it	bends
we	bend
you	bend
they	bend

Past

I	bent
you	bent
he/she/it	bent
we	bent
you	bent
they	bent

Present Perfect

I	have	bent
you	have	bent
he/she/it	has	bent
we	have	bent
you	have	bent
they	have	bent

Past Perfect

I	had	bent
you	had	bent
he/she/it	had	bent
we	had	bent
you	had	bent
they	had	bent

Will-Future

I	will	bend
you	will	bend
he/she/it	will	bend
we	will	bend
you	will	bend
they	will	bend

Going to-Future

I	am	going to	bend
you	are	going to	bend
he/she/it	is	going to	bend
we	are	going to	bend
you	are	going to	bend
they	are	going to	bend

Future Perfect

I	will have	bent
you	will have	bent
he/she/it	will have	bent
we	will have	bent
you	will have	bent
they	will have	bent

Imperative

bend

Impersonal

ing-Form

bending

Past Participle

bent

Continuous tenses

Present

I	am	bending
you	are	bending
he/she/it	is	bending
we	are	bending
you	are	bending
they	are	bending

Past

I	was	bending
you	were	bending
he/she/it	was	bending
we	were	bending
you	were	bending
they	were	bending

Present Perfect

I	have been	bending
you	have been	bending
he/she/it	has been	bending
we	have been	bending
you	have been	bending
they	have been	bending

Past Perfect

I	had been	bending
you	had been	bending
he/she/it	had been	bending
we	had been	bending
you	had been	bending
they	had been	bending

Will-Future

I	will be	bending
you	will be	bending
he/she/it	will be	bending
we	will be	bending
you	will be	bending
they	will be	bending

Going to-Future

I	am	going to be	bending
you	are	going to be	bending
he/she/it	is	going to be	bending
we	are	going to be	bending
you	are	going to be	bending
they	are	going to be	bending

Future Perfect

I	will have been	bending
you	will have been	bending
he/she/it	will have been	bending
we	will have been	bending
you	will have been	bending
they	will have been	bending

Conditional

I	would	bend
you	would	bend
he/she/it	would	bend
we	would	bend
you	would	bend
they	would	bend

Conditional Past

I	would have	bent
you	would have	bent
he/she/it	would have	bent
we	would have	bent
you	would have	bent
they	would have	bent

bet

– bet/betted – bet/betted

wetten

Konsonantenverdopplung
Unregelmäßiges Verb

Simple tenses

Present

I	bet
you	bet
he/she/it	bets
we	bet
you	bet
they	bet

Past

I	bet | betted
you	bet | betted
he/she/it	bet | betted
we	bet | betted
you	bet | betted
they	bet | betted

Present Perfect

I	have	bet | betted
you	have	bet | betted
he/she/it	has	bet | betted
we	have	bet | betted
you	have	bet | betted
they	have	bet | betted

Past Perfect

I	had	bet | betted
you	had	bet | betted
he/she/it	had	bet | betted
we	had	bet | betted
you	had	bet | betted
they	had	bet | betted

Will-Future

I	will	bet
you	will	bet
he/she/it	will	bet
we	will	bet
you	will	bet
they	will	bet

Going to-Future

I	am	going to	bet
you	are	going to	bet
he/she/it	is	going to	bet
we	are	going to	bet
you	are	going to	bet
they	are	going to	bet

Future Perfect

I	will have	bet | betted
you	will have	bet | betted
he/she/it	will have	bet | betted
we	will have	bet | betted
you	will have	bet | betted
they	will have	bet | betted

Imperative

bet

Impersonal

ing-Form

betting

Past Participle

bet | betted

Continuous tenses

Present

I	am	betting
you	are	betting
he/she/it	is	betting
we	are	betting
you	are	betting
they	are	betting

Past

I	was	betting
you	were	betting
he/she/it	was	betting
we	were	betting
you	were	betting
they	were	betting

Present Perfect

I	have been	betting
you	have been	betting
he/she/it	has been	betting
we	have been	betting
you	have been	betting
they	have been	betting

Past Perfect

I	had been	betting
you	had been	betting
he/she/it	had been	betting
we	had been	betting
you	had been	betting
they	had been	betting

Will-Future

I	will be	betting
you	will be	betting
he/she/it	will be	betting
we	will be	betting
you	will be	betting
they	will be	betting

Going to-Future

I	am	going to be	betting
you	are	going to be	betting
he/she/it	is	going to be	betting
we	are	going to be	betting
you	are	going to be	betting
they	are	going to be	betting

Future Perfect

I	will have been	betting
you	will have been	betting
he/she/it	will have been	betting
we	will have been	betting
you	will have been	betting
they	will have been	betting

Conditional

I	would	bet
you	would	bet
he/she/it	would	bet
we	would	bet
you	would	bet
they	would	bet

Conditional Past

I	would have	bet | betted
you	would have	bet | betted
he/she/it	would have	bet | betted
we	would have	bet | betted
you	would have	bet | betted
they	would have	bet | betted

bieten

bid

– bid/bade – bid/bidden

Simple tenses

Present

I	bid
you	bid
he/she/it	bids
we	bid
you	bid
they	bid

Past

I	bid | bade
you	bid | bade
he/she/it	bid | bade
we	bid | bade
you	bid | bade
they	bid | bade

Present Perfect

I	have	bid | bidden
you	have	bid | bidden
he/she/it	has	bid | bidden
we	have	bid | bidden
you	have	bid | bidden
they	have	bid | bidden

Past Perfect

I	had	bid | bidden
you	had	bid | bidden
he/she/it	had	bid | bidden
we	had	bid | bidden
you	had	bid | bidden
they	had	bid | bidden

Will-Future

I	will	bid
you	will	bid
he/she/it	will	bid
we	will	bid
you	will	bid
they	will	bid

Going to-Future

I	am	going to	bid
you	are	going to	bid
he/she/it	is	going to	bid
we	are	going to	bid
you	are	going to	bid
they	are	going to	bid

Future Perfect

I	will have	bid | bidden
you	will have	bid | bidden
he/she/it	will have	bid | bidden
we	will have	bid | bidden
you	will have	bid | bidden
they	will have	bid | bidden

Imperative

bid

Impersonal

ing-Form

bidding

Past Participle

bid | bidden

Continuous tenses

Present

I	am	bidding
you	are	bidding
he/she/it	is	bidding
we	are	bidding
you	are	bidding
they	are	bidding

Past

I	was	bidding
you	were	bidding
he/she/it	was	bidding
we	were	bidding
you	were	bidding
they	were	bidding

Present Perfect

I	have	been	bidding
you	have	been	bidding
he/she/it	has	been	bidding
we	have	been	bidding
you	have	been	bidding
they	have	been	bidding

Past Perfect

I	had been	bidding
you	had been	bidding
he/she/it	had been	bidding
we	had been	bidding
you	had been	bidding
they	had been	bidding

Will-Future

I	will be	bidding
you	will be	bidding
he/she/it	will be	bidding
we	will be	bidding
you	will be	bidding
they	will be	bidding

Going to-Future

I	am	going to be	bidding
you	are	going to be	bidding
he/she/it	is	going to be	bidding
we	are	going to be	bidding
you	are	going to be	bidding
they	are	going to be	bidding

Future Perfect

I	will have been	bidding
you	will have been	bidding
he/she/it	will have been	bidding
we	will have been	bidding
you	will have been	bidding
they	will have been	bidding

Conditional

I	would	bid
you	would	bid
he/she/it	would	bid
we	would	bid
you	would	bid
they	would	bid

Conditional Past

I	would have	bid | bidden
you	would have	bid | bidden
he/she/it	would have	bid | bidden
we	would have	bid | bidden
you	would have	bid | bidden
they	would have	bid | bidden

bind

- bound - bound

binden

Unregelmäßiges Verb

Simple tenses

Present

I	bind
you	bind
he/she/it	binds
we	bind
you	bind
they	bind

Past

I	bound
you	bound
he/she/it	bound
we	bound
you	bound
they	bound

Present Perfect

I	have	bound
you	have	bound
he/she/it	has	bound
we	have	bound
you	have	bound
they	have	bound

Past Perfect

I	had	bound
you	had	bound
he/she/it	had	bound
we	had	bound
you	had	bound
they	had	bound

***Will*-Future**

I	will	bind
you	will	bind
he/she/it	will	bind
we	will	bind
you	will	bind
they	will	bind

***Going to*-Future**

I	am	going to	bind
you	are	going to	bind
he/she/it	is	going to	bind
we	are	going to	bind
you	are	going to	bind
they	are	going to	bind

Future Perfect

I	will have	bound
you	will have	bound
he/she/it	will have	bound
we	will have	bound
you	will have	bound
they	will have	bound

Imperative

bind

Impersonal

***ing*-Form**

binding

Past Participle

bound

Continuous tenses

Present

I	am	binding
you	are	binding
he/she/it	is	binding
we	are	binding
you	are	binding
they	are	binding

Past

I	was	binding
you	were	binding
he/she/it	was	binding
we	were	binding
you	were	binding
they	were	binding

Present Perfect

I	have been	binding
you	have been	binding
he/she/it	has been	binding
we	have been	binding
you	have been	binding
they	have been	binding

Past Perfect

I	had been	binding
you	had been	binding
he/she/it	had been	binding
we	had been	binding
you	had been	binding
they	had been	binding

***Will*-Future**

I	will be	binding
you	will be	binding
he/she/it	will be	binding
we	will be	binding
you	will be	binding
they	will be	binding

***Going to*-Future**

I	am	going to be	binding
you	are	going to be	binding
he/she/it	is	going to be	binding
we	are	going to be	binding
you	are	going to be	binding
they	are	going to be	binding

Future Perfect

I	will have been	binding
you	will have been	binding
he/she/it	will have been	binding
we	will have been	binding
you	will have been	binding
they	will have been	binding

Conditional

I	would	bind
you	would	bind
he/she/it	would	bind
we	would	bind
you	would	bind
they	would	bind

Conditional Past

I	would have	bound
you	would have	bound
he/she/it	would have	bound
we	would have	bound
you	would have	bound
they	would have	bound

bleed
– bled – bled

Simple tenses

Present

I	bleed
you	bleed
he/she/it	bleeds
we	bleed
you	bleed
they	bleed

Past

I	bled
you	bled
he/she/it	bled
we	bled
you	bled
they	bled

Present Perfect

I	have	bled
you	have	bled
he/she/it	has	bled
we	have	bled
you	have	bled
they	have	bled

Past Perfect

I	had	bled
you	had	bled
he/she/it	had	bled
we	had	bled
you	had	bled
they	had	bled

Will-Future

I	will	bleed
you	will	bleed
he/she/it	will	bleed
we	will	bleed
you	will	bleed
they	will	bleed

Going to-Future

I	am	going to	bleed
you	are	going to	bleed
he/she/it	is	going to	bleed
we	are	going to	bleed
you	are	going to	bleed
they	are	going to	bleed

Future Perfect

I	will have	bled
you	will have	bled
he/she/it	will have	bled
we	will have	bled
you	will have	bled
they	will have	bled

Imperative

bleed

Impersonal

ing-Form

bleeding

Past Participle

bled

Continuous tenses

Present

I	am	bleeding
you	are	bleeding
he/she/it	is	bleeding
we	are	bleeding
you	are	bleeding
they	are	bleeding

Past

I	was	bleeding
you	were	bleeding
he/she/it	was	bleeding
we	were	bleeding
you	were	bleeding
they	were	bleeding

Present Perfect

I	have been	bleeding
you	have been	bleeding
he/she/it	has been	bleeding
we	have been	bleeding
you	have been	bleeding
they	have been	bleeding

Past Perfect

I	had been	bleeding
you	had been	bleeding
he/she/it	had been	bleeding
we	had been	bleeding
you	had been	bleeding
they	had been	bleeding

Will-Future

I	will be	bleeding
you	will be	bleeding
he/she/it	will be	bleeding
we	will be	bleeding
you	will be	bleeding
they	will be	bleeding

Going to-Future

I	am	going to be	bleeding
you	are	going to be	bleeding
he/she/it	is	going to be	bleeding
we	are	going to be	bleeding
you	are	going to be	bleeding
they	are	going to be	bleeding

Future Perfect

I	will have been	bleeding
you	will have been	bleeding
he/she/it	will have been	bleeding
we	will have been	bleeding
you	will have been	bleeding
they	will have been	bleeding

Conditional

I	would	bleed
you	would	bleed
he/she/it	would	bleed
we	would	bleed
you	would	bleed
they	would	bleed

Conditional Past

I	would have	bled
you	would have	bled
he/she/it	would have	bled
we	would have	bled
you	would have	bled
they	would have	bled

blow
- blew -blown

blasen

Unregelmäßiges Verb

Simple tenses

Present

I	blow
you	blow
he/she/it	blows
we	blow
you	blow
they	blow

Past

I	blew
you	blew
he/she/it	blew
we	blew
you	blew
they	blew

Present Perfect

I	have	blown
you	have	blown
he/she/it	has	blown
we	have	blown
you	have	blown
they	have	blown

Past Perfect

I	had	blown
you	had	blown
he/she/it	had	blown
we	had	blown
you	had	blown
they	had	blown

Will-Future

I	will	blow
you	will	blow
he/she/it	will	blow
we	will	blow
you	will	blow
they	will	blow

Going to-Future

I	am	going to	blow
you	are	going to	blow
he/she/it	is	going to	blow
we	are	going to	blow
you	are	going to	blow
they	are	going to	blow

Future Perfect

I	will have	blown
you	will have	blown
he/she/it	will have	blown
we	will have	blown
you	will have	blown
they	will have	blown

Imperative

blow

Impersonal

ing-Form

blowing

Past Participle

blown

Continuous tenses

Present

I	am	blowing
you	are	blowing
he/she/it	is	blowing
we	are	blowing
you	are	blowing
they	are	blowing

Past

I	was	blowing
you	were	blowing
he/she/it	was	blowing
we	were	blowing
you	were	blowing
they	were	blowing

Present Perfect

I	have been	blowing
you	have been	blowing
he/she/it	has been	blowing
we	have been	blowing
you	have been	blowing
they	have been	blowing

Past Perfect

I	had been	blowing
you	had been	blowing
he/she/it	had been	blowing
we	had been	blowing
you	had been	blowing
they	had been	blowing

Will-Future

I	will be	blowing
you	will be	blowing
he/she/it	will be	blowing
we	will be	blowing
you	will be	blowing
they	will be	blowing

Going to-Future

I	am	going to be	blowing
you	are	going to be	blowing
he/she/it	is	going to be	blowing
we	are	going to be	blowing
you	are	going to be	blowing
they	are	going to be	blowing

Future Perfect

I	will have been	blowing
you	will have been	blowing
he/she/it	will have been	blowing
we	will have been	blowing
you	will have been	blowing
they	will have been	blowing

Conditional

I	would	blow
you	would	blow
he/she/it	would	blow
we	would	blow
you	would	blow
they	would	blow

Conditional Past

I	would have	blown
you	would have	blown
he/she/it	would have	blown
we	would have	blown
you	would have	blown
they	would have	blown

Simple tenses

Present

I	boil
you	boil
he/she/it	boils
we	boil
you	boil
they	boil

Past

I	boiled
you	boiled
he/she/it	boiled
we	boiled
you	boiled
they	boiled

Present Perfect

I	have	boiled
you	have	boiled
he/she/it	has	boiled
we	have	boiled
you	have	boiled
they	have	boiled

Past Perfect

I	had	boiled
you	had	boiled
he/she/it	had	boiled
we	had	boiled
you	had	boiled
they	had	boiled

Will-Future

I	will	boil
you	will	boil
he/she/it	will	boil
we	will	boil
you	will	boil
they	will	boil

Going to-Future

I	am	going to	boil
you	are	going to	boil
he/she/it	is	going to	boil
we	are	going to	boil
you	are	going to	boil
they	are	going to	boil

Future Perfect

I	will have	boiled
you	will have	boiled
he/she/it	will have	boiled
we	will have	boiled
you	will have	boiled
they	will have	boiled

Imperative

boil

Impersonal

ing-Form

boiling

Past Participle

boiled

Continuous tenses

Present

I	am	boiling
you	are	boiling
he/she/it	is	boiling
we	are	boiling
you	are	boiling
they	are	boiling

Past

I	was	boiling
you	were	boiling
he/she/it	was	boiling
we	were	boiling
you	were	boiling
they	were	boiling

Present Perfect

I	have	been	boiling
you	have	been	boiling
he/she/it	has	been	boiling
we	have	been	boiling
you	have	been	boiling
they	have	been	boiling

Past Perfect

I	had been	boiling
you	had been	boiling
he/she/it	had been	boiling
we	had been	boiling
you	had been	boiling
they	had been	boiling

Will-Future

I	will be	boiling
you	will be	boiling
he/she/it	will be	boiling
we	will be	boiling
you	will be	boiling
they	will be	boiling

Going to-Future

I	am	going to be	boiling
you	are	going to be	boiling
he/she/it	is	going to be	boiling
we	are	going to be	boiling
you	are	going to be	boiling
they	are	going to be	boiling

Future Perfect

I	will have been	boiling
you	will have been	boiling
he/she/it	will have been	boiling
we	will have been	boiling
you	will have been	boiling
they	will have been	boiling

Conditional

I	would	boil
you	would	boil
he/she/it	would	boil
we	would	boil
you	would	boil
they	would	boil

Conditional Past

I	would have	boiled
you	would have	boiled
he/she/it	would have	boiled
we	would have	boiled
you	would have	boiled
they	would have	boiled

book

buchen

Regelmäßiges Verb

Simple tenses

Present

I	book
you	book
he/she/it	books
we	book
you	book
they	book

Past

I	booked
you	booked
he/she/it	booked
we	booked
you	booked
they	booked

Present Perfect

I	have	booked
you	have	booked
he/she/it	has	booked
we	have	booked
you	have	booked
they	have	booked

Past Perfect

I	had	booked
you	had	booked
he/she/it	had	booked
we	had	booked
you	had	booked
they	had	booked

Will-Future

I	will	book
you	will	book
he/she/it	will	book
we	will	book
you	will	book
they	will	book

Going to-Future

I	am	going to	book
you	are	going to	book
he/she/it	is	going to	book
we	are	going to	book
you	are	going to	book
they	are	going to	book

Future Perfect

I	will have	booked
you	will have	booked
he/she/it	will have	booked
we	will have	booked
you	will have	booked
they	will have	booked

Imperative

book

Impersonal

ing-Form

booking

Past Participle

booked

Continuous tenses

Present

I	am	booking
you	are	booking
he/she/it	is	booking
we	are	booking
you	are	booking
they	are	booking

Past

I	was	booking
you	were	booking
he/she/it	was	booking
we	were	booking
you	were	booking
they	were	booking

Present Perfect

I	have been	booking
you	have been	booking
he/she/it	has been	booking
we	have been	booking
you	have been	booking
they	have been	booking

Past Perfect

I	had been	booking
you	had been	booking
he/she/it	had been	booking
we	had been	booking
you	had been	booking
they	had been	booking

Will-Future

I	will be	booking
you	will be	booking
he/she/it	will be	booking
we	will be	booking
you	will be	booking
they	will be	booking

Going to-Future

I	am	going to be	booking
you	are	going to be	booking
he/she/it	is	going to be	booking
we	are	going to be	booking
you	are	going to be	booking
they	are	going to be	booking

Future Perfect

I	will have been	booking
you	will have been	booking
he/she/it	will have been	booking
we	will have been	booking
you	will have been	booking
they	will have been	booking

Conditional

I	would	book
you	would	book
he/she/it	would	book
we	would	book
you	would	book
they	would	book

Conditional Past

I	would have	booked
you	would have	booked
he/she/it	would have	booked
we	would have	booked
you	would have	booked
they	would have	booked

borrow

Regelmäßiges Verb

Simple tenses

Present

I	borrow
you	borrow
he/she/it	borrows
we	borrow
you	borrow
they	borrow

Past

I	borrowed
you	borrowed
he/she/it	borrowed
we	borrowed
you	borrowed
they	borrowed

Present Perfect

I	have	borrowed
you	have	borrowed
he/she/it	has	borrowed
we	have	borrowed
you	have	borrowed
they	have	borrowed

Past Perfect

I	had	borrowed
you	had	borrowed
he/she/it	had	borrowed
we	had	borrowed
you	had	borrowed
they	had	borrowed

Will-Future

I	will	borrow
you	will	borrow
he/she/it	will	borrow
we	will	borrow
you	will	borrow
they	will	borrow

Going to-Future

I	am	going to	borrow
you	are	going to	borrow
he/she/it	is	going to	borrow
we	are	going to	borrow
you	are	going to	borrow
they	are	going to	borrow

Future Perfect

I	will have	borrowed
you	will have	borrowed
he/she/it	will have	borrowed
we	will have	borrowed
you	will have	borrowed
they	will have	borrowed

Imperative

borrow

Impersonal

ing-Form

borrowing

Past Participle

borrowed

Continuous tenses

Present

I	am	borrowing
you	are	borrowing
he/she/it	is	borrowing
we	are	borrowing
you	are	borrowing
they	are	borrowing

Past

I	was	borrowing
you	were	borrowing
he/she/it	was	borrowing
we	were	borrowing
you	were	borrowing
they	were	borrowing

Present Perfect

I	have been	borrowing
you	have been	borrowing
he/she/it	has been	borrowing
we	have been	borrowing
you	have been	borrowing
they	have been	borrowing

Past Perfect

I	had been	borrowing
you	had been	borrowing
he/she/it	had been	borrowing
we	had been	borrowing
you	had been	borrowing
they	had been	borrowing

Will-Future

I	will be	borrowing
you	will be	borrowing
he/she/it	will be	borrowing
we	will be	borrowing
you	will be	borrowing
they	will be	borrowing

Going to-Future

I	am	going to be	borrowing
you	are	going to be	borrowing
he/she/it	is	going to be	borrowing
we	are	going to be	borrowing
you	are	going to be	borrowing
they	are	going to be	borrowing

Future Perfect

I	will have been	borrowing
you	will have been	borrowing
he/she/it	will have been	borrowing
we	will have been	borrowing
you	will have been	borrowing
they	will have been	borrowing

Conditional

I	would	borrow
you	would	borrow
he/she/it	would	borrow
we	would	borrow
you	would	borrow
they	would	borrow

Conditional Past

I	would have	borrowed
you	would have	borrowed
he/she/it	would have	borrowed
we	would have	borrowed
you	would have	borrowed
they	would have	borrowed

break
- broke - broken

zerbrechen

Unregelmäßiges Verb

Simple tenses

Present

I	break
you	break
he/she/it	breaks
we	break
you	break
they	break

Past

I	broke
you	broke
he/she/it	broke
we	broke
you	broke
they	broke

Present Perfect

I	have	broken
you	have	broken
he/she/it	has	broken
we	have	broken
you	have	broken
they	have	broken

Past Perfect

I	had	broken
you	had	broken
he/she/it	had	broken
we	had	broken
you	had	broken
they	had	broken

Will-Future

I	will	break
you	will	break
he/she/it	will	break
we	will	break
you	will	break
they	will	break

Going to-Future

I	am	going to	break
you	are	going to	break
he/she/it	is	going to	break
we	are	going to	break
you	are	going to	break
they	are	going to	break

Future Perfect

I	will have	broken
you	will have	broken
he/she/it	will have	broken
we	will have	broken
you	will have	broken
they	will have	broken

Imperative

break

Impersonal

ing-Form

breaking

Past Participle

broken

Continuous tenses

Present

I	am	breaking
you	are	breaking
he/she/it	is	breaking
we	are	breaking
you	are	breaking
they	are	breaking

Past

I	was	breaking
you	were	breaking
he/she/it	was	breaking
we	were	breaking
you	were	breaking
they	were	breaking

Present Perfect

I	have	been	breaking
you	have	been	breaking
he/she/it	has	been	breaking
we	have	been	breaking
you	have	been	breaking
they	have	been	breaking

Past Perfect

I	had been	breaking
you	had been	breaking
he/she/it	had been	breaking
we	had been	breaking
you	had been	breaking
they	had been	breaking

Will-Future

I	will be	breaking
you	will be	breaking
he/she/it	will be	breaking
we	will be	breaking
you	will be	breaking
they	will be	breaking

Going to-Future

I	am	going to be	breaking
you	are	going to be	breaking
he/she/it	is	going to be	breaking
we	are	going to be	breaking
you	are	going to be	breaking
they	are	going to be	breaking

Future Perfect

I	will have been	breaking
you	will have been	breaking
he/she/it	will have been	breaking
we	will have been	breaking
you	will have been	breaking
they	will have been	breaking

Conditional

I	would	break
you	would	break
he/she/it	would	break
we	would	break
you	would	break
they	would	break

Conditional Past

I	would have	broken
you	would have	broken
he/she/it	would have	broken
we	would have	broken
you	would have	broken
they	would have	broken

+ **-ing** → ~~e~~ / + **-d** nicht **-ed**
Regelmäßiges Verb

atmen

breathe

Simple tenses

Present

I	breathe
you	breathe
he/she/it	breathes
we	breathe
you	breathe
they	breathe

Past

I	breathed
you	breathed
he/she/it	breathed
we	breathed
you	breathed
they	breathed

Present Perfect

I	have	breathed
you	have	breathed
he/she/it	has	breathed
we	have	breathed
you	have	breathed
they	have	breathed

Past Perfect

I	had	breathed
you	had	breathed
he/she/it	had	breathed
we	had	breathed
you	had	breathed
they	had	breathed

Will-Future

I	will	breathe
you	will	breathe
he/she/it	will	breathe
we	will	breathe
you	will	breathe
they	will	breathe

Going to-Future

I	am	going to	breathe
you	are	going to	breathe
he/she/it	is	going to	breathe
we	are	going to	breathe
you	are	going to	breathe
they	are	going to	breathe

Future Perfect

I	will have	breathed
you	will have	breathed
he/she/it	will have	breathed
we	will have	breathed
you	will have	breathed
they	will have	breathed

Imperative

breathe

Impersonal

ing-Form

breathing

Past Participle

breathed

Continuous tenses

Present

I	am	breathing
you	are	breathing
he/she/it	is	breathing
we	are	breathing
you	are	breathing
they	are	breathing

Past

I	was	breathing
you	were	breathing
he/she/it	was	breathing
we	were	breathing
you	were	breathing
they	were	breathing

Present Perfect

I	have been	breathing
you	have been	breathing
he/she/it	has been	breathing
we	have been	breathing
you	have been	breathing
they	have been	breathing

Past Perfect

I	had been	breathing
you	had been	breathing
he/she/it	had been	breathing
we	had been	breathing
you	had been	breathing
they	had been	breathing

Will-Future

I	will be	breathing
you	will be	breathing
he/she/it	will be	breathing
we	will be	breathing
you	will be	breathing
they	will be	breathing

Going to-Future

I	am	going to be	breathing
you	are	going to be	breathing
he/she/it	is	going to be	breathing
we	are	going to be	breathing
you	are	going to be	breathing
they	are	going to be	breathing

Future Perfect

I	will have been	breathing
you	will have been	breathing
he/she/it	will have been	breathing
we	will have been	breathing
you	will have been	breathing
they	will have been	breathing

Conditional

I	would	breathe
you	would	breathe
he/she/it	would	breathe
we	would	breathe
you	would	breathe
they	would	breathe

Conditional Past

I	would have	breathed
you	would have	breathed
he/she/it	would have	breathed
we	would have	breathed
you	would have	breathed
they	would have	breathed

breed

- bred - bred

brüten

Unregelmäßiges Verb

Simple tenses

Present

I	breed
you	breed
he/she/it	breeds
we	breed
you	breed
they	breed

Past

I	bred
you	bred
he/she/it	bred
we	bred
you	bred
they	bred

Present Perfect

I	have	bred
you	have	bred
he/she/it	has	bred
we	have	bred
you	have	bred
they	have	bred

Past Perfect

I	had	bred
you	had	bred
he/she/it	had	bred
we	had	bred
you	had	bred
they	had	bred

Will-Future

I	will	breed
you	will	breed
he/she/it	will	breed
we	will	breed
you	will	breed
they	will	breed

Going to-Future

I	am	going to	breed
you	are	going to	breed
he/she/it	is	going to	breed
we	are	going to	breed
you	are	going to	breed
they	are	going to	breed

Future Perfect

I	will have	bred
you	will have	bred
he/she/it	will have	bred
we	will have	bred
you	will have	bred
they	will have	bred

Imperative

breed

Impersonal

ing-Form

breeding

Past Participle

bred

Continuous tenses

Present

I	am	breeding
you	are	breeding
he/she/it	is	breeding
we	are	breeding
you	are	breeding
they	are	breeding

Past

I	was	breeding
you	were	breeding
he/she/it	was	breeding
we	were	breeding
you	were	breeding
they	were	breeding

Present Perfect

I	have been	breeding
you	have been	breeding
he/she/it	has been	breeding
we	have been	breeding
you	have been	breeding
they	have been	breeding

Past Perfect

I	had been	breeding
you	had been	breeding
he/she/it	had been	breeding
we	had been	breeding
you	had been	breeding
they	had been	breeding

Will-Future

I	will be	breeding
you	will be	breeding
he/she/it	will be	breeding
we	will be	breeding
you	will be	breeding
they	will be	breeding

Going to-Future

I	am	going to be	breeding
you	are	going to be	breeding
he/she/it	is	going to be	breeding
we	are	going to be	breeding
you	are	going to be	breeding
they	are	going to be	breeding

Future Perfect

I	will have been	breeding
you	will have been	breeding
he/she/it	will have been	breeding
we	will have been	breeding
you	will have been	breeding
they	will have been	breeding

Conditional

I	would	breed
you	would	breed
he/she/it	would	breed
we	would	breed
you	would	breed
they	would	breed

Conditional Past

I	would have	bred
you	would have	bred
he/she/it	would have	bred
we	would have	bred
you	would have	bred
they	would have	bred

bring
– brought – brought

Simple tenses

Present

I	bring
you	bring
he/she/it	brings
we	bring
you	bring
they	bring

Past

I	brought
you	brought
he/she/it	brought
we	brought
you	brought
they	brought

Present Perfect

I	have	brought
you	have	brought
he/she/it	has	brought
we	have	brought
you	have	brought
they	have	brought

Past Perfect

I	had	brought
you	had	brought
he/she/it	had	brought
we	had	brought
you	had	brought
they	had	brought

Will-Future

I	will	bring
you	will	bring
he/she/it	will	bring
we	will	bring
you	will	bring
they	will	bring

Going to-Future

I	am	going to	bring
you	are	going to	bring
he/she/it	is	going to	bring
we	are	going to	bring
you	are	going to	bring
they	are	going to	bring

Future Perfect

I	will have	brought
you	will have	brought
he/she/it	will have	brought
we	will have	brought
you	will have	brought
they	will have	brought

Imperative

bring

Impersonal

ing-Form

bringing

Past Participle

brought

Continuous tenses

Present

I	am	bringing
you	are	bringing
he/she/it	is	bringing
we	are	bringing
you	are	bringing
they	are	bringing

Past

I	was	bringing
you	were	bringing
he/she/it	was	bringing
we	were	bringing
you	were	bringing
they	were	bringing

Present Perfect

I	have been	bringing
you	have been	bringing
he/she/it	has been	bringing
we	have been	bringing
you	have been	bringing
they	have been	bringing

Past Perfect

I	had been	bringing
you	had been	bringing
he/she/it	had been	bringing
we	had been	bringing
you	had been	bringing
they	had been	bringing

Will-Future

I	will be	bringing
you	will be	bringing
he/she/it	will be	bringing
we	will be	bringing
you	will be	bringing
they	will be	bringing

Going to-Future

I	am	going to be	bringing
you	are	going to be	bringing
he/she/it	is	going to be	bringing
we	are	going to be	bringing
you	are	going to be	bringing
they	are	going to be	bringing

Future Perfect

I	will have been	bringing
you	will have been	bringing
he/she/it	will have been	bringing
we	will have been	bringing
you	will have been	bringing
they	will have been	bringing

Conditional

I	would	bring
you	would	bring
he/she/it	would	bring
we	would	bring
you	would	bring
they	would	bring

Conditional Past

I	would have	brought
you	would have	brought
he/she/it	would have	brought
we	would have	brought
you	would have	brought
they	would have	brought

build
- built - built

bauen

Unregelmäßiges Verb

Simple tenses

Present

I	build
you	build
he/she/it	builds
we	build
you	build
they	build

Past

I	built
you	built
he/she/it	built
we	built
you	built
they	built

Present Perfect

I	have	built
you	have	built
he/she/it	has	built
we	have	built
you	have	built
they	have	built

Past Perfect

I	had	built
you	had	built
he/she/it	had	built
we	had	built
you	had	built
they	had	built

Will-Future

I	will	build
you	will	build
he/she/it	will	build
we	will	build
you	will	build
they	will	build

Going to-Future

I	am	going to	build
you	are	going to	build
he/she/it	is	going to	build
we	are	going to	build
you	are	going to	build
they	are	going to	build

Future Perfect

I	will have	built
you	will have	built
he/she/it	will have	built
we	will have	built
you	will have	built
they	will have	built

Imperative

build

Impersonal

ing-Form

building

Past Participle

built

Continuous tenses

Present

I	am	building
you	are	building
he/she/it	is	building
we	are	building
you	are	building
they	are	building

Past

I	was	building
you	were	building
he/she/it	was	building
we	were	building
you	were	building
they	were	building

Present Perfect

I	have been	building
you	have been	building
he/she/it	has been	building
we	have been	building
you	have been	building
they	have been	building

Past Perfect

I	had been	building
you	had been	building
he/she/it	had been	building
we	had been	building
you	had been	building
they	had been	building

Will-Future

I	will be	building
you	will be	building
he/she/it	will be	building
we	will be	building
you	will be	building
they	will be	building

Going to-Future

I	am	going to be	building
you	are	going to be	building
he/she/it	is	going to be	building
we	are	going to be	building
you	are	going to be	building
they	are	going to be	building

Future Perfect

I	will have been	building
you	will have been	building
he/she/it	will have been	building
we	will have been	building
you	will have been	building
they	will have been	building

Conditional

I	would	build
you	would	build
he/she/it	would	build
we	would	build
you	would	build
they	would	build

Conditional Past

I	would have	built
you	would have	built
he/she/it	would have	built
we	would have	built
you	would have	built
they	would have	built

Unregelmäßiges Verb

verbrennen

burn
- burned/burnt - burned/burnt

Simple tenses

Present

I	burn
you	burn
he/she/it	burns
we	burn
you	burn
they	burn

Past

I	burned | burnt
you	burned | burnt
he/she/it	burned | burnt
we	burned | burnt
you	burned | burnt
they	burned | burnt

Present Perfect

I	have	burned | burnt
you	have	burned | burnt
he/she/it	has	burned | burnt
we	have	burned | burnt
you	have	burned | burnt
they	have	burned | burnt

Past Perfect

I	had	burned | burnt
you	had	burned | burnt
he/she/it	had	burned | burnt
we	had	burned | burnt
you	had	burned | burnt
they	had	burned | burnt

Will-Future

I	will	burn
you	will	burn
he/she/it	will	burn
we	will	burn
you	will	burn
they	will	burn

Going to-Future

I	am	going to	burn
you	are	going to	burn
he/she/it	is	going to	burn
we	are	going to	burn
you	are	going to	burn
they	are	going to	burn

Future Perfect

I	will have	burned | burnt
you	will have	burned | burnt
he/she/it	will have	burned | burnt
we	will have	burned | burnt
you	will have	burned | burnt
they	will have	burned | burnt

Imperative

burn

Impersonal

ing-Form

burning

Past Participle

burned | burnt

Continuous tenses

Present

I	am	burning
you	are	burning
he/she/it	is	burning
we	are	burning
you	are	burning
they	are	burning

Past

I	was	burning
you	were	burning
he/she/it	was	burning
we	were	burning
you	were	burning
they	were	burning

Present Perfect

I	have been	burning
you	have been	burning
he/she/it	has been	burning
we	have been	burning
you	have been	burning
they	have been	burning

Past Perfect

I	had been	burning
you	had been	burning
he/she/it	had been	burning
we	had been	burning
you	had been	burning
they	had been	burning

Will-Future

I	will be	burning
you	will be	burning
he/she/it	will be	burning
we	will be	burning
you	will be	burning
they	will be	burning

Going to-Future

I	am	going to be	burning
you	are	going to be	burning
he/she/it	is	going to be	burning
we	are	going to be	burning
you	are	going to be	burning
they	are	going to be	burning

Future Perfect

I	will have been	burning
you	will have been	burning
he/she/it	will have been	burning
we	will have been	burning
you	will have been	burning
they	will have been	burning

Conditional

I	would	burn
you	would	burn
he/she/it	would	burn
we	would	burn
you	would	burn
they	would	burn

Conditional Past

I	would have	burned | burnt
you	would have	burned | burnt
he/she/it	would have	burned | burnt
we	would have	burned | burnt
you	would have	burned | burnt
they	would have	burned | burnt

burst
- burst - burst

platzen

Unregelmäßiges Verb

Simple tenses

Present

I	burst
you	burst
he/she/it	bursts
we	burst
you	burst
they	burst

Past

I	burst
you	burst
he/she/it	burst
we	burst
you	burst
they	burst

Present Perfect

I	have	burst
you	have	burst
he/she/it	has	burst
we	have	burst
you	have	burst
they	have	burst

Past Perfect

I	had	burst
you	had	burst
he/she/it	had	burst
we	had	burst
you	had	burst
they	had	burst

Will-Future

I	will	burst
you	will	burst
he/she/it	will	burst
we	will	burst
you	will	burst
they	will	burst

Going to-Future

I	am	going to	burst
you	are	going to	burst
he/she/it	is	going to	burst
we	are	going to	burst
you	are	going to	burst
they	are	going to	burst

Future Perfect

I	will have	burst
you	will have	burst
he/she/it	will have	burst
we	will have	burst
you	will have	burst
they	will have	burst

Imperative

burst

Impersonal

ing-Form

bursting

Past Participle

burst

Continuous tenses

Present

I	am	bursting
you	are	bursting
he/she/it	is	bursting
we	are	bursting
you	are	bursting
they	are	bursting

Past

I	was	bursting
you	were	bursting
he/she/it	was	bursting
we	were	bursting
you	were	bursting
they	were	bursting

Present Perfect

I	have been	bursting
you	have been	bursting
he/she/it	has been	bursting
we	have been	bursting
you	have been	bursting
they	have been	bursting

Past Perfect

I	had been	bursting
you	had been	bursting
he/she/it	had been	bursting
we	had been	bursting
you	had been	bursting
they	had been	bursting

Will-Future

I	will be	bursting
you	will be	bursting
he/she/it	will be	bursting
we	will be	bursting
you	will be	bursting
they	will be	bursting

Going to-Future

I	am	going to be	bursting
you	are	going to be	bursting
he/she/it	is	going to be	bursting
we	are	going to be	bursting
you	are	going to be	bursting
they	are	going to be	bursting

Future Perfect

I	will have been	bursting
you	will have been	bursting
he/she/it	will have been	bursting
we	will have been	bursting
you	will have been	bursting
they	will have been	bursting

Conditional

I	would	burst
you	would	burst
he/she/it	would	burst
we	would	burst
you	would	burst
they	would	burst

Conditional Past

I	would have	burst
you	would have	burst
he/she/it	would have	burst
we	would have	burst
you	would have	burst
they	would have	burst

Unregelmäßiges Verb

kaufen

buy
- bought -bought

Simple tenses

Present

I	buy
you	buy
he/she/it	buys
we	buy
you	buy
they	buy

Past

I	bought
you	bought
he/she/it	bought
we	bought
you	bought
they	bought

Present Perfect

I	have	bought
you	have	bought
he/she/it	has	bought
we	have	bought
you	have	bought
they	have	bought

Past Perfect

I	had	bought
you	had	bought
he/she/it	had	bought
we	had	bought
you	had	bought
they	had	bought

Will-Future

I	will	buy
you	will	buy
he/she/it	will	buy
we	will	buy
you	will	buy
they	will	buy

Going to-Future

I	am	going to	buy
you	are	going to	buy
he/she/it	is	going to	buy
we	are	going to	buy
you	are	going to	buy
they	are	going to	buy

Future Perfect

I	will have	bought
you	will have	bought
he/she/it	will have	bought
we	will have	bought
you	will have	bought
they	will have	bought

Imperative

buy

Impersonal

ing-Form

buying

Past Participle

bought

Continuous tenses

Present

I	am	buying
you	are	buying
he/she/it	is	buying
we	are	buying
you	are	buying
they	are	buying

Past

I	was	buying
you	were	buying
he/she/it	was	buying
we	were	buying
you	were	buying
they	were	buying

Present Perfect

I	have	been	buying
you	have	been	buying
he/she/it	has	been	buying
we	have	been	buying
you	have	been	buying
they	have	been	buying

Past Perfect

I	had been	buying
you	had been	buying
he/she/it	had been	buying
we	had been	buying
you	had been	buying
they	had been	buying

Will-Future

I	will be	buying
you	will be	buying
he/she/it	will be	buying
we	will be	buying
you	will be	buying
they	will be	buying

Going to-Future

I	am	going to be	buying
you	are	going to be	buying
he/she/it	is	going to be	buying
we	are	going to be	buying
you	are	going to be	buying
they	are	going to be	buying

Future Perfect

I	will have been	buying
you	will have been	buying
he/she/it	will have been	buying
we	will have been	buying
you	will have been	buying
they	will have been	buying

Conditional

I	would	buy
you	would	buy
he/she/it	would	buy
we	would	buy
you	would	buy
they	would	buy

Conditional Past

I	would have	bought
you	would have	bought
he/she/it	would have	bought
we	would have	bought
you	would have	bought
they	would have	bought

calculate

rechnen

\+ **-ing** → ~~**e**~~ / + **-d** nicht **-ed**
Regelmäßiges Verb

Simple tenses

Present
I calculate
you calculate
he/she/it calculates
we calculate
you calculate
they calculate

Past
I calculated
you calculated
he/she/it calculated
we calculated
you calculated
they calculated

Present Perfect
I have calculated
you have calculated
he/she/it has calculated
we have calculated
you have calculated
they have calculated

Past Perfect
I had calculated
you had calculated
he/she/it had calculated
we had calculated
you had calculated
they had calculated

Will-Future
I will calculate
you will calculate
he/she/it will calculate
we will calculate
you will calculate
they will calculate

Going to-Future
I am going to calculate
you are going to calculate
he/she/it is going to calculate
we are going to calculate
you are going to calculate
they are going to calculate

Future Perfect
I will have calculated
you will have calculated
he/she/it will have calculated
we will have calculated
you will have calculated
they will have calculated

Imperative
calculate

Impersonal

ing-Form
calculating

Past Participle
calculated

Continuous tenses

Present
I am calculating
you are calculating
he/she/it is calculating
we are calculating
you are calculating
they are calculating

Past
I was calculating
you were calculating
he/she/it was calculating
we were calculating
you were calculating
they were calculating

Present Perfect
I have been calculating
you have been calculating
he/she/it has been calculating
we have been calculating
you have been calculating
they have been calculating

Past Perfect
I had been calculating
you had been calculating
he/she/it had been calculating
we had been calculating
you had been calculating
they had been calculating

Will-Future
I will be calculating
you will be calculating
he/she/it will be calculating
we will be calculating
you will be calculating
they will be calculating

Going to-Future
I am going to be calculating
you are going to be calculating
he/she/it is going to be calculating
we are going to be calculating
you are going to be calculating
they are going to be calculating

Future Perfect
I will have been calculating
you will have been calculating
he/she/it will have been calculating
we will have been calculating
you will have been calculating
they will have been calculating

Conditional
I would calculate
you would calculate
he/she/it would calculate
we would calculate
you would calculate
they would calculate

Conditional Past
I would have calculated
you would have calculated
he/she/it would have calculated
we would have calculated
you would have calculated
they would have calculated

anrufen

call

Simple tenses

Present

I	call
you	call
he/she/it	calls
we	call
you	call
they	call

Past

I	called
you	called
he/she/it	called
we	called
you	called
they	called

Present Perfect

I	have	called
you	have	called
he/she/it	has	called
we	have	called
you	have	called
they	have	called

Past Perfect

I	had	called
you	had	called
he/she/it	had	called
we	had	called
you	had	called
they	had	called

Will-Future

I	will	call
you	will	call
he/she/it	will	call
we	will	call
you	will	call
they	will	call

Going to-Future

I	am	going to	call
you	are	going to	call
he/she/it	is	going to	call
we	are	going to	call
you	are	going to	call
they	are	going to	call

Future Perfect

I	will have	called
you	will have	called
he/she/it	will have	called
we	will have	called
you	will have	called
they	will have	called

Imperative

call

Impersonal

ing-Form

calling

Past Participle

called

Continuous tenses

Present

I	am	calling
you	are	calling
he/she/it	is	calling
we	are	calling
you	are	calling
they	are	calling

Past

I	was	calling
you	were	calling
he/she/it	was	calling
we	were	calling
you	were	calling
they	were	calling

Present Perfect

I	have	been	calling
you	have	been	calling
he/she/it	has	been	calling
we	have	been	calling
you	have	been	calling
they	have	been	calling

Past Perfect

I	had been	calling
you	had been	calling
he/she/it	had been	calling
we	had been	calling
you	had been	calling
they	had been	calling

Will-Future

I	will be	calling
you	will be	calling
he/she/it	will be	calling
we	will be	calling
you	will be	calling
they	will be	calling

Going to-Future

I	am	going to be	calling
you	are	going to be	calling
he/she/it	is	going to be	calling
we	are	going to be	calling
you	are	going to be	calling
they	are	going to be	calling

Future Perfect

I	will have been	calling
you	will have been	calling
he/she/it	will have been	calling
we	will have been	calling
you	will have been	calling
they	will have been	calling

Conditional

I	would	call
you	would	call
he/she/it	would	call
we	would	call
you	would	call
they	would	call

Conditional Past

I	would have	called
you	would have	called
he/she/it	would have	called
we	would have	called
you	would have	called
they	would have	called

can/to be able to
- could

können

Unvollständiges Modalverb – *Can* bzw. *could* werden nur im *Present Simple* und *Past Simple* verwendet. Es gibt keine Verlaufsform.
Unregelmäßig, Modalverb

Simple tenses

Present

I	can
you	can
he/she/it	can
we	can
you	can
they	can

Past

I	could
you	could
he/she/it	could
we	could
you	could
they	could

Present Perfect

I	have	been able to
you	have	been able to
he/she/it	has	been able to
we	have	been able to
you	have	been able to
they	have	been able to

Past Perfect

I	had	been able to
you	had	been able to
he/she/it	had	been able to
we	had	been able to
you	had	been able to
they	had	been able to

Will-Future

I	will	be able to
you	will	be able to
he/she/it	will	be able to
we	will	be able to
you	will	be able to
they	will	be able to

Going to-Future

I	am	going to	be able to
you	are	going to	be able to
he/she/it	is	going to	be able to
we	are	going to	be able to
you	are	going to	be able to
they	are	going to	be able to

Future Perfect

I	will have	been able to
you	will have	been able to
he/she/it	will have	been able to
we	will have	been able to
you	will have	been able to
they	will have	been able to

Imperative

be able to

Impersonal

ing-Form

being able to

Past Participle

been able to

Continuous tenses

Present

-
-
-
-
-
-

Past

-
-
-
-
-
-

Present Perfect

-
-
-
-
-
-

Past Perfect

-
-
-
-
-
-

Will-Future

-
-
-
-
-
-

Going to-Future

-
-
-
-
-
-

Future Perfect

-
-
-
-
-
-

Conditional

I	would	be able to
you	would	be able to
he/she/it	would	be able to
we	would	be able to
you	would	be able to
they	would	be able to

Conditional Past

I	would have	been able to
you	would have	been able to
he/she/it	would have	been able to
we	would have	been able to
you	would have	been able to
they	would have	been able to

Konsonantenverdopplung im BE
Im AE wird das **-l** nicht verdoppelt.
Regelmäßiges Verb

absagen

cancel

Simple tenses

Present

I	cancel
you	cancel
he/she/it	cancels
we	cancel
you	cancel
they	cancel

Past

I	cancelled
you	cancelled
he/she/it	cancelled
we	cancelled
you	cancelled
they	cancelled

Present Perfect

I	have	cancelled
you	have	cancelled
he/she/it	has	cancelled
we	have	cancelled
you	have	cancelled
they	have	cancelled

Past Perfect

I	had	cancelled
you	had	cancelled
he/she/it	had	cancelled
we	had	cancelled
you	had	cancelled
they	had	cancelled

Will-Future

I	will	cancel
you	will	cancel
he/she/it	will	cancel
we	will	cancel
you	will	cancel
they	will	cancel

Going to-Future

I	am	going to	cancel
you	are	going to	cancel
he/she/it	is	going to	cancel
we	are	going to	cancel
you	are	going to	cancel
they	are	going to	cancel

Future Perfect

I	will have	cancelled
you	will have	cancelled
he/she/it	will have	cancelled
we	will have	cancelled
you	will have	cancelled
they	will have	cancelled

Imperative

cancel

Impersonal

ing-Form

cancelling

Past Participle

cancelled

Continuous tenses

Present

I	am	cancelling
you	are	cancelling
he/she/it	is	cancelling
we	are	cancelling
you	are	cancelling
they	are	cancelling

Past

I	was	cancelling
you	were	cancelling
he/she/it	was	cancelling
we	were	cancelling
you	were	cancelling
they	were	cancelling

Present Perfect

I	have	been	cancelling
you	have	been	cancelling
he/she/it	has	been	cancelling
we	have	been	cancelling
you	have	been	cancelling
they	have	been	cancelling

Past Perfect

I	had been	cancelling
you	had been	cancelling
he/she/it	had been	cancelling
we	had been	cancelling
you	had been	cancelling
they	had been	cancelling

Will-Future

I	will be	cancelling
you	will be	cancelling
he/she/it	will be	cancelling
we	will be	cancelling
you	will be	cancelling
they	will be	cancelling

Going to-Future

I	am	going to be	cancelling
you	are	going to be	cancelling
he/she/it	is	going to be	cancelling
we	are	going to be	cancelling
you	are	going to be	cancelling
they	are	going to be	cancelling

Future Perfect

I	will have been cancelling
you	will have been cancelling
he/she/it	will have been cancelling
we	will have been cancelling
you	will have been cancelling
they	will have been cancelling

Conditional

I	would	cancel
you	would	cancel
he/she/it	would	cancel
we	would	cancel
you	would	cancel
they	would	cancel

Conditional Past

I	would have	cancelled
you	would have	cancelled
he/she/it	would have	cancelled
we	would have	cancelled
you	would have	cancelled
they	would have	cancelled

care

betroffen sein

+ **-ing** → ~~e~~ / + **-d** nicht **-ed**
Regelmäßiges Verb

Simple tenses

Present

I	care
you	care
he/she/it	cares
we	care
you	care
they	care

Past

I	cared
you	cared
he/she/it	cared
we	cared
you	cared
they	cared

Present Perfect

I	have	cared
you	have	cared
he/she/it	has	cared
we	have	cared
you	have	cared
they	have	cared

Past Perfect

I	had	cared
you	had	cared
he/she/it	had	cared
we	had	cared
you	had	cared
they	had	cared

Will-Future

I	will	care
you	will	care
he/she/it	will	care
we	will	care
you	will	care
they	will	care

Going to-Future

I	am	going to	care
you	are	going to	care
he/she/it	is	going to	care
we	are	going to	care
you	are	going to	care
they	are	going to	care

Future Perfect

I	will have	cared
you	will have	cared
he/she/it	will have	cared
we	will have	cared
you	will have	cared
they	will have	cared

Imperative

care

Impersonal

ing-Form

caring

Past Participle

cared

Continuous tenses

Present

I	am	caring
you	are	caring
he/she/it	is	caring
we	are	caring
you	are	caring
they	are	caring

Past

I	was	caring
you	were	caring
he/she/it	was	caring
we	were	caring
you	were	caring
they	were	caring

Present Perfect

I	have	been	caring
you	have	been	caring
he/she/it	has	been	caring
we	have	been	caring
you	have	been	caring
they	have	been	caring

Past Perfect

I	had been	caring
you	had been	caring
he/she/it	had been	caring
we	had been	caring
you	had been	caring
they	had been	caring

Will-Future

I	will be	caring
you	will be	caring
he/she/it	will be	caring
we	will be	caring
you	will be	caring
they	will be	caring

Going to-Future

I	am	going to be	caring
you	are	going to be	caring
he/she/it	is	going to be	caring
we	are	going to be	caring
you	are	going to be	caring
they	are	going to be	caring

Future Perfect

I	will have been	caring
you	will have been	caring
he/she/it	will have been	caring
we	will have been	caring
you	will have been	caring
they	will have been	caring

Conditional

I	would	care
you	would	care
he/she/it	would	care
we	would	care
you	would	care
they	would	care

Conditional Past

I	would have	cared
you	would have	cared
he/she/it	would have	cared
we	would have	cared
you	would have	cared
they	would have	cared

-y → -ie vor -s / -y → -i vor -ed
Regelmäßiges Verb

tragen

carry

Simple tenses

Present

I	carry
you	carry
he/she/it	carries
we	carry
you	carry
they	carry

Past

I	carried
you	carried
he/she/it	carried
we	carried
you	carried
they	carried

Present Perfect

I	have	carried
you	have	carried
he/she/it	has	carried
we	have	carried
you	have	carried
they	have	carried

Past Perfect

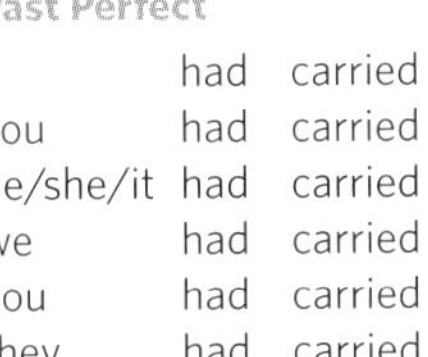

I	had	carried
you	had	carried
he/she/it	had	carried
we	had	carried
you	had	carried
they	had	carried

Will-Future

I	will	carry
you	will	carry
he/she/it	will	carry
we	will	carry
you	will	carry
they	will	carry

Going to-Future

I	am	going to	carry
you	are	going to	carry
he/she/it	is	going to	carry
we	are	going to	carry
you	are	going to	carry
they	are	going to	carry

Future Perfect

I	will have	carried
you	will have	carried
he/she/it	will have	carried
we	will have	carried
you	will have	carried
they	will have	carried

Imperative

carry

Impersonal

ing-Form

carrying

Past Participle

carried

Continuous tenses

Present

I	am	carrying
you	are	carrying
he/she/it	is	carrying
we	are	carrying
you	are	carrying
they	are	carrying

Past

I	was	carrying
you	were	carrying
he/she/it	was	carrying
we	were	carrying
you	were	carrying
they	were	carrying

Present Perfect

I	have been	carrying
you	have been	carrying
he/she/it	has been	carrying
we	have been	carrying
you	have been	carrying
they	have been	carrying

Past Perfect

I	had been	carrying
you	had been	carrying
he/she/it	had been	carrying
we	had been	carrying
you	had been	carrying
they	had been	carrying

Will-Future

I	will be	carrying
you	will be	carrying
he/she/it	will be	carrying
we	will be	carrying
you	will be	carrying
they	will be	carrying

Going to-Future

I	am	going to be	carrying
you	are	going to be	carrying
he/she/it	is	going to be	carrying
we	are	going to be	carrying
you	are	going to be	carrying
they	are	going to be	carrying

Future Perfect

I	will have been	carrying
you	will have been	carrying
he/she/it	will have been	carrying
we	will have been	carrying
you	will have been	carrying
they	will have been	carrying

Conditional

I	would	carry
you	would	carry
he/she/it	would	carry
we	would	carry
you	would	carry
they	would	carry

Conditional Past

I	would have	carried
you	would have	carried
he/she/it	would have	carried
we	would have	carried
you	would have	carried
they	would have	carried

cast

- *cast* - *cast*

werfen

Unregelmäßiges Verb

Simple tenses

Present

I	cast
you	cast
he/she/it	casts
we	cast
you	cast
they	cast

Past

I	cast
you	cast
he/she/it	cast
we	cast
you	cast
they	cast

Present Perfect

I	have	cast
you	have	cast
he/she/it	has	cast
we	have	cast
you	have	cast
they	have	cast

Past Perfect

I	had	cast
you	had	cast
he/she/it	had	cast
we	had	cast
you	had	cast
they	had	cast

Will-Future

I	will	cast
you	will	cast
he/she/it	will	cast
we	will	cast
you	will	cast
they	will	cast

Going to-Future

I	am	going to	cast
you	are	going to	cast
he/she/it	is	going to	cast
we	are	going to	cast
you	are	going to	cast
they	are	going to	cast

Future Perfect

I	will have	cast
you	will have	cast
he/she/it	will have	cast
we	will have	cast
you	will have	cast
they	will have	cast

Imperative

cast

Impersonal

ing-Form

casting

Past Participle

cast

Continuous tenses

Present

I	am	casting
you	are	casting
he/she/it	is	casting
we	are	casting
you	are	casting
they	are	casting

Past

I	was	casting
you	were	casting
he/she/it	was	casting
we	were	casting
you	were	casting
they	were	casting

Present Perfect

I	have	been	casting
you	have	been	casting
he/she/it	has	been	casting
we	have	been	casting
you	have	been	casting
they	have	been	casting

Past Perfect

I	had been	casting
you	had been	casting
he/she/it	had been	casting
we	had been	casting
you	had been	casting
they	had been	casting

Will-Future

I	will be	casting
you	will be	casting
he/she/it	will be	casting
we	will be	casting
you	will be	casting
they	will be	casting

Going to-Future

I	am	going to be	casting
you	are	going to be	casting
he/she/it	is	going to be	casting
we	are	going to be	casting
you	are	going to be	casting
they	are	going to be	casting

Future Perfect

I	will have been	casting
you	will have been	casting
he/she/it	will have been	casting
we	will have been	casting
you	will have been	casting
they	will have been	casting

Conditional

I	would	cast
you	would	cast
he/she/it	would	cast
we	would	cast
you	would	cast
they	would	cast

Conditional Past

I	would have	cast
you	would have	cast
he/she/it	would have	cast
we	would have	cast
you	would have	cast
they	would have	cast

+ **-es** in 3. Person Singular
Unregelmäßiges Verb

fangen

catch
– caught – caught

Simple tenses

Present

I	catch
you	catch
he/she/it	catches
we	catch
you	catch
they	catch

Past

I	caught
you	caught
he/she/it	caught
we	caught
you	caught
they	caught

Present Perfect

I	have	caught
you	have	caught
he/she/it	has	caught
we	have	caught
you	have	caught
they	have	caught

Past Perfect

I	had	caught
you	had	caught
he/she/it	had	caught
we	had	caught
you	had	caught
they	had	caught

Will-Future

I	will	catch
you	will	catch
he/she/it	will	catch
we	will	catch
you	will	catch
they	will	catch

Going to-Future

I	am	going to	catch
you	are	going to	catch
he/she/it	is	going to	catch
we	are	going to	catch
you	are	going to	catch
they	are	going to	catch

Future Perfect

I	will have	caught
you	will have	caught
he/she/it	will have	caught
we	will have	caught
you	will have	caught
they	will have	caught

Imperative

catch

Impersonal

ing-Form

catching

Past Participle

caught

Continuous tenses

Present

I	am	catching
you	are	catching
he/she/it	is	catching
we	are	catching
you	are	catching
they	are	catching

Past

I	was	catching
you	were	catching
he/she/it	was	catching
we	were	catching
you	were	catching
they	were	catching

Present Perfect

I	have been	catching
you	have been	catching
he/she/it	has been	catching
we	have been	catching
you	have been	catching
they	have been	catching

Past Perfect

I	had been	catching
you	had been	catching
he/she/it	had been	catching
we	had been	catching
you	had been	catching
they	had been	catching

Will-Future

I	will be	catching
you	will be	catching
he/she/it	will be	catching
we	will be	catching
you	will be	catching
they	will be	catching

Going to-Future

I	am	going to be	catching
you	are	going to be	catching
he/she/it	is	going to be	catching
we	are	going to be	catching
you	are	going to be	catching
they	are	going to be	catching

Future Perfect

I	will have been catching
you	will have been catching
he/she/it	will have been catching
we	will have been catching
you	will have been catching
they	will have been catching

Conditional

I	would	catch
you	would	catch
he/she/it	would	catch
we	would	catch
you	would	catch
they	would	catch

Conditional Past

I	would have	caught
you	would have	caught
he/she/it	would have	caught
we	would have	caught
you	would have	caught
they	would have	caught

celebrate

feiern

+ **-ing** → **e̸** / + **-d** nicht **-ed**
Regelmäßiges Verb

Simple tenses

Present

I	celebrate
you	celebrate
he/she/it	celebrates
we	celebrate
you	celebrate
they	celebrate

Past

I	celebrated
you	celebrated
he/she/it	celebrated
we	celebrated
you	celebrated
they	celebrated

Present Perfect

I	have	celebrated
you	have	celebrated
he/she/it	has	celebrated
we	have	celebrated
you	have	celebrated
they	have	celebrated

Past Perfect

I	had	celebrated
you	had	celebrated
he/she/it	had	celebrated
we	had	celebrated
you	had	celebrated
they	had	celebrated

Will-Future

I	will	celebrate
you	will	celebrate
he/she/it	will	celebrate
we	will	celebrate
you	will	celebrate
they	will	celebrate

Going to-Future

I	am	going to	celebrate
you	are	going to	celebrate
he/she/it	is	going to	celebrate
we	are	going to	celebrate
you	are	going to	celebrate
they	are	going to	celebrate

Future Perfect

I	will have	celebrated
you	will have	celebrated
he/she/it	will have	celebrated
we	will have	celebrated
you	will have	celebrated
they	will have	celebrated

Imperative

celebrate

Impersonal

ing-Form

celebrating

Past Participle

celebrated

Continuous tenses

Present

I	am	celebrating
you	are	celebrating
he/she/it	is	celebrating
we	are	celebrating
you	are	celebrating
they	are	celebrating

Past

I	was	celebrating
you	were	celebrating
he/she/it	was	celebrating
we	were	celebrating
you	were	celebrating
they	were	celebrating

Present Perfect

I	have been	celebrating
you	have been	celebrating
he/she/it	has been	celebrating
we	have been	celebrating
you	have been	celebrating
they	have been	celebrating

Past Perfect

I	had been	celebrating
you	had been	celebrating
he/she/it	had been	celebrating
we	had been	celebrating
you	had been	celebrating
they	had been	celebrating

Will-Future

I	will be	celebrating
you	will be	celebrating
he/she/it	will be	celebrating
we	will be	celebrating
you	will be	celebrating
they	will be	celebrating

Going to-Future

I	am	going to be	celebrating
you	are	going to be	celebrating
he/she/it	is	going to be	celebrating
we	are	going to be	celebrating
you	are	going to be	celebrating
they	are	going to be	celebrating

Future Perfect

I	will have been celebrating
you	will have been celebrating
he/she/it	will have been celebrating
we	will have been celebrating
you	will have been celebrating
they	will have been celebrating

Conditional

I	would	celebrate
you	would	celebrate
he/she/it	would	celebrate
we	would	celebrate
you	would	celebrate
they	would	celebrate

Conditional Past

I	would have	celebrated
you	would have	celebrated
he/she/it	would have	celebrated
we	would have	celebrated
you	would have	celebrated
they	would have	celebrated

change

ändern

+ **-ing** → ~~e~~ / + **-d** nicht **-ed**
Regelmäßiges Verb

Simple tenses

Present

I	change
you	change
he/she/it	changes
we	change
you	change
they	change

Past

I	changed
you	changed
he/she/it	changed
we	changed
you	changed
they	changed

Present Perfect

I	have	changed
you	have	changed
he/she/it	has	changed
we	have	changed
you	have	changed
they	have	changed

Past Perfect

I	had	changed
you	had	changed
he/she/it	had	changed
we	had	changed
you	had	changed
they	had	changed

Will-Future

I	will	change
you	will	change
he/she/it	will	change
we	will	change
you	will	change
they	will	change

Going to-Future

I	am	going to	change
you	are	going to	change
he/she/it	is	going to	change
we	are	going to	change
you	are	going to	change
they	are	going to	change

Future Perfect

I	will have	changed
you	will have	changed
he/she/it	will have	changed
we	will have	changed
you	will have	changed
they	will have	changed

Imperative

change

Impersonal

ing-Form

changing

Past Participle

changed

Continuous tenses

Present

I	am	changing
you	are	changing
he/she/it	is	changing
we	are	changing
you	are	changing
they	are	changing

Past

I	was	changing
you	were	changing
he/she/it	was	changing
we	were	changing
you	were	changing
they	were	changing

Present Perfect

I	have been	changing
you	have been	changing
he/she/it	has been	changing
we	have been	changing
you	have been	changing
they	have been	changing

Past Perfect

I	had been	changing
you	had been	changing
he/she/it	had been	changing
we	had been	changing
you	had been	changing
they	had been	changing

Will-Future

I	will be	changing
you	will be	changing
he/she/it	will be	changing
we	will be	changing
you	will be	changing
they	will be	changing

Going to-Future

I	am	going to be	changing
you	are	going to be	changing
he/she/it	is	going to be	changing
we	are	going to be	changing
you	are	going to be	changing
they	are	going to be	changing

Future Perfect

I	will have been	changing
you	will have been	changing
he/she/it	will have been	changing
we	will have been	changing
you	will have been	changing
they	will have been	changing

Conditional

I	would	change
you	would	change
he/she/it	would	change
we	would	change
you	would	change
they	would	change

Conditional Past

I	would have	changed
you	would have	changed
he/she/it	would have	changed
we	would have	changed
you	would have	changed
they	would have	changed

chat

plaudern, chatten

Konsonantenverdopplung
Regelmäßiges Verb

Simple tenses

Present

I	chat
you	chat
he/she/it	chats
we	chat
you	chat
they	chat

Past

I	chatted
you	chatted
he/she/it	chatted
we	chatted
you	chatted
they	chatted

Present Perfect

I	have	chatted
you	have	chatted
he/she/it	has	chatted
we	have	chatted
you	have	chatted
they	have	chatted

Past Perfect

I	had	chatted
you	had	chatted
he/she/it	had	chatted
we	had	chatted
you	had	chatted
they	had	chatted

Will-Future

I	will	chat
you	will	chat
he/she/it	will	chat
we	will	chat
you	will	chat
they	will	chat

Going to-Future

I	am	going to	chat
you	are	going to	chat
he/she/it	is	going to	chat
we	are	going to	chat
you	are	going to	chat
they	are	going to	chat

Future Perfect

I	will have	chatted
you	will have	chatted
he/she/it	will have	chatted
we	will have	chatted
you	will have	chatted
they	will have	chatted

Imperative

chat

Impersonal

ing-Form

chatting

Past Participle

chatted

Continuous tenses

Present

I	am	chatting
you	are	chatting
he/she/it	is	chatting
we	are	chatting
you	are	chatting
they	are	chatting

Past

I	was	chatting
you	were	chatting
he/she/it	was	chatting
we	were	chatting
you	were	chatting
they	were	chatting

Present Perfect

I	have been	chatting
you	have been	chatting
he/she/it	has been	chatting
we	have been	chatting
you	have been	chatting
they	have been	chatting

Past Perfect

I	had been	chatting
you	had been	chatting
he/she/it	had been	chatting
we	had been	chatting
you	had been	chatting
they	had been	chatting

Will-Future

I	will be	chatting
you	will be	chatting
he/she/it	will be	chatting
we	will be	chatting
you	will be	chatting
they	will be	chatting

Going to-Future

I	am	going to be	chatting
you	are	going to be	chatting
he/she/it	is	going to be	chatting
we	are	going to be	chatting
you	are	going to be	chatting
they	are	going to be	chatting

Future Perfect

I	will have been	chatting
you	will have been	chatting
he/she/it	will have been	chatting
we	will have been	chatting
you	will have been	chatting
they	will have been	chatting

Conditional

I	would	chat
you	would	chat
he/she/it	would	chat
we	would	chat
you	would	chat
they	would	chat

Conditional Past

I	would have	chatted
you	would have	chatted
he/she/it	would have	chatted
we	would have	chatted
you	would have	chatted
they	would have	chatted

Simple tenses

Present

I	cheat
you	cheat
he/she/it	cheats
we	cheat
you	cheat
they	cheat

Past

I	cheated
you	cheated
he/she/it	cheated
we	cheated
you	cheated
they	cheated

Present Perfect

I	have	cheated
you	have	cheated
he/she/it	has	cheated
we	have	cheated
you	have	cheated
they	have	cheated

Past Perfect

I	had	cheated
you	had	cheated
he/she/it	had	cheated
we	had	cheated
you	had	cheated
they	had	cheated

Will-Future

I	will	cheat
you	will	cheat
he/she/it	will	cheat
we	will	cheat
you	will	cheat
they	will	cheat

Going to-Future

I	am	going to	cheat
you	are	going to	cheat
he/she/it	is	going to	cheat
we	are	going to	cheat
you	are	going to	cheat
they	are	going to	cheat

Future Perfect

I	will have	cheated
you	will have	cheated
he/she/it	will have	cheated
we	will have	cheated
you	will have	cheated
they	will have	cheated

Imperative

cheat

Impersonal

ing-Form

cheating

Past Participle

cheated

Continuous tenses

Present

I	am	cheating
you	are	cheating
he/she/it	is	cheating
we	are	cheating
you	are	cheating
they	are	cheating

Past

I	was	cheating
you	were	cheating
he/she/it	was	cheating
we	were	cheating
you	were	cheating
they	were	cheating

Present Perfect

I	have been	cheating
you	have been	cheating
he/she/it	has been	cheating
we	have been	cheating
you	have been	cheating
they	have been	cheating

Past Perfect

I	had been	cheating
you	had been	cheating
he/she/it	had been	cheating
we	had been	cheating
you	had been	cheating
they	had been	cheating

Will-Future

I	will be	cheating
you	will be	cheating
he/she/it	will be	cheating
we	will be	cheating
you	will be	cheating
they	will be	cheating

Going to-Future

I	am	going to be	cheating
you	are	going to be	cheating
he/she/it	is	going to be	cheating
we	are	going to be	cheating
you	are	going to be	cheating
they	are	going to be	cheating

Future Perfect

I	will have been	cheating
you	will have been	cheating
he/she/it	will have been	cheating
we	will have been	cheating
you	will have been	cheating
they	will have been	cheating

Conditional

I	would	cheat
you	would	cheat
he/she/it	would	cheat
we	would	cheat
you	would	cheat
they	would	cheat

Conditional Past

I	would have	cheated
you	would have	cheated
he/she/it	would have	cheated
we	would have	cheated
you	would have	cheated
they	would have	cheated

chew

kauen

Regelmäßiges Verb

Simple tenses

Present

I	chew
you	chew
he/she/it	chews
we	chew
you	chew
they	chew

Past

I	chewed
you	chewed
he/she/it	chewed
we	chewed
you	chewed
they	chewed

Present Perfect

I	have	chewed
you	have	chewed
he/she/it	has	chewed
we	have	chewed
you	have	chewed
they	have	chewed

Past Perfect

I	had	chewed
you	had	chewed
he/she/it	had	chewed
we	had	chewed
you	had	chewed
they	had	chewed

Will-Future

I	will	chew
you	will	chew
he/she/it	will	chew
we	will	chew
you	will	chew
they	will	chew

Going to-Future

I	am	going to	chew
you	are	going to	chew
he/she/it	is	going to	chew
we	are	going to	chew
you	are	going to	chew
they	are	going to	chew

Future Perfect

I	will have	chewed
you	will have	chewed
he/she/it	will have	chewed
we	will have	chewed
you	will have	chewed
they	will have	chewed

Imperative

chew

Impersonal

ing-Form

chewing

Past Participle

chewed

Continuous tenses

Present

I	am	chewing
you	are	chewing
he/she/it	is	chewing
we	are	chewing
you	are	chewing
they	are	chewing

Past

I	was	chewing
you	were	chewing
he/she/it	was	chewing
we	were	chewing
you	were	chewing
they	were	chewing

Present Perfect

I	have been	chewing
you	have been	chewing
he/she/it	has been	chewing
we	have been	chewing
you	have been	chewing
they	have been	chewing

Past Perfect

I	had been	chewing
you	had been	chewing
he/she/it	had been	chewing
we	had been	chewing
you	had been	chewing
they	had been	chewing

Will-Future

I	will be	chewing
you	will be	chewing
he/she/it	will be	chewing
we	will be	chewing
you	will be	chewing
they	will be	chewing

Going to-Future

I	am	going to be	chewing
you	are	going to be	chewing
he/she/it	is	going to be	chewing
we	are	going to be	chewing
you	are	going to be	chewing
they	are	going to be	chewing

Future Perfect

I	will have been	chewing
you	will have been	chewing
he/she/it	will have been	chewing
we	will have been	chewing
you	will have been	chewing
they	will have been	chewing

Conditional

I	would	chew
you	would	chew
he/she/it	would	chew
we	would	chew
you	would	chew
they	would	chew

Conditional Past

I	would have	chewed
you	would have	chewed
he/she/it	would have	chewed
we	would have	chewed
you	would have	chewed
they	would have	chewed

+ -ing → ~~e~~
Unregelmäßiges Verb

auswählen

choose
- chose - chosen

Simple tenses

Present

I	choose
you	choose
he/she/it	chooses
we	choose
you	choose
they	choose

Past

I	chose
you	chose
he/she/it	chose
we	chose
you	chose
they	chose

Present Perfect

I	have	chosen
you	have	chosen
he/she/it	has	chosen
we	have	chosen
you	have	chosen
they	have	chosen

Past Perfect

I	had	chosen
you	had	chosen
he/she/it	had	chosen
we	had	chosen
you	had	chosen
they	had	chosen

Will-Future

I	will	choose
you	will	choose
he/she/it	will	choose
we	will	choose
you	will	choose
they	will	choose

Going to-Future

I	am	going to	choose
you	are	going to	choose
he/she/it	is	going to	choose
we	are	going to	choose
you	are	going to	choose
they	are	going to	choose

Future Perfect

I	will have	chosen
you	will have	chosen
he/she/it	will have	chosen
we	will have	chosen
you	will have	chosen
they	will have	chosen

Imperative

choose

Impersonal

ing-Form

choosing

Past Participle

chosen

Continuous tenses

Present

I	am	choosing
you	are	choosing
he/she/it	is	choosing
we	are	choosing
you	are	choosing
they	are	choosing

Past

I	was	choosing
you	were	choosing
he/she/it	was	choosing
we	were	choosing
you	were	choosing
they	were	choosing

Present Perfect

I	have	been	choosing
you	have	been	choosing
he/she/it	has	been	choosing
we	have	been	choosing
you	have	been	choosing
they	have	been	choosing

Past Perfect

I	had been	choosing
you	had been	choosing
he/she/it	had been	choosing
we	had been	choosing
you	had been	choosing
they	had been	choosing

Will-Future

I	will be	choosing
you	will be	choosing
he/she/it	will be	choosing
we	will be	choosing
you	will be	choosing
they	will be	choosing

Going to-Future

I	am	going to be	choosing
you	are	going to be	choosing
he/she/it	is	going to be	choosing
we	are	going to be	choosing
you	are	going to be	choosing
they	are	going to be	choosing

Future Perfect

I	will have been	choosing
you	will have been	choosing
he/she/it	will have been	choosing
we	will have been	choosing
you	will have been	choosing
they	will have been	choosing

Conditional

I	would	choose
you	would	choose
he/she/it	would	choose
we	would	choose
you	would	choose
they	would	choose

Conditional Past

I	would have	chosen
you	would have	chosen
he/she/it	would have	chosen
we	would have	chosen
you	would have	chosen
they	would have	chosen

claim

behaupten

Regelmäßiges Verb

Simple tenses

Present

I	claim
you	claim
he/she/it	claims
we	claim
you	claim
they	claim

Past

I	claimed
you	claimed
he/she/it	claimed
we	claimed
you	claimed
they	claimed

Present Perfect

I	have	claimed
you	have	claimed
he/she/it	has	claimed
we	have	claimed
you	have	claimed
they	have	claimed

Past Perfect

I	had	claimed
you	had	claimed
he/she/it	had	claimed
we	had	claimed
you	had	claimed
they	had	claimed

Will-Future

I	will	claim
you	will	claim
he/she/it	will	claim
we	will	claim
you	will	claim
they	will	claim

Going to-Future

I	am	going to	claim
you	are	going to	claim
he/she/it	is	going to	claim
we	are	going to	claim
you	are	going to	claim
they	are	going to	claim

Future Perfect

I	will have	claimed
you	will have	claimed
he/she/it	will have	claimed
we	will have	claimed
you	will have	claimed
they	will have	claimed

Imperative

claim

Impersonal

ing-Form

claiming

Past Participle

claimed

Continuous tenses

Present

I	am	claiming
you	are	claiming
he/she/it	is	claiming
we	are	claiming
you	are	claiming
they	are	claiming

Past

I	was	claiming
you	were	claiming
he/she/it	was	claiming
we	were	claiming
you	were	claiming
they	were	claiming

Present Perfect

I	have	been	claiming
you	have	been	claiming
he/she/it	has	been	claiming
we	have	been	claiming
you	have	been	claiming
they	have	been	claiming

Past Perfect

I	had been	claiming
you	had been	claiming
he/she/it	had been	claiming
we	had been	claiming
you	had been	claiming
they	had been	claiming

Will-Future

I	will be	claiming
you	will be	claiming
he/she/it	will be	claiming
we	will be	claiming
you	will be	claiming
they	will be	claiming

Going to-Future

I	am	going to be	claiming
you	are	going to be	claiming
he/she/it	is	going to be	claiming
we	are	going to be	claiming
you	are	going to be	claiming
they	are	going to be	claiming

Future Perfect

I	will have been	claiming
you	will have been	claiming
he/she/it	will have been	claiming
we	will have been	claiming
you	will have been	claiming
they	will have been	claiming

Conditional

I	would	claim
you	would	claim
he/she/it	would	claim
we	would	claim
you	would	claim
they	would	claim

Conditional Past

I	would have	claimed
you	would have	claimed
he/she/it	would have	claimed
we	would have	claimed
you	would have	claimed
they	would have	claimed

Konsonantenverdopplung
Regelmäßiges Verb

klatschen

Simple tenses

Present

I	clap
you	clap
he/she/it	claps
we	clap
you	clap
they	clap

Past

I	clapped
you	clapped
he/she/it	clapped
we	clapped
you	clapped
they	clapped

Present Perfect

I	have	clapped
you	have	clapped
he/she/it	has	clapped
we	have	clapped
you	have	clapped
they	have	clapped

Past Perfect

I	had	clapped
you	had	clapped
he/she/it	had	clapped
we	had	clapped
you	had	clapped
they	had	clapped

Will-Future

I	will	clap
you	will	clap
he/she/it	will	clap
we	will	clap
you	will	clap
they	will	clap

Going to-Future

I	am	going to	clap
you	are	going to	clap
he/she/it	is	going to	clap
we	are	going to	clap
you	are	going to	clap
they	are	going to	clap

Future Perfect

I	will have	clapped
you	will have	clapped
he/she/it	will have	clapped
we	will have	clapped
you	will have	clapped
they	will have	clapped

Imperative

clap

Impersonal

ing-Form

clapping

Past Participle

clapped

Continuous tenses

Present

I	am	clapping
you	are	clapping
he/she/it	is	clapping
we	are	clapping
you	are	clapping
they	are	clapping

Past

I	was	clapping
you	were	clapping
he/she/it	was	clapping
we	were	clapping
you	were	clapping
they	were	clapping

Present Perfect

I	have been	clapping
you	have been	clapping
he/she/it	has been	clapping
we	have been	clapping
you	have been	clapping
they	have been	clapping

Past Perfect

I	had been	clapping
you	had been	clapping
he/she/it	had been	clapping
we	had been	clapping
you	had been	clapping
they	had been	clapping

Will-Future

I	will be	clapping
you	will be	clapping
he/she/it	will be	clapping
we	will be	clapping
you	will be	clapping
they	will be	clapping

Going to-Future

I	am	going to be	clapping
you	are	going to be	clapping
he/she/it	is	going to be	clapping
we	are	going to be	clapping
you	are	going to be	clapping
they	are	going to be	clapping

Future Perfect

I	will have been	clapping
you	will have been	clapping
he/she/it	will have been	clapping
we	will have been	clapping
you	will have been	clapping
they	will have been	clapping

Conditional

I	would	clap
you	would	clap
he/she/it	would	clap
we	would	clap
you	would	clap
they	would	clap

Conditional Past

I	would have	clapped
you	would have	clapped
he/she/it	would have	clapped
we	would have	clapped
you	would have	clapped
they	would have	clapped

clean

reinigen

Regelmäßiges Verb

Simple tenses

Present

I	clean
you	clean
he/she/it	cleans
we	clean
you	clean
they	clean

Past

I	cleaned
you	cleaned
he/she/it	cleaned
we	cleaned
you	cleaned
they	cleaned

Present Perfect

I	have	cleaned
you	have	cleaned
he/she/it	has	cleaned
we	have	cleaned
you	have	cleaned
they	have	cleaned

Past Perfect

I	had	cleaned
you	had	cleaned
he/she/it	had	cleaned
we	had	cleaned
you	had	cleaned
they	had	cleaned

Will-Future

I	will	clean
you	will	clean
he/she/it	will	clean
we	will	clean
you	will	clean
they	will	clean

Going to-Future

I	am	going to	clean
you	are	going to	clean
he/she/it	is	going to	clean
we	are	going to	clean
you	are	going to	clean
they	are	going to	clean

Future Perfect

I	will have	cleaned
you	will have	cleaned
he/she/it	will have	cleaned
we	will have	cleaned
you	will have	cleaned
they	will have	cleaned

Imperative

clean

Impersonal

ing-Form

cleaning

Past Participle

cleaned

Continuous tenses

Present

I	am	cleaning
you	are	cleaning
he/she/it	is	cleaning
we	are	cleaning
you	are	cleaning
they	are	cleaning

Past

I	was	cleaning
you	were	cleaning
he/she/it	was	cleaning
we	were	cleaning
you	were	cleaning
they	were	cleaning

Present Perfect

I	have been	cleaning
you	have been	cleaning
he/she/it	has been	cleaning
we	have been	cleaning
you	have been	cleaning
they	have been	cleaning

Past Perfect

I	had been	cleaning
you	had been	cleaning
he/she/it	had been	cleaning
we	had been	cleaning
you	had been	cleaning
they	had been	cleaning

Will-Future

I	will be	cleaning
you	will be	cleaning
he/she/it	will be	cleaning
we	will be	cleaning
you	will be	cleaning
they	will be	cleaning

Going to-Future

I	am	going to be	cleaning
you	are	going to be	cleaning
he/she/it	is	going to be	cleaning
we	are	going to be	cleaning
you	are	going to be	cleaning
they	are	going to be	cleaning

Future Perfect

I	will have been	cleaning
you	will have been	cleaning
he/she/it	will have been	cleaning
we	will have been	cleaning
you	will have been	cleaning
they	will have been	cleaning

Conditional

I	would	clean
you	would	clean
he/she/it	would	clean
we	would	clean
you	would	clean
they	would	clean

Conditional Past

I	would have	cleaned
you	would have	cleaned
he/she/it	would have	cleaned
we	would have	cleaned
you	would have	cleaned
they	would have	cleaned

Simple tenses

Present

I	climb
you	climb
he/she/it	climbs
we	climb
you	climb
they	climb

Past

I	climbed
you	climbed
he/she/it	climbed
we	climbed
you	climbed
they	climbed

Present Perfect

I	have	climbed
you	have	climbed
he/she/it	has	climbed
we	have	climbed
you	have	climbed
they	have	climbed

Past Perfect

I	had	climbed
you	had	climbed
he/she/it	had	climbed
we	had	climbed
you	had	climbed
they	had	climbed

Will-Future

I	will	climb
you	will	climb
he/she/it	will	climb
we	will	climb
you	will	climb
they	will	climb

Going to-Future

I	am	going to	climb
you	are	going to	climb
he/she/it	is	going to	climb
we	are	going to	climb
you	are	going to	climb
they	are	going to	climb

Future Perfect

I	will have	climbed
you	will have	climbed
he/she/it	will have	climbed
we	will have	climbed
you	will have	climbed
they	will have	climbed

Imperative

climb

Impersonal

ing-Form

climbing

Past Participle

climbed

Continuous tenses

Present

I	am	climbing
you	are	climbing
he/she/it	is	climbing
we	are	climbing
you	are	climbing
they	are	climbing

Past

I	was	climbing
you	were	climbing
he/she/it	was	climbing
we	were	climbing
you	were	climbing
they	were	climbing

Present Perfect

I	have been	climbing
you	have been	climbing
he/she/it	has been	climbing
we	have been	climbing
you	have been	climbing
they	have been	climbing

Past Perfect

I	had been	climbing
you	had been	climbing
he/she/it	had been	climbing
we	had been	climbing
you	had been	climbing
they	had been	climbing

Will-Future

I	will be	climbing
you	will be	climbing
he/she/it	will be	climbing
we	will be	climbing
you	will be	climbing
they	will be	climbing

Going to-Future

I	am	going to be	climbing
you	are	going to be	climbing
he/she/it	is	going to be	climbing
we	are	going to be	climbing
you	are	going to be	climbing
they	are	going to be	climbing

Future Perfect

I	will have been	climbing
you	will have been	climbing
he/she/it	will have been	climbing
we	will have been	climbing
you	will have been	climbing
they	will have been	climbing

Conditional

I	would	climb
you	would	climb
he/she/it	would	climb
we	would	climb
you	would	climb
they	would	climb

Conditional Past

I	would have	climbed
you	would have	climbed
he/she/it	would have	climbed
we	would have	climbed
you	would have	climbed
they	would have	climbed

close

schließen

+ **-ing** → ~~e~~ / + **-d** nicht **-ed**
Regelmäßiges Verb

Simple tenses

Present

I	close
you	close
he/she/it	closes
we	close
you	close
they	close

Past

I	closed
you	closed
he/she/it	closed
we	closed
you	closed
they	closed

Present Perfect

I	have	closed
you	have	closed
he/she/it	has	closed
we	have	closed
you	have	closed
they	have	closed

Past Perfect

I	had	closed
you	had	closed
he/she/it	had	closed
we	had	closed
you	had	closed
they	had	closed

Will-Future

I	will	close
you	will	close
he/she/it	will	close
we	will	close
you	will	close
they	will	close

Going to-Future

I	am	going to	close
you	are	going to	close
he/she/it	is	going to	close
we	are	going to	close
you	are	going to	close
they	are	going to	close

Future Perfect

I	will have	closed
you	will have	closed
he/she/it	will have	closed
we	will have	closed
you	will have	closed
they	will have	closed

Imperative

close

Impersonal

ing-Form

closing

Past Participle

closed

Continuous tenses

Present

I	am	closing
you	are	closing
he/she/it	is	closing
we	are	closing
you	are	closing
they	are	closing

Past

I	was	closing
you	were	closing
he/she/it	was	closing
we	were	closing
you	were	closing
they	were	closing

Present Perfect

I	have been	closing
you	have been	closing
he/she/it	has been	closing
we	have been	closing
you	have been	closing
they	have been	closing

Past Perfect

I	had been	closing
you	had been	closing
he/she/it	had been	closing
we	had been	closing
you	had been	closing
they	had been	closing

Will-Future

I	will be	closing
you	will be	closing
he/she/it	will be	closing
we	will be	closing
you	will be	closing
they	will be	closing

Going to-Future

I	am	going to be	closing
you	are	going to be	closing
he/she/it	is	going to be	closing
we	are	going to be	closing
you	are	going to be	closing
they	are	going to be	closing

Future Perfect

I	will have been	closing
you	will have been	closing
he/she/it	will have been	closing
we	will have been	closing
you	will have been	closing
they	will have been	closing

Conditional

I	would	close
you	would	close
he/she/it	would	close
we	would	close
you	would	close
they	would	close

Conditional Past

I	would have	closed
you	would have	closed
he/she/it	would have	closed
we	would have	closed
you	would have	closed
they	would have	closed

Simple tenses

Present

I	collect
you	collect
he/she/it	collects
we	collect
you	collect
they	collect

Past

I	collected
you	collected
he/she/it	collected
we	collected
you	collected
they	collected

Present Perfect

I	have	collected
you	have	collected
he/she/it	has	collected
we	have	collected
you	have	collected
they	have	collected

Past Perfect

I	had	collected
you	had	collected
he/she/it	had	collected
we	had	collected
you	had	collected
they	had	collected

Will-Future

I	will	collect
you	will	collect
he/she/it	will	collect
we	will	collect
you	will	collect
they	will	collect

Going to-Future

I	am	going to	collect
you	are	going to	collect
he/she/it	is	going to	collect
we	are	going to	collect
you	are	going to	collect
they	are	going to	collect

Future Perfect

I	will have	collected
you	will have	collected
he/she/it	will have	collected
we	will have	collected
you	will have	collected
they	will have	collected

Imperative

collect

Impersonal

ing-Form

collecting

Past Participle

collected

Continuous tenses

Present

I	am	collecting
you	are	collecting
he/she/it	is	collecting
we	are	collecting
you	are	collecting
they	are	collecting

Past

I	was	collecting
you	were	collecting
he/she/it	was	collecting
we	were	collecting
you	were	collecting
they	were	collecting

Present Perfect

I	have been	collecting
you	have been	collecting
he/she/it	has been	collecting
we	have been	collecting
you	have been	collecting
they	have been	collecting

Past Perfect

I	had been	collecting
you	had been	collecting
he/she/it	had been	collecting
we	had been	collecting
you	had been	collecting
they	had been	collecting

Will-Future

I	will be	collecting
you	will be	collecting
he/she/it	will be	collecting
we	will be	collecting
you	will be	collecting
they	will be	collecting

Going to-Future

I	am	going to be	collecting
you	are	going to be	collecting
he/she/it	is	going to be	collecting
we	are	going to be	collecting
you	are	going to be	collecting
they	are	going to be	collecting

Future Perfect

I	will have been	collecting
you	will have been	collecting
he/she/it	will have been	collecting
we	will have been	collecting
you	will have been	collecting
they	will have been	collecting

Conditional

I	would	collect
you	would	collect
he/she/it	would	collect
we	would	collect
you	would	collect
they	would	collect

Conditional Past

I	would have	collected
you	would have	collected
he/she/it	would have	collected
we	would have	collected
you	would have	collected
they	would have	collected

combine

kombinieren

Regelmäßiges Verb

Simple tenses

Present

I	combine
you	combine
he/she/it	combines
we	combine
you	combine
they	combine

Past

I	combined
you	combined
he/she/it	combined
we	combined
you	combined
they	combined

Present Perfect

I	have	combined
you	have	combined
he/she/it	has	combined
we	have	combined
you	have	combined
they	have	combined

Past Perfect

I	had	combined
you	had	combined
he/she/it	had	combined
we	had	combined
you	had	combined
they	had	combined

Will-Future

I	will	combine
you	will	combine
he/she/it	will	combine
we	will	combine
you	will	combine
they	will	combine

Going to-Future

I	am	going to	combine
you	are	going to	combine
he/she/it	is	going to	combine
we	are	going to	combine
you	are	going to	combine
they	are	going to	combine

Future Perfect

I	will have	combined
you	will have	combined
he/she/it	will have	combined
we	will have	combined
you	will have	combined
they	will have	combined

Imperative

combine

Impersonal

ing-Form

combining

Past Participle

combined

Continuous tenses

Present

I	am	combining
you	are	combining
he/she/it	is	combining
we	are	combining
you	are	combining
they	are	combining

Past

I	was	combining
you	were	combining
he/she/it	was	combining
we	were	combining
you	were	combining
they	were	combining

Present Perfect

I	have been	combining
you	have been	combining
he/she/it	has been	combining
we	have been	combining
you	have been	combining
they	have been	combining

Past Perfect

I	had been	combining
you	had been	combining
he/she/it	had been	combining
we	had been	combining
you	had been	combining
they	had been	combining

Will-Future

I	will be	combining
you	will be	combining
he/she/it	will be	combining
we	will be	combining
you	will be	combining
they	will be	combining

Going to-Future

I	am	going to be	combining
you	are	going to be	combining
he/she/it	is	going to be	combining
we	are	going to be	combining
you	are	going to be	combining
they	are	going to be	combining

Future Perfect

I	will have been	combining
you	will have been	combining
he/she/it	will have been	combining
we	will have been	combining
you	will have been	combining
they	will have been	combining

Conditional

I	would	combine
you	would	combine
he/she/it	would	combine
we	would	combine
you	would	combine
they	would	combine

Conditional Past

I	would have	combined
you	would have	combined
he/she/it	would have	combined
we	would have	combined
you	would have	combined
they	would have	combined

Simple tenses

Present

I	come
you	come
he/she/it	comes
we	come
you	come
they	come

Past

I	came
you	came
he/she/it	came
we	came
you	came
they	came

Present Perfect

I	have	come
you	have	come
he/she/it	has	come
we	have	come
you	have	come
they	have	come

Past Perfect

I	had	come
you	had	come
he/she/it	had	come
we	had	come
you	had	come
they	had	come

Will-Future

I	will	come
you	will	come
he/she/it	will	come
we	will	come
you	will	come
they	will	come

Going to-Future

I	am	going to	come
you	are	going to	come
he/she/it	is	going to	come
we	are	going to	come
you	are	going to	come
they	are	going to	come

Future Perfect

I	will have	come
you	will have	come
he/she/it	will have	come
we	will have	come
you	will have	come
they	will have	come

Imperative

come

Impersonal

ing-Form

coming

Past Participle

come

Continuous tenses

Present

I	am	coming
you	are	coming
he/she/it	is	coming
we	are	coming
you	are	coming
they	are	coming

Past

I	was	coming
you	were	coming
he/she/it	was	coming
we	were	coming
you	were	coming
they	were	coming

Present Perfect

I	have been	coming
you	have been	coming
he/she/it	has been	coming
we	have been	coming
you	have been	coming
they	have been	coming

Past Perfect

I	had been	coming
you	had been	coming
he/she/it	had been	coming
we	had been	coming
you	had been	coming
they	had been	coming

Will-Future

I	will be	coming
you	will be	coming
he/she/it	will be	coming
we	will be	coming
you	will be	coming
they	will be	coming

Going to-Future

I	am	going to be	coming
you	are	going to be	coming
he/she/it	is	going to be	coming
we	are	going to be	coming
you	are	going to be	coming
they	are	going to be	coming

Future Perfect

I	will have been	coming
you	will have been	coming
he/she/it	will have been	coming
we	will have been	coming
you	will have been	coming
they	will have been	coming

Conditional

I	would	come
you	would	come
he/she/it	would	come
we	would	come
you	would	come
they	would	come

Conditional Past

I	would have	come
you	would have	come
he/she/it	would have	come
we	would have	come
you	would have	come
they	would have	come

comfort

trösten

Regelmäßiges Verb

Simple tenses

Present

I	comfort
you	comfort
he/she/it	comforts
we	comfort
you	comfort
they	comfort

Past

I	comforted
you	comforted
he/she/it	comforted
we	comforted
you	comforted
they	comforted

Present Perfect

I	have	comforted
you	have	comforted
he/she/it	has	comforted
we	have	comforted
you	have	comforted
they	have	comforted

Past Perfect

I	had	comforted
you	had	comforted
he/she/it	had	comforted
we	had	comforted
you	had	comforted
they	had	comforted

Will-Future

I	will	comfort
you	will	comfort
he/she/it	will	comfort
we	will	comfort
you	will	comfort
they	will	comfort

Going to-Future

I	am	going to	comfort
you	are	going to	comfort
he/she/it	is	going to	comfort
we	are	going to	comfort
you	are	going to	comfort
they	are	going to	comfort

Future Perfect

I	will have	comforted
you	will have	comforted
he/she/it	will have	comforted
we	will have	comforted
you	will have	comforted
they	will have	comforted

Imperative

comfort

Impersonal

ing-Form

comforting

Past Participle

comforted

Continuous tenses

Present

I	am	comforting
you	are	comforting
he/she/it	is	comforting
we	are	comforting
you	are	comforting
they	are	comforting

Past

I	was	comforting
you	were	comforting
he/she/it	was	comforting
we	were	comforting
you	were	comforting
they	were	comforting

Present Perfect

I	have been	comforting
you	have been	comforting
he/she/it	has been	comforting
we	have been	comforting
you	have been	comforting
they	have been	comforting

Past Perfect

I	had been	comforting
you	had been	comforting
he/she/it	had been	comforting
we	had been	comforting
you	had been	comforting
they	had been	comforting

Will-Future

I	will be	comforting
you	will be	comforting
he/she/it	will be	comforting
we	will be	comforting
you	will be	comforting
they	will be	comforting

Going to-Future

I	am	going to be	comforting
you	are	going to be	comforting
he/she/it	is	going to be	comforting
we	are	going to be	comforting
you	are	going to be	comforting
they	are	going to be	comforting

Future Perfect

I	will have been	comforting
you	will have been	comforting
he/she/it	will have been	comforting
we	will have been	comforting
you	will have been	comforting
they	will have been	comforting

Conditional

I	would	comfort
you	would	comfort
he/she/it	would	comfort
we	would	comfort
you	would	comfort
they	would	comfort

Conditional Past

I	would have	comforted
you	would have	comforted
he/she/it	would have	comforted
we	would have	comforted
you	would have	comforted
they	would have	comforted

command

Regelmäßiges Verb

Simple tenses

Present

I	command
you	command
he/she/it	commands
we	command
you	command
they	command

Past

I	commanded
you	commanded
he/she/it	commanded
we	commanded
you	commanded
they	commanded

Present Perfect

I	have	commanded
you	have	commanded
he/she/it	has	commanded
we	have	commanded
you	have	commanded
they	have	commanded

Past Perfect

I	had	commanded
you	had	commanded
he/she/it	had	commanded
we	had	commanded
you	had	commanded
they	had	commanded

Will-Future

I	will	command
you	will	command
he/she/it	will	command
we	will	command
you	will	command
they	will	command

Going to-Future

I	am	going to	command
you	are	going to	command
he/she/it	is	going to	command
we	are	going to	command
you	are	going to	command
they	are	going to	command

Future Perfect

I	will have	commanded
you	will have	commanded
he/she/it	will have	commanded
we	will have	commanded
you	will have	commanded
they	will have	commanded

Imperative

command

Impersonal

ing-Form

commanding

Past Participle

commanded

Continuous tenses

Present

I	am	commanding
you	are	commanding
he/she/it	is	commanding
we	are	commanding
you	are	commanding
they	are	commanding

Past

I	was	commanding
you	were	commanding
he/she/it	was	commanding
we	were	commanding
you	were	commanding
they	were	commanding

Present Perfect

I	have been	commanding
you	have been	commanding
he/she/it	has been	commanding
we	have been	commanding
you	have been	commanding
they	have been	commanding

Past Perfect

I	had been	commanding
you	had been	commanding
he/she/it	had been	commanding
we	had been	commanding
you	had been	commanding
they	had been	commanding

Will-Future

I	will be	commanding
you	will be	commanding
he/she/it	will be	commanding
we	will be	commanding
you	will be	commanding
they	will be	commanding

Going to-Future

I	am	going to be	commanding
you	are	going to be	commanding
he/she/it	is	going to be	commanding
we	are	going to be	commanding
you	are	going to be	commanding
they	are	going to be	commanding

Future Perfect

I	will have been	commanding
you	will have been	commanding
he/she/it	will have been	commanding
we	will have been	commanding
you	will have been	commanding
they	will have been	commanding

Conditional

I	would	command
you	would	command
he/she/it	would	command
we	would	command
you	would	command
they	would	command

Conditional Past

I	would have	commanded
you	would have	commanded
he/she/it	would have	commanded
we	would have	commanded
you	would have	commanded
they	would have	commanded

commit

begehen

Konsonantenverdopplung
Regelmäßiges Verb

Simple tenses

Present

I	commit
you	commit
he/she/it	commits
we	commit
you	commit
they	commit

Past

I	committed
you	committed
he/she/it	committed
we	committed
you	committed
they	committed

Present Perfect

I	have	committed
you	have	committed
he/she/it	has	committed
we	have	committed
you	have	committed
they	have	committed

Past Perfect

I	had	committed
you	had	committed
he/she/it	had	committed
we	had	committed
you	had	committed
they	had	committed

Will-Future

I	will	commit
you	will	commit
he/she/it	will	commit
we	will	commit
you	will	commit
they	will	commit

Going to-Future

I	am	going to	commit
you	are	going to	commit
he/she/it	is	going to	commit
we	are	going to	commit
you	are	going to	commit
they	are	going to	commit

Future Perfect

I	will have	committed
you	will have	committed
he/she/it	will have	committed
we	will have	committed
you	will have	committed
they	will have	committed

Imperative

commit

Impersonal

ing-Form

committing

Past Participle

committed

Continuous tenses

Present

I	am	committing
you	are	committing
he/she/it	is	committing
we	are	committing
you	are	committing
they	are	committing

Past

I	was	committing
you	were	committing
he/she/it	was	committing
we	were	committing
you	were	committing
they	were	committing

Present Perfect

I	have been	committing
you	have been	committing
he/she/it	has been	committing
we	have been	committing
you	have been	committing
they	have been	committing

Past Perfect

I	had been	committing
you	had been	committing
he/she/it	had been	committing
we	had been	committing
you	had been	committing
they	had been	committing

Will-Future

I	will be	committing
you	will be	committing
he/she/it	will be	committing
we	will be	committing
you	will be	committing
they	will be	committing

Going to-Future

I	am	going to be	committing
you	are	going to be	committing
he/she/it	is	going to be	committing
we	are	going to be	committing
you	are	going to be	committing
they	are	going to be	committing

Future Perfect

I	will have been committing
you	will have been committing
he/she/it	will have been committing
we	will have been committing
you	will have been committing
they	will have been committing

Conditional

I	would	commit
you	would	commit
he/she/it	would	commit
we	would	commit
you	would	commit
they	would	commit

Conditional Past

I	would have	committed
you	would have	committed
he/she/it	would have	committed
we	would have	committed
you	would have	committed
they	would have	committed

+ -ing → ~~e~~ / + -d nicht -ed
Regelmäßiges Verb

vergleichen

compare

Simple tenses

Present

I	compare
you	compare
he/she/it	compares
we	compare
you	compare
they	compare

Past

I	compared
you	compared
he/she/it	compared
we	compared
you	compared
they	compared

Present Perfect

I	have	compared
you	have	compared
he/she/it	has	compared
we	have	compared
you	have	compared
they	have	compared

Past Perfect

I	had	compared
you	had	compared
he/she/it	had	compared
we	had	compared
you	had	compared
they	had	compared

Will-Future

I	will	compare
you	will	compare
he/she/it	will	compare
we	will	compare
you	will	compare
they	will	compare

Going to-Future

I	am	going to	compare
you	are	going to	compare
he/she/it	is	going to	compare
we	are	going to	compare
you	are	going to	compare
they	are	going to	compare

Future Perfect

I	will have	compared
you	will have	compared
he/she/it	will have	compared
we	will have	compared
you	will have	compared
they	will have	compared

Imperative

compare

Impersonal

ing-Form

comparing

Past Participle

compared

Continuous tenses

Present

I	am	comparing
you	are	comparing
he/she/it	is	comparing
we	are	comparing
you	are	comparing
they	are	comparing

Past

I	was	comparing
you	were	comparing
he/she/it	was	comparing
we	were	comparing
you	were	comparing
they	were	comparing

Present Perfect

I	have been	comparing
you	have been	comparing
he/she/it	has been	comparing
we	have been	comparing
you	have been	comparing
they	have been	comparing

Past Perfect

I	had been	comparing
you	had been	comparing
he/she/it	had been	comparing
we	had been	comparing
you	had been	comparing
they	had been	comparing

Will-Future

I	will be	comparing
you	will be	comparing
he/she/it	will be	comparing
we	will be	comparing
you	will be	comparing
they	will be	comparing

Going to-Future

I	am	going to be	comparing
you	are	going to be	comparing
he/she/it	is	going to be	comparing
we	are	going to be	comparing
you	are	going to be	comparing
they	are	going to be	comparing

Future Perfect

I	will have been comparing
you	will have been comparing
he/she/it	will have been comparing
we	will have been comparing
you	will have been comparing
they	will have been comparing

Conditional

I	would	compare
you	would	compare
he/she/it	would	compare
we	would	compare
you	would	compare
they	would	compare

Conditional Past

I	would have	compared
you	would have	compared
he/she/it	would have	compared
we	would have	compared
you	would have	compared
they	would have	compared

compete

kämpfen

\+ **-ing** → ~~e~~ / + **-d** nicht **-ed**
Regelmäßiges Verb

Simple tenses

Present

I	compete
you	compete
he/she/it	competes
we	compete
you	compete
they	compete

Past

I	competed
you	competed
he/she/it	competed
we	competed
you	competed
they	competed

Present Perfect

I	have	competed
you	have	competed
he/she/it	has	competed
we	have	competed
you	have	competed
they	have	competed

Past Perfect

I	had	competed
you	had	competed
he/she/it	had	competed
we	had	competed
you	had	competed
they	had	competed

Will-Future

I	will	compete
you	will	compete
he/she/it	will	compete
we	will	compete
you	will	compete
they	will	compete

Going to-Future

I	am	going to	compete
you	are	going to	compete
he/she/it	is	going to	compete
we	are	going to	compete
you	are	going to	compete
they	are	going to	compete

Future Perfect

I	will have	competed
you	will have	competed
he/she/it	will have	competed
we	will have	competed
you	will have	competed
they	will have	competed

Imperative

compete

Impersonal

ing-Form

competing

Past Participle

competed

Continuous tenses

Present

I	am	competing
you	are	competing
he/she/it	is	competing
we	are	competing
you	are	competing
they	are	competing

Past

I	was	competing
you	were	competing
he/she/it	was	competing
we	were	competing
you	were	competing
they	were	competing

Present Perfect

I	have	been	competing
you	have	been	competing
he/she/it	has	been	competing
we	have	been	competing
you	have	been	competing
they	have	been	competing

Past Perfect

I	had been	competing
you	had been	competing
he/she/it	had been	competing
we	had been	competing
you	had been	competing
they	had been	competing

Will-Future

I	will be	competing
you	will be	competing
he/she/it	will be	competing
we	will be	competing
you	will be	competing
they	will be	competing

Going to-Future

I	am	going to be	competing
you	are	going to be	competing
he/she/it	is	going to be	competing
we	are	going to be	competing
you	are	going to be	competing
they	are	going to be	competing

Future Perfect

I	will have been	competing
you	will have been	competing
he/she/it	will have been	competing
we	will have been	competing
you	will have been	competing
they	will have been	competing

Conditional

I	would	compete
you	would	compete
he/she/it	would	compete
we	would	compete
you	would	compete
they	would	compete

Conditional Past

I	would have	competed
you	would have	competed
he/she/it	would have	competed
we	would have	competed
you	would have	competed
they	would have	competed

sich beschweren

complain

Simple tenses

Present

I	complain
you	complain
he/she/it	complains
we	complain
you	complain
they	complain

Past

I	complained
you	complained
he/she/it	complained
we	complained
you	complained
they	complained

Present Perfect

I	have	complained
you	have	complained
he/she/it	has	complained
we	have	complained
you	have	complained
they	have	complained

Past Perfect

I	had	complained
you	had	complained
he/she/it	had	complained
we	had	complained
you	had	complained
they	had	complained

Will-Future

I	will	complain
you	will	complain
he/she/it	will	complain
we	will	complain
you	will	complain
they	will	complain

Going to-Future

I	am	going to	complain
you	are	going to	complain
he/she/it	is	going to	complain
we	are	going to	complain
you	are	going to	complain
they	are	going to	complain

Future Perfect

I	will have	complained
you	will have	complained
he/she/it	will have	complained
we	will have	complained
you	will have	complained
they	will have	complained

Imperative

complain

Impersonal

ing-Form

complaining

Past Participle

complained

Continuous tenses

Present

I	am	complaining
you	are	complaining
he/she/it	is	complaining
we	are	complaining
you	are	complaining
they	are	complaining

Past

I	was	complaining
you	were	complaining
he/she/it	was	complaining
we	were	complaining
you	were	complaining
they	were	complaining

Present Perfect

I	have been	complaining
you	have been	complaining
he/she/it	has been	complaining
we	have been	complaining
you	have been	complaining
they	have been	complaining

Past Perfect

I	had been	complaining
you	had been	complaining
he/she/it	had been	complaining
we	had been	complaining
you	had been	complaining
they	had been	complaining

Will-Future

I	will be	complaining
you	will be	complaining
he/she/it	will be	complaining
we	will be	complaining
you	will be	complaining
they	will be	complaining

Going to-Future

I	am	going to be	complaining
you	are	going to be	complaining
he/she/it	is	going to be	complaining
we	are	going to be	complaining
you	are	going to be	complaining
they	are	going to be	complaining

Future Perfect

I	will have been complaining
you	will have been complaining
he/she/it	will have been complaining
we	will have been complaining
you	will have been complaining
they	will have been complaining

Conditional

I	would	complain
you	would	complain
he/she/it	would	complain
we	would	complain
you	would	complain
they	would	complain

Conditional Past

I	would have	complained
you	would have	complained
he/she/it	would have	complained
we	would have	complained
you	would have	complained
they	would have	complained

concern

angehen

Regelmäßiges Verb

Simple tenses

Present

I	concern
you	concern
he/she/it	concerns
we	concern
you	concern
they	concern

Past

I	concerned
you	concerned
he/she/it	concerned
we	concerned
you	concerned
they	concerned

Present Perfect

I	have	concerned
you	have	concerned
he/she/it	has	concerned
we	have	concerned
you	have	concerned
they	have	concerned

Past Perfect

I	had	concerned
you	had	concerned
he/she/it	had	concerned
we	had	concerned
you	had	concerned
they	had	concerned

Will-Future

I	will	concern
you	will	concern
he/she/it	will	concern
we	will	concern
you	will	concern
they	will	concern

Going to-Future

I	am	going to	concern
you	are	going to	concern
he/she/it	is	going to	concern
we	are	going to	concern
you	are	going to	concern
they	are	going to	concern

Future Perfect

I	will have	concerned
you	will have	concerned
he/she/it	will have	concerned
we	will have	concerned
you	will have	concerned
they	will have	concerned

Imperative

concern

Impersonal

ing-Form

concerning

Past Participle

concerned

Continuous tenses

Present

I	am	concerning
you	are	concerning
he/she/it	is	concerning
we	are	concerning
you	are	concerning
they	are	concerning

Past

I	was	concerning
you	were	concerning
he/she/it	was	concerning
we	were	concerning
you	were	concerning
they	were	concerning

Present Perfect

I	have been	concerning
you	have been	concerning
he/she/it	has been	concerning
we	have been	concerning
you	have been	concerning
they	have been	concerning

Past Perfect

I	had been	concerning
you	had been	concerning
he/she/it	had been	concerning
we	had been	concerning
you	had been	concerning
they	had been	concerning

Will-Future

I	will be	concerning
you	will be	concerning
he/she/it	will be	concerning
we	will be	concerning
you	will be	concerning
they	will be	concerning

Going to-Future

I	am	going to be	concerning
you	are	going to be	concerning
he/she/it	is	going to be	concerning
we	are	going to be	concerning
you	are	going to be	concerning
they	are	going to be	concerning

Future Perfect

I	will have been concerning
you	will have been concerning
he/she/it	will have been concerning
we	will have been concerning
you	will have been concerning
they	will have been concerning

Conditional

I	would	concern
you	would	concern
he/she/it	would	concern
we	would	concern
you	would	concern
they	would	concern

Conditional Past

I	would have	concerned
you	would have	concerned
he/she/it	would have	concerned
we	would have	concerned
you	would have	concerned
they	would have	concerned

+ **-ing** → ~~e~~ / + **-d** nicht **-ed**
Regelmäßiges Verb

schließen

conclude

Simple tenses

Present

I	conclude
you	conclude
he/she/it	concludes
we	conclude
you	conclude
they	conclude

Past

I	concluded
you	concluded
he/she/it	concluded
we	concluded
you	concluded
they	concluded

Present Perfect

I	have	concluded
you	have	concluded
he/she/it	has	concluded
we	have	concluded
you	have	concluded
they	have	concluded

Past Perfect

I	had	concluded
you	had	concluded
he/she/it	had	concluded
we	had	concluded
you	had	concluded
they	had	concluded

Will-Future

I	will	conclude
you	will	conclude
he/she/it	will	conclude
we	will	conclude
you	will	conclude
they	will	conclude

Going to-Future

I	am	going to	conclude
you	are	going to	conclude
he/she/it	is	going to	conclude
we	are	going to	conclude
you	are	going to	conclude
they	are	going to	conclude

Future Perfect

I	will have	concluded
you	will have	concluded
he/she/it	will have	concluded
we	will have	concluded
you	will have	concluded
they	will have	concluded

Imperative

conclude

Impersonal

ing-Form

concluding

Past Participle

concluded

Continuous tenses

Present

I	am	concluding
you	are	concluding
he/she/it	is	concluding
we	are	concluding
you	are	concluding
they	are	concluding

Past

I	was	concluding
you	were	concluding
he/she/it	was	concluding
we	were	concluding
you	were	concluding
they	were	concluding

Present Perfect

I	have been	concluding
you	have been	concluding
he/she/it	has been	concluding
we	have been	concluding
you	have been	concluding
they	have been	concluding

Past Perfect

I	had been	concluding
you	had been	concluding
he/she/it	had been	concluding
we	had been	concluding
you	had been	concluding
they	had been	concluding

Will-Future

I	will be	concluding
you	will be	concluding
he/she/it	will be	concluding
we	will be	concluding
you	will be	concluding
they	will be	concluding

Going to-Future

I	am	going to be	concluding
you	are	going to be	concluding
he/she/it	is	going to be	concluding
we	are	going to be	concluding
you	are	going to be	concluding
they	are	going to be	concluding

Future Perfect

I	will have been	concluding
you	will have been	concluding
he/she/it	will have been	concluding
we	will have been	concluding
you	will have been	concluding
they	will have been	concluding

Conditional

I	would	conclude
you	would	conclude
he/she/it	would	conclude
we	would	conclude
you	would	conclude
they	would	conclude

Conditional Past

I	would have	concluded
you	would have	concluded
he/she/it	would have	concluded
we	would have	concluded
you	would have	concluded
they	would have	concluded

conduct

durchführen

Regelmäßiges Verb

Simple tenses

Present

I	conduct
you	conduct
he/she/it	conducts
we	conduct
you	conduct
they	conduct

Past

I	conducted
you	conducted
he/she/it	conducted
we	conducted
you	conducted
they	conducted

Present Perfect

I	have	conducted
you	have	conducted
he/she/it	has	conducted
we	have	conducted
you	have	conducted
they	have	conducted

Past Perfect

I	had	conducted
you	had	conducted
he/she/it	had	conducted
we	had	conducted
you	had	conducted
they	had	conducted

Will-Future

I	will	conduct
you	will	conduct
he/she/it	will	conduct
we	will	conduct
you	will	conduct
they	will	conduct

Going to-Future

I	am	going to	conduct
you	are	going to	conduct
he/she/it	is	going to	conduct
we	are	going to	conduct
you	are	going to	conduct
they	are	going to	conduct

Future Perfect

I	will have	conducted
you	will have	conducted
he/she/it	will have	conducted
we	will have	conducted
you	will have	conducted
they	will have	conducted

Imperative

conduct

Impersonal

ing-Form

conducting

Past Participle

conducted

Continuous tenses

Present

I	am	conducting
you	are	conducting
he/she/it	is	conducting
we	are	conducting
you	are	conducting
they	are	conducting

Past

I	was	conducting
you	were	conducting
he/she/it	was	conducting
we	were	conducting
you	were	conducting
they	were	conducting

Present Perfect

I	have been	conducting
you	have been	conducting
he/she/it	has been	conducting
we	have been	conducting
you	have been	conducting
they	have been	conducting

Past Perfect

I	had been	conducting
you	had been	conducting
he/she/it	had been	conducting
we	had been	conducting
you	had been	conducting
they	had been	conducting

Will-Future

I	will be	conducting
you	will be	conducting
he/she/it	will be	conducting
we	will be	conducting
you	will be	conducting
they	will be	conducting

Going to-Future

I	am	going to be	conducting
you	are	going to be	conducting
he/she/it	is	going to be	conducting
we	are	going to be	conducting
you	are	going to be	conducting
they	are	going to be	conducting

Future Perfect

I	will have been conducting
you	will have been conducting
he/she/it	will have been conducting
we	will have been conducting
you	will have been conducting
they	will have been conducting

Conditional

I	would	conduct
you	would	conduct
he/she/it	would	conduct
we	would	conduct
you	would	conduct
they	would	conduct

Conditional Past

I	would have	conducted
you	would have	conducted
he/she/it	would have	conducted
we	would have	conducted
you	would have	conducted
they	would have	conducted

bestätigen

confirm

Simple tenses

Present

I	confirm
you	confirm
he/she/it	confirms
we	confirm
you	confirm
they	confirm

Past

I	confirmed
you	confirmed
he/she/it	confirmed
we	confirmed
you	confirmed
they	confirmed

Present Perfect

I	have	confirmed
you	have	confirmed
he/she/it	has	confirmed
we	have	confirmed
you	have	confirmed
they	have	confirmed

Past Perfect

I	had	confirmed
you	had	confirmed
he/she/it	had	confirmed
we	had	confirmed
you	had	confirmed
they	had	confirmed

Will-Future

I	will	confirm
you	will	confirm
he/she/it	will	confirm
we	will	confirm
you	will	confirm
they	will	confirm

Going to-Future

I	am	going to	confirm
you	are	going to	confirm
he/she/it	is	going to	confirm
we	are	going to	confirm
you	are	going to	confirm
they	are	going to	confirm

Future Perfect

I	will have	confirmed
you	will have	confirmed
he/she/it	will have	confirmed
we	will have	confirmed
you	will have	confirmed
they	will have	confirmed

Imperative

confirm

Impersonal

ing-Form

confirming

Past Participle

confirmed

Continuous tenses

Present

I	am	confirming
you	are	confirming
he/she/it	is	confirming
we	are	confirming
you	are	confirming
they	are	confirming

Past

I	was	confirming
you	were	confirming
he/she/it	was	confirming
we	were	confirming
you	were	confirming
they	were	confirming

Present Perfect

I	have been	confirming
you	have been	confirming
he/she/it	has been	confirming
we	have been	confirming
you	have been	confirming
they	have been	confirming

Past Perfect

I	had been	confirming
you	had been	confirming
he/she/it	had been	confirming
we	had been	confirming
you	had been	confirming
they	had been	confirming

Will-Future

I	will be	confirming
you	will be	confirming
he/she/it	will be	confirming
we	will be	confirming
you	will be	confirming
they	will be	confirming

Going to-Future

I	am	going to be	confirming
you	are	going to be	confirming
he/she/it	is	going to be	confirming
we	are	going to be	confirming
you	are	going to be	confirming
they	are	going to be	confirming

Future Perfect

I	will have been	confirming
you	will have been	confirming
he/she/it	will have been	confirming
we	will have been	confirming
you	will have been	confirming
they	will have been	confirming

Conditional

I	would	confirm
you	would	confirm
he/she/it	would	confirm
we	would	confirm
you	would	confirm
they	would	confirm

Conditional Past

I	would have	confirmed
you	would have	confirmed
he/she/it	would have	confirmed
we	would have	confirmed
you	would have	confirmed
they	would have	confirmed

confuse

verwirren

+ **-ing** → ~~e~~ / + **-d** nicht **-ed**
Regelmäßiges Verb

Simple tenses

Present

I	confuse
you	confuse
he/she/it	confuses
we	confuse
you	confuse
they	confuse

Past

I	confused
you	confused
he/she/it	confused
we	confused
you	confused
they	confused

Present Perfect

I	have	confused
you	have	confused
he/she/it	has	confused
we	have	confused
you	have	confused
they	have	confused

Past Perfect

I	had	confused
you	had	confused
he/she/it	had	confused
we	had	confused
you	had	confused
they	had	confused

Will-Future

I	will	confuse
you	will	confuse
he/she/it	will	confuse
we	will	confuse
you	will	confuse
they	will	confuse

Going to-Future

I	am	going to	confuse
you	are	going to	confuse
he/she/it	is	going to	confuse
we	are	going to	confuse
you	are	going to	confuse
they	are	going to	confuse

Future Perfect

I	will have	confused
you	will have	confused
he/she/it	will have	confused
we	will have	confused
you	will have	confused
they	will have	confused

Imperative

confuse

Impersonal

ing-Form

confusing

Past Participle

confused

Continuous tenses

Present

I	am	confusing
you	are	confusing
he/she/it	is	confusing
we	are	confusing
you	are	confusing
they	are	confusing

Past

I	was	confusing
you	were	confusing
he/she/it	was	confusing
we	were	confusing
you	were	confusing
they	were	confusing

Present Perfect

I	have	been	confusing
you	have	been	confusing
he/she/it	has	been	confusing
we	have	been	confusing
you	have	been	confusing
they	have	been	confusing

Past Perfect

I	had been	confusing
you	had been	confusing
he/she/it	had been	confusing
we	had been	confusing
you	had been	confusing
they	had been	confusing

Will-Future

I	will be	confusing
you	will be	confusing
he/she/it	will be	confusing
we	will be	confusing
you	will be	confusing
they	will be	confusing

Going to-Future

I	am	going to be	confusing
you	are	going to be	confusing
he/she/it	is	going to be	confusing
we	are	going to be	confusing
you	are	going to be	confusing
they	are	going to be	confusing

Future Perfect

I	will have been	confusing
you	will have been	confusing
he/she/it	will have been	confusing
we	will have been	confusing
you	will have been	confusing
they	will have been	confusing

Conditional

I	would	confuse
you	would	confuse
he/she/it	would	confuse
we	would	confuse
you	would	confuse
they	would	confuse

Conditional Past

I	would have	confused
you	would have	confused
he/she/it	would have	confused
we	would have	confused
you	would have	confused
they	would have	confused

Simple tenses

Present

I	connect
you	connect
he/she/it	connects
we	connect
you	connect
they	connect

Past

I	connected
you	connected
he/she/it	connected
we	connected
you	connected
they	connected

Present Perfect

I	have	connected
you	have	connected
he/she/it	has	connected
we	have	connected
you	have	connected
they	have	connected

Past Perfect

I	had	connected
you	had	connected
he/she/it	had	connected
we	had	connected
you	had	connected
they	had	connected

Will-Future

I	will	connect
you	will	connect
he/she/it	will	connect
we	will	connect
you	will	connect
they	will	connect

Going to-Future

I	am	going to	connect
you	are	going to	connect
he/she/it	is	going to	connect
we	are	going to	connect
you	are	going to	connect
they	are	going to	connect

Future Perfect

I	will have	connected
you	will have	connected
he/she/it	will have	connected
we	will have	connected
you	will have	connected
they	will have	connected

Imperative

connect

Impersonal

ing-Form

connecting

Past Participle

connected

Continuous tenses

Present

I	am	connecting
you	are	connecting
he/she/it	is	connecting
we	are	connecting
you	are	connecting
they	are	connecting

Past

I	was	connecting
you	were	connecting
he/she/it	was	connecting
we	were	connecting
you	were	connecting
they	were	connecting

Present Perfect

I	have been	connecting
you	have been	connecting
he/she/it	has been	connecting
we	have been	connecting
you	have been	connecting
they	have been	connecting

Past Perfect

I	had been	connecting
you	had been	connecting
he/she/it	had been	connecting
we	had been	connecting
you	had been	connecting
they	had been	connecting

Will-Future

I	will be	connecting
you	will be	connecting
he/she/it	will be	connecting
we	will be	connecting
you	will be	connecting
they	will be	connecting

Going to-Future

I	am	going to be	connecting
you	are	going to be	connecting
he/she/it	is	going to be	connecting
we	are	going to be	connecting
you	are	going to be	connecting
they	are	going to be	connecting

Future Perfect

I	will have been	connecting
you	will have been	connecting
he/she/it	will have been	connecting
we	will have been	connecting
you	will have been	connecting
they	will have been	connecting

Conditional

I	would	connect
you	would	connect
he/she/it	would	connect
we	would	connect
you	would	connect
they	would	connect

Conditional Past

I	would have	connected
you	would have	connected
he/she/it	would have	connected
we	would have	connected
you	would have	connected
they	would have	connected

consider

betrachten, berücksichtigen

Regelmäßiges Verb

Simple tenses

Present

I	consider
you	consider
he/she/it	considers
we	consider
you	consider
they	consider

Past

I	considered
you	considered
he/she/it	considered
we	considered
you	considered
they	considered

Present Perfect

I	have	considered
you	have	considered
he/she/it	has	considered
we	have	considered
you	have	considered
they	have	considered

Past Perfect

I	had	considered
you	had	considered
he/she/it	had	considered
we	had	considered
you	had	considered
they	had	considered

Will-Future

I	will	consider
you	will	consider
he/she/it	will	consider
we	will	consider
you	will	consider
they	will	consider

Going to-Future

I	am	going to	consider
you	are	going to	consider
he/she/it	is	going to	consider
we	are	going to	consider
you	are	going to	consider
they	are	going to	consider

Future Perfect

I	will have	considered
you	will have	considered
he/she/it	will have	considered
we	will have	considered
you	will have	considered
they	will have	considered

Imperative

consider

Impersonal

ing-Form

considering

Past Participle

considered

Continuous tenses

Present

I	am	considering
you	are	considering
he/she/it	is	considering
we	are	considering
you	are	considering
they	are	considering

Past

I	was	considering
you	were	considering
he/she/it	was	considering
we	were	considering
you	were	considering
they	were	considering

Present Perfect

I	have	been	considering
you	have	been	considering
he/she/it	has	been	considering
we	have	been	considering
you	have	been	considering
they	have	been	considering

Past Perfect

I	had been	considering
you	had been	considering
he/she/it	had been	considering
we	had been	considering
you	had been	considering
they	had been	considering

Will-Future

I	will be	considering
you	will be	considering
he/she/it	will be	considering
we	will be	considering
you	will be	considering
they	will be	considering

Going to-Future

I	am	going to be	considering
you	are	going to be	considering
he/she/it	is	going to be	considering
we	are	going to be	considering
you	are	going to be	considering
they	are	going to be	considering

Future Perfect

I	will have been considering
you	will have been considering
he/she/it	will have been considering
we	will have been considering
you	will have been considering
they	will have been considering

Conditional

I	would	consider
you	would	consider
he/she/it	would	consider
we	would	consider
you	would	consider
they	would	consider

Conditional Past

I	would have	considered
you	would have	considered
he/she/it	would have	considered
we	would have	considered
you	would have	considered
they	would have	considered

consist

Regelmäßiges Verb

Simple tenses

Present

I	consist
you	consist
he/she/it	consists
we	consist
you	consist
they	consist

Past

I	consisted
you	consisted
he/she/it	consisted
we	consisted
you	consisted
they	consisted

Present Perfect

I	have	consisted
you	have	consisted
he/she/it	has	consisted
we	have	consisted
you	have	consisted
they	have	consisted

Past Perfect

I	had	consisted
you	had	consisted
he/she/it	had	consisted
we	had	consisted
you	had	consisted
they	had	consisted

Will-Future

I	will	consist
you	will	consist
he/she/it	will	consist
we	will	consist
you	will	consist
they	will	consist

Going to-Future

I	am	going to	consist
you	are	going to	consist
he/she/it	is	going to	consist
we	are	going to	consist
you	are	going to	consist
they	are	going to	consist

Future Perfect

I	will have	consisted
you	will have	consisted
he/she/it	will have	consisted
we	will have	consisted
you	will have	consisted
they	will have	consisted

Imperative

consist

Impersonal

ing-Form

consisting

Past Participle

consisted

Continuous tenses

Present

I	am	consisting
you	are	consisting
he/she/it	is	consisting
we	are	consisting
you	are	consisting
they	are	consisting

Past

I	was	consisting
you	were	consisting
he/she/it	was	consisting
we	were	consisting
you	were	consisting
they	were	consisting

Present Perfect

I	have	been	consisting
you	have	been	consisting
he/she/it	has	been	consisting
we	have	been	consisting
you	have	been	consisting
they	have	been	consisting

Past Perfect

I	had been	consisting
you	had been	consisting
he/she/it	had been	consisting
we	had been	consisting
you	had been	consisting
they	had been	consisting

Will-Future

I	will be	consisting
you	will be	consisting
he/she/it	will be	consisting
we	will be	consisting
you	will be	consisting
they	will be	consisting

Going to-Future

I	am	going to be	consisting
you	are	going to be	consisting
he/she/it	is	going to be	consisting
we	are	going to be	consisting
you	are	going to be	consisting
they	are	going to be	consisting

Future Perfect

I	will have been	consisting
you	will have been	consisting
he/she/it	will have been	consisting
we	will have been	consisting
you	will have been	consisting
they	will have been	consisting

Conditional

I	would	consist
you	would	consist
he/she/it	would	consist
we	would	consist
you	would	consist
they	would	consist

Conditional Past

I	would have	consisted
you	would have	consisted
he/she/it	would have	consisted
we	would have	consisted
you	would have	consisted
they	would have	consisted

construct

bauen

Regelmäßiges Verb

Simple tenses

Present

I	construct
you	construct
he/she/it	constructs
we	construct
you	construct
they	construct

Past

I	constructed
you	constructed
he/she/it	constructed
we	constructed
you	constructed
they	constructed

Present Perfect

I	have	constructed
you	have	constructed
he/she/it	has	constructed
we	have	constructed
you	have	constructed
they	have	constructed

Past Perfect

I	had	constructed
you	had	constructed
he/she/it	had	constructed
we	had	constructed
you	had	constructed
they	had	constructed

Will-Future

I	will	construct
you	will	construct
he/she/it	will	construct
we	will	construct
you	will	construct
they	will	construct

Going to-Future

I	am	going to	construct
you	are	going to	construct
he/she/it	is	going to	construct
we	are	going to	construct
you	are	going to	construct
they	are	going to	construct

Future Perfect

I	will have	constructed
you	will have	constructed
he/she/it	will have	constructed
we	will have	constructed
you	will have	constructed
they	will have	constructed

Imperative

construct

Impersonal

ing-Form

constructing

Past Participle

constructed

Continuous tenses

Present

I	am	constructing
you	are	constructing
he/she/it	is	constructing
we	are	constructing
you	are	constructing
they	are	constructing

Past

I	was	constructing
you	were	constructing
he/she/it	was	constructing
we	were	constructing
you	were	constructing
they	were	constructing

Present Perfect

I	have	been	constructing
you	have	been	constructing
he/she/it	has	been	constructing
we	have	been	constructing
you	have	been	constructing
they	have	been	constructing

Past Perfect

I	had been	constructing
you	had been	constructing
he/she/it	had been	constructing
we	had been	constructing
you	had been	constructing
they	had been	constructing

Will-Future

I	will be	constructing
you	will be	constructing
he/she/it	will be	constructing
we	will be	constructing
you	will be	constructing
they	will be	constructing

Going to-Future

I	am	going to be	constructing
you	are	going to be	constructing
he/she/it	is	going to be	constructing
we	are	going to be	constructing
you	are	going to be	constructing
they	are	going to be	constructing

Future Perfect

I	will have been constructing
you	will have been constructing
he/she/it	will have been constructing
we	will have been constructing
you	will have been constructing
they	will have been constructing

Conditional

I	would	construct
you	would	construct
he/she/it	would	construct
we	would	construct
you	would	construct
they	would	construct

Conditional Past

I	would have	constructed
you	would have	constructed
he/she/it	would have	constructed
we	would have	constructed
you	would have	constructed
they	would have	constructed

enthalten

contain

Simple tenses

Present

I	contain
you	contain
he/she/it	contains
we	contain
you	contain
they	contain

Past

I	contained
you	contained
he/she/it	contained
we	contained
you	contained
they	contained

Present Perfect

I	have	contained
you	have	contained
he/she/it	has	contained
we	have	contained
you	have	contained
they	have	contained

Past Perfect

I	had	contained
you	had	contained
he/she/it	had	contained
we	had	contained
you	had	contained
they	had	contained

Will-Future

I	will	contain
you	will	contain
he/she/it	will	contain
we	will	contain
you	will	contain
they	will	contain

Going to-Future

I	am	going to	contain
you	are	going to	contain
he/she/it	is	going to	contain
we	are	going to	contain
you	are	going to	contain
they	are	going to	contain

Future Perfect

I	will have	contained
you	will have	contained
he/she/it	will have	contained
we	will have	contained
you	will have	contained
they	will have	contained

Imperative

contain

Impersonal

ing-Form

containing

Past Participle

contained

Continuous tenses

Present

I	am	containing
you	are	containing
he/she/it	is	containing
we	are	containing
you	are	containing
they	are	containing

Past

I	was	containing
you	were	containing
he/she/it	was	containing
we	were	containing
you	were	containing
they	were	containing

Present Perfect

I	have been	containing
you	have been	containing
he/she/it	has been	containing
we	have been	containing
you	have been	containing
they	have been	containing

Past Perfect

I	had been	containing
you	had been	containing
he/she/it	had been	containing
we	had been	containing
you	had been	containing
they	had been	containing

Will-Future

I	will be	containing
you	will be	containing
he/she/it	will be	containing
we	will be	containing
you	will be	containing
they	will be	containing

Going to-Future

I	am	going to be	containing
you	are	going to be	containing
he/she/it	is	going to be	containing
we	are	going to be	containing
you	are	going to be	containing
they	are	going to be	containing

Future Perfect

I	will have been containing
you	will have been containing
he/she/it	will have been containing
we	will have been containing
you	will have been containing
they	will have been containing

Conditional

I	would	contain
you	would	contain
he/she/it	would	contain
we	would	contain
you	would	contain
they	would	contain

Conditional Past

I	would have	contained
you	would have	contained
he/she/it	would have	contained
we	would have	contained
you	would have	contained
they	would have	contained

continue

andauern

+ **-ing** → ~~e~~ / + **-d** nicht **-ed**
Regelmäßiges Verb

Simple tenses

Present

I	continue
you	continue
he/she/it	continues
we	continue
you	continue
they	continue

Past

I	continued
you	continued
he/she/it	continued
we	continued
you	continued
they	continued

Present Perfect

I	have	continued
you	have	continued
he/she/it	has	continued
we	have	continued
you	have	continued
they	have	continued

Past Perfect

I	had	continued
you	had	continued
he/she/it	had	continued
we	had	continued
you	had	continued
they	had	continued

Will-Future

I	will	continue
you	will	continue
he/she/it	will	continue
we	will	continue
you	will	continue
they	will	continue

Going to-Future

I	am	going to	continue
you	are	going to	continue
he/she/it	is	going to	continue
we	are	going to	continue
you	are	going to	continue
they	are	going to	continue

Future Perfect

I	will have	continued
you	will have	continued
he/she/it	will have	continued
we	will have	continued
you	will have	continued
they	will have	continued

Imperative

continue

Impersonal

ing-Form

continuing

Past Participle

continued

Continuous tenses

Present

I	am	continuing
you	are	continuing
he/she/it	is	continuing
we	are	continuing
you	are	continuing
they	are	continuing

Past

I	was	continuing
you	were	continuing
he/she/it	was	continuing
we	were	continuing
you	were	continuing
they	were	continuing

Present Perfect

I	have	been	continuing
you	have	been	continuing
he/she/it	has	been	continuing
we	have	been	continuing
you	have	been	continuing
they	have	been	continuing

Past Perfect

I	had been	continuing
you	had been	continuing
he/she/it	had been	continuing
we	had been	continuing
you	had been	continuing
they	had been	continuing

Will-Future

I	will be	continuing
you	will be	continuing
he/she/it	will be	continuing
we	will be	continuing
you	will be	continuing
they	will be	continuing

Going to-Future

I	am	going to be	continuing
you	are	going to be	continuing
he/she/it	is	going to be	continuing
we	are	going to be	continuing
you	are	going to be	continuing
they	are	going to be	continuing

Future Perfect

I	will have been	continuing
you	will have been	continuing
he/she/it	will have been	continuing
we	will have been	continuing
you	will have been	continuing
they	will have been	continuing

Conditional

I	would	continue
you	would	continue
he/she/it	would	continue
we	would	continue
you	would	continue
they	would	continue

Conditional Past

I	would have	continued
you	would have	continued
he/she/it	would have	continued
we	would have	continued
you	would have	continued
they	would have	continued

+ **-ing** → ~~e~~ / + **-d** nicht **-ed**
Regelmäßiges Verb

beitragen

contribute

Simple tenses

Present

I	contribute
you	contribute
he/she/it	contributes
we	contribute
you	contribute
they	contribute

Past

I	contributed
you	contributed
he/she/it	contributed
we	contributed
you	contributed
they	contributed

Present Perfect

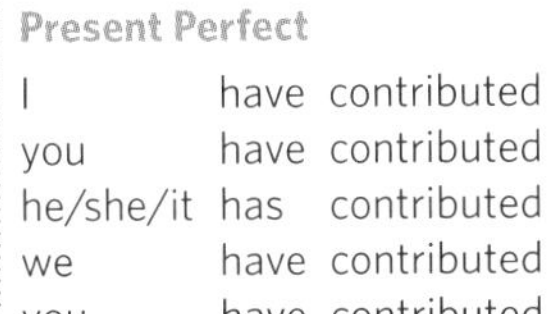

I	have	contributed
you	have	contributed
he/she/it	has	contributed
we	have	contributed
you	have	contributed
they	have	contributed

Past Perfect

I	had	contributed
you	had	contributed
he/she/it	had	contributed
we	had	contributed
you	had	contributed
they	had	contributed

Will-Future

I	will	contribute
you	will	contribute
he/she/it	will	contribute
we	will	contribute
you	will	contribute
they	will	contribute

Going to-Future

I	am	going to	contribute
you	are	going to	contribute
he/she/it	is	going to	contribute
we	are	going to	contribute
you	are	going to	contribute
they	are	going to	contribute

Future Perfect

I	will have	contributed
you	will have	contributed
he/she/it	will have	contributed
we	will have	contributed
you	will have	contributed
they	will have	contributed

Imperative

contribute

Impersonal

ing-Form

contributing

Past Participle

contributed

Continuous tenses

Present

I	am	contributing
you	are	contributing
he/she/it	is	contributing
we	are	contributing
you	are	contributing
they	are	contributing

Past

I	was	contributing
you	were	contributing
he/she/it	was	contributing
we	were	contributing
you	were	contributing
they	were	contributing

Present Perfect

I	have been	contributing
you	have been	contributing
he/she/it	has been	contributing
we	have been	contributing
you	have been	contributing
they	have been	contributing

Past Perfect

I	had been	contributing
you	had been	contributing
he/she/it	had been	contributing
we	had been	contributing
you	had been	contributing
they	had been	contributing

Will-Future

I	will be	contributing
you	will be	contributing
he/she/it	will be	contributing
we	will be	contributing
you	will be	contributing
they	will be	contributing

Going to-Future

I	am	going to be	contributing
you	are	going to be	contributing
he/she/it	is	going to be	contributing
we	are	going to be	contributing
you	are	going to be	contributing
they	are	going to be	contributing

Future Perfect

I	will have been contributing
you	will have been contributing
he/she/it	will have been contributing
we	will have been contributing
you	will have been contributing
they	will have been contributing

Conditional

I	would	contribute
you	would	contribute
he/she/it	would	contribute
we	would	contribute
you	would	contribute
they	would	contribute

Conditional Past

I	would have	contributed
you	would have	contributed
he/she/it	would have	contributed
we	would have	contributed
you	would have	contributed
they	would have	contributed

control

kontrollieren, steuern

Konsonantenverdopplung
Regelmäßiges Verb

Simple tenses

Present

I	control
you	control
he/she/it	controls
we	control
you	control
they	control

Past

I	controlled
you	controlled
he/she/it	controlled
we	controlled
you	controlled
they	controlled

Present Perfect

I	have	controlled
you	have	controlled
he/she/it	has	controlled
we	have	controlled
you	have	controlled
they	have	controlled

Past Perfect

I	had	controlled
you	had	controlled
he/she/it	had	controlled
we	had	controlled
you	had	controlled
they	had	controlled

Will-Future

I	will	control
you	will	control
he/she/it	will	control
we	will	control
you	will	control
they	will	control

Going to-Future

I	am	going to	control
you	are	going to	control
he/she/it	is	going to	control
we	are	going to	control
you	are	going to	control
they	are	going to	control

Future Perfect

I	will have	controlled
you	will have	controlled
he/she/it	will have	controlled
we	will have	controlled
you	will have	controlled
they	will have	controlled

Imperative

control

Impersonal

ing-Form

controlling

Past Participle

controlled

Continuous tenses

Present

I	am	controlling
you	are	controlling
he/she/it	is	controlling
we	are	controlling
you	are	controlling
they	are	controlling

Past

I	was	controlling
you	were	controlling
he/she/it	was	controlling
we	were	controlling
you	were	controlling
they	were	controlling

Present Perfect

I	have been	controlling
you	have been	controlling
he/she/it	has been	controlling
we	have been	controlling
you	have been	controlling
they	have been	controlling

Past Perfect

I	had been	controlling
you	had been	controlling
he/she/it	had been	controlling
we	had been	controlling
you	had been	controlling
they	had been	controlling

Will-Future

I	will be	controlling
you	will be	controlling
he/she/it	will be	controlling
we	will be	controlling
you	will be	controlling
they	will be	controlling

Going to-Future

I	am	going to be	controlling
you	are	going to be	controlling
he/she/it	is	going to be	controlling
we	are	going to be	controlling
you	are	going to be	controlling
they	are	going to be	controlling

Future Perfect

I	will have been	controlling
you	will have been	controlling
he/she/it	will have been	controlling
we	will have been	controlling
you	will have been	controlling
they	will have been	controlling

Conditional

I	would	control
you	would	control
he/she/it	would	control
we	would	control
you	would	control
they	would	control

Conditional Past

I	would have	controlled
you	would have	controlled
he/she/it	would have	controlled
we	would have	controlled
you	would have	controlled
they	would have	controlled

+ **-ing** → ~~e~~ / + **-d** nicht **-ed**
Regelmäßiges Verb

überzeugen

convince

Simple tenses

Present

I	convince
you	convince
he/she/it	convinces
we	convince
you	convince
they	convince

Past

I	convinced
you	convinced
he/she/it	convinced
we	convinced
you	convinced
they	convinced

Present Perfect

I	have	convinced
you	have	convinced
he/she/it	has	convinced
we	have	convinced
you	have	convinced
they	have	convinced

Past Perfect

I	had	convinced
you	had	convinced
he/she/it	had	convinced
we	had	convinced
you	had	convinced
they	had	convinced

Will-Future

I	will	convince
you	will	convince
he/she/it	will	convince
we	will	convince
you	will	convince
they	will	convince

Going to-Future

I	am	going to	convince
you	are	going to	convince
he/she/it	is	going to	convince
we	are	going to	convince
you	are	going to	convince
they	are	going to	convince

Future Perfect

I	will have	convinced
you	will have	convinced
he/she/it	will have	convinced
we	will have	convinced
you	will have	convinced
they	will have	convinced

Imperative

convince

Impersonal

ing-Form

convincing

Past Participle

convinced

Continuous tenses

Present

I	am	convincing
you	are	convincing
he/she/it	is	convincing
we	are	convincing
you	are	convincing
they	are	convincing

Past

I	was	convincing
you	were	convincing
he/she/it	was	convincing
we	were	convincing
you	were	convincing
they	were	convincing

Present Perfect

I	have been	convincing
you	have been	convincing
he/she/it	has been	convincing
we	have been	convincing
you	have been	convincing
they	have been	convincing

Past Perfect

I	had been	convincing
you	had been	convincing
he/she/it	had been	convincing
we	had been	convincing
you	had been	convincing
they	had been	convincing

Will-Future

I	will be	convincing
you	will be	convincing
he/she/it	will be	convincing
we	will be	convincing
you	will be	convincing
they	will be	convincing

Going to-Future

I	am	going to be	convincing
you	are	going to be	convincing
he/she/it	is	going to be	convincing
we	are	going to be	convincing
you	are	going to be	convincing
they	are	going to be	convincing

Future Perfect

I	will have been	convincing
you	will have been	convincing
he/she/it	will have been	convincing
we	will have been	convincing
you	will have been	convincing
they	will have been	convincing

Conditional

I	would	convince
you	would	convince
he/she/it	would	convince
we	would	convince
you	would	convince
they	would	convince

Conditional Past

I	would have	convinced
you	would have	convinced
he/she/it	would have	convinced
we	would have	convinced
you	would have	convinced
they	would have	convinced

cook

kochen

Regelmäßiges Verb

Simple tenses

Present

I	cook
you	cook
he/she/it	cooks
we	cook
you	cook
they	cook

Past

I	cooked
you	cooked
he/she/it	cooked
we	cooked
you	cooked
they	cooked

Present Perfect

I	have	cooked
you	have	cooked
he/she/it	has	cooked
we	have	cooked
you	have	cooked
they	have	cooked

Past Perfect

I	had	cooked
you	had	cooked
he/she/it	had	cooked
we	had	cooked
you	had	cooked
they	had	cooked

Will-Future

I	will	cook
you	will	cook
he/she/it	will	cook
we	will	cook
you	will	cook
they	will	cook

Going to-Future

I	am	going to	cook
you	are	going to	cook
he/she/it	is	going to	cook
we	are	going to	cook
you	are	going to	cook
they	are	going to	cook

Future Perfect

I	will have	cooked
you	will have	cooked
he/she/it	will have	cooked
we	will have	cooked
you	will have	cooked
they	will have	cooked

Imperative

cook

Impersonal

ing-Form

cooking

Past Participle

cooked

Continuous tenses

Present

I	am	cooking
you	are	cooking
he/she/it	is	cooking
we	are	cooking
you	are	cooking
they	are	cooking

Past

I	was	cooking
you	were	cooking
he/she/it	was	cooking
we	were	cooking
you	were	cooking
they	were	cooking

Present Perfect

I	have been	cooking
you	have been	cooking
he/she/it	has been	cooking
we	have been	cooking
you	have been	cooking
they	have been	cooking

Past Perfect

I	had been	cooking
you	had been	cooking
he/she/it	had been	cooking
we	had been	cooking
you	had been	cooking
they	had been	cooking

Will-Future

I	will be	cooking
you	will be	cooking
he/she/it	will be	cooking
we	will be	cooking
you	will be	cooking
they	will be	cooking

Going to-Future

I	am	going to be	cooking
you	are	going to be	cooking
he/she/it	is	going to be	cooking
we	are	going to be	cooking
you	are	going to be	cooking
they	are	going to be	cooking

Future Perfect

I	will have been	cooking
you	will have been	cooking
he/she/it	will have been	cooking
we	will have been	cooking
you	will have been	cooking
they	will have been	cooking

Conditional

I	would	cook
you	would	cook
he/she/it	would	cook
we	would	cook
you	would	cook
they	would	cook

Conditional Past

I	would have	cooked
you	would have	cooked
he/she/it	would have	cooked
we	would have	cooked
you	would have	cooked
they	would have	cooked

-y → -ie vor -s / -y → -i vor -ed
Regelmäßiges Verb

kopieren, abschreiben

copy

Simple tenses

Present

I	copy
you	copy
he/she/it	copies
we	copy
you	copy
they	copy

Past

I	copied
you	copied
he/she/it	copied
we	copied
you	copied
they	copied

Present Perfect

I	have	copied
you	have	copied
he/she/it	has	copied
we	have	copied
you	have	copied
they	have	copied

Past Perfect

I	had	copied
you	had	copied
he/she/it	had	copied
we	had	copied
you	had	copied
they	had	copied

Will-Future

I	will	copy
you	will	copy
he/she/it	will	copy
we	will	copy
you	will	copy
they	will	copy

Going to-Future

I	am	going to	copy
you	are	going to	copy
he/she/it	is	going to	copy
we	are	going to	copy
you	are	going to	copy
they	are	going to	copy

Future Perfect

I	will have	copied
you	will have	copied
he/she/it	will have	copied
we	will have	copied
you	will have	copied
they	will have	copied

Imperative

copy

Impersonal

ing-Form

copying

Past Participle

copied

Continuous tenses

Present

I	am	copying
you	are	copying
he/she/it	is	copying
we	are	copying
you	are	copying
they	are	copying

Past

I	was	copying
you	were	copying
he/she/it	was	copying
we	were	copying
you	were	copying
they	were	copying

Present Perfect

I	have been	copying
you	have been	copying
he/she/it	has been	copying
we	have been	copying
you	have been	copying
they	have been	copying

Past Perfect

I	had been	copying
you	had been	copying
he/she/it	had been	copying
we	had been	copying
you	had been	copying
they	had been	copying

Will-Future

I	will be	copying
you	will be	copying
he/she/it	will be	copying
we	will be	copying
you	will be	copying
they	will be	copying

Going to-Future

I	am	going to be	copying
you	are	going to be	copying
he/she/it	is	going to be	copying
we	are	going to be	copying
you	are	going to be	copying
they	are	going to be	copying

Future Perfect

I	will have been	copying
you	will have been	copying
he/she/it	will have been	copying
we	will have been	copying
you	will have been	copying
they	will have been	copying

Conditional

I	would	copy
you	would	copy
he/she/it	would	copy
we	would	copy
you	would	copy
they	would	copy

Conditional Past

I	would have	copied
you	would have	copied
he/she/it	would have	copied
we	would have	copied
you	would have	copied
they	would have	copied

correct

korrigieren

Regelmäßiges Verb

Simple tenses

Present

I	correct
you	correct
he/she/it	corrects
we	correct
you	correct
they	correct

Past

I	corrected
you	corrected
he/she/it	corrected
we	corrected
you	corrected
they	corrected

Present Perfect

I	have	corrected
you	have	corrected
he/she/it	has	corrected
we	have	corrected
you	have	corrected
they	have	corrected

Past Perfect

I	had	corrected
you	had	corrected
he/she/it	had	corrected
we	had	corrected
you	had	corrected
they	had	corrected

Will-Future

I	will	correct
you	will	correct
he/she/it	will	correct
we	will	correct
you	will	correct
they	will	correct

Going to-Future

I	am	going to	correct
you	are	going to	correct
he/she/it	is	going to	correct
we	are	going to	correct
you	are	going to	correct
they	are	going to	correct

Future Perfect

I	will have	corrected
you	will have	corrected
he/she/it	will have	corrected
we	will have	corrected
you	will have	corrected
they	will have	corrected

Imperative

correct

Impersonal

ing-Form

correcting

Past Participle

corrected

Continuous tenses

Present

I	am	correcting
you	are	correcting
he/she/it	is	correcting
we	are	correcting
you	are	correcting
they	are	correcting

Past

I	was	correcting
you	were	correcting
he/she/it	was	correcting
we	were	correcting
you	were	correcting
they	were	correcting

Present Perfect

I	have been	correcting
you	have been	correcting
he/she/it	has been	correcting
we	have been	correcting
you	have been	correcting
they	have been	correcting

Past Perfect

I	had been	correcting
you	had been	correcting
he/she/it	had been	correcting
we	had been	correcting
you	had been	correcting
they	had been	correcting

Will-Future

I	will be	correcting
you	will be	correcting
he/she/it	will be	correcting
we	will be	correcting
you	will be	correcting
they	will be	correcting

Going to-Future

I	am	going to be	correcting
you	are	going to be	correcting
he/she/it	is	going to be	correcting
we	are	going to be	correcting
you	are	going to be	correcting
they	are	going to be	correcting

Future Perfect

I	will have been	correcting
you	will have been	correcting
he/she/it	will have been	correcting
we	will have been	correcting
you	will have been	correcting
they	will have been	correcting

Conditional

I	would	correct
you	would	correct
he/she/it	would	correct
we	would	correct
you	would	correct
they	would	correct

Conditional Past

I	would have	corrected
you	would have	corrected
he/she/it	would have	corrected
we	would have	corrected
you	would have	corrected
they	would have	corrected

Simple tenses

Present

I	cost
you	cost
he/she/it	costs
we	cost
you	cost
they	cost

Past

I	cost
you	cost
he/she/it	cost
we	cost
you	cost
they	cost

Present Perfect

I	have	cost
you	have	cost
he/she/it	has	cost
we	have	cost
you	have	cost
they	have	cost

Past Perfect

I	had	cost
you	had	cost
he/she/it	had	cost
we	had	cost
you	had	cost
they	had	cost

Will-Future

I	will	cost
you	will	cost
he/she/it	will	cost
we	will	cost
you	will	cost
they	will	cost

Going to-Future

I	am	going to	cost
you	are	going to	cost
he/she/it	is	going to	cost
we	are	going to	cost
you	are	going to	cost
they	are	going to	cost

Future Perfect

I	will have	cost
you	will have	cost
he/she/it	will have	cost
we	will have	cost
you	will have	cost
they	will have	cost

Imperative

cost

Impersonal

ing-Form

costing

Past Participle

cost

Continuous tenses

Present

I	am	costing
you	are	costing
he/she/it	is	costing
we	are	costing
you	are	costing
they	are	costing

Past

I	was	costing
you	were	costing
he/she/it	was	costing
we	were	costing
you	were	costing
they	were	costing

Present Perfect

I	have	been	costing
you	have	been	costing
he/she/it	has	been	costing
we	have	been	costing
you	have	been	costing
they	have	been	costing

Past Perfect

I	had been	costing
you	had been	costing
he/she/it	had been	costing
we	had been	costing
you	had been	costing
they	had been	costing

Will-Future

I	will be	costing
you	will be	costing
he/she/it	will be	costing
we	will be	costing
you	will be	costing
they	will be	costing

Going to-Future

I	am	going to be	costing
you	are	going to be	costing
he/she/it	is	going to be	costing
we	are	going to be	costing
you	are	going to be	costing
they	are	going to be	costing

Future Perfect

I	will have been	costing
you	will have been	costing
he/she/it	will have been	costing
we	will have been	costing
you	will have been	costing
they	will have been	costing

Conditional

I	would	cost
you	would	cost
he/she/it	would	cost
we	would	cost
you	would	cost
they	would	cost

Conditional Past

I	would have	cost
you	would have	cost
he/she/it	would have	cost
we	would have	cost
you	would have	cost
they	would have	cost

cough

husten

Regelmäßiges Verb

Simple tenses

Present

I	cough
you	cough
he/she/it	coughs
we	cough
you	cough
they	cough

Past

I	coughed
you	coughed
he/she/it	coughed
we	coughed
you	coughed
they	coughed

Present Perfect

I	have	coughed
you	have	coughed
he/she/it	has	coughed
we	have	coughed
you	have	coughed
they	have	coughed

Past Perfect

I	had	coughed
you	had	coughed
he/she/it	had	coughed
we	had	coughed
you	had	coughed
they	had	coughed

Will-Future

I	will	cough
you	will	cough
he/she/it	will	cough
we	will	cough
you	will	cough
they	will	cough

Going to-Future

I	am	going to	cough
you	are	going to	cough
he/she/it	is	going to	cough
we	are	going to	cough
you	are	going to	cough
they	are	going to	cough

Future Perfect

I	will have	coughed
you	will have	coughed
he/she/it	will have	coughed
we	will have	coughed
you	will have	coughed
they	will have	coughed

Imperative

cough

Impersonal

ing-Form

coughing

Past Participle

coughed

Continuous tenses

Present

I	am	coughing
you	are	coughing
he/she/it	is	coughing
we	are	coughing
you	are	coughing
they	are	coughing

Past

I	was	coughing
you	were	coughing
he/she/it	was	coughing
we	were	coughing
you	were	coughing
they	were	coughing

Present Perfect

I	have	been	coughing
you	have	been	coughing
he/she/it	has	been	coughing
we	have	been	coughing
you	have	been	coughing
they	have	been	coughing

Past Perfect

I	had been	coughing
you	had been	coughing
he/she/it	had been	coughing
we	had been	coughing
you	had been	coughing
they	had been	coughing

Will-Future

I	will be	coughing
you	will be	coughing
he/she/it	will be	coughing
we	will be	coughing
you	will be	coughing
they	will be	coughing

Going to-Future

I	am	going to be	coughing
you	are	going to be	coughing
he/she/it	is	going to be	coughing
we	are	going to be	coughing
you	are	going to be	coughing
they	are	going to be	coughing

Future Perfect

I	will have been	coughing
you	will have been	coughing
he/she/it	will have been	coughing
we	will have been	coughing
you	will have been	coughing
they	will have been	coughing

Conditional

I	would	cough
you	would	cough
he/she/it	would	cough
we	would	cough
you	would	cough
they	would	cough

Conditional Past

I	would have	coughed
you	would have	coughed
he/she/it	would have	coughed
we	would have	coughed
you	would have	coughed
they	would have	coughed

Simple tenses

Present

I	cover
you	cover
he/she/it	covers
we	cover
you	cover
they	cover

Past

I	covered
you	covered
he/she/it	covered
we	covered
you	covered
they	covered

Present Perfect

I	have	covered
you	have	covered
he/she/it	has	covered
we	have	covered
you	have	covered
they	have	covered

Past Perfect

I	had	covered
you	had	covered
he/she/it	had	covered
we	had	covered
you	had	covered
they	had	covered

Will-Future

I	will	cover
you	will	cover
he/she/it	will	cover
we	will	cover
you	will	cover
they	will	cover

Going to-Future

I	am	going to	cover
you	are	going to	cover
he/she/it	is	going to	cover
we	are	going to	cover
you	are	going to	cover
they	are	going to	cover

Future Perfect

I	will have	covered
you	will have	covered
he/she/it	will have	covered
we	will have	covered
you	will have	covered
they	will have	covered

Imperative

cover

Impersonal

ing-Form

covering

Past Participle

covered

Continuous tenses

Present

I	am	covering
you	are	covering
he/she/it	is	covering
we	are	covering
you	are	covering
they	are	covering

Past

I	was	covering
you	were	covering
he/she/it	was	covering
we	were	covering
you	were	covering
they	were	covering

Present Perfect

I	have	been	covering
you	have	been	covering
he/she/it	has	been	covering
we	have	been	covering
you	have	been	covering
they	have	been	covering

Past Perfect

I	had been	covering
you	had been	covering
he/she/it	had been	covering
we	had been	covering
you	had been	covering
they	had been	covering

Will-Future

I	will be	covering
you	will be	covering
he/she/it	will be	covering
we	will be	covering
you	will be	covering
they	will be	covering

Going to-Future

I	am	going to be	covering
you	are	going to be	covering
he/she/it	is	going to be	covering
we	are	going to be	covering
you	are	going to be	covering
they	are	going to be	covering

Future Perfect

I	will have been	covering
you	will have been	covering
he/she/it	will have been	covering
we	will have been	covering
you	will have been	covering
they	will have been	covering

Conditional

I	would	cover
you	would	cover
he/she/it	would	cover
we	would	cover
you	would	cover
they	would	cover

Conditional Past

I	would have	covered
you	would have	covered
he/she/it	would have	covered
we	would have	covered
you	would have	covered
they	would have	covered

crash

abstürzen, aufprallen

+ -es in 3. Person Singular
Regelmäßiges Verb

Simple tenses

Present

I	crash
you	crash
he/she/it	crashes
we	crash
you	crash
they	crash

Past

I	crashed
you	crashed
he/she/it	crashed
we	crashed
you	crashed
they	crashed

Present Perfect

I	have	crashed
you	have	crashed
he/she/it	has	crashed
we	have	crashed
you	have	crashed
they	have	crashed

Past Perfect

I	had	crashed
you	had	crashed
he/she/it	had	crashed
we	had	crashed
you	had	crashed
they	had	crashed

Will-Future

I	will	crash
you	will	crash
he/she/it	will	crash
we	will	crash
you	will	crash
they	will	crash

Going to-Future

I	am	going to	crash
you	are	going to	crash
he/she/it	is	going to	crash
we	are	going to	crash
you	are	going to	crash
they	are	going to	crash

Future Perfect

I	will have	crashed
you	will have	crashed
he/she/it	will have	crashed
we	will have	crashed
you	will have	crashed
they	will have	crashed

Imperative

crash

Impersonal

ing-Form

crashing

Past Participle

crashed

Continuous tenses

Present

I	am	crashing
you	are	crashing
he/she/it	is	crashing
we	are	crashing
you	are	crashing
they	are	crashing

Past

I	was	crashing
you	were	crashing
he/she/it	was	crashing
we	were	crashing
you	were	crashing
they	were	crashing

Present Perfect

I	have been	crashing
you	have been	crashing
he/she/it	has been	crashing
we	have been	crashing
you	have been	crashing
they	have been	crashing

Past Perfect

I	had been	crashing
you	had been	crashing
he/she/it	had been	crashing
we	had been	crashing
you	had been	crashing
they	had been	crashing

Will-Future

I	will be	crashing
you	will be	crashing
he/she/it	will be	crashing
we	will be	crashing
you	will be	crashing
they	will be	crashing

Going to-Future

I	am	going to be	crashing
you	are	going to be	crashing
he/she/it	is	going to be	crashing
we	are	going to be	crashing
you	are	going to be	crashing
they	are	going to be	crashing

Future Perfect

I	will have been	crashing
you	will have been	crashing
he/she/it	will have been	crashing
we	will have been	crashing
you	will have been	crashing
they	will have been	crashing

Conditional

I	would	crash
you	would	crash
he/she/it	would	crash
we	would	crash
you	would	crash
they	would	crash

Conditional Past

I	would have	crashed
you	would have	crashed
he/she/it	would have	crashed
we	would have	crashed
you	would have	crashed
they	would have	crashed

schleichen

creep
– crept – crept

Simple tenses

Present

I	creep
you	creep
he/she/it	creeps
we	creep
you	creep
they	creep

Past

I	crept
you	crept
he/she/it	crept
we	crept
you	crept
they	crept

Present Perfect

I	have	crept
you	have	crept
he/she/it	has	crept
we	have	crept
you	have	crept
they	have	crept

Past Perfect

I	had	crept
you	had	crept
he/she/it	had	crept
we	had	crept
you	had	crept
they	had	crept

Will-Future

I	will	creep
you	will	creep
he/she/it	will	creep
we	will	creep
you	will	creep
they	will	creep

Going to-Future

I	am	going to	creep
you	are	going to	creep
he/she/it	is	going to	creep
we	are	going to	creep
you	are	going to	creep
they	are	going to	creep

Future Perfect

I	will have	crept
you	will have	crept
he/she/it	will have	crept
we	will have	crept
you	will have	crept
they	will have	crept

Imperative

creep

Impersonal

ing-Form

creeping

Past Participle

crept

Continuous tenses

Present

I	am	creeping
you	are	creeping
he/she/it	is	creeping
we	are	creeping
you	are	creeping
they	are	creeping

Past

I	was	creeping
you	were	creeping
he/she/it	was	creeping
we	were	creeping
you	were	creeping
they	were	creeping

Present Perfect

I	have been	creeping
you	have been	creeping
he/she/it	has been	creeping
we	have been	creeping
you	have been	creeping
they	have been	creeping

Past Perfect

I	had been	creeping
you	had been	creeping
he/she/it	had been	creeping
we	had been	creeping
you	had been	creeping
they	had been	creeping

Will-Future

I	will be	creeping
you	will be	creeping
he/she/it	will be	creeping
we	will be	creeping
you	will be	creeping
they	will be	creeping

Going to-Future

I	am	going to be	creeping
you	are	going to be	creeping
he/she/it	is	going to be	creeping
we	are	going to be	creeping
you	are	going to be	creeping
they	are	going to be	creeping

Future Perfect

I	will have been	creeping
you	will have been	creeping
he/she/it	will have been	creeping
we	will have been	creeping
you	will have been	creeping
they	will have been	creeping

Conditional

I	would	creep
you	would	creep
he/she/it	would	creep
we	would	creep
you	would	creep
they	would	creep

Conditional Past

I	would have	crept
you	would have	crept
he/she/it	would have	crept
we	would have	crept
you	would have	crept
they	would have	crept

cross

überqueren

+ -es in 3. Person Singular
Regelmäßiges Verb

Simple tenses

Present

I	cross
you	cross
he/she/it	crosses
we	cross
you	cross
they	cross

Past

I	crossed
you	crossed
he/she/it	crossed
we	crossed
you	crossed
they	crossed

Present Perfect

I	have	crossed
you	have	crossed
he/she/it	has	crossed
we	have	crossed
you	have	crossed
they	have	crossed

Past Perfect

I	had	crossed
you	had	crossed
he/she/it	had	crossed
we	had	crossed
you	had	crossed
they	had	crossed

Will-Future

I	will	cross
you	will	cross
he/she/it	will	cross
we	will	cross
you	will	cross
they	will	cross

Going to-Future

I	am	going to	cross
you	are	going to	cross
he/she/it	is	going to	cross
we	are	going to	cross
you	are	going to	cross
they	are	going to	cross

Future Perfect

I	will have	crossed
you	will have	crossed
he/she/it	will have	crossed
we	will have	crossed
you	will have	crossed
they	will have	crossed

Imperative

cross

Impersonal

ing-Form

crossing

Past Participle

crossed

Continuous tenses

Present

I	am	crossing
you	are	crossing
he/she/it	is	crossing
we	are	crossing
you	are	crossing
they	are	crossing

Past

I	was	crossing
you	were	crossing
he/she/it	was	crossing
we	were	crossing
you	were	crossing
they	were	crossing

Present Perfect

I	have been	crossing
you	have been	crossing
he/she/it	has been	crossing
we	have been	crossing
you	have been	crossing
they	have been	crossing

Past Perfect

I	had been	crossing
you	had been	crossing
he/she/it	had been	crossing
we	had been	crossing
you	had been	crossing
they	had been	crossing

Will-Future

I	will be	crossing
you	will be	crossing
he/she/it	will be	crossing
we	will be	crossing
you	will be	crossing
they	will be	crossing

Going to-Future

I	am	going to be	crossing
you	are	going to be	crossing
he/she/it	is	going to be	crossing
we	are	going to be	crossing
you	are	going to be	crossing
they	are	going to be	crossing

Future Perfect

I	will have been	crossing
you	will have been	crossing
he/she/it	will have been	crossing
we	will have been	crossing
you	will have been	crossing
they	will have been	crossing

Conditional

I	would	cross
you	would	cross
he/she/it	would	cross
we	would	cross
you	would	cross
they	would	cross

Conditional Past

I	would have	crossed
you	would have	crossed
he/she/it	would have	crossed
we	would have	crossed
you	would have	crossed
they	would have	crossed

weinen, schreien

cry

Simple tenses

Present

I	cry
you	cry
he/she/it	cries
we	cry
you	cry
they	cry

Past

I	cried
you	cried
he/she/it	cried
we	cried
you	cried
they	cried

Present Perfect

I	have	cried
you	have	cried
he/she/it	has	cried
we	have	cried
you	have	cried
they	have	cried

Past Perfect

I	had	cried
you	had	cried
he/she/it	had	cried
we	had	cried
you	had	cried
they	had	cried

Will-Future

I	will	cry
you	will	cry
he/she/it	will	cry
we	will	cry
you	will	cry
they	will	cry

Going to-Future

I	am	going to	cry
you	are	going to	cry
he/she/it	is	going to	cry
we	are	going to	cry
you	are	going to	cry
they	are	going to	cry

Future Perfect

I	will have	cried
you	will have	cried
he/she/it	will have	cried
we	will have	cried
you	will have	cried
they	will have	cried

Imperative

cry

Impersonal

ing-Form

crying

Past Participle

cried

Continuous tenses

Present

I	am	crying
you	are	crying
he/she/it	is	crying
we	are	crying
you	are	crying
they	are	crying

Past

I	was	crying
you	were	crying
he/she/it	was	crying
we	were	crying
you	were	crying
they	were	crying

Present Perfect

I	have been	crying
you	have been	crying
he/she/it	has been	crying
we	have been	crying
you	have been	crying
they	have been	crying

Past Perfect

I	had been	crying
you	had been	crying
he/she/it	had been	crying
we	had been	crying
you	had been	crying
they	had been	crying

Will-Future

I	will be	crying
you	will be	crying
he/she/it	will be	crying
we	will be	crying
you	will be	crying
they	will be	crying

Going to-Future

I	am	going to be	crying
you	are	going to be	crying
he/she/it	is	going to be	crying
we	are	going to be	crying
you	are	going to be	crying
they	are	going to be	crying

Future Perfect

I	will have been	crying
you	will have been	crying
he/she/it	will have been	crying
we	will have been	crying
you	will have been	crying
they	will have been	crying

Conditional

I	would	cry
you	would	cry
he/she/it	would	cry
we	would	cry
you	would	cry
they	would	cry

Conditional Past

I	would have	cried
you	would have	cried
he/she/it	would have	cried
we	would have	cried
you	would have	cried
they	would have	cried

cut

- cut - cut

schneiden

Konsonantenverdopplung
Unregelmäßiges Verb

Simple tenses

Present

I	cut
you	cut
he/she/it	cuts
we	cut
you	cut
they	cut

Past

I	cut
you	cut
he/she/it	cut
we	cut
you	cut
they	cut

Present Perfect

I	have	cut
you	have	cut
he/she/it	has	cut
we	have	cut
you	have	cut
they	have	cut

Past Perfect

I	had	cut
you	had	cut
he/she/it	had	cut
we	had	cut
you	had	cut
they	had	cut

Will-Future

I	will	cut
you	will	cut
he/she/it	will	cut
we	will	cut
you	will	cut
they	will	cut

Going to-Future

I	am	going to	cut
you	are	going to	cut
he/she/it	is	going to	cut
we	are	going to	cut
you	are	going to	cut
they	are	going to	cut

Future Perfect

I	will have	cut
you	will have	cut
he/she/it	will have	cut
we	will have	cut
you	will have	cut
they	will have	cut

Imperative

cut

Impersonal

ing-Form

cutting

Past Participle

cut

Continuous tenses

Present

I	am	cutting
you	are	cutting
he/she/it	is	cutting
we	are	cutting
you	are	cutting
they	are	cutting

Past

I	was	cutting
you	were	cutting
he/she/it	was	cutting
we	were	cutting
you	were	cutting
they	were	cutting

Present Perfect

I	have been	cutting
you	have been	cutting
he/she/it	has been	cutting
we	have been	cutting
you	have been	cutting
they	have been	cutting

Past Perfect

I	had been	cutting
you	had been	cutting
he/she/it	had been	cutting
we	had been	cutting
you	had been	cutting
they	had been	cutting

Will-Future

I	will be	cutting
you	will be	cutting
he/she/it	will be	cutting
we	will be	cutting
you	will be	cutting
they	will be	cutting

Going to-Future

I	am	going to be	cutting
you	are	going to be	cutting
he/she/it	is	going to be	cutting
we	are	going to be	cutting
you	are	going to be	cutting
they	are	going to be	cutting

Future Perfect

I	will have been	cutting
you	will have been	cutting
he/she/it	will have been	cutting
we	will have been	cutting
you	will have been	cutting
they	will have been	cutting

Conditional

I	would	cut
you	would	cut
he/she/it	would	cut
we	would	cut
you	would	cut
they	would	cut

Conditional Past

I	would have	cut
you	would have	cut
he/she/it	would have	cut
we	would have	cut
you	would have	cut
they	would have	cut

tanzen

dance

Simple tenses

Present

I	dance
you	dance
he/she/it	dances
we	dance
you	dance
they	dance

Past

I	danced
you	danced
he/she/it	danced
we	danced
you	danced
they	danced

Present Perfect

I	have	danced
you	have	danced
he/she/it	has	danced
we	have	danced
you	have	danced
they	have	danced

Past Perfect

I	had	danced
you	had	danced
he/she/it	had	danced
we	had	danced
you	had	danced
they	had	danced

Will-Future

I	will	dance
you	will	dance
he/she/it	will	dance
we	will	dance
you	will	dance
they	will	dance

Going to-Future

I	am	going to	dance
you	are	going to	dance
he/she/it	is	going to	dance
we	are	going to	dance
you	are	going to	dance
they	are	going to	dance

Future Perfect

I	will have	danced
you	will have	danced
he/she/it	will have	danced
we	will have	danced
you	will have	danced
they	will have	danced

Imperative

dance

Impersonal

ing-Form

dancing

Past Participle

danced

Continuous tenses

Present

I	am	dancing
you	are	dancing
he/she/it	is	dancing
we	are	dancing
you	are	dancing
they	are	dancing

Past

I	was	dancing
you	were	dancing
he/she/it	was	dancing
we	were	dancing
you	were	dancing
they	were	dancing

Present Perfect

I	have been	dancing
you	have been	dancing
he/she/it	has been	dancing
we	have been	dancing
you	have been	dancing
they	have been	dancing

Past Perfect

I	had been	dancing
you	had been	dancing
he/she/it	had been	dancing
we	had been	dancing
you	had been	dancing
they	had been	dancing

Will-Future

I	will be	dancing
you	will be	dancing
he/she/it	will be	dancing
we	will be	dancing
you	will be	dancing
they	will be	dancing

Going to-Future

I	am	going to be	dancing
you	are	going to be	dancing
he/she/it	is	going to be	dancing
we	are	going to be	dancing
you	are	going to be	dancing
they	are	going to be	dancing

Future Perfect

I	will have been	dancing
you	will have been	dancing
he/she/it	will have been	dancing
we	will have been	dancing
you	will have been	dancing
they	will have been	dancing

Conditional

I	would	dance
you	would	dance
he/she/it	would	dance
we	would	dance
you	would	dance
they	would	dance

Conditional Past

I	would have	danced
you	would have	danced
he/she/it	would have	danced
we	would have	danced
you	would have	danced
they	would have	danced

dare

sich trauen

+ **-ing** → ~~e~~ / + **-d** nicht **-ed**
Regelmäßiges Verb

Simple tenses

Present

I dare
you dare
he/she/it dares
we dare
you dare
they dare

Past

I dared
you dared
he/she/it dared
we dared
you dared
they dared

Present Perfect

I have dared
you have dared
he/she/it has dared
we have dared
you have dared
they have dared

Past Perfect

I had dared
you had dared
he/she/it had dared
we had dared
you had dared
they had dared

Will-Future

I will dare
you will dare
he/she/it will dare
we will dare
you will dare
they will dare

Going to-Future

I am going to dare
you are going to dare
he/she/it is going to dare
we are going to dare
you are going to dare
they are going to dare

Future Perfect

I will have dared
you will have dared
he/she/it will have dared
we will have dared
you will have dared
they will have dared

Imperative

dare

Impersonal

ing-Form

daring

Past Participle

dared

Continuous tenses

Present

I am daring
you are daring
he/she/it is daring
we are daring
you are daring
they are daring

Past

I was daring
you were daring
he/she/it was daring
we were daring
you were daring
they were daring

Present Perfect

I have been daring
you have been daring
he/she/it has been daring
we have been daring
you have been daring
they have been daring

Past Perfect

I had been daring
you had been daring
he/she/it had been daring
we had been daring
you had been daring
they had been daring

Will-Future

I will be daring
you will be daring
he/she/it will be daring
we will be daring
you will be daring
they will be daring

Going to-Future

I am going to be daring
you are going to be daring
he/she/it is going to be daring
we are going to be daring
you are going to be daring
they are going to be daring

Future Perfect

I will have been daring
you will have been daring
he/she/it will have been daring
we will have been daring
you will have been daring
they will have been daring

Conditional

I would dare
you would dare
he/she/it would dare
we would dare
you would dare
they would dare

Conditional Past

I would have dared
you would have dared
he/she/it would have dared
we would have dared
you would have dared
they would have dared

austeilen

deal
- dealt - dealt

Simple tenses

Present

I	deal
you	deal
he/she/it	deals
we	deal
you	deal
they	deal

Past

I	dealt
you	dealt
he/she/it	dealt
we	dealt
you	dealt
they	dealt

Present Perfect

I	have	dealt
you	have	dealt
he/she/it	has	dealt
we	have	dealt
you	have	dealt
they	have	dealt

Past Perfect

I	had	dealt
you	had	dealt
he/she/it	had	dealt
we	had	dealt
you	had	dealt
they	had	dealt

Will-Future

I	will	deal
you	will	deal
he/she/it	will	deal
we	will	deal
you	will	deal
they	will	deal

Going to-Future

I	am	going to	deal
you	are	going to	deal
he/she/it	is	going to	deal
we	are	going to	deal
you	are	going to	deal
they	are	going to	deal

Future Perfect

I	will have	dealt
you	will have	dealt
he/she/it	will have	dealt
we	will have	dealt
you	will have	dealt
they	will have	dealt

Imperative

deal

Impersonal

ing-Form

dealing

Past Participle

dealt

Continuous tenses

Present

I	am	dealing
you	are	dealing
he/she/it	is	dealing
we	are	dealing
you	are	dealing
they	are	dealing

Past

I	was	dealing
you	were	dealing
he/she/it	was	dealing
we	were	dealing
you	were	dealing
they	were	dealing

Present Perfect

I	have	been	dealing
you	have	been	dealing
he/she/it	has	been	dealing
we	have	been	dealing
you	have	been	dealing
they	have	been	dealing

Past Perfect

I	had been	dealing
you	had been	dealing
he/she/it	had been	dealing
we	had been	dealing
you	had been	dealing
they	had been	dealing

Will-Future

I	will be	dealing
you	will be	dealing
he/she/it	will be	dealing
we	will be	dealing
you	will be	dealing
they	will be	dealing

Going to-Future

I	am	going to be	dealing
you	are	going to be	dealing
he/she/it	is	going to be	dealing
we	are	going to be	dealing
you	are	going to be	dealing
they	are	going to be	dealing

Future Perfect

I	will have been	dealing
you	will have been	dealing
he/she/it	will have been	dealing
we	will have been	dealing
you	will have been	dealing
they	will have been	dealing

Conditional

I	would	deal
you	would	deal
he/she/it	would	deal
we	would	deal
you	would	deal
they	would	deal

Conditional Past

I	would have	dealt
you	would have	dealt
he/she/it	would have	dealt
we	would have	dealt
you	would have	dealt
they	would have	dealt

decide

entscheiden

+ **-ing** → ~~e~~ / + **-d** nicht **-ed**
Regelmäßiges Verb

Simple tenses

Present

I	decide
you	decide
he/she/it	decides
we	decide
you	decide
they	decide

Past

I	decided
you	decided
he/she/it	decided
we	decided
you	decided
they	decided

Present Perfect

I	have	decided
you	have	decided
he/she/it	has	decided
we	have	decided
you	have	decided
they	have	decided

Past Perfect

I	had	decided
you	had	decided
he/she/it	had	decided
we	had	decided
you	had	decided
they	had	decided

Will-Future

I	will	decide
you	will	decide
he/she/it	will	decide
we	will	decide
you	will	decide
they	will	decide

Going to-Future

I	am	going to	decide
you	are	going to	decide
he/she/it	is	going to	decide
we	are	going to	decide
you	are	going to	decide
they	are	going to	decide

Future Perfect

I	will have	decided
you	will have	decided
he/she/it	will have	decided
we	will have	decided
you	will have	decided
they	will have	decided

Imperative

decide

Impersonal

ing-Form

deciding

Past Participle

decided

Continuous tenses

Present

I	am	deciding
you	are	deciding
he/she/it	is	deciding
we	are	deciding
you	are	deciding
they	are	deciding

Past

I	was	deciding
you	were	deciding
he/she/it	was	deciding
we	were	deciding
you	were	deciding
they	were	deciding

Present Perfect

I	have been	deciding
you	have been	deciding
he/she/it	has been	deciding
we	have been	deciding
you	have been	deciding
they	have been	deciding

Past Perfect

I	had been	deciding
you	had been	deciding
he/she/it	had been	deciding
we	had been	deciding
you	had been	deciding
they	had been	deciding

Will-Future

I	will be	deciding
you	will be	deciding
he/she/it	will be	deciding
we	will be	deciding
you	will be	deciding
they	will be	deciding

Going to-Future

I	am	going to be	deciding
you	are	going to be	deciding
he/she/it	is	going to be	deciding
we	are	going to be	deciding
you	are	going to be	deciding
they	are	going to be	deciding

Future Perfect

I	will have been	deciding
you	will have been	deciding
he/she/it	will have been	deciding
we	will have been	deciding
you	will have been	deciding
they	will have been	deciding

Conditional

I	would	decide
you	would	decide
he/she/it	would	decide
we	would	decide
you	would	decide
they	would	decide

Conditional Past

I	would have	decided
you	would have	decided
he/she/it	would have	decided
we	would have	decided
you	would have	decided
they	would have	decided

Simple tenses

Present

I	declare
you	declare
he/she/it	declares
we	declare
you	declare
they	declare

Past

I	declared
you	declared
he/she/it	declared
we	declared
you	declared
they	declared

Present Perfect

I	have	declared
you	have	declared
he/she/it	has	declared
we	have	declared
you	have	declared
they	have	declared

Past Perfect

I	had	declared
you	had	declared
he/she/it	had	declared
we	had	declared
you	had	declared
they	had	declared

Will-Future

I	will	declare
you	will	declare
he/she/it	will	declare
we	will	declare
you	will	declare
they	will	declare

Going to-Future

I	am	going to	declare
you	are	going to	declare
he/she/it	is	going to	declare
we	are	going to	declare
you	are	going to	declare
they	are	going to	declare

Future Perfect

I	will have	declared
you	will have	declared
he/she/it	will have	declared
we	will have	declared
you	will have	declared
they	will have	declared

Imperative

declare

Impersonal

ing-Form

declaring

Past Participle

declared

Continuous tenses

Present

I	am	declaring
you	are	declaring
he/she/it	is	declaring
we	are	declaring
you	are	declaring
they	are	declaring

Past

I	was	declaring
you	were	declaring
he/she/it	was	declaring
we	were	declaring
you	were	declaring
they	were	declaring

Present Perfect

I	have	been	declaring
you	have	been	declaring
he/she/it	has	been	declaring
we	have	been	declaring
you	have	been	declaring
they	have	been	declaring

Past Perfect

I	had been	declaring
you	had been	declaring
he/she/it	had been	declaring
we	had been	declaring
you	had been	declaring
they	had been	declaring

Will-Future

I	will be	declaring
you	will be	declaring
he/she/it	will be	declaring
we	will be	declaring
you	will be	declaring
they	will be	declaring

Going to-Future

I	am	going to be	declaring
you	are	going to be	declaring
he/she/it	is	going to be	declaring
we	are	going to be	declaring
you	are	going to be	declaring
they	are	going to be	declaring

Future Perfect

I	will have been	declaring
you	will have been	declaring
he/she/it	will have been	declaring
we	will have been	declaring
you	will have been	declaring
they	will have been	declaring

Conditional

I	would	declare
you	would	declare
he/she/it	would	declare
we	would	declare
you	would	declare
they	would	declare

Conditional Past

I	would have	declared
you	would have	declared
he/she/it	would have	declared
we	would have	declared
you	would have	declared
they	would have	declared

defend

verteidigen

Regelmäßiges Verb

Simple tenses

Present

I	defend
you	defend
he/she/it	defends
we	defend
you	defend
they	defend

Past

I	defended
you	defended
he/she/it	defended
we	defended
you	defended
they	defended

Present Perfect

I	have	defended
you	have	defended
he/she/it	has	defended
we	have	defended
you	have	defended
they	have	defended

Past Perfect

I	had	defended
you	had	defended
he/she/it	had	defended
we	had	defended
you	had	defended
they	had	defended

Will-Future

I	will	defend
you	will	defend
he/she/it	will	defend
we	will	defend
you	will	defend
they	will	defend

Going to-Future

I	am	going to	defend
you	are	going to	defend
he/she/it	is	going to	defend
we	are	going to	defend
you	are	going to	defend
they	are	going to	defend

Future Perfect

I	will have	defended
you	will have	defended
he/she/it	will have	defended
we	will have	defended
you	will have	defended
they	will have	defended

Imperative

defend

Impersonal

ing-Form

defending

Past Participle

defended

Continuous tenses

Present

I	am	defending
you	are	defending
he/she/it	is	defending
we	are	defending
you	are	defending
they	are	defending

Past

I	was	defending
you	were	defending
he/she/it	was	defending
we	were	defending
you	were	defending
they	were	defending

Present Perfect

I	have been	defending
you	have been	defending
he/she/it	has been	defending
we	have been	defending
you	have been	defending
they	have been	defending

Past Perfect

I	had been	defending
you	had been	defending
he/she/it	had been	defending
we	had been	defending
you	had been	defending
they	had been	defending

Will-Future

I	will be	defending
you	will be	defending
he/she/it	will be	defending
we	will be	defending
you	will be	defending
they	will be	defending

Going to-Future

I	am	going to be	defending
you	are	going to be	defending
he/she/it	is	going to be	defending
we	are	going to be	defending
you	are	going to be	defending
they	are	going to be	defending

Future Perfect

I	will have been	defending
you	will have been	defending
he/she/it	will have been	defending
we	will have been	defending
you	will have been	defending
they	will have been	defending

Conditional

I	would	defend
you	would	defend
he/she/it	would	defend
we	would	defend
you	would	defend
they	would	defend

Conditional Past

I	would have	defended
you	would have	defended
he/she/it	would have	defended
we	would have	defended
you	would have	defended
they	would have	defended

Simple tenses

Present

I	define
you	define
he/she/it	defines
we	define
you	define
they	define

Past

I	defined
you	defined
he/she/it	defined
we	defined
you	defined
they	defined

Present Perfect

I	have	defined
you	have	defined
he/she/it	has	defined
we	have	defined
you	have	defined
they	have	defined

Past Perfect

I	had	defined
you	had	defined
he/she/it	had	defined
we	had	defined
you	had	defined
they	had	defined

Will-Future

I	will	define
you	will	define
he/she/it	will	define
we	will	define
you	will	define
they	will	define

Going to-Future

I	am	going to	define
you	are	going to	define
he/she/it	is	going to	define
we	are	going to	define
you	are	going to	define
they	are	going to	define

Future Perfect

I	will have	defined
you	will have	defined
he/she/it	will have	defined
we	will have	defined
you	will have	defined
they	will have	defined

Imperative

define

Impersonal

ing-Form

defining

Past Participle

defined

Continuous tenses

Present

I	am	defining
you	are	defining
he/she/it	is	defining
we	are	defining
you	are	defining
they	are	defining

Past

I	was	defining
you	were	defining
he/she/it	was	defining
we	were	defining
you	were	defining
they	were	defining

Present Perfect

I	have been	defining
you	have been	defining
he/she/it	has been	defining
we	have been	defining
you	have been	defining
they	have been	defining

Past Perfect

I	had been	defining
you	had been	defining
he/she/it	had been	defining
we	had been	defining
you	had been	defining
they	had been	defining

Will-Future

I	will be	defining
you	will be	defining
he/she/it	will be	defining
we	will be	defining
you	will be	defining
they	will be	defining

Going to-Future

I	am	going to be	defining
you	are	going to be	defining
he/she/it	is	going to be	defining
we	are	going to be	defining
you	are	going to be	defining
they	are	going to be	defining

Future Perfect

I	will have been	defining
you	will have been	defining
he/she/it	will have been	defining
we	will have been	defining
you	will have been	defining
they	will have been	defining

Conditional

I	would	define
you	would	define
he/she/it	would	define
we	would	define
you	would	define
they	would	define

Conditional Past

I	would have	defined
you	would have	defined
he/she/it	would have	defined
we	would have	defined
you	would have	defined
they	would have	defined

delay

verschieben

Regelmäßiges Verb

Simple tenses

Present

I	delay
you	delay
he/she/it	delays
we	delay
you	delay
they	delay

Past

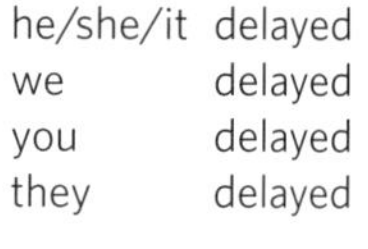

I	delayed
you	delayed
he/she/it	delayed
we	delayed
you	delayed
they	delayed

Present Perfect

I	have	delayed
you	have	delayed
he/she/it	has	delayed
we	have	delayed
you	have	delayed
they	have	delayed

Past Perfect

I	had	delayed
you	had	delayed
he/she/it	had	delayed
we	had	delayed
you	had	delayed
they	had	delayed

Will-Future

I	will	delay
you	will	delay
he/she/it	will	delay
we	will	delay
you	will	delay
they	will	delay

Going to-Future

I	am	going to	delay
you	are	going to	delay
he/she/it	is	going to	delay
we	are	going to	delay
you	are	going to	delay
they	are	going to	delay

Future Perfect

I	will have	delayed
you	will have	delayed
he/she/it	will have	delayed
we	will have	delayed
you	will have	delayed
they	will have	delayed

Imperative

delay

Impersonal

ing-Form

delaying

Past Participle

delayed

Continuous tenses

Present

I	am	delaying
you	are	delaying
he/she/it	is	delaying
we	are	delaying
you	are	delaying
they	are	delaying

Past

I	was	delaying
you	were	delaying
he/she/it	was	delaying
we	were	delaying
you	were	delaying
they	were	delaying

Present Perfect

I	have been	delaying
you	have been	delaying
he/she/it	has been	delaying
we	have been	delaying
you	have been	delaying
they	have been	delaying

Past Perfect

I	had been	delaying
you	had been	delaying
he/she/it	had been	delaying
we	had been	delaying
you	had been	delaying
they	had been	delaying

Will-Future

I	will be	delaying
you	will be	delaying
he/she/it	will be	delaying
we	will be	delaying
you	will be	delaying
they	will be	delaying

Going to-Future

I	am	going to be	delaying
you	are	going to be	delaying
he/she/it	is	going to be	delaying
we	are	going to be	delaying
you	are	going to be	delaying
they	are	going to be	delaying

Future Perfect

I	will have been	delaying
you	will have been	delaying
he/she/it	will have been	delaying
we	will have been	delaying
you	will have been	delaying
they	will have been	delaying

Conditional

I	would	delay
you	would	delay
he/she/it	would	delay
we	would	delay
you	would	delay
they	would	delay

Conditional Past

I	would have	delayed
you	would have	delayed
he/she/it	would have	delayed
we	would have	delayed
you	would have	delayed
they	would have	delayed

deliver

Regelmäßiges Verb

Simple tenses

Present

I	deliver
you	deliver
he/she/it	delivers
we	deliver
you	deliver
they	deliver

Past

I	delivered
you	delivered
he/she/it	delivered
we	delivered
you	delivered
they	delivered

Present Perfect

I	have	delivered
you	have	delivered
he/she/it	has	delivered
we	have	delivered
you	have	delivered
they	have	delivered

Past Perfect

I	had	delivered
you	had	delivered
he/she/it	had	delivered
we	had	delivered
you	had	delivered
they	had	delivered

Will-Future

I	will	deliver
you	will	deliver
he/she/it	will	deliver
we	will	deliver
you	will	deliver
they	will	deliver

Going to-Future

I	am	going to	deliver
you	are	going to	deliver
he/she/it	is	going to	deliver
we	are	going to	deliver
you	are	going to	deliver
they	are	going to	deliver

Future Perfect

I	will have	delivered
you	will have	delivered
he/she/it	will have	delivered
we	will have	delivered
you	will have	delivered
they	will have	delivered

Imperative

deliver

Impersonal

ing-Form

delivering

Past Participle

delivered

Continuous tenses

Present

I	am	delivering
you	are	delivering
he/she/it	is	delivering
we	are	delivering
you	are	delivering
they	are	delivering

Past

I	was	delivering
you	were	delivering
he/she/it	was	delivering
we	were	delivering
you	were	delivering
they	were	delivering

Present Perfect

I	have been	delivering
you	have been	delivering
he/she/it	has been	delivering
we	have been	delivering
you	have been	delivering
they	have been	delivering

Past Perfect

I	had been	delivering
you	had been	delivering
he/she/it	had been	delivering
we	had been	delivering
you	had been	delivering
they	had been	delivering

Will-Future

I	will be	delivering
you	will be	delivering
he/she/it	will be	delivering
we	will be	delivering
you	will be	delivering
they	will be	delivering

Going to-Future

I	am	going to be	delivering
you	are	going to be	delivering
he/she/it	is	going to be	delivering
we	are	going to be	delivering
you	are	going to be	delivering
they	are	going to be	delivering

Future Perfect

I	will have been	delivering
you	will have been	delivering
he/she/it	will have been	delivering
we	will have been	delivering
you	will have been	delivering
they	will have been	delivering

Conditional

I	would	deliver
you	would	deliver
he/she/it	would	deliver
we	would	deliver
you	would	deliver
they	would	deliver

Conditional Past

I	would have	delivered
you	would have	delivered
he/she/it	would have	delivered
we	would have	delivered
you	would have	delivered
they	would have	delivered

demand

verlangen

Regelmäßiges Verb

Simple tenses

Present

I	demand
you	demand
he/she/it	demands
we	demand
you	demand
they	demand

Past

I	demanded
you	demanded
he/she/it	demanded
we	demanded
you	demanded
they	demanded

Present Perfect

I	have	demanded
you	have	demanded
he/she/it	has	demanded
we	have	demanded
you	have	demanded
they	have	demanded

Past Perfect

I	had	demanded
you	had	demanded
he/she/it	had	demanded
we	had	demanded
you	had	demanded
they	had	demanded

Will-Future

I	will	demand
you	will	demand
he/she/it	will	demand
we	will	demand
you	will	demand
they	will	demand

Going to-Future

I	am	going to	demand
you	are	going to	demand
he/she/it	is	going to	demand
we	are	going to	demand
you	are	going to	demand
they	are	going to	demand

Future Perfect

I	will have	demanded
you	will have	demanded
he/she/it	will have	demanded
we	will have	demanded
you	will have	demanded
they	will have	demanded

Imperative

demand

Impersonal

ing-Form

demanding

Past Participle

demanded

Continuous tenses

Present

I	am	demanding
you	are	demanding
he/she/it	is	demanding
we	are	demanding
you	are	demanding
they	are	demanding

Past

I	was	demanding
you	were	demanding
he/she/it	was	demanding
we	were	demanding
you	were	demanding
they	were	demanding

Present Perfect

I	have been	demanding
you	have been	demanding
he/she/it	has been	demanding
we	have been	demanding
you	have been	demanding
they	have been	demanding

Past Perfect

I	had been	demanding
you	had been	demanding
he/she/it	had been	demanding
we	had been	demanding
you	had been	demanding
they	had been	demanding

Will-Future

I	will be	demanding
you	will be	demanding
he/she/it	will be	demanding
we	will be	demanding
you	will be	demanding
they	will be	demanding

Going to-Future

I	am	going to be	demanding
you	are	going to be	demanding
he/she/it	is	going to be	demanding
we	are	going to be	demanding
you	are	going to be	demanding
they	are	going to be	demanding

Future Perfect

I	will have been	demanding
you	will have been	demanding
he/she/it	will have been	demanding
we	will have been	demanding
you	will have been	demanding
they	will have been	demanding

Conditional

I	would	demand
you	would	demand
he/she/it	would	demand
we	would	demand
you	would	demand
they	would	demand

Conditional Past

I	would have	demanded
you	would have	demanded
he/she/it	would have	demanded
we	would have	demanded
you	would have	demanded
they	would have	demanded

-y → -ie vor **-s** / **-y → -i** vor **-ed**
Regelmäßiges Verb

abstreiten

deny

Simple tenses

Present

I	deny
you	deny
he/she/it	denies
we	deny
you	deny
they	deny

Past

I	denied
you	denied
he/she/it	denied
we	denied
you	denied
they	denied

Present Perfect

I	have	denied
you	have	denied
he/she/it	has	denied
we	have	denied
you	have	denied
they	have	denied

Past Perfect

I	had	denied
you	had	denied
he/she/it	had	denied
we	had	denied
you	had	denied
they	had	denied

Will-Future

I	will	deny
you	will	deny
he/she/it	will	deny
we	will	deny
you	will	deny
they	will	deny

Going to-Future

I	am	going to	deny
you	are	going to	deny
he/she/it	is	going to	deny
we	are	going to	deny
you	are	going to	deny
they	are	going to	deny

Future Perfect

I	will have	denied
you	will have	denied
he/she/it	will have	denied
we	will have	denied
you	will have	denied
they	will have	denied

Imperative

deny

Impersonal

ing-Form

denying

Past Participle

denied

Continuous tenses

Present

I	am	denying
you	are	denying
he/she/it	is	denying
we	are	denying
you	are	denying
they	are	denying

Past

I	was	denying
you	were	denying
he/she/it	was	denying
we	were	denying
you	were	denying
they	were	denying

Present Perfect

I	have been	denying
you	have been	denying
he/she/it	has been	denying
we	have been	denying
you	have been	denying
they	have been	denying

Past Perfect

I	had been	denying
you	had been	denying
he/she/it	had been	denying
we	had been	denying
you	had been	denying
they	had been	denying

Will-Future

I	will be	denying
you	will be	denying
he/she/it	will be	denying
we	will be	denying
you	will be	denying
they	will be	denying

Going to-Future

I	am	going to be	denying
you	are	going to be	denying
he/she/it	is	going to be	denying
we	are	going to be	denying
you	are	going to be	denying
they	are	going to be	denying

Future Perfect

I	will have been	denying
you	will have been	denying
he/she/it	will have been	denying
we	will have been	denying
you	will have been	denying
they	will have been	denying

Conditional

I	would	deny
you	would	deny
he/she/it	would	deny
we	would	deny
you	would	deny
they	would	deny

Conditional Past

I	would have	denied
you	would have	denied
he/she/it	would have	denied
we	would have	denied
you	would have	denied
they	would have	denied

depend

abhängen (von)

Regelmäßiges Verb

Simple tenses

Present

I	depend
you	depend
he/she/it	depends
we	depend
you	depend
they	depend

Past

I	depended
you	depended
he/she/it	depended
we	depended
you	depended
they	depended

Present Perfect

I	have	depended
you	have	depended
he/she/it	has	depended
we	have	depended
you	have	depended
they	have	depended

Past Perfect

I	had	depended
you	had	depended
he/she/it	had	depended
we	had	depended
you	had	depended
they	had	depended

Will-Future

I	will	depend
you	will	depend
he/she/it	will	depend
we	will	depend
you	will	depend
they	will	depend

Going to-Future

I	am	going to	depend
you	are	going to	depend
he/she/it	is	going to	depend
we	are	going to	depend
you	are	going to	depend
they	are	going to	depend

Future Perfect

I	will have	depended
you	will have	depended
he/she/it	will have	depended
we	will have	depended
you	will have	depended
they	will have	depended

Imperative

depend

Impersonal

ing-Form

depending

Past Participle

depended

Continuous tenses

Present

I	am	depending
you	are	depending
he/she/it	is	depending
we	are	depending
you	are	depending
they	are	depending

Past

I	was	depending
you	were	depending
he/she/it	was	depending
we	were	depending
you	were	depending
they	were	depending

Present Perfect

I	have	been	depending
you	have	been	depending
he/she/it	has	been	depending
we	have	been	depending
you	have	been	depending
they	have	been	depending

Past Perfect

I	had been	depending
you	had been	depending
he/she/it	had been	depending
we	had been	depending
you	had been	depending
they	had been	depending

Will-Future

I	will be	depending
you	will be	depending
he/she/it	will be	depending
we	will be	depending
you	will be	depending
they	will be	depending

Going to-Future

I	am	going to be	depending
you	are	going to be	depending
he/she/it	is	going to be	depending
we	are	going to be	depending
you	are	going to be	depending
they	are	going to be	depending

Future Perfect

I	will have been	depending
you	will have been	depending
he/she/it	will have been	depending
we	will have been	depending
you	will have been	depending
they	will have been	depending

Conditional

I	would	depend
you	would	depend
he/she/it	would	depend
we	would	depend
you	would	depend
they	would	depend

Conditional Past

I	would have	depended
you	would have	depended
he/she/it	would have	depended
we	would have	depended
you	would have	depended
they	would have	depended

+ **-ing** → ~~e~~ / + **-d** nicht **-ed**
Regelmäßiges Verb

beschreiben

describe

Simple tenses

Present

I	describe
you	describe
he/she/it	describes
we	describe
you	describe
they	describe

Past

I	described
you	described
he/she/it	described
we	described
you	described
they	described

Present Perfect

I	have	described
you	have	described
he/she/it	has	described
we	have	described
you	have	described
they	have	described

Past Perfect

I	had	described
you	had	described
he/she/it	had	described
we	had	described
you	had	described
they	had	described

Will-Future

I	will	describe
you	will	describe
he/she/it	will	describe
we	will	describe
you	will	describe
they	will	describe

Going to-Future

I	am	going to	describe
you	are	going to	describe
he/she/it	is	going to	describe
we	are	going to	describe
you	are	going to	describe
they	are	going to	describe

Future Perfect

I	will have	described
you	will have	described
he/she/it	will have	described
we	will have	described
you	will have	described
they	will have	described

Imperative

describe

Impersonal

ing-Form

describing

Past Participle

described

Continuous tenses

Present

I	am	describing
you	are	describing
he/she/it	is	describing
we	are	describing
you	are	describing
they	are	describing

Past

I	was	describing
you	were	describing
he/she/it	was	describing
we	were	describing
you	were	describing
they	were	describing

Present Perfect

I	have been	describing
you	have been	describing
he/she/it	has been	describing
we	have been	describing
you	have been	describing
they	have been	describing

Past Perfect

I	had been	describing
you	had been	describing
he/she/it	had been	describing
we	had been	describing
you	had been	describing
they	had been	describing

Will-Future

I	will be	describing
you	will be	describing
he/she/it	will be	describing
we	will be	describing
you	will be	describing
they	will be	describing

Going to-Future

I	am	going to be	describing
you	are	going to be	describing
he/she/it	is	going to be	describing
we	are	going to be	describing
you	are	going to be	describing
they	are	going to be	describing

Future Perfect

I	will have been	describing
you	will have been	describing
he/she/it	will have been	describing
we	will have been	describing
you	will have been	describing
they	will have been	describing

Conditional

I	would	describe
you	would	describe
he/she/it	would	describe
we	would	describe
you	would	describe
they	would	describe

Conditional Past

I	would have	described
you	would have	described
he/she/it	would have	described
we	would have	described
you	would have	described
they	would have	described

design

entwerfen

Regelmäßiges Verb

Simple tenses

Present

I	design
you	design
he/she/it	designs
we	design
you	design
they	design

Past

I	designed
you	designed
he/she/it	designed
we	designed
you	designed
they	designed

Present Perfect

I	have	designed
you	have	designed
he/she/it	has	designed
we	have	designed
you	have	designed
they	have	designed

Past Perfect

I	had	designed
you	had	designed
he/she/it	had	designed
we	had	designed
you	had	designed
they	had	designed

Will-Future

I	will	design
you	will	design
he/she/it	will	design
we	will	design
you	will	design
they	will	design

Going to-Future

I	am	going to	design
you	are	going to	design
he/she/it	is	going to	design
we	are	going to	design
you	are	going to	design
they	are	going to	design

Future Perfect

I	will have	designed
you	will have	designed
he/she/it	will have	designed
we	will have	designed
you	will have	designed
they	will have	designed

Imperative

design

Impersonal

ing-Form

designing

Past Participle

designed

Continuous tenses

Present

I	am	designing
you	are	designing
he/she/it	is	designing
we	are	designing
you	are	designing
they	are	designing

Past

I	was	designing
you	were	designing
he/she/it	was	designing
we	were	designing
you	were	designing
they	were	designing

Present Perfect

I	have been	designing
you	have been	designing
he/she/it	has been	designing
we	have been	designing
you	have been	designing
they	have been	designing

Past Perfect

I	had been	designing
you	had been	designing
he/she/it	had been	designing
we	had been	designing
you	had been	designing
they	had been	designing

Will-Future

I	will be	designing
you	will be	designing
he/she/it	will be	designing
we	will be	designing
you	will be	designing
they	will be	designing

Going to-Future

I	am	going to be	designing
you	are	going to be	designing
he/she/it	is	going to be	designing
we	are	going to be	designing
you	are	going to be	designing
they	are	going to be	designing

Future Perfect

I	will have been	designing
you	will have been	designing
he/she/it	will have been	designing
we	will have been	designing
you	will have been	designing
they	will have been	designing

Conditional

I	would	design
you	would	design
he/she/it	would	design
we	would	design
you	would	design
they	would	design

Conditional Past

I	would have	designed
you	would have	designed
he/she/it	would have	designed
we	would have	designed
you	would have	designed
they	would have	designed

Simple tenses

Present

I	desire
you	desire
he/she/it	desires
we	desire
you	desire
they	desire

Past

I	desired
you	desired
he/she/it	desired
we	desired
you	desired
they	desired

Present Perfect

I	have	desired
you	have	desired
he/she/it	has	desired
we	have	desired
you	have	desired
they	have	desired

Past Perfect

I	had	desired
you	had	desired
he/she/it	had	desired
we	had	desired
you	had	desired
they	had	desired

Will-Future

I	will	desire
you	will	desire
he/she/it	will	desire
we	will	desire
you	will	desire
they	will	desire

Going to-Future

I	am	going to	desire
you	are	going to	desire
he/she/it	is	going to	desire
we	are	going to	desire
you	are	going to	desire
they	are	going to	desire

Future Perfect

I	will have	desired
you	will have	desired
he/she/it	will have	desired
we	will have	desired
you	will have	desired
they	will have	desired

Imperative

desire

Impersonal

ing-Form

desiring

Past Participle

desired

Continuous tenses

Present

I	am	desiring
you	are	desiring
he/she/it	is	desiring
we	are	desiring
you	are	desiring
they	are	desiring

Past

I	was	desiring
you	were	desiring
he/she/it	was	desiring
we	were	desiring
you	were	desiring
they	were	desiring

Present Perfect

I	have been	desiring
you	have been	desiring
he/she/it	has been	desiring
we	have been	desiring
you	have been	desiring
they	have been	desiring

Past Perfect

I	had been	desiring
you	had been	desiring
he/she/it	had been	desiring
we	had been	desiring
you	had been	desiring
they	had been	desiring

Will-Future

I	will be	desiring
you	will be	desiring
he/she/it	will be	desiring
we	will be	desiring
you	will be	desiring
they	will be	desiring

Going to-Future

I	am	going to be	desiring
you	are	going to be	desiring
he/she/it	is	going to be	desiring
we	are	going to be	desiring
you	are	going to be	desiring
they	are	going to be	desiring

Future Perfect

I	will have been desiring
you	will have been desiring
he/she/it	will have been desiring
we	will have been desiring
you	will have been desiring
they	will have been desiring

Conditional

I	would	desire
you	would	desire
he/she/it	would	desire
we	would	desire
you	would	desire
they	would	desire

Conditional Past

I	would have	desired
you	would have	desired
he/she/it	would have	desired
we	would have	desired
you	would have	desired
they	would have	desired

destroy

zerstören

Regelmäßiges Verb

Simple tenses

Present

I	destroy
you	destroy
he/she/it	destroys
we	destroy
you	destroy
they	destroy

Past

I	destroyed
you	destroyed
he/she/it	destroyed
we	destroyed
you	destroyed
they	destroyed

Present Perfect

I	have	destroyed
you	have	destroyed
he/she/it	has	destroyed
we	have	destroyed
you	have	destroyed
they	have	destroyed

Past Perfect

I	had	destroyed
you	had	destroyed
he/she/it	had	destroyed
we	had	destroyed
you	had	destroyed
they	had	destroyed

Will-Future

I	will	destroy
you	will	destroy
he/she/it	will	destroy
we	will	destroy
you	will	destroy
they	will	destroy

Going to-Future

I	am	going to	destroy
you	are	going to	destroy
he/she/it	is	going to	destroy
we	are	going to	destroy
you	are	going to	destroy
they	are	going to	destroy

Future Perfect

I	will have	destroyed
you	will have	destroyed
he/she/it	will have	destroyed
we	will have	destroyed
you	will have	destroyed
they	will have	destroyed

Imperative

destroy

Impersonal

ing-Form

destroying

Past Participle

destroyed

Continuous tenses

Present

I	am	destroying
you	are	destroying
he/she/it	is	destroying
we	are	destroying
you	are	destroying
they	are	destroying

Past

I	was	destroying
you	were	destroying
he/she/it	was	destroying
we	were	destroying
you	were	destroying
they	were	destroying

Present Perfect

I	have been	destroying
you	have been	destroying
he/she/it	has been	destroying
we	have been	destroying
you	have been	destroying
they	have been	destroying

Past Perfect

I	had been	destroying
you	had been	destroying
he/she/it	had been	destroying
we	had been	destroying
you	had been	destroying
they	had been	destroying

Will-Future

I	will be	destroying
you	will be	destroying
he/she/it	will be	destroying
we	will be	destroying
you	will be	destroying
they	will be	destroying

Going to-Future

I	am	going to be	destroying
you	are	going to be	destroying
he/she/it	is	going to be	destroying
we	are	going to be	destroying
you	are	going to be	destroying
they	are	going to be	destroying

Future Perfect

I	will have been	destroying
you	will have been	destroying
he/she/it	will have been	destroying
we	will have been	destroying
you	will have been	destroying
they	will have been	destroying

Conditional

I	would	destroy
you	would	destroy
he/she/it	would	destroy
we	would	destroy
you	would	destroy
they	would	destroy

Conditional Past

I	would have	destroyed
you	would have	destroyed
he/she/it	would have	destroyed
we	would have	destroyed
you	would have	destroyed
they	would have	destroyed

Simple tenses

Present

I	develop
you	develop
he/she/it	develops
we	develop
you	develop
they	develop

Past

I	developed
you	developed
he/she/it	developed
we	developed
you	developed
they	developed

Present Perfect

I	have	developed
you	have	developed
he/she/it	has	developed
we	have	developed
you	have	developed
they	have	developed

Past Perfect

I	had	developed
you	had	developed
he/she/it	had	developed
we	had	developed
you	had	developed
they	had	developed

Will-Future

I	will	develop
you	will	develop
he/she/it	will	develop
we	will	develop
you	will	develop
they	will	develop

Going to-Future

I	am	going to	develop
you	are	going to	develop
he/she/it	is	going to	develop
we	are	going to	develop
you	are	going to	develop
they	are	going to	develop

Future Perfect

I	will have	developed
you	will have	developed
he/she/it	will have	developed
we	will have	developed
you	will have	developed
they	will have	developed

Imperative

develop

Impersonal

ing-Form

developing

Past Participle

developed

Continuous tenses

Present

I	am	developing
you	are	developing
he/she/it	is	developing
we	are	developing
you	are	developing
they	are	developing

Past

I	was	developing
you	were	developing
he/she/it	was	developing
we	were	developing
you	were	developing
they	were	developing

Present Perfect

I	have	been	developing
you	have	been	developing
he/she/it	has	been	developing
we	have	been	developing
you	have	been	developing
they	have	been	developing

Past Perfect

I	had been	developing
you	had been	developing
he/she/it	had been	developing
we	had been	developing
you	had been	developing
they	had been	developing

Will-Future

I	will be	developing
you	will be	developing
he/she/it	will be	developing
we	will be	developing
you	will be	developing
they	will be	developing

Going to-Future

I	am	going to be	developing
you	are	going to be	developing
he/she/it	is	going to be	developing
we	are	going to be	developing
you	are	going to be	developing
they	are	going to be	developing

Future Perfect

I	will have been developing
you	will have been developing
he/she/it	will have been developing
we	will have been developing
you	will have been developing
they	will have been developing

Conditional

I	would	develop
you	would	develop
he/she/it	would	develop
we	would	develop
you	would	develop
they	would	develop

Conditional Past

I	would have	developed
you	would have	developed
he/she/it	would have	developed
we	would have	developed
you	would have	developed
they	would have	developed

disagree

nicht übereinstimmen

\+ **-d** nicht **-ed**
Regelmäßiges Verb

Simple tenses

Present

I	disagree
you	disagree
he/she/it	disagrees
we	disagree
you	disagree
they	disagree

Past

I	disagreed
you	disagreed
he/she/it	disagreed
we	disagreed
you	disagreed
they	disagreed

Present Perfect

I	have	disagreed
you	have	disagreed
he/she/it	has	disagreed
we	have	disagreed
you	have	disagreed
they	have	disagreed

Past Perfect

I	had	disagreed
you	had	disagreed
he/she/it	had	disagreed
we	had	disagreed
you	had	disagreed
they	had	disagreed

Will-Future

I	will	disagree
you	will	disagree
he/she/it	will	disagree
we	will	disagree
you	will	disagree
they	will	disagree

Going to-Future

I	am	going to	disagree
you	are	going to	disagree
he/she/it	is	going to	disagree
we	are	going to	disagree
you	are	going to	disagree
they	are	going to	disagree

Future Perfect

I	will have	disagreed
you	will have	disagreed
he/she/it	will have	disagreed
we	will have	disagreed
you	will have	disagreed
they	will have	disagreed

Imperative

disagree

Impersonal

ing-Form

disagreeing

Past Participle

disagreed

Continuous tenses

Present

I	am	disagreeing
you	are	disagreeing
he/she/it	is	disagreeing
we	are	disagreeing
you	are	disagreeing
they	are	disagreeing

Past

I	was	disagreeing
you	were	disagreeing
he/she/it	was	disagreeing
we	were	disagreeing
you	were	disagreeing
they	were	disagreeing

Present Perfect

I	have been	disagreeing
you	have been	disagreeing
he/she/it	has been	disagreeing
we	have been	disagreeing
you	have been	disagreeing
they	have been	disagreeing

Past Perfect

I	had been	disagreeing
you	had been	disagreeing
he/she/it	had been	disagreeing
we	had been	disagreeing
you	had been	disagreeing
they	had been	disagreeing

Will-Future

I	will be	disagreeing
you	will be	disagreeing
he/she/it	will be	disagreeing
we	will be	disagreeing
you	will be	disagreeing
they	will be	disagreeing

Going to-Future

I	am	going to be	disagreeing
you	are	going to be	disagreeing
he/she/it	is	going to be	disagreeing
we	are	going to be	disagreeing
you	are	going to be	disagreeing
they	are	going to be	disagreeing

Future Perfect

I	will have been	disagreeing
you	will have been	disagreeing
he/she/it	will have been	disagreeing
we	will have been	disagreeing
you	will have been	disagreeing
they	will have been	disagreeing

Conditional

I	would	disagree
you	would	disagree
he/she/it	would	disagree
we	would	disagree
you	would	disagree
they	would	disagree

Conditional Past

I	would have	disagreed
you	would have	disagreed
he/she/it	would have	disagreed
we	would have	disagreed
you	would have	disagreed
they	would have	disagreed

Simple tenses

Present

I	disappear
you	disappear
he/she/it	disappears
we	disappear
you	disappear
they	disappear

Past

I	disappeared
you	disappeared
he/she/it	disappeared
we	disappeared
you	disappeared
they	disappeared

Present Perfect

I	have	disappeared
you	have	disappeared
he/she/it	has	disappeared
we	have	disappeared
you	have	disappeared
they	have	disappeared

Past Perfect

I	had	disappeared
you	had	disappeared
he/she/it	had	disappeared
we	had	disappeared
you	had	disappeared
they	had	disappeared

Will-Future

I	will	disappear
you	will	disappear
he/she/it	will	disappear
we	will	disappear
you	will	disappear
they	will	disappear

Going to-Future

I	am	going to	disappear
you	are	going to	disappear
he/she/it	is	going to	disappear
we	are	going to	disappear
you	are	going to	disappear
they	are	going to	disappear

Future Perfect

I	will have	disappeared
you	will have	disappeared
he/she/it	will have	disappeared
we	will have	disappeared
you	will have	disappeared
they	will have	disappeared

Imperative

disappear

Impersonal

ing-Form

disappearing

Past Participle

disappeared

Continuous tenses

Present

I	am	disappearing
you	are	disappearing
he/she/it	is	disappearing
we	are	disappearing
you	are	disappearing
they	are	disappearing

Past

I	was	disappearing
you	were	disappearing
he/she/it	was	disappearing
we	were	disappearing
you	were	disappearing
they	were	disappearing

Present Perfect

I	have been	disappearing
you	have been	disappearing
he/she/it	has been	disappearing
we	have been	disappearing
you	have been	disappearing
they	have been	disappearing

Past Perfect

I	had been	disappearing
you	had been	disappearing
he/she/it	had been	disappearing
we	had been	disappearing
you	had been	disappearing
they	had been	disappearing

Will-Future

I	will be	disappearing
you	will be	disappearing
he/she/it	will be	disappearing
we	will be	disappearing
you	will be	disappearing
they	will be	disappearing

Going to-Future

I	am	going to be	disappearing
you	are	going to be	disappearing
he/she/it	is	going to be	disappearing
we	are	going to be	disappearing
you	are	going to be	disappearing
they	are	going to be	disappearing

Future Perfect

I	will have been	disappearing
you	will have been	disappearing
he/she/it	will have been	disappearing
we	will have been	disappearing
you	will have been	disappearing
they	will have been	disappearing

Conditional

I	would	disappear
you	would	disappear
he/she/it	would	disappear
we	would	disappear
you	would	disappear
they	would	disappear

Conditional Past

I	would have	disappeared
you	would have	disappeared
he/she/it	would have	disappeared
we	would have	disappeared
you	would have	disappeared
they	would have	disappeared

discover

herausfinden

Regelmäßiges Verb

Simple tenses

Present

I	discover
you	discover
he/she/it	discovers
we	discover
you	discover
they	discover

Past

I	discovered
you	discovered
he/she/it	discovered
we	discovered
you	discovered
they	discovered

Present Perfect

I	have	discovered
you	have	discovered
he/she/it	has	discovered
we	have	discovered
you	have	discovered
they	have	discovered

Past Perfect

I	had	discovered
you	had	discovered
he/she/it	had	discovered
we	had	discovered
you	had	discovered
they	had	discovered

Will-Future

I	will	discover
you	will	discover
he/she/it	will	discover
we	will	discover
you	will	discover
they	will	discover

Going to-Future

I	am	going to	discover
you	are	going to	discover
he/she/it	is	going to	discover
we	are	going to	discover
you	are	going to	discover
they	are	going to	discover

Future Perfect

I	will have	discovered
you	will have	discovered
he/she/it	will have	discovered
we	will have	discovered
you	will have	discovered
they	will have	discovered

Imperative

discover

Impersonal

ing-Form

discovering

Past Participle

discovered

Continuous tenses

Present

I	am	discovering
you	are	discovering
he/she/it	is	discovering
we	are	discovering
you	are	discovering
they	are	discovering

Past

I	was	discovering
you	were	discovering
he/she/it	was	discovering
we	were	discovering
you	were	discovering
they	were	discovering

Present Perfect

I	have been	discovering
you	have been	discovering
he/she/it	has been	discovering
we	have been	discovering
you	have been	discovering
they	have been	discovering

Past Perfect

I	had been	discovering
you	had been	discovering
he/she/it	had been	discovering
we	had been	discovering
you	had been	discovering
they	had been	discovering

Will-Future

I	will be	discovering
you	will be	discovering
he/she/it	will be	discovering
we	will be	discovering
you	will be	discovering
they	will be	discovering

Going to-Future

I	am	going to be	discovering
you	are	going to be	discovering
he/she/it	is	going to be	discovering
we	are	going to be	discovering
you	are	going to be	discovering
they	are	going to be	discovering

Future Perfect

I	will have been discovering
you	will have been discovering
he/she/it	will have been discovering
we	will have been discovering
you	will have been discovering
they	will have been discovering

Conditional

I	would	discover
you	would	discover
he/she/it	would	discover
we	would	discover
you	would	discover
they	would	discover

Conditional Past

I	would have	discovered
you	would have	discovered
he/she/it	would have	discovered
we	would have	discovered
you	would have	discovered
they	would have	discovered

diskutieren

discuss

Simple tenses

Present

I	discuss
you	discuss
he/she/it	discusses
we	discuss
you	discuss
they	discuss

Past

I	discussed
you	discussed
he/she/it	discussed
we	discussed
you	discussed
they	discussed

Present Perfect

I	have	discussed
you	have	discussed
he/she/it	has	discussed
we	have	discussed
you	have	discussed
they	have	discussed

Past Perfect

I	had	discussed
you	had	discussed
he/she/it	had	discussed
we	had	discussed
you	had	discussed
they	had	discussed

Will-Future

I	will	discuss
you	will	discuss
he/she/it	will	discuss
we	will	discuss
you	will	discuss
they	will	discuss

Going to-Future

I	am	going to	discuss
you	are	going to	discuss
he/she/it	is	going to	discuss
we	are	going to	discuss
you	are	going to	discuss
they	are	going to	discuss

Future Perfect

I	will have	discussed
you	will have	discussed
he/she/it	will have	discussed
we	will have	discussed
you	will have	discussed
they	will have	discussed

Imperative

discuss

Impersonal

ing-Form

discussing

Past Participle

discussed

Continuous tenses

Present

I	am	discussing
you	are	discussing
he/she/it	is	discussing
we	are	discussing
you	are	discussing
they	are	discussing

Past

I	was	discussing
you	were	discussing
he/she/it	was	discussing
we	were	discussing
you	were	discussing
they	were	discussing

Present Perfect

I	have been	discussing
you	have been	discussing
he/she/it	has been	discussing
we	have been	discussing
you	have been	discussing
they	have been	discussing

Past Perfect

I	had been	discussing
you	had been	discussing
he/she/it	had been	discussing
we	had been	discussing
you	had been	discussing
they	had been	discussing

Will-Future

I	will be	discussing
you	will be	discussing
he/she/it	will be	discussing
we	will be	discussing
you	will be	discussing
they	will be	discussing

Going to-Future

I	am	going to be	discussing
you	are	going to be	discussing
he/she/it	is	going to be	discussing
we	are	going to be	discussing
you	are	going to be	discussing
they	are	going to be	discussing

Future Perfect

I	will have been discussing
you	will have been discussing
he/she/it	will have been discussing
we	will have been discussing
you	will have been discussing
they	will have been discussing

Conditional

I	would	discuss
you	would	discuss
he/she/it	would	discuss
we	would	discuss
you	would	discuss
they	would	discuss

Conditional Past

I	would have	discussed
you	would have	discussed
he/she/it	would have	discussed
we	would have	discussed
you	would have	discussed
they	would have	discussed

distribute

verteilen

+ **-ing** → ~~e~~ / + **-d** nicht **-ed**
Regelmäßiges Verb

Simple tenses

Present

I	distribute
you	distribute
he/she/it	distributes
we	distribute
you	distribute
they	distribute

Past

I	distributed
you	distributed
he/she/it	distributed
we	distributed
you	distributed
they	distributed

Present Perfect

I	have	distributed
you	have	distributed
he/she/it	has	distributed
we	have	distributed
you	have	distributed
they	have	distributed

Past Perfect

I	had	distributed
you	had	distributed
he/she/it	had	distributed
we	had	distributed
you	had	distributed
they	had	distributed

Will-Future

I	will	distribute
you	will	distribute
he/she/it	will	distribute
we	will	distribute
you	will	distribute
they	will	distribute

Going to-Future

I	am	going to	distribute
you	are	going to	distribute
he/she/it	is	going to	distribute
we	are	going to	distribute
you	are	going to	distribute
they	are	going to	distribute

Future Perfect

I	will have	distributed
you	will have	distributed
he/she/it	will have	distributed
we	will have	distributed
you	will have	distributed
they	will have	distributed

Imperative

distribute

Impersonal

ing-Form

distributing

Past Participle

distributed

Continuous tenses

Present

I	am	distributing
you	are	distributing
he/she/it	is	distributing
we	are	distributing
you	are	distributing
they	are	distributing

Past

I	was	distributing
you	were	distributing
he/she/it	was	distributing
we	were	distributing
you	were	distributing
they	were	distributing

Present Perfect

I	have been	distributing
you	have been	distributing
he/she/it	has been	distributing
we	have been	distributing
you	have been	distributing
they	have been	distributing

Past Perfect

I	had been	distributing
you	had been	distributing
he/she/it	had been	distributing
we	had been	distributing
you	had been	distributing
they	had been	distributing

Will-Future

I	will be	distributing
you	will be	distributing
he/she/it	will be	distributing
we	will be	distributing
you	will be	distributing
they	will be	distributing

Going to-Future

I	am	going to be	distributing
you	are	going to be	distributing
he/she/it	is	going to be	distributing
we	are	going to be	distributing
you	are	going to be	distributing
they	are	going to be	distributing

Future Perfect

I	will have been distributing
you	will have been distributing
he/she/it	will have been distributing
we	will have been distributing
you	will have been distributing
they	will have been distributing

Conditional

I	would	distribute
you	would	distribute
he/she/it	would	distribute
we	would	distribute
you	would	distribute
they	would	distribute

Conditional Past

I	would have	distributed
you	would have	distributed
he/she/it	would have	distributed
we	would have	distributed
you	would have	distributed
they	would have	distributed

Simple tenses

Present

I	disturb
you	disturb
he/she/it	disturbs
we	disturb
you	disturb
they	disturb

Past

I	disturbed
you	disturbed
he/she/it	disturbed
we	disturbed
you	disturbed
they	disturbed

Present Perfect

I	have	disturbed
you	have	disturbed
he/she/it	has	disturbed
we	have	disturbed
you	have	disturbed
they	have	disturbed

Past Perfect

I	had	disturbed
you	had	disturbed
he/she/it	had	disturbed
we	had	disturbed
you	had	disturbed
they	had	disturbed

Will-Future

I	will	disturb
you	will	disturb
he/she/it	will	disturb
we	will	disturb
you	will	disturb
they	will	disturb

Going to-Future

I	am	going to	disturb
you	are	going to	disturb
he/she/it	is	going to	disturb
we	are	going to	disturb
you	are	going to	disturb
they	are	going to	disturb

Future Perfect

I	will have	disturbed
you	will have	disturbed
he/she/it	will have	disturbed
we	will have	disturbed
you	will have	disturbed
they	will have	disturbed

Imperative

disturb

Impersonal

ing-Form

disturbing

Past Participle

disturbed

Continuous tenses

Present

I	am	disturbing
you	are	disturbing
he/she/it	is	disturbing
we	are	disturbing
you	are	disturbing
they	are	disturbing

Past

I	was	disturbing
you	were	disturbing
he/she/it	was	disturbing
we	were	disturbing
you	were	disturbing
they	were	disturbing

Present Perfect

I	have been	disturbing
you	have been	disturbing
he/she/it	has been	disturbing
we	have been	disturbing
you	have been	disturbing
they	have been	disturbing

Past Perfect

I	had been	disturbing
you	had been	disturbing
he/she/it	had been	disturbing
we	had been	disturbing
you	had been	disturbing
they	had been	disturbing

Will-Future

I	will be	disturbing
you	will be	disturbing
he/she/it	will be	disturbing
we	will be	disturbing
you	will be	disturbing
they	will be	disturbing

Going to-Future

I	am	going to be	disturbing
you	are	going to be	disturbing
he/she/it	is	going to be	disturbing
we	are	going to be	disturbing
you	are	going to be	disturbing
they	are	going to be	disturbing

Future Perfect

I	will have been	disturbing
you	will have been	disturbing
he/she/it	will have been	disturbing
we	will have been	disturbing
you	will have been	disturbing
they	will have been	disturbing

Conditional

I	would	disturb
you	would	disturb
he/she/it	would	disturb
we	would	disturb
you	would	disturb
they	would	disturb

Conditional Past

I	would have	disturbed
you	would have	disturbed
he/she/it	would have	disturbed
we	would have	disturbed
you	would have	disturbed
they	would have	disturbed

divide

teilen

\+ **-ing** → ~~e~~ / + **-d** nicht **-ed**
Regelmäßiges Verb

Simple tenses

Present

I	divide
you	divide
he/she/it	divides
we	divide
you	divide
they	divide

Past

I	divided
you	divided
he/she/it	divided
we	divided
you	divided
they	divided

Present Perfect

I	have	divided
you	have	divided
he/she/it	has	divided
we	have	divided
you	have	divided
they	have	divided

Past Perfect

I	had	divided
you	had	divided
he/she/it	had	divided
we	had	divided
you	had	divided
they	had	divided

Will-Future

I	will	divide
you	will	divide
he/she/it	will	divide
we	will	divide
you	will	divide
they	will	divide

Going to-Future

I	am	going to	divide
you	are	going to	divide
he/she/it	is	going to	divide
we	are	going to	divide
you	are	going to	divide
they	are	going to	divide

Future Perfect

I	will have	divided
you	will have	divided
he/she/it	will have	divided
we	will have	divided
you	will have	divided
they	will have	divided

Imperative

divide

Impersonal

ing-Form

dividing

Past Participle

divided

Continuous tenses

Present

I	am	dividing
you	are	dividing
he/she/it	is	dividing
we	are	dividing
you	are	dividing
they	are	dividing

Past

I	was	dividing
you	were	dividing
he/she/it	was	dividing
we	were	dividing
you	were	dividing
they	were	dividing

Present Perfect

I	have	been	dividing
you	have	been	dividing
he/she/it	has	been	dividing
we	have	been	dividing
you	have	been	dividing
they	have	been	dividing

Past Perfect

I	had been	dividing
you	had been	dividing
he/she/it	had been	dividing
we	had been	dividing
you	had been	dividing
they	had been	dividing

Will-Future

I	will be	dividing
you	will be	dividing
he/she/it	will be	dividing
we	will be	dividing
you	will be	dividing
they	will be	dividing

Going to-Future

I	am	going to be	dividing
you	are	going to be	dividing
he/she/it	is	going to be	dividing
we	are	going to be	dividing
you	are	going to be	dividing
they	are	going to be	dividing

Future Perfect

I	will have been	dividing
you	will have been	dividing
he/she/it	will have been	dividing
we	will have been	dividing
you	will have been	dividing
they	will have been	dividing

Conditional

I	would	divide
you	would	divide
he/she/it	would	divide
we	would	divide
you	would	divide
they	would	divide

Conditional Past

I	would have	divided
you	would have	divided
he/she/it	would have	divided
we	would have	divided
you	would have	divided
they	would have	divided

tun

do

- did - done

Simple tenses

Present

I	do
you	do
he/she/it	does
we	do
you	do
they	do

Past

I	did
you	did
he/she/it	did
we	did
you	did
they	did

Present Perfect

I	have	done
you	have	done
he/she/it	has	done
we	have	done
you	have	done
they	have	done

Past Perfect

I	had	done
you	had	done
he/she/it	had	done
we	had	done
you	had	done
they	had	done

Will-Future

I	will	do
you	will	do
he/she/it	will	do
we	will	do
you	will	do
they	will	do

Going to-Future

I	am	going to	do
you	are	going to	do
he/she/it	is	going to	do
we	are	going to	do
you	are	going to	do
they	are	going to	do

Future Perfect

I	will have	done
you	will have	done
he/she/it	will have	done
we	will have	done
you	will have	done
they	will have	done

Imperative

do

Impersonal

ing-Form

doing

Past Participle

done

Continuous tenses

Present

I	am	doing
you	are	doing
he/she/it	is	doing
we	are	doing
you	are	doing
they	are	doing

Past

I	was	doing
you	were	doing
he/she/it	was	doing
we	were	doing
you	were	doing
they	were	doing

Present Perfect

I	have been	doing
you	have been	doing
he/she/it	has been	doing
we	have been	doing
you	have been	doing
they	have been	doing

Past Perfect

I	had been	doing
you	had been	doing
he/she/it	had been	doing
we	had been	doing
you	had been	doing
they	had been	doing

Will-Future

I	will be	doing
you	will be	doing
he/she/it	will be	doing
we	will be	doing
you	will be	doing
they	will be	doing

Going to-Future

I	am	going to be	doing
you	are	going to be	doing
he/she/it	is	going to be	doing
we	are	going to be	doing
you	are	going to be	doing
they	are	going to be	doing

Future Perfect

I	will have been	doing
you	will have been	doing
he/she/it	will have been	doing
we	will have been	doing
you	will have been	doing
they	will have been	doing

Conditional

I	would	do
you	would	do
he/she/it	would	do
we	would	do
you	would	do
they	would	do

Conditional Past

I	would have	done
you	would have	done
he/she/it	would have	done
we	would have	done
you	would have	done
they	would have	done

draw

- drew - drawn

zeichnen

Unregelmäßiges Verb

Simple tenses

Present

I	draw
you	draw
he/she/it	draws
we	draw
you	draw
they	draw

Past

I	drew
you	drew
he/she/it	drew
we	drew
you	drew
they	drew

Present Perfect

I	have	drawn
you	have	drawn
he/she/it	has	drawn
we	have	drawn
you	have	drawn
they	have	drawn

Past Perfect

I	had	drawn
you	had	drawn
he/she/it	had	drawn
we	had	drawn
you	had	drawn
they	had	drawn

***Will*-Future**

I	will	draw
you	will	draw
he/she/it	will	draw
we	will	draw
you	will	draw
they	will	draw

***Going to*-Future**

I	am	going to	draw
you	are	going to	draw
he/she/it	is	going to	draw
we	are	going to	draw
you	are	going to	draw
they	are	going to	draw

Future Perfect

I	will have	drawn
you	will have	drawn
he/she/it	will have	drawn
we	will have	drawn
you	will have	drawn
they	will have	drawn

Imperative

draw

Impersonal

***ing*-Form**

drawing

Past Participle

drawn

Continuous tenses

Present

I	am	drawing
you	are	drawing
he/she/it	is	drawing
we	are	drawing
you	are	drawing
they	are	drawing

Past

I	was	drawing
you	were	drawing
he/she/it	was	drawing
we	were	drawing
you	were	drawing
they	were	drawing

Present Perfect

I	have been	drawing
you	have been	drawing
he/she/it	has been	drawing
we	have been	drawing
you	have been	drawing
they	have been	drawing

Past Perfect

I	had been	drawing
you	had been	drawing
he/she/it	had been	drawing
we	had been	drawing
you	had been	drawing
they	had been	drawing

***Will*-Future**

I	will be	drawing
you	will be	drawing
he/she/it	will be	drawing
we	will be	drawing
you	will be	drawing
they	will be	drawing

***Going to*-Future**

I	am	going to be	drawing
you	are	going to be	drawing
he/she/it	is	going to be	drawing
we	are	going to be	drawing
you	are	going to be	drawing
they	are	going to be	drawing

Future Perfect

I	will have been	drawing
you	will have been	drawing
he/she/it	will have been	drawing
we	will have been	drawing
you	will have been	drawing
they	will have been	drawing

Conditional

I	would	draw
you	would	draw
he/she/it	would	draw
we	would	draw
you	would	draw
they	would	draw

Conditional Past

I	would have	drawn
you	would have	drawn
he/she/it	would have	drawn
we	would have	drawn
you	would have	drawn
they	would have	drawn

dream - dreamed/dreamt - dreamed/dreamt

träumen

Unregelmäßiges Verb

Simple tenses

Present

I	dream
you	dream
he/she/it	dreams
we	dream
you	dream
they	dream

Past

I	dreamed | dreamt
you	dreamed | dreamt
he/she/it	dreamed | dreamt
we	dreamed | dreamt
you	dreamed | dreamt
they	dreamed | dreamt

Present Perfect

I	have	dreamed | dreamt
you	have	dreamed | dreamt
he/she/it	has	dreamed | dreamt
we	have	dreamed | dreamt
you	have	dreamed | dreamt
they	have	dreamed | dreamt

Past Perfect

I	had	dreamed | dreamt
you	had	dreamed | dreamt
he/she/it	had	dreamed | dreamt
we	had	dreamed | dreamt
you	had	dreamed | dreamt
they	had	dreamed | dreamt

Will-Future

I	will	dream
you	will	dream
he/she/it	will	dream
we	will	dream
you	will	dream
they	will	dream

Going to-Future

I	am	going to	dream
you	are	going to	dream
he/she/it	is	going to	dream
we	are	going to	dream
you	are	going to	dream
they	are	going to	dream

Future Perfect

I	will have	dreamed | dreamt
you	will have	dreamed | dreamt
he/she/it	will have	dreamed | dreamt
we	will have	dreamed | dreamt
you	will have	dreamed | dreamt
they	will have	dreamed | dreamt

Imperative

dream

Impersonal

ing-Form

dreaming

Past Participle

dreamed | dreamt

Continuous tenses

Present

I	am	dreaming
you	are	dreaming
he/she/it	is	dreaming
we	are	dreaming
you	are	dreaming
they	are	dreaming

Past

I	was	dreaming
you	were	dreaming
he/she/it	was	dreaming
we	were	dreaming
you	were	dreaming
they	were	dreaming

Present Perfect

I	have been	dreaming
you	have been	dreaming
he/she/it	has been	dreaming
we	have been	dreaming
you	have been	dreaming
they	have been	dreaming

Past Perfect

I	had been	dreaming
you	had been	dreaming
he/she/it	had been	dreaming
we	had been	dreaming
you	had been	dreaming
they	had been	dreaming

Will-Future

I	will be	dreaming
you	will be	dreaming
he/she/it	will be	dreaming
we	will be	dreaming
you	will be	dreaming
they	will be	dreaming

Going to-Future

I	am	going to be	dreaming
you	are	going to be	dreaming
he/she/it	is	going to be	dreaming
we	are	going to be	dreaming
you	are	going to be	dreaming
they	are	going to be	dreaming

Future Perfect

I	will have been	dreaming
you	will have been	dreaming
he/she/it	will have been	dreaming
we	will have been	dreaming
you	will have been	dreaming
they	will have been	dreaming

Conditional

I	would	dream
you	would	dream
he/she/it	would	dream
we	would	dream
you	would	dream
they	would	dream

Conditional Past

I	would have	dreamed | dreamt
you	would have	dreamed | dreamt
he/she/it	would have	dreamed | dreamt
we	would have	dreamed | dreamt
you	would have	dreamed | dreamt
they	would have	dreamed | dreamt

dress

jemanden/sich anziehen

+ **-es** in 3. Person Singular
Regelmäßiges Verb

Simple tenses

Present

I	dress
you	dress
he/she/it	dresses
we	dress
you	dress
they	dress

Past

I	dressed
you	dressed
he/she/it	dressed
we	dressed
you	dressed
they	dressed

Present Perfect

I	have	dressed
you	have	dressed
he/she/it	has	dressed
we	have	dressed
you	have	dressed
they	have	dressed

Past Perfect

I	had	dressed
you	had	dressed
he/she/it	had	dressed
we	had	dressed
you	had	dressed
they	had	dressed

Will-Future

I	will	dress
you	will	dress
he/she/it	will	dress
we	will	dress
you	will	dress
they	will	dress

Going to-Future

I	am	going to	dress
you	are	going to	dress
he/she/it	is	going to	dress
we	are	going to	dress
you	are	going to	dress
they	are	going to	dress

Future Perfect

I	will have	dressed
you	will have	dressed
he/she/it	will have	dressed
we	will have	dressed
you	will have	dressed
they	will have	dressed

Imperative

dress

Impersonal

ing-Form

dressing

Past Participle

dressed

Continuous tenses

Present

I	am	dressing
you	are	dressing
he/she/it	is	dressing
we	are	dressing
you	are	dressing
they	are	dressing

Past

I	was	dressing
you	were	dressing
he/she/it	was	dressing
we	were	dressing
you	were	dressing
they	were	dressing

Present Perfect

I	have been	dressing
you	have been	dressing
he/she/it	has been	dressing
we	have been	dressing
you	have been	dressing
they	have been	dressing

Past Perfect

I	had been	dressing
you	had been	dressing
he/she/it	had been	dressing
we	had been	dressing
you	had been	dressing
they	had been	dressing

Will-Future

I	will be	dressing
you	will be	dressing
he/she/it	will be	dressing
we	will be	dressing
you	will be	dressing
they	will be	dressing

Going to-Future

I	am	going to be	dressing
you	are	going to be	dressing
he/she/it	is	going to be	dressing
we	are	going to be	dressing
you	are	going to be	dressing
they	are	going to be	dressing

Future Perfect

I	will have been	dressing
you	will have been	dressing
he/she/it	will have been	dressing
we	will have been	dressing
you	will have been	dressing
they	will have been	dressing

Conditional

I	would	dress
you	would	dress
he/she/it	would	dress
we	would	dress
you	would	dress
they	would	dress

Conditional Past

I	would have	dressed
you	would have	dressed
he/she/it	would have	dressed
we	would have	dressed
you	would have	dressed
they	would have	dressed

Simple tenses

Present

I	drink
you	drink
he/she/it	drinks
we	drink
you	drink
they	drink

Past

I	drank
you	drank
he/she/it	drank
we	drank
you	drank
they	drank

Present Perfect

I	have	drunk
you	have	drunk
he/she/it	has	drunk
we	have	drunk
you	have	drunk
they	have	drunk

Past Perfect

I	had	drunk
you	had	drunk
he/she/it	had	drunk
we	had	drunk
you	had	drunk
they	had	drunk

Will-Future

I	will	drink
you	will	drink
he/she/it	will	drink
we	will	drink
you	will	drink
they	will	drink

Going to-Future

I	am	going to	drink
you	are	going to	drink
he/she/it	is	going to	drink
we	are	going to	drink
you	are	going to	drink
they	are	going to	drink

Future Perfect

I	will have	drunk
you	will have	drunk
he/she/it	will have	drunk
we	will have	drunk
you	will have	drunk
they	will have	drunk

Imperative

drink

Impersonal

ing-Form

drinking

Past Participle

drunk

Continuous tenses

Present

I	am	drinking
you	are	drinking
he/she/it	is	drinking
we	are	drinking
you	are	drinking
they	are	drinking

Past

I	was	drinking
you	were	drinking
he/she/it	was	drinking
we	were	drinking
you	were	drinking
they	were	drinking

Present Perfect

I	have been	drinking
you	have been	drinking
he/she/it	has been	drinking
we	have been	drinking
you	have been	drinking
they	have been	drinking

Past Perfect

I	had been	drinking
you	had been	drinking
he/she/it	had been	drinking
we	had been	drinking
you	had been	drinking
they	had been	drinking

Will-Future

I	will be	drinking
you	will be	drinking
he/she/it	will be	drinking
we	will be	drinking
you	will be	drinking
they	will be	drinking

Going to-Future

I	am	going to be	drinking
you	are	going to be	drinking
he/she/it	is	going to be	drinking
we	are	going to be	drinking
you	are	going to be	drinking
they	are	going to be	drinking

Future Perfect

I	will have been	drinking
you	will have been	drinking
he/she/it	will have been	drinking
we	will have been	drinking
you	will have been	drinking
they	will have been	drinking

Conditional

I	would	drink
you	would	drink
he/she/it	would	drink
we	would	drink
you	would	drink
they	would	drink

Conditional Past

I	would have	drunk
you	would have	drunk
he/she/it	would have	drunk
we	would have	drunk
you	would have	drunk
they	would have	drunk

drive

- drove - driven

fahren

+ -ing → ~~e~~
Unregelmäßiges Verb

Simple tenses

Present

I	drive
you	drive
he/she/it	drives
we	drive
you	drive
they	drive

Past

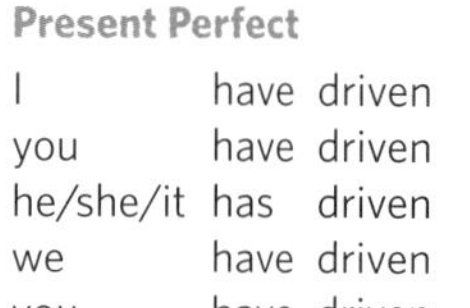

I	drove
you	drove
he/she/it	drove
we	drove
you	drove
they	drove

Present Perfect

I	have	driven
you	have	driven
he/she/it	has	driven
we	have	driven
you	have	driven
they	have	driven

Past Perfect

I	had	driven
you	had	driven
he/she/it	had	driven
we	had	driven
you	had	driven
they	had	driven

Will-Future

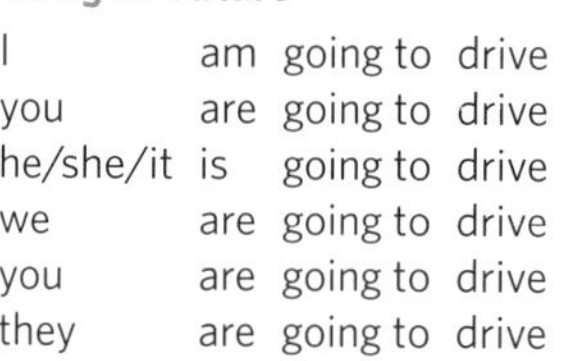

I	will	drive
you	will	drive
he/she/it	will	drive
we	will	drive
you	will	drive
they	will	drive

Going to-Future

I	am	going to	drive
you	are	going to	drive
he/she/it	is	going to	drive
we	are	going to	drive
you	are	going to	drive
they	are	going to	drive

Future Perfect

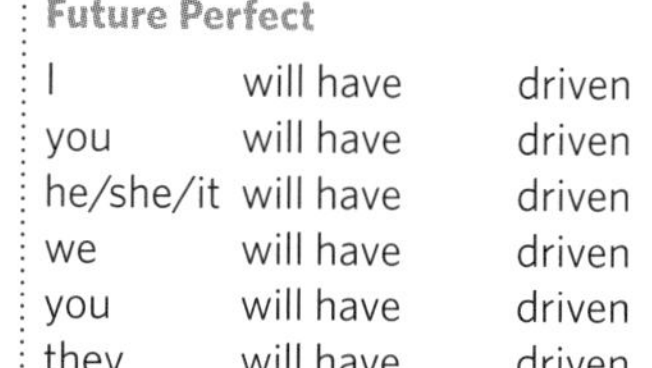

I	will have	driven
you	will have	driven
he/she/it	will have	driven
we	will have	driven
you	will have	driven
they	will have	driven

Imperative

drive

Impersonal

ing-Form

driving

Past Participle

driven

Continuous tenses

Present

I	am	driving
you	are	driving
he/she/it	is	driving
we	are	driving
you	are	driving
they	are	driving

Past

I	was	driving
you	were	driving
he/she/it	was	driving
we	were	driving
you	were	driving
they	were	driving

Present Perfect

I	have been	driving
you	have been	driving
he/she/it	has been	driving
we	have been	driving
you	have been	driving
they	have been	driving

Past Perfect

I	had been	driving
you	had been	driving
he/she/it	had been	driving
we	had been	driving
you	had been	driving
they	had been	driving

Will-Future

I	will be	driving
you	will be	driving
he/she/it	will be	driving
we	will be	driving
you	will be	driving
they	will be	driving

Going to-Future

I	am	going to be	driving
you	are	going to be	driving
he/she/it	is	going to be	driving
we	are	going to be	driving
you	are	going to be	driving
they	are	going to be	driving

Future Perfect

I	will have been	driving
you	will have been	driving
he/she/it	will have been	driving
we	will have been	driving
you	will have been	driving
they	will have been	driving

Conditional

I	would	drive
you	would	drive
he/she/it	would	drive
we	would	drive
you	would	drive
they	would	drive

Conditional Past

I	would have	driven
you	would have	driven
he/she/it	would have	driven
we	would have	driven
you	would have	driven
they	would have	driven

Konsonantenverdopplung
Regelmäßiges Verb

fallen lassen

drop

Simple tenses

Present

I	drop
you	drop
he/she/it	drops
we	drop
you	drop
they	drop

Past

I	dropped
you	dropped
he/she/it	dropped
we	dropped
you	dropped
they	dropped

Present Perfect

I	have	dropped
you	have	dropped
he/she/it	has	dropped
we	have	dropped
you	have	dropped
they	have	dropped

Past Perfect

I	had	dropped
you	had	dropped
he/she/it	had	dropped
we	had	dropped
you	had	dropped
they	had	dropped

Will-Future

I	will	drop
you	will	drop
he/she/it	will	drop
we	will	drop
you	will	drop
they	will	drop

Going to-Future

I	am	going to	drop
you	are	going to	drop
he/she/it	is	going to	drop
we	are	going to	drop
you	are	going to	drop
they	are	going to	drop

Future Perfect

I	will have	dropped
you	will have	dropped
he/she/it	will have	dropped
we	will have	dropped
you	will have	dropped
they	will have	dropped

Imperative

drop

Impersonal

ing-Form

dropping

Past Participle

dropped

Continuous tenses

Present

I	am	dropping
you	are	dropping
he/she/it	is	dropping
we	are	dropping
you	are	dropping
they	are	dropping

Past

I	was	dropping
you	were	dropping
he/she/it	was	dropping
we	were	dropping
you	were	dropping
they	were	dropping

Present Perfect

I	have been	dropping
you	have been	dropping
he/she/it	has been	dropping
we	have been	dropping
you	have been	dropping
they	have been	dropping

Past Perfect

I	had been	dropping
you	had been	dropping
he/she/it	had been	dropping
we	had been	dropping
you	had been	dropping
they	had been	dropping

Will-Future

I	will be	dropping
you	will be	dropping
he/she/it	will be	dropping
we	will be	dropping
you	will be	dropping
they	will be	dropping

Going to-Future

I	am	going to be	dropping
you	are	going to be	dropping
he/she/it	is	going to be	dropping
we	are	going to be	dropping
you	are	going to be	dropping
they	are	going to be	dropping

Future Perfect

I	will have been	dropping
you	will have been	dropping
he/she/it	will have been	dropping
we	will have been	dropping
you	will have been	dropping
they	will have been	dropping

Conditional

I	would	drop
you	would	drop
he/she/it	would	drop
we	would	drop
you	would	drop
they	would	drop

Conditional Past

I	would have	dropped
you	would have	dropped
he/she/it	would have	dropped
we	would have	dropped
you	would have	dropped
they	would have	dropped

earn

verdienen

Regelmäßiges Verb

Simple tenses

Present

I	earn
you	earn
he/she/it	earns
we	earn
you	earn
they	earn

Past

I	earned
you	earned
he/she/it	earned
we	earned
you	earned
they	earned

Present Perfect

I	have	earned
you	have	earned
he/she/it	has	earned
we	have	earned
you	have	earned
they	have	earned

Past Perfect

I	had	earned
you	had	earned
he/she/it	had	earned
we	had	earned
you	had	earned
they	had	earned

Will-Future

I	will	earn
you	will	earn
he/she/it	will	earn
we	will	earn
you	will	earn
they	will	earn

Going to-Future

I	am	going to	earn
you	are	going to	earn
he/she/it	is	going to	earn
we	are	going to	earn
you	are	going to	earn
they	are	going to	earn

Future Perfect

I	will have	earned
you	will have	earned
he/she/it	will have	earned
we	will have	earned
you	will have	earned
they	will have	earned

Imperative

earn

Impersonal

ing-Form

earning

Past Participle

earned

Continuous tenses

Present

I	am	earning
you	are	earning
he/she/it	is	earning
we	are	earning
you	are	earning
they	are	earning

Past

I	was	earning
you	were	earning
he/she/it	was	earning
we	were	earning
you	were	earning
they	were	earning

Present Perfect

I	have	been	earning
you	have	been	earning
he/she/it	has	been	earning
we	have	been	earning
you	have	been	earning
they	have	been	earning

Past Perfect

I	had been	earning
you	had been	earning
he/she/it	had been	earning
we	had been	earning
you	had been	earning
they	had been	earning

Will-Future

I	will be	earning
you	will be	earning
he/she/it	will be	earning
we	will be	earning
you	will be	earning
they	will be	earning

Going to-Future

I	am	going to be	earning
you	are	going to be	earning
he/she/it	is	going to be	earning
we	are	going to be	earning
you	are	going to be	earning
they	are	going to be	earning

Future Perfect

I	will have been	earning
you	will have been	earning
he/she/it	will have been	earning
we	will have been	earning
you	will have been	earning
they	will have been	earning

Conditional

I	would	earn
you	would	earn
he/she/it	would	earn
we	would	earn
you	would	earn
they	would	earn

Conditional Past

I	would have	earned
you	would have	earned
he/she/it	would have	earned
we	would have	earned
you	would have	earned
they	would have	earned

Simple tenses

Present

I	eat
you	eat
he/she/it	eats
we	eat
you	eat
they	eat

Past

I	ate
you	ate
he/she/it	ate
we	ate
you	ate
they	ate

Present Perfect

I	have	eaten
you	have	eaten
he/she/it	has	eaten
we	have	eaten
you	have	eaten
they	have	eaten

Past Perfect

I	had	eaten
you	had	eaten
he/she/it	had	eaten
we	had	eaten
you	had	eaten
they	had	eaten

Will-Future

I	will	eat
you	will	eat
he/she/it	will	eat
we	will	eat
you	will	eat
they	will	eat

Going to-Future

I	am	going to	eat
you	are	going to	eat
he/she/it	is	going to	eat
we	are	going to	eat
you	are	going to	eat
they	are	going to	eat

Future Perfect

I	will have	eaten
you	will have	eaten
he/she/it	will have	eaten
we	will have	eaten
you	will have	eaten
they	will have	eaten

Imperative

eat

Impersonal

ing-Form

eating

Past Participle

eaten

Continuous tenses

Present

I	am	eating
you	are	eating
he/she/it	is	eating
we	are	eating
you	are	eating
they	are	eating

Past

I	was	eating
you	were	eating
he/she/it	was	eating
we	were	eating
you	were	eating
they	were	eating

Present Perfect

I	have been	eating
you	have been	eating
he/she/it	has been	eating
we	have been	eating
you	have been	eating
they	have been	eating

Past Perfect

I	had been	eating
you	had been	eating
he/she/it	had been	eating
we	had been	eating
you	had been	eating
they	had been	eating

Will-Future

I	will be	eating
you	will be	eating
he/she/it	will be	eating
we	will be	eating
you	will be	eating
they	will be	eating

Going to-Future

I	am	going to be	eating
you	are	going to be	eating
he/she/it	is	going to be	eating
we	are	going to be	eating
you	are	going to be	eating
they	are	going to be	eating

Future Perfect

I	will have been	eating
you	will have been	eating
he/she/it	will have been	eating
we	will have been	eating
you	will have been	eating
they	will have been	eating

Conditional

I	would	eat
you	would	eat
he/she/it	would	eat
we	would	eat
you	would	eat
they	would	eat

Conditional Past

I	would have	eaten
you	would have	eaten
he/she/it	would have	eaten
we	would have	eaten
you	would have	eaten
they	would have	eaten

educate

erziehen

\+ **-ing** → ~~e~~ / + **-d** nicht **-ed**
Regelmäßiges Verb

Simple tenses

Present

I	educate
you	educate
he/she/it	educates
we	educate
you	educate
they	educate

Past

I	educated
you	educated
he/she/it	educated
we	educated
you	educated
they	educated

Present Perfect

I	have	educated
you	have	educated
he/she/it	has	educated
we	have	educated
you	have	educated
they	have	educated

Past Perfect

I	had	educated
you	had	educated
he/she/it	had	educated
we	had	educated
you	had	educated
they	had	educated

Will-Future

I	will	educate
you	will	educate
he/she/it	will	educate
we	will	educate
you	will	educate
they	will	educate

Going to-Future

I	am	going to	educate
you	are	going to	educate
he/she/it	is	going to	educate
we	are	going to	educate
you	are	going to	educate
they	are	going to	educate

Future Perfect

I	will have	educated
you	will have	educated
he/she/it	will have	educated
we	will have	educated
you	will have	educated
they	will have	educated

Imperative

educate

Impersonal

ing-Form

educating

Past Participle

educated

Continuous tenses

Present

I	am	educating
you	are	educating
he/she/it	is	educating
we	are	educating
you	are	educating
they	are	educating

Past

I	was	educating
you	were	educating
he/she/it	was	educating
we	were	educating
you	were	educating
they	were	educating

Present Perfect

I	have	been	educating
you	have	been	educating
he/she/it	has	been	educating
we	have	been	educating
you	have	been	educating
they	have	been	educating

Past Perfect

I	had been	educating
you	had been	educating
he/she/it	had been	educating
we	had been	educating
you	had been	educating
they	had been	educating

Will-Future

I	will be	educating
you	will be	educating
he/she/it	will be	educating
we	will be	educating
you	will be	educating
they	will be	educating

Going to-Future

I	am	going to be	educating
you	are	going to be	educating
he/she/it	is	going to be	educating
we	are	going to be	educating
you	are	going to be	educating
they	are	going to be	educating

Future Perfect

I	will have been	educating
you	will have been	educating
he/she/it	will have been	educating
we	will have been	educating
you	will have been	educating
they	will have been	educating

Conditional

I	would	educate
you	would	educate
he/she/it	would	educate
we	would	educate
you	would	educate
they	would	educate

Conditional Past

I	would have	educated
you	would have	educated
he/she/it	would have	educated
we	would have	educated
you	would have	educated
they	would have	educated

Simple tenses

Present

I	elect
you	elect
he/she/it	elects
we	elect
you	elect
they	elect

Past

I	elected
you	elected
he/she/it	elected
we	elected
you	elected
they	elected

Present Perfect

I	have	elected
you	have	elected
he/she/it	has	elected
we	have	elected
you	have	elected
they	have	elected

Past Perfect

I	had	elected
you	had	elected
he/she/it	had	elected
we	had	elected
you	had	elected
they	had	elected

Will-Future

I	will	elect
you	will	elect
he/she/it	will	elect
we	will	elect
you	will	elect
they	will	elect

Going to-Future

I	am	going to	elect
you	are	going to	elect
he/she/it	is	going to	elect
we	are	going to	elect
you	are	going to	elect
they	are	going to	elect

Future Perfect

I	will have	elected
you	will have	elected
he/she/it	will have	elected
we	will have	elected
you	will have	elected
they	will have	elected

Imperative

elect

Impersonal

ing-Form

electing

Past Participle

elected

Continuous tenses

Present

I	am	electing
you	are	electing
he/she/it	is	electing
we	are	electing
you	are	electing
they	are	electing

Past

I	was	electing
you	were	electing
he/she/it	was	electing
we	were	electing
you	were	electing
they	were	electing

Present Perfect

I	have been	electing
you	have been	electing
he/she/it	has been	electing
we	have been	electing
you	have been	electing
they	have been	electing

Past Perfect

I	had been	electing
you	had been	electing
he/she/it	had been	electing
we	had been	electing
you	had been	electing
they	had been	electing

Will-Future

I	will be	electing
you	will be	electing
he/she/it	will be	electing
we	will be	electing
you	will be	electing
they	will be	electing

Going to-Future

I	am	going to be	electing
you	are	going to be	electing
he/she/it	is	going to be	electing
we	are	going to be	electing
you	are	going to be	electing
they	are	going to be	electing

Future Perfect

I	will have been	electing
you	will have been	electing
he/she/it	will have been	electing
we	will have been	electing
you	will have been	electing
they	will have been	electing

Conditional

I	would	elect
you	would	elect
he/she/it	would	elect
we	would	elect
you	would	elect
they	would	elect

Conditional Past

I	would have	elected
you	would have	elected
he/she/it	would have	elected
we	would have	elected
you	would have	elected
they	would have	elected

emphasize

betonen

+ **-ing** → ~~e~~ / + **-d** nicht **-ed**
im BE auch **emphasise**
Regelmäßiges Verb

Simple tenses

Present

I	emphasize
you	emphasize
he/she/it	emphasizes
we	emphasize
you	emphasize
they	emphasize

Past

I	emphasized
you	emphasized
he/she/it	emphasized
we	emphasized
you	emphasized
they	emphasized

Present Perfect

I	have	emphasized
you	have	emphasized
he/she/it	has	emphasized
we	have	emphasized
you	have	emphasized
they	have	emphasized

Past Perfect

I	had	emphasized
you	had	emphasized
he/she/it	had	emphasized
we	had	emphasized
you	had	emphasized
they	had	emphasized

Will-Future

I	will	emphasize
you	will	emphasize
he/she/it	will	emphasize
we	will	emphasize
you	will	emphasize
they	will	emphasize

Going to-Future

I	am	going to	emphasize
you	are	going to	emphasize
he/she/it	is	going to	emphasize
we	are	going to	emphasize
you	are	going to	emphasize
they	are	going to	emphasize

Future Perfect

I	will have	emphasized
you	will have	emphasized
he/she/it	will have	emphasized
we	will have	emphasized
you	will have	emphasized
they	will have	emphasized

Imperative

emphasize

Impersonal

ing-Form

emphasizing

Past Participle

emphasized

Continuous tenses

Present

I	am	emphasizing
you	are	emphasizing
he/she/it	is	emphasizing
we	are	emphasizing
you	are	emphasizing
they	are	emphasizing

Past

I	was	emphasizing
you	were	emphasizing
he/she/it	was	emphasizing
we	were	emphasizing
you	were	emphasizing
they	were	emphasizing

Present Perfect

I	have been	emphasizing
you	have been	emphasizing
he/she/it	has been	emphasizing
we	have been	emphasizing
you	have been	emphasizing
they	have been	emphasizing

Past Perfect

I	had been	emphasizing
you	had been	emphasizing
he/she/it	had been	emphasizing
we	had been	emphasizing
you	had been	emphasizing
they	had been	emphasizing

Will-Future

I	will be	emphasizing
you	will be	emphasizing
he/she/it	will be	emphasizing
we	will be	emphasizing
you	will be	emphasizing
they	will be	emphasizing

Going to-Future

I	am	going to be	emphasizing
you	are	going to be	emphasizing
he/she/it	is	going to be	emphasizing
we	are	going to be	emphasizing
you	are	going to be	emphasizing
they	are	going to be	emphasizing

Future Perfect

I	will have been	emphasizing
you	will have been	emphasizing
he/she/it	will have been	emphasizing
we	will have been	emphasizing
you	will have been	emphasizing
they	will have been	emphasizing

Conditional

I	would	emphasize
you	would	emphasize
he/she/it	would	emphasize
we	would	emphasize
you	would	emphasize
they	would	emphasize

Conditional Past

I	would have	emphasized
you	would have	emphasized
he/she/it	would have	emphasized
we	would have	emphasized
you	would have	emphasized
they	would have	emphasized

employ

Regelmäßiges Verb

Simple tenses

Present

I	employ
you	employ
he/she/it	employs
we	employ
you	employ
they	employ

Past

I	employed
you	employed
he/she/it	employed
we	employed
you	employed
they	employed

Present Perfect

I	have	employed
you	have	employed
he/she/it	has	employed
we	have	employed
you	have	employed
they	have	employed

Past Perfect

I	had	employed
you	had	employed
he/she/it	had	employed
we	had	employed
you	had	employed
they	had	employed

Will-Future

I	will	employ
you	will	employ
he/she/it	will	employ
we	will	employ
you	will	employ
they	will	employ

Going to-Future

I	am	going to	employ
you	are	going to	employ
he/she/it	is	going to	employ
we	are	going to	employ
you	are	going to	employ
they	are	going to	employ

Future Perfect

I	will have	employed
you	will have	employed
he/she/it	will have	employed
we	will have	employed
you	will have	employed
they	will have	employed

Imperative

employ

Impersonal

ing-Form

employing

Past Participle

employed

Continuous tenses

Present

I	am	employing
you	are	employing
he/she/it	is	employing
we	are	employing
you	are	employing
they	are	employing

Past

I	was	employing
you	were	employing
he/she/it	was	employing
we	were	employing
you	were	employing
they	were	employing

Present Perfect

I	have been	employing
you	have been	employing
he/she/it	has been	employing
we	have been	employing
you	have been	employing
they	have been	employing

Past Perfect

I	had been	employing
you	had been	employing
he/she/it	had been	employing
we	had been	employing
you	had been	employing
they	had been	employing

Will-Future

I	will be	employing
you	will be	employing
he/she/it	will be	employing
we	will be	employing
you	will be	employing
they	will be	employing

Going to-Future

I	am	going to be	employing
you	are	going to be	employing
he/she/it	is	going to be	employing
we	are	going to be	employing
you	are	going to be	employing
they	are	going to be	employing

Future Perfect

I	will have been employing
you	will have been employing
he/she/it	will have been employing
we	will have been employing
you	will have been employing
they	will have been employing

Conditional

I	would	employ
you	would	employ
he/she/it	would	employ
we	would	employ
you	would	employ
they	would	employ

Conditional Past

I	would have	employed
you	would have	employed
he/she/it	would have	employed
we	would have	employed
you	would have	employed
they	would have	employed

encourage

ermutigen

+ **-ing** → ~~e~~ / + **-d** nicht **-ed**
Regelmäßiges Verb

Simple tenses

Present

I	encourage
you	encourage
he/she/it	encourages
we	encourage
you	encourage
they	encourage

Past

I	encouraged
you	encouraged
he/she/it	encouraged
we	encouraged
you	encouraged
they	encouraged

Present Perfect

I	have	encouraged
you	have	encouraged
he/she/it	has	encouraged
we	have	encouraged
you	have	encouraged
they	have	encouraged

Past Perfect

I	had	encouraged
you	had	encouraged
he/she/it	had	encouraged
we	had	encouraged
you	had	encouraged
they	had	encouraged

Will-Future

I	will	encourage
you	will	encourage
he/she/it	will	encourage
we	will	encourage
you	will	encourage
they	will	encourage

Going to-Future

I	am	going to	encourage
you	are	going to	encourage
he/she/it	is	going to	encourage
we	are	going to	encourage
you	are	going to	encourage
they	are	going to	encourage

Future Perfect

I	will have	encouraged
you	will have	encouraged
he/she/it	will have	encouraged
we	will have	encouraged
you	will have	encouraged
they	will have	encouraged

Imperative

encourage

Impersonal

ing-Form

encouraging

Past Participle

encouraged

Continuous tenses

Present

I	am	encouraging
you	are	encouraging
he/she/it	is	encouraging
we	are	encouraging
you	are	encouraging
they	are	encouraging

Past

I	was	encouraging
you	were	encouraging
he/she/it	was	encouraging
we	were	encouraging
you	were	encouraging
they	were	encouraging

Present Perfect

I	have been	encouraging
you	have been	encouraging
he/she/it	has been	encouraging
we	have been	encouraging
you	have been	encouraging
they	have been	encouraging

Past Perfect

I	had been	encouraging
you	had been	encouraging
he/she/it	had been	encouraging
we	had been	encouraging
you	had been	encouraging
they	had been	encouraging

Will-Future

I	will be	encouraging
you	will be	encouraging
he/she/it	will be	encouraging
we	will be	encouraging
you	will be	encouraging
they	will be	encouraging

Going to-Future

I	am	going to be	encouraging
you	are	going to be	encouraging
he/she/it	is	going to be	encouraging
we	are	going to be	encouraging
you	are	going to be	encouraging
they	are	going to be	encouraging

Future Perfect

I	will have been encouraging
you	will have been encouraging
he/she/it	will have been encouraging
we	will have been encouraging
you	will have been encouraging
they	will have been encouraging

Conditional

I	would	encourage
you	would	encourage
he/she/it	would	encourage
we	would	encourage
you	would	encourage
they	would	encourage

Conditional Past

I	would have	encouraged
you	would have	encouraged
he/she/it	would have	encouraged
we	would have	encouraged
you	would have	encouraged
they	would have	encouraged

Simple tenses

Present

I	end
you	end
he/she/it	ends
we	end
you	end
they	end

Past

I	ended
you	ended
he/she/it	ended
we	ended
you	ended
they	ended

Present Perfect

I	have	ended
you	have	ended
he/she/it	has	ended
we	have	ended
you	have	ended
they	have	ended

Past Perfect

I	had	ended
you	had	ended
he/she/it	had	ended
we	had	ended
you	had	ended
they	had	ended

Will-Future

I	will	end
you	will	end
he/she/it	will	end
we	will	end
you	will	end
they	will	end

Going to-Future

I	am	going to	end
you	are	going to	end
he/she/it	is	going to	end
we	are	going to	end
you	are	going to	end
they	are	going to	end

Future Perfect

I	will have	ended
you	will have	ended
he/she/it	will have	ended
we	will have	ended
you	will have	ended
they	will have	ended

Imperative

end

Impersonal

ing-Form

ending

Past Participle

ended

Continuous tenses

Present

I	am	ending
you	are	ending
he/she/it	is	ending
we	are	ending
you	are	ending
they	are	ending

Past

I	was	ending
you	were	ending
he/she/it	was	ending
we	were	ending
you	were	ending
they	were	ending

Present Perfect

I	have been	ending
you	have been	ending
he/she/it	has been	ending
we	have been	ending
you	have been	ending
they	have been	ending

Past Perfect

I	had been	ending
you	had been	ending
he/she/it	had been	ending
we	had been	ending
you	had been	ending
they	had been	ending

Will-Future

I	will be	ending
you	will be	ending
he/she/it	will be	ending
we	will be	ending
you	will be	ending
they	will be	ending

Going to-Future

I	am	going to be	ending
you	are	going to be	ending
he/she/it	is	going to be	ending
we	are	going to be	ending
you	are	going to be	ending
they	are	going to be	ending

Future Perfect

I	will have been	ending
you	will have been	ending
he/she/it	will have been	ending
we	will have been	ending
you	will have been	ending
they	will have been	ending

Conditional

I	would	end
you	would	end
he/she/it	would	end
we	would	end
you	would	end
they	would	end

Conditional Past

I	would have	ended
you	would have	ended
he/she/it	would have	ended
we	would have	ended
you	would have	ended
they	would have	ended

enjoy

genießen

Regelmäßiges Verb

Simple tenses

Present

I	enjoy
you	enjoy
he/she/it	enjoys
we	enjoy
you	enjoy
they	enjoy

Past

I	enjoyed
you	enjoyed
he/she/it	enjoyed
we	enjoyed
you	enjoyed
they	enjoyed

Present Perfect

I	have	enjoyed
you	have	enjoyed
he/she/it	has	enjoyed
we	have	enjoyed
you	have	enjoyed
they	have	enjoyed

Past Perfect

I	had	enjoyed
you	had	enjoyed
he/she/it	had	enjoyed
we	had	enjoyed
you	had	enjoyed
they	had	enjoyed

Will-Future

I	will	enjoy
you	will	enjoy
he/she/it	will	enjoy
we	will	enjoy
you	will	enjoy
they	will	enjoy

Going to-Future

I	am	going to	enjoy
you	are	going to	enjoy
he/she/it	is	going to	enjoy
we	are	going to	enjoy
you	are	going to	enjoy
they	are	going to	enjoy

Future Perfect

I	will have	enjoyed
you	will have	enjoyed
he/she/it	will have	enjoyed
we	will have	enjoyed
you	will have	enjoyed
they	will have	enjoyed

Imperative

enjoy

Impersonal

ing-Form

enjoying

Past Participle

enjoyed

Continuous tenses

Present

I	am	enjoying
you	are	enjoying
he/she/it	is	enjoying
we	are	enjoying
you	are	enjoying
they	are	enjoying

Past

I	was	enjoying
you	were	enjoying
he/she/it	was	enjoying
we	were	enjoying
you	were	enjoying
they	were	enjoying

Present Perfect

I	have been	enjoying
you	have been	enjoying
he/she/it	has been	enjoying
we	have been	enjoying
you	have been	enjoying
they	have been	enjoying

Past Perfect

I	had been	enjoying
you	had been	enjoying
he/she/it	had been	enjoying
we	had been	enjoying
you	had been	enjoying
they	had been	enjoying

Will-Future

I	will be	enjoying
you	will be	enjoying
he/she/it	will be	enjoying
we	will be	enjoying
you	will be	enjoying
they	will be	enjoying

Going to-Future

I	am	going to be	enjoying
you	are	going to be	enjoying
he/she/it	is	going to be	enjoying
we	are	going to be	enjoying
you	are	going to be	enjoying
they	are	going to be	enjoying

Future Perfect

I	will have been	enjoying
you	will have been	enjoying
he/she/it	will have been	enjoying
we	will have been	enjoying
you	will have been	enjoying
they	will have been	enjoying

Conditional

I	would	enjoy
you	would	enjoy
he/she/it	would	enjoy
we	would	enjoy
you	would	enjoy
they	would	enjoy

Conditional Past

I	would have	enjoyed
you	would have	enjoyed
he/she/it	would have	enjoyed
we	would have	enjoyed
you	would have	enjoyed
they	would have	enjoyed

Simple tenses

Present

I	enter
you	enter
he/she/it	enters
we	enter
you	enter
they	enter

Past

I	entered
you	entered
he/she/it	entered
we	entered
you	entered
they	entered

Present Perfect

I	have	entered
you	have	entered
he/she/it	has	entered
we	have	entered
you	have	entered
they	have	entered

Past Perfect

I	had	entered
you	had	entered
he/she/it	had	entered
we	had	entered
you	had	entered
they	had	entered

Will-Future

I	will	enter
you	will	enter
he/she/it	will	enter
we	will	enter
you	will	enter
they	will	enter

Going to-Future

I	am	going to	enter
you	are	going to	enter
he/she/it	is	going to	enter
we	are	going to	enter
you	are	going to	enter
they	are	going to	enter

Future Perfect

I	will have	entered
you	will have	entered
he/she/it	will have	entered
we	will have	entered
you	will have	entered
they	will have	entered

Imperative

enter

Impersonal

ing-Form

entering

Past Participle

entered

Continuous tenses

Present

I	am	entering
you	are	entering
he/she/it	is	entering
we	are	entering
you	are	entering
they	are	entering

Past

I	was	entering
you	were	entering
he/she/it	was	entering
we	were	entering
you	were	entering
they	were	entering

Present Perfect

I	have	been	entering
you	have	been	entering
he/she/it	has	been	entering
we	have	been	entering
you	have	been	entering
they	have	been	entering

Past Perfect

I	had been	entering
you	had been	entering
he/she/it	had been	entering
we	had been	entering
you	had been	entering
they	had been	entering

Will-Future

I	will be	entering
you	will be	entering
he/she/it	will be	entering
we	will be	entering
you	will be	entering
they	will be	entering

Going to-Future

I	am	going to be	entering
you	are	going to be	entering
he/she/it	is	going to be	entering
we	are	going to be	entering
you	are	going to be	entering
they	are	going to be	entering

Future Perfect

I	will have been entering
you	will have been entering
he/she/it	will have been entering
we	will have been entering
you	will have been entering
they	will have been entering

Conditional

I	would	enter
you	would	enter
he/she/it	would	enter
we	would	enter
you	would	enter
they	would	enter

Conditional Past

I	would have	entered
you	would have	entered
he/she/it	would have	entered
we	would have	entered
you	would have	entered
they	would have	entered

entertain

unterhalten

Regelmäßiges Verb

Simple tenses

Present

I	entertain
you	entertain
he/she/it	entertains
we	entertain
you	entertain
they	entertain

Past

I	entertained
you	entertained
he/she/it	entertained
we	entertained
you	entertained
they	entertained

Present Perfect

I	have	entertained
you	have	entertained
he/she/it	has	entertained
we	have	entertained
you	have	entertained
they	have	entertained

Past Perfect

I	had	entertained
you	had	entertained
he/she/it	had	entertained
we	had	entertained
you	had	entertained
they	had	entertained

Will-Future

I	will	entertain
you	will	entertain
he/she/it	will	entertain
we	will	entertain
you	will	entertain
they	will	entertain

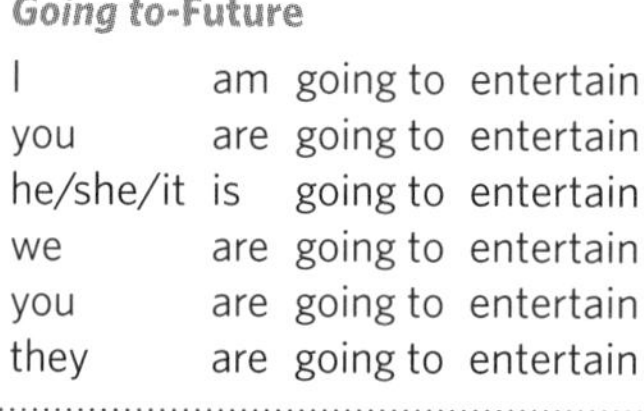

Going to-Future

I	am	going to	entertain
you	are	going to	entertain
he/she/it	is	going to	entertain
we	are	going to	entertain
you	are	going to	entertain
they	are	going to	entertain

Future Perfect

I	will have	entertained
you	will have	entertained
he/she/it	will have	entertained
we	will have	entertained
you	will have	entertained
they	will have	entertained

Imperative

entertain

Impersonal

ing-Form

entertaining

Past Participle

entertained

Continuous tenses

Present

I	am	entertaining
you	are	entertaining
he/she/it	is	entertaining
we	are	entertaining
you	are	entertaining
they	are	entertaining

Past

I	was	entertaining
you	were	entertaining
he/she/it	was	entertaining
we	were	entertaining
you	were	entertaining
they	were	entertaining

Present Perfect

I	have been	entertaining
you	have been	entertaining
he/she/it	has been	entertaining
we	have been	entertaining
you	have been	entertaining
they	have been	entertaining

Past Perfect

I	had been	entertaining
you	had been	entertaining
he/she/it	had been	entertaining
we	had been	entertaining
you	had been	entertaining
they	had been	entertaining

Will-Future

I	will be	entertaining
you	will be	entertaining
he/she/it	will be	entertaining
we	will be	entertaining
you	will be	entertaining
they	will be	entertaining

Going to-Future

I	am	going to be	entertaining
you	are	going to be	entertaining
he/she/it	is	going to be	entertaining
we	are	going to be	entertaining
you	are	going to be	entertaining
they	are	going to be	entertaining

Future Perfect

I	will have been entertaining
you	will have been entertaining
he/she/it	will have been entertaining
we	will have been entertaining
you	will have been entertaining
they	will have been entertaining

Conditional

I	would	entertain
you	would	entertain
he/she/it	would	entertain
we	would	entertain
you	would	entertain
they	would	entertain

Conditional Past

I	would have	entertained
you	would have	entertained
he/she/it	would have	entertained
we	would have	entertained
you	would have	entertained
they	would have	entertained

Simple tenses

Present

I	escape
you	escape
he/she/it	escapes
we	escape
you	escape
they	escape

Past

I	escaped
you	escaped
he/she/it	escaped
we	escaped
you	escaped
they	escaped

Present Perfect

I	have	escaped
you	have	escaped
he/she/it	has	escaped
we	have	escaped
you	have	escaped
they	have	escaped

Past Perfect

I	had	escaped
you	had	escaped
he/she/it	had	escaped
we	had	escaped
you	had	escaped
they	had	escaped

Will-Future

I	will	escape
you	will	escape
he/she/it	will	escape
we	will	escape
you	will	escape
they	will	escape

Going to-Future

I	am	going to	escape
you	are	going to	escape
he/she/it	is	going to	escape
we	are	going to	escape
you	are	going to	escape
they	are	going to	escape

Future Perfect

I	will have	escaped
you	will have	escaped
he/she/it	will have	escaped
we	will have	escaped
you	will have	escaped
they	will have	escaped

Imperative

escape

Impersonal

ing-Form

escaping

Past Participle

escaped

Continuous tenses

Present

I	am	escaping
you	are	escaping
he/she/it	is	escaping
we	are	escaping
you	are	escaping
they	are	escaping

Past

I	was	escaping
you	were	escaping
he/she/it	was	escaping
we	were	escaping
you	were	escaping
they	were	escaping

Present Perfect

I	have been	escaping
you	have been	escaping
he/she/it	has been	escaping
we	have been	escaping
you	have been	escaping
they	have been	escaping

Past Perfect

I	had been	escaping
you	had been	escaping
he/she/it	had been	escaping
we	had been	escaping
you	had been	escaping
they	had been	escaping

Will-Future

I	will be	escaping
you	will be	escaping
he/she/it	will be	escaping
we	will be	escaping
you	will be	escaping
they	will be	escaping

Going to-Future

I	am	going to be	escaping
you	are	going to be	escaping
he/she/it	is	going to be	escaping
we	are	going to be	escaping
you	are	going to be	escaping
they	are	going to be	escaping

Future Perfect

I	will have been	escaping
you	will have been	escaping
he/she/it	will have been	escaping
we	will have been	escaping
you	will have been	escaping
they	will have been	escaping

Conditional

I	would	escape
you	would	escape
he/she/it	would	escape
we	would	escape
you	would	escape
they	would	escape

Conditional Past

I	would have	escaped
you	would have	escaped
he/she/it	would have	escaped
we	would have	escaped
you	would have	escaped
they	would have	escaped

establish

gründen

+ **-es** in 3. Person Singular
Regelmäßiges Verb

Simple tenses

Present

I	establish
you	establish
he/she/it	establishes
we	establish
you	establish
they	establish

Past

I	established
you	established
he/she/it	established
we	established
you	established
they	established

Present Perfect

I	have	established
you	have	established
he/she/it	has	established
we	have	established
you	have	established
they	have	established

Past Perfect

I	had	established
you	had	established
he/she/it	had	established
we	had	established
you	had	established
they	had	established

Will-Future

I	will	establish
you	will	establish
he/she/it	will	establish
we	will	establish
you	will	establish
they	will	establish

Going to-Future

I	am	going to	establish
you	are	going to	establish
he/she/it	is	going to	establish
we	are	going to	establish
you	are	going to	establish
they	are	going to	establish

Future Perfect

I	will have	established
you	will have	established
he/she/it	will have	established
we	will have	established
you	will have	established
they	will have	established

Imperative

establish

Impersonal

ing-Form

establishing

Past Participle

established

Continuous tenses

Present

I	am	establishing
you	are	establishing
he/she/it	is	establishing
we	are	establishing
you	are	establishing
they	are	establishing

Past

I	was	establishing
you	were	establishing
he/she/it	was	establishing
we	were	establishing
you	were	establishing
they	were	establishing

Present Perfect

I	have been	establishing
you	have been	establishing
he/she/it	has been	establishing
we	have been	establishing
you	have been	establishing
they	have been	establishing

Past Perfect

I	had been	establishing
you	had been	establishing
he/she/it	had been	establishing
we	had been	establishing
you	had been	establishing
they	had been	establishing

Will-Future

I	will be	establishing
you	will be	establishing
he/she/it	will be	establishing
we	will be	establishing
you	will be	establishing
they	will be	establishing

Going to-Future

I	am	going to be	establishing
you	are	going to be	establishing
he/she/it	is	going to be	establishing
we	are	going to be	establishing
you	are	going to be	establishing
they	are	going to be	establishing

Future Perfect

I	will have been establishing
you	will have been establishing
he/she/it	will have been establishing
we	will have been establishing
you	will have been establishing
they	will have been establishing

Conditional

I	would	establish
you	would	establish
he/she/it	would	establish
we	would	establish
you	would	establish
they	would	establish

Conditional Past

I	would have	established
you	would have	established
he/she/it	would have	established
we	would have	established
you	would have	established
they	would have	established

einschätzen

estimate

Simple tenses

Present

I	estimate
you	estimate
he/she/it	estimates
we	estimate
you	estimate
they	estimate

Past

I	estimated
you	estimated
he/she/it	estimated
we	estimated
you	estimated
they	estimated

Present Perfect

I	have	estimated
you	have	estimated
he/she/it	has	estimated
we	have	estimated
you	have	estimated
they	have	estimated

Past Perfect

I	had	estimated
you	had	estimated
he/she/it	had	estimated
we	had	estimated
you	had	estimated
they	had	estimated

Will-Future

I	will	estimate
you	will	estimate
he/she/it	will	estimate
we	will	estimate
you	will	estimate
they	will	estimate

Going to-Future

I	am	going to	estimate
you	are	going to	estimate
he/she/it	is	going to	estimate
we	are	going to	estimate
you	are	going to	estimate
they	are	going to	estimate

Future Perfect

I	will have	estimated
you	will have	estimated
he/she/it	will have	estimated
we	will have	estimated
you	will have	estimated
they	will have	estimated

Imperative

estimate

Impersonal

ing-Form

estimating

Past Participle

estimated

Continuous tenses

Present

I	am	estimating
you	are	estimating
he/she/it	is	estimating
we	are	estimating
you	are	estimating
they	are	estimating

Past

I	was	estimating
you	were	estimating
he/she/it	was	estimating
we	were	estimating
you	were	estimating
they	were	estimating

Present Perfect

I	have	been	estimating
you	have	been	estimating
he/she/it	has	been	estimating
we	have	been	estimating
you	have	been	estimating
they	have	been	estimating

Past Perfect

I	had been	estimating
you	had been	estimating
he/she/it	had been	estimating
we	had been	estimating
you	had been	estimating
they	had been	estimating

Will-Future

I	will be	estimating
you	will be	estimating
he/she/it	will be	estimating
we	will be	estimating
you	will be	estimating
they	will be	estimating

Going to-Future

I	am	going to be	estimating
you	are	going to be	estimating
he/she/it	is	going to be	estimating
we	are	going to be	estimating
you	are	going to be	estimating
they	are	going to be	estimating

Future Perfect

I	will have been estimating
you	will have been estimating
he/she/it	will have been estimating
we	will have been estimating
you	will have been estimating
they	will have been estimating

Conditional

I	would	estimate
you	would	estimate
he/she/it	would	estimate
we	would	estimate
you	would	estimate
they	would	estimate

Conditional Past

I	would have	estimated
you	would have	estimated
he/she/it	would have	estimated
we	would have	estimated
you	would have	estimated
they	would have	estimated

exaggerate

übertreiben

+ **-ing** → ~~e~~ / + -d nicht -ed
Regelmäßiges Verb

Simple tenses

Present

I	exaggerate
you	exaggerate
he/she/it	exaggerates
we	exaggerate
you	exaggerate
they	exaggerate

Past

I	exaggerated
you	exaggerated
he/she/it	exaggerated
we	exaggerated
you	exaggerated
they	exaggerated

Present Perfect

I	have	exaggerated
you	have	exaggerated
he/she/it	has	exaggerated
we	have	exaggerated
you	have	exaggerated
they	have	exaggerated

Past Perfect

I	had	exaggerated
you	had	exaggerated
he/she/it	had	exaggerated
we	had	exaggerated
you	had	exaggerated
they	had	exaggerated

Will-Future

I	will	exaggerate
you	will	exaggerate
he/she/it	will	exaggerate
we	will	exaggerate
you	will	exaggerate
they	will	exaggerate

Going to-Future

I	am	going to	exaggerate
you	are	going to	exaggerate
he/she/it	is	going to	exaggerate
we	are	going to	exaggerate
you	are	going to	exaggerate
they	are	going to	exaggerate

Future Perfect

I	will have	exaggerated
you	will have	exaggerated
he/she/it	will have	exaggerated
we	will have	exaggerated
you	will have	exaggerated
they	will have	exaggerated

Imperative

exaggerate

Impersonal

ing-Form

exaggerating

Past Participle

exaggerated

Continuous tenses

Present

I	am	exaggerating
you	are	exaggerating
he/she/it	is	exaggerating
we	are	exaggerating
you	are	exaggerating
they	are	exaggerating

Past

I	was	exaggerating
you	were	exaggerating
he/she/it	was	exaggerating
we	were	exaggerating
you	were	exaggerating
they	were	exaggerating

Present Perfect

I	have been	exaggerating
you	have been	exaggerating
he/she/it	has been	exaggerating
we	have been	exaggerating
you	have been	exaggerating
they	have been	exaggerating

Past Perfect

I	had been	exaggerating
you	had been	exaggerating
he/she/it	had been	exaggerating
we	had been	exaggerating
you	had been	exaggerating
they	had been	exaggerating

Will-Future

I	will be	exaggerating
you	will be	exaggerating
he/she/it	will be	exaggerating
we	will be	exaggerating
you	will be	exaggerating
they	will be	exaggerating

Going to-Future

I	am	going to be	exaggerating
you	are	going to be	exaggerating
he/she/it	is	going to be	exaggerating
we	are	going to be	exaggerating
you	are	going to be	exaggerating
they	are	going to be	exaggerating

Future Perfect

I	will have been	exaggerating
you	will have been	exaggerating
he/she/it	will have been	exaggerating
we	will have been	exaggerating
you	will have been	exaggerating
they	will have been	exaggerating

Conditional

I	would	exaggerate
you	would	exaggerate
he/she/it	would	exaggerate
we	would	exaggerate
you	would	exaggerate
they	would	exaggerate

Conditional Past

I	would have	exaggerated
you	would have	exaggerated
he/she/it	would have	exaggerated
we	would have	exaggerated
you	would have	exaggerated
they	would have	exaggerated

Simple tenses

Present

I	examine
you	examine
he/she/it	examines
we	examine
you	examine
they	examine

Past

I	examined
you	examined
he/she/it	examined
we	examined
you	examined
they	examined

Present Perfect

I	have	examined
you	have	examined
he/she/it	has	examined
we	have	examined
you	have	examined
they	have	examined

Past Perfect

I	had	examined
you	had	examined
he/she/it	had	examined
we	had	examined
you	had	examined
they	had	examined

Will-Future

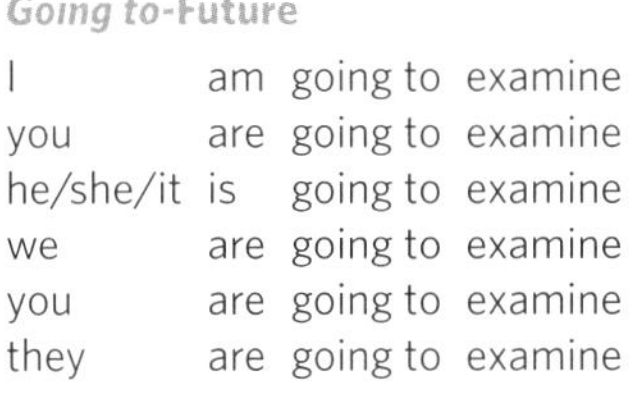

I	will	examine
you	will	examine
he/she/it	will	examine
we	will	examine
you	will	examine
they	will	examine

Going to-Future

I	am	going to	examine
you	are	going to	examine
he/she/it	is	going to	examine
we	are	going to	examine
you	are	going to	examine
they	are	going to	examine

Future Perfect

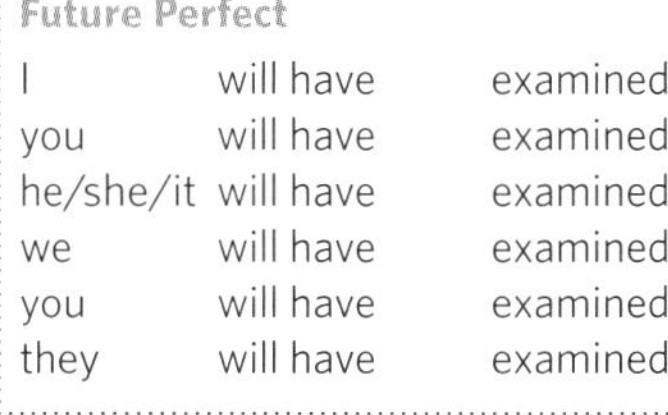

I	will have	examined
you	will have	examined
he/she/it	will have	examined
we	will have	examined
you	will have	examined
they	will have	examined

Imperative

examine

Impersonal

ing-Form

examining

Past Participle

examined

Continuous tenses

Present

I	am	examining
you	are	examining
he/she/it	is	examining
we	are	examining
you	are	examining
they	are	examining

Past

I	was	examining
you	were	examining
he/she/it	was	examining
we	were	examining
you	were	examining
they	were	examining

Present Perfect

I	have been	examining
you	have been	examining
he/she/it	has been	examining
we	have been	examining
you	have been	examining
they	have been	examining

Past Perfect

I	had been	examining
you	had been	examining
he/she/it	had been	examining
we	had been	examining
you	had been	examining
they	had been	examining

Will-Future

I	will be	examining
you	will be	examining
he/she/it	will be	examining
we	will be	examining
you	will be	examining
they	will be	examining

Going to-Future

I	am	going to be	examining
you	are	going to be	examining
he/she/it	is	going to be	examining
we	are	going to be	examining
you	are	going to be	examining
they	are	going to be	examining

Future Perfect

I	will have been examining
you	will have been examining
he/she/it	will have been examining
we	will have been examining
you	will have been examining
they	will have been examining

Conditional

I	would	examine
you	would	examine
he/she/it	would	examine
we	would	examine
you	would	examine
they	would	examine

Conditional Past

I	would have	examined
you	would have	examined
he/she/it	would have	examined
we	would have	examined
you	would have	examined
they	would have	examined

exchange

austauschen

+ **-ing** → ~~e~~ / + -d nicht -ed
Regelmäßiges Verb

Simple tenses

Present

I	exchange
you	exchange
he/she/it	exchanges
we	exchange
you	exchange
they	exchange

Past

I	exchanged
you	exchanged
he/she/it	exchanged
we	exchanged
you	exchanged
they	exchanged

Present Perfect

I	have	exchanged
you	have	exchanged
he/she/it	has	exchanged
we	have	exchanged
you	have	exchanged
they	have	exchanged

Past Perfect

I	had	exchanged
you	had	exchanged
he/she/it	had	exchanged
we	had	exchanged
you	had	exchanged
they	had	exchanged

Will-Future

I	will	exchange
you	will	exchange
he/she/it	will	exchange
we	will	exchange
you	will	exchange
they	will	exchange

Going to-Future

I	am	going to	exchange
you	are	going to	exchange
he/she/it	is	going to	exchange
we	are	going to	exchange
you	are	going to	exchange
they	are	going to	exchange

Future Perfect

I	will have	exchanged
you	will have	exchanged
he/she/it	will have	exchanged
we	will have	exchanged
you	will have	exchanged
they	will have	exchanged

Imperative

exchange

Impersonal

ing-Form

exchanging

Past Participle

exchanged

Continuous tenses

Present

I	am	exchanging
you	are	exchanging
he/she/it	is	exchanging
we	are	exchanging
you	are	exchanging
they	are	exchanging

Past

I	was	exchanging
you	were	exchanging
he/she/it	was	exchanging
we	were	exchanging
you	were	exchanging
they	were	exchanging

Present Perfect

I	have been	exchanging
you	have been	exchanging
he/she/it	has been	exchanging
we	have been	exchanging
you	have been	exchanging
they	have been	exchanging

Past Perfect

I	had been	exchanging
you	had been	exchanging
he/she/it	had been	exchanging
we	had been	exchanging
you	had been	exchanging
they	had been	exchanging

Will-Future

I	will be	exchanging
you	will be	exchanging
he/she/it	will be	exchanging
we	will be	exchanging
you	will be	exchanging
they	will be	exchanging

Going to-Future

I	am	going to be	exchanging
you	are	going to be	exchanging
he/she/it	is	going to be	exchanging
we	are	going to be	exchanging
you	are	going to be	exchanging
they	are	going to be	exchanging

Future Perfect

I	will have been exchanging
you	will have been exchanging
he/she/it	will have been exchanging
we	will have been exchanging
you	will have been exchanging
they	will have been exchanging

Conditional

I	would	exchange
you	would	exchange
he/she/it	would	exchange
we	would	exchange
you	would	exchange
they	would	exchange

Conditional Past

I	would have	exchanged
you	would have	exchanged
he/she/it	would have	exchanged
we	would have	exchanged
you	would have	exchanged
they	would have	exchanged

+ **-ing** → e̸ / + -d nicht -ed
Regelmäßiges Verb

entschuldigen

excuse

Simple tenses

Present

I	excuse
you	excuse
he/she/it	excuses
we	excuse
you	excuse
they	excuse

Past

I	excused
you	excused
he/she/it	excused
we	excused
you	excused
they	excused

Present Perfect

I	have	excused
you	have	excused
he/she/it	has	excused
we	have	excused
you	have	excused
they	have	excused

Past Perfect

I	had	excused
you	had	excused
he/she/it	had	excused
we	had	excused
you	had	excused
they	had	excused

Will-Future

I	will	excuse
you	will	excuse
he/she/it	will	excuse
we	will	excuse
you	will	excuse
they	will	excuse

Going to-Future

I	am	going to	excuse
you	are	going to	excuse
he/she/it	is	going to	excuse
we	are	going to	excuse
you	are	going to	excuse
they	are	going to	excuse

Future Perfect

I	will have	excused
you	will have	excused
he/she/it	will have	excused
we	will have	excused
you	will have	excused
they	will have	excused

Imperative

excuse

Impersonal

ing-Form

excusing

Past Participle

excused

Continuous tenses

Present

I	am	excusing
you	are	excusing
he/she/it	is	excusing
we	are	excusing
you	are	excusing
they	are	excusing

Past

I	was	excusing
you	were	excusing
he/she/it	was	excusing
we	were	excusing
you	were	excusing
they	were	excusing

Present Perfect

I	have been	excusing
you	have been	excusing
he/she/it	has been	excusing
we	have been	excusing
you	have been	excusing
they	have been	excusing

Past Perfect

I	had been	excusing
you	had been	excusing
he/she/it	had been	excusing
we	had been	excusing
you	had been	excusing
they	had been	excusing

Will-Future

I	will be	excusing
you	will be	excusing
he/she/it	will be	excusing
we	will be	excusing
you	will be	excusing
they	will be	excusing

Going to-Future

I	am	going to be	excusing
you	are	going to be	excusing
he/she/it	is	going to be	excusing
we	are	going to be	excusing
you	are	going to be	excusing
they	are	going to be	excusing

Future Perfect

I	will have been	excusing
you	will have been	excusing
he/she/it	will have been	excusing
we	will have been	excusing
you	will have been	excusing
they	will have been	excusing

Conditional

I	would	excuse
you	would	excuse
he/she/it	would	excuse
we	would	excuse
you	would	excuse
they	would	excuse

Conditional Past

I	would have	excused
you	would have	excused
he/she/it	would have	excused
we	would have	excused
you	would have	excused
they	would have	excused

exercise

trainieren

+ **-ing** → ~~e~~ / + -d nicht -ed
Regelmäßiges Verb

Simple tenses

Present

I	exercise
you	exercise
he/she/it	exercises
we	exercise
you	exercise
they	exercise

Past

I	exercised
you	exercised
he/she/it	exercised
we	exercised
you	exercised
they	exercised

Present Perfect

I	have	exercised
you	have	exercised
he/she/it	has	exercised
we	have	exercised
you	have	exercised
they	have	exercised

Past Perfect

I	had	exercised
you	had	exercised
he/she/it	had	exercised
we	had	exercised
you	had	exercised
they	had	exercised

Will-Future

I	will	exercise
you	will	exercise
he/she/it	will	exercise
we	will	exercise
you	will	exercise
they	will	exercise

Going to-Future

I	am	going to	exercise
you	are	going to	exercise
he/she/it	is	going to	exercise
we	are	going to	exercise
you	are	going to	exercise
they	are	going to	exercise

Future Perfect

I	will have	exercised
you	will have	exercised
he/she/it	will have	exercised
we	will have	exercised
you	will have	exercised
they	will have	exercised

Imperative

exercise

Impersonal

ing-Form

exercising

Past Participle

exercised

Continuous tenses

Present

I	am	exercising
you	are	exercising
he/she/it	is	exercising
we	are	exercising
you	are	exercising
they	are	exercising

Past

I	was	exercising
you	were	exercising
he/she/it	was	exercising
we	were	exercising
you	were	exercising
they	were	exercising

Present Perfect

I	have been	exercising
you	have been	exercising
he/she/it	has been	exercising
we	have been	exercising
you	have been	exercising
they	have been	exercising

Past Perfect

I	had been	exercising
you	had been	exercising
he/she/it	had been	exercising
we	had been	exercising
you	had been	exercising
they	had been	exercising

Will-Future

I	will be	exercising
you	will be	exercising
he/she/it	will be	exercising
we	will be	exercising
you	will be	exercising
they	will be	exercising

Going to-Future

I	am	going to be	exercising
you	are	going to be	exercising
he/she/it	is	going to be	exercising
we	are	going to be	exercising
you	are	going to be	exercising
they	are	going to be	exercising

Future Perfect

I	will have been	exercising
you	will have been	exercising
he/she/it	will have been	exercising
we	will have been	exercising
you	will have been	exercising
they	will have been	exercising

Conditional

I	would	exercise
you	would	exercise
he/she/it	would	exercise
we	would	exercise
you	would	exercise
they	would	exercise

Conditional Past

I	would have	exercised
you	would have	exercised
he/she/it	would have	exercised
we	would have	exercised
you	would have	exercised
they	would have	exercised

existieren **exist**

Simple tenses

Present

I	exist
you	exist
he/she/it	exists
we	exist
you	exist
they	exist

Past

I	existed
you	existed
he/she/it	existed
we	existed
you	existed
they	existed

Present Perfect

I	have	existed
you	have	existed
he/she/it	has	existed
we	have	existed
you	have	existed
they	have	existed

Past Perfect

I	had	existed
you	had	existed
he/she/it	had	existed
we	had	existed
you	had	existed
they	had	existed

Will-Future

I	will	exist
you	will	exist
he/she/it	will	exist
we	will	exist
you	will	exist
they	will	exist

Going to-Future

I	am	going to	exist
you	are	going to	exist
he/she/it	is	going to	exist
we	are	going to	exist
you	are	going to	exist
they	are	going to	exist

Future Perfect

I	will have	existed
you	will have	existed
he/she/it	will have	existed
we	will have	existed
you	will have	existed
they	will have	existed

Imperative

exist

Impersonal

ing-Form

existing

Past Participle

existed

Continuous tenses

Present

I	am	existing
you	are	existing
he/she/it	is	existing
we	are	existing
you	are	existing
they	are	existing

Past

I	was	existing
you	were	existing
he/she/it	was	existing
we	were	existing
you	were	existing
they	were	existing

Present Perfect

I	have been	existing
you	have been	existing
he/she/it	has been	existing
we	have been	existing
you	have been	existing
they	have been	existing

Past Perfect

I	had been	existing
you	had been	existing
he/she/it	had been	existing
we	had been	existing
you	had been	existing
they	had been	existing

Will-Future

I	will be	existing
you	will be	existing
he/she/it	will be	existing
we	will be	existing
you	will be	existing
they	will be	existing

Going to-Future

I	am	going to be	existing
you	are	going to be	existing
he/she/it	is	going to be	existing
we	are	going to be	existing
you	are	going to be	existing
they	are	going to be	existing

Future Perfect

I	will have been	existing
you	will have been	existing
he/she/it	will have been	existing
we	will have been	existing
you	will have been	existing
they	will have been	existing

Conditional

I	would	exist
you	would	exist
he/she/it	would	exist
we	would	exist
you	would	exist
they	would	exist

Conditional Past

I	would have	existed
you	would have	existed
he/she/it	would have	existed
we	would have	existed
you	would have	existed
they	would have	existed

exit

hinausgehen

Regelmäßiges Verb

Simple tenses

Present

I	exit
you	exit
he/she/it	exits
we	exit
you	exit
they	exit

Past

I	exited
you	exited
he/she/it	exited
we	exited
you	exited
they	exited

Present Perfect

I	have	exited
you	have	exited
he/she/it	has	exited
we	have	exited
you	have	exited
they	have	exited

Past Perfect

I	had	exited
you	had	exited
he/she/it	had	exited
we	had	exited
you	had	exited
they	had	exited

Will-Future

I	will	exit
you	will	exit
he/she/it	will	exit
we	will	exit
you	will	exit
they	will	exit

Going to-Future

I	am	going to	exit
you	are	going to	exit
he/she/it	is	going to	exit
we	are	going to	exit
you	are	going to	exit
they	are	going to	exit

Future Perfect

I	will have	exited
you	will have	exited
he/she/it	will have	exited
we	will have	exited
you	will have	exited
they	will have	exited

Imperative

exit

Impersonal

ing-Form

exiting

Past Participle

exited

Continuous tenses

Present

I	am	exiting
you	are	exiting
he/she/it	is	exiting
we	are	exiting
you	are	exiting
they	are	exiting

Past

I	was	exiting
you	were	exiting
he/she/it	was	exiting
we	were	exiting
you	were	exiting
they	were	exiting

Present Perfect

I	have	been	exiting
you	have	been	exiting
he/she/it	has	been	exiting
we	have	been	exiting
you	have	been	exiting
they	have	been	exiting

Past Perfect

I	had been	exiting
you	had been	exiting
he/she/it	had been	exiting
we	had been	exiting
you	had been	exiting
they	had been	exiting

Will-Future

I	will be	exiting
you	will be	exiting
he/she/it	will be	exiting
we	will be	exiting
you	will be	exiting
they	will be	exiting

Going to-Future

I	am	going to be	exiting
you	are	going to be	exiting
he/she/it	is	going to be	exiting
we	are	going to be	exiting
you	are	going to be	exiting
they	are	going to be	exiting

Future Perfect

I	will have been	exiting
you	will have been	exiting
he/she/it	will have been	exiting
we	will have been	exiting
you	will have been	exiting
they	will have been	exiting

Conditional

I	would	exit
you	would	exit
he/she/it	would	exit
we	would	exit
you	would	exit
they	would	exit

Conditional Past

I	would have	exited
you	would have	exited
he/she/it	would have	exited
we	would have	exited
you	would have	exited
they	would have	exited

Simple tenses

Present

I	expand
you	expand
he/she/it	expands
we	expand
you	expand
they	expand

Past

I	expanded
you	expanded
he/she/it	expanded
we	expanded
you	expanded
they	expanded

Present Perfect

I	have	expanded
you	have	expanded
he/she/it	has	expanded
we	have	expanded
you	have	expanded
they	have	expanded

Past Perfect

I	had	expanded
you	had	expanded
he/she/it	had	expanded
we	had	expanded
you	had	expanded
they	had	expanded

Will-Future

I	will	expand
you	will	expand
he/she/it	will	expand
we	will	expand
you	will	expand
they	will	expand

Going to-Future

I	am	going to	expand
you	are	going to	expand
he/she/it	is	going to	expand
we	are	going to	expand
you	are	going to	expand
they	are	going to	expand

Future Perfect

I	will have	expanded
you	will have	expanded
he/she/it	will have	expanded
we	will have	expanded
you	will have	expanded
they	will have	expanded

Imperative

expand

Impersonal

ing-Form

expanding

Past Participle

expanded

Continuous tenses

Present

I	am	expanding
you	are	expanding
he/she/it	is	expanding
we	are	expanding
you	are	expanding
they	are	expanding

Past

I	was	expanding
you	were	expanding
he/she/it	was	expanding
we	were	expanding
you	were	expanding
they	were	expanding

Present Perfect

I	have been	expanding
you	have been	expanding
he/she/it	has been	expanding
we	have been	expanding
you	have been	expanding
they	have been	expanding

Past Perfect

I	had been	expanding
you	had been	expanding
he/she/it	had been	expanding
we	had been	expanding
you	had been	expanding
they	had been	expanding

Will-Future

I	will be	expanding
you	will be	expanding
he/she/it	will be	expanding
we	will be	expanding
you	will be	expanding
they	will be	expanding

Going to-Future

I	am	going to be	expanding
you	are	going to be	expanding
he/she/it	is	going to be	expanding
we	are	going to be	expanding
you	are	going to be	expanding
they	are	going to be	expanding

Future Perfect

I	will have been	expanding
you	will have been	expanding
he/she/it	will have been	expanding
we	will have been	expanding
you	will have been	expanding
they	will have been	expanding

Conditional

I	would	expand
you	would	expand
he/she/it	would	expand
we	would	expand
you	would	expand
they	would	expand

Conditional Past

I	would have	expanded
you	would have	expanded
he/she/it	would have	expanded
we	would have	expanded
you	would have	expanded
they	would have	expanded

expect

erwarten

Regelmäßiges Verb

Simple tenses

Present

I	expect
you	expect
he/she/it	expects
we	expect
you	expect
they	expect

Past

I	expected
you	expected
he/she/it	expected
we	expected
you	expected
they	expected

Present Perfect

I	have	expected
you	have	expected
he/she/it	has	expected
we	have	expected
you	have	expected
they	have	expected

Past Perfect

I	had	expected
you	had	expected
he/she/it	had	expected
we	had	expected
you	had	expected
they	had	expected

***Will*-Future**

I	will	expect
you	will	expect
he/she/it	will	expect
we	will	expect
you	will	expect
they	will	expect

***Going to*-Future**

I	am	going to	expect
you	are	going to	expect
he/she/it	is	going to	expect
we	are	going to	expect
you	are	going to	expect
they	are	going to	expect

Future Perfect

I	will have	expected
you	will have	expected
he/she/it	will have	expected
we	will have	expected
you	will have	expected
they	will have	expected

Imperative

expect

Impersonal

***ing*-Form**

expecting

Past Participle

expected

Continuous tenses

Present

I	am	expecting
you	are	expecting
he/she/it	is	expecting
we	are	expecting
you	are	expecting
they	are	expecting

Past

I	was	expecting
you	were	expecting
he/she/it	was	expecting
we	were	expecting
you	were	expecting
they	were	expecting

Present Perfect

I	have been	expecting
you	have been	expecting
he/she/it	has been	expecting
we	have been	expecting
you	have been	expecting
they	have been	expecting

Past Perfect

I	had been	expecting
you	had been	expecting
he/she/it	had been	expecting
we	had been	expecting
you	had been	expecting
they	had been	expecting

***Will*-Future**

I	will be	expecting
you	will be	expecting
he/she/it	will be	expecting
we	will be	expecting
you	will be	expecting
they	will be	expecting

***Going to*-Future**

I	am	going to be	expecting
you	are	going to be	expecting
he/she/it	is	going to be	expecting
we	are	going to be	expecting
you	are	going to be	expecting
they	are	going to be	expecting

Future Perfect

I	will have been	expecting
you	will have been	expecting
he/she/it	will have been	expecting
we	will have been	expecting
you	will have been	expecting
they	will have been	expecting

Conditional

I	would	expect
you	would	expect
he/she/it	would	expect
we	would	expect
you	would	expect
they	would	expect

Conditional Past

I	would have	expected
you	would have	expected
he/she/it	would have	expected
we	would have	expected
you	would have	expected
they	would have	expected

erleben

experience

Simple tenses

Present

I	experience
you	experience
he/she/it	experiences
we	experience
you	experience
they	experience

Past

I	experienced
you	experienced
he/she/it	experienced
we	experienced
you	experienced
they	experienced

Present Perfect

I	have	experienced
you	have	experienced
he/she/it	has	experienced
we	have	experienced
you	have	experienced
they	have	experienced

Past Perfect

I	had	experienced
you	had	experienced
he/she/it	had	experienced
we	had	experienced
you	had	experienced
they	had	experienced

Will-Future

I	will	experience
you	will	experience
he/she/it	will	experience
we	will	experience
you	will	experience
they	will	experience

Going to-Future

I	am	going to	experience
you	are	going to	experience
he/she/it	is	going to	experience
we	are	going to	experience
you	are	going to	experience
they	are	going to	experience

Future Perfect

I	will have	experienced
you	will have	experienced
he/she/it	will have	experienced
we	will have	experienced
you	will have	experienced
they	will have	experienced

Imperative

experience

Impersonal

ing-Form

experiencing

Past Participle

experienced

Continuous tenses

Present

I	am	experiencing
you	are	experiencing
he/she/it	is	experiencing
we	are	experiencing
you	are	experiencing
they	are	experiencing

Past

I	was	experiencing
you	were	experiencing
he/she/it	was	experiencing
we	were	experiencing
you	were	experiencing
they	were	experiencing

Present Perfect

I	have	been experiencing
you	have	been experiencing
he/she/it	has	been experiencing
we	have	been experiencing
you	have	been experiencing
they	have	been experiencing

Past Perfect

I	had been	experiencing
you	had been	experiencing
he/she/it	had been	experiencing
we	had been	experiencing
you	had been	experiencing
they	had been	experiencing

Will-Future

I	will be	experiencing
you	will be	experiencing
he/she/it	will be	experiencing
we	will be	experiencing
you	will be	experiencing
they	will be	experiencing

Going to-Future

I	am	going to be	experiencing
you	are	going to be	experiencing
he/she/it	is	going to be	experiencing
we	are	going to be	experiencing
you	are	going to be	experiencing
they	are	going to be	experiencing

Future Perfect

I	will have been experiencing
you	will have been experiencing
he/she/it	will have been experiencing
we	will have been experiencing
you	will have been experiencing
they	will have been experiencing

Conditional

I	would	experience
you	would	experience
he/she/it	would	experience
we	would	experience
you	would	experience
they	would	experience

Conditional Past

I	would have	experienced
you	would have	experienced
he/she/it	would have	experienced
we	would have	experienced
you	would have	experienced
they	would have	experienced

explain

erklären

Regelmäßiges Verb

Simple tenses

Present

I	explain
you	explain
he/she/it	explains
we	explain
you	explain
they	explain

Past

I	explained
you	explained
he/she/it	explained
we	explained
you	explained
they	explained

Present Perfect

I	have	explained
you	have	explained
he/she/it	has	explained
we	have	explained
you	have	explained
they	have	explained

Past Perfect

I	had	explained
you	had	explained
he/she/it	had	explained
we	had	explained
you	had	explained
they	had	explained

Will-Future

I	will	explain
you	will	explain
he/she/it	will	explain
we	will	explain
you	will	explain
they	will	explain

Going to-Future

I	am	going to	explain
you	are	going to	explain
he/she/it	is	going to	explain
we	are	going to	explain
you	are	going to	explain
they	are	going to	explain

Future Perfect

I	will have	explained
you	will have	explained
he/she/it	will have	explained
we	will have	explained
you	will have	explained
they	will have	explained

Imperative

explain

Impersonal

ing-Form

explaining

Past Participle

explained

Continuous tenses

Present

I	am	explaining
you	are	explaining
he/she/it	is	explaining
we	are	explaining
you	are	explaining
they	are	explaining

Past

I	was	explaining
you	were	explaining
he/she/it	was	explaining
we	were	explaining
you	were	explaining
they	were	explaining

Present Perfect

I	have	been	explaining
you	have	been	explaining
he/she/it	has	been	explaining
we	have	been	explaining
you	have	been	explaining
they	have	been	explaining

Past Perfect

I	had been	explaining
you	had been	explaining
he/she/it	had been	explaining
we	had been	explaining
you	had been	explaining
they	had been	explaining

Will-Future

I	will be	explaining
you	will be	explaining
he/she/it	will be	explaining
we	will be	explaining
you	will be	explaining
they	will be	explaining

Going to-Future

I	am	going to be	explaining
you	are	going to be	explaining
he/she/it	is	going to be	explaining
we	are	going to be	explaining
you	are	going to be	explaining
they	are	going to be	explaining

Future Perfect

I	will have been	explaining
you	will have been	explaining
he/she/it	will have been	explaining
we	will have been	explaining
you	will have been	explaining
they	will have been	explaining

Conditional

I	would	explain
you	would	explain
he/she/it	would	explain
we	would	explain
you	would	explain
they	would	explain

Conditional Past

I	would have	explained
you	would have	explained
he/she/it	would have	explained
we	would have	explained
you	would have	explained
they	would have	explained

+ -ing → ~~e~~ / + -d nicht -ed
Regelmäßiges Verb

explodieren

explode

Simple tenses

Present

I	explode
you	explode
he/she/it	explodes
we	explode
you	explode
they	explode

Past

I	exploded
you	exploded
he/she/it	exploded
we	exploded
you	exploded
they	exploded

Present Perfect

I	have	exploded
you	have	exploded
he/she/it	has	exploded
we	have	exploded
you	have	exploded
they	have	exploded

Past Perfect

I	had	exploded
you	had	exploded
he/she/it	had	exploded
we	had	exploded
you	had	exploded
they	had	exploded

Will-Future

I	will	explode
you	will	explode
he/she/it	will	explode
we	will	explode
you	will	explode
they	will	explode

Going to-Future

I	am	going to	explode
you	are	going to	explode
he/she/it	is	going to	explode
we	are	going to	explode
you	are	going to	explode
they	are	going to	explode

Future Perfect

I	will have	exploded
you	will have	exploded
he/she/it	will have	exploded
we	will have	exploded
you	will have	exploded
they	will have	exploded

Imperative

explode

Impersonal

ing-Form

exploding

Past Participle

exploded

Continuous tenses

Present

I	am	exploding
you	are	exploding
he/she/it	is	exploding
we	are	exploding
you	are	exploding
they	are	exploding

Past

I	was	exploding
you	were	exploding
he/she/it	was	exploding
we	were	exploding
you	were	exploding
they	were	exploding

Present Perfect

I	have been	exploding
you	have been	exploding
he/she/it	has been	exploding
we	have been	exploding
you	have been	exploding
they	have been	exploding

Past Perfect

I	had been	exploding
you	had been	exploding
he/she/it	had been	exploding
we	had been	exploding
you	had been	exploding
they	had been	exploding

Will-Future

I	will be	exploding
you	will be	exploding
he/she/it	will be	exploding
we	will be	exploding
you	will be	exploding
they	will be	exploding

Going to-Future

I	am	going to be	exploding
you	are	going to be	exploding
he/she/it	is	going to be	exploding
we	are	going to be	exploding
you	are	going to be	exploding
they	are	going to be	exploding

Future Perfect

I	will have been exploding
you	will have been exploding
he/she/it	will have been exploding
we	will have been exploding
you	will have been exploding
they	will have been exploding

Conditional

I	would	explode
you	would	explode
he/she/it	would	explode
we	would	explode
you	would	explode
they	would	explode

Conditional Past

I	would have	exploded
you	would have	exploded
he/she/it	would have	exploded
we	would have	exploded
you	would have	exploded
they	would have	exploded

explore

erforschen

+ **-ing** → ~~e~~ / + **-d** nicht **-ed**
Regelmäßiges Verb

Simple tenses

Present

I	explore
you	explore
he/she/it	explores
we	explore
you	explore
they	explore

Past

I	explored
you	explored
he/she/it	explored
we	explored
you	explored
they	explored

Present Perfect

I	have	explored
you	have	explored
he/she/it	has	explored
we	have	explored
you	have	explored
they	have	explored

Past Perfect

I	had	explored
you	had	explored
he/she/it	had	explored
we	had	explored
you	had	explored
they	had	explored

Will-Future

I	will	explore
you	will	explore
he/she/it	will	explore
we	will	explore
you	will	explore
they	will	explore

Going to-Future

I	am	going to	explore
you	are	going to	explore
he/she/it	is	going to	explore
we	are	going to	explore
you	are	going to	explore
they	are	going to	explore

Future Perfect

I	will have	explored
you	will have	explored
he/she/it	will have	explored
we	will have	explored
you	will have	explored
they	will have	explored

Imperative

explore

Impersonal

ing-Form

exploring

Past Participle

explored

Continuous tenses

Present

I	am	exploring
you	are	exploring
he/she/it	is	exploring
we	are	exploring
you	are	exploring
they	are	exploring

Past

I	was	exploring
you	were	exploring
he/she/it	was	exploring
we	were	exploring
you	were	exploring
they	were	exploring

Present Perfect

I	have been	exploring
you	have been	exploring
he/she/it	has been	exploring
we	have been	exploring
you	have been	exploring
they	have been	exploring

Past Perfect

I	had been	exploring
you	had been	exploring
he/she/it	had been	exploring
we	had been	exploring
you	had been	exploring
they	had been	exploring

Will-Future

I	will be	exploring
you	will be	exploring
he/she/it	will be	exploring
we	will be	exploring
you	will be	exploring
they	will be	exploring

Going to-Future

I	am	going to be	exploring
you	are	going to be	exploring
he/she/it	is	going to be	exploring
we	are	going to be	exploring
you	are	going to be	exploring
they	are	going to be	exploring

Future Perfect

I	will have been	exploring
you	will have been	exploring
he/she/it	will have been	exploring
we	will have been	exploring
you	will have been	exploring
they	will have been	exploring

Conditional

I	would	explore
you	would	explore
he/she/it	would	explore
we	would	explore
you	would	explore
they	would	explore

Conditional Past

I	would have	explored
you	would have	explored
he/she/it	would have	explored
we	would have	explored
you	would have	explored
they	would have	explored

Simple tenses

Present

I	export
you	export
he/she/it	exports
we	export
you	export
they	export

Past

I	exported
you	exported
he/she/it	exported
we	exported
you	exported
they	exported

Present Perfect

I	have	exported
you	have	exported
he/she/it	has	exported
we	have	exported
you	have	exported
they	have	exported

Past Perfect

I	had	exported
you	had	exported
he/she/it	had	exported
we	had	exported
you	had	exported
they	had	exported

Will-Future

I	will	export
you	will	export
he/she/it	will	export
we	will	export
you	will	export
they	will	export

Going to-Future

I	am	going to	export
you	are	going to	export
he/she/it	is	going to	export
we	are	going to	export
you	are	going to	export
they	are	going to	export

Future Perfect

I	will have	exported
you	will have	exported
he/she/it	will have	exported
we	will have	exported
you	will have	exported
they	will have	exported

Imperative

export

Impersonal

ing-Form

exporting

Past Participle

exported

Continuous tenses

Present

I	am	exporting
you	are	exporting
he/she/it	is	exporting
we	are	exporting
you	are	exporting
they	are	exporting

Past

I	was	exporting
you	were	exporting
he/she/it	was	exporting
we	were	exporting
you	were	exporting
they	were	exporting

Present Perfect

I	have	been	exporting
you	have	been	exporting
he/she/it	has	been	exporting
we	have	been	exporting
you	have	been	exporting
they	have	been	exporting

Past Perfect

I	had been	exporting
you	had been	exporting
he/she/it	had been	exporting
we	had been	exporting
you	had been	exporting
they	had been	exporting

Will-Future

I	will be	exporting
you	will be	exporting
he/she/it	will be	exporting
we	will be	exporting
you	will be	exporting
they	will be	exporting

Going to-Future

I	am	going to be	exporting
you	are	going to be	exporting
he/she/it	is	going to be	exporting
we	are	going to be	exporting
you	are	going to be	exporting
they	are	going to be	exporting

Future Perfect

I	will have been	exporting
you	will have been	exporting
he/she/it	will have been	exporting
we	will have been	exporting
you	will have been	exporting
they	will have been	exporting

Conditional

I	would	export
you	would	export
he/she/it	would	export
we	would	export
you	would	export
they	would	export

Conditional Past

I	would have	exported
you	would have	exported
he/she/it	would have	exported
we	would have	exported
you	would have	exported
they	would have	exported

express

ausdrücken

\+ **-es** in 3. Person Singular
Regelmäßiges Verb

Simple tenses

Present

I	express
you	express
he/she/it	expresses
we	express
you	express
they	express

Past

I	expressed
you	expressed
he/she/it	expressed
we	expressed
you	expressed
they	expressed

Present Perfect

I	have	expressed
you	have	expressed
he/she/it	has	expressed
we	have	expressed
you	have	expressed
they	have	expressed

Past Perfect

I	had	expressed
you	had	expressed
he/she/it	had	expressed
we	had	expressed
you	had	expressed
they	had	expressed

Will-Future

I	will	express
you	will	express
he/she/it	will	express
we	will	express
you	will	express
they	will	express

Going to-Future

I	am	going to	express
you	are	going to	express
he/she/it	is	going to	express
we	are	going to	express
you	are	going to	express
they	are	going to	express

Future Perfect

I	will have	expressed
you	will have	expressed
he/she/it	will have	expressed
we	will have	expressed
you	will have	expressed
they	will have	expressed

Imperative

express

Impersonal

ing-Form

expressing

Past Participle

expressed

Continuous tenses

Present

I	am	expressing
you	are	expressing
he/she/it	is	expressing
we	are	expressing
you	are	expressing
they	are	expressing

Past

I	was	expressing
you	were	expressing
he/she/it	was	expressing
we	were	expressing
you	were	expressing
they	were	expressing

Present Perfect

I	have been	expressing
you	have been	expressing
he/she/it	has been	expressing
we	have been	expressing
you	have been	expressing
they	have been	expressing

Past Perfect

I	had been	expressing
you	had been	expressing
he/she/it	had been	expressing
we	had been	expressing
you	had been	expressing
they	had been	expressing

Will-Future

I	will be	expressing
you	will be	expressing
he/she/it	will be	expressing
we	will be	expressing
you	will be	expressing
they	will be	expressing

Going to-Future

I	am	going to be	expressing
you	are	going to be	expressing
he/she/it	is	going to be	expressing
we	are	going to be	expressing
you	are	going to be	expressing
they	are	going to be	expressing

Future Perfect

I	will have been	expressing
you	will have been	expressing
he/she/it	will have been	expressing
we	will have been	expressing
you	will have been	expressing
they	will have been	expressing

Conditional

I	would	express
you	would	express
he/she/it	would	express
we	would	express
you	would	express
they	would	express

Conditional Past

I	would have	expressed
you	would have	expressed
he/she/it	would have	expressed
we	would have	expressed
you	would have	expressed
they	would have	expressed

Simple tenses

Present

I	fail
you	fail
he/she/it	fails
we	fail
you	fail
they	fail

Past

I	failed
you	failed
he/she/it	failed
we	failed
you	failed
they	failed

Present Perfect

I	have	failed
you	have	failed
he/she/it	has	failed
we	have	failed
you	have	failed
they	have	failed

Past Perfect

I	had	failed
you	had	failed
he/she/it	had	failed
we	had	failed
you	had	failed
they	had	failed

Will-Future

I	will	fail
you	will	fail
he/she/it	will	fail
we	will	fail
you	will	fail
they	will	fail

Going to-Future

I	am going to	fail
you	are going to	fail
he/she/it	is going to	fail
we	are going to	fail
you	are going to	fail
they	are going to	fail

Future Perfect

I	will have	failed
you	will have	failed
he/she/it	will have	failed
we	will have	failed
you	will have	failed
they	will have	failed

Imperative

fail

Impersonal

ing-Form

failing

Past Participle

failed

Continuous tenses

Present

I	am	failing
you	are	failing
he/she/it	is	failing
we	are	failing
you	are	failing
they	are	failing

Past

I	was	failing
you	were	failing
he/she/it	was	failing
we	were	failing
you	were	failing
they	were	failing

Present Perfect

I	have been	failing
you	have been	failing
he/she/it	has been	failing
we	have been	failing
you	have been	failing
they	have been	failing

Past Perfect

I	had been	failing
you	had been	failing
he/she/it	had been	failing
we	had been	failing
you	had been	failing
they	had been	failing

Will-Future

I	will be	failing
you	will be	failing
he/she/it	will be	failing
we	will be	failing
you	will be	failing
they	will be	failing

Going to-Future

I	am going to be	failing
you	are going to be	failing
he/she/it	is going to be	failing
we	are going to be	failing
you	are going to be	failing
they	are going to be	failing

Future Perfect

I	will have been	failing
you	will have been	failing
he/she/it	will have been	failing
we	will have been	failing
you	will have been	failing
they	will have been	failing

Conditional

I	would	fail
you	would	fail
he/she/it	would	fail
we	would	fail
you	would	fail
they	would	fail

Conditional Past

I	would have	failed
you	would have	failed
he/she/it	would have	failed
we	would have	failed
you	would have	failed
they	would have	failed

fall
- fell - fallen

fallen

Unregelmäßiges Verb

Simple tenses

Present

I	fall
you	fall
he/she/it	falls
we	fall
you	fall
they	fall

Past

I	fell
you	fell
he/she/it	fell
we	fell
you	fell
they	fell

Present Perfect

I	have	fallen
you	have	fallen
he/she/it	has	fallen
we	have	fallen
you	have	fallen
they	have	fallen

Past Perfect

I	had	fallen
you	had	fallen
he/she/it	had	fallen
we	had	fallen
you	had	fallen
they	had	fallen

Will-Future

I	will	fall
you	will	fall
he/she/it	will	fall
we	will	fall
you	will	fall
they	will	fall

Going to-Future

I	am	going to	fall
you	are	going to	fall
he/she/it	is	going to	fall
we	are	going to	fall
you	are	going to	fall
they	are	going to	fall

Future Perfect

I	will have	fallen
you	will have	fallen
he/she/it	will have	fallen
we	will have	fallen
you	will have	fallen
they	will have	fallen

Imperative

fall

Impersonal

ing-Form

falling

Past Participle

fallen

Continuous tenses

Present

I	am	falling
you	are	falling
he/she/it	is	falling
we	are	falling
you	are	falling
they	are	falling

Past

I	was	falling
you	were	falling
he/she/it	was	falling
we	were	falling
you	were	falling
they	were	falling

Present Perfect

I	have been	falling
you	have been	falling
he/she/it	has been	falling
we	have been	falling
you	have been	falling
they	have been	falling

Past Perfect

I	had been	falling
you	had been	falling
he/she/it	had been	falling
we	had been	falling
you	had been	falling
they	had been	falling

Will-Future

I	will be	falling
you	will be	falling
he/she/it	will be	falling
we	will be	falling
you	will be	falling
they	will be	falling

Going to-Future

I	am	going to be	falling
you	are	going to be	falling
he/she/it	is	going to be	falling
we	are	going to be	falling
you	are	going to be	falling
they	are	going to be	falling

Future Perfect

I	will have been	falling
you	will have been	falling
he/she/it	will have been	falling
we	will have been	falling
you	will have been	falling
they	will have been	falling

Conditional

I	would	fall
you	would	fall
he/she/it	would	fall
we	would	fall
you	would	fall
they	would	fall

Conditional Past

I	would have	fallen
you	would have	fallen
he/she/it	would have	fallen
we	would have	fallen
you	would have	fallen
they	would have	fallen

Simple tenses

Present

I	fasten
you	fasten
he/she/it	fastens
we	fasten
you	fasten
they	fasten

Past

I	fastened
you	fastened
he/she/it	fastened
we	fastened
you	fastened
they	fastened

Present Perfect

I	have	fastened
you	have	fastened
he/she/it	has	fastened
we	have	fastened
you	have	fastened
they	have	fastened

Past Perfect

I	had	fastened
you	had	fastened
he/she/it	had	fastened
we	had	fastened
you	had	fastened
they	had	fastened

Will-Future

I	will	fasten
you	will	fasten
he/she/it	will	fasten
we	will	fasten
you	will	fasten
they	will	fasten

Going to-Future

I	am	going to	fasten
you	are	going to	fasten
he/she/it	is	going to	fasten
we	are	going to	fasten
you	are	going to	fasten
they	are	going to	fasten

Future Perfect

I	will have	fastened
you	will have	fastened
he/she/it	will have	fastened
we	will have	fastened
you	will have	fastened
they	will have	fastened

Imperative

fasten

Impersonal

ing-Form

fastening

Past Participle

fastened

Continuous tenses

Present

I	am	fastening
you	are	fastening
he/she/it	is	fastening
we	are	fastening
you	are	fastening
they	are	fastening

Past

I	was	fastening
you	were	fastening
he/she/it	was	fastening
we	were	fastening
you	were	fastening
they	were	fastening

Present Perfect

I	have been	fastening
you	have been	fastening
he/she/it	has been	fastening
we	have been	fastening
you	have been	fastening
they	have been	fastening

Past Perfect

I	had been	fastening
you	had been	fastening
he/she/it	had been	fastening
we	had been	fastening
you	had been	fastening
they	had been	fastening

Will-Future

I	will be	fastening
you	will be	fastening
he/she/it	will be	fastening
we	will be	fastening
you	will be	fastening
they	will be	fastening

Going to-Future

I	am	going to be	fastening
you	are	going to be	fastening
he/she/it	is	going to be	fastening
we	are	going to be	fastening
you	are	going to be	fastening
they	are	going to be	fastening

Future Perfect

I	will have been	fastening
you	will have been	fastening
he/she/it	will have been	fastening
we	will have been	fastening
you	will have been	fastening
they	will have been	fastening

Conditional

I	would	fasten
you	would	fasten
he/she/it	would	fasten
we	would	fasten
you	would	fasten
they	would	fasten

Conditional Past

I	would have	fastened
you	would have	fastened
he/she/it	would have	fastened
we	would have	fastened
you	would have	fastened
they	would have	fastened

fear

fürchten

Regelmäßiges Verb

Simple tenses

Present

I	fear
you	fear
he/she/it	fears
we	fear
you	fear
they	fear

Past

I	feared
you	feared
he/she/it	feared
we	feared
you	feared
they	feared

Present Perfect

I	have	feared
you	have	feared
he/she/it	has	feared
we	have	feared
you	have	feared
they	have	feared

Past Perfect

I	had	feared
you	had	feared
he/she/it	had	feared
we	had	feared
you	had	feared
they	had	feared

Will-Future

I	will	fear
you	will	fear
he/she/it	will	fear
we	will	fear
you	will	fear
they	will	fear

Going to-Future

I	am	going to	fear
you	are	going to	fear
he/she/it	is	going to	fear
we	are	going to	fear
you	are	going to	fear
they	are	going to	fear

Future Perfect

I	will have	feared
you	will have	feared
he/she/it	will have	feared
we	will have	feared
you	will have	feared
they	will have	feared

Imperative

fear

Impersonal

ing-Form

fearing

Past Participle

feared

Continuous tenses

Present

I	am	fearing
you	are	fearing
he/she/it	is	fearing
we	are	fearing
you	are	fearing
they	are	fearing

Past

I	was	fearing
you	were	fearing
he/she/it	was	fearing
we	were	fearing
you	were	fearing
they	were	fearing

Present Perfect

I	have been	fearing
you	have been	fearing
he/she/it	has been	fearing
we	have been	fearing
you	have been	fearing
they	have been	fearing

Past Perfect

I	had been	fearing
you	had been	fearing
he/she/it	had been	fearing
we	had been	fearing
you	had been	fearing
they	had been	fearing

Will-Future

I	will be	fearing
you	will be	fearing
he/she/it	will be	fearing
we	will be	fearing
you	will be	fearing
they	will be	fearing

Going to-Future

I	am	going to be	fearing
you	are	going to be	fearing
he/she/it	is	going to be	fearing
we	are	going to be	fearing
you	are	going to be	fearing
they	are	going to be	fearing

Future Perfect

I	will have been	fearing
you	will have been	fearing
he/she/it	will have been	fearing
we	will have been	fearing
you	will have been	fearing
they	will have been	fearing

Conditional

I	would	fear
you	would	fear
he/she/it	would	fear
we	would	fear
you	would	fear
they	would	fear

Conditional Past

I	would have	feared
you	would have	feared
he/she/it	would have	feared
we	would have	feared
you	would have	feared
they	would have	feared

+ **-ing** → ~~e~~ / + **-d** nicht **-ed**
Regelmäßiges Verb

aufweisen, herausbringen

feature

Simple tenses

Present

I	feature
you	feature
he/she/it	features
we	feature
you	feature
they	feature

Past

I	featured
you	featured
he/she/it	featured
we	featured
you	featured
they	featured

Present Perfect

I	have	featured
you	have	featured
he/she/it	has	featured
we	have	featured
you	have	featured
they	have	featured

Past Perfect

I	had	featured
you	had	featured
he/she/it	had	featured
we	had	featured
you	had	featured
they	had	featured

Will-Future

I	will	feature
you	will	feature
he/she/it	will	feature
we	will	feature
you	will	feature
they	will	feature

Going to-Future

I	am	going to	feature
you	are	going to	feature
he/she/it	is	going to	feature
we	are	going to	feature
you	are	going to	feature
they	are	going to	feature

Future Perfect

I	will have	featured
you	will have	featured
he/she/it	will have	featured
we	will have	featured
you	will have	featured
they	will have	featured

Imperative

feature

Impersonal

ing-Form

featuring

Past Participle

featured

Continuous tenses

Present

I	am	featuring
you	are	featuring
he/she/it	is	featuring
we	are	featuring
you	are	featuring
they	are	featuring

Past

I	was	featuring
you	were	featuring
he/she/it	was	featuring
we	were	featuring
you	were	featuring
they	were	featuring

Present Perfect

I	have been	featuring
you	have been	featuring
he/she/it	has been	featuring
we	have been	featuring
you	have been	featuring
they	have been	featuring

Past Perfect

I	had been	featuring
you	had been	featuring
he/she/it	had been	featuring
we	had been	featuring
you	had been	featuring
they	had been	featuring

Will-Future

I	will be	featuring
you	will be	featuring
he/she/it	will be	featuring
we	will be	featuring
you	will be	featuring
they	will be	featuring

Going to-Future

I	am	going to be	featuring
you	are	going to be	featuring
he/she/it	is	going to be	featuring
we	are	going to be	featuring
you	are	going to be	featuring
they	are	going to be	featuring

Future Perfect

I	will have been	featuring
you	will have been	featuring
he/she/it	will have been	featuring
we	will have been	featuring
you	will have been	featuring
they	will have been	featuring

Conditional

I	would	feature
you	would	feature
he/she/it	would	feature
we	would	feature
you	would	feature
they	would	feature

Conditional Past

I	would have	featured
you	would have	featured
he/she/it	would have	featured
we	would have	featured
you	would have	featured
they	would have	featured

feed – *fed* – *fed*

füttern

Unregelmäßiges Verb

Simple tenses

Present

I	feed
you	feed
he/she/it	feeds
we	feed
you	feed
they	feed

Past

I	fed
you	fed
he/she/it	fed
we	fed
you	fed
they	fed

Present Perfect

I	have	fed
you	have	fed
he/she/it	has	fed
we	have	fed
you	have	fed
they	have	fed

Past Perfect

I	had	fed
you	had	fed
he/she/it	had	fed
we	had	fed
you	had	fed
they	had	fed

Will-Future

I	will	feed
you	will	feed
he/she/it	will	feed
we	will	feed
you	will	feed
they	will	feed

Going to-Future

I	am	going to	feed
you	are	going to	feed
he/she/it	is	going to	feed
we	are	going to	feed
you	are	going to	feed
they	are	going to	feed

Future Perfect

I	will have	fed
you	will have	fed
he/she/it	will have	fed
we	will have	fed
you	will have	fed
they	will have	fed

Imperative

feed

Impersonal

ing-Form

feeding

Past Participle

fed

Continuous tenses

Present

I	am	feeding
you	are	feeding
he/she/it	is	feeding
we	are	feeding
you	are	feeding
they	are	feeding

Past

I	was	feeding
you	were	feeding
he/she/it	was	feeding
we	were	feeding
you	were	feeding
they	were	feeding

Present Perfect

I	have been	feeding
you	have been	feeding
he/she/it	has been	feeding
we	have been	feeding
you	have been	feeding
they	have been	feeding

Past Perfect

I	had been	feeding
you	had been	feeding
he/she/it	had been	feeding
we	had been	feeding
you	had been	feeding
they	had been	feeding

Will-Future

I	will be	feeding
you	will be	feeding
he/she/it	will be	feeding
we	will be	feeding
you	will be	feeding
they	will be	feeding

Going to-Future

I	am	going to be	feeding
you	are	going to be	feeding
he/she/it	is	going to be	feeding
we	are	going to be	feeding
you	are	going to be	feeding
they	are	going to be	feeding

Future Perfect

I	will have been	feeding
you	will have been	feeding
he/she/it	will have been	feeding
we	will have been	feeding
you	will have been	feeding
they	will have been	feeding

Conditional

I	would	feed
you	would	feed
he/she/it	would	feed
we	would	feed
you	would	feed
they	would	feed

Conditional Past

I	would have	fed
you	would have	fed
he/she/it	would have	fed
we	would have	fed
you	would have	fed
they	would have	fed

Simple tenses

Present

I	feel
you	feel
he/she/it	feels
we	feel
you	feel
they	feel

Past

I	felt
you	felt
he/she/it	felt
we	felt
you	felt
they	felt

Present Perfect

I	have	felt
you	have	felt
he/she/it	has	felt
we	have	felt
you	have	felt
they	have	felt

Past Perfect

I	had	felt
you	had	felt
he/she/it	had	felt
we	had	felt
you	had	felt
they	had	felt

Will-Future

I	will	feel
you	will	feel
he/she/it	will	feel
we	will	feel
you	will	feel
they	will	feel

Going to-Future

I	am	going to	feel
you	are	going to	feel
he/she/it	is	going to	feel
we	are	going to	feel
you	are	going to	feel
they	are	going to	feel

Future Perfect

I	will have	felt
you	will have	felt
he/she/it	will have	felt
we	will have	felt
you	will have	felt
they	will have	felt

Imperative

feel

Impersonal

ing-Form

feeling

Past Participle

felt

Continuous tenses

Present

I	am	feeling
you	are	feeling
he/she/it	is	feeling
we	are	feeling
you	are	feeling
they	are	feeling

Past

I	was	feeling
you	were	feeling
he/she/it	was	feeling
we	were	feeling
you	were	feeling
they	were	feeling

Present Perfect

I	have been	feeling
you	have been	feeling
he/she/it	has been	feeling
we	have been	feeling
you	have been	feeling
they	have been	feeling

Past Perfect

I	had been	feeling
you	had been	feeling
he/she/it	had been	feeling
we	had been	feeling
you	had been	feeling
they	had been	feeling

Will-Future

I	will be	feeling
you	will be	feeling
he/she/it	will be	feeling
we	will be	feeling
you	will be	feeling
they	will be	feeling

Going to-Future

I	am	going to be	feeling
you	are	going to be	feeling
he/she/it	is	going to be	feeling
we	are	going to be	feeling
you	are	going to be	feeling
they	are	going to be	feeling

Future Perfect

I	will have been	feeling
you	will have been	feeling
he/she/it	will have been	feeling
we	will have been	feeling
you	will have been	feeling
they	will have been	feeling

Conditional

I	would	feel
you	would	feel
he/she/it	would	feel
we	would	feel
you	would	feel
they	would	feel

Conditional Past

I	would have	felt
you	would have	felt
he/she/it	would have	felt
we	would have	felt
you	would have	felt
they	would have	felt

fight
- fought - fought

kämpfen

Unregelmäßiges Verb

Simple tenses

Present

I	fight
you	fight
he/she/it	fights
we	fight
you	fight
they	fight

Past

I	fought
you	fought
he/she/it	fought
we	fought
you	fought
they	fought

Present Perfect

I	have	fought
you	have	fought
he/she/it	has	fought
we	have	fought
you	have	fought
they	have	fought

Past Perfect

I	had	fought
you	had	fought
he/she/it	had	fought
we	had	fought
you	had	fought
they	had	fought

Will-Future

I	will	fight
you	will	fight
he/she/it	will	fight
we	will	fight
you	will	fight
they	will	fight

Going to-Future

I	am	going to	fight
you	are	going to	fight
he/she/it	is	going to	fight
we	are	going to	fight
you	are	going to	fight
they	are	going to	fight

Future Perfect

I	will have	fought
you	will have	fought
he/she/it	will have	fought
we	will have	fought
you	will have	fought
they	will have	fought

Imperative

fight

Impersonal

ing-Form

fighting

Past Participle

fought

Continuous tenses

Present

I	am	fighting
you	are	fighting
he/she/it	is	fighting
we	are	fighting
you	are	fighting
they	are	fighting

Past

I	was	fighting
you	were	fighting
he/she/it	was	fighting
we	were	fighting
you	were	fighting
they	were	fighting

Present Perfect

I	have been	fighting
you	have been	fighting
he/she/it	has been	fighting
we	have been	fighting
you	have been	fighting
they	have been	fighting

Past Perfect

I	had been	fighting
you	had been	fighting
he/she/it	had been	fighting
we	had been	fighting
you	had been	fighting
they	had been	fighting

Will-Future

I	will be	fighting
you	will be	fighting
he/she/it	will be	fighting
we	will be	fighting
you	will be	fighting
they	will be	fighting

Going to-Future

I	am	going to be	fighting
you	are	going to be	fighting
he/she/it	is	going to be	fighting
we	are	going to be	fighting
you	are	going to be	fighting
they	are	going to be	fighting

Future Perfect

I	will have been	fighting
you	will have been	fighting
he/she/it	will have been	fighting
we	will have been	fighting
you	will have been	fighting
they	will have been	fighting

Conditional

I	would	fight
you	would	fight
he/she/it	would	fight
we	would	fight
you	would	fight
they	would	fight

Conditional Past

I	would have	fought
you	would have	fought
he/she/it	would have	fought
we	would have	fought
you	would have	fought
they	would have	fought

Simple tenses

Present

I	file
you	file
he/she/it	files
we	file
you	file
they	file

Past

I	filed
you	filed
he/she/it	filed
we	filed
you	filed
they	filed

Present Perfect

I	have	filed
you	have	filed
he/she/it	has	filed
we	have	filed
you	have	filed
they	have	filed

Past Perfect

I	had	filed
you	had	filed
he/she/it	had	filed
we	had	filed
you	had	filed
they	had	filed

Will-Future

I	will	file
you	will	file
he/she/it	will	file
we	will	file
you	will	file
they	will	file

Going to-Future

I	am	going to	file
you	are	going to	file
he/she/it	is	going to	file
we	are	going to	file
you	are	going to	file
they	are	going to	file

Future Perfect

I	will have	filed
you	will have	filed
he/she/it	will have	filed
we	will have	filed
you	will have	filed
they	will have	filed

Imperative

file

Impersonal

ing-Form

filing

Past Participle

filed

Continuous tenses

Present

I	am	filing
you	are	filing
he/she/it	is	filing
we	are	filing
you	are	filing
they	are	filing

Past

I	was	filing
you	were	filing
he/she/it	was	filing
we	were	filing
you	were	filing
they	were	filing

Present Perfect

I	have been	filing
you	have been	filing
he/she/it	has been	filing
we	have been	filing
you	have been	filing
they	have been	filing

Past Perfect

I	had been	filing
you	had been	filing
he/she/it	had been	filing
we	had been	filing
you	had been	filing
they	had been	filing

Will-Future

I	will be	filing
you	will be	filing
he/she/it	will be	filing
we	will be	filing
you	will be	filing
they	will be	filing

Going to-Future

I	am	going to be	filing
you	are	going to be	filing
he/she/it	is	going to be	filing
we	are	going to be	filing
you	are	going to be	filing
they	are	going to be	filing

Future Perfect

I	will have been	filing
you	will have been	filing
he/she/it	will have been	filing
we	will have been	filing
you	will have been	filing
they	will have been	filing

Conditional

I	would	file
you	would	file
he/she/it	would	file
we	would	file
you	would	file
they	would	file

Conditional Past

I	would have	filed
you	would have	filed
he/she/it	would have	filed
we	would have	filed
you	would have	filed
they	would have	filed

füllen

+ **-ing** → ~~e~~ / + **-d** nicht **-ed**
Regelmäßiges Verb

Simple tenses

Present

I	fill
you	fill
he/she/it	fills
we	fill
you	fill
they	fill

Past

I	filled
you	filled
he/she/it	filled
we	filled
you	filled
they	filled

Present Perfect

I	have	filled
you	have	filled
he/she/it	has	filled
we	have	filled
you	have	filled
they	have	filled

Past Perfect

I	had	filled
you	had	filled
he/she/it	had	filled
we	had	filled
you	had	filled
they	had	filled

Will-Future

I	will	fill
you	will	fill
he/she/it	will	fill
we	will	fill
you	will	fill
they	will	fill

Going to-Future

I	am	going to	fill
you	are	going to	fill
he/she/it	is	going to	fill
we	are	going to	fill
you	are	going to	fill
they	are	going to	fill

Future Perfect

I	will have	filled
you	will have	filled
he/she/it	will have	filled
we	will have	filled
you	will have	filled
they	will have	filled

Imperative

fill

Impersonal

ing-Form

filling

Past Participle

filled

Continuous tenses

Present

I	am	filling
you	are	filling
he/she/it	is	filling
we	are	filling
you	are	filling
they	are	filling

Past

I	was	filling
you	were	filling
he/she/it	was	filling
we	were	filling
you	were	filling
they	were	filling

Present Perfect

I	have been	filling
you	have been	filling
he/she/it	has been	filling
we	have been	filling
you	have been	filling
they	have been	filling

Past Perfect

I	had been	filling
you	had been	filling
he/she/it	had been	filling
we	had been	filling
you	had been	filling
they	had been	filling

Will-Future

I	will be	filling
you	will be	filling
he/she/it	will be	filling
we	will be	filling
you	will be	filling
they	will be	filling

Going to-Future

I	am	going to be	filling
you	are	going to be	filling
he/she/it	is	going to be	filling
we	are	going to be	filling
you	are	going to be	filling
they	are	going to be	filling

Future Perfect

I	will have been	filling
you	will have been	filling
he/she/it	will have been	filling
we	will have been	filling
you	will have been	filling
they	will have been	filling

Conditional

I	would	fill
you	would	fill
he/she/it	would	fill
we	would	fill
you	would	fill
they	would	fill

Conditional Past

I	would have	filled
you	would have	filled
he/she/it	would have	filled
we	would have	filled
you	would have	filled
they	would have	filled

Simple tenses

Present

I	film
you	film
he/she/it	films
we	film
you	film
they	film

Past

I	filmed
you	filmed
he/she/it	filmed
we	filmed
you	filmed
they	filmed

Present Perfect

I	have	filmed
you	have	filmed
he/she/it	has	filmed
we	have	filmed
you	have	filmed
they	have	filmed

Past Perfect

I	had	filmed
you	had	filmed
he/she/it	had	filmed
we	had	filmed
you	had	filmed
they	had	filmed

Will-Future

I	will	film
you	will	film
he/she/it	will	film
we	will	film
you	will	film
they	will	film

Going to-Future

I	am	going to	film
you	are	going to	film
he/she/it	is	going to	film
we	are	going to	film
you	are	going to	film
they	are	going to	film

Future Perfect

I	will have	filmed
you	will have	filmed
he/she/it	will have	filmed
we	will have	filmed
you	will have	filmed
they	will have	filmed

Imperative

film

Impersonal

ing-Form

filming

Past Participle

filmed

Continuous tenses

Present

I	am	filming
you	are	filming
he/she/it	is	filming
we	are	filming
you	are	filming
they	are	filming

Past

I	was	filming
you	were	filming
he/she/it	was	filming
we	were	filming
you	were	filming
they	were	filming

Present Perfect

I	have been	filming
you	have been	filming
he/she/it	has been	filming
we	have been	filming
you	have been	filming
they	have been	filming

Past Perfect

I	had been	filming
you	had been	filming
he/she/it	had been	filming
we	had been	filming
you	had been	filming
they	had been	filming

Will-Future

I	will be	filming
you	will be	filming
he/she/it	will be	filming
we	will be	filming
you	will be	filming
they	will be	filming

Going to-Future

I	am	going to be	filming
you	are	going to be	filming
he/she/it	is	going to be	filming
we	are	going to be	filming
you	are	going to be	filming
they	are	going to be	filming

Future Perfect

I	will have been	filming
you	will have been	filming
he/she/it	will have been	filming
we	will have been	filming
you	will have been	filming
they	will have been	filming

Conditional

I	would	film
you	would	film
he/she/it	would	film
we	would	film
you	would	film
they	would	film

Conditional Past

I	would have	filmed
you	would have	filmed
he/she/it	would have	filmed
we	would have	filmed
you	would have	filmed
they	would have	filmed

find

- found - found

finden

Unregelmäßiges Verb

Simple tenses

Present

I	find
you	find
he/she/it	finds
we	find
you	find
they	find

Past

I	found
you	found
he/she/it	found
we	found
you	found
they	found

Present Perfect

I	have	found
you	have	found
he/she/it	has	found
we	have	found
you	have	found
they	have	found

Past Perfect

I	had	found
you	had	found
he/she/it	had	found
we	had	found
you	had	found
they	had	found

Will-Future

I	will	find
you	will	find
he/she/it	will	find
we	will	find
you	will	find
they	will	find

Going to-Future

I	am	going to	find
you	are	going to	find
he/she/it	is	going to	find
we	are	going to	find
you	are	going to	find
they	are	going to	find

Future Perfect

I	will have	found
you	will have	found
he/she/it	will have	found
we	will have	found
you	will have	found
they	will have	found

Imperative

find

Impersonal

ing-Form

finding

Past Participle

found

Continuous tenses

Present

I	am	finding
you	are	finding
he/she/it	is	finding
we	are	finding
you	are	finding
they	are	finding

Past

I	was	finding
you	were	finding
he/she/it	was	finding
we	were	finding
you	were	finding
they	were	finding

Present Perfect

I	have been	finding
you	have been	finding
he/she/it	has been	finding
we	have been	finding
you	have been	finding
they	have been	finding

Past Perfect

I	had been	finding
you	had been	finding
he/she/it	had been	finding
we	had been	finding
you	had been	finding
they	had been	finding

Will-Future

I	will be	finding
you	will be	finding
he/she/it	will be	finding
we	will be	finding
you	will be	finding
they	will be	finding

Going to-Future

I	am	going to be	finding
you	are	going to be	finding
he/she/it	is	going to be	finding
we	are	going to be	finding
you	are	going to be	finding
they	are	going to be	finding

Future Perfect

I	will have been	finding
you	will have been	finding
he/she/it	will have been	finding
we	will have been	finding
you	will have been	finding
they	will have been	finding

Conditional

I	would	find
you	would	find
he/she/it	would	find
we	would	find
you	would	find
they	would	find

Conditional Past

I	would have	found
you	would have	found
he/she/it	would have	found
we	would have	found
you	would have	found
they	would have	found

Simple tenses

Present

I	finish
you	finish
he/she/it	finishes
we	finish
you	finish
they	finish

Past

I	finished
you	finished
he/she/it	finished
we	finished
you	finished
they	finished

Present Perfect

I	have	finished
you	have	finished
he/she/it	has	finished
we	have	finished
you	have	finished
they	have	finished

Past Perfect

I	had	finished
you	had	finished
he/she/it	had	finished
we	had	finished
you	had	finished
they	had	finished

Will-Future

I	will	finish
you	will	finish
he/she/it	will	finish
we	will	finish
you	will	finish
they	will	finish

Going to-Future

I	am	going to	finish
you	are	going to	finish
he/she/it	is	going to	finish
we	are	going to	finish
you	are	going to	finish
they	are	going to	finish

Future Perfect

I	will have	finished
you	will have	finished
he/she/it	will have	finished
we	will have	finished
you	will have	finished
they	will have	finished

Imperative

finish

Impersonal

ing-Form

finishing

Past Participle

finished

Continuous tenses

Present

I	am	finishing
you	are	finishing
he/she/it	is	finishing
we	are	finishing
you	are	finishing
they	are	finishing

Past

I	was	finishing
you	were	finishing
he/she/it	was	finishing
we	were	finishing
you	were	finishing
they	were	finishing

Present Perfect

I	have	been	finishing
you	have	been	finishing
he/she/it	has	been	finishing
we	have	been	finishing
you	have	been	finishing
they	have	been	finishing

Past Perfect

I	had been	finishing
you	had been	finishing
he/she/it	had been	finishing
we	had been	finishing
you	had been	finishing
they	had been	finishing

Will-Future

I	will be	finishing
you	will be	finishing
he/she/it	will be	finishing
we	will be	finishing
you	will be	finishing
they	will be	finishing

Going to-Future

I	am	going to be	finishing
you	are	going to be	finishing
he/she/it	is	going to be	finishing
we	are	going to be	finishing
you	are	going to be	finishing
they	are	going to be	finishing

Future Perfect

I	will have been	finishing
you	will have been	finishing
he/she/it	will have been	finishing
we	will have been	finishing
you	will have been	finishing
they	will have been	finishing

Conditional

I	would	finish
you	would	finish
he/she/it	would	finish
we	would	finish
you	would	finish
they	would	finish

Conditional Past

I	would have	finished
you	would have	finished
he/she/it	would have	finished
we	would have	finished
you	would have	finished
they	would have	finished

fish

fischen

+ **-es** in 3. Person Singular
Regelmäßiges Verb

Simple tenses

Present

I	fish
you	fish
he/she/it	fishes
we	fish
you	fish
they	fish

Past

I	fished
you	fished
he/she/it	fished
we	fished
you	fished
they	fished

Present Perfect

I	have	fished
you	have	fished
he/she/it	has	fished
we	have	fished
you	have	fished
they	have	fished

Past Perfect

I	had	fished
you	had	fished
he/she/it	had	fished
we	had	fished
you	had	fished
they	had	fished

Will-Future

I	will	fish
you	will	fish
he/she/it	will	fish
we	will	fish
you	will	fish
they	will	fish

Going to-Future

I	am	going to	fish
you	are	going to	fish
he/she/it	is	going to	fish
we	are	going to	fish
you	are	going to	fish
they	are	going to	fish

Future Perfect

I	will have	fished
you	will have	fished
he/she/it	will have	fished
we	will have	fished
you	will have	fished
they	will have	fished

Imperative

fish

Impersonal

ing-Form

fishing

Past Participle

fished

Continuous tenses

Present

I	am	fishing
you	are	fishing
he/she/it	is	fishing
we	are	fishing
you	are	fishing
they	are	fishing

Past

I	was	fishing
you	were	fishing
he/she/it	was	fishing
we	were	fishing
you	were	fishing
they	were	fishing

Present Perfect

I	have been	fishing
you	have been	fishing
he/she/it	has been	fishing
we	have been	fishing
you	have been	fishing
they	have been	fishing

Past Perfect

I	had been	fishing
you	had been	fishing
he/she/it	had been	fishing
we	had been	fishing
you	had been	fishing
they	had been	fishing

Will-Future

I	will be	fishing
you	will be	fishing
he/she/it	will be	fishing
we	will be	fishing
you	will be	fishing
they	will be	fishing

Going to-Future

I	am	going to be	fishing
you	are	going to be	fishing
he/she/it	is	going to be	fishing
we	are	going to be	fishing
you	are	going to be	fishing
they	are	going to be	fishing

Future Perfect

I	will have been	fishing
you	will have been	fishing
he/she/it	will have been	fishing
we	will have been	fishing
you	will have been	fishing
they	will have been	fishing

Conditional

I	would	fish
you	would	fish
he/she/it	would	fish
we	would	fish
you	would	fish
they	would	fish

Conditional Past

I	would have	fished
you	would have	fished
he/she/it	would have	fished
we	would have	fished
you	would have	fished
they	would have	fished

Simple tenses

Present

I	fix
you	fix
he/she/it	fixes
we	fix
you	fix
they	fix

Past

I	fixed
you	fixed
he/she/it	fixed
we	fixed
you	fixed
they	fixed

Present Perfect

I	have	fixed
you	have	fixed
he/she/it	has	fixed
we	have	fixed
you	have	fixed
they	have	fixed

Past Perfect

I	had	fixed
you	had	fixed
he/she/it	had	fixed
we	had	fixed
you	had	fixed
they	had	fixed

Will-Future

I	will	fix
you	will	fix
he/she/it	will	fix
we	will	fix
you	will	fix
they	will	fix

Going to-Future

I	am	going to	fix
you	are	going to	fix
he/she/it	is	going to	fix
we	are	going to	fix
you	are	going to	fix
they	are	going to	fix

Future Perfect

I	will have	fixed
you	will have	fixed
he/she/it	will have	fixed
we	will have	fixed
you	will have	fixed
they	will have	fixed

Imperative

fix

Impersonal

ing-Form

fixing

Past Participle

fixed

Continuous tenses

Present

I	am	fixing
you	are	fixing
he/she/it	is	fixing
we	are	fixing
you	are	fixing
they	are	fixing

Past

I	was	fixing
you	were	fixing
he/she/it	was	fixing
we	were	fixing
you	were	fixing
they	were	fixing

Present Perfect

I	have	been	fixing
you	have	been	fixing
he/she/it	has	been	fixing
we	have	been	fixing
you	have	been	fixing
they	have	been	fixing

Past Perfect

I	had been	fixing
you	had been	fixing
he/she/it	had been	fixing
we	had been	fixing
you	had been	fixing
they	had been	fixing

Will-Future

I	will be	fixing
you	will be	fixing
he/she/it	will be	fixing
we	will be	fixing
you	will be	fixing
they	will be	fixing

Going to-Future

I	am	going to be	fixing
you	are	going to be	fixing
he/she/it	is	going to be	fixing
we	are	going to be	fixing
you	are	going to be	fixing
they	are	going to be	fixing

Future Perfect

I	will have been	fixing
you	will have been	fixing
he/she/it	will have been	fixing
we	will have been	fixing
you	will have been	fixing
they	will have been	fixing

Conditional

I	would	fix
you	would	fix
he/she/it	would	fix
we	would	fix
you	would	fix
they	would	fix

Conditional Past

I	would have	fixed
you	would have	fixed
he/she/it	would have	fixed
we	would have	fixed
you	would have	fixed
they	would have	fixed

flash

blitzen

+ **-es** in 3. Person Singular
Regelmäßiges Verb

Simple tenses

Present

I	flash
you	flash
he/she/it	flashes
we	flash
you	flash
they	flash

Past

I	flashed
you	flashed
he/she/it	flashed
we	flashed
you	flashed
they	flashed

Present Perfect

I	have	flashed
you	have	flashed
he/she/it	has	flashed
we	have	flashed
you	have	flashed
they	have	flashed

Past Perfect

I	had	flashed
you	had	flashed
he/she/it	had	flashed
we	had	flashed
you	had	flashed
they	had	flashed

Will-Future

I	will	flash
you	will	flash
he/she/it	will	flash
we	will	flash
you	will	flash
they	will	flash

Going to-Future

I	am	going to	flash
you	are	going to	flash
he/she/it	is	going to	flash
we	are	going to	flash
you	are	going to	flash
they	are	going to	flash

Future Perfect

I	will have	flashed
you	will have	flashed
he/she/it	will have	flashed
we	will have	flashed
you	will have	flashed
they	will have	flashed

Imperative

flash

Impersonal

ing-Form

flashing

Past Participle

flashed

Continuous tenses

Present

I	am	flashing
you	are	flashing
he/she/it	is	flashing
we	are	flashing
you	are	flashing
they	are	flashing

Past

I	was	flashing
you	were	flashing
he/she/it	was	flashing
we	were	flashing
you	were	flashing
they	were	flashing

Present Perfect

I	have been	flashing
you	have been	flashing
he/she/it	has been	flashing
we	have been	flashing
you	have been	flashing
they	have been	flashing

Past Perfect

I	had been	flashing
you	had been	flashing
he/she/it	had been	flashing
we	had been	flashing
you	had been	flashing
they	had been	flashing

Will-Future

I	will be	flashing
you	will be	flashing
he/she/it	will be	flashing
we	will be	flashing
you	will be	flashing
they	will be	flashing

Going to-Future

I	am	going to be	flashing
you	are	going to be	flashing
he/she/it	is	going to be	flashing
we	are	going to be	flashing
you	are	going to be	flashing
they	are	going to be	flashing

Future Perfect

I	will have been	flashing
you	will have been	flashing
he/she/it	will have been	flashing
we	will have been	flashing
you	will have been	flashing
they	will have been	flashing

Conditional

I	would	flash
you	would	flash
he/she/it	would	flash
we	would	flash
you	would	flash
they	would	flash

Conditional Past

I	would have	flashed
you	would have	flashed
he/she/it	would have	flashed
we	would have	flashed
you	would have	flashed
they	would have	flashed

Simple tenses

Present

I	fly
you	fly
he/she/it	flies
we	fly
you	fly
they	fly

Past

I	flew
you	flew
he/she/it	flew
we	flew
you	flew
they	flew

Present Perfect

I	have	flown
you	have	flown
he/she/it	has	flown
we	have	flown
you	have	flown
they	have	flown

Past Perfect

I	had	flown
you	had	flown
he/she/it	had	flown
we	had	flown
you	had	flown
they	had	flown

Will-Future

I	will	fly
you	will	fly
he/she/it	will	fly
we	will	fly
you	will	fly
they	will	fly

Going to-Future

I	am	going to	fly
you	are	going to	fly
he/she/it	is	going to	fly
we	are	going to	fly
you	are	going to	fly
they	are	going to	fly

Future Perfect

I	will have	flown
you	will have	flown
he/she/it	will have	flown
we	will have	flown
you	will have	flown
they	will have	flown

Imperative

fly

Impersonal

ing-Form

flying

Past Participle

flown

Continuous tenses

Present

I	am	flying
you	are	flying
he/she/it	is	flying
we	are	flying
you	are	flying
they	are	flying

Past

I	was	flying
you	were	flying
he/she/it	was	flying
we	were	flying
you	were	flying
they	were	flying

Present Perfect

I	have	been	flying
you	have	been	flying
he/she/it	has	been	flying
we	have	been	flying
you	have	been	flying
they	have	been	flying

Past Perfect

I	had been	flying
you	had been	flying
he/she/it	had been	flying
we	had been	flying
you	had been	flying
they	had been	flying

Will-Future

I	will be	flying
you	will be	flying
he/she/it	will be	flying
we	will be	flying
you	will be	flying
they	will be	flying

Going to-Future

I	am	going to be	flying
you	are	going to be	flying
he/she/it	is	going to be	flying
we	are	going to be	flying
you	are	going to be	flying
they	are	going to be	flying

Future Perfect

I	will have been flying
you	will have been flying
he/she/it	will have been flying
we	will have been flying
you	will have been flying
they	will have been flying

Conditional

I	would	fly
you	would	fly
he/she/it	would	fly
we	would	fly
you	would	fly
they	would	fly

Conditional Past

I	would have	flown
you	would have	flown
he/she/it	would have	flown
we	would have	flown
you	would have	flown
they	would have	flown

fold

falten

Regelmäßiges Verb

Simple tenses

Present

I	fold
you	fold
he/she/it	folds
we	fold
you	fold
they	fold

Past

I	folded
you	folded
he/she/it	folded
we	folded
you	folded
they	folded

Present Perfect

I	have	folded
you	have	folded
he/she/it	has	folded
we	have	folded
you	have	folded
they	have	folded

Past Perfect

I	had	folded
you	had	folded
he/she/it	had	folded
we	had	folded
you	had	folded
they	had	folded

Will-Future

I	will	fold
you	will	fold
he/she/it	will	fold
we	will	fold
you	will	fold
they	will	fold

Going to-Future

I	am	going to	fold
you	are	going to	fold
he/she/it	is	going to	fold
we	are	going to	fold
you	are	going to	fold
they	are	going to	fold

Future Perfect

I	will have	folded
you	will have	folded
he/she/it	will have	folded
we	will have	folded
you	will have	folded
they	will have	folded

Imperative

fold

Impersonal

ing-Form

folding

Past Participle

folded

Continuous tenses

Present

I	am	folding
you	are	folding
he/she/it	is	folding
we	are	folding
you	are	folding
they	are	folding

Past

I	was	folding
you	were	folding
he/she/it	was	folding
we	were	folding
you	were	folding
they	were	folding

Present Perfect

I	have been	folding
you	have been	folding
he/she/it	has been	folding
we	have been	folding
you	have been	folding
they	have been	folding

Past Perfect

I	had been	folding
you	had been	folding
he/she/it	had been	folding
we	had been	folding
you	had been	folding
they	had been	folding

Will-Future

I	will be	folding
you	will be	folding
he/she/it	will be	folding
we	will be	folding
you	will be	folding
they	will be	folding

Going to-Future

I	am	going to be	folding
you	are	going to be	folding
he/she/it	is	going to be	folding
we	are	going to be	folding
you	are	going to be	folding
they	are	going to be	folding

Future Perfect

I	will have been	folding
you	will have been	folding
he/she/it	will have been	folding
we	will have been	folding
you	will have been	folding
they	will have been	folding

Conditional

I	would	fold
you	would	fold
he/she/it	would	fold
we	would	fold
you	would	fold
they	would	fold

Conditional Past

I	would have	folded
you	would have	folded
he/she/it	would have	folded
we	would have	folded
you	would have	folded
they	would have	folded

Simple tenses

Present

I	follow
you	follow
he/she/it	follows
we	follow
you	follow
they	follow

Past

I	followed
you	followed
he/she/it	followed
we	followed
you	followed
they	followed

Present Perfect

I	have	followed
you	have	followed
he/she/it	has	followed
we	have	followed
you	have	followed
they	have	followed

Past Perfect

I	had	followed
you	had	followed
he/she/it	had	followed
we	had	followed
you	had	followed
they	had	followed

Will-Future

I	will	follow
you	will	follow
he/she/it	will	follow
we	will	follow
you	will	follow
they	will	follow

Going to-Future

I	am	going to	follow
you	are	going to	follow
he/she/it	is	going to	follow
we	are	going to	follow
you	are	going to	follow
they	are	going to	follow

Future Perfect

I	will have	followed
you	will have	followed
he/she/it	will have	followed
we	will have	followed
you	will have	followed
they	will have	followed

Imperative

follow

Impersonal

ing-Form

following

Past Participle

followed

Continuous tenses

Present

I	am	following
you	are	following
he/she/it	is	following
we	are	following
you	are	following
they	are	following

Past

I	was	following
you	were	following
he/she/it	was	following
we	were	following
you	were	following
they	were	following

Present Perfect

I	have been	following
you	have been	following
he/she/it	has been	following
we	have been	following
you	have been	following
they	have been	following

Past Perfect

I	had been	following
you	had been	following
he/she/it	had been	following
we	had been	following
you	had been	following
they	had been	following

Will-Future

I	will be	following
you	will be	following
he/she/it	will be	following
we	will be	following
you	will be	following
they	will be	following

Going to-Future

I	am	going to be	following
you	are	going to be	following
he/she/it	is	going to be	following
we	are	going to be	following
you	are	going to be	following
they	are	going to be	following

Future Perfect

I	will have been	following
you	will have been	following
he/she/it	will have been	following
we	will have been	following
you	will have been	following
they	will have been	following

Conditional

I	would	follow
you	would	follow
he/she/it	would	follow
we	would	follow
you	would	follow
they	would	follow

Conditional Past

I	would have	followed
you	would have	followed
he/she/it	would have	followed
we	would have	followed
you	would have	followed
they	would have	followed

force

zwingen

+ **-ing** → ~~e~~ / + **-d** nicht **-ed**
Regelmäßiges Verb

Simple tenses

Present

I	force
you	force
he/she/it	forces
we	force
you	force
they	force

Past

I	forced
you	forced
he/she/it	forced
we	forced
you	forced
they	forced

Present Perfect

I	have	forced
you	have	forced
he/she/it	has	forced
we	have	forced
you	have	forced
they	have	forced

Past Perfect

I	had	forced
you	had	forced
he/she/it	had	forced
we	had	forced
you	had	forced
they	had	forced

Will-Future

I	will	force
you	will	force
he/she/it	will	force
we	will	force
you	will	force
they	will	force

Going to-Future

I	am	going to	force
you	are	going to	force
he/she/it	is	going to	force
we	are	going to	force
you	are	going to	force
they	are	going to	force

Future Perfect

I	will have	forced
you	will have	forced
he/she/it	will have	forced
we	will have	forced
you	will have	forced
they	will have	forced

Imperative

force

Impersonal

ing-Form

forcing

Past Participle

forced

Continuous tenses

Present

I	am	forcing
you	are	forcing
he/she/it	is	forcing
we	are	forcing
you	are	forcing
they	are	forcing

Past

I	was	forcing
you	were	forcing
he/she/it	was	forcing
we	were	forcing
you	were	forcing
they	were	forcing

Present Perfect

I	have been	forcing
you	have been	forcing
he/she/it	has been	forcing
we	have been	forcing
you	have been	forcing
they	have been	forcing

Past Perfect

I	had been	forcing
you	had been	forcing
he/she/it	had been	forcing
we	had been	forcing
you	had been	forcing
they	had been	forcing

Will-Future

I	will be	forcing
you	will be	forcing
he/she/it	will be	forcing
we	will be	forcing
you	will be	forcing
they	will be	forcing

Going to-Future

I	am	going to be	forcing
you	are	going to be	forcing
he/she/it	is	going to be	forcing
we	are	going to be	forcing
you	are	going to be	forcing
they	are	going to be	forcing

Future Perfect

I	will have been	forcing
you	will have been	forcing
he/she/it	will have been	forcing
we	will have been	forcing
you	will have been	forcing
they	will have been	forcing

Conditional

I	would	force
you	would	force
he/she/it	would	force
we	would	force
you	would	force
they	would	force

Conditional Past

I	would have	forced
you	would have	forced
he/she/it	would have	forced
we	would have	forced
you	would have	forced
they	would have	forced

Konsonantenverdopplung
Unregelmäßiges Verb

vergessen

forget
– forgot – forgotten

Simple tenses

Present

I	forget
you	forget
he/she/it	forgets
we	forget
you	forget
they	forget

Past

I	forgot
you	forgot
he/she/it	forgot
we	forgot
you	forgot
they	forgot

Present Perfect

I	have	forgotten
you	have	forgotten
he/she/it	has	forgotten
we	have	forgotten
you	have	forgotten
they	have	forgotten

Past Perfect

I	had	forgotten
you	had	forgotten
he/she/it	had	forgotten
we	had	forgotten
you	had	forgotten
they	had	forgotten

Will-Future

I	will	forget
you	will	forget
he/she/it	will	forget
we	will	forget
you	will	forget
they	will	forget

Going to-Future

I	am	going to	forget
you	are	going to	forget
he/she/it	is	going to	forget
we	are	going to	forget
you	are	going to	forget
they	are	going to	forget

Future Perfect

I	will have	forgotten
you	will have	forgotten
he/she/it	will have	forgotten
we	will have	forgotten
you	will have	forgotten
they	will have	forgotten

Imperative

forget

Impersonal

ing-Form

forgetting

Past Participle

forgotten

Continuous tenses

Present

I	am	forgetting
you	are	forgetting
he/she/it	is	forgetting
we	are	forgetting
you	are	forgetting
they	are	forgetting

Past

I	was	forgetting
you	were	forgetting
he/she/it	was	forgetting
we	were	forgetting
you	were	forgetting
they	were	forgetting

Present Perfect

I	have been	forgetting
you	have been	forgetting
he/she/it	has been	forgetting
we	have been	forgetting
you	have been	forgetting
they	have been	forgetting

Past Perfect

I	had been	forgetting
you	had been	forgetting
he/she/it	had been	forgetting
we	had been	forgetting
you	had been	forgetting
they	had been	forgetting

Will-Future

I	will be	forgetting
you	will be	forgetting
he/she/it	will be	forgetting
we	will be	forgetting
you	will be	forgetting
they	will be	forgetting

Going to-Future

I	am	going to be	forgetting
you	are	going to be	forgetting
he/she/it	is	going to be	forgetting
we	are	going to be	forgetting
you	are	going to be	forgetting
they	are	going to be	forgetting

Future Perfect

I	will have been	forgetting
you	will have been	forgetting
he/she/it	will have been	forgetting
we	will have been	forgetting
you	will have been	forgetting
they	will have been	forgetting

Conditional

I	would	forget
you	would	forget
he/she/it	would	forget
we	would	forget
you	would	forget
they	would	forget

Conditional Past

I	would have	forgotten
you	would have	forgotten
he/she/it	would have	forgotten
we	would have	forgotten
you	would have	forgotten
they	would have	forgotten

forgive

– forgave – forgiven

verzeihen

+ -ing → e̸
Unregelmäßiges Verb

Simple tenses

Present

I	forgive
you	forgive
he/she/it	forgives
we	forgive
you	forgive
they	forgive

Past

I	forgave
you	forgave
he/she/it	forgave
we	forgave
you	forgave
they	forgave

Present Perfect

I	have	forgiven
you	have	forgiven
he/she/it	has	forgiven
we	have	forgiven
you	have	forgiven
they	have	forgiven

Past Perfect

I	had	forgiven
you	had	forgiven
he/she/it	had	forgiven
we	had	forgiven
you	had	forgiven
they	had	forgiven

Will-Future

I	will	forgive
you	will	forgive
he/she/it	will	forgive
we	will	forgive
you	will	forgive
they	will	forgive

Going to-Future

I	am	going to	forgive
you	are	going to	forgive
he/she/it	is	going to	forgive
we	are	going to	forgive
you	are	going to	forgive
they	are	going to	forgive

Future Perfect

I	will have	forgiven
you	will have	forgiven
he/she/it	will have	forgiven
we	will have	forgiven
you	will have	forgiven
they	will have	forgiven

Imperative

forgive

Impersonal

ing-Form

forgiving

Past Participle

forgiven

Continuous tenses

Present

I	am	forgiving
you	are	forgiving
he/she/it	is	forgiving
we	are	forgiving
you	are	forgiving
they	are	forgiving

Past

I	was	forgiving
you	were	forgiving
he/she/it	was	forgiving
we	were	forgiving
you	were	forgiving
they	were	forgiving

Present Perfect

I	have been	forgiving
you	have been	forgiving
he/she/it	has been	forgiving
we	have been	forgiving
you	have been	forgiving
they	have been	forgiving

Past Perfect

I	had been	forgiving
you	had been	forgiving
he/she/it	had been	forgiving
we	had been	forgiving
you	had been	forgiving
they	had been	forgiving

Will-Future

I	will be	forgiving
you	will be	forgiving
he/she/it	will be	forgiving
we	will be	forgiving
you	will be	forgiving
they	will be	forgiving

Going to-Future

I	am	going to be	forgiving
you	are	going to be	forgiving
he/she/it	is	going to be	forgiving
we	are	going to be	forgiving
you	are	going to be	forgiving
they	are	going to be	forgiving

Future Perfect

I	will have been	forgiving
you	will have been	forgiving
he/she/it	will have been	forgiving
we	will have been	forgiving
you	will have been	forgiving
they	will have been	forgiving

Conditional

I	would	forgive
you	would	forgive
he/she/it	would	forgive
we	would	forgive
you	would	forgive
they	would	forgive

Conditional Past

I	would have	forgiven
you	would have	forgiven
he/she/it	would have	forgiven
we	would have	forgiven
you	would have	forgiven
they	would have	forgiven

Simple tenses

Present
I	form
you	form
he/she/it	forms
we	form
you	form
they	form

Past
I	formed
you	formed
he/she/it	formed
we	formed
you	formed
they	formed

Present Perfect
I	have	formed
you	have	formed
he/she/it	has	formed
we	have	formed
you	have	formed
they	have	formed

Past Perfect
I	had	formed
you	had	formed
he/she/it	had	formed
we	had	formed
you	had	formed
they	had	formed

Will-Future
I	will	form
you	will	form
he/she/it	will	form
we	will	form
you	will	form
they	will	form

Going to-Future
I	am	going to	form
you	are	going to	form
he/she/it	is	going to	form
we	are	going to	form
you	are	going to	form
they	are	going to	form

Future Perfect
I	will have	formed
you	will have	formed
he/she/it	will have	formed
we	will have	formed
you	will have	formed
they	will have	formed

Imperative
form

Impersonal

ing-Form
forming

Past Participle
formed

Continuous tenses

Present
I	am	forming
you	are	forming
he/she/it	is	forming
we	are	forming
you	are	forming
they	are	forming

Past
I	was	forming
you	were	forming
he/she/it	was	forming
we	were	forming
you	were	forming
they	were	forming

Present Perfect
I	have been	forming
you	have been	forming
he/she/it	has been	forming
we	have been	forming
you	have been	forming
they	have been	forming

Past Perfect
I	had been	forming
you	had been	forming
he/she/it	had been	forming
we	had been	forming
you	had been	forming
they	had been	forming

Will-Future
I	will be	forming
you	will be	forming
he/she/it	will be	forming
we	will be	forming
you	will be	forming
they	will be	forming

Going to-Future
I	am	going to be	forming
you	are	going to be	forming
he/she/it	is	going to be	forming
we	are	going to be	forming
you	are	going to be	forming
they	are	going to be	forming

Future Perfect
I	will have been	forming
you	will have been	forming
he/she/it	will have been	forming
we	will have been	forming
you	will have been	forming
they	will have been	forming

Conditional
I	would	form
you	would	form
he/she/it	would	form
we	would	form
you	would	form
they	would	form

Conditional Past
I	would have	formed
you	would have	formed
he/she/it	would have	formed
we	would have	formed
you	would have	formed
they	would have	formed

forsake

- forsook - forsaken

verlassen

+ **-ing** → ~~e~~
Unregelmäßiges Verb

Simple tenses

Present

I	forsake
you	forsake
he/she/it	forsakes
we	forsake
you	forsake
they	forsake

Past

I	forsook
you	forsook
he/she/it	forsook
we	forsook
you	forsook
they	forsook

Present Perfect

I	have	forsaken
you	have	forsaken
he/she/it	has	forsaken
we	have	forsaken
you	have	forsaken
they	have	forsaken

Past Perfect

I	had	forsaken
you	had	forsaken
he/she/it	had	forsaken
we	had	forsaken
you	had	forsaken
they	had	forsaken

Will-Future

I	will	forsake
you	will	forsake
he/she/it	will	forsake
we	will	forsake
you	will	forsake
they	will	forsake

Going to-Future

I	am	going to	forsake
you	are	going to	forsake
he/she/it	is	going to	forsake
we	are	going to	forsake
you	are	going to	forsake
they	are	going to	forsake

Future Perfect

I	will have	forsaken
you	will have	forsaken
he/she/it	will have	forsaken
we	will have	forsaken
you	will have	forsaken
they	will have	forsaken

Imperative

forsake

Impersonal

ing-Form

forsaking

Past Participle

forsaken

Continuous tenses

Present

I	am	forsaking
you	are	forsaking
he/she/it	is	forsaking
we	are	forsaking
you	are	forsaking
they	are	forsaking

Past

I	was	forsaking
you	were	forsaking
he/she/it	was	forsaking
we	were	forsaking
you	were	forsaking
they	were	forsaking

Present Perfect

I	have been	forsaking
you	have been	forsaking
he/she/it	has been	forsaking
we	have been	forsaking
you	have been	forsaking
they	have been	forsaking

Past Perfect

I	had been	forsaking
you	had been	forsaking
he/she/it	had been	forsaking
we	had been	forsaking
you	had been	forsaking
they	had been	forsaking

Will-Future

I	will be	forsaking
you	will be	forsaking
he/she/it	will be	forsaking
we	will be	forsaking
you	will be	forsaking
they	will be	forsaking

Going to-Future

I	am	going to be	forsaking
you	are	going to be	forsaking
he/she/it	is	going to be	forsaking
we	are	going to be	forsaking
you	are	going to be	forsaking
they	are	going to be	forsaking

Future Perfect

I	will have been	forsaking
you	will have been	forsaking
he/she/it	will have been	forsaking
we	will have been	forsaking
you	will have been	forsaking
they	will have been	forsaking

Conditional

I	would	forsake
you	would	forsake
he/she/it	would	forsake
we	would	forsake
you	would	forsake
they	would	forsake

Conditional Past

I	would have	forsaken
you	would have	forsaken
he/she/it	would have	forsaken
we	would have	forsaken
you	would have	forsaken
they	would have	forsaken

freeze
- froze - frozen

Simple tenses

Present

I	freeze
you	freeze
he/she/it	freezes
we	freeze
you	freeze
they	freeze

Past

I	froze
you	froze
he/she/it	froze
we	froze
you	froze
they	froze

Present Perfect

I	have	frozen
you	have	frozen
he/she/it	has	frozen
we	have	frozen
you	have	frozen
they	have	frozen

Past Perfect

I	had	frozen
you	had	frozen
he/she/it	had	frozen
we	had	frozen
you	had	frozen
they	had	frozen

Will-Future

I	will	freeze
you	will	freeze
he/she/it	will	freeze
we	will	freeze
you	will	freeze
they	will	freeze

Going to-Future

I	am	going to	freeze
you	are	going to	freeze
he/she/it	is	going to	freeze
we	are	going to	freeze
you	are	going to	freeze
they	are	going to	freeze

Future Perfect

I	will have	frozen
you	will have	frozen
he/she/it	will have	frozen
we	will have	frozen
you	will have	frozen
they	will have	frozen

Imperative

freeze

Impersonal

ing-Form

freezing

Past Participle

frozen

Continuous tenses

Present

I	am	freezing
you	are	freezing
he/she/it	is	freezing
we	are	freezing
you	are	freezing
they	are	freezing

Past

I	was	freezing
you	were	freezing
he/she/it	was	freezing
we	were	freezing
you	were	freezing
they	were	freezing

Present Perfect

I	have	been	freezing
you	have	been	freezing
he/she/it	has	been	freezing
we	have	been	freezing
you	have	been	freezing
they	have	been	freezing

Past Perfect

I	had been	freezing
you	had been	freezing
he/she/it	had been	freezing
we	had been	freezing
you	had been	freezing
they	had been	freezing

Will-Future

I	will be	freezing
you	will be	freezing
he/she/it	will be	freezing
we	will be	freezing
you	will be	freezing
they	will be	freezing

Going to-Future

I	am	going to be	freezing
you	are	going to be	freezing
he/she/it	is	going to be	freezing
we	are	going to be	freezing
you	are	going to be	freezing
they	are	going to be	freezing

Future Perfect

I	will have been	freezing
you	will have been	freezing
he/she/it	will have been	freezing
we	will have been	freezing
you	will have been	freezing
they	will have been	freezing

Conditional

I	would	freeze
you	would	freeze
he/she/it	would	freeze
we	would	freeze
you	would	freeze
they	would	freeze

Conditional Past

I	would have	frozen
you	would have	frozen
he/she/it	would have	frozen
we	would have	frozen
you	would have	frozen
they	would have	frozen

gain

gewinnen

Regelmäßiges Verb

Simple tenses

Present

I	gain
you	gain
he/she/it	gains
we	gain
you	gain
they	gain

Past

I	gained
you	gained
he/she/it	gained
we	gained
you	gained
they	gained

Present Perfect

I	have	gained
you	have	gained
he/she/it	has	gained
we	have	gained
you	have	gained
they	have	gained

Past Perfect

I	had	gained
you	had	gained
he/she/it	had	gained
we	had	gained
you	had	gained
they	had	gained

Will-Future

I	will	gain
you	will	gain
he/she/it	will	gain
we	will	gain
you	will	gain
they	will	gain

Going to-Future

I	am	going to	gain
you	are	going to	gain
he/she/it	is	going to	gain
we	are	going to	gain
you	are	going to	gain
they	are	going to	gain

Future Perfect

I	will have	gained
you	will have	gained
he/she/it	will have	gained
we	will have	gained
you	will have	gained
they	will have	gained

Imperative

gain

Impersonal

ing-Form

gaining

Past Participle

gained

Continuous tenses

Present

I	am	gaining
you	are	gaining
he/she/it	is	gaining
we	are	gaining
you	are	gaining
they	are	gaining

Past

I	was	gaining
you	were	gaining
he/she/it	was	gaining
we	were	gaining
you	were	gaining
they	were	gaining

Present Perfect

I	have been	gaining
you	have been	gaining
he/she/it	has been	gaining
we	have been	gaining
you	have been	gaining
they	have been	gaining

Past Perfect

I	had been	gaining
you	had been	gaining
he/she/it	had been	gaining
we	had been	gaining
you	had been	gaining
they	had been	gaining

Will-Future

I	will be	gaining
you	will be	gaining
he/she/it	will be	gaining
we	will be	gaining
you	will be	gaining
they	will be	gaining

Going to-Future

I	am	going to be	gaining
you	are	going to be	gaining
he/she/it	is	going to be	gaining
we	are	going to be	gaining
you	are	going to be	gaining
they	are	going to be	gaining

Future Perfect

I	will have been	gaining
you	will have been	gaining
he/she/it	will have been	gaining
we	will have been	gaining
you	will have been	gaining
they	will have been	gaining

Conditional

I	would	gain
you	would	gain
he/she/it	would	gain
we	would	gain
you	would	gain
they	would	gain

Conditional Past

I	would have	gained
you	would have	gained
he/she/it	would have	gained
we	would have	gained
you	would have	gained
they	would have	gained

Im AE ist das Partizip Perfekt *gotten.* /
Konsonantenverdopplung
Unregelmäßiges Verb

bekommen

get
- got - got

Simple tenses

Present

I	get
you	get
he/she/it	gets
we	get
you	get
they	get

Past

I	got
you	got
he/she/it	got
we	got
you	got
they	got

Present Perfect

I	have	got
you	have	got
he/she/it	has	got
we	have	got
you	have	got
they	have	got

Past Perfect

I	had	got
you	had	got
he/she/it	had	got
we	had	got
you	had	got
they	had	got

Will-Future

I	will	get
you	will	get
he/she/it	will	get
we	will	get
you	will	get
they	will	get

Going to-Future

I	am	going to	get
you	are	going to	get
he/she/it	is	going to	get
we	are	going to	get
you	are	going to	get
they	are	going to	get

Future Perfect

I	will have	got
you	will have	got
he/she/it	will have	got
we	will have	got
you	will have	got
they	will have	got

Imperative

get

Impersonal

ing-Form

getting

Past Participle

got

Continuous tenses

Present

I	am	getting
you	are	getting
he/she/it	is	getting
we	are	getting
you	are	getting
they	are	getting

Past

I	was	getting
you	were	getting
he/she/it	was	getting
we	were	getting
you	were	getting
they	were	getting

Present Perfect

I	have been	getting
you	have been	getting
he/she/it	has been	getting
we	have been	getting
you	have been	getting
they	have been	getting

Past Perfect

I	had been	getting
you	had been	getting
he/she/it	had been	getting
we	had been	getting
you	had been	getting
they	had been	getting

Will-Future

I	will be	getting
you	will be	getting
he/she/it	will be	getting
we	will be	getting
you	will be	getting
they	will be	getting

Going to-Future

I	am	going to be	getting
you	are	going to be	getting
he/she/it	is	going to be	getting
we	are	going to be	getting
you	are	going to be	getting
they	are	going to be	getting

Future Perfect

I	will have been	getting
you	will have been	getting
he/she/it	will have been	getting
we	will have been	getting
you	will have been	getting
they	will have been	getting

Conditional

I	would	get
you	would	get
he/she/it	would	get
we	would	get
you	would	get
they	would	get

Conditional Past

I	would have	got
you	would have	got
he/she/it	would have	got
we	would have	got
you	would have	got
they	would have	got

give

- gave - given

geben

+ -ing → e̸
Unregelmäßiges Verb

Simple tenses

Present

I	give
you	give
he/she/it	gives
we	give
you	give
they	give

Past

I	gave
you	gave
he/she/it	gave
we	gave
you	gave
they	gave

Present Perfect

I	have	given
you	have	given
he/she/it	has	given
we	have	given
you	have	given
they	have	given

Past Perfect

I	had	given
you	had	given
he/she/it	had	given
we	had	given
you	had	given
they	had	given

Will-Future

I	will	give
you	will	give
he/she/it	will	give
we	will	give
you	will	give
they	will	give

Going to-Future

I	am	going to	give
you	are	going to	give
he/she/it	is	going to	give
we	are	going to	give
you	are	going to	give
they	are	going to	give

Future Perfect

I	will have	given
you	will have	given
he/she/it	will have	given
we	will have	given
you	will have	given
they	will have	given

Imperative

give

Impersonal

ing-Form

giving

Past Participle

given

Continuous tenses

Present

I	am	giving
you	are	giving
he/she/it	is	giving
we	are	giving
you	are	giving
they	are	giving

Past

I	was	giving
you	were	giving
he/she/it	was	giving
we	were	giving
you	were	giving
they	were	giving

Present Perfect

I	have been	giving
you	have been	giving
he/she/it	has been	giving
we	have been	giving
you	have been	giving
they	have been	giving

Past Perfect

I	had been	giving
you	had been	giving
he/she/it	had been	giving
we	had been	giving
you	had been	giving
they	had been	giving

Will-Future

I	will be	giving
you	will be	giving
he/she/it	will be	giving
we	will be	giving
you	will be	giving
they	will be	giving

Going to-Future

I	am	going to be	giving
you	are	going to be	giving
he/she/it	is	going to be	giving
we	are	going to be	giving
you	are	going to be	giving
they	are	going to be	giving

Future Perfect

I	will have been	giving
you	will have been	giving
he/she/it	will have been	giving
we	will have been	giving
you	will have been	giving
they	will have been	giving

Conditional

I	would	give
you	would	give
he/she/it	would	give
we	would	give
you	would	give
they	would	give

Conditional Past

I	would have	given
you	would have	given
he/she/it	would have	given
we	would have	given
you	would have	given
they	would have	given

go
– went – gone

Simple tenses

Present

I	go
you	go
he/she/it	goes
we	go
you	go
they	go

Past

I	went
you	went
he/she/it	went
we	went
you	went
they	went

Present Perfect

I	have	gone
you	have	gone
he/she/it	has	gone
we	have	gone
you	have	gone
they	have	gone

Past Perfect

I	had	gone
you	had	gone
he/she/it	had	gone
we	had	gone
you	had	gone
they	had	gone

Will-Future

I	will	go
you	will	go
he/she/it	will	go
we	will	go
you	will	go
they	will	go

Going to-Future

I	am	going to	go
you	are	going to	go
he/she/it	is	going to	go
we	are	going to	go
you	are	going to	go
they	are	going to	go

Future Perfect

I	will have	gone
you	will have	gone
he/she/it	will have	gone
we	will have	gone
you	will have	gone
they	will have	gone

Imperative

go

Impersonal

ing-Form

going

Past Participle

gone

Continuous tenses

Present

I	am	going
you	are	going
he/she/it	is	going
we	are	going
you	are	going
they	are	going

Past

I	was	going
you	were	going
he/she/it	was	going
we	were	going
you	were	going
they	were	going

Present Perfect

I	have been	going
you	have been	going
he/she/it	has been	going
we	have been	going
you	have been	going
they	have been	going

Past Perfect

I	had been	going
you	had been	going
he/she/it	had been	going
we	had been	going
you	had been	going
they	had been	going

Will-Future

I	will be	going
you	will be	going
he/she/it	will be	going
we	will be	going
you	will be	going
they	will be	going

Going to-Future

I	am	going to be	going
you	are	going to be	going
he/she/it	is	going to be	going
we	are	going to be	going
you	are	going to be	going
they	are	going to be	going

Future Perfect

I	will have been	going
you	will have been	going
he/she/it	will have been	going
we	will have been	going
you	will have been	going
they	will have been	going

Conditional

I	would	go
you	would	go
he/she/it	would	go
we	would	go
you	would	go
they	would	go

Conditional Past

I	would have	gone
you	would have	gone
he/she/it	would have	gone
we	would have	gone
you	would have	gone
they	would have	gone

govern

regieren

Regelmäßiges Verb

Simple tenses

Present

I	govern
you	govern
he/she/it	governs
we	govern
you	govern
they	govern

Past

I	governed
you	governed
he/she/it	governed
we	governed
you	governed
they	governed

Present Perfect

I	have	governed
you	have	governed
he/she/it	has	governed
we	have	governed
you	have	governed
they	have	governed

Past Perfect

I	had	governed
you	had	governed
he/she/it	had	governed
we	had	governed
you	had	governed
they	had	governed

Will-Future

I	will	govern
you	will	govern
he/she/it	will	govern
we	will	govern
you	will	govern
they	will	govern

Going to-Future

I	am	going to	govern
you	are	going to	govern
he/she/it	is	going to	govern
we	are	going to	govern
you	are	going to	govern
they	are	going to	govern

Future Perfect

I	will have	governed
you	will have	governed
he/she/it	will have	governed
we	will have	governed
you	will have	governed
they	will have	governed

Imperative

govern

Impersonal

ing-Form

governing

Past Participle

governed

Continuous tenses

Present

I	am	governing
you	are	governing
he/she/it	is	governing
we	are	governing
you	are	governing
they	are	governing

Past

I	was	governing
you	were	governing
he/she/it	was	governing
we	were	governing
you	were	governing
they	were	governing

Present Perfect

I	have been	governing
you	have been	governing
he/she/it	has been	governing
we	have been	governing
you	have been	governing
they	have been	governing

Past Perfect

I	had been	governing
you	had been	governing
he/she/it	had been	governing
we	had been	governing
you	had been	governing
they	had been	governing

Will-Future

I	will be	governing
you	will be	governing
he/she/it	will be	governing
we	will be	governing
you	will be	governing
they	will be	governing

Going to-Future

I	am	going to be	governing
you	are	going to be	governing
he/she/it	is	going to be	governing
we	are	going to be	governing
you	are	going to be	governing
they	are	going to be	governing

Future Perfect

I	will have been	governing
you	will have been	governing
he/she/it	will have been	governing
we	will have been	governing
you	will have been	governing
they	will have been	governing

Conditional

I	would	govern
you	would	govern
he/she/it	would	govern
we	would	govern
you	would	govern
they	would	govern

Conditional Past

I	would have	governed
you	would have	governed
he/she/it	would have	governed
we	would have	governed
you	would have	governed
they	would have	governed

schnappen

grab

Simple tenses

Present

I	grab
you	grab
he/she/it	grabs
we	grab
you	grab
they	grab

Past

I	grabbed
you	grabbed
he/she/it	grabbed
we	grabbed
you	grabbed
they	grabbed

Present Perfect

I	have	grabbed
you	have	grabbed
he/she/it	has	grabbed
we	have	grabbed
you	have	grabbed
they	have	grabbed

Past Perfect

I	had	grabbed
you	had	grabbed
he/she/it	had	grabbed
we	had	grabbed
you	had	grabbed
they	had	grabbed

Will-Future

I	will	grab
you	will	grab
he/she/it	will	grab
we	will	grab
you	will	grab
they	will	grab

Going to-Future

I	am	going to	grab
you	are	going to	grab
he/she/it	is	going to	grab
we	are	going to	grab
you	are	going to	grab
they	are	going to	grab

Future Perfect

I	will have	grabbed
you	will have	grabbed
he/she/it	will have	grabbed
we	will have	grabbed
you	will have	grabbed
they	will have	grabbed

Imperative

grab

Impersonal

ing-Form

grabbing

Past Participle

grabbed

Continuous tenses

Present

I	am	grabbing
you	are	grabbing
he/she/it	is	grabbing
we	are	grabbing
you	are	grabbing
they	are	grabbing

Past

I	was	grabbing
you	were	grabbing
he/she/it	was	grabbing
we	were	grabbing
you	were	grabbing
they	were	grabbing

Present Perfect

I	have been	grabbing
you	have been	grabbing
he/she/it	has been	grabbing
we	have been	grabbing
you	have been	grabbing
they	have been	grabbing

Past Perfect

I	had been	grabbing
you	had been	grabbing
he/she/it	had been	grabbing
we	had been	grabbing
you	had been	grabbing
they	had been	grabbing

Will-Future

I	will be	grabbing
you	will be	grabbing
he/she/it	will be	grabbing
we	will be	grabbing
you	will be	grabbing
they	will be	grabbing

Going to-Future

I	am	going to be	grabbing
you	are	going to be	grabbing
he/she/it	is	going to be	grabbing
we	are	going to be	grabbing
you	are	going to be	grabbing
they	are	going to be	grabbing

Future Perfect

I	will have been	grabbing
you	will have been	grabbing
he/she/it	will have been	grabbing
we	will have been	grabbing
you	will have been	grabbing
they	will have been	grabbing

Conditional

I	would	grab
you	would	grab
he/she/it	would	grab
we	would	grab
you	would	grab
they	would	grab

Conditional Past

I	would have	grabbed
you	would have	grabbed
he/she/it	would have	grabbed
we	would have	grabbed
you	would have	grabbed
they	would have	grabbed

grant

gewähren

Regelmäßiges Verb

Simple tenses

Present

I	grant
you	grant
he/she/it	grants
we	grant
you	grant
they	grant

Past

I	granted
you	granted
he/she/it	granted
we	granted
you	granted
they	granted

Present Perfect

I	have	granted
you	have	granted
he/she/it	has	granted
we	have	granted
you	have	granted
they	have	granted

Past Perfect

I	had	granted
you	had	granted
he/she/it	had	granted
we	had	granted
you	had	granted
they	had	granted

Will-Future

I	will	grant
you	will	grant
he/she/it	will	grant
we	will	grant
you	will	grant
they	will	grant

Going to-Future

I	am	going to	grant
you	are	going to	grant
he/she/it	is	going to	grant
we	are	going to	grant
you	are	going to	grant
they	are	going to	grant

Future Perfect

I	will have	granted
you	will have	granted
he/she/it	will have	granted
we	will have	granted
you	will have	granted
they	will have	granted

Imperative

grant

Impersonal

ing-Form

granting

Past Participle

granted

Continuous tenses

Present

I	am	granting
you	are	granting
he/she/it	is	granting
we	are	granting
you	are	granting
they	are	granting

Past

I	was	granting
you	were	granting
he/she/it	was	granting
we	were	granting
you	were	granting
they	were	granting

Present Perfect

I	have been	granting
you	have been	granting
he/she/it	has been	granting
we	have been	granting
you	have been	granting
they	have been	granting

Past Perfect

I	had been	granting
you	had been	granting
he/she/it	had been	granting
we	had been	granting
you	had been	granting
they	had been	granting

Will-Future

I	will be	granting
you	will be	granting
he/she/it	will be	granting
we	will be	granting
you	will be	granting
they	will be	granting

Going to-Future

I	am	going to be	granting
you	are	going to be	granting
he/she/it	is	going to be	granting
we	are	going to be	granting
you	are	going to be	granting
they	are	going to be	granting

Future Perfect

I	will have been	granting
you	will have been	granting
he/she/it	will have been	granting
we	will have been	granting
you	will have been	granting
they	will have been	granting

Conditional

I	would	grant
you	would	grant
he/she/it	would	grant
we	would	grant
you	would	grant
they	would	grant

Conditional Past

I	would have	granted
you	would have	granted
he/she/it	would have	granted
we	would have	granted
you	would have	granted
they	would have	granted

grind
- ground - ground

Simple tenses

Present

I	grind
you	grind
he/she/it	grinds
we	grind
you	grind
they	grind

Past

I	ground
you	ground
he/she/it	ground
we	ground
you	ground
they	ground

Present Perfect

I	have	ground
you	have	ground
he/she/it	has	ground
we	have	ground
you	have	ground
they	have	ground

Past Perfect

I	had	ground
you	had	ground
he/she/it	had	ground
we	had	ground
you	had	ground
they	had	ground

Will-Future

I	will	grind
you	will	grind
he/she/it	will	grind
we	will	grind
you	will	grind
they	will	grind

Going to-Future

I	am	going to	grind
you	are	going to	grind
he/she/it	is	going to	grind
we	are	going to	grind
you	are	going to	grind
they	are	going to	grind

Future Perfect

I	will have	ground
you	will have	ground
he/she/it	will have	ground
we	will have	ground
you	will have	ground
they	will have	ground

Imperative

grind

Impersonal

ing-Form

grinding

Past Participle

ground

Continuous tenses

Present

I	am	grinding
you	are	grinding
he/she/it	is	grinding
we	are	grinding
you	are	grinding
they	are	grinding

Past

I	was	grinding
you	were	grinding
he/she/it	was	grinding
we	were	grinding
you	were	grinding
they	were	grinding

Present Perfect

I	have been	grinding
you	have been	grinding
he/she/it	has been	grinding
we	have been	grinding
you	have been	grinding
they	have been	grinding

Past Perfect

I	had been	grinding
you	had been	grinding
he/she/it	had been	grinding
we	had been	grinding
you	had been	grinding
they	had been	grinding

Will-Future

I	will be	grinding
you	will be	grinding
he/she/it	will be	grinding
we	will be	grinding
you	will be	grinding
they	will be	grinding

Going to-Future

I	am	going to be	grinding
you	are	going to be	grinding
he/she/it	is	going to be	grinding
we	are	going to be	grinding
you	are	going to be	grinding
they	are	going to be	grinding

Future Perfect

I	will have been	grinding
you	will have been	grinding
he/she/it	will have been	grinding
we	will have been	grinding
you	will have been	grinding
they	will have been	grinding

Conditional

I	would	grind
you	would	grind
he/she/it	would	grind
we	would	grind
you	would	grind
they	would	grind

Conditional Past

I	would have	ground
you	would have	ground
he/she/it	would have	ground
we	would have	ground
you	would have	ground
they	would have	ground

grow
- grew - grown

wachsen

Unregelmäßiges Verb

Simple tenses

Present

I	grow
you	grow
he/she/it	grows
we	grow
you	grow
they	grow

Past

I	grew
you	grew
he/she/it	grew
we	grew
you	grew
they	grew

Present Perfect

I	have	grown
you	have	grown
he/she/it	has	grown
we	have	grown
you	have	grown
they	have	grown

Past Perfect

I	had	grown
you	had	grown
he/she/it	had	grown
we	had	grown
you	had	grown
they	had	grown

Will-Future

I	will	grow
you	will	grow
he/she/it	will	grow
we	will	grow
you	will	grow
they	will	grow

Going to-Future

I	am	going to	grow
you	are	going to	grow
he/she/it	is	going to	grow
we	are	going to	grow
you	are	going to	grow
they	are	going to	grow

Future Perfect

I	will have	grown
you	will have	grown
he/she/it	will have	grown
we	will have	grown
you	will have	grown
they	will have	grown

Imperative

grow

Impersonal

ing-Form

growing

Past Participle

grown

Continuous tenses

Present

I	am	growing
you	are	growing
he/she/it	is	growing
we	are	growing
you	are	growing
they	are	growing

Past

I	was	growing
you	were	growing
he/she/it	was	growing
we	were	growing
you	were	growing
they	were	growing

Present Perfect

I	have been	growing
you	have been	growing
he/she/it	has been	growing
we	have been	growing
you	have been	growing
they	have been	growing

Past Perfect

I	had been	growing
you	had been	growing
he/she/it	had been	growing
we	had been	growing
you	had been	growing
they	had been	growing

Will-Future

I	will be	growing
you	will be	growing
he/she/it	will be	growing
we	will be	growing
you	will be	growing
they	will be	growing

Going to-Future

I	am	going to be	growing
you	are	going to be	growing
he/she/it	is	going to be	growing
we	are	going to be	growing
you	are	going to be	growing
they	are	going to be	growing

Future Perfect

I	will have been	growing
you	will have been	growing
he/she/it	will have been	growing
we	will have been	growing
you	will have been	growing
they	will have been	growing

Conditional

I	would	grow
you	would	grow
he/she/it	would	grow
we	would	grow
you	would	grow
they	would	grow

Conditional Past

I	would have	grown
you	would have	grown
he/she/it	would have	grown
we	would have	grown
you	would have	grown
they	would have	grown

Simple tenses

Present

I	guarantee
you	guarantee
he/she/it	guarantees
we	guarantee
you	guarantee
they	guarantee

Past

I	guaranteed
you	guaranteed
he/she/it	guaranteed
we	guaranteed
you	guaranteed
they	guaranteed

Present Perfect

I	have	guaranteed
you	have	guaranteed
he/she/it	has	guaranteed
we	have	guaranteed
you	have	guaranteed
they	have	guaranteed

Past Perfect

I	had	guaranteed
you	had	guaranteed
he/she/it	had	guaranteed
we	had	guaranteed
you	had	guaranteed
they	had	guaranteed

Will-Future

I	will	guarantee
you	will	guarantee
he/she/it	will	guarantee
we	will	guarantee
you	will	guarantee
they	will	guarantee

Going to-Future

I	am	going to	guarantee
you	are	going to	guarantee
he/she/it	is	going to	guarantee
we	are	going to	guarantee
you	are	going to	guarantee
they	are	going to	guarantee

Future Perfect

I	will have	guaranteed
you	will have	guaranteed
he/she/it	will have	guaranteed
we	will have	guaranteed
you	will have	guaranteed
they	will have	guaranteed

Imperative

guarantee

Impersonal

ing-Form

guaranteeing

Past Participle

guaranteed

Continuous tenses

Present

I	am	guaranteeing
you	are	guaranteeing
he/she/it	is	guaranteeing
we	are	guaranteeing
you	are	guaranteeing
they	are	guaranteeing

Past

I	was	guaranteeing
you	were	guaranteeing
he/she/it	was	guaranteeing
we	were	guaranteeing
you	were	guaranteeing
they	were	guaranteeing

Present Perfect

I	have been	guaranteeing
you	have been	guaranteeing
he/she/it	has been	guaranteeing
we	have been	guaranteeing
you	have been	guaranteeing
they	have been	guaranteeing

Past Perfect

I	had been	guaranteeing
you	had been	guaranteeing
he/she/it	had been	guaranteeing
we	had been	guaranteeing
you	had been	guaranteeing
they	had been	guaranteeing

Will-Future

I	will be	guaranteeing
you	will be	guaranteeing
he/she/it	will be	guaranteeing
we	will be	guaranteeing
you	will be	guaranteeing
they	will be	guaranteeing

Going to-Future

I	am	going to be	guaranteeing
you	are	going to be	guaranteeing
he/she/it	is	going to be	guaranteeing
we	are	going to be	guaranteeing
you	are	going to be	guaranteeing
they	are	going to be	guaranteeing

Future Perfect

I	will have been	guaranteeing
you	will have been	guaranteeing
he/she/it	will have been	guaranteeing
we	will have been	guaranteeing
you	will have been	guaranteeing
they	will have been	guaranteeing

Conditional

I	would	guarantee
you	would	guarantee
he/she/it	would	guarantee
we	would	guarantee
you	would	guarantee
they	would	guarantee

Conditional Past

I	would have	guaranteed
you	would have	guaranteed
he/she/it	would have	guaranteed
we	would have	guaranteed
you	would have	guaranteed
they	would have	guaranteed

guard

bewachen

Regelmäßiges Verb

Simple tenses

Present

I	guard
you	guard
he/she/it	guards
we	guard
you	guard
they	guard

Past

I	guarded
you	guarded
he/she/it	guarded
we	guarded
you	guarded
they	guarded

Present Perfect

I	have	guarded
you	have	guarded
he/she/it	has	guarded
we	have	guarded
you	have	guarded
they	have	guarded

Past Perfect

I	had	guarded
you	had	guarded
he/she/it	had	guarded
we	had	guarded
you	had	guarded
they	had	guarded

Will-Future

I	will	guard
you	will	guard
he/she/it	will	guard
we	will	guard
you	will	guard
they	will	guard

Going to-Future

I	am	going to	guard
you	are	going to	guard
he/she/it	is	going to	guard
we	are	going to	guard
you	are	going to	guard
they	are	going to	guard

Future Perfect

I	will have	guarded
you	will have	guarded
he/she/it	will have	guarded
we	will have	guarded
you	will have	guarded
they	will have	guarded

Imperative

guard

Impersonal

ing-Form

guarding

Past Participle

guarded

Continuous tenses

Present

I	am	guarding
you	are	guarding
he/she/it	is	guarding
we	are	guarding
you	are	guarding
they	are	guarding

Past

I	was	guarding
you	were	guarding
he/she/it	was	guarding
we	were	guarding
you	were	guarding
they	were	guarding

Present Perfect

I	have been	guarding
you	have been	guarding
he/she/it	has been	guarding
we	have been	guarding
you	have been	guarding
they	have been	guarding

Past Perfect

I	had been	guarding
you	had been	guarding
he/she/it	had been	guarding
we	had been	guarding
you	had been	guarding
they	had been	guarding

Will-Future

I	will be	guarding
you	will be	guarding
he/she/it	will be	guarding
we	will be	guarding
you	will be	guarding
they	will be	guarding

Going to-Future

I	am	going to be	guarding
you	are	going to be	guarding
he/she/it	is	going to be	guarding
we	are	going to be	guarding
you	are	going to be	guarding
they	are	going to be	guarding

Future Perfect

I	will have been	guarding
you	will have been	guarding
he/she/it	will have been	guarding
we	will have been	guarding
you	will have been	guarding
they	will have been	guarding

Conditional

I	would	guard
you	would	guard
he/she/it	would	guard
we	would	guard
you	would	guard
they	would	guard

Conditional Past

I	would have	guarded
you	would have	guarded
he/she/it	would have	guarded
we	would have	guarded
you	would have	guarded
they	would have	guarded

Simple tenses

Present

I	guess
you	guess
he/she/it	guesses
we	guess
you	guess
they	guess

Past

I	guessed
you	guessed
he/she/it	guessed
we	guessed
you	guessed
they	guessed

Present Perfect

I	have	guessed
you	have	guessed
he/she/it	has	guessed
we	have	guessed
you	have	guessed
they	have	guessed

Past Perfect

I	had	guessed
you	had	guessed
he/she/it	had	guessed
we	had	guessed
you	had	guessed
they	had	guessed

Will-Future

I	will	guess
you	will	guess
he/she/it	will	guess
we	will	guess
you	will	guess
they	will	guess

Going to-Future

I	am	going to	guess
you	are	going to	guess
he/she/it	is	going to	guess
we	are	going to	guess
you	are	going to	guess
they	are	going to	guess

Future Perfect

I	will have	guessed
you	will have	guessed
he/she/it	will have	guessed
we	will have	guessed
you	will have	guessed
they	will have	guessed

Imperative

guess

Impersonal

ing-Form

guessing

Past Participle

guessed

Continuous tenses

Present

I	am	guessing
you	are	guessing
he/she/it	is	guessing
we	are	guessing
you	are	guessing
they	are	guessing

Past

I	was	guessing
you	were	guessing
he/she/it	was	guessing
we	were	guessing
you	were	guessing
they	were	guessing

Present Perfect

I	have	been	guessing
you	have	been	guessing
he/she/it	has	been	guessing
we	have	been	guessing
you	have	been	guessing
they	have	been	guessing

Past Perfect

I	had been	guessing
you	had been	guessing
he/she/it	had been	guessing
we	had been	guessing
you	had been	guessing
they	had been	guessing

Will-Future

I	will be	guessing
you	will be	guessing
he/she/it	will be	guessing
we	will be	guessing
you	will be	guessing
they	will be	guessing

Going to-Future

I	am	going to be	guessing
you	are	going to be	guessing
he/she/it	is	going to be	guessing
we	are	going to be	guessing
you	are	going to be	guessing
they	are	going to be	guessing

Future Perfect

I	will have been	guessing
you	will have been	guessing
he/she/it	will have been	guessing
we	will have been	guessing
you	will have been	guessing
they	will have been	guessing

Conditional

I	would	guess
you	would	guess
he/she/it	would	guess
we	would	guess
you	would	guess
they	would	guess

Conditional Past

I	would have	guessed
you	would have	guessed
he/she/it	would have	guessed
we	would have	guessed
you	would have	guessed
they	would have	guessed

guide

führen

+ **-ing** → ~~e~~ / + **-d** nicht **-ed**
Regelmäßiges Verb

Simple tenses

Present

I	guide
you	guide
he/she/it	guides
we	guide
you	guide
they	guide

Past

I	guided
you	guided
he/she/it	guided
we	guided
you	guided
they	guided

Present Perfect

I	have	guided
you	have	guided
he/she/it	has	guided
we	have	guided
you	have	guided
they	have	guided

Past Perfect

I	had	guided
you	had	guided
he/she/it	had	guided
we	had	guided
you	had	guided
they	had	guided

Will-Future

I	will	guide
you	will	guide
he/she/it	will	guide
we	will	guide
you	will	guide
they	will	guide

Going to-Future

I	am	going to	guide
you	are	going to	guide
he/she/it	is	going to	guide
we	are	going to	guide
you	are	going to	guide
they	are	going to	guide

Future Perfect

I	will have	guided
you	will have	guided
he/she/it	will have	guided
we	will have	guided
you	will have	guided
they	will have	guided

Imperative

guide

Impersonal

ing-Form

guiding

Past Participle

guided

Continuous tenses

Present

I	am	guiding
you	are	guiding
he/she/it	is	guiding
we	are	guiding
you	are	guiding
they	are	guiding

Past

I	was	guiding
you	were	guiding
he/she/it	was	guiding
we	were	guiding
you	were	guiding
they	were	guiding

Present Perfect

I	have been	guiding
you	have been	guiding
he/she/it	has been	guiding
we	have been	guiding
you	have been	guiding
they	have been	guiding

Past Perfect

I	had been	guiding
you	had been	guiding
he/she/it	had been	guiding
we	had been	guiding
you	had been	guiding
they	had been	guiding

Will-Future

I	will be	guiding
you	will be	guiding
he/she/it	will be	guiding
we	will be	guiding
you	will be	guiding
they	will be	guiding

Going to-Future

I	am	going to be	guiding
you	are	going to be	guiding
he/she/it	is	going to be	guiding
we	are	going to be	guiding
you	are	going to be	guiding
they	are	going to be	guiding

Future Perfect

I	will have been	guiding
you	will have been	guiding
he/she/it	will have been	guiding
we	will have been	guiding
you	will have been	guiding
they	will have been	guiding

Conditional

I	would	guide
you	would	guide
he/she/it	would	guide
we	would	guide
you	would	guide
they	would	guide

Conditional Past

I	would have	guided
you	would have	guided
he/she/it	would have	guided
we	would have	guided
you	would have	guided
they	would have	guided

+ **-ing** → ~~e~~ / + **-d** nicht **-ed**
Regelmäßiges Verb

bewältigen

handle

Simple tenses

Present

I	handle
you	handle
he/she/it	handles
we	handle
you	handle
they	handle

Past

I	handled
you	handled
he/she/it	handled
we	handled
you	handled
they	handled

Present Perfect

I	have	handled
you	have	handled
he/she/it	has	handled
we	have	handled
you	have	handled
they	have	handled

Past Perfect

I	had	handled
you	had	handled
he/she/it	had	handled
we	had	handled
you	had	handled
they	had	handled

Will-Future

I	will	handle
you	will	handle
he/she/it	will	handle
we	will	handle
you	will	handle
they	will	handle

Going to-Future

I	am	going to	handle
you	are	going to	handle
he/she/it	is	going to	handle
we	are	going to	handle
you	are	going to	handle
they	are	going to	handle

Future Perfect

I	will have	handled
you	will have	handled
he/she/it	will have	handled
we	will have	handled
you	will have	handled
they	will have	handled

Imperative

handle

Impersonal

ing-Form

handling

Past Participle

handled

Continuous tenses

Present

I	am	handling
you	are	handling
he/she/it	is	handling
we	are	handling
you	are	handling
they	are	handling

Past

I	was	handling
you	were	handling
he/she/it	was	handling
we	were	handling
you	were	handling
they	were	handling

Present Perfect

I	have been	handling
you	have been	handling
he/she/it	has been	handling
we	have been	handling
you	have been	handling
they	have been	handling

Past Perfect

I	had been	handling
you	had been	handling
he/she/it	had been	handling
we	had been	handling
you	had been	handling
they	had been	handling

Will-Future

I	will be	handling
you	will be	handling
he/she/it	will be	handling
we	will be	handling
you	will be	handling
they	will be	handling

Going to-Future

I	am	going to be	handling
you	are	going to be	handling
he/she/it	is	going to be	handling
we	are	going to be	handling
you	are	going to be	handling
they	are	going to be	handling

Future Perfect

I	will have been	handling
you	will have been	handling
he/she/it	will have been	handling
we	will have been	handling
you	will have been	handling
they	will have been	handling

Conditional

I	would	handle
you	would	handle
he/she/it	would	handle
we	would	handle
you	would	handle
they	would	handle

Conditional Past

I	would have	handled
you	would have	handled
he/she/it	would have	handled
we	would have	handled
you	would have	handled
they	would have	handled

hang

- hung - hung

aufhängen

Unregelmäßiges Verb

Simple tenses

Present

I	hang
you	hang
he/she/it	hangs
we	hang
you	hang
they	hang

Past

I	hung
you	hung
he/she/it	hung
we	hung
you	hung
they	hung

Present Perfect

I	have	hung
you	have	hung
he/she/it	has	hung
we	have	hung
you	have	hung
they	have	hung

Past Perfect

I	had	hung
you	had	hung
he/she/it	had	hung
we	had	hung
you	had	hung
they	had	hung

Will-Future

I	will	hang
you	will	hang
he/she/it	will	hang
we	will	hang
you	will	hang
they	will	hang

Going to-Future

I	am	going to	hang
you	are	going to	hang
he/she/it	is	going to	hang
we	are	going to	hang
you	are	going to	hang
they	are	going to	hang

Future Perfect

I	will have	hung
you	will have	hung
he/she/it	will have	hung
we	will have	hung
you	will have	hung
they	will have	hung

Imperative

hang

Impersonal

ing-Form

hanging

Past Participle

hung

Continuous tenses

Present

I	am	hanging
you	are	hanging
he/she/it	is	hanging
we	are	hanging
you	are	hanging
they	are	hanging

Past

I	was	hanging
you	were	hanging
he/she/it	was	hanging
we	were	hanging
you	were	hanging
they	were	hanging

Present Perfect

I	have been	hanging
you	have been	hanging
he/she/it	has been	hanging
we	have been	hanging
you	have been	hanging
they	have been	hanging

Past Perfect

I	had been	hanging
you	had been	hanging
he/she/it	had been	hanging
we	had been	hanging
you	had been	hanging
they	had been	hanging

Will-Future

I	will be	hanging
you	will be	hanging
he/she/it	will be	hanging
we	will be	hanging
you	will be	hanging
they	will be	hanging

Going to-Future

I	am	going to be	hanging
you	are	going to be	hanging
he/she/it	is	going to be	hanging
we	are	going to be	hanging
you	are	going to be	hanging
they	are	going to be	hanging

Future Perfect

I	will have been	hanging
you	will have been	hanging
he/she/it	will have been	hanging
we	will have been	hanging
you	will have been	hanging
they	will have been	hanging

Conditional

I	would	hang
you	would	hang
he/she/it	would	hang
we	would	hang
you	would	hang
they	would	hang

Conditional Past

I	would have	hung
you	would have	hung
he/she/it	would have	hung
we	would have	hung
you	would have	hung
they	would have	hung

Regelmäßiges Verb

Simple tenses

Present

I	happen
you	happen
he/she/it	happens
we	happen
you	happen
they	happen

Past

I	happened
you	happened
he/she/it	happened
we	happened
you	happened
they	happened

Present Perfect

I	have	happened
you	have	happened
he/she/it	has	happened
we	have	happened
you	have	happened
they	have	happened

Past Perfect

I	had	happened
you	had	happened
he/she/it	had	happened
we	had	happened
you	had	happened
they	had	happened

Will-Future

I	will	happen
you	will	happen
he/she/it	will	happen
we	will	happen
you	will	happen
they	will	happen

Going to-Future

I	am	going to	happen
you	are	going to	happen
he/she/it	is	going to	happen
we	are	going to	happen
you	are	going to	happen
they	are	going to	happen

Future Perfect

I	will have	happened
you	will have	happened
he/she/it	will have	happened
we	will have	happened
you	will have	happened
they	will have	happened

Imperative

happen

Impersonal

ing-Form

happening

Past Participle

happened

Continuous tenses

Present

I	am	happening
you	are	happening
he/she/it	is	happening
we	are	happening
you	are	happening
they	are	happening

Past

I	was	happening
you	were	happening
he/she/it	was	happening
we	were	happening
you	were	happening
they	were	happening

Present Perfect

I	have	been	happening
you	have	been	happening
he/she/it	has	been	happening
we	have	been	happening
you	have	been	happening
they	have	been	happening

Past Perfect

I	had been	happening
you	had been	happening
he/she/it	had been	happening
we	had been	happening
you	had been	happening
they	had been	happening

Will-Future

I	will be	happening
you	will be	happening
he/she/it	will be	happening
we	will be	happening
you	will be	happening
they	will be	happening

Going to-Future

I	am	going to be	happening
you	are	going to be	happening
he/she/it	is	going to be	happening
we	are	going to be	happening
you	are	going to be	happening
they	are	going to be	happening

Future Perfect

I	will have been happening
you	will have been happening
he/she/it	will have been happening
we	will have been happening
you	will have been happening
they	will have been happening

Conditional

I	would	happen
you	would	happen
he/she/it	would	happen
we	would	happen
you	would	happen
they	would	happen

Conditional Past

I	would have	happened
you	would have	happened
he/she/it	would have	happened
we	would have	happened
you	would have	happened
they	would have	happened

hate

hassen

+ **-ing** → ~~e~~ / + **-d** nicht **-ed**
Regelmäßiges Verb

Simple tenses

Present

I	hate
you	hate
he/she/it	hates
we	hate
you	hate
they	hate

Past

I	hated
you	hated
he/she/it	hated
we	hated
you	hated
they	hated

Present Perfect

I	have	hated
you	have	hated
he/she/it	has	hated
we	have	hated
you	have	hated
they	have	hated

Past Perfect

I	had	hated
you	had	hated
he/she/it	had	hated
we	had	hated
you	had	hated
they	had	hated

Will-Future

I	will	hate
you	will	hate
he/she/it	will	hate
we	will	hate
you	will	hate
they	will	hate

Going to-Future

I	am	going to	hate
you	are	going to	hate
he/she/it	is	going to	hate
we	are	going to	hate
you	are	going to	hate
they	are	going to	hate

Future Perfect

I	will have	hated
you	will have	hated
he/she/it	will have	hated
we	will have	hated
you	will have	hated
they	will have	hated

Imperative

hate

Impersonal

ing-Form

hating

Past Participle

hated

Continuous tenses

Present

I	am	hating
you	are	hating
he/she/it	is	hating
we	are	hating
you	are	hating
they	are	hating

Past

I	was	hating
you	were	hating
he/she/it	was	hating
we	were	hating
you	were	hating
they	were	hating

Present Perfect

I	have been	hating
you	have been	hating
he/she/it	has been	hating
we	have been	hating
you	have been	hating
they	have been	hating

Past Perfect

I	had been	hating
you	had been	hating
he/she/it	had been	hating
we	had been	hating
you	had been	hating
they	had been	hating

Will-Future

I	will be	hating
you	will be	hating
he/she/it	will be	hating
we	will be	hating
you	will be	hating
they	will be	hating

Going to-Future

I	am	going to be	hating
you	are	going to be	hating
he/she/it	is	going to be	hating
we	are	going to be	hating
you	are	going to be	hating
they	are	going to be	hating

Future Perfect

I	will have been	hating
you	will have been	hating
he/she/it	will have been	hating
we	will have been	hating
you	will have been	hating
they	will have been	hating

Conditional

I	would	hate
you	would	hate
he/she/it	would	hate
we	would	hate
you	would	hate
they	would	hate

Conditional Past

I	would have	hated
you	would have	hated
he/she/it	would have	hated
we	would have	hated
you	would have	hated
they	would have	hated

Simple tenses

Present

I	have
you	have
he/she/it	has
we	have
you	have
they	have

Past

I	had
you	had
he/she/it	had
we	had
you	had
they	had

Present Perfect

I	have	had
you	have	had
he/she/it	has	had
we	have	had
you	have	had
they	have	had

Past Perfect

I	had	had
you	had	had
he/she/it	had	had
we	had	had
you	had	had
they	had	had

Will-Future

I	will	have
you	will	have
he/she/it	will	have
we	will	have
you	will	have
they	will	have

Going to-Future

I	am	going to	have
you	are	going to	have
he/she/it	is	going to	have
we	are	going to	have
you	are	going to	have
they	are	going to	have

Future Perfect

I	will have	had
you	will have	had
he/she/it	will have	had
we	will have	had
you	will have	had
they	will have	had

Imperative

have

Impersonal

ing-Form

having

Past Participle

had

Continuous tenses

Present

I	am	having
you	are	having
he/she/it	is	having
we	are	having
you	are	having
they	are	having

Past

I	was	having
you	were	having
he/she/it	was	having
we	were	having
you	were	having
they	were	having

Present Perfect

I	have been	having
you	have been	having
he/she/it	has been	having
we	have been	having
you	have been	having
they	have been	having

Past Perfect

I	had been	having
you	had been	having
he/she/it	had been	having
we	had been	having
you	had been	having
they	had been	having

Will-Future

I	will be	having
you	will be	having
he/she/it	will be	having
we	will be	having
you	will be	having
they	will be	having

Going to-Future

I	am	going to be	having
you	are	going to be	having
he/she/it	is	going to be	having
we	are	going to be	having
you	are	going to be	having
they	are	going to be	having

Future Perfect

I	will have been	having
you	will have been	having
he/she/it	will have been	having
we	will have been	having
you	will have been	having
they	will have been	having

Conditional

I	would	have
you	would	have
he/she/it	would	have
we	would	have
you	would	have
they	would	have

Conditional Past

I	would have	had
you	would have	had
he/she/it	would have	had
we	would have	had
you	would have	had
they	would have	had

hear

- heard - heard

hören

Unregelmäßiges Verb

Simple tenses

Present

I	hear
you	hear
he/she/it	hears
we	hear
you	hear
they	hear

Past

I	heard
you	heard
he/she/it	heard
we	heard
you	heard
they	heard

Present Perfect

I	have	heard
you	have	heard
he/she/it	has	heard
we	have	heard
you	have	heard
they	have	heard

Past Perfect

I	had	heard
you	had	heard
he/she/it	had	heard
we	had	heard
you	had	heard
they	had	heard

Will-Future

I	will	hear
you	will	hear
he/she/it	will	hear
we	will	hear
you	will	hear
they	will	hear

Going to-Future

I	am	going to	hear
you	are	going to	hear
he/she/it	is	going to	hear
we	are	going to	hear
you	are	going to	hear
they	are	going to	hear

Future Perfect

I	will have	heard
you	will have	heard
he/she/it	will have	heard
we	will have	heard
you	will have	heard
they	will have	heard

Imperative

hear

Impersonal

ing-Form

hearing

Past Participle

heard

Continuous tenses

Present

I	am	hearing
you	are	hearing
he/she/it	is	hearing
we	are	hearing
you	are	hearing
they	are	hearing

Past

I	was	hearing
you	were	hearing
he/she/it	was	hearing
we	were	hearing
you	were	hearing
they	were	hearing

Present Perfect

I	have been	hearing
you	have been	hearing
he/she/it	has been	hearing
we	have been	hearing
you	have been	hearing
they	have been	hearing

Past Perfect

I	had been	hearing
you	had been	hearing
he/she/it	had been	hearing
we	had been	hearing
you	had been	hearing
they	had been	hearing

Will-Future

I	will be	hearing
you	will be	hearing
he/she/it	will be	hearing
we	will be	hearing
you	will be	hearing
they	will be	hearing

Going to-Future

I	am	going to be	hearing
you	are	going to be	hearing
he/she/it	is	going to be	hearing
we	are	going to be	hearing
you	are	going to be	hearing
they	are	going to be	hearing

Future Perfect

I	will have been	hearing
you	will have been	hearing
he/she/it	will have been	hearing
we	will have been	hearing
you	will have been	hearing
they	will have been	hearing

Conditional

I	would	hear
you	would	hear
he/she/it	would	hear
we	would	hear
you	would	hear
they	would	hear

Conditional Past

I	would have	heard
you	would have	heard
he/she/it	would have	heard
we	would have	heard
you	would have	heard
they	would have	heard

Simple tenses

Present

I	heat
you	heat
he/she/it	heats
we	heat
you	heat
they	heat

Past

I	heated
you	heated
he/she/it	heated
we	heated
you	heated
they	heated

Present Perfect

I	have	heated
you	have	heated
he/she/it	has	heated
we	have	heated
you	have	heated
they	have	heated

Past Perfect

I	had	heated
you	had	heated
he/she/it	had	heated
we	had	heated
you	had	heated
they	had	heated

Will-Future

I	will	heat
you	will	heat
he/she/it	will	heat
we	will	heat
you	will	heat
they	will	heat

Going to-Future

I	am	going to	heat
you	are	going to	heat
he/she/it	is	going to	heat
we	are	going to	heat
you	are	going to	heat
they	are	going to	heat

Future Perfect

I	will have	heated
you	will have	heated
he/she/it	will have	heated
we	will have	heated
you	will have	heated
they	will have	heated

Imperative

heat

Impersonal

ing-Form

heating

Past Participle

heated

Continuous tenses

Present

I	am	heating
you	are	heating
he/she/it	is	heating
we	are	heating
you	are	heating
they	are	heating

Past

I	was	heating
you	were	heating
he/she/it	was	heating
we	were	heating
you	were	heating
they	were	heating

Present Perfect

I	have	been	heating
you	have	been	heating
he/she/it	has	been	heating
we	have	been	heating
you	have	been	heating
they	have	been	heating

Past Perfect

I	had been	heating
you	had been	heating
he/she/it	had been	heating
we	had been	heating
you	had been	heating
they	had been	heating

Will-Future

I	will be	heating
you	will be	heating
he/she/it	will be	heating
we	will be	heating
you	will be	heating
they	will be	heating

Going to-Future

I	am	going to be	heating
you	are	going to be	heating
he/she/it	is	going to be	heating
we	are	going to be	heating
you	are	going to be	heating
they	are	going to be	heating

Future Perfect

I	will have been	heating
you	will have been	heating
he/she/it	will have been	heating
we	will have been	heating
you	will have been	heating
they	will have been	heating

Conditional

I	would	heat
you	would	heat
he/she/it	would	heat
we	would	heat
you	would	heat
they	would	heat

Conditional Past

I	would have	heated
you	would have	heated
he/she/it	would have	heated
we	would have	heated
you	would have	heated
they	would have	heated

help

helfen

Regelmäßiges Verb

Simple tenses

Present

I	help
you	help
he/she/it	helps
we	help
you	help
they	help

Past

I	helped
you	helped
he/she/it	helped
we	helped
you	helped
they	helped

Present Perfect

I	have	helped
you	have	helped
he/she/it	has	helped
we	have	helped
you	have	helped
they	have	helped

Past Perfect

I	had	helped
you	had	helped
he/she/it	had	helped
we	had	helped
you	had	helped
they	had	helped

Will-Future

I	will	help
you	will	help
he/she/it	will	help
we	will	help
you	will	help
they	will	help

Going to-Future

I	am	going to	help
you	are	going to	help
he/she/it	is	going to	help
we	are	going to	help
you	are	going to	help
they	are	going to	help

Future Perfect

I	will have	helped
you	will have	helped
he/she/it	will have	helped
we	will have	helped
you	will have	helped
they	will have	helped

Imperative

help

Impersonal

ing-Form

helping

Past Participle

helped

Continuous tenses

Present

I	am	helping
you	are	helping
he/she/it	is	helping
we	are	helping
you	are	helping
they	are	helping

Past

I	was	helping
you	were	helping
he/she/it	was	helping
we	were	helping
you	were	helping
they	were	helping

Present Perfect

I	have been	helping
you	have been	helping
he/she/it	has been	helping
we	have been	helping
you	have been	helping
they	have been	helping

Past Perfect

I	had been	helping
you	had been	helping
he/she/it	had been	helping
we	had been	helping
you	had been	helping
they	had been	helping

Will-Future

I	will be	helping
you	will be	helping
he/she/it	will be	helping
we	will be	helping
you	will be	helping
they	will be	helping

Going to-Future

I	am	going to be	helping
you	are	going to be	helping
he/she/it	is	going to be	helping
we	are	going to be	helping
you	are	going to be	helping
they	are	going to be	helping

Future Perfect

I	will have been	helping
you	will have been	helping
he/she/it	will have been	helping
we	will have been	helping
you	will have been	helping
they	will have been	helping

Conditional

I	would	help
you	would	help
he/she/it	would	help
we	would	help
you	would	help
they	would	help

Conditional Past

I	would have	helped
you	would have	helped
he/she/it	would have	helped
we	would have	helped
you	would have	helped
they	would have	helped

Simple tenses

Present

I	hire
you	hire
he/she/it	hires
we	hire
you	hire
they	hire

Past

I	hired
you	hired
he/she/it	hired
we	hired
you	hired
they	hired

Present Perfect

I	have	hired
you	have	hired
he/she/it	has	hired
we	have	hired
you	have	hired
they	have	hired

Past Perfect

I	had	hired
you	had	hired
he/she/it	had	hired
we	had	hired
you	had	hired
they	had	hired

Will-Future

I	will	hire
you	will	hire
he/she/it	will	hire
we	will	hire
you	will	hire
they	will	hire

Going to-Future

I	am	going to	hire
you	are	going to	hire
he/she/it	is	going to	hire
we	are	going to	hire
you	are	going to	hire
they	are	going to	hire

Future Perfect

I	will have	hired
you	will have	hired
he/she/it	will have	hired
we	will have	hired
you	will have	hired
they	will have	hired

Imperative

hire

Impersonal

ing-Form

hiring

Past Participle

hired

Continuous tenses

Present

I	am	hiring
you	are	hiring
he/she/it	is	hiring
we	are	hiring
you	are	hiring
they	are	hiring

Past

I	was	hiring
you	were	hiring
he/she/it	was	hiring
we	were	hiring
you	were	hiring
they	were	hiring

Present Perfect

I	have been	hiring
you	have been	hiring
he/she/it	has been	hiring
we	have been	hiring
you	have been	hiring
they	have been	hiring

Past Perfect

I	had been	hiring
you	had been	hiring
he/she/it	had been	hiring
we	had been	hiring
you	had been	hiring
they	had been	hiring

Will-Future

I	will be	hiring
you	will be	hiring
he/she/it	will be	hiring
we	will be	hiring
you	will be	hiring
they	will be	hiring

Going to-Future

I	am	going to be	hiring
you	are	going to be	hiring
he/she/it	is	going to be	hiring
we	are	going to be	hiring
you	are	going to be	hiring
they	are	going to be	hiring

Future Perfect

I	will have been	hiring
you	will have been	hiring
he/she/it	will have been	hiring
we	will have been	hiring
you	will have been	hiring
they	will have been	hiring

Conditional

I	would	hire
you	would	hire
he/she/it	would	hire
we	would	hire
you	would	hire
they	would	hire

Conditional Past

I	would have	hired
you	would have	hired
he/she/it	would have	hired
we	would have	hired
you	would have	hired
they	would have	hired

hit
- hit - hit

schlagen

Konsonantenverdopplung
Unregelmäßiges Verb

Simple tenses

Present

I	hit
you	hit
he/she/it	hits
we	hit
you	hit
they	hit

Past

I	hit
you	hit
he/she/it	hit
we	hit
you	hit
they	hit

Present Perfect

I	have	hit
you	have	hit
he/she/it	has	hit
we	have	hit
you	have	hit
they	have	hit

Past Perfect

I	had	hit
you	had	hit
he/she/it	had	hit
we	had	hit
you	had	hit
they	had	hit

Will-Future

I	will	hit
you	will	hit
he/she/it	will	hit
we	will	hit
you	will	hit
they	will	hit

Going to-Future

I	am	going to	hit
you	are	going to	hit
he/she/it	is	going to	hit
we	are	going to	hit
you	are	going to	hit
they	are	going to	hit

Future Perfect

I	will have	hit
you	will have	hit
he/she/it	will have	hit
we	will have	hit
you	will have	hit
they	will have	hit

Imperative

hit

Impersonal

ing-Form

hitting

Past Participle

hit

Continuous tenses

Present

I	am	hitting
you	are	hitting
he/she/it	is	hitting
we	are	hitting
you	are	hitting
they	are	hitting

Past

I	was	hitting
you	were	hitting
he/she/it	was	hitting
we	were	hitting
you	were	hitting
they	were	hitting

Present Perfect

I	have been	hitting
you	have been	hitting
he/she/it	has been	hitting
we	have been	hitting
you	have been	hitting
they	have been	hitting

Past Perfect

I	had been	hitting
you	had been	hitting
he/she/it	had been	hitting
we	had been	hitting
you	had been	hitting
they	had been	hitting

Will-Future

I	will be	hitting
you	will be	hitting
he/she/it	will be	hitting
we	will be	hitting
you	will be	hitting
they	will be	hitting

Going to-Future

I	am	going to be	hitting
you	are	going to be	hitting
he/she/it	is	going to be	hitting
we	are	going to be	hitting
you	are	going to be	hitting
they	are	going to be	hitting

Future Perfect

I	will have been	hitting
you	will have been	hitting
he/she/it	will have been	hitting
we	will have been	hitting
you	will have been	hitting
they	will have been	hitting

Conditional

I	would	hit
you	would	hit
he/she/it	would	hit
we	would	hit
you	would	hit
they	would	hit

Conditional Past

I	would have	hit
you	would have	hit
he/she/it	would have	hit
we	would have	hit
you	would have	hit
they	would have	hit

Simple tenses

Present

I	hold
you	hold
he/she/it	holds
we	hold
you	hold
they	hold

Past

I	held
you	held
he/she/it	held
we	held
you	held
they	held

Present Perfect

I	have	held
you	have	held
he/she/it	has	held
we	have	held
you	have	held
they	have	held

Past Perfect

I	had	held
you	had	held
he/she/it	had	held
we	had	held
you	had	held
they	had	held

Will-Future

I	will	hold
you	will	hold
he/she/it	will	hold
we	will	hold
you	will	hold
they	will	hold

Going to-Future

I	am	going to	hold
you	are	going to	hold
he/she/it	is	going to	hold
we	are	going to	hold
you	are	going to	hold
they	are	going to	hold

Future Perfect

I	will have	held
you	will have	held
he/she/it	will have	held
we	will have	held
you	will have	held
they	will have	held

Imperative

hold

Impersonal

ing-Form

holding

Past Participle

held

Continuous tenses

Present

I	am	holding
you	are	holding
he/she/it	is	holding
we	are	holding
you	are	holding
they	are	holding

Past

I	was	holding
you	were	holding
he/she/it	was	holding
we	were	holding
you	were	holding
they	were	holding

Present Perfect

I	have been	holding
you	have been	holding
he/she/it	has been	holding
we	have been	holding
you	have been	holding
they	have been	holding

Past Perfect

I	had been	holding
you	had been	holding
he/she/it	had been	holding
we	had been	holding
you	had been	holding
they	had been	holding

Will-Future

I	will be	holding
you	will be	holding
he/she/it	will be	holding
we	will be	holding
you	will be	holding
they	will be	holding

Going to-Future

I	am	going to be	holding
you	are	going to be	holding
he/she/it	is	going to be	holding
we	are	going to be	holding
you	are	going to be	holding
they	are	going to be	holding

Future Perfect

I	will have been	holding
you	will have been	holding
he/she/it	will have been	holding
we	will have been	holding
you	will have been	holding
they	will have been	holding

Conditional

I	would	hold
you	would	hold
he/she/it	would	hold
we	would	hold
you	would	hold
they	would	hold

Conditional Past

I	would have	held
you	would have	held
he/she/it	would have	held
we	would have	held
you	would have	held
they	would have	held

hope

hoffen

\+ **-ing** → ~~e~~ / + **-d** nicht **-ed**
Regelmäßiges Verb

Simple tenses

Present

I	hope
you	hope
he/she/it	hopes
we	hope
you	hope
they	hope

Past

I	hoped
you	hoped
he/she/it	hoped
we	hoped
you	hoped
they	hoped

Present Perfect

I	have	hoped
you	have	hoped
he/she/it	has	hoped
we	have	hoped
you	have	hoped
they	have	hoped

Past Perfect

I	had	hoped
you	had	hoped
he/she/it	had	hoped
we	had	hoped
you	had	hoped
they	had	hoped

Will-Future

I	will	hope
you	will	hope
he/she/it	will	hope
we	will	hope
you	will	hope
they	will	hope

Going to-Future

I	am	going to	hope
you	are	going to	hope
he/she/it	is	going to	hope
we	are	going to	hope
you	are	going to	hope
they	are	going to	hope

Future Perfect

I	will have	hoped
you	will have	hoped
he/she/it	will have	hoped
we	will have	hoped
you	will have	hoped
they	will have	hoped

Imperative

hope

Impersonal

ing-Form

hoping

Past Participle

hoped

Continuous tenses

Present

I	am	hoping
you	are	hoping
he/she/it	is	hoping
we	are	hoping
you	are	hoping
they	are	hoping

Past

I	was	hoping
you	were	hoping
he/she/it	was	hoping
we	were	hoping
you	were	hoping
they	were	hoping

Present Perfect

I	have	been	hoping
you	have	been	hoping
he/she/it	has	been	hoping
we	have	been	hoping
you	have	been	hoping
they	have	been	hoping

Past Perfect

I	had been	hoping
you	had been	hoping
he/she/it	had been	hoping
we	had been	hoping
you	had been	hoping
they	had been	hoping

Will-Future

I	will be	hoping
you	will be	hoping
he/she/it	will be	hoping
we	will be	hoping
you	will be	hoping
they	will be	hoping

Going to-Future

I	am	going to be	hoping
you	are	going to be	hoping
he/she/it	is	going to be	hoping
we	are	going to be	hoping
you	are	going to be	hoping
they	are	going to be	hoping

Future Perfect

I	will have been	hoping
you	will have been	hoping
he/she/it	will have been	hoping
we	will have been	hoping
you	will have been	hoping
they	will have been	hoping

Conditional

I	would	hope
you	would	hope
he/she/it	would	hope
we	would	hope
you	would	hope
they	would	hope

Conditional Past

I	would have	hoped
you	would have	hoped
he/she/it	would have	hoped
we	would have	hoped
you	would have	hoped
they	would have	hoped

Simple tenses

Present

I	host
you	host
he/she/it	hosts
we	host
you	host
they	host

Past

I	hosted
you	hosted
he/she/it	hosted
we	hosted
you	hosted
they	hosted

Present Perfect

I	have	hosted
you	have	hosted
he/she/it	has	hosted
we	have	hosted
you	have	hosted
they	have	hosted

Past Perfect

I	had	hosted
you	had	hosted
he/she/it	had	hosted
we	had	hosted
you	had	hosted
they	had	hosted

Will-Future

I	will	host
you	will	host
he/she/it	will	host
we	will	host
you	will	host
they	will	host

Going to-Future

I	am	going to	host
you	are	going to	host
he/she/it	is	going to	host
we	are	going to	host
you	are	going to	host
they	are	going to	host

Future Perfect

I	will have	hosted
you	will have	hosted
he/she/it	will have	hosted
we	will have	hosted
you	will have	hosted
they	will have	hosted

Imperative

host

Impersonal

ing-Form

hosting

Past Participle

hosted

Continuous tenses

Present

I	am	hosting
you	are	hosting
he/she/it	is	hosting
we	are	hosting
you	are	hosting
they	are	hosting

Past

I	was	hosting
you	were	hosting
he/she/it	was	hosting
we	were	hosting
you	were	hosting
they	were	hosting

Present Perfect

I	have	been	hosting
you	have	been	hosting
he/she/it	has	been	hosting
we	have	been	hosting
you	have	been	hosting
they	have	been	hosting

Past Perfect

I	had been	hosting
you	had been	hosting
he/she/it	had been	hosting
we	had been	hosting
you	had been	hosting
they	had been	hosting

Will-Future

I	will be	hosting
you	will be	hosting
he/she/it	will be	hosting
we	will be	hosting
you	will be	hosting
they	will be	hosting

Going to-Future

I	am	going to be	hosting
you	are	going to be	hosting
he/she/it	is	going to be	hosting
we	are	going to be	hosting
you	are	going to be	hosting
they	are	going to be	hosting

Future Perfect

I	will have been	hosting
you	will have been	hosting
he/she/it	will have been	hosting
we	will have been	hosting
you	will have been	hosting
they	will have been	hosting

Conditional

I	would	host
you	would	host
he/she/it	would	host
we	would	host
you	would	host
they	would	host

Conditional Past

I	would have	hosted
you	would have	hosted
he/she/it	would have	hosted
we	would have	hosted
you	would have	hosted
they	would have	hosted

hurry

sich beeilen

-y → **-ie** vor **-s** / **-y** → **-i** vor **-ed**
Regelmäßiges Verb

Simple tenses

Present

I	hurry
you	hurry
he/she/it	hurries
we	hurry
you	hurry
they	hurry

Past

I	hurried
you	hurried
he/she/it	hurried
we	hurried
you	hurried
they	hurried

Present Perfect

I	have	hurried
you	have	hurried
he/she/it	has	hurried
we	have	hurried
you	have	hurried
they	have	hurried

Past Perfect

I	had	hurried
you	had	hurried
he/she/it	had	hurried
we	had	hurried
you	had	hurried
they	had	hurried

Will-Future

I	will	hurry
you	will	hurry
he/she/it	will	hurry
we	will	hurry
you	will	hurry
they	will	hurry

Going to-Future

I	am	going to	hurry
you	are	going to	hurry
he/she/it	is	going to	hurry
we	are	going to	hurry
you	are	going to	hurry
they	are	going to	hurry

Future Perfect

I	will have	hurried
you	will have	hurried
he/she/it	will have	hurried
we	will have	hurried
you	will have	hurried
they	will have	hurried

Imperative

hurry

Impersonal

ing-Form

hurrying

Past Participle

hurried

Continuous tenses

Present

I	am	hurrying
you	are	hurrying
he/she/it	is	hurrying
we	are	hurrying
you	are	hurrying
they	are	hurrying

Past

I	was	hurrying
you	were	hurrying
he/she/it	was	hurrying
we	were	hurrying
you	were	hurrying
they	were	hurrying

Present Perfect

I	have been	hurrying
you	have been	hurrying
he/she/it	has been	hurrying
we	have been	hurrying
you	have been	hurrying
they	have been	hurrying

Past Perfect

I	had been	hurrying
you	had been	hurrying
he/she/it	had been	hurrying
we	had been	hurrying
you	had been	hurrying
they	had been	hurrying

Will-Future

I	will be	hurrying
you	will be	hurrying
he/she/it	will be	hurrying
we	will be	hurrying
you	will be	hurrying
they	will be	hurrying

Going to-Future

I	am	going to be	hurrying
you	are	going to be	hurrying
he/she/it	is	going to be	hurrying
we	are	going to be	hurrying
you	are	going to be	hurrying
they	are	going to be	hurrying

Future Perfect

I	will have been	hurrying
you	will have been	hurrying
he/she/it	will have been	hurrying
we	will have been	hurrying
you	will have been	hurrying
they	will have been	hurrying

Conditional

I	would	hurry
you	would	hurry
he/she/it	would	hurry
we	would	hurry
you	would	hurry
they	would	hurry

Conditional Past

I	would have	hurried
you	would have	hurried
he/she/it	would have	hurried
we	would have	hurried
you	would have	hurried
they	would have	hurried

wehtun

hurt

- hurt - hurt

Simple tenses

Present

I	hurt
you	hurt
he/she/it	hurts
we	hurt
you	hurt
they	hurt

Past

I	hurt
you	hurt
he/she/it	hurt
we	hurt
you	hurt
they	hurt

Present Perfect

I	have	hurt
you	have	hurt
he/she/it	has	hurt
we	have	hurt
you	have	hurt
they	have	hurt

Past Perfect

I	had	hurt
you	had	hurt
he/she/it	had	hurt
we	had	hurt
you	had	hurt
they	had	hurt

Will-Future

I	will	hurt
you	will	hurt
he/she/it	will	hurt
we	will	hurt
you	will	hurt
they	will	hurt

Going to-Future

I	am	going to	hurt
you	are	going to	hurt
he/she/it	is	going to	hurt
we	are	going to	hurt
you	are	going to	hurt
they	are	going to	hurt

Future Perfect

I	will have	hurt
you	will have	hurt
he/she/it	will have	hurt
we	will have	hurt
you	will have	hurt
they	will have	hurt

Imperative

hurt

Impersonal

ing-Form

hurting

Past Participle

hurt

Continuous tenses

Present

I	am	hurting
you	are	hurting
he/she/it	is	hurting
we	are	hurting
you	are	hurting
they	are	hurting

Past

I	was	hurting
you	were	hurting
he/she/it	was	hurting
we	were	hurting
you	were	hurting
they	were	hurting

Present Perfect

I	have been	hurting
you	have been	hurting
he/she/it	has been	hurting
we	have been	hurting
you	have been	hurting
they	have been	hurting

Past Perfect

I	had been	hurting
you	had been	hurting
he/she/it	had been	hurting
we	had been	hurting
you	had been	hurting
they	had been	hurting

Will-Future

I	will be	hurting
you	will be	hurting
he/she/it	will be	hurting
we	will be	hurting
you	will be	hurting
they	will be	hurting

Going to-Future

I	am	going to be	hurting
you	are	going to be	hurting
he/she/it	is	going to be	hurting
we	are	going to be	hurting
you	are	going to be	hurting
they	are	going to be	hurting

Future Perfect

I	will have been	hurting
you	will have been	hurting
he/she/it	will have been	hurting
we	will have been	hurting
you	will have been	hurting
they	will have been	hurting

Conditional

I	would	hurt
you	would	hurt
he/she/it	would	hurt
we	would	hurt
you	would	hurt
they	would	hurt

Conditional Past

I	would have	hurt
you	would have	hurt
he/she/it	would have	hurt
we	would have	hurt
you	would have	hurt
they	would have	hurt

imagine

sich vorstellen

+ **-ing** → ~~e~~ / + **-d** nicht **-ed**
Regelmäßiges Verb

Simple tenses

Present

I	imagine
you	imagine
he/she/it	imagines
we	imagine
you	imagine
they	imagine

Past

I	imagined
you	imagined
he/she/it	imagined
we	imagined
you	imagined
they	imagined

Present Perfect

I	have	imagined
you	have	imagined
he/she/it	has	imagined
we	have	imagined
you	have	imagined
they	have	imagined

Past Perfect

I	had	imagined
you	had	imagined
he/she/it	had	imagined
we	had	imagined
you	had	imagined
they	had	imagined

Will-Future

I	will	imagine
you	will	imagine
he/she/it	will	imagine
we	will	imagine
you	will	imagine
they	will	imagine

Going to-Future

I	am	going to	imagine
you	are	going to	imagine
he/she/it	is	going to	imagine
we	are	going to	imagine
you	are	going to	imagine
they	are	going to	imagine

Future Perfect

I	will have	imagined
you	will have	imagined
he/she/it	will have	imagined
we	will have	imagined
you	will have	imagined
they	will have	imagined

Imperative

imagine

Impersonal

ing-Form

imagining

Past Participle

imagined

Continuous tenses

Present

I	am	imagining
you	are	imagining
he/she/it	is	imagining
we	are	imagining
you	are	imagining
they	are	imagining

Past

I	was	imagining
you	were	imagining
he/she/it	was	imagining
we	were	imagining
you	were	imagining
they	were	imagining

Present Perfect

I	have been	imagining
you	have been	imagining
he/she/it	has been	imagining
we	have been	imagining
you	have been	imagining
they	have been	imagining

Past Perfect

I	had been	imagining
you	had been	imagining
he/she/it	had been	imagining
we	had been	imagining
you	had been	imagining
they	had been	imagining

Will-Future

I	will be	imagining
you	will be	imagining
he/she/it	will be	imagining
we	will be	imagining
you	will be	imagining
they	will be	imagining

Going to-Future

I	am	going to be	imagining
you	are	going to be	imagining
he/she/it	is	going to be	imagining
we	are	going to be	imagining
you	are	going to be	imagining
they	are	going to be	imagining

Future Perfect

I	will have been	imagining
you	will have been	imagining
he/she/it	will have been	imagining
we	will have been	imagining
you	will have been	imagining
they	will have been	imagining

Conditional

I	would	imagine
you	would	imagine
he/she/it	would	imagine
we	would	imagine
you	would	imagine
they	would	imagine

Conditional Past

I	would have	imagined
you	would have	imagined
he/she/it	would have	imagined
we	would have	imagined
you	would have	imagined
they	would have	imagined

andeuten

imply

Simple tenses

Present

I	imply
you	imply
he/she/it	implies
we	imply
you	imply
they	imply

Past

I	implied
you	implied
he/she/it	implied
we	implied
you	implied
they	implied

Present Perfect

I	have	implied
you	have	implied
he/she/it	has	implied
we	have	implied
you	have	implied
they	have	implied

Past Perfect

I	had	implied
you	had	implied
he/she/it	had	implied
we	had	implied
you	had	implied
they	had	implied

Will-Future

I	will	imply
you	will	imply
he/she/it	will	imply
we	will	imply
you	will	imply
they	will	imply

Going to-Future

I	am	going to	imply
you	are	going to	imply
he/she/it	is	going to	imply
we	are	going to	imply
you	are	going to	imply
they	are	going to	imply

Future Perfect

I	will have	implied
you	will have	implied
he/she/it	will have	implied
we	will have	implied
you	will have	implied
they	will have	implied

Imperative

imply

Impersonal

ing-Form

implying

Past Participle

implied

Continuous tenses

Present

I	am	implying
you	are	implying
he/she/it	is	implying
we	are	implying
you	are	implying
they	are	implying

Past

I	was	implying
you	were	implying
he/she/it	was	implying
we	were	implying
you	were	implying
they	were	implying

Present Perfect

I	have been	implying
you	have been	implying
he/she/it	has been	implying
we	have been	implying
you	have been	implying
they	have been	implying

Past Perfect

I	had been	implying
you	had been	implying
he/she/it	had been	implying
we	had been	implying
you	had been	implying
they	had been	implying

Will-Future

I	will be	implying
you	will be	implying
he/she/it	will be	implying
we	will be	implying
you	will be	implying
they	will be	implying

Going to-Future

I	am	going to be	implying
you	are	going to be	implying
he/she/it	is	going to be	implying
we	are	going to be	implying
you	are	going to be	implying
they	are	going to be	implying

Future Perfect

I	will have been	implying
you	will have been	implying
he/she/it	will have been	implying
we	will have been	implying
you	will have been	implying
they	will have been	implying

Conditional

I	would	imply
you	would	imply
he/she/it	would	imply
we	would	imply
you	would	imply
they	would	imply

Conditional Past

I	would have	implied
you	would have	implied
he/she/it	would have	implied
we	would have	implied
you	would have	implied
they	would have	implied

import

importieren

Regelmäßiges Verb

Simple tenses

Present

I	import
you	import
he/she/it	imports
we	import
you	import
they	import

Past

I	imported
you	imported
he/she/it	imported
we	imported
you	imported
they	imported

Present Perfect

I	have	imported
you	have	imported
he/she/it	has	imported
we	have	imported
you	have	imported
they	have	imported

Past Perfect

I	had	imported
you	had	imported
he/she/it	had	imported
we	had	imported
you	had	imported
they	had	imported

Will-Future

I	will	import
you	will	import
he/she/it	will	import
we	will	import
you	will	import
they	will	import

Going to-Future

I	am	going to	import
you	are	going to	import
he/she/it	is	going to	import
we	are	going to	import
you	are	going to	import
they	are	going to	import

Future Perfect

I	will have	imported
you	will have	imported
he/she/it	will have	imported
we	will have	imported
you	will have	imported
they	will have	imported

Imperative

import

Impersonal

ing-Form

importing

Past Participle

imported

Continuous tenses

Present

I	am	importing
you	are	importing
he/she/it	is	importing
we	are	importing
you	are	importing
they	are	importing

Past

I	was	importing
you	were	importing
he/she/it	was	importing
we	were	importing
you	were	importing
they	were	importing

Present Perfect

I	have	been	importing
you	have	been	importing
he/she/it	has	been	importing
we	have	been	importing
you	have	been	importing
they	have	been	importing

Past Perfect

I	had been	importing
you	had been	importing
he/she/it	had been	importing
we	had been	importing
you	had been	importing
they	had been	importing

Will-Future

I	will be	importing
you	will be	importing
he/she/it	will be	importing
we	will be	importing
you	will be	importing
they	will be	importing

Going to-Future

I	am	going to be	importing
you	are	going to be	importing
he/she/it	is	going to be	importing
we	are	going to be	importing
you	are	going to be	importing
they	are	going to be	importing

Future Perfect

I	will have been	importing
you	will have been	importing
he/she/it	will have been	importing
we	will have been	importing
you	will have been	importing
they	will have been	importing

Conditional

I	would	import
you	would	import
he/she/it	would	import
we	would	import
you	would	import
they	would	import

Conditional Past

I	would have	imported
you	would have	imported
he/she/it	would have	imported
we	would have	imported
you	would have	imported
they	would have	imported

+ **-ing** → ~~e~~ / + **-d** nicht **-ed**
Regelmäßiges Verb

durchsetzen

impose

Simple tenses

Present

I	impose
you	impose
he/she/it	imposes
we	impose
you	impose
they	impose

Past

I	imposed
you	imposed
he/she/it	imposed
we	imposed
you	imposed
they	imposed

Present Perfect

I	have	imposed
you	have	imposed
he/she/it	has	imposed
we	have	imposed
you	have	imposed
they	have	imposed

Past Perfect

I	had	imposed
you	had	imposed
he/she/it	had	imposed
we	had	imposed
you	had	imposed
they	had	imposed

Will-Future

I	will	impose
you	will	impose
he/she/it	will	impose
we	will	impose
you	will	impose
they	will	impose

Going to-Future

I	am	going to	impose
you	are	going to	impose
he/she/it	is	going to	impose
we	are	going to	impose
you	are	going to	impose
they	are	going to	impose

Future Perfect

I	will have	imposed
you	will have	imposed
he/she/it	will have	imposed
we	will have	imposed
you	will have	imposed
they	will have	imposed

Imperative

impose

Impersonal

ing-Form

imposing

Past Participle

imposed

Continuous tenses

Present

I	am	imposing
you	are	imposing
he/she/it	is	imposing
we	are	imposing
you	are	imposing
they	are	imposing

Past

I	was	imposing
you	were	imposing
he/she/it	was	imposing
we	were	imposing
you	were	imposing
they	were	imposing

Present Perfect

I	have been	imposing
you	have been	imposing
he/she/it	has been	imposing
we	have been	imposing
you	have been	imposing
they	have been	imposing

Past Perfect

I	had been	imposing
you	had been	imposing
he/she/it	had been	imposing
we	had been	imposing
you	had been	imposing
they	had been	imposing

Will-Future

I	will be	imposing
you	will be	imposing
he/she/it	will be	imposing
we	will be	imposing
you	will be	imposing
they	will be	imposing

Going to-Future

I	am	going to be	imposing
you	are	going to be	imposing
he/she/it	is	going to be	imposing
we	are	going to be	imposing
you	are	going to be	imposing
they	are	going to be	imposing

Future Perfect

I	will have been	imposing
you	will have been	imposing
he/she/it	will have been	imposing
we	will have been	imposing
you	will have been	imposing
they	will have been	imposing

Conditional

I	would	impose
you	would	impose
he/she/it	would	impose
we	would	impose
you	would	impose
they	would	impose

Conditional Past

I	would have	imposed
you	would have	imposed
he/she/it	would have	imposed
we	would have	imposed
you	would have	imposed
they	would have	imposed

impress

beeindrucken

\+ **-es** in 3. Person Singular
Regelmäßiges Verb

Simple tenses

Present

I	impress
you	impress
he/she/it	impresses
we	impress
you	impress
they	impress

Past

I	impressed
you	impressed
he/she/it	impressed
we	impressed
you	impressed
they	impressed

Present Perfect

I	have	impressed
you	have	impressed
he/she/it	has	impressed
we	have	impressed
you	have	impressed
they	have	impressed

Past Perfect

I	had	impressed
you	had	impressed
he/she/it	had	impressed
we	had	impressed
you	had	impressed
they	had	impressed

Will-Future

I	will	impress
you	will	impress
he/she/it	will	impress
we	will	impress
you	will	impress
they	will	impress

Going to-Future

I	am	going to	impress
you	are	going to	impress
he/she/it	is	going to	impress
we	are	going to	impress
you	are	going to	impress
they	are	going to	impress

Future Perfect

I	will have	impressed
you	will have	impressed
he/she/it	will have	impressed
we	will have	impressed
you	will have	impressed
they	will have	impressed

Imperative

impress

Impersonal

ing-Form

impressing

Past Participle

impressed

Continuous tenses

Present

I	am	impressing
you	are	impressing
he/she/it	is	impressing
we	are	impressing
you	are	impressing
they	are	impressing

Past

I	was	impressing
you	were	impressing
he/she/it	was	impressing
we	were	impressing
you	were	impressing
they	were	impressing

Present Perfect

I	have been	impressing
you	have been	impressing
he/she/it	has been	impressing
we	have been	impressing
you	have been	impressing
they	have been	impressing

Past Perfect

I	had been	impressing
you	had been	impressing
he/she/it	had been	impressing
we	had been	impressing
you	had been	impressing
they	had been	impressing

Will-Future

I	will be	impressing
you	will be	impressing
he/she/it	will be	impressing
we	will be	impressing
you	will be	impressing
they	will be	impressing

Going to-Future

I	am	going to be	impressing
you	are	going to be	impressing
he/she/it	is	going to be	impressing
we	are	going to be	impressing
you	are	going to be	impressing
they	are	going to be	impressing

Future Perfect

I	will have been	impressing
you	will have been	impressing
he/she/it	will have been	impressing
we	will have been	impressing
you	will have been	impressing
they	will have been	impressing

Conditional

I	would	impress
you	would	impress
he/she/it	would	impress
we	would	impress
you	would	impress
they	would	impress

Conditional Past

I	would have	impressed
you	would have	impressed
he/she/it	would have	impressed
we	would have	impressed
you	would have	impressed
they	would have	impressed

+ **-ing** → ~~**e**~~ / + **-d** nicht **-ed**
Regelmäßiges Verb

verbessern

improve

Simple tenses

Present

I	improve
you	improve
he/she/it	improves
we	improve
you	improve
they	improve

Past

I	improved
you	improved
he/she/it	improved
we	improved
you	improved
they	improved

Present Perfect

I	have	improved
you	have	improved
he/she/it	has	improved
we	have	improved
you	have	improved
they	have	improved

Past Perfect

I	had	improved
you	had	improved
he/she/it	had	improved
we	had	improved
you	had	improved
they	had	improved

Will-Future

I	will	improve
you	will	improve
he/she/it	will	improve
we	will	improve
you	will	improve
they	will	improve

Going to-Future

I	am	going to	improve
you	are	going to	improve
he/she/it	is	going to	improve
we	are	going to	improve
you	are	going to	improve
they	are	going to	improve

Future Perfect

I	will have	improved
you	will have	improved
he/she/it	will have	improved
we	will have	improved
you	will have	improved
they	will have	improved

Imperative

improve

Impersonal

ing-Form

improving

Past Participle

improved

Continuous tenses

Present

I	am	improving
you	are	improving
he/she/it	is	improving
we	are	improving
you	are	improving
they	are	improving

Past

I	was	improving
you	were	improving
he/she/it	was	improving
we	were	improving
you	were	improving
they	were	improving

Present Perfect

I	have been	improving
you	have been	improving
he/she/it	has been	improving
we	have been	improving
you	have been	improving
they	have been	improving

Past Perfect

I	had been	improving
you	had been	improving
he/she/it	had been	improving
we	had been	improving
you	had been	improving
they	had been	improving

Will-Future

I	will be	improving
you	will be	improving
he/she/it	will be	improving
we	will be	improving
you	will be	improving
they	will be	improving

Going to-Future

I	am	going to be	improving
you	are	going to be	improving
he/she/it	is	going to be	improving
we	are	going to be	improving
you	are	going to be	improving
they	are	going to be	improving

Future Perfect

I	will have been	improving
you	will have been	improving
he/she/it	will have been	improving
we	will have been	improving
you	will have been	improving
they	will have been	improving

Conditional

I	would	improve
you	would	improve
he/she/it	would	improve
we	would	improve
you	would	improve
they	would	improve

Conditional Past

I	would have	improved
you	would have	improved
he/she/it	would have	improved
we	would have	improved
you	would have	improved
they	would have	improved

include

beinhalten

+ **-ing** → ~~e~~ / + -d nicht -ed
Regelmäßiges Verb

Simple tenses

Present

I	include
you	include
he/she/it	includes
we	include
you	include
they	include

Past

I	included
you	included
he/she/it	included
we	included
you	included
they	included

Present Perfect

I	have	included
you	have	included
he/she/it	has	included
we	have	included
you	have	included
they	have	included

Past Perfect

I	had	included
you	had	included
he/she/it	had	included
we	had	included
you	had	included
they	had	included

Will-Future

I	will	include
you	will	include
he/she/it	will	include
we	will	include
you	will	include
they	will	include

Going to-Future

I	am	going to	include
you	are	going to	include
he/she/it	is	going to	include
we	are	going to	include
you	are	going to	include
they	are	going to	include

Future Perfect

I	will have	included
you	will have	included
he/she/it	will have	included
we	will have	included
you	will have	included
they	will have	included

Imperative

include

Impersonal

ing-Form

including

Past Participle

included

Continuous tenses

Present

I	am	including
you	are	including
he/she/it	is	including
we	are	including
you	are	including
they	are	including

Past

I	was	including
you	were	including
he/she/it	was	including
we	were	including
you	were	including
they	were	including

Present Perfect

I	have been	including
you	have been	including
he/she/it	has been	including
we	have been	including
you	have been	including
they	have been	including

Past Perfect

I	had been	including
you	had been	including
he/she/it	had been	including
we	had been	including
you	had been	including
they	had been	including

Will-Future

I	will be	including
you	will be	including
he/she/it	will be	including
we	will be	including
you	will be	including
they	will be	including

Going to-Future

I	am	going to be	including
you	are	going to be	including
he/she/it	is	going to be	including
we	are	going to be	including
you	are	going to be	including
they	are	going to be	including

Future Perfect

I	will have been	including
you	will have been	including
he/she/it	will have been	including
we	will have been	including
you	will have been	including
they	will have been	including

Conditional

I	would	include
you	would	include
he/she/it	would	include
we	would	include
you	would	include
they	would	include

Conditional Past

I	would have	included
you	would have	included
he/she/it	would have	included
we	would have	included
you	would have	included
they	would have	included

ansteigen

increase

Simple tenses

Present

I	increase
you	increase
he/she/it	increases
we	increase
you	increase
they	increase

Past

I	increased
you	increased
he/she/it	increased
we	increased
you	increased
they	increased

Present Perfect

I	have	increased
you	have	increased
he/she/it	has	increased
we	have	increased
you	have	increased
they	have	increased

Past Perfect

I	had	increased
you	had	increased
he/she/it	had	increased
we	had	increased
you	had	increased
they	had	increased

Will-Future

I	will	increase
you	will	increase
he/she/it	will	increase
we	will	increase
you	will	increase
they	will	increase

Going to-Future

I	am	going to	increase
you	are	going to	increase
he/she/it	is	going to	increase
we	are	going to	increase
you	are	going to	increase
they	are	going to	increase

Future Perfect

I	will have	increased
you	will have	increased
he/she/it	will have	increased
we	will have	increased
you	will have	increased
they	will have	increased

Imperative

increase

Impersonal

ing-Form

increasing

Past Participle

increased

Continuous tenses

Present

I	am	increasing
you	are	increasing
he/she/it	is	increasing
we	are	increasing
you	are	increasing
they	are	increasing

Past

I	was	increasing
you	were	increasing
he/she/it	was	increasing
we	were	increasing
you	were	increasing
they	were	increasing

Present Perfect

I	have	been	increasing
you	have	been	increasing
he/she/it	has	been	increasing
we	have	been	increasing
you	have	been	increasing
they	have	been	increasing

Past Perfect

I	had been	increasing
you	had been	increasing
he/she/it	had been	increasing
we	had been	increasing
you	had been	increasing
they	had been	increasing

Will-Future

I	will be	increasing
you	will be	increasing
he/she/it	will be	increasing
we	will be	increasing
you	will be	increasing
they	will be	increasing

Going to-Future

I	am	going to be	increasing
you	are	going to be	increasing
he/she/it	is	going to be	increasing
we	are	going to be	increasing
you	are	going to be	increasing
they	are	going to be	increasing

Future Perfect

I	will have been increasing
you	will have been increasing
he/she/it	will have been increasing
we	will have been increasing
you	will have been increasing
they	will have been increasing

Conditional

I	would	increase
you	would	increase
he/she/it	would	increase
we	would	increase
you	would	increase
they	would	increase

Conditional Past

I	would have	increased
you	would have	increased
he/she/it	would have	increased
we	would have	increased
you	would have	increased
they	would have	increased

indicate

zeigen

+ **-ing** → ~~e~~ / + **-d** nicht **-ed**
Regelmäßiges Verb

Simple tenses

Present

I indicate
you indicate
he/she/it indicates
we indicate
you indicate
they indicate

Past

I indicated
you indicated
he/she/it indicated
we indicated
you indicated
they indicated

Present Perfect

I have indicated
you have indicated
he/she/it has indicated
we have indicated
you have indicated
they have indicated

Past Perfect

I had indicated
you had indicated
he/she/it had indicated
we had indicated
you had indicated
they had indicated

Will-Future

I will indicate
you will indicate
he/she/it will indicate
we will indicate
you will indicate
they will indicate

Going to-Future

I am going to indicate
you are going to indicate
he/she/it is going to indicate
we are going to indicate
you are going to indicate
they are going to indicate

Future Perfect

I will have indicated
you will have indicated
he/she/it will have indicated
we will have indicated
you will have indicated
they will have indicated

Imperative

indicate

Impersonal

ing-Form

indicating

Past Participle

indicated

Continuous tenses

Present

I am indicating
you are indicating
he/she/it is indicating
we are indicating
you are indicating
they are indicating

Past

I was indicating
you were indicating
he/she/it was indicating
we were indicating
you were indicating
they were indicating

Present Perfect

I have been indicating
you have been indicating
he/she/it has been indicating
we have been indicating
you have been indicating
they have been indicating

Past Perfect

I had been indicating
you had been indicating
he/she/it had been indicating
we had been indicating
you had been indicating
they had been indicating

Will-Future

I will be indicating
you will be indicating
he/she/it will be indicating
we will be indicating
you will be indicating
they will be indicating

Going to-Future

I am going to be indicating
you are going to be indicating
he/she/it is going to be indicating
we are going to be indicating
you are going to be indicating
they are going to be indicating

Future Perfect

I will have been indicating
you will have been indicating
he/she/it will have been indicating
we will have been indicating
you will have been indicating
they will have been indicating

Conditional

I would indicate
you would indicate
he/she/it would indicate
we would indicate
you would indicate
they would indicate

Conditional Past

I would have indicated
you would have indicated
he/she/it would have indicated
we would have indicated
you would have indicated
they would have indicated

Simple tenses

Present

I	inform
you	inform
he/she/it	informs
we	inform
you	inform
they	inform

Past

I	informed
you	informed
he/she/it	informed
we	informed
you	informed
they	informed

Present Perfect

I	have	informed
you	have	informed
he/she/it	has	informed
we	have	informed
you	have	informed
they	have	informed

Past Perfect

I	had	informed
you	had	informed
he/she/it	had	informed
we	had	informed
you	had	informed
they	had	informed

Will-Future

I	will	inform
you	will	inform
he/she/it	will	inform
we	will	inform
you	will	inform
they	will	inform

Going to-Future

I	am	going to	inform
you	are	going to	inform
he/she/it	is	going to	inform
we	are	going to	inform
you	are	going to	inform
they	are	going to	inform

Future Perfect

I	will have	informed
you	will have	informed
he/she/it	will have	informed
we	will have	informed
you	will have	informed
they	will have	informed

Imperative

inform

Impersonal

ing-Form

informing

Past Participle

informed

Continuous tenses

Present

I	am	informing
you	are	informing
he/she/it	is	informing
we	are	informing
you	are	informing
they	are	informing

Past

I	was	informing
you	were	informing
he/she/it	was	informing
we	were	informing
you	were	informing
they	were	informing

Present Perfect

I	have	been	informing
you	have	been	informing
he/she/it	has	been	informing
we	have	been	informing
you	have	been	informing
they	have	been	informing

Past Perfect

I	had been	informing
you	had been	informing
he/she/it	had been	informing
we	had been	informing
you	had been	informing
they	had been	informing

Will-Future

I	will be	informing
you	will be	informing
he/she/it	will be	informing
we	will be	informing
you	will be	informing
they	will be	informing

Going to-Future

I	am	going to be	informing
you	are	going to be	informing
he/she/it	is	going to be	informing
we	are	going to be	informing
you	are	going to be	informing
they	are	going to be	informing

Future Perfect

I	will have been	informing
you	will have been	informing
he/she/it	will have been	informing
we	will have been	informing
you	will have been	informing
they	will have been	informing

Conditional

I	would	inform
you	would	inform
he/she/it	would	inform
we	would	inform
you	would	inform
they	would	inform

Conditional Past

I	would have	informed
you	would have	informed
he/she/it	would have	informed
we	would have	informed
you	would have	informed
they	would have	informed

injure

verletzen

+ **-ing** → ~~e~~ / + **-d** nicht **-ed**
Regelmäßiges Verb

Simple tenses

Present

I	injure
you	injure
he/she/it	injures
we	injure
you	injure
they	injure

Past

I	injured
you	injured
he/she/it	injured
we	injured
you	injured
they	injured

Present Perfect

I	have	injured
you	have	injured
he/she/it	has	injured
we	have	injured
you	have	injured
they	have	injured

Past Perfect

I	had	injured
you	had	injured
he/she/it	had	injured
we	had	injured
you	had	injured
they	had	injured

Will-Future

I	will	injure
you	will	injure
he/she/it	will	injure
we	will	injure
you	will	injure
they	will	injure

Going to-Future

I	am	going to	injure
you	are	going to	injure
he/she/it	is	going to	injure
we	are	going to	injure
you	are	going to	injure
they	are	going to	injure

Future Perfect

I	will have	injured
you	will have	injured
he/she/it	will have	injured
we	will have	injured
you	will have	injured
they	will have	injured

Imperative

injure

Impersonal

ing-Form

injuring

Past Participle

injured

Continuous tenses

Present

I	am	injuring
you	are	injuring
he/she/it	is	injuring
we	are	injuring
you	are	injuring
they	are	injuring

Past

I	was	injuring
you	were	injuring
he/she/it	was	injuring
we	were	injuring
you	were	injuring
they	were	injuring

Present Perfect

I	have been	injuring
you	have been	injuring
he/she/it	has been	injuring
we	have been	injuring
you	have been	injuring
they	have been	injuring

Past Perfect

I	had been	injuring
you	had been	injuring
he/she/it	had been	injuring
we	had been	injuring
you	had been	injuring
they	had been	injuring

Will-Future

I	will be	injuring
you	will be	injuring
he/she/it	will be	injuring
we	will be	injuring
you	will be	injuring
they	will be	injuring

Going to-Future

I	am	going to be	injuring
you	are	going to be	injuring
he/she/it	is	going to be	injuring
we	are	going to be	injuring
you	are	going to be	injuring
they	are	going to be	injuring

Future Perfect

I	will have been	injuring
you	will have been	injuring
he/she/it	will have been	injuring
we	will have been	injuring
you	will have been	injuring
they	will have been	injuring

Conditional

I	would	injure
you	would	injure
he/she/it	would	injure
we	would	injure
you	would	injure
they	would	injure

Conditional Past

I	would have	injured
you	would have	injured
he/she/it	would have	injured
we	would have	injured
you	would have	injured
they	would have	injured

insert

Regelmäßiges Verb

Simple tenses

Present

I	insert
you	insert
he/she/it	inserts
we	insert
you	insert
they	insert

Past

I	inserted
you	inserted
he/she/it	inserted
we	inserted
you	inserted
they	inserted

Present Perfect

I	have	inserted
you	have	inserted
he/she/it	has	inserted
we	have	inserted
you	have	inserted
they	have	inserted

Past Perfect

I	had	inserted
you	had	inserted
he/she/it	had	inserted
we	had	inserted
you	had	inserted
they	had	inserted

Will-Future

I	will	insert
you	will	insert
he/she/it	will	insert
we	will	insert
you	will	insert
they	will	insert

Going to-Future

I	am	going to	insert
you	are	going to	insert
he/she/it	is	going to	insert
we	are	going to	insert
you	are	going to	insert
they	are	going to	insert

Future Perfect

I	will have	inserted
you	will have	inserted
he/she/it	will have	inserted
we	will have	inserted
you	will have	inserted
they	will have	inserted

Imperative

insert

Impersonal

ing-Form

inserting

Past Participle

inserted

Continuous tenses

Present

I	am	inserting
you	are	inserting
he/she/it	is	inserting
we	are	inserting
you	are	inserting
they	are	inserting

Past

I	was	inserting
you	were	inserting
he/she/it	was	inserting
we	were	inserting
you	were	inserting
they	were	inserting

Present Perfect

I	have been	inserting
you	have been	inserting
he/she/it	has been	inserting
we	have been	inserting
you	have been	inserting
they	have been	inserting

Past Perfect

I	had been	inserting
you	had been	inserting
he/she/it	had been	inserting
we	had been	inserting
you	had been	inserting
they	had been	inserting

Will-Future

I	will be	inserting
you	will be	inserting
he/she/it	will be	inserting
we	will be	inserting
you	will be	inserting
they	will be	inserting

Going to-Future

I	am	going to be	inserting
you	are	going to be	inserting
he/she/it	is	going to be	inserting
we	are	going to be	inserting
you	are	going to be	inserting
they	are	going to be	inserting

Future Perfect

I	will have been	inserting
you	will have been	inserting
he/she/it	will have been	inserting
we	will have been	inserting
you	will have been	inserting
they	will have been	inserting

Conditional

I	would	insert
you	would	insert
he/she/it	would	insert
we	would	insert
you	would	insert
they	would	insert

Conditional Past

I	would have	inserted
you	would have	inserted
he/she/it	would have	inserted
we	would have	inserted
you	would have	inserted
they	would have	inserted

insult

beleidigen

Regelmäßiges Verb

Simple tenses

Present

I	insult
you	insult
he/she/it	insults
we	insult
you	insult
they	insult

Past

I	insulted
you	insulted
he/she/it	insulted
we	insulted
you	insulted
they	insulted

Present Perfect

I	have	insulted
you	have	insulted
he/she/it	has	insulted
we	have	insulted
you	have	insulted
they	have	insulted

Past Perfect

I	had	insulted
you	had	insulted
he/she/it	had	insulted
we	had	insulted
you	had	insulted
they	had	insulted

Will-Future

I	will	insult
you	will	insult
he/she/it	will	insult
we	will	insult
you	will	insult
they	will	insult

Going to-Future

I	am	going to	insult
you	are	going to	insult
he/she/it	is	going to	insult
we	are	going to	insult
you	are	going to	insult
they	are	going to	insult

Future Perfect

I	will have	insulted
you	will have	insulted
he/she/it	will have	insulted
we	will have	insulted
you	will have	insulted
they	will have	insulted

Imperative

insult

Impersonal

ing-Form

insulting

Past Participle

insulted

Continuous tenses

Present

I	am	insulting
you	are	insulting
he/she/it	is	insulting
we	are	insulting
you	are	insulting
they	are	insulting

Past

I	was	insulting
you	were	insulting
he/she/it	was	insulting
we	were	insulting
you	were	insulting
they	were	insulting

Present Perfect

I	have been	insulting
you	have been	insulting
he/she/it	has been	insulting
we	have been	insulting
you	have been	insulting
they	have been	insulting

Past Perfect

I	had been	insulting
you	had been	insulting
he/she/it	had been	insulting
we	had been	insulting
you	had been	insulting
they	had been	insulting

Will-Future

I	will be	insulting
you	will be	insulting
he/she/it	will be	insulting
we	will be	insulting
you	will be	insulting
they	will be	insulting

Going to-Future

I	am	going to be	insulting
you	are	going to be	insulting
he/she/it	is	going to be	insulting
we	are	going to be	insulting
you	are	going to be	insulting
they	are	going to be	insulting

Future Perfect

I	will have been	insulting
you	will have been	insulting
he/she/it	will have been	insulting
we	will have been	insulting
you	will have been	insulting
they	will have been	insulting

Conditional

I	would	insult
you	would	insult
he/she/it	would	insult
we	would	insult
you	would	insult
they	would	insult

Conditional Past

I	would have	insulted
you	would have	insulted
he/she/it	would have	insulted
we	would have	insulted
you	would have	insulted
they	would have	insulted

Simple tenses

Present

I	intend
you	intend
he/she/it	intends
we	intend
you	intend
they	intend

Past

I	intended
you	intended
he/she/it	intended
we	intended
you	intended
they	intended

Present Perfect

I	have	intended
you	have	intended
he/she/it	has	intended
we	have	intended
you	have	intended
they	have	intended

Past Perfect

I	had	intended
you	had	intended
he/she/it	had	intended
we	had	intended
you	had	intended
they	had	intended

Will-Future

I	will	intend
you	will	intend
he/she/it	will	intend
we	will	intend
you	will	intend
they	will	intend

Going to-Future

I	am	going to	intend
you	are	going to	intend
he/she/it	is	going to	intend
we	are	going to	intend
you	are	going to	intend
they	are	going to	intend

Future Perfect

I	will have	intended
you	will have	intended
he/she/it	will have	intended
we	will have	intended
you	will have	intended
they	will have	intended

Imperative

intend

Impersonal

ing-Form

intending

Past Participle

intended

Continuous tenses

Present

I	am	intending
you	are	intending
he/she/it	is	intending
we	are	intending
you	are	intending
they	are	intending

Past

I	was	intending
you	were	intending
he/she/it	was	intending
we	were	intending
you	were	intending
they	were	intending

Present Perfect

I	have been	intending
you	have been	intending
he/she/it	has been	intending
we	have been	intending
you	have been	intending
they	have been	intending

Past Perfect

I	had been	intending
you	had been	intending
he/she/it	had been	intending
we	had been	intending
you	had been	intending
they	had been	intending

Will-Future

I	will be	intending
you	will be	intending
he/she/it	will be	intending
we	will be	intending
you	will be	intending
they	will be	intending

Going to-Future

I	am	going to be	intending
you	are	going to be	intending
he/she/it	is	going to be	intending
we	are	going to be	intending
you	are	going to be	intending
they	are	going to be	intending

Future Perfect

I	will have been	intending
you	will have been	intending
he/she/it	will have been	intending
we	will have been	intending
you	will have been	intending
they	will have been	intending

Conditional

I	would	intend
you	would	intend
he/she/it	would	intend
we	would	intend
you	would	intend
they	would	intend

Conditional Past

I	would have	intended
you	would have	intended
he/she/it	would have	intended
we	would have	intended
you	would have	intended
they	would have	intended

interrupt

unterbrechen

Regelmäßiges Verb

Simple tenses

Present

I	interrupt
you	interrupt
he/she/it	interrupts
we	interrupt
you	interrupt
they	interrupt

Past

I	interrupted
you	interrupted
he/she/it	interrupted
we	interrupted
you	interrupted
they	interrupted

Present Perfect

I	have	interrupted
you	have	interrupted
he/she/it	has	interrupted
we	have	interrupted
you	have	interrupted
they	have	interrupted

Past Perfect

I	had	interrupted
you	had	interrupted
he/she/it	had	interrupted
we	had	interrupted
you	had	interrupted
they	had	interrupted

Will-Future

I	will	interrupt
you	will	interrupt
he/she/it	will	interrupt
we	will	interrupt
you	will	interrupt
they	will	interrupt

Going to-Future

I	am	going to	interrupt
you	are	going to	interrupt
he/she/it	is	going to	interrupt
we	are	going to	interrupt
you	are	going to	interrupt
they	are	going to	interrupt

Future Perfect

I	will have	interrupted
you	will have	interrupted
he/she/it	will have	interrupted
we	will have	interrupted
you	will have	interrupted
they	will have	interrupted

Imperative

interrupt

Impersonal

ing-Form

interrupting

Past Participle

interrupted

Continuous tenses

Present

I	am	interrupting
you	are	interrupting
he/she/it	is	interrupting
we	are	interrupting
you	are	interrupting
they	are	interrupting

Past

I	was	interrupting
you	were	interrupting
he/she/it	was	interrupting
we	were	interrupting
you	were	interrupting
they	were	interrupting

Present Perfect

I	have been	interrupting
you	have been	interrupting
he/she/it	has been	interrupting
we	have been	interrupting
you	have been	interrupting
they	have been	interrupting

Past Perfect

I	had been	interrupting
you	had been	interrupting
he/she/it	had been	interrupting
we	had been	interrupting
you	had been	interrupting
they	had been	interrupting

Will-Future

I	will be	interrupting
you	will be	interrupting
he/she/it	will be	interrupting
we	will be	interrupting
you	will be	interrupting
they	will be	interrupting

Going to-Future

I	am	going to be	interrupting
you	are	going to be	interrupting
he/she/it	is	going to be	interrupting
we	are	going to be	interrupting
you	are	going to be	interrupting
they	are	going to be	interrupting

Future Perfect

I	will have been interrupting
you	will have been interrupting
he/she/it	will have been interrupting
we	will have been interrupting
you	will have been interrupting
they	will have been interrupting

Conditional

I	would	interrupt
you	would	interrupt
he/she/it	would	interrupt
we	would	interrupt
you	would	interrupt
they	would	interrupt

Conditional Past

I	would have	interrupted
you	would have	interrupted
he/she/it	would have	interrupted
we	would have	interrupted
you	would have	interrupted
they	would have	interrupted

+ **-ing** → ~~e~~ / + **-d** nicht **-ed**
Regelmäßiges Verb

vorstellen

introduce

Simple tenses

Present

I	introduce
you	introduce
he/she/it	introduces
we	introduce
you	introduce
they	introduce

Past

I	introduced
you	introduced
he/she/it	introduced
we	introduced
you	introduced
they	introduced

Present Perfect

I	have	introduced
you	have	introduced
he/she/it	has	introduced
we	have	introduced
you	have	introduced
they	have	introduced

Past Perfect

I	had	introduced
you	had	introduced
he/she/it	had	introduced
we	had	introduced
you	had	introduced
they	had	introduced

Will-Future

I	will	introduce
you	will	introduce
he/she/it	will	introduce
we	will	introduce
you	will	introduce
they	will	introduce

Going to-Future

I	am	going to	introduce
you	are	going to	introduce
he/she/it	is	going to	introduce
we	are	going to	introduce
you	are	going to	introduce
they	are	going to	introduce

Future Perfect

I	will have	introduced
you	will have	introduced
he/she/it	will have	introduced
we	will have	introduced
you	will have	introduced
they	will have	introduced

Imperative

introduce

Impersonal

ing-Form

introducing

Past Participle

introduced

Continuous tenses

Present

I	am	introducing
you	are	introducing
he/she/it	is	introducing
we	are	introducing
you	are	introducing
they	are	introducing

Past

I	was	introducing
you	were	introducing
he/she/it	was	introducing
we	were	introducing
you	were	introducing
they	were	introducing

Present Perfect

I	have been	introducing
you	have been	introducing
he/she/it	has been	introducing
we	have been	introducing
you	have been	introducing
they	have been	introducing

Past Perfect

I	had been	introducing
you	had been	introducing
he/she/it	had been	introducing
we	had been	introducing
you	had been	introducing
they	had been	introducing

Will-Future

I	will be	introducing
you	will be	introducing
he/she/it	will be	introducing
we	will be	introducing
you	will be	introducing
they	will be	introducing

Going to-Future

I	am	going to be	introducing
you	are	going to be	introducing
he/she/it	is	going to be	introducing
we	are	going to be	introducing
you	are	going to be	introducing
they	are	going to be	introducing

Future Perfect

I	will have been introducing
you	will have been introducing
he/she/it	will have been introducing
we	will have been introducing
you	will have been introducing
they	will have been introducing

Conditional

I	would	introduce
you	would	introduce
he/she/it	would	introduce
we	would	introduce
you	would	introduce
they	would	introduce

Conditional Past

I	would have	introduced
you	would have	introduced
he/she/it	would have	introduced
we	would have	introduced
you	would have	introduced
they	would have	introduced

invent

erfinden

Regelmäßiges Verb

Simple tenses

Present

I	invent
you	invent
he/she/it	invents
we	invent
you	invent
they	invent

Past

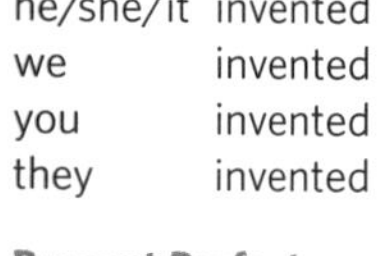

I	invented
you	invented
he/she/it	invented
we	invented
you	invented
they	invented

Present Perfect

I	have	invented
you	have	invented
he/she/it	has	invented
we	have	invented
you	have	invented
they	have	invented

Past Perfect

I	had	invented
you	had	invented
he/she/it	had	invented
we	had	invented
you	had	invented
they	had	invented

Will-Future

I	will	invent
you	will	invent
he/she/it	will	invent
we	will	invent
you	will	invent
they	will	invent

Going to-Future

I	am	going to	invent
you	are	going to	invent
he/she/it	is	going to	invent
we	are	going to	invent
you	are	going to	invent
they	are	going to	invent

Future Perfect

I	will have	invented
you	will have	invented
he/she/it	will have	invented
we	will have	invented
you	will have	invented
they	will have	invented

Imperative

invent

Impersonal

ing-Form

inventing

Past Participle

invented

Continuous tenses

Present

I	am	inventing
you	are	inventing
he/she/it	is	inventing
we	are	inventing
you	are	inventing
they	are	inventing

Past

I	was	inventing
you	were	inventing
he/she/it	was	inventing
we	were	inventing
you	were	inventing
they	were	inventing

Present Perfect

I	have been	inventing
you	have been	inventing
he/she/it	has been	inventing
we	have been	inventing
you	have been	inventing
they	have been	inventing

Past Perfect

I	had been	inventing
you	had been	inventing
he/she/it	had been	inventing
we	had been	inventing
you	had been	inventing
they	had been	inventing

Will-Future

I	will be	inventing
you	will be	inventing
he/she/it	will be	inventing
we	will be	inventing
you	will be	inventing
they	will be	inventing

Going to-Future

I	am	going to be	inventing
you	are	going to be	inventing
he/she/it	is	going to be	inventing
we	are	going to be	inventing
you	are	going to be	inventing
they	are	going to be	inventing

Future Perfect

I	will have been	inventing
you	will have been	inventing
he/she/it	will have been	inventing
we	will have been	inventing
you	will have been	inventing
they	will have been	inventing

Conditional

I	would	invent
you	would	invent
he/she/it	would	invent
we	would	invent
you	would	invent
they	would	invent

Conditional Past

I	would have	invented
you	would have	invented
he/she/it	would have	invented
we	would have	invented
you	would have	invented
they	would have	invented

Simple tenses

Present

I	invest
you	invest
he/she/it	invests
we	invest
you	invest
they	invest

Past

I	invested
you	invested
he/she/it	invested
we	invested
you	invested
they	invested

Present Perfect

I	have	invested
you	have	invested
he/she/it	has	invested
we	have	invested
you	have	invested
they	have	invested

Past Perfect

I	had	invested
you	had	invested
he/she/it	had	invested
we	had	invested
you	had	invested
they	had	invested

Will-Future

I	will	invest
you	will	invest
he/she/it	will	invest
we	will	invest
you	will	invest
they	will	invest

Going to-Future

I	am	going to	invest
you	are	going to	invest
he/she/it	is	going to	invest
we	are	going to	invest
you	are	going to	invest
they	are	going to	invest

Future Perfect

I	will have	invested
you	will have	invested
he/she/it	will have	invested
we	will have	invested
you	will have	invested
they	will have	invested

Imperative

invest

Impersonal

ing-Form

investing

Past Participle

invested

Continuous tenses

Present

I	am	investing
you	are	investing
he/she/it	is	investing
we	are	investing
you	are	investing
they	are	investing

Past

I	was	investing
you	were	investing
he/she/it	was	investing
we	were	investing
you	were	investing
they	were	investing

Present Perfect

I	have	been	investing
you	have	been	investing
he/she/it	has	been	investing
we	have	been	investing
you	have	been	investing
they	have	been	investing

Past Perfect

I	had been	investing
you	had been	investing
he/she/it	had been	investing
we	had been	investing
you	had been	investing
they	had been	investing

Will-Future

I	will be	investing
you	will be	investing
he/she/it	will be	investing
we	will be	investing
you	will be	investing
they	will be	investing

Going to-Future

I	am	going to be	investing
you	are	going to be	investing
he/she/it	is	going to be	investing
we	are	going to be	investing
you	are	going to be	investing
they	are	going to be	investing

Future Perfect

I	will have been	investing
you	will have been	investing
he/she/it	will have been	investing
we	will have been	investing
you	will have been	investing
they	will have been	investing

Conditional

I	would	invest
you	would	invest
he/she/it	would	invest
we	would	invest
you	would	invest
they	would	invest

Conditional Past

I	would have	invested
you	would have	invested
he/she/it	would have	invested
we	would have	invested
you	would have	invested
they	would have	invested

investigate

untersuchen

+ **-ing** → ~~e~~ / + **-d** nicht **-ed**
Regelmäßiges Verb

Simple tenses

Present

I	investigate
you	investigate
he/she/it	investigates
we	investigate
you	investigate
they	investigate

Past

I	investigated
you	investigated
he/she/it	investigated
we	investigated
you	investigated
they	investigated

Present Perfect

I	have	investigated
you	have	investigated
he/she/it	has	investigated
we	have	investigated
you	have	investigated
they	have	investigated

Past Perfect

I	had	investigated
you	had	investigated
he/she/it	had	investigated
we	had	investigated
you	had	investigated
they	had	investigated

Will-Future

I	will	investigate
you	will	investigate
he/she/it	will	investigate
we	will	investigate
you	will	investigate
they	will	investigate

Going to-Future

I	am	going to	investigate
you	are	going to	investigate
he/she/it	is	going to	investigate
we	are	going to	investigate
you	are	going to	investigate
they	are	going to	investigate

Future Perfect

I	will have	investigated
you	will have	investigated
he/she/it	will have	investigated
we	will have	investigated
you	will have	investigated
they	will have	investigated

Imperative

investigate

Impersonal

ing-Form

investigating

Past Participle

investigated

Continuous tenses

Present

I	am	investigating
you	are	investigating
he/she/it	is	investigating
we	are	investigating
you	are	investigating
they	are	investigating

Past

I	was	investigating
you	were	investigating
he/she/it	was	investigating
we	were	investigating
you	were	investigating
they	were	investigating

Present Perfect

I	have been	investigating
you	have been	investigating
he/she/it	has been	investigating
we	have been	investigating
you	have been	investigating
they	have been	investigating

Past Perfect

I	had been	investigating
you	had been	investigating
he/she/it	had been	investigating
we	had been	investigating
you	had been	investigating
they	had been	investigating

Will-Future

I	will be	investigating
you	will be	investigating
he/she/it	will be	investigating
we	will be	investigating
you	will be	investigating
they	will be	investigating

Going to-Future

I	am	going to be	investigating
you	are	going to be	investigating
he/she/it	is	going to be	investigating
we	are	going to be	investigating
you	are	going to be	investigating
they	are	going to be	investigating

Future Perfect

I	will have been	investigating
you	will have been	investigating
he/she/it	will have been	investigating
we	will have been	investigating
you	will have been	investigating
they	will have been	investigating

Conditional

I	would	investigate
you	would	investigate
he/she/it	would	investigate
we	would	investigate
you	would	investigate
they	would	investigate

Conditional Past

I	would have	investigated
you	would have	investigated
he/she/it	would have	investigated
we	would have	investigated
you	would have	investigated
they	would have	investigated

Simple tenses

Present

I	invite
you	invite
he/she/it	invites
we	invite
you	invite
they	invite

Past

I	invited
you	invited
he/she/it	invited
we	invited
you	invited
they	invited

Present Perfect

I	have	invited
you	have	invited
he/she/it	has	invited
we	have	invited
you	have	invited
they	have	invited

Past Perfect

I	had	invited
you	had	invited
he/she/it	had	invited
we	had	invited
you	had	invited
they	had	invited

Will-Future

I	will	invite
you	will	invite
he/she/it	will	invite
we	will	invite
you	will	invite
they	will	invite

Going to-Future

I	am	going to	invite
you	are	going to	invite
he/she/it	is	going to	invite
we	are	going to	invite
you	are	going to	invite
they	are	going to	invite

Future Perfect

I	will have	invited
you	will have	invited
he/she/it	will have	invited
we	will have	invited
you	will have	invited
they	will have	invited

Imperative

invite

Impersonal

ing-Form

inviting

Past Participle

invited

Continuous tenses

Present

I	am	inviting
you	are	inviting
he/she/it	is	inviting
we	are	inviting
you	are	inviting
they	are	inviting

Past

I	was	inviting
you	were	inviting
he/she/it	was	inviting
we	were	inviting
you	were	inviting
they	were	inviting

Present Perfect

I	have been	inviting
you	have been	inviting
he/she/it	has been	inviting
we	have been	inviting
you	have been	inviting
they	have been	inviting

Past Perfect

I	had been	inviting
you	had been	inviting
he/she/it	had been	inviting
we	had been	inviting
you	had been	inviting
they	had been	inviting

Will-Future

I	will be	inviting
you	will be	inviting
he/she/it	will be	inviting
we	will be	inviting
you	will be	inviting
they	will be	inviting

Going to-Future

I	am	going to be	inviting
you	are	going to be	inviting
he/she/it	is	going to be	inviting
we	are	going to be	inviting
you	are	going to be	inviting
they	are	going to be	inviting

Future Perfect

I	will have been	inviting
you	will have been	inviting
he/she/it	will have been	inviting
we	will have been	inviting
you	will have been	inviting
they	will have been	inviting

Conditional

I	would	invite
you	would	invite
he/she/it	would	invite
we	would	invite
you	would	invite
they	would	invite

Conditional Past

I	would have	invited
you	would have	invited
he/she/it	would have	invited
we	would have	invited
you	would have	invited
they	would have	invited

involve

beinhalten

+ **-ing** → ~~e~~ / + **-d** nicht **-ed**
Regelmäßiges Verb

Simple tenses

Present

I	involve
you	involve
he/she/it	involves
we	involve
you	involve
they	involve

Past

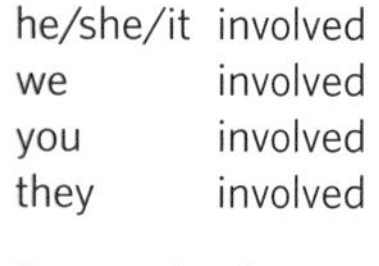

I	involved
you	involved
he/she/it	involved
we	involved
you	involved
they	involved

Present Perfect

I	have	involved
you	have	involved
he/she/it	has	involved
we	have	involved
you	have	involved
they	have	involved

Past Perfect

I	had	involved
you	had	involved
he/she/it	had	involved
we	had	involved
you	had	involved
they	had	involved

Will-Future

I	will	involve
you	will	involve
he/she/it	will	involve
we	will	involve
you	will	involve
they	will	involve

Going to-Future

I	am	going to	involve
you	are	going to	involve
he/she/it	is	going to	involve
we	are	going to	involve
you	are	going to	involve
they	are	going to	involve

Future Perfect

I	will have	involved
you	will have	involved
he/she/it	will have	involved
we	will have	involved
you	will have	involved
they	will have	involved

Imperative

involve

Impersonal

ing-Form

involving

Past Participle

involved

Continuous tenses

Present

I	am	involving
you	are	involving
he/she/it	is	involving
we	are	involving
you	are	involving
they	are	involving

Past

I	was	involving
you	were	involving
he/she/it	was	involving
we	were	involving
you	were	involving
they	were	involving

Present Perfect

I	have been	involving
you	have been	involving
he/she/it	has been	involving
we	have been	involving
you	have been	involving
they	have been	involving

Past Perfect

I	had been	involving
you	had been	involving
he/she/it	had been	involving
we	had been	involving
you	had been	involving
they	had been	involving

Will-Future

I	will be	involving
you	will be	involving
he/she/it	will be	involving
we	will be	involving
you	will be	involving
they	will be	involving

Going to-Future

I	am	going to be	involving
you	are	going to be	involving
he/she/it	is	going to be	involving
we	are	going to be	involving
you	are	going to be	involving
they	are	going to be	involving

Future Perfect

I	will have been	involving
you	will have been	involving
he/she/it	will have been	involving
we	will have been	involving
you	will have been	involving
they	will have been	involving

Conditional

I	would	involve
you	would	involve
he/she/it	would	involve
we	would	involve
you	would	involve
they	would	involve

Conditional Past

I	would have	involved
you	would have	involved
he/she/it	would have	involved
we	would have	involved
you	would have	involved
they	would have	involved

Simple tenses

Present

I	iron
you	iron
he/she/it	irons
we	iron
you	iron
they	iron

Past

I	ironed
you	ironed
he/she/it	ironed
we	ironed
you	ironed
they	ironed

Present Perfect

I	have	ironed
you	have	ironed
he/she/it	has	ironed
we	have	ironed
you	have	ironed
they	have	ironed

Past Perfect

I	had	ironed
you	had	ironed
he/she/it	had	ironed
we	had	ironed
you	had	ironed
they	had	ironed

Will-Future

I	will	iron
you	will	iron
he/she/it	will	iron
we	will	iron
you	will	iron
they	will	iron

Going to-Future

I	am	going to	iron
you	are	going to	iron
he/she/it	is	going to	iron
we	are	going to	iron
you	are	going to	iron
they	are	going to	iron

Future Perfect

I	will have	ironed
you	will have	ironed
he/she/it	will have	ironed
we	will have	ironed
you	will have	ironed
they	will have	ironed

Imperative

iron

Impersonal

ing-Form

ironing

Past Participle

ironed

Continuous tenses

Present

I	am	ironing
you	are	ironing
he/she/it	is	ironing
we	are	ironing
you	are	ironing
they	are	ironing

Past

I	was	ironing
you	were	ironing
he/she/it	was	ironing
we	were	ironing
you	were	ironing
they	were	ironing

Present Perfect

I	have been	ironing
you	have been	ironing
he/she/it	has been	ironing
we	have been	ironing
you	have been	ironing
they	have been	ironing

Past Perfect

I	had been	ironing
you	had been	ironing
he/she/it	had been	ironing
we	had been	ironing
you	had been	ironing
they	had been	ironing

Will-Future

I	will be	ironing
you	will be	ironing
he/she/it	will be	ironing
we	will be	ironing
you	will be	ironing
they	will be	ironing

Going to-Future

I	am	going to be	ironing
you	are	going to be	ironing
he/she/it	is	going to be	ironing
we	are	going to be	ironing
you	are	going to be	ironing
they	are	going to be	ironing

Future Perfect

I	will have been	ironing
you	will have been	ironing
he/she/it	will have been	ironing
we	will have been	ironing
you	will have been	ironing
they	will have been	ironing

Conditional

I	would	iron
you	would	iron
he/she/it	would	iron
we	would	iron
you	would	iron
they	would	iron

Conditional Past

I	would have	ironed
you	would have	ironed
he/she/it	would have	ironed
we	would have	ironed
you	would have	ironed
they	would have	ironed

join

verbinden

Regelmäßiges Verb

Simple tenses

Present

I	join
you	join
he/she/it	joins
we	join
you	join
they	join

Past

I	joined
you	joined
he/she/it	joined
we	joined
you	joined
they	joined

Present Perfect

I	have	joined
you	have	joined
he/she/it	has	joined
we	have	joined
you	have	joined
they	have	joined

Past Perfect

I	had	joined
you	had	joined
he/she/it	had	joined
we	had	joined
you	had	joined
they	had	joined

Will-Future

I	will	join
you	will	join
he/she/it	will	join
we	will	join
you	will	join
they	will	join

Going to-Future

I	am	going to	join
you	are	going to	join
he/she/it	is	going to	join
we	are	going to	join
you	are	going to	join
they	are	going to	join

Future Perfect

I	will have	joined
you	will have	joined
he/she/it	will have	joined
we	will have	joined
you	will have	joined
they	will have	joined

Imperative

join

Impersonal

ing-Form

joining

Past Participle

joined

Continuous tenses

Present

I	am	joining
you	are	joining
he/she/it	is	joining
we	are	joining
you	are	joining
they	are	joining

Past

I	was	joining
you	were	joining
he/she/it	was	joining
we	were	joining
you	were	joining
they	were	joining

Present Perfect

I	have	been	joining
you	have	been	joining
he/she/it	has	been	joining
we	have	been	joining
you	have	been	joining
they	have	been	joining

Past Perfect

I	had been	joining
you	had been	joining
he/she/it	had been	joining
we	had been	joining
you	had been	joining
they	had been	joining

Will-Future

I	will be	joining
you	will be	joining
he/she/it	will be	joining
we	will be	joining
you	will be	joining
they	will be	joining

Going to-Future

I	am	going to be	joining
you	are	going to be	joining
he/she/it	is	going to be	joining
we	are	going to be	joining
you	are	going to be	joining
they	are	going to be	joining

Future Perfect

I	will have been	joining
you	will have been	joining
he/she/it	will have been	joining
we	will have been	joining
you	will have been	joining
they	will have been	joining

Conditional

I	would	join
you	would	join
he/she/it	would	join
we	would	join
you	would	join
they	would	join

Conditional Past

I	would have	joined
you	would have	joined
he/she/it	would have	joined
we	would have	joined
you	would have	joined
they	would have	joined

scherzen

joke

Simple tenses

Present

I	joke
you	joke
he/she/it	jokes
we	joke
you	joke
they	joke

Past

I	joked
you	joked
he/she/it	joked
we	joked
you	joked
they	joked

Present Perfect

I	have	joked
you	have	joked
he/she/it	has	joked
we	have	joked
you	have	joked
they	have	joked

Past Perfect

I	had	joked
you	had	joked
he/she/it	had	joked
we	had	joked
you	had	joked
they	had	joked

Will-Future

I	will	joke
you	will	joke
he/she/it	will	joke
we	will	joke
you	will	joke
they	will	joke

Going to-Future

I	am	going to	joke
you	are	going to	joke
he/she/it	is	going to	joke
we	are	going to	joke
you	are	going to	joke
they	are	going to	joke

Future Perfect

I	will have	joked
you	will have	joked
he/she/it	will have	joked
we	will have	joked
you	will have	joked
they	will have	joked

Imperative

joke

Impersonal

ing-Form

joking

Past Participle

joked

Continuous tenses

Present

I	am	joking
you	are	joking
he/she/it	is	joking
we	are	joking
you	are	joking
they	are	joking

Past

I	was	joking
you	were	joking
he/she/it	was	joking
we	were	joking
you	were	joking
they	were	joking

Present Perfect

I	have been	joking
you	have been	joking
he/she/it	has been	joking
we	have been	joking
you	have been	joking
they	have been	joking

Past Perfect

I	had been	joking
you	had been	joking
he/she/it	had been	joking
we	had been	joking
you	had been	joking
they	had been	joking

Will-Future

I	will be	joking
you	will be	joking
he/she/it	will be	joking
we	will be	joking
you	will be	joking
they	will be	joking

Going to-Future

I	am	going to be	joking
you	are	going to be	joking
he/she/it	is	going to be	joking
we	are	going to be	joking
you	are	going to be	joking
they	are	going to be	joking

Future Perfect

I	will have been	joking
you	will have been	joking
he/she/it	will have been	joking
we	will have been	joking
you	will have been	joking
they	will have been	joking

Conditional

I	would	joke
you	would	joke
he/she/it	would	joke
we	would	joke
you	would	joke
they	would	joke

Conditional Past

I	would have	joked
you	would have	joked
he/she/it	would have	joked
we	would have	joked
you	would have	joked
they	would have	joked

beurteilen

+ **-ing** → ~~e~~ / + **-d** nicht **-ed**
Regelmäßiges Verb

Simple tenses

Present

I	judge
you	judge
he/she/it	judges
we	judge
you	judge
they	judge

Past

I	judged
you	judged
he/she/it	judged
we	judged
you	judged
they	judged

Present Perfect

I	have	judged
you	have	judged
he/she/it	has	judged
we	have	judged
you	have	judged
they	have	judged

Past Perfect

I	had	judged
you	had	judged
he/she/it	had	judged
we	had	judged
you	had	judged
they	had	judged

Will-Future

I	will	judge
you	will	judge
he/she/it	will	judge
we	will	judge
you	will	judge
they	will	judge

Going to-Future

I	am	going to	judge
you	are	going to	judge
he/she/it	is	going to	judge
we	are	going to	judge
you	are	going to	judge
they	are	going to	judge

Future Perfect

I	will have	judged
you	will have	judged
he/she/it	will have	judged
we	will have	judged
you	will have	judged
they	will have	judged

Imperative

judge

Impersonal

ing-Form

judging

Past Participle

judged

Continuous tenses

Present

I	am	judging
you	are	judging
he/she/it	is	judging
we	are	judging
you	are	judging
they	are	judging

Past

I	was	judging
you	were	judging
he/she/it	was	judging
we	were	judging
you	were	judging
they	were	judging

Present Perfect

I	have been	judging
you	have been	judging
he/she/it	has been	judging
we	have been	judging
you	have been	judging
they	have been	judging

Past Perfect

I	had been	judging
you	had been	judging
he/she/it	had been	judging
we	had been	judging
you	had been	judging
they	had been	judging

Will-Future

I	will be	judging
you	will be	judging
he/she/it	will be	judging
we	will be	judging
you	will be	judging
they	will be	judging

Going to-Future

I	am	going to be	judging
you	are	going to be	judging
he/she/it	is	going to be	judging
we	are	going to be	judging
you	are	going to be	judging
they	are	going to be	judging

Future Perfect

I	will have been	judging
you	will have been	judging
he/she/it	will have been	judging
we	will have been	judging
you	will have been	judging
they	will have been	judging

Conditional

I	would	judge
you	would	judge
he/she/it	would	judge
we	would	judge
you	would	judge
they	would	judge

Conditional Past

I	would have	judged
you	would have	judged
he/she/it	would have	judged
we	would have	judged
you	would have	judged
they	would have	judged

springen

Regelmäßiges Verb

Simple tenses

Present

I	jump
you	jump
he/she/it	jumps
we	jump
you	jump
they	jump

Past

I	jumped
you	jumped
he/she/it	jumped
we	jumped
you	jumped
they	jumped

Present Perfect

I	have	jumped
you	have	jumped
he/she/it	has	jumped
we	have	jumped
you	have	jumped
they	have	jumped

Past Perfect

I	had	jumped
you	had	jumped
he/she/it	had	jumped
we	had	jumped
you	had	jumped
they	had	jumped

Will-Future

I	will	jump
you	will	jump
he/she/it	will	jump
we	will	jump
you	will	jump
they	will	jump

Going to-Future

I	am	going to	jump
you	are	going to	jump
he/she/it	is	going to	jump
we	are	going to	jump
you	are	going to	jump
they	are	going to	jump

Future Perfect

I	will have	jumped
you	will have	jumped
he/she/it	will have	jumped
we	will have	jumped
you	will have	jumped
they	will have	jumped

Imperative

jump

Impersonal

ing-Form

jumping

Past Participle

jumped

Continuous tenses

Present

I	am	jumping
you	are	jumping
he/she/it	is	jumping
we	are	jumping
you	are	jumping
they	are	jumping

Past

I	was	jumping
you	were	jumping
he/she/it	was	jumping
we	were	jumping
you	were	jumping
they	were	jumping

Present Perfect

I	have been	jumping
you	have been	jumping
he/she/it	has been	jumping
we	have been	jumping
you	have been	jumping
they	have been	jumping

Past Perfect

I	had been	jumping
you	had been	jumping
he/she/it	had been	jumping
we	had been	jumping
you	had been	jumping
they	had been	jumping

Will-Future

I	will be	jumping
you	will be	jumping
he/she/it	will be	jumping
we	will be	jumping
you	will be	jumping
they	will be	jumping

Going to-Future

I	am	going to be	jumping
you	are	going to be	jumping
he/she/it	is	going to be	jumping
we	are	going to be	jumping
you	are	going to be	jumping
they	are	going to be	jumping

Future Perfect

I	will have been	jumping
you	will have been	jumping
he/she/it	will have been	jumping
we	will have been	jumping
you	will have been	jumping
they	will have been	jumping

Conditional

I	would	jump
you	would	jump
he/she/it	would	jump
we	would	jump
you	would	jump
they	would	jump

Conditional Past

I	would have	jumped
you	would have	jumped
he/she/it	would have	jumped
we	would have	jumped
you	would have	jumped
they	would have	jumped

justify

rechtfertigen

-y → **-ie** vor **-s** / **-y** → **-i** vor **-ed**
Regelmäßiges Verb

Simple tenses

Present

I	justify
you	justify
he/she/it	justifies
we	justify
you	justify
they	justify

Past

I	justified
you	justified
he/she/it	justified
we	justified
you	justified
they	justified

Present Perfect

I	have	justified
you	have	justified
he/she/it	has	justified
we	have	justified
you	have	justified
they	have	justified

Past Perfect

I	had	justified
you	had	justified
he/she/it	had	justified
we	had	justified
you	had	justified
they	had	justified

Will-Future

I	will	justify
you	will	justify
he/she/it	will	justify
we	will	justify
you	will	justify
they	will	justify

Going to-Future

I	am	going to	justify
you	are	going to	justify
he/she/it	is	going to	justify
we	are	going to	justify
you	are	going to	justify
they	are	going to	justify

Future Perfect

I	will have	justified
you	will have	justified
he/she/it	will have	justified
we	will have	justified
you	will have	justified
they	will have	justified

Imperative

justify

Impersonal

ing-Form

justifying

Past Participle

justified

Continuous tenses

Present

I	am	justifying
you	are	justifying
he/she/it	is	justifying
we	are	justifying
you	are	justifying
they	are	justifying

Past

I	was	justifying
you	were	justifying
he/she/it	was	justifying
we	were	justifying
you	were	justifying
they	were	justifying

Present Perfect

I	have been	justifying
you	have been	justifying
he/she/it	has been	justifying
we	have been	justifying
you	have been	justifying
they	have been	justifying

Past Perfect

I	had been	justifying
you	had been	justifying
he/she/it	had been	justifying
we	had been	justifying
you	had been	justifying
they	had been	justifying

Will-Future

I	will be	justifying
you	will be	justifying
he/she/it	will be	justifying
we	will be	justifying
you	will be	justifying
they	will be	justifying

Going to-Future

I	am	going to be	justifying
you	are	going to be	justifying
he/she/it	is	going to be	justifying
we	are	going to be	justifying
you	are	going to be	justifying
they	are	going to be	justifying

Future Perfect

I	will have been	justifying
you	will have been	justifying
he/she/it	will have been	justifying
we	will have been	justifying
you	will have been	justifying
they	will have been	justifying

Conditional

I	would	justify
you	would	justify
he/she/it	would	justify
we	would	justify
you	would	justify
they	would	justify

Conditional Past

I	would have	justified
you	would have	justified
he/she/it	would have	justified
we	would have	justified
you	would have	justified
they	would have	justified

Unregelmäßiges Verb

behalten

keep

- kept - kept

Simple tenses

Present

I	keep
you	keep
he/she/it	keeps
we	keep
you	keep
they	keep

Past

I	kept
you	kept
he/she/it	kept
we	kept
you	kept
they	kept

Present Perfect

I	have	kept
you	have	kept
he/she/it	has	kept
we	have	kept
you	have	kept
they	have	kept

Past Perfect

I	had	kept
you	had	kept
he/she/it	had	kept
we	had	kept
you	had	kept
they	had	kept

Will-Future

I	will	keep
you	will	keep
he/she/it	will	keep
we	will	keep
you	will	keep
they	will	keep

Going to-Future

I	am	going to	keep
you	are	going to	keep
he/she/it	is	going to	keep
we	are	going to	keep
you	are	going to	keep
they	are	going to	keep

Future Perfect

I	will have	kept
you	will have	kept
he/she/it	will have	kept
we	will have	kept
you	will have	kept
they	will have	kept

Imperative

keep

Impersonal

ing-Form

keeping

Past Participle

kept

Continuous tenses

Present

I	am	keeping
you	are	keeping
he/she/it	is	keeping
we	are	keeping
you	are	keeping
they	are	keeping

Past

I	was	keeping
you	were	keeping
he/she/it	was	keeping
we	were	keeping
you	were	keeping
they	were	keeping

Present Perfect

I	have been	keeping
you	have been	keeping
he/she/it	has been	keeping
we	have been	keeping
you	have been	keeping
they	have been	keeping

Past Perfect

I	had been	keeping
you	had been	keeping
he/she/it	had been	keeping
we	had been	keeping
you	had been	keeping
they	had been	keeping

Will-Future

I	will be	keeping
you	will be	keeping
he/she/it	will be	keeping
we	will be	keeping
you	will be	keeping
they	will be	keeping

Going to-Future

I	am	going to be	keeping
you	are	going to be	keeping
he/she/it	is	going to be	keeping
we	are	going to be	keeping
you	are	going to be	keeping
they	are	going to be	keeping

Future Perfect

I	will have been	keeping
you	will have been	keeping
he/she/it	will have been	keeping
we	will have been	keeping
you	will have been	keeping
they	will have been	keeping

Conditional

I	would	keep
you	would	keep
he/she/it	would	keep
we	would	keep
you	would	keep
they	would	keep

Conditional Past

I	would have	kept
you	would have	kept
he/she/it	would have	kept
we	would have	kept
you	would have	kept
they	would have	kept

kick

treten

Regelmäßiges Verb

Simple tenses

Present

I	kick
you	kick
he/she/it	kicks
we	kick
you	kick
they	kick

Past

I	kicked
you	kicked
he/she/it	kicked
we	kicked
you	kicked
they	kicked

Present Perfect

I	have	kicked
you	have	kicked
he/she/it	has	kicked
we	have	kicked
you	have	kicked
they	have	kicked

Past Perfect

I	had	kicked
you	had	kicked
he/she/it	had	kicked
we	had	kicked
you	had	kicked
they	had	kicked

Will-Future

I	will	kick
you	will	kick
he/she/it	will	kick
we	will	kick
you	will	kick
they	will	kick

Going to-Future

I	am	going to	kick
you	are	going to	kick
he/she/it	is	going to	kick
we	are	going to	kick
you	are	going to	kick
they	are	going to	kick

Future Perfect

I	will have	kicked
you	will have	kicked
he/she/it	will have	kicked
we	will have	kicked
you	will have	kicked
they	will have	kicked

Imperative

kick

Impersonal

ing-Form

kicking

Past Participle

kicked

Continuous tenses

Present

I	am	kicking
you	are	kicking
he/she/it	is	kicking
we	are	kicking
you	are	kicking
they	are	kicking

Past

I	was	kicking
you	were	kicking
he/she/it	was	kicking
we	were	kicking
you	were	kicking
they	were	kicking

Present Perfect

I	have	been	kicking
you	have	been	kicking
he/she/it	has	been	kicking
we	have	been	kicking
you	have	been	kicking
they	have	been	kicking

Past Perfect

I	had been	kicking
you	had been	kicking
he/she/it	had been	kicking
we	had been	kicking
you	had been	kicking
they	had been	kicking

Will-Future

I	will be	kicking
you	will be	kicking
he/she/it	will be	kicking
we	will be	kicking
you	will be	kicking
they	will be	kicking

Going to-Future

I	am	going to be	kicking
you	are	going to be	kicking
he/she/it	is	going to be	kicking
we	are	going to be	kicking
you	are	going to be	kicking
they	are	going to be	kicking

Future Perfect

I	will have been	kicking
you	will have been	kicking
he/she/it	will have been	kicking
we	will have been	kicking
you	will have been	kicking
they	will have been	kicking

Conditional

I	would	kick
you	would	kick
he/she/it	would	kick
we	would	kick
you	would	kick
they	would	kick

Conditional Past

I	would have	kicked
you	would have	kicked
he/she/it	would have	kicked
we	would have	kicked
you	would have	kicked
they	would have	kicked

Simple tenses

Present

I	kill
you	kill
he/she/it	kills
we	kill
you	kill
they	kill

Past

I	killed
you	killed
he/she/it	killed
we	killed
you	killed
they	killed

Present Perfect

I	have	killed
you	have	killed
he/she/it	has	killed
we	have	killed
you	have	killed
they	have	killed

Past Perfect

I	had	killed
you	had	killed
he/she/it	had	killed
we	had	killed
you	had	killed
they	had	killed

Will-Future

I	will	kill
you	will	kill
he/she/it	will	kill
we	will	kill
you	will	kill
they	will	kill

Going to-Future

I	am	going to	kill
you	are	going to	kill
he/she/it	is	going to	kill
we	are	going to	kill
you	are	going to	kill
they	are	going to	kill

Future Perfect

I	will have	killed
you	will have	killed
he/she/it	will have	killed
we	will have	killed
you	will have	killed
they	will have	killed

Imperative

kill

Impersonal

ing-Form

killing

Past Participle

killed

Continuous tenses

Present

I	am	killing
you	are	killing
he/she/it	is	killing
we	are	killing
you	are	killing
they	are	killing

Past

I	was	killing
you	were	killing
he/she/it	was	killing
we	were	killing
you	were	killing
they	were	killing

Present Perfect

I	have	been	killing
you	have	been	killing
he/she/it	has	been	killing
we	have	been	killing
you	have	been	killing
they	have	been	killing

Past Perfect

I	had been	killing
you	had been	killing
he/she/it	had been	killing
we	had been	killing
you	had been	killing
they	had been	killing

Will-Future

I	will be	killing
you	will be	killing
he/she/it	will be	killing
we	will be	killing
you	will be	killing
they	will be	killing

Going to-Future

I	am	going to be	killing
you	are	going to be	killing
he/she/it	is	going to be	killing
we	are	going to be	killing
you	are	going to be	killing
they	are	going to be	killing

Future Perfect

I	will have been	killing
you	will have been	killing
he/she/it	will have been	killing
we	will have been	killing
you	will have been	killing
they	will have been	killing

Conditional

I	would	kill
you	would	kill
he/she/it	would	kill
we	would	kill
you	would	kill
they	would	kill

Conditional Past

I	would have	killed
you	would have	killed
he/she/it	would have	killed
we	would have	killed
you	would have	killed
they	would have	killed

kiss

küssen

+ -es in 3. Person Singular
Regelmäßiges Verb

Simple tenses

Present

I	kiss
you	kiss
he/she/it	kisses
we	kiss
you	kiss
they	kiss

Past

I	kissed
you	kissed
he/she/it	kissed
we	kissed
you	kissed
they	kissed

Present Perfect

I	have	kissed
you	have	kissed
he/she/it	has	kissed
we	have	kissed
you	have	kissed
they	have	kissed

Past Perfect

I	had	kissed
you	had	kissed
he/she/it	had	kissed
we	had	kissed
you	had	kissed
they	had	kissed

Will-Future

I	will	kiss
you	will	kiss
he/she/it	will	kiss
we	will	kiss
you	will	kiss
they	will	kiss

Going to-Future

I	am	going to	kiss
you	are	going to	kiss
he/she/it	is	going to	kiss
we	are	going to	kiss
you	are	going to	kiss
they	are	going to	kiss

Future Perfect

I	will have	kissed
you	will have	kissed
he/she/it	will have	kissed
we	will have	kissed
you	will have	kissed
they	will have	kissed

Imperative

kiss

Impersonal

ing-Form

kissing

Past Participle

kissed

Continuous tenses

Present

I	am	kissing
you	are	kissing
he/she/it	is	kissing
we	are	kissing
you	are	kissing
they	are	kissing

Past

I	was	kissing
you	were	kissing
he/she/it	was	kissing
we	were	kissing
you	were	kissing
they	were	kissing

Present Perfect

I	have	been	kissing
you	have	been	kissing
he/she/it	has	been	kissing
we	have	been	kissing
you	have	been	kissing
they	have	been	kissing

Past Perfect

I	had been	kissing
you	had been	kissing
he/she/it	had been	kissing
we	had been	kissing
you	had been	kissing
they	had been	kissing

Will-Future

I	will be	kissing
you	will be	kissing
he/she/it	will be	kissing
we	will be	kissing
you	will be	kissing
they	will be	kissing

Going to-Future

I	am	going to be	kissing
you	are	going to be	kissing
he/she/it	is	going to be	kissing
we	are	going to be	kissing
you	are	going to be	kissing
they	are	going to be	kissing

Future Perfect

I	will have been	kissing
you	will have been	kissing
he/she/it	will have been	kissing
we	will have been	kissing
you	will have been	kissing
they	will have been	kissing

Conditional

I	would	kiss
you	would	kiss
he/she/it	would	kiss
we	would	kiss
you	would	kiss
they	would	kiss

Conditional Past

I	would have	kissed
you	would have	kissed
he/she/it	would have	kissed
we	would have	kissed
you	would have	kissed
they	would have	kissed

knien

kneel

- knelt/kneeled - knelt/kneeled

Simple tenses

Present

I	kneel
you	kneel
he/she/it	kneels
we	kneel
you	kneel
they	kneel

Past

I	knelt | kneeled
you	knelt | kneeled
he/she/it	knelt | kneeled
we	knelt | kneeled
you	knelt | kneeled
they	knelt | kneeled

Present Perfect

I	have	knelt | kneeled
you	have	knelt | kneeled
he/she/it	has	knelt | kneeled
we	have	knelt | kneeled
you	have	knelt | kneeled
they	have	knelt | kneeled

Past Perfect

I	had	knelt | kneeled
you	had	knelt | kneeled
he/she/it	had	knelt | kneeled
we	had	knelt | kneeled
you	had	knelt | kneeled
they	had	knelt | kneeled

Will-Future

I	will	kneel
you	will	kneel
he/she/it	will	kneel
we	will	kneel
you	will	kneel
they	will	kneel

Going to-Future

I	am	going to	kneel
you	are	going to	kneel
he/she/it	is	going to	kneel
we	are	going to	kneel
you	are	going to	kneel
they	are	going to	kneel

Future Perfect

I	will have	knelt | kneeled
you	will have	knelt | kneeled
he/she/it	will have	knelt | kneeled
we	will have	knelt | kneeled
you	will have	knelt | kneeled
they	will have	knelt | kneeled

Imperative

kneel

Impersonal

ing-Form

kneeling

Past Participle

knelt | kneeled

Continuous tenses

Present

I	am	kneeling
you	are	kneeling
he/she/it	is	kneeling
we	are	kneeling
you	are	kneeling
they	are	kneeling

Past

I	was	kneeling
you	were	kneeling
he/she/it	was	kneeling
we	were	kneeling
you	were	kneeling
they	were	kneeling

Present Perfect

I	have been	kneeling
you	have been	kneeling
he/she/it	has been	kneeling
we	have been	kneeling
you	have been	kneeling
they	have been	kneeling

Past Perfect

I	had been	kneeling
you	had been	kneeling
he/she/it	had been	kneeling
we	had been	kneeling
you	had been	kneeling
they	had been	kneeling

Will-Future

I	will be	kneeling
you	will be	kneeling
he/she/it	will be	kneeling
we	will be	kneeling
you	will be	kneeling
they	will be	kneeling

Going to-Future

I	am	going to be	kneeling
you	are	going to be	kneeling
he/she/it	is	going to be	kneeling
we	are	going to be	kneeling
you	are	going to be	kneeling
they	are	going to be	kneeling

Future Perfect

I	will have been	kneeling
you	will have been	kneeling
he/she/it	will have been	kneeling
we	will have been	kneeling
you	will have been	kneeling
they	will have been	kneeling

Conditional

I	would	kneel
you	would	kneel
he/she/it	would	kneel
we	would	kneel
you	would	kneel
they	would	kneel

Conditional Past

I	would have	knelt | kneeled
you	would have	knelt | kneeled
he/she/it	would have	knelt | kneeled
we	would have	knelt | kneeled
you	would have	knelt | kneeled
they	would have	knelt | kneeled

knock

klopfen

Regelmäßiges Verb

Simple tenses

Present

I	knock
you	knock
he/she/it	knocks
we	knock
you	knock
they	knock

Past

I	knocked
you	knocked
he/she/it	knocked
we	knocked
you	knocked
they	knocked

Present Perfect

I	have	knocked
you	have	knocked
he/she/it	has	knocked
we	have	knocked
you	have	knocked
they	have	knocked

Past Perfect

I	had	knocked
you	had	knocked
he/she/it	had	knocked
we	had	knocked
you	had	knocked
they	had	knocked

Will-Future

I	will	knock
you	will	knock
he/she/it	will	knock
we	will	knock
you	will	knock
they	will	knock

Going to-Future

I	am	going to	knock
you	are	going to	knock
he/she/it	is	going to	knock
we	are	going to	knock
you	are	going to	knock
they	are	going to	knock

Future Perfect

I	will have	knocked
you	will have	knocked
he/she/it	will have	knocked
we	will have	knocked
you	will have	knocked
they	will have	knocked

Imperative

knock

Impersonal

ing-Form

knocking

Past Participle

knocked

Continuous tenses

Present

I	am	knocking
you	are	knocking
he/she/it	is	knocking
we	are	knocking
you	are	knocking
they	are	knocking

Past

I	was	knocking
you	were	knocking
he/she/it	was	knocking
we	were	knocking
you	were	knocking
they	were	knocking

Present Perfect

I	have been	knocking
you	have been	knocking
he/she/it	has been	knocking
we	have been	knocking
you	have been	knocking
they	have been	knocking

Past Perfect

I	had been	knocking
you	had been	knocking
he/she/it	had been	knocking
we	had been	knocking
you	had been	knocking
they	had been	knocking

Will-Future

I	will be	knocking
you	will be	knocking
he/she/it	will be	knocking
we	will be	knocking
you	will be	knocking
they	will be	knocking

Going to-Future

I	am	going to be	knocking
you	are	going to be	knocking
he/she/it	is	going to be	knocking
we	are	going to be	knocking
you	are	going to be	knocking
they	are	going to be	knocking

Future Perfect

I	will have been	knocking
you	will have been	knocking
he/she/it	will have been	knocking
we	will have been	knocking
you	will have been	knocking
they	will have been	knocking

Conditional

I	would	knock
you	would	knock
he/she/it	would	knock
we	would	knock
you	would	knock
they	would	knock

Conditional Past

I	would have	knocked
you	would have	knocked
he/she/it	would have	knocked
we	would have	knocked
you	would have	knocked
they	would have	knocked

Know hat keine Verlaufsform.
Unregelmäßiges Verb

wissen

know

- knew - known

Simple tenses

Present

I	know
you	know
he/she/it	knows
we	know
you	know
they	know

Past

I	knew
you	knew
he/she/it	knew
we	knew
you	knew
they	knew

Present Perfect

I	have	known
you	have	known
he/she/it	has	known
we	have	known
you	have	known
they	have	known

Past Perfect

I	had	known
you	had	known
he/she/it	had	known
we	had	known
you	had	known
they	had	known

Will-Future

I	will	know
you	will	know
he/she/it	will	know
we	will	know
you	will	know
they	will	know

Going to-Future

I	am	going to	know
you	are	going to	know
he/she/it	is	going to	know
we	are	going to	know
you	are	going to	know
they	are	going to	know

Future Perfect

I	will have	known
you	will have	known
he/she/it	will have	known
we	will have	known
you	will have	known
they	will have	known

Imperative

know

Impersonal

ing-Form

knowing

Past Participle

known

Continuous tenses

Present

I	am	knowing
you	are	knowing
he/she/it	is	knowing
we	are	knowing
you	are	knowing
they	are	knowing

Past

I	was	knowing
you	were	knowing
he/she/it	was	knowing
we	were	knowing
you	were	knowing
they	were	knowing

Present Perfect

I	have been	knowing
you	have been	knowing
he/she/it	has been	knowing
we	have been	knowing
you	have been	knowing
they	have been	knowing

Past Perfect

I	had been	knowing
you	had been	knowing
he/she/it	had been	knowing
we	had been	knowing
you	had been	knowing
they	had been	knowing

Will-Future

I	will be	knowing
you	will be	knowing
he/she/it	will be	knowing
we	will be	knowing
you	will be	knowing
they	will be	knowing

Going to-Future

I	am	going to be	knowing
you	are	going to be	knowing
he/she/it	is	going to be	knowing
we	are	going to be	knowing
you	are	going to be	knowing
they	are	going to be	knowing

Future Perfect

I	will have been	knowing
you	will have been	knowing
he/she/it	will have been	knowing
we	will have been	knowing
you	will have been	knowing
they	will have been	knowing

Conditional

I	would	know
you	would	know
he/she/it	would	know
we	would	know
you	would	know
they	would	know

Conditional Past

I	would have	known
you	would have	known
he/she/it	would have	known
we	would have	known
you	would have	known
they	would have	known

lack

nicht haben

Regelmäßiges Verb

Simple tenses

Present

I	lack
you	lack
he/she/it	lacks
we	lack
you	lack
they	lack

Past

I	lacked
you	lacked
he/she/it	lacked
we	lacked
you	lacked
they	lacked

Present Perfect

I	have	lacked
you	have	lacked
he/she/it	has	lacked
we	have	lacked
you	have	lacked
they	have	lacked

Past Perfect

I	had	lacked
you	had	lacked
he/she/it	had	lacked
we	had	lacked
you	had	lacked
they	had	lacked

Will-Future

I	will	lack
you	will	lack
he/she/it	will	lack
we	will	lack
you	will	lack
they	will	lack

Going to-Future

I	am	going to	lack
you	are	going to	lack
he/she/it	is	going to	lack
we	are	going to	lack
you	are	going to	lack
they	are	going to	lack

Future Perfect

I	will have	lacked
you	will have	lacked
he/she/it	will have	lacked
we	will have	lacked
you	will have	lacked
they	will have	lacked

Imperative

lack

Impersonal

ing-Form

lacking

Past Participle

lacked

Continuous tenses

Present

I	am	lacking
you	are	lacking
he/she/it	is	lacking
we	are	lacking
you	are	lacking
they	are	lacking

Past

I	was	lacking
you	were	lacking
he/she/it	was	lacking
we	were	lacking
you	were	lacking
they	were	lacking

Present Perfect

I	have been	lacking
you	have been	lacking
he/she/it	has been	lacking
we	have been	lacking
you	have been	lacking
they	have been	lacking

Past Perfect

I	had been	lacking
you	had been	lacking
he/she/it	had been	lacking
we	had been	lacking
you	had been	lacking
they	had been	lacking

Will-Future

I	will be	lacking
you	will be	lacking
he/she/it	will be	lacking
we	will be	lacking
you	will be	lacking
they	will be	lacking

Going to-Future

I	am	going to be	lacking
you	are	going to be	lacking
he/she/it	is	going to be	lacking
we	are	going to be	lacking
you	are	going to be	lacking
they	are	going to be	lacking

Future Perfect

I	will have been	lacking
you	will have been	lacking
he/she/it	will have been	lacking
we	will have been	lacking
you	will have been	lacking
they	will have been	lacking

Conditional

I	would	lack
you	would	lack
he/she/it	would	lack
we	would	lack
you	would	lack
they	would	lack

Conditional Past

I	would have	lacked
you	would have	lacked
he/she/it	would have	lacked
we	would have	lacked
you	would have	lacked
they	would have	lacked

Simple tenses

Present

I	land
you	land
he/she/it	lands
we	land
you	land
they	land

Past

I	landed
you	landed
he/she/it	landed
we	landed
you	landed
they	landed

Present Perfect

I	have	landed
you	have	landed
he/she/it	has	landed
we	have	landed
you	have	landed
they	have	landed

Past Perfect

I	had	landed
you	had	landed
he/she/it	had	landed
we	had	landed
you	had	landed
they	had	landed

Will-Future

I	will	land
you	will	land
he/she/it	will	land
we	will	land
you	will	land
they	will	land

Going to-Future

I	am	going to	land
you	are	going to	land
he/she/it	is	going to	land
we	are	going to	land
you	are	going to	land
they	are	going to	land

Future Perfect

I	will have	landed
you	will have	landed
he/she/it	will have	landed
we	will have	landed
you	will have	landed
they	will have	landed

Imperative

land

Impersonal

ing-Form

landing

Past Participle

landed

Continuous tenses

Present

I	am	landing
you	are	landing
he/she/it	is	landing
we	are	landing
you	are	landing
they	are	landing

Past

I	was	landing
you	were	landing
he/she/it	was	landing
we	were	landing
you	were	landing
they	were	landing

Present Perfect

I	have been	landing
you	have been	landing
he/she/it	has been	landing
we	have been	landing
you	have been	landing
they	have been	landing

Past Perfect

I	had been	landing
you	had been	landing
he/she/it	had been	landing
we	had been	landing
you	had been	landing
they	had been	landing

Will-Future

I	will be	landing
you	will be	landing
he/she/it	will be	landing
we	will be	landing
you	will be	landing
they	will be	landing

Going to-Future

I	am	going to be	landing
you	are	going to be	landing
he/she/it	is	going to be	landing
we	are	going to be	landing
you	are	going to be	landing
they	are	going to be	landing

Future Perfect

I	will have been	landing
you	will have been	landing
he/she/it	will have been	landing
we	will have been	landing
you	will have been	landing
they	will have been	landing

Conditional

I	would	land
you	would	land
he/she/it	would	land
we	would	land
you	would	land
they	would	land

Conditional Past

I	would have	landed
you	would have	landed
he/she/it	would have	landed
we	would have	landed
you	would have	landed
they	would have	landed

laugh

lachen

Regelmäßiges Verb

Simple tenses

Present

I	laugh
you	laugh
he/she/it	laughs
we	laugh
you	laugh
they	laugh

Past

I	laughed
you	laughed
he/she/it	laughed
we	laughed
you	laughed
they	laughed

Present Perfect

I	have	laughed
you	have	laughed
he/she/it	has	laughed
we	have	laughed
you	have	laughed
they	have	laughed

Past Perfect

I	had	laughed
you	had	laughed
he/she/it	had	laughed
we	had	laughed
you	had	laughed
they	had	laughed

Will-Future

I	will	laugh
you	will	laugh
he/she/it	will	laugh
we	will	laugh
you	will	laugh
they	will	laugh

Going to-Future

I	am	going to	laugh
you	are	going to	laugh
he/she/it	is	going to	laugh
we	are	going to	laugh
you	are	going to	laugh
they	are	going to	laugh

Future Perfect

I	will have	laughed
you	will have	laughed
he/she/it	will have	laughed
we	will have	laughed
you	will have	laughed
they	will have	laughed

Imperative

laugh

Impersonal

ing-Form

laughing

Past Participle

laughed

Continuous tenses

Present

I	am	laughing
you	are	laughing
he/she/it	is	laughing
we	are	laughing
you	are	laughing
they	are	laughing

Past

I	was	laughing
you	were	laughing
he/she/it	was	laughing
we	were	laughing
you	were	laughing
they	were	laughing

Present Perfect

I	have been	laughing
you	have been	laughing
he/she/it	has been	laughing
we	have been	laughing
you	have been	laughing
they	have been	laughing

Past Perfect

I	had been	laughing
you	had been	laughing
he/she/it	had been	laughing
we	had been	laughing
you	had been	laughing
they	had been	laughing

Will-Future

I	will be	laughing
you	will be	laughing
he/she/it	will be	laughing
we	will be	laughing
you	will be	laughing
they	will be	laughing

Going to-Future

I	am	going to be	laughing
you	are	going to be	laughing
he/she/it	is	going to be	laughing
we	are	going to be	laughing
you	are	going to be	laughing
they	are	going to be	laughing

Future Perfect

I	will have been	laughing
you	will have been	laughing
he/she/it	will have been	laughing
we	will have been	laughing
you	will have been	laughing
they	will have been	laughing

Conditional

I	would	laugh
you	would	laugh
he/she/it	would	laugh
we	would	laugh
you	would	laugh
they	would	laugh

Conditional Past

I	would have	laughed
you	would have	laughed
he/she/it	would have	laughed
we	would have	laughed
you	would have	laughed
they	would have	laughed

Simple tenses

Present

I	launch
you	launch
he/she/it	launches
we	launch
you	launch
they	launch

Past

I	launched
you	launched
he/she/it	launched
we	launched
you	launched
they	launched

Present Perfect

I	have	launched
you	have	launched
he/she/it	has	launched
we	have	launched
you	have	launched
they	have	launched

Past Perfect

I	had	launched
you	had	launched
he/she/it	had	launched
we	had	launched
you	had	launched
they	had	launched

Will-Future

I	will	launch
you	will	launch
he/she/it	will	launch
we	will	launch
you	will	launch
they	will	launch

Going to-Future

I	am	going to	launch
you	are	going to	launch
he/she/it	is	going to	launch
we	are	going to	launch
you	are	going to	launch
they	are	going to	launch

Future Perfect

I	will have	launched
you	will have	launched
he/she/it	will have	launched
we	will have	launched
you	will have	launched
they	will have	launched

Imperative

launch

Impersonal

ing-Form

launching

Past Participle

launched

Continuous tenses

Present

I	am	launching
you	are	launching
he/she/it	is	launching
we	are	launching
you	are	launching
they	are	launching

Past

I	was	launching
you	were	launching
he/she/it	was	launching
we	were	launching
you	were	launching
they	were	launching

Present Perfect

I	have been	launching
you	have been	launching
he/she/it	has been	launching
we	have been	launching
you	have been	launching
they	have been	launching

Past Perfect

I	had been	launching
you	had been	launching
he/she/it	had been	launching
we	had been	launching
you	had been	launching
they	had been	launching

Will-Future

I	will be	launching
you	will be	launching
he/she/it	will be	launching
we	will be	launching
you	will be	launching
they	will be	launching

Going to-Future

I	am	going to be	launching
you	are	going to be	launching
he/she/it	is	going to be	launching
we	are	going to be	launching
you	are	going to be	launching
they	are	going to be	launching

Future Perfect

I	will have been	launching
you	will have been	launching
he/she/it	will have been	launching
we	will have been	launching
you	will have been	launching
they	will have been	launching

Conditional

I	would	launch
you	would	launch
he/she/it	would	launch
we	would	launch
you	would	launch
they	would	launch

Conditional Past

I	would have	launched
you	would have	launched
he/she/it	would have	launched
we	would have	launched
you	would have	launched
they	would have	launched

lay

- laid - laid

legen

Unregelmäßiges Verb

Simple tenses

Present

I	lay
you	lay
he/she/it	lays
we	lay
you	lay
they	lay

Past

I	laid
you	laid
he/she/it	laid
we	laid
you	laid
they	laid

Present Perfect

I	have	laid
you	have	laid
he/she/it	has	laid
we	have	laid
you	have	laid
they	have	laid

Past Perfect

I	had	laid
you	had	laid
he/she/it	had	laid
we	had	laid
you	had	laid
they	had	laid

Will-Future

I	will	lay
you	will	lay
he/she/it	will	lay
we	will	lay
you	will	lay
they	will	lay

Going to-Future

I	am	going to	lay
you	are	going to	lay
he/she/it	is	going to	lay
we	are	going to	lay
you	are	going to	lay
they	are	going to	lay

Future Perfect

I	will have	laid
you	will have	laid
he/she/it	will have	laid
we	will have	laid
you	will have	laid
they	will have	laid

Imperative

lay

Impersonal

ing-Form

laying

Past Participle

laid

Continuous tenses

Present

I	am	laying
you	are	laying
he/she/it	is	laying
we	are	laying
you	are	laying
they	are	laying

Past

I	was	laying
you	were	laying
he/she/it	was	laying
we	were	laying
you	were	laying
they	were	laying

Present Perfect

I	have been	laying
you	have been	laying
he/she/it	has been	laying
we	have been	laying
you	have been	laying
they	have been	laying

Past Perfect

I	had been	laying
you	had been	laying
he/she/it	had been	laying
we	had been	laying
you	had been	laying
they	had been	laying

Will-Future

I	will be	laying
you	will be	laying
he/she/it	will be	laying
we	will be	laying
you	will be	laying
they	will be	laying

Going to-Future

I	am	going to be	laying
you	are	going to be	laying
he/she/it	is	going to be	laying
we	are	going to be	laying
you	are	going to be	laying
they	are	going to be	laying

Future Perfect

I	will have been	laying
you	will have been	laying
he/she/it	will have been	laying
we	will have been	laying
you	will have been	laying
they	will have been	laying

Conditional

I	would	lay
you	would	lay
he/she/it	would	lay
we	would	lay
you	would	lay
they	would	lay

Conditional Past

I	would have	laid
you	would have	laid
he/she/it	would have	laid
we	would have	laid
you	would have	laid
they	would have	laid

führen

lead
- led - led

Simple tenses

Present

I	lead
you	lead
he/she/it	leads
we	lead
you	lead
they	lead

Past

I	led
you	led
he/she/it	led
we	led
you	led
they	led

Present Perfect

I	have	led
you	have	led
he/she/it	has	led
we	have	led
you	have	led
they	have	led

Past Perfect

I	had	led
you	had	led
he/she/it	had	led
we	had	led
you	had	led
they	had	led

Will-Future

I	will	lead
you	will	lead
he/she/it	will	lead
we	will	lead
you	will	lead
they	will	lead

Going to-Future

I	am	going to	lead
you	are	going to	lead
he/she/it	is	going to	lead
we	are	going to	lead
you	are	going to	lead
they	are	going to	lead

Future Perfect

I	will have	led
you	will have	led
he/she/it	will have	led
we	will have	led
you	will have	led
they	will have	led

Imperative

lead

Impersonal

ing-Form

leading

Past Participle

led

Continuous tenses

Present

I	am	leading
you	are	leading
he/she/it	is	leading
we	are	leading
you	are	leading
they	are	leading

Past

I	was	leading
you	were	leading
he/she/it	was	leading
we	were	leading
you	were	leading
they	were	leading

Present Perfect

I	have been	leading
you	have been	leading
he/she/it	has been	leading
we	have been	leading
you	have been	leading
they	have been	leading

Past Perfect

I	had been	leading
you	had been	leading
he/she/it	had been	leading
we	had been	leading
you	had been	leading
they	had been	leading

Will-Future

I	will be	leading
you	will be	leading
he/she/it	will be	leading
we	will be	leading
you	will be	leading
they	will be	leading

Going to-Future

I	am	going to be	leading
you	are	going to be	leading
he/she/it	is	going to be	leading
we	are	going to be	leading
you	are	going to be	leading
they	are	going to be	leading

Future Perfect

I	will have been	leading
you	will have been	leading
he/she/it	will have been	leading
we	will have been	leading
you	will have been	leading
they	will have been	leading

Conditional

I	would	lead
you	would	lead
he/she/it	would	lead
we	would	lead
you	would	lead
they	would	lead

Conditional Past

I	would have	led
you	would have	led
he/she/it	would have	led
we	would have	led
you	would have	led
they	would have	led

learn
- learned/learnt - learned/learnt

lernen

Im AE ist das Partizip Perfekt *learned.*
Unregelmäßiges Verb

Simple tenses

Present

I	learn
you	learn
he/she/it	learns
we	learn
you	learn
they	learn

Past

I	learned | learnt
you	learned | learnt
he/she/it	learned | learnt
we	learned | learnt
you	learned | learnt
they	learned | learnt

Present Perfect

I	have	learned | learnt
you	have	learned | learnt
he/she/it	has	learned | learnt
we	have	learned | learnt
you	have	learned | learnt
they	have	learned | learnt

Past Perfect

I	had	learned | learnt
you	had	learned | learnt
he/she/it	had	learned | learnt
we	had	learned | learnt
you	had	learned | learnt
they	had	learned | learnt

Will-Future

I	will	learn
you	will	learn
he/she/it	will	learn
we	will	learn
you	will	learn
they	will	learn

Going to-Future

I	am	going to learn
you	are	going to learn
he/she/it	is	going to learn
we	are	going to learn
you	are	going to learn
they	are	going to learn

Future Perfect

I	will have	learned | learnt
you	will have	learned | learnt
he/she/it	will have	learned | learnt
we	will have	learned | learnt
you	will have	learned | learnt
they	will have	learned | learnt

Imperative

learn

Impersonal

ing-Form

learning

Past Participle

learned | learnt

Continuous tenses

Present

I	am	learning
you	are	learning
he/she/it	is	learning
we	are	learning
you	are	learning
they	are	learning

Past

I	was	learning
you	were	learning
he/she/it	was	learning
we	were	learning
you	were	learning
they	were	learning

Present Perfect

I	have been	learning
you	have been	learning
he/she/it	has been	learning
we	have been	learning
you	have been	learning
they	have been	learning

Past Perfect

I	had been	learning
you	had been	learning
he/she/it	had been	learning
we	had been	learning
you	had been	learning
they	had been	learning

Will-Future

I	will be	learning
you	will be	learning
he/she/it	will be	learning
we	will be	learning
you	will be	learning
they	will be	learning

Going to-Future

I	am	going to be learning
you	are	going to be learning
he/she/it	is	going to be learning
we	are	going to be learning
you	are	going to be learning
they	are	going to be learning

Future Perfect

I	will have been	learning
you	will have been	learning
he/she/it	will have been	learning
we	will have been	learning
you	will have been	learning
they	will have been	learning

Conditional

I	would	learn
you	would	learn
he/she/it	would	learn
we	would	learn
you	would	learn
they	would	learn

Conditional Past

I	would have	learned | learnt
you	would have	learned | learnt
he/she/it	would have	learned | learnt
we	would have	learned | learnt
you	would have	learned | learnt
they	would have	learned | learnt

+ -ing → ~~e~~
Unregelmäßiges Verb

verlassen

leave
- left - left

Simple tenses

Present

I	leave
you	leave
he/she/it	leaves
we	leave
you	leave
they	leave

Past

I	left
you	left
he/she/it	left
we	left
you	left
they	left

Present Perfect

I	have	left
you	have	left
he/she/it	has	left
we	have	left
you	have	left
they	have	left

Past Perfect

I	had	left
you	had	left
he/she/it	had	left
we	had	left
you	had	left
they	had	left

Will-Future

I	will	leave
you	will	leave
he/she/it	will	leave
we	will	leave
you	will	leave
they	will	leave

Going to-Future

I	am	going to	leave
you	are	going to	leave
he/she/it	is	going to	leave
we	are	going to	leave
you	are	going to	leave
they	are	going to	leave

Future Perfect

I	will have	left
you	will have	left
he/she/it	will have	left
we	will have	left
you	will have	left
they	will have	left

Imperative

leave

Impersonal

ing-Form

leaving

Past Participle

left

Continuous tenses

Present

I	am	leaving
you	are	leaving
he/she/it	is	leaving
we	are	leaving
you	are	leaving
they	are	leaving

Past

I	was	leaving
you	were	leaving
he/she/it	was	leaving
we	were	leaving
you	were	leaving
they	were	leaving

Present Perfect

I	have been	leaving
you	have been	leaving
he/she/it	has been	leaving
we	have been	leaving
you	have been	leaving
they	have been	leaving

Past Perfect

I	had been	leaving
you	had been	leaving
he/she/it	had been	leaving
we	had been	leaving
you	had been	leaving
they	had been	leaving

Will-Future

I	will be	leaving
you	will be	leaving
he/she/it	will be	leaving
we	will be	leaving
you	will be	leaving
they	will be	leaving

Going to-Future

I	am	going to be	leaving
you	are	going to be	leaving
he/she/it	is	going to be	leaving
we	are	going to be	leaving
you	are	going to be	leaving
they	are	going to be	leaving

Future Perfect

I	will have been	leaving
you	will have been	leaving
he/she/it	will have been	leaving
we	will have been	leaving
you	will have been	leaving
they	will have been	leaving

Conditional

I	would	leave
you	would	leave
he/she/it	would	leave
we	would	leave
you	would	leave
they	would	leave

Conditional Past

I	would have	left
you	would have	left
he/she/it	would have	left
we	would have	left
you	would have	left
they	would have	left

lend
- lent - lent

ausleihen

Unregelmäßiges Verb

Simple tenses

Present

I	lend
you	lend
he/she/it	lends
we	lend
you	lend
they	lend

Past

I	lent
you	lent
he/she/it	lent
we	lent
you	lent
they	lent

Present Perfect

I	have	lent
you	have	lent
he/she/it	has	lent
we	have	lent
you	have	lent
they	have	lent

Past Perfect

I	had	lent
you	had	lent
he/she/it	had	lent
we	had	lent
you	had	lent
they	had	lent

Will-Future

I	will	lend
you	will	lend
he/she/it	will	lend
we	will	lend
you	will	lend
they	will	lend

Going to-Future

I	am	going to	lend
you	are	going to	lend
he/she/it	is	going to	lend
we	are	going to	lend
you	are	going to	lend
they	are	going to	lend

Future Perfect

I	will have	lent
you	will have	lent
he/she/it	will have	lent
we	will have	lent
you	will have	lent
they	will have	lent

Imperative

lend

Impersonal

ing-Form

lending

Past Participle

lent

Continuous tenses

Present

I	am	lending
you	are	lending
he/she/it	is	lending
we	are	lending
you	are	lending
they	are	lending

Past

I	was	lending
you	were	lending
he/she/it	was	lending
we	were	lending
you	were	lending
they	were	lending

Present Perfect

I	have	been	lending
you	have	been	lending
he/she/it	has	been	lending
we	have	been	lending
you	have	been	lending
they	have	been	lending

Past Perfect

I	had been	lending
you	had been	lending
he/she/it	had been	lending
we	had been	lending
you	had been	lending
they	had been	lending

Will-Future

I	will be	lending
you	will be	lending
he/she/it	will be	lending
we	will be	lending
you	will be	lending
they	will be	lending

Going to-Future

I	am	going to be	lending
you	are	going to be	lending
he/she/it	is	going to be	lending
we	are	going to be	lending
you	are	going to be	lending
they	are	going to be	lending

Future Perfect

I	will have been	lending
you	will have been	lending
he/she/it	will have been	lending
we	will have been	lending
you	will have been	lending
they	will have been	lending

Conditional

I	would	lend
you	would	lend
he/she/it	would	lend
we	would	lend
you	would	lend
they	would	lend

Conditional Past

I	would have	lent
you	would have	lent
he/she/it	would have	lent
we	would have	lent
you	would have	lent
they	would have	lent

lassen

let

- let - let

Simple tenses

Present

I	let
you	let
he/she/it	lets
we	let
you	let
they	let

Past

I	let
you	let
he/she/it	let
we	let
you	let
they	let

Present Perfect

I	have	let
you	have	let
he/she/it	has	let
we	have	let
you	have	let
they	have	let

Past Perfect

I	had	let
you	had	let
he/she/it	had	let
we	had	let
you	had	let
they	had	let

Will-Future

I	will	let
you	will	let
he/she/it	will	let
we	will	let
you	will	let
they	will	let

Going to-Future

I	am	going to	let
you	are	going to	let
he/she/it	is	going to	let
we	are	going to	let
you	are	going to	let
they	are	going to	let

Future Perfect

I	will have	let
you	will have	let
he/she/it	will have	let
we	will have	let
you	will have	let
they	will have	let

Imperative

let

Impersonal

ing-Form

letting

Past Participle

let

Continuous tenses

Present

I	am	letting
you	are	letting
he/she/it	is	letting
we	are	letting
you	are	letting
they	are	letting

Past

I	was	letting
you	were	letting
he/she/it	was	letting
we	were	letting
you	were	letting
they	were	letting

Present Perfect

I	have been	letting
you	have been	letting
he/she/it	has been	letting
we	have been	letting
you	have been	letting
they	have been	letting

Past Perfect

I	had been	letting
you	had been	letting
he/she/it	had been	letting
we	had been	letting
you	had been	letting
they	had been	letting

Will-Future

I	will be	letting
you	will be	letting
he/she/it	will be	letting
we	will be	letting
you	will be	letting
they	will be	letting

Going to-Future

I	am	going to be	letting
you	are	going to be	letting
he/she/it	is	going to be	letting
we	are	going to be	letting
you	are	going to be	letting
they	are	going to be	letting

Future Perfect

I	will have been	letting
you	will have been	letting
he/she/it	will have been	letting
we	will have been	letting
you	will have been	letting
they	will have been	letting

Conditional

I	would	let
you	would	let
he/she/it	would	let
we	would	let
you	would	let
they	would	let

Conditional Past

I	would have	let
you	would have	let
he/she/it	would have	let
we	would have	let
you	would have	let
they	would have	let

lie
- lay - lain

liegen

Unregelmäßiges Verb

Simple tenses

Present

I	lie
you	lie
he/she/it	lies
we	lie
you	lie
they	lie

Past

I	lay
you	lay
he/she/it	lay
we	lay
you	lay
they	lay

Present Perfect

I	have	lain
you	have	lain
he/she/it	has	lain
we	have	lain
you	have	lain
they	have	lain

Past Perfect

I	had	lain
you	had	lain
he/she/it	had	lain
we	had	lain
you	had	lain
they	had	lain

Will-Future

I	will	lie
you	will	lie
he/she/it	will	lie
we	will	lie
you	will	lie
they	will	lie

Going to-Future

I	am	going to	lie
you	are	going to	lie
he/she/it	is	going to	lie
we	are	going to	lie
you	are	going to	lie
they	are	going to	lie

Future Perfect

I	will have	lain
you	will have	lain
he/she/it	will have	lain
we	will have	lain
you	will have	lain
they	will have	lain

Imperative

lie

Impersonal

ing-Form

lying

Past Participle

lain

Continuous tenses

Present

I	am	lying
you	are	lying
he/she/it	is	lying
we	are	lying
you	are	lying
they	are	lying

Past

I	was	lying
you	were	lying
he/she/it	was	lying
we	were	lying
you	were	lying
they	were	lying

Present Perfect

I	have	been	lying
you	have	been	lying
he/she/it	has	been	lying
we	have	been	lying
you	have	been	lying
they	have	been	lying

Past Perfect

I	had been	lying
you	had been	lying
he/she/it	had been	lying
we	had been	lying
you	had been	lying
they	had been	lying

Will-Future

I	will be	lying
you	will be	lying
he/she/it	will be	lying
we	will be	lying
you	will be	lying
they	will be	lying

Going to-Future

I	am	going to be	lying
you	are	going to be	lying
he/she/it	is	going to be	lying
we	are	going to be	lying
you	are	going to be	lying
they	are	going to be	lying

Future Perfect

I	will have been	lying
you	will have been	lying
he/she/it	will have been	lying
we	will have been	lying
you	will have been	lying
they	will have been	lying

Conditional

I	would	lie
you	would	lie
he/she/it	would	lie
we	would	lie
you	would	lie
they	would	lie

Conditional Past

I	would have	lain
you	would have	lain
he/she/it	would have	lain
we	would have	lain
you	would have	lain
they	would have	lain

lie
- lied - lied

Simple tenses

Present

I	lie
you	lie
he/she/it	lies
we	lie
you	lie
they	lie

Past

I	lied
you	lied
he/she/it	lied
we	lied
you	lied
they	lied

Present Perfect

I	have	lied
you	have	lied
he/she/it	has	lied
we	have	lied
you	have	lied
they	have	lied

Past Perfect

I	had	lied
you	had	lied
he/she/it	had	lied
we	had	lied
you	had	lied
they	had	lied

Will-Future

I	will	lie
you	will	lie
he/she/it	will	lie
we	will	lie
you	will	lie
they	will	lie

Going to-Future

I	am	going to	lie
you	are	going to	lie
he/she/it	is	going to	lie
we	are	going to	lie
you	are	going to	lie
they	are	going to	lie

Future Perfect

I	will have	lied
you	will have	lied
he/she/it	will have	lied
we	will have	lied
you	will have	lied
they	will have	lied

Imperative

lie

Impersonal

ing-Form

lying

Past Participle

lied

Continuous tenses

Present

I	am	lying
you	are	lying
he/she/it	is	lying
we	are	lying
you	are	lying
they	are	lying

Past

I	was	lying
you	were	lying
he/she/it	was	lying
we	were	lying
you	were	lying
they	were	lying

Present Perfect

I	have been	lying
you	have been	lying
he/she/it	has been	lying
we	have been	lying
you	have been	lying
they	have been	lying

Past Perfect

I	had been	lying
you	had been	lying
he/she/it	had been	lying
we	had been	lying
you	had been	lying
they	had been	lying

Will-Future

I	will be	lying
you	will be	lying
he/she/it	will be	lying
we	will be	lying
you	will be	lying
they	will be	lying

Going to-Future

I	am	going to be	lying
you	are	going to be	lying
he/she/it	is	going to be	lying
we	are	going to be	lying
you	are	going to be	lying
they	are	going to be	lying

Future Perfect

I	will have been	lying
you	will have been	lying
he/she/it	will have been	lying
we	will have been	lying
you	will have been	lying
they	will have been	lying

Conditional

I	would	lie
you	would	lie
he/she/it	would	lie
we	would	lie
you	would	lie
they	would	lie

Conditional Past

I	would have	lied
you	would have	lied
he/she/it	would have	lied
we	would have	lied
you	would have	lied
they	would have	lied

lift

hochheben

Regelmäßiges Verb

Simple tenses

Present

I	lift
you	lift
he/she/it	lifts
we	lift
you	lift
they	lift

Past

I	lifted
you	lifted
he/she/it	lifted
we	lifted
you	lifted
they	lifted

Present Perfect

I	have	lifted
you	have	lifted
he/she/it	has	lifted
we	have	lifted
you	have	lifted
they	have	lifted

Past Perfect

I	had	lifted
you	had	lifted
he/she/it	had	lifted
we	had	lifted
you	had	lifted
they	had	lifted

Will-Future

I	will	lift
you	will	lift
he/she/it	will	lift
we	will	lift
you	will	lift
they	will	lift

Going to-Future

I	am	going to	lift
you	are	going to	lift
he/she/it	is	going to	lift
we	are	going to	lift
you	are	going to	lift
they	are	going to	lift

Future Perfect

I	will have	lifted
you	will have	lifted
he/she/it	will have	lifted
we	will have	lifted
you	will have	lifted
they	will have	lifted

Imperative

lift

Impersonal

ing-Form

lifting

Past Participle

lifted

Continuous tenses

Present

I	am	lifting
you	are	lifting
he/she/it	is	lifting
we	are	lifting
you	are	lifting
they	are	lifting

Past

I	was	lifting
you	were	lifting
he/she/it	was	lifting
we	were	lifting
you	were	lifting
they	were	lifting

Present Perfect

I	have been	lifting
you	have been	lifting
he/she/it	has been	lifting
we	have been	lifting
you	have been	lifting
they	have been	lifting

Past Perfect

I	had been	lifting
you	had been	lifting
he/she/it	had been	lifting
we	had been	lifting
you	had been	lifting
they	had been	lifting

Will-Future

I	will be	lifting
you	will be	lifting
he/she/it	will be	lifting
we	will be	lifting
you	will be	lifting
they	will be	lifting

Going to-Future

I	am	going to be	lifting
you	are	going to be	lifting
he/she/it	is	going to be	lifting
we	are	going to be	lifting
you	are	going to be	lifting
they	are	going to be	lifting

Future Perfect

I	will have been	lifting
you	will have been	lifting
he/she/it	will have been	lifting
we	will have been	lifting
you	will have been	lifting
they	will have been	lifting

Conditional

I	would	lift
you	would	lift
he/she/it	would	lift
we	would	lift
you	would	lift
they	would	lift

Conditional Past

I	would have	lifted
you	would have	lifted
he/she/it	would have	lifted
we	would have	lifted
you	would have	lifted
they	would have	lifted

Simple tenses

Present

I	like
you	like
he/she/it	likes
we	like
you	like
they	like

Past

I	liked
you	liked
he/she/it	liked
we	liked
you	liked
they	liked

Present Perfect

I	have	liked
you	have	liked
he/she/it	has	liked
we	have	liked
you	have	liked
they	have	liked

Past Perfect

I	had	liked
you	had	liked
he/she/it	had	liked
we	had	liked
you	had	liked
they	had	liked

Will-Future

I	will	like
you	will	like
he/she/it	will	like
we	will	like
you	will	like
they	will	like

Going to-Future

I	am	going to	like
you	are	going to	like
he/she/it	is	going to	like
we	are	going to	like
you	are	going to	like
they	are	going to	like

Future Perfect

I	will have	liked
you	will have	liked
he/she/it	will have	liked
we	will have	liked
you	will have	liked
they	will have	liked

Imperative

like

Impersonal

ing-Form

liking

Past Participle

liked

Continuous tenses

Present

I	am	liking
you	are	liking
he/she/it	is	liking
we	are	liking
you	are	liking
they	are	liking

Past

I	was	liking
you	were	liking
he/she/it	was	liking
we	were	liking
you	were	liking
they	were	liking

Present Perfect

I	have been	liking
you	have been	liking
he/she/it	has been	liking
we	have been	liking
you	have been	liking
they	have been	liking

Past Perfect

I	had been	liking
you	had been	liking
he/she/it	had been	liking
we	had been	liking
you	had been	liking
they	had been	liking

Will-Future

I	will be	liking
you	will be	liking
he/she/it	will be	liking
we	will be	liking
you	will be	liking
they	will be	liking

Going to-Future

I	am	going to be	liking
you	are	going to be	liking
he/she/it	is	going to be	liking
we	are	going to be	liking
you	are	going to be	liking
they	are	going to be	liking

Future Perfect

I	will have been	liking
you	will have been	liking
he/she/it	will have been	liking
we	will have been	liking
you	will have been	liking
they	will have been	liking

Conditional

I	would	like
you	would	like
he/she/it	would	like
we	would	like
you	would	like
they	would	like

Conditional Past

I	would have	liked
you	would have	liked
he/she/it	would have	liked
we	would have	liked
you	would have	liked
they	would have	liked

limit

einschränken

Regelmäßiges Verb

Simple tenses

Present

I	limit
you	limit
he/she/it	limits
we	limit
you	limit
they	limit

Past

I	limited
you	limited
he/she/it	limited
we	limited
you	limited
they	limited

Present Perfect

I	have	limited
you	have	limited
he/she/it	has	limited
we	have	limited
you	have	limited
they	have	limited

Past Perfect

I	had	limited
you	had	limited
he/she/it	had	limited
we	had	limited
you	had	limited
they	had	limited

Will-Future

I	will	limit
you	will	limit
he/she/it	will	limit
we	will	limit
you	will	limit
they	will	limit

Going to-Future

I	am	going to	limit
you	are	going to	limit
he/she/it	is	going to	limit
we	are	going to	limit
you	are	going to	limit
they	are	going to	limit

Future Perfect

I	will have	limited
you	will have	limited
he/she/it	will have	limited
we	will have	limited
you	will have	limited
they	will have	limited

Imperative

limit

Impersonal

ing-Form

limiting

Past Participle

limited

Continuous tenses

Present

I	am	limiting
you	are	limiting
he/she/it	is	limiting
we	are	limiting
you	are	limiting
they	are	limiting

Past

I	was	limiting
you	were	limiting
he/she/it	was	limiting
we	were	limiting
you	were	limiting
they	were	limiting

Present Perfect

I	have been	limiting
you	have been	limiting
he/she/it	has been	limiting
we	have been	limiting
you	have been	limiting
they	have been	limiting

Past Perfect

I	had been	limiting
you	had been	limiting
he/she/it	had been	limiting
we	had been	limiting
you	had been	limiting
they	had been	limiting

Will-Future

I	will be	limiting
you	will be	limiting
he/she/it	will be	limiting
we	will be	limiting
you	will be	limiting
they	will be	limiting

Going to-Future

I	am	going to be	limiting
you	are	going to be	limiting
he/she/it	is	going to be	limiting
we	are	going to be	limiting
you	are	going to be	limiting
they	are	going to be	limiting

Future Perfect

I	will have been	limiting
you	will have been	limiting
he/she/it	will have been	limiting
we	will have been	limiting
you	will have been	limiting
they	will have been	limiting

Conditional

I	would	limit
you	would	limit
he/she/it	would	limit
we	would	limit
you	would	limit
they	would	limit

Conditional Past

I	would have	limited
you	would have	limited
he/she/it	would have	limited
we	would have	limited
you	would have	limited
they	would have	limited

Simple tenses

Present

I	listen
you	listen
he/she/it	listens
we	listen
you	listen
they	listen

Past

I	listened
you	listened
he/she/it	listened
we	listened
you	listened
they	listened

Present Perfect

I	have	listened
you	have	listened
he/she/it	has	listened
we	have	listened
you	have	listened
they	have	listened

Past Perfect

I	had	listened
you	had	listened
he/she/it	had	listened
we	had	listened
you	had	listened
they	had	listened

Will-Future

I	will	listen
you	will	listen
he/she/it	will	listen
we	will	listen
you	will	listen
they	will	listen

Going to-Future

I	am	going to	listen
you	are	going to	listen
he/she/it	is	going to	listen
we	are	going to	listen
you	are	going to	listen
they	are	going to	listen

Future Perfect

I	will have	listened
you	will have	listened
he/she/it	will have	listened
we	will have	listened
you	will have	listened
they	will have	listened

Imperative

listen

Impersonal

ing-Form

listening

Past Participle

listened

Continuous tenses

Present

I	am	listening
you	are	listening
he/she/it	is	listening
we	are	listening
you	are	listening
they	are	listening

Past

I	was	listening
you	were	listening
he/she/it	was	listening
we	were	listening
you	were	listening
they	were	listening

Present Perfect

I	have been	listening
you	have been	listening
he/she/it	has been	listening
we	have been	listening
you	have been	listening
they	have been	listening

Past Perfect

I	had been	listening
you	had been	listening
he/she/it	had been	listening
we	had been	listening
you	had been	listening
they	had been	listening

Will-Future

I	will be	listening
you	will be	listening
he/she/it	will be	listening
we	will be	listening
you	will be	listening
they	will be	listening

Going to-Future

I	am	going to be	listening
you	are	going to be	listening
he/she/it	is	going to be	listening
we	are	going to be	listening
you	are	going to be	listening
they	are	going to be	listening

Future Perfect

I	will have been	listening
you	will have been	listening
he/she/it	will have been	listening
we	will have been	listening
you	will have been	listening
they	will have been	listening

Conditional

I	would	listen
you	would	listen
he/she/it	would	listen
we	would	listen
you	would	listen
they	would	listen

Conditional Past

I	would have	listened
you	would have	listened
he/she/it	would have	listened
we	would have	listened
you	would have	listened
they	would have	listened

live

leben

\+ **-ing** → ~~e~~ / + **-d** nicht **-ed**
Regelmäßiges Verb

Simple tenses

Present

I	live
you	live
he/she/it	lives
we	live
you	live
they	live

Past

I	lived
you	lived
he/she/it	lived
we	lived
you	lived
they	lived

Present Perfect

I	have	lived
you	have	lived
he/she/it	has	lived
we	have	lived
you	have	lived
they	have	lived

Past Perfect

I	had	lived
you	had	lived
he/she/it	had	lived
we	had	lived
you	had	lived
they	had	lived

Will-Future

I	will	live
you	will	live
he/she/it	will	live
we	will	live
you	will	live
they	will	live

Going to-Future

I	am	going to	live
you	are	going to	live
he/she/it	is	going to	live
we	are	going to	live
you	are	going to	live
they	are	going to	live

Future Perfect

I	will have	lived
you	will have	lived
he/she/it	will have	lived
we	will have	lived
you	will have	lived
they	will have	lived

Imperative

live

Impersonal

ing-Form

living

Past Participle

lived

Continuous tenses

Present

I	am	living
you	are	living
he/she/it	is	living
we	are	living
you	are	living
they	are	living

Past

I	was	living
you	were	living
he/she/it	was	living
we	were	living
you	were	living
they	were	living

Present Perfect

I	have been	living
you	have been	living
he/she/it	has been	living
we	have been	living
you	have been	living
they	have been	living

Past Perfect

I	had been	living
you	had been	living
he/she/it	had been	living
we	had been	living
you	had been	living
they	had been	living

Will-Future

I	will be	living
you	will be	living
he/she/it	will be	living
we	will be	living
you	will be	living
they	will be	living

Going to-Future

I	am	going to be	living
you	are	going to be	living
he/she/it	is	going to be	living
we	are	going to be	living
you	are	going to be	living
they	are	going to be	living

Future Perfect

I	will have been	living
you	will have been	living
he/she/it	will have been	living
we	will have been	living
you	will have been	living
they	will have been	living

Conditional

I	would	live
you	would	live
he/she/it	would	live
we	would	live
you	would	live
they	would	live

Conditional Past

I	would have	lived
you	would have	lived
he/she/it	would have	lived
we	would have	lived
you	would have	lived
they	would have	lived

load

Regelmäßiges Verb

Simple tenses

Present

I	load
you	load
he/she/it	loads
we	load
you	load
they	load

Past

I	loaded
you	loaded
he/she/it	loaded
we	loaded
you	loaded
they	loaded

Present Perfect

I	have	loaded
you	have	loaded
he/she/it	has	loaded
we	have	loaded
you	have	loaded
they	have	loaded

Past Perfect

I	had	loaded
you	had	loaded
he/she/it	had	loaded
we	had	loaded
you	had	loaded
they	had	loaded

Will-Future

I	will	load
you	will	load
he/she/it	will	load
we	will	load
you	will	load
they	will	load

Going to-Future

I	am	going to	load
you	are	going to	load
he/she/it	is	going to	load
we	are	going to	load
you	are	going to	load
they	are	going to	load

Future Perfect

I	will have	loaded
you	will have	loaded
he/she/it	will have	loaded
we	will have	loaded
you	will have	loaded
they	will have	loaded

Imperative

load

Impersonal

ing-Form

loading

Past Participle

loaded

Continuous tenses

Present

I	am	loading
you	are	loading
he/she/it	is	loading
we	are	loading
you	are	loading
they	are	loading

Past

I	was	loading
you	were	loading
he/she/it	was	loading
we	were	loading
you	were	loading
they	were	loading

Present Perfect

I	have been	loading
you	have been	loading
he/she/it	has been	loading
we	have been	loading
you	have been	loading
they	have been	loading

Past Perfect

I	had been	loading
you	had been	loading
he/she/it	had been	loading
we	had been	loading
you	had been	loading
they	had been	loading

Will-Future

I	will be	loading
you	will be	loading
he/she/it	will be	loading
we	will be	loading
you	will be	loading
they	will be	loading

Going to-Future

I	am	going to be	loading
you	are	going to be	loading
he/she/it	is	going to be	loading
we	are	going to be	loading
you	are	going to be	loading
they	are	going to be	loading

Future Perfect

I	will have been	loading
you	will have been	loading
he/she/it	will have been	loading
we	will have been	loading
you	will have been	loading
they	will have been	loading

Conditional

I	would	load
you	would	load
he/she/it	would	load
we	would	load
you	would	load
they	would	load

Conditional Past

I	would have	loaded
you	would have	loaded
he/she/it	would have	loaded
we	would have	loaded
you	would have	loaded
they	would have	loaded

loan

leihen

Regelmäßiges Verb

Simple tenses

Present

I	loan
you	loan
he/she/it	loans
we	loan
you	loan
they	loan

Past

I	loaned
you	loaned
he/she/it	loaned
we	loaned
you	loaned
they	loaned

Present Perfect

I	have	loaned
you	have	loaned
he/she/it	has	loaned
we	have	loaned
you	have	loaned
they	have	loaned

Past Perfect

I	had	loaned
you	had	loaned
he/she/it	had	loaned
we	had	loaned
you	had	loaned
they	had	loaned

Will-Future

I	will	loan
you	will	loan
he/she/it	will	loan
we	will	loan
you	will	loan
they	will	loan

Going to-Future

I	am	going to	loan
you	are	going to	loan
he/she/it	is	going to	loan
we	are	going to	loan
you	are	going to	loan
they	are	going to	loan

Future Perfect

I	will have	loaned
you	will have	loaned
he/she/it	will have	loaned
we	will have	loaned
you	will have	loaned
they	will have	loaned

Imperative

loan

Impersonal

ing-Form

loaning

Past Participle

loaned

Continuous tenses

Present

I	am	loaning
you	are	loaning
he/she/it	is	loaning
we	are	loaning
you	are	loaning
they	are	loaning

Past

I	was	loaning
you	were	loaning
he/she/it	was	loaning
we	were	loaning
you	were	loaning
they	were	loaning

Present Perfect

I	have	been	loaning
you	have	been	loaning
he/she/it	has	been	loaning
we	have	been	loaning
you	have	been	loaning
they	have	been	loaning

Past Perfect

I	had been	loaning
you	had been	loaning
he/she/it	had been	loaning
we	had been	loaning
you	had been	loaning
they	had been	loaning

Will-Future

I	will be	loaning
you	will be	loaning
he/she/it	will be	loaning
we	will be	loaning
you	will be	loaning
they	will be	loaning

Going to-Future

I	am	going to be	loaning
you	are	going to be	loaning
he/she/it	is	going to be	loaning
we	are	going to be	loaning
you	are	going to be	loaning
they	are	going to be	loaning

Future Perfect

I	will have been	loaning
you	will have been	loaning
he/she/it	will have been	loaning
we	will have been	loaning
you	will have been	loaning
they	will have been	loaning

Conditional

I	would	loan
you	would	loan
he/she/it	would	loan
we	would	loan
you	would	loan
they	would	loan

Conditional Past

I	would have	loaned
you	would have	loaned
he/she/it	would have	loaned
we	would have	loaned
you	would have	loaned
they	would have	loaned

Simple tenses

Present

I	lock
you	lock
he/she/it	locks
we	lock
you	lock
they	lock

Past

I	locked
you	locked
he/she/it	locked
we	locked
you	locked
they	locked

Present Perfect

I	have	locked
you	have	locked
he/she/it	has	locked
we	have	locked
you	have	locked
they	have	locked

Past Perfect

I	had	locked
you	had	locked
he/she/it	had	locked
we	had	locked
you	had	locked
they	had	locked

Will-Future

I	will	lock
you	will	lock
he/she/it	will	lock
we	will	lock
you	will	lock
they	will	lock

Going to-Future

I	am	going to	lock
you	are	going to	lock
he/she/it	is	going to	lock
we	are	going to	lock
you	are	going to	lock
they	are	going to	lock

Future Perfect

I	will have	locked
you	will have	locked
he/she/it	will have	locked
we	will have	locked
you	will have	locked
they	will have	locked

Imperative

lock

Impersonal

ing-Form

locking

Past Participle

locked

Continuous tenses

Present

I	am	locking
you	are	locking
he/she/it	is	locking
we	are	locking
you	are	locking
they	are	locking

Past

I	was	locking
you	were	locking
he/she/it	was	locking
we	were	locking
you	were	locking
they	were	locking

Present Perfect

I	have	been	locking
you	have	been	locking
he/she/it	has	been	locking
we	have	been	locking
you	have	been	locking
they	have	been	locking

Past Perfect

I	had been	locking
you	had been	locking
he/she/it	had been	locking
we	had been	locking
you	had been	locking
they	had been	locking

Will-Future

I	will be	locking
you	will be	locking
he/she/it	will be	locking
we	will be	locking
you	will be	locking
they	will be	locking

Going to-Future

I	am	going to be	locking
you	are	going to be	locking
he/she/it	is	going to be	locking
we	are	going to be	locking
you	are	going to be	locking
they	are	going to be	locking

Future Perfect

I	will have been	locking
you	will have been	locking
he/she/it	will have been	locking
we	will have been	locking
you	will have been	locking
they	will have been	locking

Conditional

I	would	lock
you	would	lock
he/she/it	would	lock
we	would	lock
you	would	lock
they	would	lock

Conditional Past

I	would have	locked
you	would have	locked
he/she/it	would have	locked
we	would have	locked
you	would have	locked
they	would have	locked

look

sehen

Regelmäßiges Verb

Simple tenses

Present

I	look
you	look
he/she/it	looks
we	look
you	look
they	look

Past

I	looked
you	looked
he/she/it	looked
we	looked
you	looked
they	looked

Present Perfect

I	have	looked
you	have	looked
he/she/it	has	looked
we	have	looked
you	have	looked
they	have	looked

Past Perfect

I	had	looked
you	had	looked
he/she/it	had	looked
we	had	looked
you	had	looked
they	had	looked

Will-Future

I	will	look
you	will	look
he/she/it	will	look
we	will	look
you	will	look
they	will	look

Going to-Future

I	am	going to	look
you	are	going to	look
he/she/it	is	going to	look
we	are	going to	look
you	are	going to	look
they	are	going to	look

Future Perfect

I	will have	looked
you	will have	looked
he/she/it	will have	looked
we	will have	looked
you	will have	looked
they	will have	looked

Imperative

look

Impersonal

ing-Form

looking

Past Participle

looked

Continuous tenses

Present

I	am	looking
you	are	looking
he/she/it	is	looking
we	are	looking
you	are	looking
they	are	looking

Past

I	was	looking
you	were	looking
he/she/it	was	looking
we	were	looking
you	were	looking
they	were	looking

Present Perfect

I	have	been	looking
you	have	been	looking
he/she/it	has	been	looking
we	have	been	looking
you	have	been	looking
they	have	been	looking

Past Perfect

I	had been	looking
you	had been	looking
he/she/it	had been	looking
we	had been	looking
you	had been	looking
they	had been	looking

Will-Future

I	will be	looking
you	will be	looking
he/she/it	will be	looking
we	will be	looking
you	will be	looking
they	will be	looking

Going to-Future

I	am	going to be	looking
you	are	going to be	looking
he/she/it	is	going to be	looking
we	are	going to be	looking
you	are	going to be	looking
they	are	going to be	looking

Future Perfect

I	will have been	looking
you	will have been	looking
he/she/it	will have been	looking
we	will have been	looking
you	will have been	looking
they	will have been	looking

Conditional

I	would	look
you	would	look
he/she/it	would	look
we	would	look
you	would	look
they	would	look

Conditional Past

I	would have	looked
you	would have	looked
he/she/it	would have	looked
we	would have	looked
you	would have	looked
they	would have	looked

+ -ing → ~~e~~
Unregelmäßiges Verb

verlieren

lose
- lost - lost

Simple tenses

Present
I	lose
you	lose
he/she/it	loses
we	lose
you	lose
they	lose

Past
I	lost
you	lost
he/she/it	lost
we	lost
you	lost
they	lost

Present Perfect
I	have	lost
you	have	lost
he/she/it	has	lost
we	have	lost
you	have	lost
they	have	lost

Past Perfect
I	had	lost
you	had	lost
he/she/it	had	lost
we	had	lost
you	had	lost
they	had	lost

Will-Future
I	will	lose
you	will	lose
he/she/it	will	lose
we	will	lose
you	will	lose
they	will	lose

Going to-Future
I	am	going to	lose
you	are	going to	lose
he/she/it	is	going to	lose
we	are	going to	lose
you	are	going to	lose
they	are	going to	lose

Future Perfect
I	will have	lost
you	will have	lost
he/she/it	will have	lost
we	will have	lost
you	will have	lost
they	will have	lost

Imperative
lose

Impersonal

ing-Form
losing

Past Participle
lost

Continuous tenses

Present
I	am	losing
you	are	losing
he/she/it	is	losing
we	are	losing
you	are	losing
they	are	losing

Past
I	was	losing
you	were	losing
he/she/it	was	losing
we	were	losing
you	were	losing
they	were	losing

Present Perfect
I	have	been	losing
you	have	been	losing
he/she/it	has	been	losing
we	have	been	losing
you	have	been	losing
they	have	been	losing

Past Perfect
I	had been	losing
you	had been	losing
he/she/it	had been	losing
we	had been	losing
you	had been	losing
they	had been	losing

Will-Future
I	will be	losing
you	will be	losing
he/she/it	will be	losing
we	will be	losing
you	will be	losing
they	will be	losing

Going to-Future
I	am	going to be	losing
you	are	going to be	losing
he/she/it	is	going to be	losing
we	are	going to be	losing
you	are	going to be	losing
they	are	going to be	losing

Future Perfect
I	will have been	losing
you	will have been	losing
he/she/it	will have been	losing
we	will have been	losing
you	will have been	losing
they	will have been	losing

Conditional
I	would	lose
you	would	lose
he/she/it	would	lose
we	would	lose
you	would	lose
they	would	lose

Conditional Past
I	would have	lost
you	would have	lost
he/she/it	would have	lost
we	would have	lost
you	would have	lost
they	would have	lost

love

lieben

+ **-ing** → ~~e~~ / + **-d** nicht **-ed**
Regelmäßiges Verb

Simple tenses

Present

I	love
you	love
he/she/it	loves
we	love
you	love
they	love

Past

I	loved
you	loved
he/she/it	loved
we	loved
you	loved
they	loved

Present Perfect

I	have	loved
you	have	loved
he/she/it	has	loved
we	have	loved
you	have	loved
they	have	loved

Past Perfect

I	had	loved
you	had	loved
he/she/it	had	loved
we	had	loved
you	had	loved
they	had	loved

Will-Future

I	will	love
you	will	love
he/she/it	will	love
we	will	love
you	will	love
they	will	love

Going to-Future

I	am	going to	love
you	are	going to	love
he/she/it	is	going to	love
we	are	going to	love
you	are	going to	love
they	are	going to	love

Future Perfect

I	will have	loved
you	will have	loved
he/she/it	will have	loved
we	will have	loved
you	will have	loved
they	will have	loved

Imperative

love

Impersonal

ing-Form

loving

Past Participle

loved

Continuous tenses

Present

I	am	loving
you	are	loving
he/she/it	is	loving
we	are	loving
you	are	loving
they	are	loving

Past

I	was	loving
you	were	loving
he/she/it	was	loving
we	were	loving
you	were	loving
they	were	loving

Present Perfect

I	have been	loving
you	have been	loving
he/she/it	has been	loving
we	have been	loving
you	have been	loving
they	have been	loving

Past Perfect

I	had been	loving
you	had been	loving
he/she/it	had been	loving
we	had been	loving
you	had been	loving
they	had been	loving

Will-Future

I	will be	loving
you	will be	loving
he/she/it	will be	loving
we	will be	loving
you	will be	loving
they	will be	loving

Going to-Future

I	am	going to be	loving
you	are	going to be	loving
he/she/it	is	going to be	loving
we	are	going to be	loving
you	are	going to be	loving
they	are	going to be	loving

Future Perfect

I	will have been	loving
you	will have been	loving
he/she/it	will have been	loving
we	will have been	loving
you	will have been	loving
they	will have been	loving

Conditional

I	would	love
you	would	love
he/she/it	would	love
we	would	love
you	would	love
they	would	love

Conditional Past

I	would have	loved
you	would have	loved
he/she/it	would have	loved
we	would have	loved
you	would have	loved
they	would have	loved

Simple tenses

Present

I	maintain
you	maintain
he/she/it	maintains
we	maintain
you	maintain
they	maintain

Past

I	maintained
you	maintained
he/she/it	maintained
we	maintained
you	maintained
they	maintained

Present Perfect

I	have	maintained
you	have	maintained
he/she/it	has	maintained
we	have	maintained
you	have	maintained
they	have	maintained

Past Perfect

I	had	maintained
you	had	maintained
he/she/it	had	maintained
we	had	maintained
you	had	maintained
they	had	maintained

Will-Future

I	will	maintain
you	will	maintain
he/she/it	will	maintain
we	will	maintain
you	will	maintain
they	will	maintain

Going to-Future

I	am	going to	maintain
you	are	going to	maintain
he/she/it	is	going to	maintain
we	are	going to	maintain
you	are	going to	maintain
they	are	going to	maintain

Future Perfect

I	will have	maintained
you	will have	maintained
he/she/it	will have	maintained
we	will have	maintained
you	will have	maintained
they	will have	maintained

Imperative

maintain

Impersonal

ing-Form

maintaining

Past Participle

maintained

Continuous tenses

Present

I	am	maintaining
you	are	maintaining
he/she/it	is	maintaining
we	are	maintaining
you	are	maintaining
they	are	maintaining

Past

I	was	maintaining
you	were	maintaining
he/she/it	was	maintaining
we	were	maintaining
you	were	maintaining
they	were	maintaining

Present Perfect

I	have been	maintaining
you	have been	maintaining
he/she/it	has been	maintaining
we	have been	maintaining
you	have been	maintaining
they	have been	maintaining

Past Perfect

I	had been	maintaining
you	had been	maintaining
he/she/it	had been	maintaining
we	had been	maintaining
you	had been	maintaining
they	had been	maintaining

Will-Future

I	will be	maintaining
you	will be	maintaining
he/she/it	will be	maintaining
we	will be	maintaining
you	will be	maintaining
they	will be	maintaining

Going to-Future

I	am	going to be	maintaining
you	are	going to be	maintaining
he/she/it	is	going to be	maintaining
we	are	going to be	maintaining
you	are	going to be	maintaining
they	are	going to be	maintaining

Future Perfect

I	will have been maintaining
you	will have been maintaining
he/she/it	will have been maintaining
we	will have been maintaining
you	will have been maintaining
they	will have been maintaining

Conditional

I	would	maintain
you	would	maintain
he/she/it	would	maintain
we	would	maintain
you	would	maintain
they	would	maintain

Conditional Past

I	would have	maintained
you	would have	maintained
he/she/it	would have	maintained
we	would have	maintained
you	would have	maintained
they	would have	maintained

make
- made - made

machen

\+ **-ing** → ~~e~~
Unregelmäßiges Verb

Simple tenses

Present

I	make
you	make
he/she/it	makes
we	make
you	make
they	make

Past

I	made
you	made
he/she/it	made
we	made
you	made
they	made

Present Perfect

I	have	made
you	have	made
he/she/it	has	made
we	have	made
you	have	made
they	have	made

Past Perfect

I	had	made
you	had	made
he/she/it	had	made
we	had	made
you	had	made
they	had	made

Will-Future

I	will	make
you	will	make
he/she/it	will	make
we	will	make
you	will	make
they	will	make

Going to-Future

I	am	going to	make
you	are	going to	make
he/she/it	is	going to	make
we	are	going to	make
you	are	going to	make
they	are	going to	make

Future Perfect

I	will have	made
you	will have	made
he/she/it	will have	made
we	will have	made
you	will have	made
they	will have	made

Imperative

make

Impersonal

ing-Form

making

Past Participle

made

Continuous tenses

Present

I	am	making
you	are	making
he/she/it	is	making
we	are	making
you	are	making
they	are	making

Past

I	was	making
you	were	making
he/she/it	was	making
we	were	making
you	were	making
they	were	making

Present Perfect

I	have been	making
you	have been	making
he/she/it	has been	making
we	have been	making
you	have been	making
they	have been	making

Past Perfect

I	had been	making
you	had been	making
he/she/it	had been	making
we	had been	making
you	had been	making
they	had been	making

Will-Future

I	will be	making
you	will be	making
he/she/it	will be	making
we	will be	making
you	will be	making
they	will be	making

Going to-Future

I	am	going to be	making
you	are	going to be	making
he/she/it	is	going to be	making
we	are	going to be	making
you	are	going to be	making
they	are	going to be	making

Future Perfect

I	will have been	making
you	will have been	making
he/she/it	will have been	making
we	will have been	making
you	will have been	making
they	will have been	making

Conditional

I	would	make
you	would	make
he/she/it	would	make
we	would	make
you	would	make
they	would	make

Conditional Past

I	would have	made
you	would have	made
he/she/it	would have	made
we	would have	made
you	would have	made
they	would have	made

Simple tenses

Present

I	manage
you	manage
he/she/it	manages
we	manage
you	manage
they	manage

Past

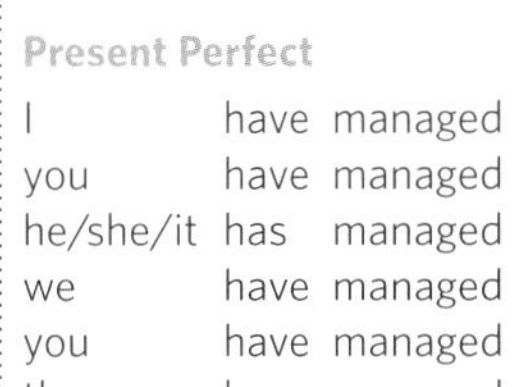

I	managed
you	managed
he/she/it	managed
we	managed
you	managed
they	managed

Present Perfect

I	have	managed
you	have	managed
he/she/it	has	managed
we	have	managed
you	have	managed
they	have	managed

Past Perfect

I	had	managed
you	had	managed
he/she/it	had	managed
we	had	managed
you	had	managed
they	had	managed

Will-Future

I	will	manage
you	will	manage
he/she/it	will	manage
we	will	manage
you	will	manage
they	will	manage

Going to-Future

I	am	going to	manage
you	are	going to	manage
he/she/it	is	going to	manage
we	are	going to	manage
you	are	going to	manage
they	are	going to	manage

Future Perfect

I	will have	managed
you	will have	managed
he/she/it	will have	managed
we	will have	managed
you	will have	managed
they	will have	managed

Imperative

manage

Impersonal

ing-Form

managing

Past Participle

managed

Continuous tenses

Present

I	am	managing
you	are	managing
he/she/it	is	managing
we	are	managing
you	are	managing
they	are	managing

Past

I	was	managing
you	were	managing
he/she/it	was	managing
we	were	managing
you	were	managing
they	were	managing

Present Perfect

I	have been	managing
you	have been	managing
he/she/it	has been	managing
we	have been	managing
you	have been	managing
they	have been	managing

Past Perfect

I	had been	managing
you	had been	managing
he/she/it	had been	managing
we	had been	managing
you	had been	managing
they	had been	managing

Will-Future

I	will be	managing
you	will be	managing
he/she/it	will be	managing
we	will be	managing
you	will be	managing
they	will be	managing

Going to-Future

I	am	going to be	managing
you	are	going to be	managing
he/she/it	is	going to be	managing
we	are	going to be	managing
you	are	going to be	managing
they	are	going to be	managing

Future Perfect

I	will have been	managing
you	will have been	managing
he/she/it	will have been	managing
we	will have been	managing
you	will have been	managing
they	will have been	managing

Conditional

I	would	manage
you	would	manage
he/she/it	would	manage
we	would	manage
you	would	manage
they	would	manage

Conditional Past

I	would have	managed
you	would have	managed
he/she/it	would have	managed
we	would have	managed
you	would have	managed
they	would have	managed

manufacture

herstellen

+ **-ing** → ~~e~~ / + **-d** nicht **-ed**
Regelmäßiges Verb

Simple tenses

Present

I	manufacture
you	manufacture
he/she/it	manufactures
we	manufacture
you	manufacture
they	manufacture

Past

I	manufactured
you	manufactured
he/she/it	manufactured
we	manufactured
you	manufactured
they	manufactured

Present Perfect

I	have	manufactured
you	have	manufactured
he/she/it	has	manufactured
we	have	manufactured
you	have	manufactured
they	have	manufactured

Past Perfect

I	had	manufactured
you	had	manufactured
he/she/it	had	manufactured
we	had	manufactured
you	had	manufactured
they	had	manufactured

Will-Future

I	will	manufacture
you	will	manufacture
he/she/it	will	manufacture
we	will	manufacture
you	will	manufacture
they	will	manufacture

Going to-Future

I	am	going to	manufacture
you	are	going to	manufacture
he/she/it	is	going to	manufacture
we	are	going to	manufacture
you	are	going to	manufacture
they	are	going to	manufacture

Future Perfect

I	will have	manufactured
you	will have	manufactured
he/she/it	will have	manufactured
we	will have	manufactured
you	will have	manufactured
they	will have	manufactured

Imperative

manufacture

Impersonal

ing-Form

manufacturing

Past Participle

manufactured

Continuous tenses

Present

I	am	manufacturing
you	are	manufacturing
he/she/it	is	manufacturing
we	are	manufacturing
you	are	manufacturing
they	are	manufacturing

Past

I	was	manufacturing
you	were	manufacturing
he/she/it	was	manufacturing
we	were	manufacturing
you	were	manufacturing
they	were	manufacturing

Present Perfect

I	have been	manufacturing
you	have been	manufacturing
he/she/it	has been	manufacturing
we	have been	manufacturing
you	have been	manufacturing
they	have been	manufacturing

Past Perfect

I	had been	manufacturing
you	had been	manufacturing
he/she/it	had been	manufacturing
we	had been	manufacturing
you	had been	manufacturing
they	had been	manufacturing

Will-Future

I	will be	manufacturing
you	will be	manufacturing
he/she/it	will be	manufacturing
we	will be	manufacturing
you	will be	manufacturing
they	will be	manufacturing

Going to-Future

I	am going to be	manufacturing
you	are going to be	manufacturing
he/she/it	is going to be	manufacturing
we	are going to be	manufacturing
you	are going to be	manufacturing
they	are going to be	manufacturing

Future Perfect

I	will have been	manufacturing
you	will have been	manufacturing
he/she/it	will have been	manufacturing
we	will have been	manufacturing
you	will have been	manufacturing
they	will have been	manufacturing

Conditional

I	would	manufacture
you	would	manufacture
he/she/it	would	manufacture
we	would	manufacture
you	would	manufacture
they	would	manufacture

Conditional Past

I	would have	manufactured
you	would have	manufactured
he/she/it	would have	manufactured
we	would have	manufactured
you	would have	manufactured
they	would have	manufactured

marschieren

march

Simple tenses

Present

I	march
you	march
he/she/it	marches
we	march
you	march
they	march

Past

I	marched
you	marched
he/she/it	marched
we	marched
you	marched
they	marched

Present Perfect

I	have	marched
you	have	marched
he/she/it	has	marched
we	have	marched
you	have	marched
they	have	marched

Past Perfect

I	had	marched
you	had	marched
he/she/it	had	marched
we	had	marched
you	had	marched
they	had	marched

Will-Future

I	will	march
you	will	march
he/she/it	will	march
we	will	march
you	will	march
they	will	march

Going to-Future

I	am	going to	march
you	are	going to	march
he/she/it	is	going to	march
we	are	going to	march
you	are	going to	march
they	are	going to	march

Future Perfect

I	will have	marched
you	will have	marched
he/she/it	will have	marched
we	will have	marched
you	will have	marched
they	will have	marched

Imperative

march

Impersonal

ing-Form

marching

Past Participle

marched

Continuous tenses

Present

I	am	marching
you	are	marching
he/she/it	is	marching
we	are	marching
you	are	marching
they	are	marching

Past

I	was	marching
you	were	marching
he/she/it	was	marching
we	were	marching
you	were	marching
they	were	marching

Present Perfect

I	have been	marching
you	have been	marching
he/she/it	has been	marching
we	have been	marching
you	have been	marching
they	have been	marching

Past Perfect

I	had been	marching
you	had been	marching
he/she/it	had been	marching
we	had been	marching
you	had been	marching
they	had been	marching

Will-Future

I	will be	marching
you	will be	marching
he/she/it	will be	marching
we	will be	marching
you	will be	marching
they	will be	marching

Going to-Future

I	am	going to be	marching
you	are	going to be	marching
he/she/it	is	going to be	marching
we	are	going to be	marching
you	are	going to be	marching
they	are	going to be	marching

Future Perfect

I	will have been	marching
you	will have been	marching
he/she/it	will have been	marching
we	will have been	marching
you	will have been	marching
they	will have been	marching

Conditional

I	would	march
you	would	march
he/she/it	would	march
we	would	march
you	would	march
they	would	march

Conditional Past

I	would have	marched
you	would have	marched
he/she/it	would have	marched
we	would have	marched
you	would have	marched
they	would have	marched

marry

heiraten

-y → **-ie** vor **-s** / **-y** → **-i** vor **-ed**
Regelmäßiges Verb

Simple tenses

Present

I	marry
you	marry
he/she/it	marries
we	marry
you	marry
they	marry

Past

I	married
you	married
he/she/it	married
we	married
you	married
they	married

Present Perfect

I	have	married
you	have	married
he/she/it	has	married
we	have	married
you	have	married
they	have	married

Past Perfect

I	had	married
you	had	married
he/she/it	had	married
we	had	married
you	had	married
they	had	married

Will-Future

I	will	marry
you	will	marry
he/she/it	will	marry
we	will	marry
you	will	marry
they	will	marry

Going to-Future

I	am	going to	marry
you	are	going to	marry
he/she/it	is	going to	marry
we	are	going to	marry
you	are	going to	marry
they	are	going to	marry

Future Perfect

I	will have	married
you	will have	married
he/she/it	will have	married
we	will have	married
you	will have	married
they	will have	married

Imperative

marry

Impersonal

ing-Form

marrying

Past Participle

married

Continuous tenses

Present

I	am	marrying
you	are	marrying
he/she/it	is	marrying
we	are	marrying
you	are	marrying
they	are	marrying

Past

I	was	marrying
you	were	marrying
he/she/it	was	marrying
we	were	marrying
you	were	marrying
they	were	marrying

Present Perfect

I	have been	marrying
you	have been	marrying
he/she/it	has been	marrying
we	have been	marrying
you	have been	marrying
they	have been	marrying

Past Perfect

I	had been	marrying
you	had been	marrying
he/she/it	had been	marrying
we	had been	marrying
you	had been	marrying
they	had been	marrying

Will-Future

I	will be	marrying
you	will be	marrying
he/she/it	will be	marrying
we	will be	marrying
you	will be	marrying
they	will be	marrying

Going to-Future

I	am	going to be	marrying
you	are	going to be	marrying
he/she/it	is	going to be	marrying
we	are	going to be	marrying
you	are	going to be	marrying
they	are	going to be	marrying

Future Perfect

I	will have been	marrying
you	will have been	marrying
he/she/it	will have been	marrying
we	will have been	marrying
you	will have been	marrying
they	will have been	marrying

Conditional

I	would	marry
you	would	marry
he/she/it	would	marry
we	would	marry
you	would	marry
they	would	marry

Conditional Past

I	would have	married
you	would have	married
he/she/it	would have	married
we	would have	married
you	would have	married
they	would have	married

Simple tenses

Present

I	matter
you	matter
he/she/it	matters
we	matter
you	matter
they	matter

Past

I	mattered
you	mattered
he/she/it	mattered
we	mattered
you	mattered
they	mattered

Present Perfect

I	have	mattered
you	have	mattered
he/she/it	has	mattered
we	have	mattered
you	have	mattered
they	have	mattered

Past Perfect

I	had	mattered
you	had	mattered
he/she/it	had	mattered
we	had	mattered
you	had	mattered
they	had	mattered

Will-Future

I	will	matter
you	will	matter
he/she/it	will	matter
we	will	matter
you	will	matter
they	will	matter

Going to-Future

I	am	going to	matter
you	are	going to	matter
he/she/it	is	going to	matter
we	are	going to	matter
you	are	going to	matter
they	are	going to	matter

Future Perfect

I	will have	mattered
you	will have	mattered
he/she/it	will have	mattered
we	will have	mattered
you	will have	mattered
they	will have	mattered

Imperative

matter

Impersonal

ing-Form

mattering

Past Participle

mattered

Continuous tenses

Present

I	am	mattering
you	are	mattering
he/she/it	is	mattering
we	are	mattering
you	are	mattering
they	are	mattering

Past

I	was	mattering
you	were	mattering
he/she/it	was	mattering
we	were	mattering
you	were	mattering
they	were	mattering

Present Perfect

I	have been	mattering
you	have been	mattering
he/she/it	has been	mattering
we	have been	mattering
you	have been	mattering
they	have been	mattering

Past Perfect

I	had been	mattering
you	had been	mattering
he/she/it	had been	mattering
we	had been	mattering
you	had been	mattering
they	had been	mattering

Will-Future

I	will be	mattering
you	will be	mattering
he/she/it	will be	mattering
we	will be	mattering
you	will be	mattering
they	will be	mattering

Going to-Future

I	am	going to be	mattering
you	are	going to be	mattering
he/she/it	is	going to be	mattering
we	are	going to be	mattering
you	are	going to be	mattering
they	are	going to be	mattering

Future Perfect

I	will have been	mattering
you	will have been	mattering
he/she/it	will have been	mattering
we	will have been	mattering
you	will have been	mattering
they	will have been	mattering

Conditional

I	would	matter
you	would	matter
he/she/it	would	matter
we	would	matter
you	would	matter
they	would	matter

Conditional Past

I	would have	mattered
you	would have	mattered
he/she/it	would have	mattered
we	would have	mattered
you	would have	mattered
they	would have	mattered

mean

- *meant* - *meant*

bedeuten

Unregelmäßiges Verb

Simple tenses

Present

I	mean
you	mean
he/she/it	means
we	mean
you	mean
they	mean

Past

I	meant
you	meant
he/she/it	meant
we	meant
you	meant
they	meant

Present Perfect

I	have	meant
you	have	meant
he/she/it	has	meant
we	have	meant
you	have	meant
they	have	meant

Past Perfect

I	had	meant
you	had	meant
he/she/it	had	meant
we	had	meant
you	had	meant
they	had	meant

Will-Future

I	will	mean
you	will	mean
he/she/it	will	mean
we	will	mean
you	will	mean
they	will	mean

Going to-Future

I	am	going to	mean
you	are	going to	mean
he/she/it	is	going to	mean
we	are	going to	mean
you	are	going to	mean
they	are	going to	mean

Future Perfect

I	will have	meant
you	will have	meant
he/she/it	will have	meant
we	will have	meant
you	will have	meant
they	will have	meant

Imperative

mean

Impersonal

ing-Form

meaning

Past Participle

meant

Continuous tenses

Present

I	am	meaning
you	are	meaning
he/she/it	is	meaning
we	are	meaning
you	are	meaning
they	are	meaning

Past

I	was	meaning
you	were	meaning
he/she/it	was	meaning
we	were	meaning
you	were	meaning
they	were	meaning

Present Perfect

I	have been	meaning
you	have been	meaning
he/she/it	has been	meaning
we	have been	meaning
you	have been	meaning
they	have been	meaning

Past Perfect

I	had been	meaning
you	had been	meaning
he/she/it	had been	meaning
we	had been	meaning
you	had been	meaning
they	had been	meaning

Will-Future

I	will be	meaning
you	will be	meaning
he/she/it	will be	meaning
we	will be	meaning
you	will be	meaning
they	will be	meaning

Going to-Future

I	am	going to be	meaning
you	are	going to be	meaning
he/she/it	is	going to be	meaning
we	are	going to be	meaning
you	are	going to be	meaning
they	are	going to be	meaning

Future Perfect

I	will have been	meaning
you	will have been	meaning
he/she/it	will have been	meaning
we	will have been	meaning
you	will have been	meaning
they	will have been	meaning

Conditional

I	would	mean
you	would	mean
he/she/it	would	mean
we	would	mean
you	would	mean
they	would	mean

Conditional Past

I	would have	meant
you	would have	meant
he/she/it	would have	meant
we	would have	meant
you	would have	meant
they	would have	meant

+ **-ing** → ~~e~~ / + **-d** nicht **-ed**
Regelmäßiges Verb

messen

measure

Simple tenses

Present

I	measure
you	measure
he/she/it	measures
we	measure
you	measure
they	measure

Past

I	measured
you	measured
he/she/it	measured
we	measured
you	measured
they	measured

Present Perfect

I	have	measured
you	have	measured
he/she/it	has	measured
we	have	measured
you	have	measured
they	have	measured

Past Perfect

I	had	measured
you	had	measured
he/she/it	had	measured
we	had	measured
you	had	measured
they	had	measured

Will-Future

I	will	measure
you	will	measure
he/she/it	will	measure
we	will	measure
you	will	measure
they	will	measure

Going to-Future

I	am	going to	measure
you	are	going to	measure
he/she/it	is	going to	measure
we	are	going to	measure
you	are	going to	measure
they	are	going to	measure

Future Perfect

I	will have	measured
you	will have	measured
he/she/it	will have	measured
we	will have	measured
you	will have	measured
they	will have	measured

Imperative

measure

Impersonal

ing-Form

measuring

Past Participle

measured

Continuous tenses

Present

I	am	measuring
you	are	measuring
he/she/it	is	measuring
we	are	measuring
you	are	measuring
they	are	measuring

Past

I	was	measuring
you	were	measuring
he/she/it	was	measuring
we	were	measuring
you	were	measuring
they	were	measuring

Present Perfect

I	have been	measuring
you	have been	measuring
he/she/it	has been	measuring
we	have been	measuring
you	have been	measuring
they	have been	measuring

Past Perfect

I	had been	measuring
you	had been	measuring
he/she/it	had been	measuring
we	had been	measuring
you	had been	measuring
they	had been	measuring

Will-Future

I	will be	measuring
you	will be	measuring
he/she/it	will be	measuring
we	will be	measuring
you	will be	measuring
they	will be	measuring

Going to-Future

I	am	going to be	measuring
you	are	going to be	measuring
he/she/it	is	going to be	measuring
we	are	going to be	measuring
you	are	going to be	measuring
they	are	going to be	measuring

Future Perfect

I	will have been	measuring
you	will have been	measuring
he/she/it	will have been	measuring
we	will have been	measuring
you	will have been	measuring
they	will have been	measuring

Conditional

I	would	measure
you	would	measure
he/she/it	would	measure
we	would	measure
you	would	measure
they	would	measure

Conditional Past

I	would have	measured
you	would have	measured
he/she/it	would have	measured
we	would have	measured
you	would have	measured
they	would have	measured

meet
- met - met

treffen

Unregelmäßiges Verb

Simple tenses

Present

I	meet
you	meet
he/she/it	meets
we	meet
you	meet
they	meet

Past

I	met
you	met
he/she/it	met
we	met
you	met
they	met

Present Perfect

I	have	met
you	have	met
he/she/it	has	met
we	have	met
you	have	met
they	have	met

Past Perfect

I	had	met
you	had	met
he/she/it	had	met
we	had	met
you	had	met
they	had	met

***Will*-Future**

I	will	meet
you	will	meet
he/she/it	will	meet
we	will	meet
you	will	meet
they	will	meet

***Going to*-Future**

I	am	going to	meet
you	are	going to	meet
he/she/it	is	going to	meet
we	are	going to	meet
you	are	going to	meet
they	are	going to	meet

Future Perfect

I	will have	met
you	will have	met
he/she/it	will have	met
we	will have	met
you	will have	met
they	will have	met

Imperative

meet

Impersonal

***ing*-Form**

meeting

Past Participle

met

Continuous tenses

Present

I	am	meeting
you	are	meeting
he/she/it	is	meeting
we	are	meeting
you	are	meeting
they	are	meeting

Past

I	was	meeting
you	were	meeting
he/she/it	was	meeting
we	were	meeting
you	were	meeting
they	were	meeting

Present Perfect

I	have	been	meeting
you	have	been	meeting
he/she/it	has	been	meeting
we	have	been	meeting
you	have	been	meeting
they	have	been	meeting

Past Perfect

I	had been	meeting
you	had been	meeting
he/she/it	had been	meeting
we	had been	meeting
you	had been	meeting
they	had been	meeting

***Will*-Future**

I	will be	meeting
you	will be	meeting
he/she/it	will be	meeting
we	will be	meeting
you	will be	meeting
they	will be	meeting

***Going to*-Future**

I	am	going to be	meeting
you	are	going to be	meeting
he/she/it	is	going to be	meeting
we	are	going to be	meeting
you	are	going to be	meeting
they	are	going to be	meeting

Future Perfect

I	will have been	meeting
you	will have been	meeting
he/she/it	will have been	meeting
we	will have been	meeting
you	will have been	meeting
they	will have been	meeting

Conditional

I	would	meet
you	would	meet
he/she/it	would	meet
we	would	meet
you	would	meet
they	would	meet

Conditional Past

I	would have	met
you	would have	met
he/she/it	would have	met
we	would have	met
you	would have	met
they	would have	met

Unregelmäßiges Verb

schmelzen

melt
- melted - melted

Simple tenses

Present

I	melt
you	melt
he/she/it	melts
we	melt
you	melt
they	melt

Past

I	melted
you	melted
he/she/it	melted
we	melted
you	melted
they	melted

Present Perfect

I	have	melted
you	have	melted
he/she/it	has	melted
we	have	melted
you	have	melted
they	have	melted

Past Perfect

I	had	melted
you	had	melted
he/she/it	had	melted
we	had	melted
you	had	melted
they	had	melted

Will-Future

I	will	melt
you	will	melt
he/she/it	will	melt
we	will	melt
you	will	melt
they	will	melt

Going to-Future

I	am	going to	melt
you	are	going to	melt
he/she/it	is	going to	melt
we	are	going to	melt
you	are	going to	melt
they	are	going to	melt

Future Perfect

I	will have	melted
you	will have	melted
he/she/it	will have	melted
we	will have	melted
you	will have	melted
they	will have	melted

Imperative

melt

Impersonal

ing-Form

melting

Past Participle

melted

Continuous tenses

Present

I	am	melting
you	are	melting
he/she/it	is	melting
we	are	melting
you	are	melting
they	are	melting

Past

I	was	melting
you	were	melting
he/she/it	was	melting
we	were	melting
you	were	melting
they	were	melting

Present Perfect

I	have been	melting
you	have been	melting
he/she/it	has been	melting
we	have been	melting
you	have been	melting
they	have been	melting

Past Perfect

I	had been	melting
you	had been	melting
he/she/it	had been	melting
we	had been	melting
you	had been	melting
they	had been	melting

Will-Future

I	will be	melting
you	will be	melting
he/she/it	will be	melting
we	will be	melting
you	will be	melting
they	will be	melting

Going to-Future

I	am	going to be	melting
you	are	going to be	melting
he/she/it	is	going to be	melting
we	are	going to be	melting
you	are	going to be	melting
they	are	going to be	melting

Future Perfect

I	will have been	melting
you	will have been	melting
he/she/it	will have been	melting
we	will have been	melting
you	will have been	melting
they	will have been	melting

Conditional

I	would	melt
you	would	melt
he/she/it	would	melt
we	would	melt
you	would	melt
they	would	melt

Conditional Past

I	would have	melted
you	would have	melted
he/she/it	would have	melted
we	would have	melted
you	would have	melted
they	would have	melted

mention

erwähnen

Regelmäßiges Verb

Simple tenses

Present

I	mention
you	mention
he/she/it	mentions
we	mention
you	mention
they	mention

Past

I	mentioned
you	mentioned
he/she/it	mentioned
we	mentioned
you	mentioned
they	mentioned

Present Perfect

I	have	mentioned
you	have	mentioned
he/she/it	has	mentioned
we	have	mentioned
you	have	mentioned
they	have	mentioned

Past Perfect

I	had	mentioned
you	had	mentioned
he/she/it	had	mentioned
we	had	mentioned
you	had	mentioned
they	had	mentioned

Will-Future

I	will	mention
you	will	mention
he/she/it	will	mention
we	will	mention
you	will	mention
they	will	mention

Going to-Future

I	am	going to	mention
you	are	going to	mention
he/she/it	is	going to	mention
we	are	going to	mention
you	are	going to	mention
they	are	going to	mention

Future Perfect

I	will have	mentioned
you	will have	mentioned
he/she/it	will have	mentioned
we	will have	mentioned
you	will have	mentioned
they	will have	mentioned

Imperative

mention

Impersonal

ing-Form

mentioning

Past Participle

mentioned

Continuous tenses

Present

I	am	mentioning
you	are	mentioning
he/she/it	is	mentioning
we	are	mentioning
you	are	mentioning
they	are	mentioning

Past

I	was	mentioning
you	were	mentioning
he/she/it	was	mentioning
we	were	mentioning
you	were	mentioning
they	were	mentioning

Present Perfect

I	have been	mentioning
you	have been	mentioning
he/she/it	has been	mentioning
we	have been	mentioning
you	have been	mentioning
they	have been	mentioning

Past Perfect

I	had been	mentioning
you	had been	mentioning
he/she/it	had been	mentioning
we	had been	mentioning
you	had been	mentioning
they	had been	mentioning

Will-Future

I	will be	mentioning
you	will be	mentioning
he/she/it	will be	mentioning
we	will be	mentioning
you	will be	mentioning
they	will be	mentioning

Going to-Future

I	am	going to be	mentioning
you	are	going to be	mentioning
he/she/it	is	going to be	mentioning
we	are	going to be	mentioning
you	are	going to be	mentioning
they	are	going to be	mentioning

Future Perfect

I	will have been mentioning
you	will have been mentioning
he/she/it	will have been mentioning
we	will have been mentioning
you	will have been mentioning
they	will have been mentioning

Conditional

I	would	mention
you	would	mention
he/she/it	would	mention
we	would	mention
you	would	mention
they	would	mention

Conditional Past

I	would have	mentioned
you	would have	mentioned
he/she/it	would have	mentioned
we	would have	mentioned
you	would have	mentioned
they	would have	mentioned

mind

Regelmäßiges Verb

Simple tenses

Present

I	mind
you	mind
he/she/it	minds
we	mind
you	mind
they	mind

Past

I	minded
you	minded
he/she/it	minded
we	minded
you	minded
they	minded

Present Perfect

I	have	minded
you	have	minded
he/she/it	has	minded
we	have	minded
you	have	minded
they	have	minded

Past Perfect

I	had	minded
you	had	minded
he/she/it	had	minded
we	had	minded
you	had	minded
they	had	minded

Will-Future

I	will	mind
you	will	mind
he/she/it	will	mind
we	will	mind
you	will	mind
they	will	mind

Going to-Future

I	am	going to	mind
you	are	going to	mind
he/she/it	is	going to	mind
we	are	going to	mind
you	are	going to	mind
they	are	going to	mind

Future Perfect

I	will have	minded
you	will have	minded
he/she/it	will have	minded
we	will have	minded
you	will have	minded
they	will have	minded

Imperative

mind

Impersonal

ing-Form

minding

Past Participle

minded

Continuous tenses

Present

I	am	minding
you	are	minding
he/she/it	is	minding
we	are	minding
you	are	minding
they	are	minding

Past

I	was	minding
you	were	minding
he/she/it	was	minding
we	were	minding
you	were	minding
they	were	minding

Present Perfect

I	have been	minding
you	have been	minding
he/she/it	has been	minding
we	have been	minding
you	have been	minding
they	have been	minding

Past Perfect

I	had been	minding
you	had been	minding
he/she/it	had been	minding
we	had been	minding
you	had been	minding
they	had been	minding

Will-Future

I	will be	minding
you	will be	minding
he/she/it	will be	minding
we	will be	minding
you	will be	minding
they	will be	minding

Going to-Future

I	am	going to be	minding
you	are	going to be	minding
he/she/it	is	going to be	minding
we	are	going to be	minding
you	are	going to be	minding
they	are	going to be	minding

Future Perfect

I	will have been	minding
you	will have been	minding
he/she/it	will have been	minding
we	will have been	minding
you	will have been	minding
they	will have been	minding

Conditional

I	would	mind
you	would	mind
he/she/it	would	mind
we	would	mind
you	would	mind
they	would	mind

Conditional Past

I	would have	minded
you	would have	minded
he/she/it	would have	minded
we	would have	minded
you	would have	minded
they	would have	minded

mix

vermischen

+ **-es** in 3. Person Singular
Regelmäßiges Verb

Simple tenses

Present

I	mix
you	mix
he/she/it	mixes
we	mix
you	mix
they	mix

Past

I	mixed
you	mixed
he/she/it	mixed
we	mixed
you	mixed
they	mixed

Present Perfect

I	have	mixed
you	have	mixed
he/she/it	has	mixed
we	have	mixed
you	have	mixed
they	have	mixed

Past Perfect

I	had	mixed
you	had	mixed
he/she/it	had	mixed
we	had	mixed
you	had	mixed
they	had	mixed

Will-Future

I	will	mix
you	will	mix
he/she/it	will	mix
we	will	mix
you	will	mix
they	will	mix

Going to-Future

I	am	going to	mix
you	are	going to	mix
he/she/it	is	going to	mix
we	are	going to	mix
you	are	going to	mix
they	are	going to	mix

Future Perfect

I	will have	mixed
you	will have	mixed
he/she/it	will have	mixed
we	will have	mixed
you	will have	mixed
they	will have	mixed

Imperative

mix

Impersonal

ing-Form

mixing

Past Participle

mixed

Continuous tenses

Present

I	am	mixing
you	are	mixing
he/she/it	is	mixing
we	are	mixing
you	are	mixing
they	are	mixing

Past

I	was	mixing
you	were	mixing
he/she/it	was	mixing
we	were	mixing
you	were	mixing
they	were	mixing

Present Perfect

I	have been	mixing
you	have been	mixing
he/she/it	has been	mixing
we	have been	mixing
you	have been	mixing
they	have been	mixing

Past Perfect

I	had been	mixing
you	had been	mixing
he/she/it	had been	mixing
we	had been	mixing
you	had been	mixing
they	had been	mixing

Will-Future

I	will be	mixing
you	will be	mixing
he/she/it	will be	mixing
we	will be	mixing
you	will be	mixing
they	will be	mixing

Going to-Future

I	am	going to be	mixing
you	are	going to be	mixing
he/she/it	is	going to be	mixing
we	are	going to be	mixing
you	are	going to be	mixing
they	are	going to be	mixing

Future Perfect

I	will have been	mixing
you	will have been	mixing
he/she/it	will have been	mixing
we	will have been	mixing
you	will have been	mixing
they	will have been	mixing

Conditional

I	would	mix
you	would	mix
he/she/it	would	mix
we	would	mix
you	would	mix
they	would	mix

Conditional Past

I	would have	mixed
you	would have	mixed
he/she/it	would have	mixed
we	would have	mixed
you	would have	mixed
they	would have	mixed

bewegen

move

Simple tenses

Present

I	move
you	move
he/she/it	moves
we	move
you	move
they	move

Past

I	moved
you	moved
he/she/it	moved
we	moved
you	moved
they	moved

Present Perfect

I	have	moved
you	have	moved
he/she/it	has	moved
we	have	moved
you	have	moved
they	have	moved

Past Perfect

I	had	moved
you	had	moved
he/she/it	had	moved
we	had	moved
you	had	moved
they	had	moved

Will-Future

I	will	move
you	will	move
he/she/it	will	move
we	will	move
you	will	move
they	will	move

Going to-Future

I	am	going to	move
you	are	going to	move
he/she/it	is	going to	move
we	are	going to	move
you	are	going to	move
they	are	going to	move

Future Perfect

I	will have	moved
you	will have	moved
he/she/it	will have	moved
we	will have	moved
you	will have	moved
they	will have	moved

Imperative

move

Impersonal

ing-Form

moving

Past Participle

moved

Continuous tenses

Present

I	am	moving
you	are	moving
he/she/it	is	moving
we	are	moving
you	are	moving
they	are	moving

Past

I	was	moving
you	were	moving
he/she/it	was	moving
we	were	moving
you	were	moving
they	were	moving

Present Perfect

I	have been	moving
you	have been	moving
he/she/it	has been	moving
we	have been	moving
you	have been	moving
they	have been	moving

Past Perfect

I	had been	moving
you	had been	moving
he/she/it	had been	moving
we	had been	moving
you	had been	moving
they	had been	moving

Will-Future

I	will be	moving
you	will be	moving
he/she/it	will be	moving
we	will be	moving
you	will be	moving
they	will be	moving

Going to-Future

I	am	going to be	moving
you	are	going to be	moving
he/she/it	is	going to be	moving
we	are	going to be	moving
you	are	going to be	moving
they	are	going to be	moving

Future Perfect

I	will have been	moving
you	will have been	moving
he/she/it	will have been	moving
we	will have been	moving
you	will have been	moving
they	will have been	moving

Conditional

I	would	move
you	would	move
he/she/it	would	move
we	would	move
you	would	move
they	would	move

Conditional Past

I	would have	moved
you	would have	moved
he/she/it	would have	moved
we	would have	moved
you	would have	moved
they	would have	moved

name

nennen

\+ **-ing** → ~~e~~ / + **-d** nicht **-ed**
Regelmäßiges Verb

Simple tenses

Present

I	name
you	name
he/she/it	names
we	name
you	name
they	name

Past

I	named
you	named
he/she/it	named
we	named
you	named
they	named

Present Perfect

I	have	named
you	have	named
he/she/it	has	named
we	have	named
you	have	named
they	have	named

Past Perfect

I	had	named
you	had	named
he/she/it	had	named
we	had	named
you	had	named
they	had	named

Will-Future

I	will	name
you	will	name
he/she/it	will	name
we	will	name
you	will	name
they	will	name

Going to-Future

I	am	going to	name
you	are	going to	name
he/she/it	is	going to	name
we	are	going to	name
you	are	going to	name
they	are	going to	name

Future Perfect

I	will have	named
you	will have	named
he/she/it	will have	named
we	will have	named
you	will have	named
they	will have	named

Imperative

name

Impersonal

ing-Form

naming

Past Participle

named

Continuous tenses

Present

I	am	naming
you	are	naming
he/she/it	is	naming
we	are	naming
you	are	naming
they	are	naming

Past

I	was	naming
you	were	naming
he/she/it	was	naming
we	were	naming
you	were	naming
they	were	naming

Present Perfect

I	have been	naming
you	have been	naming
he/she/it	has been	naming
we	have been	naming
you	have been	naming
they	have been	naming

Past Perfect

I	had been	naming
you	had been	naming
he/she/it	had been	naming
we	had been	naming
you	had been	naming
they	had been	naming

Will-Future

I	will be	naming
you	will be	naming
he/she/it	will be	naming
we	will be	naming
you	will be	naming
they	will be	naming

Going to-Future

I	am	going to be	naming
you	are	going to be	naming
he/she/it	is	going to be	naming
we	are	going to be	naming
you	are	going to be	naming
they	are	going to be	naming

Future Perfect

I	will have been	naming
you	will have been	naming
he/she/it	will have been	naming
we	will have been	naming
you	will have been	naming
they	will have been	naming

Conditional

I	would	name
you	would	name
he/she/it	would	name
we	would	name
you	would	name
they	would	name

Conditional Past

I	would have	named
you	would have	named
he/she/it	would have	named
we	would have	named
you	would have	named
they	would have	named

Simple tenses

Present

I	need
you	need
he/she/it	needs
we	need
you	need
they	need

Past

I	needed
you	needed
he/she/it	needed
we	needed
you	needed
they	needed

Present Perfect

I	have	needed
you	have	needed
he/she/it	has	needed
we	have	needed
you	have	needed
they	have	needed

Past Perfect

I	had	needed
you	had	needed
he/she/it	had	needed
we	had	needed
you	had	needed
they	had	needed

Will-Future

I	will	need
you	will	need
he/she/it	will	need
we	will	need
you	will	need
they	will	need

Going to-Future

I	am	going to	need
you	are	going to	need
he/she/it	is	going to	need
we	are	going to	need
you	are	going to	need
they	are	going to	need

Future Perfect

I	will have	needed
you	will have	needed
he/she/it	will have	needed
we	will have	needed
you	will have	needed
they	will have	needed

Imperative

need

Impersonal

ing-Form

needing

Past Participle

needed

Continuous tenses

Present

I	am	needing
you	are	needing
he/she/it	is	needing
we	are	needing
you	are	needing
they	are	needing

Past

I	was	needing
you	were	needing
he/she/it	was	needing
we	were	needing
you	were	needing
they	were	needing

Present Perfect

I	have been	needing
you	have been	needing
he/she/it	has been	needing
we	have been	needing
you	have been	needing
they	have been	needing

Past Perfect

I	had been	needing
you	had been	needing
he/she/it	had been	needing
we	had been	needing
you	had been	needing
they	had been	needing

Will-Future

I	will be	needing
you	will be	needing
he/she/it	will be	needing
we	will be	needing
you	will be	needing
they	will be	needing

Going to-Future

I	am	going to be	needing
you	are	going to be	needing
he/she/it	is	going to be	needing
we	are	going to be	needing
you	are	going to be	needing
they	are	going to be	needing

Future Perfect

I	will have been	needing
you	will have been	needing
he/she/it	will have been	needing
we	will have been	needing
you	will have been	needing
they	will have been	needing

Conditional

I	would	need
you	would	need
he/she/it	would	need
we	would	need
you	would	need
they	would	need

Conditional Past

I	would have	needed
you	would have	needed
he/she/it	would have	needed
we	would have	needed
you	would have	needed
they	would have	needed

note

wahrnehmen

+ **-ing** → ~~e~~ / + **-d** nicht **-ed**
Regelmäßiges Verb

Simple tenses

Present

I	note
you	note
he/she/it	notes
we	note
you	note
they	note

Past

I	noted
you	noted
he/she/it	noted
we	noted
you	noted
they	noted

Present Perfect

I	have	noted
you	have	noted
he/she/it	has	noted
we	have	noted
you	have	noted
they	have	noted

Past Perfect

I	had	noted
you	had	noted
he/she/it	had	noted
we	had	noted
you	had	noted
they	had	noted

Will-Future

I	will	note
you	will	note
he/she/it	will	note
we	will	note
you	will	note
they	will	note

Going to-Future

I	am	going to	note
you	are	going to	note
he/she/it	is	going to	note
we	are	going to	note
you	are	going to	note
they	are	going to	note

Future Perfect

I	will have	noted
you	will have	noted
he/she/it	will have	noted
we	will have	noted
you	will have	noted
they	will have	noted

Imperative

note

Impersonal

ing-Form

noting

Past Participle

noted

Continuous tenses

Present

I	am	noting
you	are	noting
he/she/it	is	noting
we	are	noting
you	are	noting
they	are	noting

Past

I	was	noting
you	were	noting
he/she/it	was	noting
we	were	noting
you	were	noting
they	were	noting

Present Perfect

I	have been	noting
you	have been	noting
he/she/it	has been	noting
we	have been	noting
you	have been	noting
they	have been	noting

Past Perfect

I	had been	noting
you	had been	noting
he/she/it	had been	noting
we	had been	noting
you	had been	noting
they	had been	noting

Will-Future

I	will be	noting
you	will be	noting
he/she/it	will be	noting
we	will be	noting
you	will be	noting
they	will be	noting

Going to-Future

I	am	going to be	noting
you	are	going to be	noting
he/she/it	is	going to be	noting
we	are	going to be	noting
you	are	going to be	noting
they	are	going to be	noting

Future Perfect

I	will have been	noting
you	will have been	noting
he/she/it	will have been	noting
we	will have been	noting
you	will have been	noting
they	will have been	noting

Conditional

I	would	note
you	would	note
he/she/it	would	note
we	would	note
you	would	note
they	would	note

Conditional Past

I	would have	noted
you	would have	noted
he/she/it	would have	noted
we	would have	noted
you	would have	noted
they	would have	noted

+ **-ing** → ~~e~~ / + **-d** nicht **-ed**
Regelmäßiges Verb

bemerken

notice

Simple tenses

Present

I	notice
you	notice
he/she/it	notices
we	notice
you	notice
they	notice

Past

I	noticed
you	noticed
he/she/it	noticed
we	noticed
you	noticed
they	noticed

Present Perfect

I	have	noticed
you	have	noticed
he/she/it	has	noticed
we	have	noticed
you	have	noticed
they	have	noticed

Past Perfect

I	had	noticed
you	had	noticed
he/she/it	had	noticed
we	had	noticed
you	had	noticed
they	had	noticed

Will-Future

I	will	notice
you	will	notice
he/she/it	will	notice
we	will	notice
you	will	notice
they	will	notice

Going to-Future

I	am	going to	notice
you	are	going to	notice
he/she/it	is	going to	notice
we	are	going to	notice
you	are	going to	notice
they	are	going to	notice

Future Perfect

I	will have	noticed
you	will have	noticed
he/she/it	will have	noticed
we	will have	noticed
you	will have	noticed
they	will have	noticed

Imperative

notice

Impersonal

ing-Form

noticing

Past Participle

noticed

Continuous tenses

Present

I	am	noticing
you	are	noticing
he/she/it	is	noticing
we	are	noticing
you	are	noticing
they	are	noticing

Past

I	was	noticing
you	were	noticing
he/she/it	was	noticing
we	were	noticing
you	were	noticing
they	were	noticing

Present Perfect

I	have been	noticing
you	have been	noticing
he/she/it	has been	noticing
we	have been	noticing
you	have been	noticing
they	have been	noticing

Past Perfect

I	had been	noticing
you	had been	noticing
he/she/it	had been	noticing
we	had been	noticing
you	had been	noticing
they	had been	noticing

Will-Future

I	will be	noticing
you	will be	noticing
he/she/it	will be	noticing
we	will be	noticing
you	will be	noticing
they	will be	noticing

Going to-Future

I	am	going to be	noticing
you	are	going to be	noticing
he/she/it	is	going to be	noticing
we	are	going to be	noticing
you	are	going to be	noticing
they	are	going to be	noticing

Future Perfect

I	will have been	noticing
you	will have been	noticing
he/she/it	will have been	noticing
we	will have been	noticing
you	will have been	noticing
they	will have been	noticing

Conditional

I	would	notice
you	would	notice
he/she/it	would	notice
we	would	notice
you	would	notice
they	would	notice

Conditional Past

I	would have	noticed
you	would have	noticed
he/she/it	would have	noticed
we	would have	noticed
you	would have	noticed
they	would have	noticed

obey

gehorchen

Regelmäßiges Verb

Simple tenses

Present

I	obey
you	obey
he/she/it	obeys
we	obey
you	obey
they	obey

Past

I	obeyed
you	obeyed
he/she/it	obeyed
we	obeyed
you	obeyed
they	obeyed

Present Perfect

I	have	obeyed
you	have	obeyed
he/she/it	has	obeyed
we	have	obeyed
you	have	obeyed
they	have	obeyed

Past Perfect

I	had	obeyed
you	had	obeyed
he/she/it	had	obeyed
we	had	obeyed
you	had	obeyed
they	had	obeyed

Will-Future

I	will	obey
you	will	obey
he/she/it	will	obey
we	will	obey
you	will	obey
they	will	obey

Going to-Future

I	am	going to	obey
you	are	going to	obey
he/she/it	is	going to	obey
we	are	going to	obey
you	are	going to	obey
they	are	going to	obey

Future Perfect

I	will have	obeyed
you	will have	obeyed
he/she/it	will have	obeyed
we	will have	obeyed
you	will have	obeyed
they	will have	obeyed

Imperative

obey

Impersonal

ing-Form

obeying

Past Participle

obeyed

Continuous tenses

Present

I	am	obeying
you	are	obeying
he/she/it	is	obeying
we	are	obeying
you	are	obeying
they	are	obeying

Past

I	was	obeying
you	were	obeying
he/she/it	was	obeying
we	were	obeying
you	were	obeying
they	were	obeying

Present Perfect

I	have been	obeying
you	have been	obeying
he/she/it	has been	obeying
we	have been	obeying
you	have been	obeying
they	have been	obeying

Past Perfect

I	had been	obeying
you	had been	obeying
he/she/it	had been	obeying
we	had been	obeying
you	had been	obeying
they	had been	obeying

Will-Future

I	will be	obeying
you	will be	obeying
he/she/it	will be	obeying
we	will be	obeying
you	will be	obeying
they	will be	obeying

Going to-Future

I	am	going to be	obeying
you	are	going to be	obeying
he/she/it	is	going to be	obeying
we	are	going to be	obeying
you	are	going to be	obeying
they	are	going to be	obeying

Future Perfect

I	will have been	obeying
you	will have been	obeying
he/she/it	will have been	obeying
we	will have been	obeying
you	will have been	obeying
they	will have been	obeying

Conditional

I	would	obey
you	would	obey
he/she/it	would	obey
we	would	obey
you	would	obey
they	would	obey

Conditional Past

I	would have	obeyed
you	would have	obeyed
he/she/it	would have	obeyed
we	would have	obeyed
you	would have	obeyed
they	would have	obeyed

Simple tenses

Present

I	object
you	object
he/she/it	objects
we	object
you	object
they	object

Past

I	objected
you	objected
he/she/it	objected
we	objected
you	objected
they	objected

Present Perfect

I	have	objected
you	have	objected
he/she/it	has	objected
we	have	objected
you	have	objected
they	have	objected

Past Perfect

I	had	objected
you	had	objected
he/she/it	had	objected
we	had	objected
you	had	objected
they	had	objected

Will-Future

I	will	object
you	will	object
he/she/it	will	object
we	will	object
you	will	object
they	will	object

Going to-Future

I	am	going to	object
you	are	going to	object
he/she/it	is	going to	object
we	are	going to	object
you	are	going to	object
they	are	going to	object

Future Perfect

I	will have	objected
you	will have	objected
he/she/it	will have	objected
we	will have	objected
you	will have	objected
they	will have	objected

Imperative

object

Impersonal

ing-Form

objecting

Past Participle

objected

Continuous tenses

Present

I	am	objecting
you	are	objecting
he/she/it	is	objecting
we	are	objecting
you	are	objecting
they	are	objecting

Past

I	was	objecting
you	were	objecting
he/she/it	was	objecting
we	were	objecting
you	were	objecting
they	were	objecting

Present Perfect

I	have been	objecting
you	have been	objecting
he/she/it	has been	objecting
we	have been	objecting
you	have been	objecting
they	have been	objecting

Past Perfect

I	had been	objecting
you	had been	objecting
he/she/it	had been	objecting
we	had been	objecting
you	had been	objecting
they	had been	objecting

Will-Future

I	will be	objecting
you	will be	objecting
he/she/it	will be	objecting
we	will be	objecting
you	will be	objecting
they	will be	objecting

Going to-Future

I	am	going to be	objecting
you	are	going to be	objecting
he/she/it	is	going to be	objecting
we	are	going to be	objecting
you	are	going to be	objecting
they	are	going to be	objecting

Future Perfect

I	will have been	objecting
you	will have been	objecting
he/she/it	will have been	objecting
we	will have been	objecting
you	will have been	objecting
they	will have been	objecting

Conditional

I	would	object
you	would	object
he/she/it	would	object
we	would	object
you	would	object
they	would	object

Conditional Past

I	would have	objected
you	would have	objected
he/she/it	would have	objected
we	would have	objected
you	would have	objected
they	would have	objected

observe

beobachten

+ **-ing** → ~~e~~ / + **-d** nicht **-ed**
Regelmäßiges Verb

Simple tenses

Present

I	observe
you	observe
he/she/it	observes
we	observe
you	observe
they	observe

Past

I	observed
you	observed
he/she/it	observed
we	observed
you	observed
they	observed

Present Perfect

I	have	observed
you	have	observed
he/she/it	has	observed
we	have	observed
you	have	observed
they	have	observed

Past Perfect

I	had	observed
you	had	observed
he/she/it	had	observed
we	had	observed
you	had	observed
they	had	observed

Will-Future

I	will	observe
you	will	observe
he/she/it	will	observe
we	will	observe
you	will	observe
they	will	observe

Going to-Future

I	am	going to	observe
you	are	going to	observe
he/she/it	is	going to	observe
we	are	going to	observe
you	are	going to	observe
they	are	going to	observe

Future Perfect

I	will have	observed
you	will have	observed
he/she/it	will have	observed
we	will have	observed
you	will have	observed
they	will have	observed

Imperative

observe

Impersonal

ing-Form

observing

Past Participle

observed

Continuous tenses

Present

I	am	observing
you	are	observing
he/she/it	is	observing
we	are	observing
you	are	observing
they	are	observing

Past

I	was	observing
you	were	observing
he/she/it	was	observing
we	were	observing
you	were	observing
they	were	observing

Present Perfect

I	have been	observing
you	have been	observing
he/she/it	has been	observing
we	have been	observing
you	have been	observing
they	have been	observing

Past Perfect

I	had been	observing
you	had been	observing
he/she/it	had been	observing
we	had been	observing
you	had been	observing
they	had been	observing

Will-Future

I	will be	observing
you	will be	observing
he/she/it	will be	observing
we	will be	observing
you	will be	observing
they	will be	observing

Going to-Future

I	am	going to be	observing
you	are	going to be	observing
he/she/it	is	going to be	observing
we	are	going to be	observing
you	are	going to be	observing
they	are	going to be	observing

Future Perfect

I	will have been	observing
you	will have been	observing
he/she/it	will have been	observing
we	will have been	observing
you	will have been	observing
they	will have been	observing

Conditional

I	would	observe
you	would	observe
he/she/it	would	observe
we	would	observe
you	would	observe
they	would	observe

Conditional Past

I	would have	observed
you	would have	observed
he/she/it	would have	observed
we	would have	observed
you	would have	observed
they	would have	observed

Simple tenses

Present

I	obtain
you	obtain
he/she/it	obtains
we	obtain
you	obtain
they	obtain

Past

I	obtained
you	obtained
he/she/it	obtained
we	obtained
you	obtained
they	obtained

Present Perfect

I	have	obtained
you	have	obtained
he/she/it	has	obtained
we	have	obtained
you	have	obtained
they	have	obtained

Past Perfect

I	had	obtained
you	had	obtained
he/she/it	had	obtained
we	had	obtained
you	had	obtained
they	had	obtained

Will-Future

I	will	obtain
you	will	obtain
he/she/it	will	obtain
we	will	obtain
you	will	obtain
they	will	obtain

Going to-Future

I	am	going to	obtain
you	are	going to	obtain
he/she/it	is	going to	obtain
we	are	going to	obtain
you	are	going to	obtain
they	are	going to	obtain

Future Perfect

I	will have	obtained
you	will have	obtained
he/she/it	will have	obtained
we	will have	obtained
you	will have	obtained
they	will have	obtained

Imperative

obtain

Impersonal

ing-Form

obtaining

Past Participle

obtained

Continuous tenses

Present

I	am	obtaining
you	are	obtaining
he/she/it	is	obtaining
we	are	obtaining
you	are	obtaining
they	are	obtaining

Past

I	was	obtaining
you	were	obtaining
he/she/it	was	obtaining
we	were	obtaining
you	were	obtaining
they	were	obtaining

Present Perfect

I	have been	obtaining
you	have been	obtaining
he/she/it	has been	obtaining
we	have been	obtaining
you	have been	obtaining
they	have been	obtaining

Past Perfect

I	had been	obtaining
you	had been	obtaining
he/she/it	had been	obtaining
we	had been	obtaining
you	had been	obtaining
they	had been	obtaining

Will-Future

I	will be	obtaining
you	will be	obtaining
he/she/it	will be	obtaining
we	will be	obtaining
you	will be	obtaining
they	will be	obtaining

Going to-Future

I	am	going to be	obtaining
you	are	going to be	obtaining
he/she/it	is	going to be	obtaining
we	are	going to be	obtaining
you	are	going to be	obtaining
they	are	going to be	obtaining

Future Perfect

I	will have been	obtaining
you	will have been	obtaining
he/she/it	will have been	obtaining
we	will have been	obtaining
you	will have been	obtaining
they	will have been	obtaining

Conditional

I	would	obtain
you	would	obtain
he/she/it	would	obtain
we	would	obtain
you	would	obtain
they	would	obtain

Conditional Past

I	would have	obtained
you	would have	obtained
he/she/it	would have	obtained
we	would have	obtained
you	would have	obtained
they	would have	obtained

occupy

ausfüllen

-y → -ie vor **-s** / **-y → -i** vor **-ed**
Regelmäßiges Verb

Simple tenses

Present

I	occupy
you	occupy
he/she/it	occupies
we	occupy
you	occupy
they	occupy

Past

I	occupied
you	occupied
he/she/it	occupied
we	occupied
you	occupied
they	occupied

Present Perfect

I	have	occupied
you	have	occupied
he/she/it	has	occupied
we	have	occupied
you	have	occupied
they	have	occupied

Past Perfect

I	had	occupied
you	had	occupied
he/she/it	had	occupied
we	had	occupied
you	had	occupied
they	had	occupied

Will-Future

I	will	occupy
you	will	occupy
he/she/it	will	occupy
we	will	occupy
you	will	occupy
they	will	occupy

Going to-Future

I	am	going to	occupy
you	are	going to	occupy
he/she/it	is	going to	occupy
we	are	going to	occupy
you	are	going to	occupy
they	are	going to	occupy

Future Perfect

I	will have	occupied
you	will have	occupied
he/she/it	will have	occupied
we	will have	occupied
you	will have	occupied
they	will have	occupied

Imperative

occupy

Impersonal

ing-Form

occupying

Past Participle

occupied

Continuous tenses

Present

I	am	occupying
you	are	occupying
he/she/it	is	occupying
we	are	occupying
you	are	occupying
they	are	occupying

Past

I	was	occupying
you	were	occupying
he/she/it	was	occupying
we	were	occupying
you	were	occupying
they	were	occupying

Present Perfect

I	have been	occupying
you	have been	occupying
he/she/it	has been	occupying
we	have been	occupying
you	have been	occupying
they	have been	occupying

Past Perfect

I	had been	occupying
you	had been	occupying
he/she/it	had been	occupying
we	had been	occupying
you	had been	occupying
they	had been	occupying

Will-Future

I	will be	occupying
you	will be	occupying
he/she/it	will be	occupying
we	will be	occupying
you	will be	occupying
they	will be	occupying

Going to-Future

I	am	going to be	occupying
you	are	going to be	occupying
he/she/it	is	going to be	occupying
we	are	going to be	occupying
you	are	going to be	occupying
they	are	going to be	occupying

Future Perfect

I	will have been	occupying
you	will have been	occupying
he/she/it	will have been	occupying
we	will have been	occupying
you	will have been	occupying
they	will have been	occupying

Conditional

I	would	occupy
you	would	occupy
he/she/it	would	occupy
we	would	occupy
you	would	occupy
they	would	occupy

Conditional Past

I	would have	occupied
you	would have	occupied
he/she/it	would have	occupied
we	would have	occupied
you	would have	occupied
they	would have	occupied

Simple tenses

Present

I	occur
you	occur
he/she/it	occurs
we	occur
you	occur
they	occur

Past

I	occurred
you	occurred
he/she/it	occurred
we	occurred
you	occurred
they	occurred

Present Perfect

I	have	occurred
you	have	occurred
he/she/it	has	occurred
we	have	occurred
you	have	occurred
they	have	occurred

Past Perfect

I	had	occurred
you	had	occurred
he/she/it	had	occurred
we	had	occurred
you	had	occurred
they	had	occurred

Will-Future

I	will	occur
you	will	occur
he/she/it	will	occur
we	will	occur
you	will	occur
they	will	occur

Going to-Future

I	am	going to	occur
you	are	going to	occur
he/she/it	is	going to	occur
we	are	going to	occur
you	are	going to	occur
they	are	going to	occur

Future Perfect

I	will have	occurred
you	will have	occurred
he/she/it	will have	occurred
we	will have	occurred
you	will have	occurred
they	will have	occurred

Imperative

occur

Impersonal

ing-Form

occurring

Past Participle

occurred

Continuous tenses

Present

I	am	occurring
you	are	occurring
he/she/it	is	occurring
we	are	occurring
you	are	occurring
they	are	occurring

Past

I	was	occurring
you	were	occurring
he/she/it	was	occurring
we	were	occurring
you	were	occurring
they	were	occurring

Present Perfect

I	have been	occurring
you	have been	occurring
he/she/it	has been	occurring
we	have been	occurring
you	have been	occurring
they	have been	occurring

Past Perfect

I	had been	occurring
you	had been	occurring
he/she/it	had been	occurring
we	had been	occurring
you	had been	occurring
they	had been	occurring

Will-Future

I	will be	occurring
you	will be	occurring
he/she/it	will be	occurring
we	will be	occurring
you	will be	occurring
they	will be	occurring

Going to-Future

I	am	going to be	occurring
you	are	going to be	occurring
he/she/it	is	going to be	occurring
we	are	going to be	occurring
you	are	going to be	occurring
they	are	going to be	occurring

Future Perfect

I	will have been	occurring
you	will have been	occurring
he/she/it	will have been	occurring
we	will have been	occurring
you	will have been	occurring
they	will have been	occurring

Conditional

I	would	occur
you	would	occur
he/she/it	would	occur
we	would	occur
you	would	occur
they	would	occur

Conditional Past

I	would have	occurred
you	would have	occurred
he/she/it	would have	occurred
we	would have	occurred
you	would have	occurred
they	would have	occurred

offer

anbieten

Regelmäßiges Verb

Simple tenses

Present

I	offer
you	offer
he/she/it	offers
we	offer
you	offer
they	offer

Past

I	offered
you	offered
he/she/it	offered
we	offered
you	offered
they	offered

Present Perfect

I	have	offered
you	have	offered
he/she/it	has	offered
we	have	offered
you	have	offered
they	have	offered

Past Perfect

I	had	offered
you	had	offered
he/she/it	had	offered
we	had	offered
you	had	offered
they	had	offered

Will-Future

I	will	offer
you	will	offer
he/she/it	will	offer
we	will	offer
you	will	offer
they	will	offer

Going to-Future

I	am	going to	offer
you	are	going to	offer
he/she/it	is	going to	offer
we	are	going to	offer
you	are	going to	offer
they	are	going to	offer

Future Perfect

I	will have	offered
you	will have	offered
he/she/it	will have	offered
we	will have	offered
you	will have	offered
they	will have	offered

Imperative

offer

Impersonal

ing-Form

offering

Past Participle

offered

Continuous tenses

Present

I	am	offering
you	are	offering
he/she/it	is	offering
we	are	offering
you	are	offering
they	are	offering

Past

I	was	offering
you	were	offering
he/she/it	was	offering
we	were	offering
you	were	offering
they	were	offering

Present Perfect

I	have been	offering
you	have been	offering
he/she/it	has been	offering
we	have been	offering
you	have been	offering
they	have been	offering

Past Perfect

I	had been	offering
you	had been	offering
he/she/it	had been	offering
we	had been	offering
you	had been	offering
they	had been	offering

Will-Future

I	will be	offering
you	will be	offering
he/she/it	will be	offering
we	will be	offering
you	will be	offering
they	will be	offering

Going to-Future

I	am	going to be	offering
you	are	going to be	offering
he/she/it	is	going to be	offering
we	are	going to be	offering
you	are	going to be	offering
they	are	going to be	offering

Future Perfect

I	will have been	offering
you	will have been	offering
he/she/it	will have been	offering
we	will have been	offering
you	will have been	offering
they	will have been	offering

Conditional

I	would	offer
you	would	offer
he/she/it	would	offer
we	would	offer
you	would	offer
they	would	offer

Conditional Past

I	would have	offered
you	would have	offered
he/she/it	would have	offered
we	would have	offered
you	would have	offered
they	would have	offered

open

Regelmäßiges Verb

Simple tenses

Present

I	open
you	open
he/she/it	opens
we	open
you	open
they	open

Past

I	opened
you	opened
he/she/it	opened
we	opened
you	opened
they	opened

Present Perfect

I	have	opened
you	have	opened
he/she/it	has	opened
we	have	opened
you	have	opened
they	have	opened

Past Perfect

I	had	opened
you	had	opened
he/she/it	had	opened
we	had	opened
you	had	opened
they	had	opened

Will-Future

I	will	open
you	will	open
he/she/it	will	open
we	will	open
you	will	open
they	will	open

Going to-Future

I	am	going to	open
you	are	going to	open
he/she/it	is	going to	open
we	are	going to	open
you	are	going to	open
they	are	going to	open

Future Perfect

I	will have	opened
you	will have	opened
he/she/it	will have	opened
we	will have	opened
you	will have	opened
they	will have	opened

Imperative

open

Impersonal

ing-Form

opening

Past Participle

opened

Continuous tenses

Present

I	am	opening
you	are	opening
he/she/it	is	opening
we	are	opening
you	are	opening
they	are	opening

Past

I	was	opening
you	were	opening
he/she/it	was	opening
we	were	opening
you	were	opening
they	were	opening

Present Perfect

I	have been	opening
you	have been	opening
he/she/it	has been	opening
we	have been	opening
you	have been	opening
they	have been	opening

Past Perfect

I	had been	opening
you	had been	opening
he/she/it	had been	opening
we	had been	opening
you	had been	opening
they	had been	opening

Will-Future

I	will be	opening
you	will be	opening
he/she/it	will be	opening
we	will be	opening
you	will be	opening
they	will be	opening

Going to-Future

I	am	going to be	opening
you	are	going to be	opening
he/she/it	is	going to be	opening
we	are	going to be	opening
you	are	going to be	opening
they	are	going to be	opening

Future Perfect

I	will have been opening
you	will have been opening
he/she/it	will have been opening
we	will have been opening
you	will have been opening
they	will have been opening

Conditional

I	would	open
you	would	open
he/she/it	would	open
we	would	open
you	would	open
they	would	open

Conditional Past

I	would have	opened
you	would have	opened
he/she/it	would have	opened
we	would have	opened
you	would have	opened
they	would have	opened

operate

funktionieren

+ **-ing** → ~~e~~ / + **-d** nicht **-ed**
Regelmäßiges Verb

Simple tenses

Present

I operate
you operate
he/she/it operates
we operate
you operate
they operate

Past

I operated
you operated
he/she/it operated
we operated
you operated
they operated

Present Perfect

I have operated
you have operated
he/she/it has operated
we have operated
you have operated
they have operated

Past Perfect

I had operated
you had operated
he/she/it had operated
we had operated
you had operated
they had operated

Will-Future

I will operate
you will operate
he/she/it will operate
we will operate
you will operate
they will operate

Going to-Future

I am going to operate
you are going to operate
he/she/it is going to operate
we are going to operate
you are going to operate
they are going to operate

Future Perfect

I will have operated
you will have operated
he/she/it will have operated
we will have operated
you will have operated
they will have operated

Imperative

operate

Impersonal

ing-Form

operating

Past Participle

operated

Continuous tenses

Present

I am operating
you are operating
he/she/it is operating
we are operating
you are operating
they are operating

Past

I was operating
you were operating
he/she/it was operating
we were operating
you were operating
they were operating

Present Perfect

I have been operating
you have been operating
he/she/it has been operating
we have been operating
you have been operating
they have been operating

Past Perfect

I had been operating
you had been operating
he/she/it had been operating
we had been operating
you had been operating
they had been operating

Will-Future

I will be operating
you will be operating
he/she/it will be operating
we will be operating
you will be operating
they will be operating

Going to-Future

I am going to be operating
you are going to be operating
he/she/it is going to be operating
we are going to be operating
you are going to be operating
they are going to be operating

Future Perfect

I will have been operating
you will have been operating
he/she/it will have been operating
we will have been operating
you will have been operating
they will have been operating

Conditional

I would operate
you would operate
he/she/it would operate
we would operate
you would operate
they would operate

Conditional Past

I would have operated
you would have operated
he/she/it would have operated
we would have operated
you would have operated
they would have operated

Simple tenses

Present

I	oppose
you	oppose
he/she/it	opposes
we	oppose
you	oppose
they	oppose

Past

I	opposed
you	opposed
he/she/it	opposed
we	opposed
you	opposed
they	opposed

Present Perfect

I	have	opposed
you	have	opposed
he/she/it	has	opposed
we	have	opposed
you	have	opposed
they	have	opposed

Past Perfect

I	had	opposed
you	had	opposed
he/she/it	had	opposed
we	had	opposed
you	had	opposed
they	had	opposed

Will-Future

I	will	oppose
you	will	oppose
he/she/it	will	oppose
we	will	oppose
you	will	oppose
they	will	oppose

Going to-Future

I	am	going to	oppose
you	are	going to	oppose
he/she/it	is	going to	oppose
we	are	going to	oppose
you	are	going to	oppose
they	are	going to	oppose

Future Perfect

I	will have	opposed
you	will have	opposed
he/she/it	will have	opposed
we	will have	opposed
you	will have	opposed
they	will have	opposed

Imperative

oppose

Impersonal

ing-Form

opposing

Past Participle

opposed

Continuous tenses

Present

I	am	opposing
you	are	opposing
he/she/it	is	opposing
we	are	opposing
you	are	opposing
they	are	opposing

Past

I	was	opposing
you	were	opposing
he/she/it	was	opposing
we	were	opposing
you	were	opposing
they	were	opposing

Present Perfect

I	have been	opposing
you	have been	opposing
he/she/it	has been	opposing
we	have been	opposing
you	have been	opposing
they	have been	opposing

Past Perfect

I	had been	opposing
you	had been	opposing
he/she/it	had been	opposing
we	had been	opposing
you	had been	opposing
they	had been	opposing

Will-Future

I	will be	opposing
you	will be	opposing
he/she/it	will be	opposing
we	will be	opposing
you	will be	opposing
they	will be	opposing

Going to-Future

I	am	going to be	opposing
you	are	going to be	opposing
he/she/it	is	going to be	opposing
we	are	going to be	opposing
you	are	going to be	opposing
they	are	going to be	opposing

Future Perfect

I	will have been	opposing
you	will have been	opposing
he/she/it	will have been	opposing
we	will have been	opposing
you	will have been	opposing
they	will have been	opposing

Conditional

I	would	oppose
you	would	oppose
he/she/it	would	oppose
we	would	oppose
you	would	oppose
they	would	oppose

Conditional Past

I	would have	opposed
you	would have	opposed
he/she/it	would have	opposed
we	would have	opposed
you	would have	opposed
they	would have	opposed

order

bestellen

Regelmäßiges Verb

Simple tenses

Present

I	order
you	order
he/she/it	orders
we	order
you	order
they	order

Past

I	ordered
you	ordered
he/she/it	ordered
we	ordered
you	ordered
they	ordered

Present Perfect

I	have	ordered
you	have	ordered
he/she/it	has	ordered
we	have	ordered
you	have	ordered
they	have	ordered

Past Perfect

I	had	ordered
you	had	ordered
he/she/it	had	ordered
we	had	ordered
you	had	ordered
they	had	ordered

Will-Future

I	will	order
you	will	order
he/she/it	will	order
we	will	order
you	will	order
they	will	order

Going to-Future

I	am	going to	order
you	are	going to	order
he/she/it	is	going to	order
we	are	going to	order
you	are	going to	order
they	are	going to	order

Future Perfect

I	will have	ordered
you	will have	ordered
he/she/it	will have	ordered
we	will have	ordered
you	will have	ordered
they	will have	ordered

Imperative

order

Impersonal

ing-Form

ordering

Past Participle

ordered

Continuous tenses

Present

I	am	ordering
you	are	ordering
he/she/it	is	ordering
we	are	ordering
you	are	ordering
they	are	ordering

Past

I	was	ordering
you	were	ordering
he/she/it	was	ordering
we	were	ordering
you	were	ordering
they	were	ordering

Present Perfect

I	have been	ordering
you	have been	ordering
he/she/it	has been	ordering
we	have been	ordering
you	have been	ordering
they	have been	ordering

Past Perfect

I	had been	ordering
you	had been	ordering
he/she/it	had been	ordering
we	had been	ordering
you	had been	ordering
they	had been	ordering

Will-Future

I	will be	ordering
you	will be	ordering
he/she/it	will be	ordering
we	will be	ordering
you	will be	ordering
they	will be	ordering

Going to-Future

I	am	going to be	ordering
you	are	going to be	ordering
he/she/it	is	going to be	ordering
we	are	going to be	ordering
you	are	going to be	ordering
they	are	going to be	ordering

Future Perfect

I	will have been	ordering
you	will have been	ordering
he/she/it	will have been	ordering
we	will have been	ordering
you	will have been	ordering
they	will have been	ordering

Conditional

I	would	order
you	would	order
he/she/it	would	order
we	would	order
you	would	order
they	would	order

Conditional Past

I	would have	ordered
you	would have	ordered
he/she/it	would have	ordered
we	would have	ordered
you	would have	ordered
they	would have	ordered

+ **-ing** → ~~e~~ / + **-d** nicht **-ed**
im BE auch **organise**
Regelmäßiges Verb

organisieren

organize

Simple tenses

Present

I organize
you organize
he/she/it organizes
we organize
you organize
they organize

Past

I organized
you organized
he/she/it organized
we organized
you organized
they organized

Present Perfect

I have organized
you have organized
he/she/it has organized
we have organized
you have organized
they have organized

Past Perfect

I had organized
you had organized
he/she/it had organized
we had organized
you had organized
they had organized

Will-Future

I will organize
you will organize
he/she/it will organize
we will organize
you will organize
they will organize

Going to-Future

I am going to organize
you are going to organize
he/she/it is going to organize
we are going to organize
you are going to organize
they are going to organize

Future Perfect

I will have organized
you will have organized
he/she/it will have organized
we will have organized
you will have organized
they will have organized

Imperative

organize

Impersonal

ing-Form

organizing

Past Participle

organized

Continuous tenses

Present

I am organizing
you are organizing
he/she/it is organizing
we are organizing
you are organizing
they are organizing

Past

I was organizing
you were organizing
he/she/it was organizing
we were organizing
you were organizing
they were organizing

Present Perfect

I have been organizing
you have been organizing
he/she/it has been organizing
we have been organizing
you have been organizing
they have been organizing

Past Perfect

I had been organizing
you had been organizing
he/she/it had been organizing
we had been organizing
you had been organizing
they had been organizing

Will-Future

I will be organizing
you will be organizing
he/she/it will be organizing
we will be organizing
you will be organizing
they will be organizing

Going to-Future

I am going to be organizing
you are going to be organizing
he/she/it is going to be organizing
we are going to be organizing
you are going to be organizing
they are going to be organizing

Future Perfect

I will have been organizing
you will have been organizing
he/she/it will have been organizing
we will have been organizing
you will have been organizing
they will have been organizing

Conditional

I would organize
you would organize
he/she/it would organize
we would organize
you would organize
they would organize

Conditional Past

I would have organized
you would have organized
he/she/it would have organized
we would have organized
you would have organized
they would have organized

outline

umreißen

\+ **-ing** → ~~e~~ / + **-d** nicht **-ed**
Regelmäßiges Verb

Simple tenses

Present

I	outline
you	outline
he/she/it	outlines
we	outline
you	outline
they	outline

Past

I	outlined
you	outlined
he/she/it	outlined
we	outlined
you	outlined
they	outlined

Present Perfect

I	have	outlined
you	have	outlined
he/she/it	has	outlined
we	have	outlined
you	have	outlined
they	have	outlined

Past Perfect

I	had	outlined
you	had	outlined
he/she/it	had	outlined
we	had	outlined
you	had	outlined
they	had	outlined

Will-Future

I	will	outline
you	will	outline
he/she/it	will	outline
we	will	outline
you	will	outline
they	will	outline

Going to-Future

I	am	going to	outline
you	are	going to	outline
he/she/it	is	going to	outline
we	are	going to	outline
you	are	going to	outline
they	are	going to	outline

Future Perfect

I	will have	outlined
you	will have	outlined
he/she/it	will have	outlined
we	will have	outlined
you	will have	outlined
they	will have	outlined

Imperative

outline

Impersonal

ing-Form

outlining

Past Participle

outlined

Continuous tenses

Present

I	am	outlining
you	are	outlining
he/she/it	is	outlining
we	are	outlining
you	are	outlining
they	are	outlining

Past

I	was	outlining
you	were	outlining
he/she/it	was	outlining
we	were	outlining
you	were	outlining
they	were	outlining

Present Perfect

I	have been	outlining
you	have been	outlining
he/she/it	has been	outlining
we	have been	outlining
you	have been	outlining
they	have been	outlining

Past Perfect

I	had been	outlining
you	had been	outlining
he/she/it	had been	outlining
we	had been	outlining
you	had been	outlining
they	had been	outlining

Will-Future

I	will be	outlining
you	will be	outlining
he/she/it	will be	outlining
we	will be	outlining
you	will be	outlining
they	will be	outlining

Going to-Future

I	am	going to be	outlining
you	are	going to be	outlining
he/she/it	is	going to be	outlining
we	are	going to be	outlining
you	are	going to be	outlining
they	are	going to be	outlining

Future Perfect

I	will have been	outlining
you	will have been	outlining
he/she/it	will have been	outlining
we	will have been	outlining
you	will have been	outlining
they	will have been	outlining

Conditional

I	would	outline
you	would	outline
he/she/it	would	outline
we	would	outline
you	would	outline
they	would	outline

Conditional Past

I	would have	outlined
you	would have	outlined
he/she/it	would have	outlined
we	would have	outlined
you	would have	outlined
they	would have	outlined

Simple tenses

Present

I	overload
you	overload
he/she/it	overloads
we	overload
you	overload
they	overload

Past

I	overloaded
you	overloaded
he/she/it	overloaded
we	overloaded
you	overloaded
they	overloaded

Present Perfect

I	have	overloaded
you	have	overloaded
he/she/it	has	overloaded
we	have	overloaded
you	have	overloaded
they	have	overloaded

Past Perfect

I	had	overloaded
you	had	overloaded
he/she/it	had	overloaded
we	had	overloaded
you	had	overloaded
they	had	overloaded

Will-Future

I	will	overload
you	will	overload
he/she/it	will	overload
we	will	overload
you	will	overload
they	will	overload

Going to-Future

I	am	going to	overload
you	are	going to	overload
he/she/it	is	going to	overload
we	are	going to	overload
you	are	going to	overload
they	are	going to	overload

Future Perfect

I	will have	overloaded
you	will have	overloaded
he/she/it	will have	overloaded
we	will have	overloaded
you	will have	overloaded
they	will have	overloaded

Imperative

overload

Impersonal

ing-Form

overloading

Past Participle

overloaded

Continuous tenses

Present

I	am	overloading
you	are	overloading
he/she/it	is	overloading
we	are	overloading
you	are	overloading
they	are	overloading

Past

I	was	overloading
you	were	overloading
he/she/it	was	overloading
we	were	overloading
you	were	overloading
they	were	overloading

Present Perfect

I	have been	overloading
you	have been	overloading
he/she/it	has been	overloading
we	have been	overloading
you	have been	overloading
they	have been	overloading

Past Perfect

I	had been	overloading
you	had been	overloading
he/she/it	had been	overloading
we	had been	overloading
you	had been	overloading
they	had been	overloading

Will-Future

I	will be	overloading
you	will be	overloading
he/she/it	will be	overloading
we	will be	overloading
you	will be	overloading
they	will be	overloading

Going to-Future

I	am	going to be	overloading
you	are	going to be	overloading
he/she/it	is	going to be	overloading
we	are	going to be	overloading
you	are	going to be	overloading
they	are	going to be	overloading

Future Perfect

I	will have been overloading
you	will have been overloading
he/she/it	will have been overloading
we	will have been overloading
you	will have been overloading
they	will have been overloading

Conditional

I	would	overload
you	would	overload
he/she/it	would	overload
we	would	overload
you	would	overload
they	would	overload

Conditional Past

I	would have	overloaded
you	would have	overloaded
he/she/it	would have	overloaded
we	would have	overloaded
you	would have	overloaded
they	would have	overloaded

overreact

überreagieren

Regelmäßiges Verb

Simple tenses

Present

I	overreact
you	overreact
he/she/it	overreacts
we	overreact
you	overreact
they	overreact

Past

I	overreacted
you	overreacted
he/she/it	overreacted
we	overreacted
you	overreacted
they	overreacted

Present Perfect

I	have	overreacted
you	have	overreacted
he/she/it	has	overreacted
we	have	overreacted
you	have	overreacted
they	have	overreacted

Past Perfect

I	had	overreacted
you	had	overreacted
he/she/it	had	overreacted
we	had	overreacted
you	had	overreacted
they	had	overreacted

Will-Future

I	will	overreact
you	will	overreact
he/she/it	will	overreact
we	will	overreact
you	will	overreact
they	will	overreact

Going to-Future

I	am	going to	overreact
you	are	going to	overreact
he/she/it	is	going to	overreact
we	are	going to	overreact
you	are	going to	overreact
they	are	going to	overreact

Future Perfect

I	will have	overreacted
you	will have	overreacted
he/she/it	will have	overreacted
we	will have	overreacted
you	will have	overreacted
they	will have	overreacted

Imperative

overreact

Impersonal

ing-Form

overreacting

Past Participle

overreacted

Continuous tenses

Present

I	am	overreacting
you	are	overreacting
he/she/it	is	overreacting
we	are	overreacting
you	are	overreacting
they	are	overreacting

Past

I	was	overreacting
you	were	overreacting
he/she/it	was	overreacting
we	were	overreacting
you	were	overreacting
they	were	overreacting

Present Perfect

I	have been	overreacting
you	have been	overreacting
he/she/it	has been	overreacting
we	have been	overreacting
you	have been	overreacting
they	have been	overreacting

Past Perfect

I	had been	overreacting
you	had been	overreacting
he/she/it	had been	overreacting
we	had been	overreacting
you	had been	overreacting
they	had been	overreacting

Will-Future

I	will be	overreacting
you	will be	overreacting
he/she/it	will be	overreacting
we	will be	overreacting
you	will be	overreacting
they	will be	overreacting

Going to-Future

I	am	going to be	overreacting
you	are	going to be	overreacting
he/she/it	is	going to be	overreacting
we	are	going to be	overreacting
you	are	going to be	overreacting
they	are	going to be	overreacting

Future Perfect

I	will have been overreacting
you	will have been overreacting
he/she/it	will have been overreacting
we	will have been overreacting
you	will have been overreacting
they	will have been overreacting

Conditional

I	would	overreact
you	would	overreact
he/she/it	would	overreact
we	would	overreact
you	would	overreact
they	would	overreact

Conditional Past

I	would have	overreacted
you	would have	overreacted
he/she/it	would have	overreacted
we	would have	overreacted
you	would have	overreacted
they	would have	overreacted

+ **-ing** → ~~e~~ / + **-d** nicht **-ed**
Regelmäßiges Verb

schulden

owe

Simple tenses

Present

I	owe
you	owe
he/she/it	owes
we	owe
you	owe
they	owe

Past

I	owed
you	owed
he/she/it	owed
we	owed
you	owed
they	owed

Present Perfect

I	have	owed
you	have	owed
he/she/it	has	owed
we	have	owed
you	have	owed
they	have	owed

Past Perfect

I	had	owed
you	had	owed
he/she/it	had	owed
we	had	owed
you	had	owed
they	had	owed

Will-Future

I	will	owe
you	will	owe
he/she/it	will	owe
we	will	owe
you	will	owe
they	will	owe

Going to-Future

I	am	going to	owe
you	are	going to	owe
he/she/it	is	going to	owe
we	are	going to	owe
you	are	going to	owe
they	are	going to	owe

Future Perfect

I	will have	owed
you	will have	owed
he/she/it	will have	owed
we	will have	owed
you	will have	owed
they	will have	owed

Imperative

owe

Impersonal

ing-Form

owing

Past Participle

owed

Continuous tenses

Present

I	am	owing
you	are	owing
he/she/it	is	owing
we	are	owing
you	are	owing
they	are	owing

Past

I	was	owing
you	were	owing
he/she/it	was	owing
we	were	owing
you	were	owing
they	were	owing

Present Perfect

I	have been	owing
you	have been	owing
he/she/it	has been	owing
we	have been	owing
you	have been	owing
they	have been	owing

Past Perfect

I	had been	owing
you	had been	owing
he/she/it	had been	owing
we	had been	owing
you	had been	owing
they	had been	owing

Will-Future

I	will be	owing
you	will be	owing
he/she/it	will be	owing
we	will be	owing
you	will be	owing
they	will be	owing

Going to-Future

I	am	going to be	owing
you	are	going to be	owing
he/she/it	is	going to be	owing
we	are	going to be	owing
you	are	going to be	owing
they	are	going to be	owing

Future Perfect

I	will have been	owing
you	will have been	owing
he/she/it	will have been	owing
we	will have been	owing
you	will have been	owing
they	will have been	owing

Conditional

I	would	owe
you	would	owe
he/she/it	would	owe
we	would	owe
you	would	owe
they	would	owe

Conditional Past

I	would have	owed
you	would have	owed
he/she/it	would have	owed
we	would have	owed
you	would have	owed
they	would have	owed

own

besitzen

Regelmäßiges Verb

Simple tenses

Present

I	own
you	own
he/she/it	owns
we	own
you	own
they	own

Past

I	owned
you	owned
he/she/it	owned
we	owned
you	owned
they	owned

Present Perfect

I	have	owned
you	have	owned
he/she/it	has	owned
we	have	owned
you	have	owned
they	have	owned

Past Perfect

I	had	owned
you	had	owned
he/she/it	had	owned
we	had	owned
you	had	owned
they	had	owned

Will-Future

I	will	own
you	will	own
he/she/it	will	own
we	will	own
you	will	own
they	will	own

Going to-Future

I	am	going to	own
you	are	going to	own
he/she/it	is	going to	own
we	are	going to	own
you	are	going to	own
they	are	going to	own

Future Perfect

I	will have	owned
you	will have	owned
he/she/it	will have	owned
we	will have	owned
you	will have	owned
they	will have	owned

Imperative

own

Impersonal

ing-Form

owning

Past Participle

owned

Continuous tenses

Present

I	am	owning
you	are	owning
he/she/it	is	owning
we	are	owning
you	are	owning
they	are	owning

Past

I	was	owning
you	were	owning
he/she/it	was	owning
we	were	owning
you	were	owning
they	were	owning

Present Perfect

I	have been	owning
you	have been	owning
he/she/it	has been	owning
we	have been	owning
you	have been	owning
they	have been	owning

Past Perfect

I	had been	owning
you	had been	owning
he/she/it	had been	owning
we	had been	owning
you	had been	owning
they	had been	owning

Will-Future

I	will be	owning
you	will be	owning
he/she/it	will be	owning
we	will be	owning
you	will be	owning
they	will be	owning

Going to-Future

I	am	going to be	owning
you	are	going to be	owning
he/she/it	is	going to be	owning
we	are	going to be	owning
you	are	going to be	owning
they	are	going to be	owning

Future Perfect

I	will have been	owning
you	will have been	owning
he/she/it	will have been	owning
we	will have been	owning
you	will have been	owning
they	will have been	owning

Conditional

I	would	own
you	would	own
he/she/it	would	own
we	would	own
you	would	own
they	would	own

Conditional Past

I	would have	owned
you	would have	owned
he/she/it	would have	owned
we	would have	owned
you	would have	owned
they	would have	owned

Simple tenses

Present

I	pack
you	pack
he/she/it	packs
we	pack
you	pack
they	pack

Past

I	packed
you	packed
he/she/it	packed
we	packed
you	packed
they	packed

Present Perfect

I	have	packed
you	have	packed
he/she/it	has	packed
we	have	packed
you	have	packed
they	have	packed

Past Perfect

I	had	packed
you	had	packed
he/she/it	had	packed
we	had	packed
you	had	packed
they	had	packed

Will-Future

I	will	pack
you	will	pack
he/she/it	will	pack
we	will	pack
you	will	pack
they	will	pack

Going to-Future

I	am	going to	pack
you	are	going to	pack
he/she/it	is	going to	pack
we	are	going to	pack
you	are	going to	pack
they	are	going to	pack

Future Perfect

I	will have	packed
you	will have	packed
he/she/it	will have	packed
we	will have	packed
you	will have	packed
they	will have	packed

Imperative

pack

Impersonal

ing-Form

packing

Past Participle

packed

Continuous tenses

Present

I	am	packing
you	are	packing
he/she/it	is	packing
we	are	packing
you	are	packing
they	are	packing

Past

I	was	packing
you	were	packing
he/she/it	was	packing
we	were	packing
you	were	packing
they	were	packing

Present Perfect

I	have	been	packing
you	have	been	packing
he/she/it	has	been	packing
we	have	been	packing
you	have	been	packing
they	have	been	packing

Past Perfect

I	had been	packing
you	had been	packing
he/she/it	had been	packing
we	had been	packing
you	had been	packing
they	had been	packing

Will-Future

I	will be	packing
you	will be	packing
he/she/it	will be	packing
we	will be	packing
you	will be	packing
they	will be	packing

Going to-Future

I	am	going to be	packing
you	are	going to be	packing
he/she/it	is	going to be	packing
we	are	going to be	packing
you	are	going to be	packing
they	are	going to be	packing

Future Perfect

I	will have been packing
you	will have been packing
he/she/it	will have been packing
we	will have been packing
you	will have been packing
they	will have been packing

Conditional

I	would	pack
you	would	pack
he/she/it	would	pack
we	would	pack
you	would	pack
they	would	pack

Conditional Past

I	would have	packed
you	would have	packed
he/she/it	would have	packed
we	would have	packed
you	would have	packed
they	would have	packed

paint

malen

Regelmäßiges Verb

Simple tenses

Present

I	paint
you	paint
he/she/it	paints
we	paint
you	paint
they	paint

Past

I	painted
you	painted
he/she/it	painted
we	painted
you	painted
they	painted

Present Perfect

I	have	painted
you	have	painted
he/she/it	has	painted
we	have	painted
you	have	painted
they	have	painted

Past Perfect

I	had	painted
you	had	painted
he/she/it	had	painted
we	had	painted
you	had	painted
they	had	painted

Will-Future

I	will	paint
you	will	paint
he/she/it	will	paint
we	will	paint
you	will	paint
they	will	paint

Going to-Future

I	am	going to	paint
you	are	going to	paint
he/she/it	is	going to	paint
we	are	going to	paint
you	are	going to	paint
they	are	going to	paint

Future Perfect

I	will have	painted
you	will have	painted
he/she/it	will have	painted
we	will have	painted
you	will have	painted
they	will have	painted

Imperative

paint

Impersonal

ing-Form

painting

Past Participle

painted

Continuous tenses

Present

I	am	painting
you	are	painting
he/she/it	is	painting
we	are	painting
you	are	painting
they	are	painting

Past

I	was	painting
you	were	painting
he/she/it	was	painting
we	were	painting
you	were	painting
they	were	painting

Present Perfect

I	have been	painting
you	have been	painting
he/she/it	has been	painting
we	have been	painting
you	have been	painting
they	have been	painting

Past Perfect

I	had been	painting
you	had been	painting
he/she/it	had been	painting
we	had been	painting
you	had been	painting
they	had been	painting

Will-Future

I	will be	painting
you	will be	painting
he/she/it	will be	painting
we	will be	painting
you	will be	painting
they	will be	painting

Going to-Future

I	am	going to be	painting
you	are	going to be	painting
he/she/it	is	going to be	painting
we	are	going to be	painting
you	are	going to be	painting
they	are	going to be	painting

Future Perfect

I	will have been	painting
you	will have been	painting
he/she/it	will have been	painting
we	will have been	painting
you	will have been	painting
they	will have been	painting

Conditional

I	would	paint
you	would	paint
he/she/it	would	paint
we	would	paint
you	would	paint
they	would	paint

Conditional Past

I	would have	painted
you	would have	painted
he/she/it	would have	painted
we	would have	painted
you	would have	painted
they	would have	painted

Simple tenses

Present

I	park
you	park
he/she/it	parks
we	park
you	park
they	park

Past

I	parked
you	parked
he/she/it	parked
we	parked
you	parked
they	parked

Present Perfect

I	have	parked
you	have	parked
he/she/it	has	parked
we	have	parked
you	have	parked
they	have	parked

Past Perfect

I	had	parked
you	had	parked
he/she/it	had	parked
we	had	parked
you	had	parked
they	had	parked

Will-Future

I	will	park
you	will	park
he/she/it	will	park
we	will	park
you	will	park
they	will	park

Going to-Future

I	am	going to	park
you	are	going to	park
he/she/it	is	going to	park
we	are	going to	park
you	are	going to	park
they	are	going to	park

Future Perfect

I	will have	parked
you	will have	parked
he/she/it	will have	parked
we	will have	parked
you	will have	parked
they	will have	parked

Imperative

park

Impersonal

ing-Form

parking

Past Participle

parked

Continuous tenses

Present

I	am	parking
you	are	parking
he/she/it	is	parking
we	are	parking
you	are	parking
they	are	parking

Past

I	was	parking
you	were	parking
he/she/it	was	parking
we	were	parking
you	were	parking
they	were	parking

Present Perfect

I	have been	parking
you	have been	parking
he/she/it	has been	parking
we	have been	parking
you	have been	parking
they	have been	parking

Past Perfect

I	had been	parking
you	had been	parking
he/she/it	had been	parking
we	had been	parking
you	had been	parking
they	had been	parking

Will-Future

I	will be	parking
you	will be	parking
he/she/it	will be	parking
we	will be	parking
you	will be	parking
they	will be	parking

Going to-Future

I	am	going to be	parking
you	are	going to be	parking
he/she/it	is	going to be	parking
we	are	going to be	parking
you	are	going to be	parking
they	are	going to be	parking

Future Perfect

I	will have been	parking
you	will have been	parking
he/she/it	will have been	parking
we	will have been	parking
you	will have been	parking
they	will have been	parking

Conditional

I	would	park
you	would	park
he/she/it	would	park
we	would	park
you	would	park
they	would	park

Conditional Past

I	would have	parked
you	would have	parked
he/she/it	would have	parked
we	would have	parked
you	would have	parked
they	would have	parked

pass

vorbeigehen

+ **-es** in 3. Person Singular
Regelmäßiges Verb

Simple tenses

Present

I	pass
you	pass
he/she/it	passes
we	pass
you	pass
they	pass

Past

I	passed
you	passed
he/she/it	passed
we	passed
you	passed
they	passed

Present Perfect

I	have	passed
you	have	passed
he/she/it	has	passed
we	have	passed
you	have	passed
they	have	passed

Past Perfect

I	had	passed
you	had	passed
he/she/it	had	passed
we	had	passed
you	had	passed
they	had	passed

Will-Future

I	will	pass
you	will	pass
he/she/it	will	pass
we	will	pass
you	will	pass
they	will	pass

Going to-Future

I	am	going to	pass
you	are	going to	pass
he/she/it	is	going to	pass
we	are	going to	pass
you	are	going to	pass
they	are	going to	pass

Future Perfect

I	will have	passed
you	will have	passed
he/she/it	will have	passed
we	will have	passed
you	will have	passed
they	will have	passed

Imperative

pass

Impersonal

ing-Form

passing

Past Participle

passed

Continuous tenses

Present

I	am	passing
you	are	passing
he/she/it	is	passing
we	are	passing
you	are	passing
they	are	passing

Past

I	was	passing
you	were	passing
he/she/it	was	passing
we	were	passing
you	were	passing
they	were	passing

Present Perfect

I	have	been	passing
you	have	been	passing
he/she/it	has	been	passing
we	have	been	passing
you	have	been	passing
they	have	been	passing

Past Perfect

I	had been	passing
you	had been	passing
he/she/it	had been	passing
we	had been	passing
you	had been	passing
they	had been	passing

Will-Future

I	will be	passing
you	will be	passing
he/she/it	will be	passing
we	will be	passing
you	will be	passing
they	will be	passing

Going to-Future

I	am	going to be	passing
you	are	going to be	passing
he/she/it	is	going to be	passing
we	are	going to be	passing
you	are	going to be	passing
they	are	going to be	passing

Future Perfect

I	will have been	passing
you	will have been	passing
he/she/it	will have been	passing
we	will have been	passing
you	will have been	passing
they	will have been	passing

Conditional

I	would	pass
you	would	pass
he/she/it	would	pass
we	would	pass
you	would	pass
they	would	pass

Conditional Past

I	would have	passed
you	would have	passed
he/she/it	would have	passed
we	would have	passed
you	would have	passed
they	would have	passed

Simple tenses

Present

I	pause
you	pause
he/she/it	pauses
we	pause
you	pause
they	pause

Past

I	paused
you	paused
he/she/it	paused
we	paused
you	paused
they	paused

Present Perfect

I	have	paused
you	have	paused
he/she/it	has	paused
we	have	paused
you	have	paused
they	have	paused

Past Perfect

I	had	paused
you	had	paused
he/she/it	had	paused
we	had	paused
you	had	paused
they	had	paused

Will-Future

I	will	pause
you	will	pause
he/she/it	will	pause
we	will	pause
you	will	pause
they	will	pause

Going to-Future

I	am	going to	pause
you	are	going to	pause
he/she/it	is	going to	pause
we	are	going to	pause
you	are	going to	pause
they	are	going to	pause

Future Perfect

I	will have	paused
you	will have	paused
he/she/it	will have	paused
we	will have	paused
you	will have	paused
they	will have	paused

Imperative

pause

Impersonal

ing-Form

pausing

Past Participle

paused

Continuous tenses

Present

I	am	pausing
you	are	pausing
he/she/it	is	pausing
we	are	pausing
you	are	pausing
they	are	pausing

Past

I	was	pausing
you	were	pausing
he/she/it	was	pausing
we	were	pausing
you	were	pausing
they	were	pausing

Present Perfect

I	have been	pausing
you	have been	pausing
he/she/it	has been	pausing
we	have been	pausing
you	have been	pausing
they	have been	pausing

Past Perfect

I	had been	pausing
you	had been	pausing
he/she/it	had been	pausing
we	had been	pausing
you	had been	pausing
they	had been	pausing

Will-Future

I	will be	pausing
you	will be	pausing
he/she/it	will be	pausing
we	will be	pausing
you	will be	pausing
they	will be	pausing

Going to-Future

I	am	going to be	pausing
you	are	going to be	pausing
he/she/it	is	going to be	pausing
we	are	going to be	pausing
you	are	going to be	pausing
they	are	going to be	pausing

Future Perfect

I	will have been pausing
you	will have been pausing
he/she/it	will have been pausing
we	will have been pausing
you	will have been pausing
they	will have been pausing

Conditional

I	would	pause
you	would	pause
he/she/it	would	pause
we	would	pause
you	would	pause
they	would	pause

Conditional Past

I	would have	paused
you	would have	paused
he/she/it	would have	paused
we	would have	paused
you	would have	paused
they	would have	paused

pay
- paid - paid

zahlen

Unregelmäßiges Verb

Simple tenses

Present

I	pay
you	pay
he/she/it	pays
we	pay
you	pay
they	pay

Past

I	paid
you	paid
he/she/it	paid
we	paid
you	paid
they	paid

Present Perfect

I	have	paid
you	have	paid
he/she/it	has	paid
we	have	paid
you	have	paid
they	have	paid

Past Perfect

I	had	paid
you	had	paid
he/she/it	had	paid
we	had	paid
you	had	paid
they	had	paid

Will-Future

I	will	pay
you	will	pay
he/she/it	will	pay
we	will	pay
you	will	pay
they	will	pay

Going to-Future

I	am	going to	pay
you	are	going to	pay
he/she/it	is	going to	pay
we	are	going to	pay
you	are	going to	pay
they	are	going to	pay

Future Perfect

I	will have	paid
you	will have	paid
he/she/it	will have	paid
we	will have	paid
you	will have	paid
they	will have	paid

Imperative

pay

Impersonal

ing-Form

paying

Past Participle

paid

Continuous tenses

Present

I	am	paying
you	are	paying
he/she/it	is	paying
we	are	paying
you	are	paying
they	are	paying

Past

I	was	paying
you	were	paying
he/she/it	was	paying
we	were	paying
you	were	paying
they	were	paying

Present Perfect

I	have been	paying
you	have been	paying
he/she/it	has been	paying
we	have been	paying
you	have been	paying
they	have been	paying

Past Perfect

I	had been	paying
you	had been	paying
he/she/it	had been	paying
we	had been	paying
you	had been	paying
they	had been	paying

Will-Future

I	will be	paying
you	will be	paying
he/she/it	will be	paying
we	will be	paying
you	will be	paying
they	will be	paying

Going to-Future

I	am	going to be	paying
you	are	going to be	paying
he/she/it	is	going to be	paying
we	are	going to be	paying
you	are	going to be	paying
they	are	going to be	paying

Future Perfect

I	will have been	paying
you	will have been	paying
he/she/it	will have been	paying
we	will have been	paying
you	will have been	paying
they	will have been	paying

Conditional

I	would	pay
you	would	pay
he/she/it	would	pay
we	would	pay
you	would	pay
they	would	pay

Conditional Past

I	would have	paid
you	would have	paid
he/she/it	would have	paid
we	would have	paid
you	would have	paid
they	would have	paid

Present

I	perform
you	perform
he/she/it	performs
we	perform
you	perform
they	perform

Past

I	performed
you	performed
he/she/it	performed
we	performed
you	performed
they	performed

Present Perfect

I	have	performed
you	have	performed
he/she/it	has	performed
we	have	performed
you	have	performed
they	have	performed

Past Perfect

I	had	performed
you	had	performed
he/she/it	had	performed
we	had	performed
you	had	performed
they	had	performed

Will-Future

I	will	perform
you	will	perform
he/she/it	will	perform
we	will	perform
you	will	perform
they	will	perform

Going to-Future

I	am	going to	perform
you	are	going to	perform
he/she/it	is	going to	perform
we	are	going to	perform
you	are	going to	perform
they	are	going to	perform

Future Perfect

I	will have	performed
you	will have	performed
he/she/it	will have	performed
we	will have	performed
you	will have	performed
they	will have	performed

Imperative

perform

Impersonal

ing-Form

performing

Past Participle

performed

Continuous tenses

Present

I	am	performing
you	are	performing
he/she/it	is	performing
we	are	performing
you	are	performing
they	are	performing

Past

I	was	performing
you	were	performing
he/she/it	was	performing
we	were	performing
you	were	performing
they	were	performing

Present Perfect

I	have	been	performing
you	have	been	performing
he/she/it	has	been	performing
we	have	been	performing
you	have	been	performing
they	have	been	performing

Past Perfect

I	had been	performing
you	had been	performing
he/she/it	had been	performing
we	had been	performing
you	had been	performing
they	had been	performing

Will-Future

I	will be	performing
you	will be	performing
he/she/it	will be	performing
we	will be	performing
you	will be	performing
they	will be	performing

Going to-Future

I	am	going to be	performing
you	are	going to be	performing
he/she/it	is	going to be	performing
we	are	going to be	performing
you	are	going to be	performing
they	are	going to be	performing

Future Perfect

I	will have been performing
you	will have been performing
he/she/it	will have been performing
we	will have been performing
you	will have been performing
they	will have been performing

Conditional

I	would	perform
you	would	perform
he/she/it	would	perform
we	would	perform
you	would	perform
they	would	perform

Conditional Past

I	would have	performed
you	would have	performed
he/she/it	would have	performed
we	would have	performed
you	would have	performed
they	would have	performed

permit

erlauben

Konsonantenverdopplung
Regelmäßiges Verb

Simple tenses

Present

I	permit
you	permit
he/she/it	permits
we	permit
you	permit
they	permit

Past

I	permitted
you	permitted
he/she/it	permitted
we	permitted
you	permitted
they	permitted

Present Perfect

I	have	permitted
you	have	permitted
he/she/it	has	permitted
we	have	permitted
you	have	permitted
they	have	permitted

Past Perfect

I	had	permitted
you	had	permitted
he/she/it	had	permitted
we	had	permitted
you	had	permitted
they	had	permitted

Will-Future

I	will	permit
you	will	permit
he/she/it	will	permit
we	will	permit
you	will	permit
they	will	permit

Going to-Future

I	am	going to	permit
you	are	going to	permit
he/she/it	is	going to	permit
we	are	going to	permit
you	are	going to	permit
they	are	going to	permit

Future Perfect

I	will have	permitted
you	will have	permitted
he/she/it	will have	permitted
we	will have	permitted
you	will have	permitted
they	will have	permitted

Imperative

permit

Impersonal

ing-Form

permitting

Past Participle

permitted

Continuous tenses

Present

I	am	permitting
you	are	permitting
he/she/it	is	permitting
we	are	permitting
you	are	permitting
they	are	permitting

Past

I	was	permitting
you	were	permitting
he/she/it	was	permitting
we	were	permitting
you	were	permitting
they	were	permitting

Present Perfect

I	have been	permitting
you	have been	permitting
he/she/it	has been	permitting
we	have been	permitting
you	have been	permitting
they	have been	permitting

Past Perfect

I	had been	permitting
you	had been	permitting
he/she/it	had been	permitting
we	had been	permitting
you	had been	permitting
they	had been	permitting

Will-Future

I	will be	permitting
you	will be	permitting
he/she/it	will be	permitting
we	will be	permitting
you	will be	permitting
they	will be	permitting

Going to-Future

I	am	going to be	permitting
you	are	going to be	permitting
he/she/it	is	going to be	permitting
we	are	going to be	permitting
you	are	going to be	permitting
they	are	going to be	permitting

Future Perfect

I	will have been	permitting
you	will have been	permitting
he/she/it	will have been	permitting
we	will have been	permitting
you	will have been	permitting
they	will have been	permitting

Conditional

I	would	permit
you	would	permit
he/she/it	would	permit
we	would	permit
you	would	permit
they	would	permit

Conditional Past

I	would have	permitted
you	would have	permitted
he/she/it	would have	permitted
we	would have	permitted
you	would have	permitted
they	would have	permitted

+ -ing → ~~e~~ / + -d nicht **-ed**
Regelmäßiges Verb

überzeugen

persuade

Simple tenses

Present

I	persuade
you	persuade
he/she/it	persuades
we	persuade
you	persuade
they	persuade

Past

I	persuaded
you	persuaded
he/she/it	persuaded
we	persuaded
you	persuaded
they	persuaded

Present Perfect

I	have	persuaded
you	have	persuaded
he/she/it	has	persuaded
we	have	persuaded
you	have	persuaded
they	have	persuaded

Past Perfect

I	had	persuaded
you	had	persuaded
he/she/it	had	persuaded
we	had	persuaded
you	had	persuaded
they	had	persuaded

Will-Future

I	will	persuade
you	will	persuade
he/she/it	will	persuade
we	will	persuade
you	will	persuade
they	will	persuade

Going to-Future

I	am	going to	persuade
you	are	going to	persuade
he/she/it	is	going to	persuade
we	are	going to	persuade
you	are	going to	persuade
they	are	going to	persuade

Future Perfect

I	will have	persuaded
you	will have	persuaded
he/she/it	will have	persuaded
we	will have	persuaded
you	will have	persuaded
they	will have	persuaded

Imperative

persuade

Impersonal

ing-Form

persuading

Past Participle

persuaded

Continuous tenses

Present

I	am	persuading
you	are	persuading
he/she/it	is	persuading
we	are	persuading
you	are	persuading
they	are	persuading

Past

I	was	persuading
you	were	persuading
he/she/it	was	persuading
we	were	persuading
you	were	persuading
they	were	persuading

Present Perfect

I	have	been	persuading
you	have	been	persuading
he/she/it	has	been	persuading
we	have	been	persuading
you	have	been	persuading
they	have	been	persuading

Past Perfect

I	had been	persuading
you	had been	persuading
he/she/it	had been	persuading
we	had been	persuading
you	had been	persuading
they	had been	persuading

Will-Future

I	will be	persuading
you	will be	persuading
he/she/it	will be	persuading
we	will be	persuading
you	will be	persuading
they	will be	persuading

Going to-Future

I	am	going to be	persuading
you	are	going to be	persuading
he/she/it	is	going to be	persuading
we	are	going to be	persuading
you	are	going to be	persuading
they	are	going to be	persuading

Future Perfect

I	will have been persuading
you	will have been persuading
he/she/it	will have been persuading
we	will have been persuading
you	will have been persuading
they	will have been persuading

Conditional

I	would	persuade
you	would	persuade
he/she/it	would	persuade
we	would	persuade
you	would	persuade
they	would	persuade

Conditional Past

I	would have	persuaded
you	would have	persuaded
he/she/it	would have	persuaded
we	would have	persuaded
you	would have	persuaded
they	would have	persuaded

phone

anrufen

+ **-ing** → ~~e~~ / + **-d** nicht **-ed**
Regelmäßiges Verb

Simple tenses

Present

I	phone
you	phone
he/she/it	phones
we	phone
you	phone
they	phone

Past

I	phoned
you	phoned
he/she/it	phoned
we	phoned
you	phoned
they	phoned

Present Perfect

I	have	phoned
you	have	phoned
he/she/it	has	phoned
we	have	phoned
you	have	phoned
they	have	phoned

Past Perfect

I	had	phoned
you	had	phoned
he/she/it	had	phoned
we	had	phoned
you	had	phoned
they	had	phoned

Will-Future

I	will	phone
you	will	phone
he/she/it	will	phone
we	will	phone
you	will	phone
they	will	phone

Going to-Future

I	am	going to	phone
you	are	going to	phone
he/she/it	is	going to	phone
we	are	going to	phone
you	are	going to	phone
they	are	going to	phone

Future Perfect

I	will have	phoned
you	will have	phoned
he/she/it	will have	phoned
we	will have	phoned
you	will have	phoned
they	will have	phoned

Imperative

phone

Impersonal

ing-Form

phoning

Past Participle

phoned

Continuous tenses

Present

I	am	phoning
you	are	phoning
he/she/it	is	phoning
we	are	phoning
you	are	phoning
they	are	phoning

Past

I	was	phoning
you	were	phoning
he/she/it	was	phoning
we	were	phoning
you	were	phoning
they	were	phoning

Present Perfect

I	have been	phoning
you	have been	phoning
he/she/it	has been	phoning
we	have been	phoning
you	have been	phoning
they	have been	phoning

Past Perfect

I	had been	phoning
you	had been	phoning
he/she/it	had been	phoning
we	had been	phoning
you	had been	phoning
they	had been	phoning

Will-Future

I	will be	phoning
you	will be	phoning
he/she/it	will be	phoning
we	will be	phoning
you	will be	phoning
they	will be	phoning

Going to-Future

I	am	going to be	phoning
you	are	going to be	phoning
he/she/it	is	going to be	phoning
we	are	going to be	phoning
you	are	going to be	phoning
they	are	going to be	phoning

Future Perfect

I	will have been	phoning
you	will have been	phoning
he/she/it	will have been	phoning
we	will have been	phoning
you	will have been	phoning
they	will have been	phoning

Conditional

I	would	phone
you	would	phone
he/she/it	would	phone
we	would	phone
you	would	phone
they	would	phone

Conditional Past

I	would have	phoned
you	would have	phoned
he/she/it	would have	phoned
we	would have	phoned
you	would have	phoned
they	would have	phoned

Simple tenses

Present

I	pick
you	pick
he/she/it	picks
we	pick
you	pick
they	pick

Past

I	picked
you	picked
he/she/it	picked
we	picked
you	picked
they	picked

Present Perfect

I	have	picked
you	have	picked
he/she/it	has	picked
we	have	picked
you	have	picked
they	have	picked

Past Perfect

I	had	picked
you	had	picked
he/she/it	had	picked
we	had	picked
you	had	picked
they	had	picked

Will-Future

I	will	pick
you	will	pick
he/she/it	will	pick
we	will	pick
you	will	pick
they	will	pick

Going to-Future

I	am	going to	pick
you	are	going to	pick
he/she/it	is	going to	pick
we	are	going to	pick
you	are	going to	pick
they	are	going to	pick

Future Perfect

I	will have	picked
you	will have	picked
he/she/it	will have	picked
we	will have	picked
you	will have	picked
they	will have	picked

Imperative

pick

Impersonal

ing-Form

picking

Past Participle

picked

Continuous tenses

Present

I	am	picking
you	are	picking
he/she/it	is	picking
we	are	picking
you	are	picking
they	are	picking

Past

I	was	picking
you	were	picking
he/she/it	was	picking
we	were	picking
you	were	picking
they	were	picking

Present Perfect

I	have	been	picking
you	have	been	picking
he/she/it	has	been	picking
we	have	been	picking
you	have	been	picking
they	have	been	picking

Past Perfect

I	had been	picking
you	had been	picking
he/she/it	had been	picking
we	had been	picking
you	had been	picking
they	had been	picking

Will-Future

I	will be	picking
you	will be	picking
he/she/it	will be	picking
we	will be	picking
you	will be	picking
they	will be	picking

Going to-Future

I	am	going to be	picking
you	are	going to be	picking
he/she/it	is	going to be	picking
we	are	going to be	picking
you	are	going to be	picking
they	are	going to be	picking

Future Perfect

I	will have been	picking
you	will have been	picking
he/she/it	will have been	picking
we	will have been	picking
you	will have been	picking
they	will have been	picking

Conditional

I	would	pick
you	would	pick
he/she/it	would	pick
we	would	pick
you	would	pick
they	would	pick

Conditional Past

I	would have	picked
you	would have	picked
he/she/it	would have	picked
we	would have	picked
you	would have	picked
they	would have	picked

pin

befestigen

Konsonantenverdopplung
Regelmäßiges Verb

Simple tenses

Present
I	pin
you	pin
he/she/it	pins
we	pin
you	pin
they	pin

Past
I	pinned
you	pinned
he/she/it	pinned
we	pinned
you	pinned
they	pinned

Present Perfect
I	have	pinned
you	have	pinned
he/she/it	has	pinned
we	have	pinned
you	have	pinned
they	have	pinned

Past Perfect
I	had	pinned
you	had	pinned
he/she/it	had	pinned
we	had	pinned
you	had	pinned
they	had	pinned

Will-Future
I	will	pin
you	will	pin
he/she/it	will	pin
we	will	pin
you	will	pin
they	will	pin

Going to-Future
I	am	going to	pin
you	are	going to	pin
he/she/it	is	going to	pin
we	are	going to	pin
you	are	going to	pin
they	are	going to	pin

Future Perfect
I	will have	pinned
you	will have	pinned
he/she/it	will have	pinned
we	will have	pinned
you	will have	pinned
they	will have	pinned

Imperative
pin

Impersonal

ing-Form
pinning

Past Participle
pinned

Continuous tenses

Present
I	am	pinning
you	are	pinning
he/she/it	is	pinning
we	are	pinning
you	are	pinning
they	are	pinning

Past
I	was	pinning
you	were	pinning
he/she/it	was	pinning
we	were	pinning
you	were	pinning
they	were	pinning

Present Perfect
I	have	been	pinning
you	have	been	pinning
he/she/it	has	been	pinning
we	have	been	pinning
you	have	been	pinning
they	have	been	pinning

Past Perfect
I	had been	pinning
you	had been	pinning
he/she/it	had been	pinning
we	had been	pinning
you	had been	pinning
they	had been	pinning

Will-Future
I	will be	pinning
you	will be	pinning
he/she/it	will be	pinning
we	will be	pinning
you	will be	pinning
they	will be	pinning

Going to-Future
I	am	going to be	pinning
you	are	going to be	pinning
he/she/it	is	going to be	pinning
we	are	going to be	pinning
you	are	going to be	pinning
they	are	going to be	pinning

Future Perfect
I	will have been	pinning
you	will have been	pinning
he/she/it	will have been	pinning
we	will have been	pinning
you	will have been	pinning
they	will have been	pinning

Conditional
I	would	pin
you	would	pin
he/she/it	would	pin
we	would	pin
you	would	pin
they	would	pin

Conditional Past
I	would have	pinned
you	would have	pinned
he/she/it	would have	pinned
we	would have	pinned
you	would have	pinned
they	would have	pinned

Simple tenses

Present

I	pipe
you	pipe
he/she/it	pipes
we	pipe
you	pipe
they	pipe

Past

I	piped
you	piped
he/she/it	piped
we	piped
you	piped
they	piped

Present Perfect

I	have	piped
you	have	piped
he/she/it	has	piped
we	have	piped
you	have	piped
they	have	piped

Past Perfect

I	had	piped
you	had	piped
he/she/it	had	piped
we	had	piped
you	had	piped
they	had	piped

Will-Future

I	will	pipe
you	will	pipe
he/she/it	will	pipe
we	will	pipe
you	will	pipe
they	will	pipe

Going to-Future

I	am	going to	pipe
you	are	going to	pipe
he/she/it	is	going to	pipe
we	are	going to	pipe
you	are	going to	pipe
they	are	going to	pipe

Future Perfect

I	will have	piped
you	will have	piped
he/she/it	will have	piped
we	will have	piped
you	will have	piped
they	will have	piped

Imperative

pipe

Impersonal

ing-Form

piping

Past Participle

piped

Continuous tenses

Present

I	am	piping
you	are	piping
he/she/it	is	piping
we	are	piping
you	are	piping
they	are	piping

Past

I	was	piping
you	were	piping
he/she/it	was	piping
we	were	piping
you	were	piping
they	were	piping

Present Perfect

I	have been	piping
you	have been	piping
he/she/it	has been	piping
we	have been	piping
you	have been	piping
they	have been	piping

Past Perfect

I	had been	piping
you	had been	piping
he/she/it	had been	piping
we	had been	piping
you	had been	piping
they	had been	piping

Will-Future

I	will be	piping
you	will be	piping
he/she/it	will be	piping
we	will be	piping
you	will be	piping
they	will be	piping

Going to-Future

I	am	going to be	piping
you	are	going to be	piping
he/she/it	is	going to be	piping
we	are	going to be	piping
you	are	going to be	piping
they	are	going to be	piping

Future Perfect

I	will have been	piping
you	will have been	piping
he/she/it	will have been	piping
we	will have been	piping
you	will have been	piping
they	will have been	piping

Conditional

I	would	pipe
you	would	pipe
he/she/it	would	pipe
we	would	pipe
you	would	pipe
they	would	pipe

Conditional Past

I	would have	piped
you	would have	piped
he/she/it	would have	piped
we	would have	piped
you	would have	piped
they	would have	piped

plant

pflanzen

Regelmäßiges Verb

Simple tenses

Present

I	plant
you	plant
he/she/it	plants
we	plant
you	plant
they	plant

Past

I	planted
you	planted
he/she/it	planted
we	planted
you	planted
they	planted

Present Perfect

I	have	planted
you	have	planted
he/she/it	has	planted
we	have	planted
you	have	planted
they	have	planted

Past Perfect

I	had	planted
you	had	planted
he/she/it	had	planted
we	had	planted
you	had	planted
they	had	planted

Will-Future

I	will	plant
you	will	plant
he/she/it	will	plant
we	will	plant
you	will	plant
they	will	plant

Going to-Future

I	am	going to	plant
you	are	going to	plant
he/she/it	is	going to	plant
we	are	going to	plant
you	are	going to	plant
they	are	going to	plant

Future Perfect

I	will have	planted
you	will have	planted
he/she/it	will have	planted
we	will have	planted
you	will have	planted
they	will have	planted

Imperative

plant

Impersonal

ing-Form

planting

Past Participle

planted

Continuous tenses

Present

I	am	planting
you	are	planting
he/she/it	is	planting
we	are	planting
you	are	planting
they	are	planting

Past

I	was	planting
you	were	planting
he/she/it	was	planting
we	were	planting
you	were	planting
they	were	planting

Present Perfect

I	have been	planting
you	have been	planting
he/she/it	has been	planting
we	have been	planting
you	have been	planting
they	have been	planting

Past Perfect

I	had been	planting
you	had been	planting
he/she/it	had been	planting
we	had been	planting
you	had been	planting
they	had been	planting

Will-Future

I	will be	planting
you	will be	planting
he/she/it	will be	planting
we	will be	planting
you	will be	planting
they	will be	planting

Going to-Future

I	am	going to be	planting
you	are	going to be	planting
he/she/it	is	going to be	planting
we	are	going to be	planting
you	are	going to be	planting
they	are	going to be	planting

Future Perfect

I	will have been	planting
you	will have been	planting
he/she/it	will have been	planting
we	will have been	planting
you	will have been	planting
they	will have been	planting

Conditional

I	would	plant
you	would	plant
he/she/it	would	plant
we	would	plant
you	would	plant
they	would	plant

Conditional Past

I	would have	planted
you	would have	planted
he/she/it	would have	planted
we	would have	planted
you	would have	planted
they	would have	planted

Simple tenses

Present

I	play
you	play
he/she/it	plays
we	play
you	play
they	play

Past

I	played
you	played
he/she/it	played
we	played
you	played
they	played

Present Perfect

I	have	played
you	have	played
he/she/it	has	played
we	have	played
you	have	played
they	have	played

Past Perfect

I	had	played
you	had	played
he/she/it	had	played
we	had	played
you	had	played
they	had	played

Will-Future

I	will	play
you	will	play
he/she/it	will	play
we	will	play
you	will	play
they	will	play

Going to-Future

I	am	going to	play
you	are	going to	play
he/she/it	is	going to	play
we	are	going to	play
you	are	going to	play
they	are	going to	play

Future Perfect

I	will have	played
you	will have	played
he/she/it	will have	played
we	will have	played
you	will have	played
they	will have	played

Imperative

play

Impersonal

ing-Form

playing

Past Participle

played

Continuous tenses

Present

I	am	playing
you	are	playing
he/she/it	is	playing
we	are	playing
you	are	playing
they	are	playing

Past

I	was	playing
you	were	playing
he/she/it	was	playing
we	were	playing
you	were	playing
they	were	playing

Present Perfect

I	have been	playing
you	have been	playing
he/she/it	has been	playing
we	have been	playing
you	have been	playing
they	have been	playing

Past Perfect

I	had been	playing
you	had been	playing
he/she/it	had been	playing
we	had been	playing
you	had been	playing
they	had been	playing

Will-Future

I	will be	playing
you	will be	playing
he/she/it	will be	playing
we	will be	playing
you	will be	playing
they	will be	playing

Going to-Future

I	am	going to be	playing
you	are	going to be	playing
he/she/it	is	going to be	playing
we	are	going to be	playing
you	are	going to be	playing
they	are	going to be	playing

Future Perfect

I	will have been	playing
you	will have been	playing
he/she/it	will have been	playing
we	will have been	playing
you	will have been	playing
they	will have been	playing

Conditional

I	would	play
you	would	play
he/she/it	would	play
we	would	play
you	would	play
they	would	play

Conditional Past

I	would have	played
you	would have	played
he/she/it	would have	played
we	would have	played
you	would have	played
they	would have	played

please

gefallen

+ **-ing** → ~~e~~ / + **-d** nicht **-ed**
Regelmäßiges Verb

Simple tenses

Present

I	please
you	please
he/she/it	pleases
we	please
you	please
they	please

Past

I	pleased
you	pleased
he/she/it	pleased
we	pleased
you	pleased
they	pleased

Present Perfect

I	have	pleased
you	have	pleased
he/she/it	has	pleased
we	have	pleased
you	have	pleased
they	have	pleased

Past Perfect

I	had	pleased
you	had	pleased
he/she/it	had	pleased
we	had	pleased
you	had	pleased
they	had	pleased

Will-Future

I	will	please
you	will	please
he/she/it	will	please
we	will	please
you	will	please
they	will	please

Going to-Future

I	am	going to	please
you	are	going to	please
he/she/it	is	going to	please
we	are	going to	please
you	are	going to	please
they	are	going to	please

Future Perfect

I	will have	pleased
you	will have	pleased
he/she/it	will have	pleased
we	will have	pleased
you	will have	pleased
they	will have	pleased

Imperative

please

Impersonal

ing-Form

pleasing

Past Participle

pleased

Continuous tenses

Present

I	am	pleasing
you	are	pleasing
he/she/it	is	pleasing
we	are	pleasing
you	are	pleasing
they	are	pleasing

Past

I	was	pleasing
you	were	pleasing
he/she/it	was	pleasing
we	were	pleasing
you	were	pleasing
they	were	pleasing

Present Perfect

I	have been	pleasing
you	have been	pleasing
he/she/it	has been	pleasing
we	have been	pleasing
you	have been	pleasing
they	have been	pleasing

Past Perfect

I	had been	pleasing
you	had been	pleasing
he/she/it	had been	pleasing
we	had been	pleasing
you	had been	pleasing
they	had been	pleasing

Will-Future

I	will be	pleasing
you	will be	pleasing
he/she/it	will be	pleasing
we	will be	pleasing
you	will be	pleasing
they	will be	pleasing

Going to-Future

I	am	going to be	pleasing
you	are	going to be	pleasing
he/she/it	is	going to be	pleasing
we	are	going to be	pleasing
you	are	going to be	pleasing
they	are	going to be	pleasing

Future Perfect

I	will have been	pleasing
you	will have been	pleasing
he/she/it	will have been	pleasing
we	will have been	pleasing
you	will have been	pleasing
they	will have been	pleasing

Conditional

I	would	please
you	would	please
he/she/it	would	please
we	would	please
you	would	please
they	would	please

Conditional Past

I	would have	pleased
you	would have	pleased
he/she/it	would have	pleased
we	would have	pleased
you	would have	pleased
they	would have	pleased

Simple tenses

Present

I	point
you	point
he/she/it	points
we	point
you	point
they	point

Past

I	pointed
you	pointed
he/she/it	pointed
we	pointed
you	pointed
they	pointed

Present Perfect

I	have	pointed
you	have	pointed
he/she/it	has	pointed
we	have	pointed
you	have	pointed
they	have	pointed

Past Perfect

I	had	pointed
you	had	pointed
he/she/it	had	pointed
we	had	pointed
you	had	pointed
they	had	pointed

Will-Future

I	will	point
you	will	point
he/she/it	will	point
we	will	point
you	will	point
they	will	point

Going to-Future

I	am	going to	point
you	are	going to	point
he/she/it	is	going to	point
we	are	going to	point
you	are	going to	point
they	are	going to	point

Future Perfect

I	will have	pointed
you	will have	pointed
he/she/it	will have	pointed
we	will have	pointed
you	will have	pointed
they	will have	pointed

Imperative

point

Impersonal

ing-Form

pointing

Past Participle

pointed

Continuous tenses

Present

I	am	pointing
you	are	pointing
he/she/it	is	pointing
we	are	pointing
you	are	pointing
they	are	pointing

Past

I	was	pointing
you	were	pointing
he/she/it	was	pointing
we	were	pointing
you	were	pointing
they	were	pointing

Present Perfect

I	have been	pointing
you	have been	pointing
he/she/it	has been	pointing
we	have been	pointing
you	have been	pointing
they	have been	pointing

Past Perfect

I	had been	pointing
you	had been	pointing
he/she/it	had been	pointing
we	had been	pointing
you	had been	pointing
they	had been	pointing

Will-Future

I	will be	pointing
you	will be	pointing
he/she/it	will be	pointing
we	will be	pointing
you	will be	pointing
they	will be	pointing

Going to-Future

I	am	going to be	pointing
you	are	going to be	pointing
he/she/it	is	going to be	pointing
we	are	going to be	pointing
you	are	going to be	pointing
they	are	going to be	pointing

Future Perfect

I	will have been	pointing
you	will have been	pointing
he/she/it	will have been	pointing
we	will have been	pointing
you	will have been	pointing
they	will have been	pointing

Conditional

I	would	point
you	would	point
he/she/it	would	point
we	would	point
you	would	point
they	would	point

Conditional Past

I	would have	pointed
you	would have	pointed
he/she/it	would have	pointed
we	would have	pointed
you	would have	pointed
they	would have	pointed

possess

besitzen

+ **-es** in 3. Person Singular
Regelmäßiges Verb

Simple tenses

Present

I	possess
you	possess
he/she/it	possesses
we	possess
you	possess
they	possess

Past

I	possessed
you	possessed
he/she/it	possessed
we	possessed
you	possessed
they	possessed

Present Perfect

I	have	possessed
you	have	possessed
he/she/it	has	possessed
we	have	possessed
you	have	possessed
they	have	possessed

Past Perfect

I	had	possessed
you	had	possessed
he/she/it	had	possessed
we	had	possessed
you	had	possessed
they	had	possessed

Will-Future

I	will	possess
you	will	possess
he/she/it	will	possess
we	will	possess
you	will	possess
they	will	possess

Going to-Future

I	am	going to	possess
you	are	going to	possess
he/she/it	is	going to	possess
we	are	going to	possess
you	are	going to	possess
they	are	going to	possess

Future Perfect

I	will have	possessed
you	will have	possessed
he/she/it	will have	possessed
we	will have	possessed
you	will have	possessed
they	will have	possessed

Imperative

possess

Impersonal

ing-Form

possessing

Past Participle

possessed

Continuous tenses

Present

I	am	possessing
you	are	possessing
he/she/it	is	possessing
we	are	possessing
you	are	possessing
they	are	possessing

Past

I	was	possessing
you	were	possessing
he/she/it	was	possessing
we	were	possessing
you	were	possessing
they	were	possessing

Present Perfect

I	have	been	possessing
you	have	been	possessing
he/she/it	has	been	possessing
we	have	been	possessing
you	have	been	possessing
they	have	been	possessing

Past Perfect

I	had been	possessing
you	had been	possessing
he/she/it	had been	possessing
we	had been	possessing
you	had been	possessing
they	had been	possessing

Will-Future

I	will be	possessing
you	will be	possessing
he/she/it	will be	possessing
we	will be	possessing
you	will be	possessing
they	will be	possessing

Going to-Future

I	am	going to be	possessing
you	are	going to be	possessing
he/she/it	is	going to be	possessing
we	are	going to be	possessing
you	are	going to be	possessing
they	are	going to be	possessing

Future Perfect

I	will have been	possessing
you	will have been	possessing
he/she/it	will have been	possessing
we	will have been	possessing
you	will have been	possessing
they	will have been	possessing

Conditional

I	would	possess
you	would	possess
he/she/it	would	possess
we	would	possess
you	would	possess
they	would	possess

Conditional Past

I	would have	possessed
you	would have	possessed
he/she/it	would have	possessed
we	would have	possessed
you	would have	possessed
they	would have	possessed

Simple tenses

Present

I	post
you	post
he/she/it	posts
we	post
you	post
they	post

Past

I	posted
you	posted
he/she/it	posted
we	posted
you	posted
they	posted

Present Perfect

I	have	posted
you	have	posted
he/she/it	has	posted
we	have	posted
you	have	posted
they	have	posted

Past Perfect

I	had	posted
you	had	posted
he/she/it	had	posted
we	had	posted
you	had	posted
they	had	posted

Will-Future

I	will	post
you	will	post
he/she/it	will	post
we	will	post
you	will	post
they	will	post

Going to-Future

I	am	going to	post
you	are	going to	post
he/she/it	is	going to	post
we	are	going to	post
you	are	going to	post
they	are	going to	post

Future Perfect

I	will have	posted
you	will have	posted
he/she/it	will have	posted
we	will have	posted
you	will have	posted
they	will have	posted

Imperative

post

Impersonal

ing-Form

posting

Past Participle

posted

Continuous tenses

Present

I	am	posting
you	are	posting
he/she/it	is	posting
we	are	posting
you	are	posting
they	are	posting

Past

I	was	posting
you	were	posting
he/she/it	was	posting
we	were	posting
you	were	posting
they	were	posting

Present Perfect

I	have been	posting
you	have been	posting
he/she/it	has been	posting
we	have been	posting
you	have been	posting
they	have been	posting

Past Perfect

I	had been	posting
you	had been	posting
he/she/it	had been	posting
we	had been	posting
you	had been	posting
they	had been	posting

Will-Future

I	will be	posting
you	will be	posting
he/she/it	will be	posting
we	will be	posting
you	will be	posting
they	will be	posting

Going to-Future

I	am	going to be	posting
you	are	going to be	posting
he/she/it	is	going to be	posting
we	are	going to be	posting
you	are	going to be	posting
they	are	going to be	posting

Future Perfect

I	will have been	posting
you	will have been	posting
he/she/it	will have been	posting
we	will have been	posting
you	will have been	posting
they	will have been	posting

Conditional

I	would	post
you	would	post
he/she/it	would	post
we	would	post
you	would	post
they	would	post

Conditional Past

I	would have	posted
you	would have	posted
he/she/it	would have	posted
we	would have	posted
you	would have	posted
they	would have	posted

practise

üben

+ **-ing** → ~~e~~ / + **-d** nicht **-ed**
Regelmäßiges Verb

Simple tenses

Present

I	practise
you	practise
he/she/it	practises
we	practise
you	practise
they	practise

Past

I	practised
you	practised
he/she/it	practised
we	practised
you	practised
they	practised

Present Perfect

I	have	practised
you	have	practised
he/she/it	has	practised
we	have	practised
you	have	practised
they	have	practised

Past Perfect

I	had	practised
you	had	practised
he/she/it	had	practised
we	had	practised
you	had	practised
they	had	practised

Will-Future

I	will	practise
you	will	practise
he/she/it	will	practise
we	will	practise
you	will	practise
they	will	practise

Going to-Future

I	am	going to	practise
you	are	going to	practise
he/she/it	is	going to	practise
we	are	going to	practise
you	are	going to	practise
they	are	going to	practise

Future Perfect

I	will have	practised
you	will have	practised
he/she/it	will have	practised
we	will have	practised
you	will have	practised
they	will have	practised

Imperative

practise

Impersonal

ing-Form

practising

Past Participle

practised

Continuous tenses

Present

I	am	practising
you	are	practising
he/she/it	is	practising
we	are	practising
you	are	practising
they	are	practising

Past

I	was	practising
you	were	practising
he/she/it	was	practising
we	were	practising
you	were	practising
they	were	practising

Present Perfect

I	have been	practising
you	have been	practising
he/she/it	has been	practising
we	have been	practising
you	have been	practising
they	have been	practising

Past Perfect

I	had been	practising
you	had been	practising
he/she/it	had been	practising
we	had been	practising
you	had been	practising
they	had been	practising

Will-Future

I	will be	practising
you	will be	practising
he/she/it	will be	practising
we	will be	practising
you	will be	practising
they	will be	practising

Going to-Future

I	am	going to be	practising
you	are	going to be	practising
he/she/it	is	going to be	practising
we	are	going to be	practising
you	are	going to be	practising
they	are	going to be	practising

Future Perfect

I	will have been	practising
you	will have been	practising
he/she/it	will have been	practising
we	will have been	practising
you	will have been	practising
they	will have been	practising

Conditional

I	would	practise
you	would	practise
he/she/it	would	practise
we	would	practise
you	would	practise
they	would	practise

Conditional Past

I	would have	practised
you	would have	practised
he/she/it	would have	practised
we	would have	practised
you	would have	practised
they	would have	practised

Simple tenses

Present

I	pray
you	pray
he/she/it	prays
we	pray
you	pray
they	pray

Past

I	prayed
you	prayed
he/she/it	prayed
we	prayed
you	prayed
they	prayed

Present Perfect

I	have	prayed
you	have	prayed
he/she/it	has	prayed
we	have	prayed
you	have	prayed
they	have	prayed

Past Perfect

I	had	prayed
you	had	prayed
he/she/it	had	prayed
we	had	prayed
you	had	prayed
they	had	prayed

Will-Future

I	will	pray
you	will	pray
he/she/it	will	pray
we	will	pray
you	will	pray
they	will	pray

Going to-Future

I	am	going to	pray
you	are	going to	pray
he/she/it	is	going to	pray
we	are	going to	pray
you	are	going to	pray
they	are	going to	pray

Future Perfect

I	will have	prayed
you	will have	prayed
he/she/it	will have	prayed
we	will have	prayed
you	will have	prayed
they	will have	prayed

Imperative

pray

Impersonal

ing-Form

praying

Past Participle

prayed

Continuous tenses

Present

I	am	praying
you	are	praying
he/she/it	is	praying
we	are	praying
you	are	praying
they	are	praying

Past

I	was	praying
you	were	praying
he/she/it	was	praying
we	were	praying
you	were	praying
they	were	praying

Present Perfect

I	have been	praying
you	have been	praying
he/she/it	has been	praying
we	have been	praying
you	have been	praying
they	have been	praying

Past Perfect

I	had been	praying
you	had been	praying
he/she/it	had been	praying
we	had been	praying
you	had been	praying
they	had been	praying

Will-Future

I	will be	praying
you	will be	praying
he/she/it	will be	praying
we	will be	praying
you	will be	praying
they	will be	praying

Going to-Future

I	am	going to be	praying
you	are	going to be	praying
he/she/it	is	going to be	praying
we	are	going to be	praying
you	are	going to be	praying
they	are	going to be	praying

Future Perfect

I	will have been	praying
you	will have been	praying
he/she/it	will have been	praying
we	will have been	praying
you	will have been	praying
they	will have been	praying

Conditional

I	would	pray
you	would	pray
he/she/it	would	pray
we	would	pray
you	would	pray
they	would	pray

Conditional Past

I	would have	prayed
you	would have	prayed
he/she/it	would have	prayed
we	would have	prayed
you	would have	prayed
they	would have	prayed

predict

vorhersagen

Regelmäßiges Verb

Simple tenses

Present

I	predict
you	predict
he/she/it	predicts
we	predict
you	predict
they	predict

Past

I	predicted
you	predicted
he/she/it	predicted
we	predicted
you	predicted
they	predicted

Present Perfect

I	have	predicted
you	have	predicted
he/she/it	has	predicted
we	have	predicted
you	have	predicted
they	have	predicted

Past Perfect

I	had	predicted
you	had	predicted
he/she/it	had	predicted
we	had	predicted
you	had	predicted
they	had	predicted

Will-Future

I	will	predict
you	will	predict
he/she/it	will	predict
we	will	predict
you	will	predict
they	will	predict

Going to-Future

I	am	going to	predict
you	are	going to	predict
he/she/it	is	going to	predict
we	are	going to	predict
you	are	going to	predict
they	are	going to	predict

Future Perfect

I	will have	predicted
you	will have	predicted
he/she/it	will have	predicted
we	will have	predicted
you	will have	predicted
they	will have	predicted

Imperative

predict

Impersonal

ing-Form

predicting

Past Participle

predicted

Continuous tenses

Present

I	am	predicting
you	are	predicting
he/she/it	is	predicting
we	are	predicting
you	are	predicting
they	are	predicting

Past

I	was	predicting
you	were	predicting
he/she/it	was	predicting
we	were	predicting
you	were	predicting
they	were	predicting

Present Perfect

I	have been	predicting
you	have been	predicting
he/she/it	has been	predicting
we	have been	predicting
you	have been	predicting
they	have been	predicting

Past Perfect

I	had been	predicting
you	had been	predicting
he/she/it	had been	predicting
we	had been	predicting
you	had been	predicting
they	had been	predicting

Will-Future

I	will be	predicting
you	will be	predicting
he/she/it	will be	predicting
we	will be	predicting
you	will be	predicting
they	will be	predicting

Going to-Future

I	am	going to be	predicting
you	are	going to be	predicting
he/she/it	is	going to be	predicting
we	are	going to be	predicting
you	are	going to be	predicting
they	are	going to be	predicting

Future Perfect

I	will have been	predicting
you	will have been	predicting
he/she/it	will have been	predicting
we	will have been	predicting
you	will have been	predicting
they	will have been	predicting

Conditional

I	would	predict
you	would	predict
he/she/it	would	predict
we	would	predict
you	would	predict
they	would	predict

Conditional Past

I	would have	predicted
you	would have	predicted
he/she/it	would have	predicted
we	would have	predicted
you	would have	predicted
they	would have	predicted

Konsonantenverdopplung
Regelmäßiges Verb

bevorzugen

prefer

Simple tenses

Present

I	prefer
you	prefer
he/she/it	prefers
we	prefer
you	prefer
they	prefer

Past

I	preferred
you	preferred
he/she/it	preferred
we	preferred
you	preferred
they	preferred

Present Perfect

I	have	preferred
you	have	preferred
he/she/it	has	preferred
we	have	preferred
you	have	preferred
they	have	preferred

Past Perfect

I	had	preferred
you	had	preferred
he/she/it	had	preferred
we	had	preferred
you	had	preferred
they	had	preferred

Will-Future

I	will	prefer
you	will	prefer
he/she/it	will	prefer
we	will	prefer
you	will	prefer
they	will	prefer

Going to-Future

I	am	going to	prefer
you	are	going to	prefer
he/she/it	is	going to	prefer
we	are	going to	prefer
you	are	going to	prefer
they	are	going to	prefer

Future Perfect

I	will have	preferred
you	will have	preferred
he/she/it	will have	preferred
we	will have	preferred
you	will have	preferred
they	will have	preferred

Imperative

prefer

Impersonal

ing-Form

preferring

Past Participle

preferred

Continuous tenses

Present

I	am	preferring
you	are	preferring
he/she/it	is	preferring
we	are	preferring
you	are	preferring
they	are	preferring

Past

I	was	preferring
you	were	preferring
he/she/it	was	preferring
we	were	preferring
you	were	preferring
they	were	preferring

Present Perfect

I	have been	preferring
you	have been	preferring
he/she/it	has been	preferring
we	have been	preferring
you	have been	preferring
they	have been	preferring

Past Perfect

I	had been	preferring
you	had been	preferring
he/she/it	had been	preferring
we	had been	preferring
you	had been	preferring
they	had been	preferring

Will-Future

I	will be	preferring
you	will be	preferring
he/she/it	will be	preferring
we	will be	preferring
you	will be	preferring
they	will be	preferring

Going to-Future

I	am	going to be	preferring
you	are	going to be	preferring
he/she/it	is	going to be	preferring
we	are	going to be	preferring
you	are	going to be	preferring
they	are	going to be	preferring

Future Perfect

I	will have been preferring
you	will have been preferring
he/she/it	will have been preferring
we	will have been preferring
you	will have been preferring
they	will have been preferring

Conditional

I	would	prefer
you	would	prefer
he/she/it	would	prefer
we	would	prefer
you	would	prefer
they	would	prefer

Conditional Past

I	would have	preferred
you	would have	preferred
he/she/it	would have	preferred
we	would have	preferred
you	would have	preferred
they	would have	preferred

prepare

vorbereiten

+ **-ing** → ~~e~~ / + **-d** nicht **-ed**
Regelmäßiges Verb

Simple tenses

Present

I	prepare
you	prepare
he/she/it	prepares
we	prepare
you	prepare
they	prepare

Past

I	prepared
you	prepared
he/she/it	prepared
we	prepared
you	prepared
they	prepared

Present Perfect

I	have	prepared
you	have	prepared
he/she/it	has	prepared
we	have	prepared
you	have	prepared
they	have	prepared

Past Perfect

I	had	prepared
you	had	prepared
he/she/it	had	prepared
we	had	prepared
you	had	prepared
they	had	prepared

Will-Future

I	will	prepare
you	will	prepare
he/she/it	will	prepare
we	will	prepare
you	will	prepare
they	will	prepare

Going to-Future

I	am	going to	prepare
you	are	going to	prepare
he/she/it	is	going to	prepare
we	are	going to	prepare
you	are	going to	prepare
they	are	going to	prepare

Future Perfect

I	will have	prepared
you	will have	prepared
he/she/it	will have	prepared
we	will have	prepared
you	will have	prepared
they	will have	prepared

Imperative

prepare

Impersonal

ing-Form

preparing

Past Participle

prepared

Continuous tenses

Present

I	am	preparing
you	are	preparing
he/she/it	is	preparing
we	are	preparing
you	are	preparing
they	are	preparing

Past

I	was	preparing
you	were	preparing
he/she/it	was	preparing
we	were	preparing
you	were	preparing
they	were	preparing

Present Perfect

I	have been	preparing
you	have been	preparing
he/she/it	has been	preparing
we	have been	preparing
you	have been	preparing
they	have been	preparing

Past Perfect

I	had been	preparing
you	had been	preparing
he/she/it	had been	preparing
we	had been	preparing
you	had been	preparing
they	had been	preparing

Will-Future

I	will be	preparing
you	will be	preparing
he/she/it	will be	preparing
we	will be	preparing
you	will be	preparing
they	will be	preparing

Going to-Future

I	am	going to be	preparing
you	are	going to be	preparing
he/she/it	is	going to be	preparing
we	are	going to be	preparing
you	are	going to be	preparing
they	are	going to be	preparing

Future Perfect

I	will have been	preparing
you	will have been	preparing
he/she/it	will have been	preparing
we	will have been	preparing
you	will have been	preparing
they	will have been	preparing

Conditional

I	would	prepare
you	would	prepare
he/she/it	would	prepare
we	would	prepare
you	would	prepare
they	would	prepare

Conditional Past

I	would have	prepared
you	would have	prepared
he/she/it	would have	prepared
we	would have	prepared
you	would have	prepared
they	would have	prepared

Simple tenses

Present

I	present
you	present
he/she/it	presents
we	present
you	present
they	present

Past

I	presented
you	presented
he/she/it	presented
we	presented
you	presented
they	presented

Present Perfect

I	have	presented
you	have	presented
he/she/it	has	presented
we	have	presented
you	have	presented
they	have	presented

Past Perfect

I	had	presented
you	had	presented
he/she/it	had	presented
we	had	presented
you	had	presented
they	had	presented

Will-Future

I	will	present
you	will	present
he/she/it	will	present
we	will	present
you	will	present
they	will	present

Going to-Future

I	am	going to	present
you	are	going to	present
he/she/it	is	going to	present
we	are	going to	present
you	are	going to	present
they	are	going to	present

Future Perfect

I	will have	presented
you	will have	presented
he/she/it	will have	presented
we	will have	presented
you	will have	presented
they	will have	presented

Imperative

present

Impersonal

ing-Form

presenting

Past Participle

presented

Continuous tenses

Present

I	am	presenting
you	are	presenting
he/she/it	is	presenting
we	are	presenting
you	are	presenting
they	are	presenting

Past

I	was	presenting
you	were	presenting
he/she/it	was	presenting
we	were	presenting
you	were	presenting
they	were	presenting

Present Perfect

I	have been	presenting
you	have been	presenting
he/she/it	has been	presenting
we	have been	presenting
you	have been	presenting
they	have been	presenting

Past Perfect

I	had been	presenting
you	had been	presenting
he/she/it	had been	presenting
we	had been	presenting
you	had been	presenting
they	had been	presenting

Will-Future

I	will be	presenting
you	will be	presenting
he/she/it	will be	presenting
we	will be	presenting
you	will be	presenting
they	will be	presenting

Going to-Future

I	am	going to be	presenting
you	are	going to be	presenting
he/she/it	is	going to be	presenting
we	are	going to be	presenting
you	are	going to be	presenting
they	are	going to be	presenting

Future Perfect

I	will have been	presenting
you	will have been	presenting
he/she/it	will have been	presenting
we	will have been	presenting
you	will have been	presenting
they	will have been	presenting

Conditional

I	would	present
you	would	present
he/she/it	would	present
we	would	present
you	would	present
they	would	present

Conditional Past

I	would have	presented
you	would have	presented
he/she/it	would have	presented
we	would have	presented
you	would have	presented
they	would have	presented

preserve

erhalten

\+ **-ing** → ~~e~~ / + **-d** nicht **-ed**
Regelmäßiges Verb

Simple tenses

Present

I	preserve
you	preserve
he/she/it	preserves
we	preserve
you	preserve
they	preserve

Past

I	preserved
you	preserved
he/she/it	preserved
we	preserved
you	preserved
they	preserved

Present Perfect

I	have	preserved
you	have	preserved
he/she/it	has	preserved
we	have	preserved
you	have	preserved
they	have	preserved

Past Perfect

I	had	preserved
you	had	preserved
he/she/it	had	preserved
we	had	preserved
you	had	preserved
they	had	preserved

Will-Future

I	will	preserve
you	will	preserve
he/she/it	will	preserve
we	will	preserve
you	will	preserve
they	will	preserve

Going to-Future

I	am	going to	preserve
you	are	going to	preserve
he/she/it	is	going to	preserve
we	are	going to	preserve
you	are	going to	preserve
they	are	going to	preserve

Future Perfect

I	will have	preserved
you	will have	preserved
he/she/it	will have	preserved
we	will have	preserved
you	will have	preserved
they	will have	preserved

Imperative

preserve

Impersonal

ing-Form

preserving

Past Participle

preserved

Continuous tenses

Present

I	am	preserving
you	are	preserving
he/she/it	is	preserving
we	are	preserving
you	are	preserving
they	are	preserving

Past

I	was	preserving
you	were	preserving
he/she/it	was	preserving
we	were	preserving
you	were	preserving
they	were	preserving

Present Perfect

I	have been	preserving
you	have been	preserving
he/she/it	has been	preserving
we	have been	preserving
you	have been	preserving
they	have been	preserving

Past Perfect

I	had been	preserving
you	had been	preserving
he/she/it	had been	preserving
we	had been	preserving
you	had been	preserving
they	had been	preserving

Will-Future

I	will be	preserving
you	will be	preserving
he/she/it	will be	preserving
we	will be	preserving
you	will be	preserving
they	will be	preserving

Going to-Future

I	am	going to be	preserving
you	are	going to be	preserving
he/she/it	is	going to be	preserving
we	are	going to be	preserving
you	are	going to be	preserving
they	are	going to be	preserving

Future Perfect

I	will have been	preserving
you	will have been	preserving
he/she/it	will have been	preserving
we	will have been	preserving
you	will have been	preserving
they	will have been	preserving

Conditional

I	would	preserve
you	would	preserve
he/she/it	would	preserve
we	would	preserve
you	would	preserve
they	would	preserve

Conditional Past

I	would have	preserved
you	would have	preserved
he/she/it	would have	preserved
we	would have	preserved
you	would have	preserved
they	would have	preserved

Simple tenses

Present

I	press
you	press
he/she/it	presses
we	press
you	press
they	press

Past

I	pressed
you	pressed
he/she/it	pressed
we	pressed
you	pressed
they	pressed

Present Perfect

I	have	pressed
you	have	pressed
he/she/it	has	pressed
we	have	pressed
you	have	pressed
they	have	pressed

Past Perfect

I	had	pressed
you	had	pressed
he/she/it	had	pressed
we	had	pressed
you	had	pressed
they	had	pressed

Will-Future

I	will	press
you	will	press
he/she/it	will	press
we	will	press
you	will	press
they	will	press

Going to-Future

I	am	going to	press
you	are	going to	press
he/she/it	is	going to	press
we	are	going to	press
you	are	going to	press
they	are	going to	press

Future Perfect

I	will have	pressed
you	will have	pressed
he/she/it	will have	pressed
we	will have	pressed
you	will have	pressed
they	will have	pressed

Imperative

press

Impersonal

ing-Form

pressing

Past Participle

pressed

Continuous tenses

Present

I	am	pressing
you	are	pressing
he/she/it	is	pressing
we	are	pressing
you	are	pressing
they	are	pressing

Past

I	was	pressing
you	were	pressing
he/she/it	was	pressing
we	were	pressing
you	were	pressing
they	were	pressing

Present Perfect

I	have been	pressing
you	have been	pressing
he/she/it	has been	pressing
we	have been	pressing
you	have been	pressing
they	have been	pressing

Past Perfect

I	had been	pressing
you	had been	pressing
he/she/it	had been	pressing
we	had been	pressing
you	had been	pressing
they	had been	pressing

Will-Future

I	will be	pressing
you	will be	pressing
he/she/it	will be	pressing
we	will be	pressing
you	will be	pressing
they	will be	pressing

Going to-Future

I	am	going to be	pressing
you	are	going to be	pressing
he/she/it	is	going to be	pressing
we	are	going to be	pressing
you	are	going to be	pressing
they	are	going to be	pressing

Future Perfect

I	will have been	pressing
you	will have been	pressing
he/she/it	will have been	pressing
we	will have been	pressing
you	will have been	pressing
they	will have been	pressing

Conditional

I	would	press
you	would	press
he/she/it	would	press
we	would	press
you	would	press
they	would	press

Conditional Past

I	would have	pressed
you	would have	pressed
he/she/it	would have	pressed
we	would have	pressed
you	would have	pressed
they	would have	pressed

prevent

verhindern

Regelmäßiges Verb

Simple tenses

Present

I	prevent
you	prevent
he/she/it	prevents
we	prevent
you	prevent
they	prevent

Past

I	prevented
you	prevented
he/she/it	prevented
we	prevented
you	prevented
they	prevented

Present Perfect

I	have	prevented
you	have	prevented
he/she/it	has	prevented
we	have	prevented
you	have	prevented
they	have	prevented

Past Perfect

I	had	prevented
you	had	prevented
he/she/it	had	prevented
we	had	prevented
you	had	prevented
they	had	prevented

Will-Future

I	will	prevent
you	will	prevent
he/she/it	will	prevent
we	will	prevent
you	will	prevent
they	will	prevent

Going to-Future

I	am	going to	prevent
you	are	going to	prevent
he/she/it	is	going to	prevent
we	are	going to	prevent
you	are	going to	prevent
they	are	going to	prevent

Future Perfect

I	will have	prevented
you	will have	prevented
he/she/it	will have	prevented
we	will have	prevented
you	will have	prevented
they	will have	prevented

Imperative

prevent

Impersonal

ing-Form

preventing

Past Participle

prevented

Continuous tenses

Present

I	am	preventing
you	are	preventing
he/she/it	is	preventing
we	are	preventing
you	are	preventing
they	are	preventing

Past

I	was	preventing
you	were	preventing
he/she/it	was	preventing
we	were	preventing
you	were	preventing
they	were	preventing

Present Perfect

I	have	been	preventing
you	have	been	preventing
he/she/it	has	been	preventing
we	have	been	preventing
you	have	been	preventing
they	have	been	preventing

Past Perfect

I	had been	preventing
you	had been	preventing
he/she/it	had been	preventing
we	had been	preventing
you	had been	preventing
they	had been	preventing

Will-Future

I	will be	preventing
you	will be	preventing
he/she/it	will be	preventing
we	will be	preventing
you	will be	preventing
they	will be	preventing

Going to-Future

I	am	going to be	preventing
you	are	going to be	preventing
he/she/it	is	going to be	preventing
we	are	going to be	preventing
you	are	going to be	preventing
they	are	going to be	preventing

Future Perfect

I	will have been	preventing
you	will have been	preventing
he/she/it	will have been	preventing
we	will have been	preventing
you	will have been	preventing
they	will have been	preventing

Conditional

I	would	prevent
you	would	prevent
he/she/it	would	prevent
we	would	prevent
you	would	prevent
they	would	prevent

Conditional Past

I	would have	prevented
you	would have	prevented
he/she/it	would have	prevented
we	would have	prevented
you	would have	prevented
they	would have	prevented

Simple tenses

Present

I	print
you	print
he/she/it	prints
we	print
you	print
they	print

Past

I	printed
you	printed
he/she/it	printed
we	printed
you	printed
they	printed

Present Perfect

I	have	printed
you	have	printed
he/she/it	has	printed
we	have	printed
you	have	printed
they	have	printed

Past Perfect

I	had	printed
you	had	printed
he/she/it	had	printed
we	had	printed
you	had	printed
they	had	printed

Will-Future

I	will	print
you	will	print
he/she/it	will	print
we	will	print
you	will	print
they	will	print

Going to-Future

I	am	going to	print
you	are	going to	print
he/she/it	is	going to	print
we	are	going to	print
you	are	going to	print
they	are	going to	print

Future Perfect

I	will have	printed
you	will have	printed
he/she/it	will have	printed
we	will have	printed
you	will have	printed
they	will have	printed

Imperative

print

Impersonal

ing-Form

printing

Past Participle

printed

Continuous tenses

Present

I	am	printing
you	are	printing
he/she/it	is	printing
we	are	printing
you	are	printing
they	are	printing

Past

I	was	printing
you	were	printing
he/she/it	was	printing
we	were	printing
you	were	printing
they	were	printing

Present Perfect

I	have been	printing
you	have been	printing
he/she/it	has been	printing
we	have been	printing
you	have been	printing
they	have been	printing

Past Perfect

I	had been	printing
you	had been	printing
he/she/it	had been	printing
we	had been	printing
you	had been	printing
they	had been	printing

Will-Future

I	will be	printing
you	will be	printing
he/she/it	will be	printing
we	will be	printing
you	will be	printing
they	will be	printing

Going to-Future

I	am	going to be	printing
you	are	going to be	printing
he/she/it	is	going to be	printing
we	are	going to be	printing
you	are	going to be	printing
they	are	going to be	printing

Future Perfect

I	will have been	printing
you	will have been	printing
he/she/it	will have been	printing
we	will have been	printing
you	will have been	printing
they	will have been	printing

Conditional

I	would	print
you	would	print
he/she/it	would	print
we	would	print
you	would	print
they	would	print

Conditional Past

I	would have	printed
you	would have	printed
he/she/it	would have	printed
we	would have	printed
you	would have	printed
they	would have	printed

process

bearbeiten

+ **-es** in 3. Person Singular
Regelmäßiges Verb

Simple tenses

Present

I	process
you	process
he/she/it	processes
we	process
you	process
they	process

Past

I	processed
you	processed
he/she/it	processed
we	processed
you	processed
they	processed

Present Perfect

I	have	processed
you	have	processed
he/she/it	has	processed
we	have	processed
you	have	processed
they	have	processed

Past Perfect

I	had	processed
you	had	processed
he/she/it	had	processed
we	had	processed
you	had	processed
they	had	processed

Will-Future

I	will	process
you	will	process
he/she/it	will	process
we	will	process
you	will	process
they	will	process

Going to-Future

I	am	going to	process
you	are	going to	process
he/she/it	is	going to	process
we	are	going to	process
you	are	going to	process
they	are	going to	process

Future Perfect

I	will have	processed
you	will have	processed
he/she/it	will have	processed
we	will have	processed
you	will have	processed
they	will have	processed

Imperative

process

Impersonal

ing-Form

processing

Past Participle

processed

Continuous tenses

Present

I	am	processing
you	are	processing
he/she/it	is	processing
we	are	processing
you	are	processing
they	are	processing

Past

I	was	processing
you	were	processing
he/she/it	was	processing
we	were	processing
you	were	processing
they	were	processing

Present Perfect

I	have been	processing
you	have been	processing
he/she/it	has been	processing
we	have been	processing
you	have been	processing
they	have been	processing

Past Perfect

I	had been	processing
you	had been	processing
he/she/it	had been	processing
we	had been	processing
you	had been	processing
they	had been	processing

Will-Future

I	will be	processing
you	will be	processing
he/she/it	will be	processing
we	will be	processing
you	will be	processing
they	will be	processing

Going to-Future

I	am	going to be	processing
you	are	going to be	processing
he/she/it	is	going to be	processing
we	are	going to be	processing
you	are	going to be	processing
they	are	going to be	processing

Future Perfect

I	will have been	processing
you	will have been	processing
he/she/it	will have been	processing
we	will have been	processing
you	will have been	processing
they	will have been	processing

Conditional

I	would	process
you	would	process
he/she/it	would	process
we	would	process
you	would	process
they	would	process

Conditional Past

I	would have	processed
you	would have	processed
he/she/it	would have	processed
we	would have	processed
you	would have	processed
they	would have	processed

+ **-ing** → ~~e~~ / + **-d** nicht **-ed**
Regelmäßiges Verb

herstellen

produce

Simple tenses

Present

I	produce
you	produce
he/she/it	produces
we	produce
you	produce
they	produce

Past

I	produced
you	produced
he/she/it	produced
we	produced
you	produced
they	produced

Present Perfect

I	have	produced
you	have	produced
he/she/it	has	produced
we	have	produced
you	have	produced
they	have	produced

Past Perfect

I	had	produced
you	had	produced
he/she/it	had	produced
we	had	produced
you	had	produced
they	had	produced

Will-Future

I	will	produce
you	will	produce
he/she/it	will	produce
we	will	produce
you	will	produce
they	will	produce

Going to-Future

I	am	going to	produce
you	are	going to	produce
he/she/it	is	going to	produce
we	are	going to	produce
you	are	going to	produce
they	are	going to	produce

Future Perfect

I	will have	produced
you	will have	produced
he/she/it	will have	produced
we	will have	produced
you	will have	produced
they	will have	produced

Imperative

produce

Impersonal

ing-Form

producing

Past Participle

produced

Continuous tenses

Present

I	am	producing
you	are	producing
he/she/it	is	producing
we	are	producing
you	are	producing
they	are	producing

Past

I	was	producing
you	were	producing
he/she/it	was	producing
we	were	producing
you	were	producing
they	were	producing

Present Perfect

I	have been	producing
you	have been	producing
he/she/it	has been	producing
we	have been	producing
you	have been	producing
they	have been	producing

Past Perfect

I	had been	producing
you	had been	producing
he/she/it	had been	producing
we	had been	producing
you	had been	producing
they	had been	producing

Will-Future

I	will be	producing
you	will be	producing
he/she/it	will be	producing
we	will be	producing
you	will be	producing
they	will be	producing

Going to-Future

I	am	going to be	producing
you	are	going to be	producing
he/she/it	is	going to be	producing
we	are	going to be	producing
you	are	going to be	producing
they	are	going to be	producing

Future Perfect

I	will have been	producing
you	will have been	producing
he/she/it	will have been	producing
we	will have been	producing
you	will have been	producing
they	will have been	producing

Conditional

I	would	produce
you	would	produce
he/she/it	would	produce
we	would	produce
you	would	produce
they	would	produce

Conditional Past

I	would have	produced
you	would have	produced
he/she/it	would have	produced
we	would have	produced
you	would have	produced
they	would have	produced

profit

profitieren

Regelmäßiges Verb

Simple tenses

Present

I	profit
you	profit
he/she/it	profits
we	profit
you	profit
they	profit

Past

I	profited
you	profited
he/she/it	profited
we	profited
you	profited
they	profited

Present Perfect

I	have	profited
you	have	profited
he/she/it	has	profited
we	have	profited
you	have	profited
they	have	profited

Past Perfect

I	had	profited
you	had	profited
he/she/it	had	profited
we	had	profited
you	had	profited
they	had	profited

Will-Future

I	will	profit
you	will	profit
he/she/it	will	profit
we	will	profit
you	will	profit
they	will	profit

Going to-Future

I	am	going to	profit
you	are	going to	profit
he/she/it	is	going to	profit
we	are	going to	profit
you	are	going to	profit
they	are	going to	profit

Future Perfect

I	will have	profited
you	will have	profited
he/she/it	will have	profited
we	will have	profited
you	will have	profited
they	will have	profited

Imperative

profit

Impersonal

ing-Form

profiting

Past Participle

profited

Continuous tenses

Present

I	am	profiting
you	are	profiting
he/she/it	is	profiting
we	are	profiting
you	are	profiting
they	are	profiting

Past

I	was	profiting
you	were	profiting
he/she/it	was	profiting
we	were	profiting
you	were	profiting
they	were	profiting

Present Perfect

I	have been	profiting
you	have been	profiting
he/she/it	has been	profiting
we	have been	profiting
you	have been	profiting
they	have been	profiting

Past Perfect

I	had been	profiting
you	had been	profiting
he/she/it	had been	profiting
we	had been	profiting
you	had been	profiting
they	had been	profiting

Will-Future

I	will be	profiting
you	will be	profiting
he/she/it	will be	profiting
we	will be	profiting
you	will be	profiting
they	will be	profiting

Going to-Future

I	am	going to be	profiting
you	are	going to be	profiting
he/she/it	is	going to be	profiting
we	are	going to be	profiting
you	are	going to be	profiting
they	are	going to be	profiting

Future Perfect

I	will have been	profiting
you	will have been	profiting
he/she/it	will have been	profiting
we	will have been	profiting
you	will have been	profiting
they	will have been	profiting

Conditional

I	would	profit
you	would	profit
he/she/it	would	profit
we	would	profit
you	would	profit
they	would	profit

Conditional Past

I	would have	profited
you	would have	profited
he/she/it	would have	profited
we	would have	profited
you	would have	profited
they	would have	profited

Simple tenses

Present

I	promise
you	promise
he/she/it	promises
we	promise
you	promise
they	promise

Past

I	promised
you	promised
he/she/it	promised
we	promised
you	promised
they	promised

Present Perfect

I	have	promised
you	have	promised
he/she/it	has	promised
we	have	promised
you	have	promised
they	have	promised

Past Perfect

I	had	promised
you	had	promised
he/she/it	had	promised
we	had	promised
you	had	promised
they	had	promised

Will-Future

I	will	promise
you	will	promise
he/she/it	will	promise
we	will	promise
you	will	promise
they	will	promise

Going to-Future

I	am	going to	promise
you	are	going to	promise
he/she/it	is	going to	promise
we	are	going to	promise
you	are	going to	promise
they	are	going to	promise

Future Perfect

I	will have	promised
you	will have	promised
he/she/it	will have	promised
we	will have	promised
you	will have	promised
they	will have	promised

Imperative

promise

Impersonal

ing-Form

promising

Past Participle

promised

Continuous tenses

Present

I	am	promising
you	are	promising
he/she/it	is	promising
we	are	promising
you	are	promising
they	are	promising

Past

I	was	promising
you	were	promising
he/she/it	was	promising
we	were	promising
you	were	promising
they	were	promising

Present Perfect

I	have been	promising
you	have been	promising
he/she/it	has been	promising
we	have been	promising
you	have been	promising
they	have been	promising

Past Perfect

I	had been	promising
you	had been	promising
he/she/it	had been	promising
we	had been	promising
you	had been	promising
they	had been	promising

Will-Future

I	will be	promising
you	will be	promising
he/she/it	will be	promising
we	will be	promising
you	will be	promising
they	will be	promising

Going to-Future

I	am	going to be	promising
you	are	going to be	promising
he/she/it	is	going to be	promising
we	are	going to be	promising
you	are	going to be	promising
they	are	going to be	promising

Future Perfect

I	will have been	promising
you	will have been	promising
he/she/it	will have been	promising
we	will have been	promising
you	will have been	promising
they	will have been	promising

Conditional

I	would	promise
you	would	promise
he/she/it	would	promise
we	would	promise
you	would	promise
they	would	promise

Conditional Past

I	would have	promised
you	would have	promised
he/she/it	would have	promised
we	would have	promised
you	would have	promised
they	would have	promised

promote

befördern

+ **-ing** → ~~e~~ / + **-d** nicht **-ed**
Regelmäßiges Verb

Simple tenses

Present

I	promote
you	promote
he/she/it	promotes
we	promote
you	promote
they	promote

Past

I	promoted
you	promoted
he/she/it	promoted
we	promoted
you	promoted
they	promoted

Present Perfect

I	have	promoted
you	have	promoted
he/she/it	has	promoted
we	have	promoted
you	have	promoted
they	have	promoted

Past Perfect

I	had	promoted
you	had	promoted
he/she/it	had	promoted
we	had	promoted
you	had	promoted
they	had	promoted

Will-Future

I	will	promote
you	will	promote
he/she/it	will	promote
we	will	promote
you	will	promote
they	will	promote

Going to-Future

I	am	going to	promote
you	are	going to	promote
he/she/it	is	going to	promote
we	are	going to	promote
you	are	going to	promote
they	are	going to	promote

Future Perfect

I	will have	promoted
you	will have	promoted
he/she/it	will have	promoted
we	will have	promoted
you	will have	promoted
they	will have	promoted

Imperative

promote

Impersonal

ing-Form

promoting

Past Participle

promoted

Continuous tenses

Present

I	am	promoting
you	are	promoting
he/she/it	is	promoting
we	are	promoting
you	are	promoting
they	are	promoting

Past

I	was	promoting
you	were	promoting
he/she/it	was	promoting
we	were	promoting
you	were	promoting
they	were	promoting

Present Perfect

I	have been	promoting
you	have been	promoting
he/she/it	has been	promoting
we	have been	promoting
you	have been	promoting
they	have been	promoting

Past Perfect

I	had been	promoting
you	had been	promoting
he/she/it	had been	promoting
we	had been	promoting
you	had been	promoting
they	had been	promoting

Will-Future

I	will be	promoting
you	will be	promoting
he/she/it	will be	promoting
we	will be	promoting
you	will be	promoting
they	will be	promoting

Going to-Future

I	am	going to be	promoting
you	are	going to be	promoting
he/she/it	is	going to be	promoting
we	are	going to be	promoting
you	are	going to be	promoting
they	are	going to be	promoting

Future Perfect

I	will have been	promoting
you	will have been	promoting
he/she/it	will have been	promoting
we	will have been	promoting
you	will have been	promoting
they	will have been	promoting

Conditional

I	would	promote
you	would	promote
he/she/it	would	promote
we	would	promote
you	would	promote
they	would	promote

Conditional Past

I	would have	promoted
you	would have	promoted
he/she/it	would have	promoted
we	would have	promoted
you	would have	promoted
they	would have	promoted

+ **-ing** → ~~e~~ / + **-d** nicht **-ed**
Regelmäßiges Verb

aussprechen

pronounce

Simple tenses

Present

I	pronounce
you	pronounce
he/she/it	pronounces
we	pronounce
you	pronounce
they	pronounce

Past

I	pronounced
you	pronounced
he/she/it	pronounced
we	pronounced
you	pronounced
they	pronounced

Present Perfect

I	have	pronounced
you	have	pronounced
he/she/it	has	pronounced
we	have	pronounced
you	have	pronounced
they	have	pronounced

Past Perfect

I	had	pronounced
you	had	pronounced
he/she/it	had	pronounced
we	had	pronounced
you	had	pronounced
they	had	pronounced

Will-Future

I	will	pronounce
you	will	pronounce
he/she/it	will	pronounce
we	will	pronounce
you	will	pronounce
they	will	pronounce

Going to-Future

I	am	going to	pronounce
you	are	going to	pronounce
he/she/it	is	going to	pronounce
we	are	going to	pronounce
you	are	going to	pronounce
they	are	going to	pronounce

Future Perfect

I	will have	pronounced
you	will have	pronounced
he/she/it	will have	pronounced
we	will have	pronounced
you	will have	pronounced
they	will have	pronounced

Imperative

pronounce

Impersonal

ing-Form

pronouncing

Past Participle

pronounced

Continuous tenses

Present

I	am	pronouncing
you	are	pronouncing
he/she/it	is	pronouncing
we	are	pronouncing
you	are	pronouncing
they	are	pronouncing

Past

I	was	pronouncing
you	were	pronouncing
he/she/it	was	pronouncing
we	were	pronouncing
you	were	pronouncing
they	were	pronouncing

Present Perfect

I	have been	pronouncing
you	have been	pronouncing
he/she/it	has been	pronouncing
we	have been	pronouncing
you	have been	pronouncing
they	have been	pronouncing

Past Perfect

I	had been	pronouncing
you	had been	pronouncing
he/she/it	had been	pronouncing
we	had been	pronouncing
you	had been	pronouncing
they	had been	pronouncing

Will-Future

I	will be	pronouncing
you	will be	pronouncing
he/she/it	will be	pronouncing
we	will be	pronouncing
you	will be	pronouncing
they	will be	pronouncing

Going to-Future

I	am	going to be	pronouncing
you	are	going to be	pronouncing
he/she/it	is	going to be	pronouncing
we	are	going to be	pronouncing
you	are	going to be	pronouncing
they	are	going to be	pronouncing

Future Perfect

I	will have been pronouncing
you	will have been pronouncing
he/she/it	will have been pronouncing
we	will have been pronouncing
you	will have been pronouncing
they	will have been pronouncing

Conditional

I	would	pronounce
you	would	pronounce
he/she/it	would	pronounce
we	would	pronounce
you	would	pronounce
they	would	pronounce

Conditional Past

I	would have	pronounced
you	would have	pronounced
he/she/it	would have	pronounced
we	would have	pronounced
you	would have	pronounced
they	would have	pronounced

propose

vorschlagen

\+ **-ing** → ~~e~~ / + **-d** nicht **-ed**
Regelmäßiges Verb

Simple tenses

Present

I	propose
you	propose
he/she/it	proposes
we	propose
you	propose
they	propose

Past

I	proposed
you	proposed
he/she/it	proposed
we	proposed
you	proposed
they	proposed

Present Perfect

I	have	proposed
you	have	proposed
he/she/it	has	proposed
we	have	proposed
you	have	proposed
they	have	proposed

Past Perfect

I	had	proposed
you	had	proposed
he/she/it	had	proposed
we	had	proposed
you	had	proposed
they	had	proposed

Will-Future

I	will	propose
you	will	propose
he/she/it	will	propose
we	will	propose
you	will	propose
they	will	propose

Going to-Future

I	am	going to	propose
you	are	going to	propose
he/she/it	is	going to	propose
we	are	going to	propose
you	are	going to	propose
they	are	going to	propose

Future Perfect

I	will have	proposed
you	will have	proposed
he/she/it	will have	proposed
we	will have	proposed
you	will have	proposed
they	will have	proposed

Imperative

propose

Impersonal

ing-Form

proposing

Past Participle

proposed

Continuous tenses

Present

I	am	proposing
you	are	proposing
he/she/it	is	proposing
we	are	proposing
you	are	proposing
they	are	proposing

Past

I	was	proposing
you	were	proposing
he/she/it	was	proposing
we	were	proposing
you	were	proposing
they	were	proposing

Present Perfect

I	have been	proposing
you	have been	proposing
he/she/it	has been	proposing
we	have been	proposing
you	have been	proposing
they	have been	proposing

Past Perfect

I	had been	proposing
you	had been	proposing
he/she/it	had been	proposing
we	had been	proposing
you	had been	proposing
they	had been	proposing

Will-Future

I	will be	proposing
you	will be	proposing
he/she/it	will be	proposing
we	will be	proposing
you	will be	proposing
they	will be	proposing

Going to-Future

I	am	going to be	proposing
you	are	going to be	proposing
he/she/it	is	going to be	proposing
we	are	going to be	proposing
you	are	going to be	proposing
they	are	going to be	proposing

Future Perfect

I	will have been	proposing
you	will have been	proposing
he/she/it	will have been	proposing
we	will have been	proposing
you	will have been	proposing
they	will have been	proposing

Conditional

I	would	propose
you	would	propose
he/she/it	would	propose
we	would	propose
you	would	propose
they	would	propose

Conditional Past

I	would have	proposed
you	would have	proposed
he/she/it	would have	proposed
we	would have	proposed
you	would have	proposed
they	would have	proposed

Simple tenses

Present

I	protect
you	protect
he/she/it	protects
we	protect
you	protect
they	protect

Past

I	protected
you	protected
he/she/it	protected
we	protected
you	protected
they	protected

Present Perfect

I	have	protected
you	have	protected
he/she/it	has	protected
we	have	protected
you	have	protected
they	have	protected

Past Perfect

I	had	protected
you	had	protected
he/she/it	had	protected
we	had	protected
you	had	protected
they	had	protected

Will-Future

I	will	protect
you	will	protect
he/she/it	will	protect
we	will	protect
you	will	protect
they	will	protect

Going to-Future

I	am	going to	protect
you	are	going to	protect
he/she/it	is	going to	protect
we	are	going to	protect
you	are	going to	protect
they	are	going to	protect

Future Perfect

I	will have	protected
you	will have	protected
he/she/it	will have	protected
we	will have	protected
you	will have	protected
they	will have	protected

Imperative

protect

Impersonal

ing-Form

protecting

Past Participle

protected

Continuous tenses

Present

I	am	protecting
you	are	protecting
he/she/it	is	protecting
we	are	protecting
you	are	protecting
they	are	protecting

Past

I	was	protecting
you	were	protecting
he/she/it	was	protecting
we	were	protecting
you	were	protecting
they	were	protecting

Present Perfect

I	have been	protecting
you	have been	protecting
he/she/it	has been	protecting
we	have been	protecting
you	have been	protecting
they	have been	protecting

Past Perfect

I	had been	protecting
you	had been	protecting
he/she/it	had been	protecting
we	had been	protecting
you	had been	protecting
they	had been	protecting

Will-Future

I	will be	protecting
you	will be	protecting
he/she/it	will be	protecting
we	will be	protecting
you	will be	protecting
they	will be	protecting

Going to-Future

I	am	going to be	protecting
you	are	going to be	protecting
he/she/it	is	going to be	protecting
we	are	going to be	protecting
you	are	going to be	protecting
they	are	going to be	protecting

Future Perfect

I	will have been	protecting
you	will have been	protecting
he/she/it	will have been	protecting
we	will have been	protecting
you	will have been	protecting
they	will have been	protecting

Conditional

I	would	protect
you	would	protect
he/she/it	would	protect
we	would	protect
you	would	protect
they	would	protect

Conditional Past

I	would have	protected
you	would have	protected
he/she/it	would have	protected
we	would have	protected
you	would have	protected
they	would have	protected

protest

protestieren

Regelmäßiges Verb

Simple tenses

Present

I	protest
you	protest
he/she/it	protests
we	protest
you	protest
they	protest

Past

I	protested
you	protested
he/she/it	protested
we	protested
you	protested
they	protested

Present Perfect

I	have	protested
you	have	protested
he/she/it	has	protested
we	have	protested
you	have	protested
they	have	protested

Past Perfect

I	had	protested
you	had	protested
he/she/it	had	protested
we	had	protested
you	had	protested
they	had	protested

Will-Future

I	will	protest
you	will	protest
he/she/it	will	protest
we	will	protest
you	will	protest
they	will	protest

Going to-Future

I	am	going to	protest
you	are	going to	protest
he/she/it	is	going to	protest
we	are	going to	protest
you	are	going to	protest
they	are	going to	protest

Future Perfect

I	will have	protested
you	will have	protested
he/she/it	will have	protested
we	will have	protested
you	will have	protested
they	will have	protested

Imperative

protest

Impersonal

ing-Form

protesting

Past Participle

protested

Continuous tenses

Present

I	am	protesting
you	are	protesting
he/she/it	is	protesting
we	are	protesting
you	are	protesting
they	are	protesting

Past

I	was	protesting
you	were	protesting
he/she/it	was	protesting
we	were	protesting
you	were	protesting
they	were	protesting

Present Perfect

I	have been	protesting
you	have been	protesting
he/she/it	has been	protesting
we	have been	protesting
you	have been	protesting
they	have been	protesting

Past Perfect

I	had been	protesting
you	had been	protesting
he/she/it	had been	protesting
we	had been	protesting
you	had been	protesting
they	had been	protesting

Will-Future

I	will be	protesting
you	will be	protesting
he/she/it	will be	protesting
we	will be	protesting
you	will be	protesting
they	will be	protesting

Going to-Future

I	am	going to be	protesting
you	are	going to be	protesting
he/she/it	is	going to be	protesting
we	are	going to be	protesting
you	are	going to be	protesting
they	are	going to be	protesting

Future Perfect

I	will have been	protesting
you	will have been	protesting
he/she/it	will have been	protesting
we	will have been	protesting
you	will have been	protesting
they	will have been	protesting

Conditional

I	would	protest
you	would	protest
he/she/it	would	protest
we	would	protest
you	would	protest
they	would	protest

Conditional Past

I	would have	protested
you	would have	protested
he/she/it	would have	protested
we	would have	protested
you	would have	protested
they	would have	protested

+ **-ing** → ~~e~~ / + **-d** nicht **-ed**
Unregelmäßiges Verb

beweisen

prove
- proved - proved/proven

Simple tenses

Present

I	prove
you	prove
he/she/it	proves
we	prove
you	prove
they	prove

Past

I	proved
you	proved
he/she/it	proved
we	proved
you	proved
they	proved

Present Perfect

I	have	proved | proven
you	have	proved | proven
he/she/it	has	proved | proven
we	have	proved | proven
you	have	proved | proven
they	have	proved | proven

Past Perfect

I	had	proved | proven
you	had	proved | proven
he/she/it	had	proved | proven
we	had	proved | proven
you	had	proved | proven
they	had	proved | proven

Will-Future

I	will	prove
you	will	prove
he/she/it	will	prove
we	will	prove
you	will	prove
they	will	prove

Going to-Future

I	am	going to	prove
you	are	going to	prove
he/she/it	is	going to	prove
we	are	going to	prove
you	are	going to	prove
they	are	going to	prove

Future Perfect

I	will have	proved | proven
you	will have	proved | proven
he/she/it	will have	proved | proven
we	will have	proved | proven
you	will have	proved | proven
they	will have	proved | proven

Imperative

prove

Impersonal

ing-Form

proving

Past Participle

proved | proven

Continuous tenses

Present

I	am	proving
you	are	proving
he/she/it	is	proving
we	are	proving
you	are	proving
they	are	proving

Past

I	was	proving
you	were	proving
he/she/it	was	proving
we	were	proving
you	were	proving
they	were	proving

Present Perfect

I	have been	proving
you	have been	proving
he/she/it	has been	proving
we	have been	proving
you	have been	proving
they	have been	proving

Past Perfect

I	had been	proving
you	had been	proving
he/she/it	had been	proving
we	had been	proving
you	had been	proving
they	had been	proving

Will-Future

I	will be	proving
you	will be	proving
he/she/it	will be	proving
we	will be	proving
you	will be	proving
they	will be	proving

Going to-Future

I	am	going to be	proving
you	are	going to be	proving
he/she/it	is	going to be	proving
we	are	going to be	proving
you	are	going to be	proving
they	are	going to be	proving

Future Perfect

I	will have been	proving
you	will have been	proving
he/she/it	will have been	proving
we	will have been	proving
you	will have been	proving
they	will have been	proving

Conditional

I	would	prove
you	would	prove
he/she/it	would	prove
we	would	prove
you	would	prove
they	would	prove

Conditional Past

I	would have	proved | proven
you	would have	proved | proven
he/she/it	would have	proved | proven
we	would have	proved | proven
you	would have	proved | proven
they	would have	proved | proven

provide

bereitstellen

+ **-ing** → ~~e~~ / + **-d** nicht **-ed**
Regelmäßiges Verb

Simple tenses

Present

I	provide
you	provide
he/she/it	provides
we	provide
you	provide
they	provide

Past

I	provided
you	provided
he/she/it	provided
we	provided
you	provided
they	provided

Present Perfect

I	have	provided
you	have	provided
he/she/it	has	provided
we	have	provided
you	have	provided
they	have	provided

Past Perfect

I	had	provided
you	had	provided
he/she/it	had	provided
we	had	provided
you	had	provided
they	had	provided

Will-Future

I	will	provide
you	will	provide
he/she/it	will	provide
we	will	provide
you	will	provide
they	will	provide

Going to-Future

I	am	going to	provide
you	are	going to	provide
he/she/it	is	going to	provide
we	are	going to	provide
you	are	going to	provide
they	are	going to	provide

Future Perfect

I	will have	provided
you	will have	provided
he/she/it	will have	provided
we	will have	provided
you	will have	provided
they	will have	provided

Imperative

provide

Impersonal

ing-Form

providing

Past Participle

provided

Continuous tenses

Present

I	am	providing
you	are	providing
he/she/it	is	providing
we	are	providing
you	are	providing
they	are	providing

Past

I	was	providing
you	were	providing
he/she/it	was	providing
we	were	providing
you	were	providing
they	were	providing

Present Perfect

I	have been	providing
you	have been	providing
he/she/it	has been	providing
we	have been	providing
you	have been	providing
they	have been	providing

Past Perfect

I	had been	providing
you	had been	providing
he/she/it	had been	providing
we	had been	providing
you	had been	providing
they	had been	providing

Will-Future

I	will be	providing
you	will be	providing
he/she/it	will be	providing
we	will be	providing
you	will be	providing
they	will be	providing

Going to-Future

I	am	going to be	providing
you	are	going to be	providing
he/she/it	is	going to be	providing
we	are	going to be	providing
you	are	going to be	providing
they	are	going to be	providing

Future Perfect

I	will have been	providing
you	will have been	providing
he/she/it	will have been	providing
we	will have been	providing
you	will have been	providing
they	will have been	providing

Conditional

I	would	provide
you	would	provide
he/she/it	would	provide
we	would	provide
you	would	provide
they	would	provide

Conditional Past

I	would have	provided
you	would have	provided
he/she/it	would have	provided
we	would have	provided
you	would have	provided
they	would have	provided

Simple tenses

Present

I	publish
you	publish
he/she/it	publishes
we	publish
you	publish
they	publish

Past

I	published
you	published
he/she/it	published
we	published
you	published
they	published

Present Perfect

I	have	published
you	have	published
he/she/it	has	published
we	have	published
you	have	published
they	have	published

Past Perfect

I	had	published
you	had	published
he/she/it	had	published
we	had	published
you	had	published
they	had	published

Will-Future

I	will	publish
you	will	publish
he/she/it	will	publish
we	will	publish
you	will	publish
they	will	publish

Going to-Future

I	am	going to	publish
you	are	going to	publish
he/she/it	is	going to	publish
we	are	going to	publish
you	are	going to	publish
they	are	going to	publish

Future Perfect

I	will have	published
you	will have	published
he/she/it	will have	published
we	will have	published
you	will have	published
they	will have	published

Imperative

publish

Impersonal

ing-Form

publishing

Past Participle

published

Continuous tenses

Present

I	am	publishing
you	are	publishing
he/she/it	is	publishing
we	are	publishing
you	are	publishing
they	are	publishing

Past

I	was	publishing
you	were	publishing
he/she/it	was	publishing
we	were	publishing
you	were	publishing
they	were	publishing

Present Perfect

I	have	been	publishing
you	have	been	publishing
he/she/it	has	been	publishing
we	have	been	publishing
you	have	been	publishing
they	have	been	publishing

Past Perfect

I	had been	publishing
you	had been	publishing
he/she/it	had been	publishing
we	had been	publishing
you	had been	publishing
they	had been	publishing

Will-Future

I	will be	publishing
you	will be	publishing
he/she/it	will be	publishing
we	will be	publishing
you	will be	publishing
they	will be	publishing

Going to-Future

I	am	going to be	publishing
you	are	going to be	publishing
he/she/it	is	going to be	publishing
we	are	going to be	publishing
you	are	going to be	publishing
they	are	going to be	publishing

Future Perfect

I	will have been	publishing
you	will have been	publishing
he/she/it	will have been	publishing
we	will have been	publishing
you	will have been	publishing
they	will have been	publishing

Conditional

I	would	publish
you	would	publish
he/she/it	would	publish
we	would	publish
you	would	publish
they	would	publish

Conditional Past

I	would have	published
you	would have	published
he/she/it	would have	published
we	would have	published
you	would have	published
they	would have	published

punish

bestrafen

\+ **-es** in 3. Person Singular
Regelmäßiges Verb

Simple tenses

Present

I	punish
you	punish
he/she/it	punishes
we	punish
you	punish
they	punish

Past

I	punished
you	punished
he/she/it	punished
we	punished
you	punished
they	punished

Present Perfect

I	have	punished
you	have	punished
he/she/it	has	punished
we	have	punished
you	have	punished
they	have	punished

Past Perfect

I	had	punished
you	had	punished
he/she/it	had	punished
we	had	punished
you	had	punished
they	had	punished

Will-Future

I	will	punish
you	will	punish
he/she/it	will	punish
we	will	punish
you	will	punish
they	will	punish

Going to-Future

I	am	going to	punish
you	are	going to	punish
he/she/it	is	going to	punish
we	are	going to	punish
you	are	going to	punish
they	are	going to	punish

Future Perfect

I	will have	punished
you	will have	punished
he/she/it	will have	punished
we	will have	punished
you	will have	punished
they	will have	punished

Imperative

punish

Impersonal

ing-Form

punishing

Past Participle

punished

Continuous tenses

Present

I	am	punishing
you	are	punishing
he/she/it	is	punishing
we	are	punishing
you	are	punishing
they	are	punishing

Past

I	was	punishing
you	were	punishing
he/she/it	was	punishing
we	were	punishing
you	were	punishing
they	were	punishing

Present Perfect

I	have been	punishing
you	have been	punishing
he/she/it	has been	punishing
we	have been	punishing
you	have been	punishing
they	have been	punishing

Past Perfect

I	had been	punishing
you	had been	punishing
he/she/it	had been	punishing
we	had been	punishing
you	had been	punishing
they	had been	punishing

Will-Future

I	will be	punishing
you	will be	punishing
he/she/it	will be	punishing
we	will be	punishing
you	will be	punishing
they	will be	punishing

Going to-Future

I	am	going to be	punishing
you	are	going to be	punishing
he/she/it	is	going to be	punishing
we	are	going to be	punishing
you	are	going to be	punishing
they	are	going to be	punishing

Future Perfect

I	will have been	punishing
you	will have been	punishing
he/she/it	will have been	punishing
we	will have been	punishing
you	will have been	punishing
they	will have been	punishing

Conditional

I	would	punish
you	would	punish
he/she/it	would	punish
we	would	punish
you	would	punish
they	would	punish

Conditional Past

I	would have	punished
you	would have	punished
he/she/it	would have	punished
we	would have	punished
you	would have	punished
they	would have	punished

Simple tenses

Present

I	push
you	push
he/she/it	pushes
we	push
you	push
they	push

Past

I	pushed
you	pushed
he/she/it	pushed
we	pushed
you	pushed
they	pushed

Present Perfect

I	have	pushed
you	have	pushed
he/she/it	has	pushed
we	have	pushed
you	have	pushed
they	have	pushed

Past Perfect

I	had	pushed
you	had	pushed
he/she/it	had	pushed
we	had	pushed
you	had	pushed
they	had	pushed

Will-Future

I	will	push
you	will	push
he/she/it	will	push
we	will	push
you	will	push
they	will	push

Going to-Future

I	am	going to	push
you	are	going to	push
he/she/it	is	going to	push
we	are	going to	push
you	are	going to	push
they	are	going to	push

Future Perfect

I	will have	pushed
you	will have	pushed
he/she/it	will have	pushed
we	will have	pushed
you	will have	pushed
they	will have	pushed

Imperative

push

Impersonal

ing-Form

pushing

Past Participle

pushed

Continuous tenses

Present

I	am	pushing
you	are	pushing
he/she/it	is	pushing
we	are	pushing
you	are	pushing
they	are	pushing

Past

I	was	pushing
you	were	pushing
he/she/it	was	pushing
we	were	pushing
you	were	pushing
they	were	pushing

Present Perfect

I	have	been	pushing
you	have	been	pushing
he/she/it	has	been	pushing
we	have	been	pushing
you	have	been	pushing
they	have	been	pushing

Past Perfect

I	had been	pushing
you	had been	pushing
he/she/it	had been	pushing
we	had been	pushing
you	had been	pushing
they	had been	pushing

Will-Future

I	will be	pushing
you	will be	pushing
he/she/it	will be	pushing
we	will be	pushing
you	will be	pushing
they	will be	pushing

Going to-Future

I	am	going to be	pushing
you	are	going to be	pushing
he/she/it	is	going to be	pushing
we	are	going to be	pushing
you	are	going to be	pushing
they	are	going to be	pushing

Future Perfect

I	will have been	pushing
you	will have been	pushing
he/she/it	will have been	pushing
we	will have been	pushing
you	will have been	pushing
they	will have been	pushing

Conditional

I	would	push
you	would	push
he/she/it	would	push
we	would	push
you	would	push
they	would	push

Conditional Past

I	would have	pushed
you	would have	pushed
he/she/it	would have	pushed
we	would have	pushed
you	would have	pushed
they	would have	pushed

put
- put - put

stellen

Konsonantenverdopplung
Unregelmäßiges Verb

Simple tenses

Present

I	put
you	put
he/she/it	puts
we	put
you	put
they	put

Past

I	put
you	put
he/she/it	put
we	put
you	put
they	put

Present Perfect

I	have	put
you	have	put
he/she/it	has	put
we	have	put
you	have	put
they	have	put

Past Perfect

I	had	put
you	had	put
he/she/it	had	put
we	had	put
you	had	put
they	had	put

Will-Future

I	will	put
you	will	put
he/she/it	will	put
we	will	put
you	will	put
they	will	put

Going to-Future

I	am	going to	put
you	are	going to	put
he/she/it	is	going to	put
we	are	going to	put
you	are	going to	put
they	are	going to	put

Future Perfect

I	will have	put
you	will have	put
he/she/it	will have	put
we	will have	put
you	will have	put
they	will have	put

Imperative

put

Impersonal

ing-Form

putting

Past Participle

put

Continuous tenses

Present

I	am	putting
you	are	putting
he/she/it	is	putting
we	are	putting
you	are	putting
they	are	putting

Past

I	was	putting
you	were	putting
he/she/it	was	putting
we	were	putting
you	were	putting
they	were	putting

Present Perfect

I	have been	putting
you	have been	putting
he/she/it	has been	putting
we	have been	putting
you	have been	putting
they	have been	putting

Past Perfect

I	had been	putting
you	had been	putting
he/she/it	had been	putting
we	had been	putting
you	had been	putting
they	had been	putting

Will-Future

I	will be	putting
you	will be	putting
he/she/it	will be	putting
we	will be	putting
you	will be	putting
they	will be	putting

Going to-Future

I	am	going to be	putting
you	are	going to be	putting
he/she/it	is	going to be	putting
we	are	going to be	putting
you	are	going to be	putting
they	are	going to be	putting

Future Perfect

I	will have been	putting
you	will have been	putting
he/she/it	will have been	putting
we	will have been	putting
you	will have been	putting
they	will have been	putting

Conditional

I	would	put
you	would	put
he/she/it	would	put
we	would	put
you	would	put
they	would	put

Conditional Past

I	would have	put
you	would have	put
he/she/it	would have	put
we	would have	put
you	would have	put
they	would have	put

-y → -ie vor **-s** / **-y → -i** vor **-ed**
Regelmäßiges Verb

qualifizieren

qualify

Simple tenses

Present

I	qualify
you	qualify
he/she/it	qualifies
we	qualify
you	qualify
they	qualify

Past

I	qualified
you	qualified
he/she/it	qualified
we	qualified
you	qualified
they	qualified

Present Perfect

I	have	qualified
you	have	qualified
he/she/it	has	qualified
we	have	qualified
you	have	qualified
they	have	qualified

Past Perfect

I	had	qualified
you	had	qualified
he/she/it	had	qualified
we	had	qualified
you	had	qualified
they	had	qualified

Will-Future

I	will	qualify
you	will	qualify
he/she/it	will	qualify
we	will	qualify
you	will	qualify
they	will	qualify

Going to-Future

I	am	going to	qualify
you	are	going to	qualify
he/she/it	is	going to	qualify
we	are	going to	qualify
you	are	going to	qualify
they	are	going to	qualify

Future Perfect

I	will have	qualified
you	will have	qualified
he/she/it	will have	qualified
we	will have	qualified
you	will have	qualified
they	will have	qualified

Imperative

qualify

Impersonal

ing-Form

qualifying

Past Participle

qualified

Continuous tenses

Present

I	am	qualifying
you	are	qualifying
he/she/it	is	qualifying
we	are	qualifying
you	are	qualifying
they	are	qualifying

Past

I	was	qualifying
you	were	qualifying
he/she/it	was	qualifying
we	were	qualifying
you	were	qualifying
they	were	qualifying

Present Perfect

I	have been	qualifying
you	have been	qualifying
he/she/it	has been	qualifying
we	have been	qualifying
you	have been	qualifying
they	have been	qualifying

Past Perfect

I	had been	qualifying
you	had been	qualifying
he/she/it	had been	qualifying
we	had been	qualifying
you	had been	qualifying
they	had been	qualifying

Will-Future

I	will be	qualifying
you	will be	qualifying
he/she/it	will be	qualifying
we	will be	qualifying
you	will be	qualifying
they	will be	qualifying

Going to-Future

I	am	going to be	qualifying
you	are	going to be	qualifying
he/she/it	is	going to be	qualifying
we	are	going to be	qualifying
you	are	going to be	qualifying
they	are	going to be	qualifying

Future Perfect

I	will have been	qualifying
you	will have been	qualifying
he/she/it	will have been	qualifying
we	will have been	qualifying
you	will have been	qualifying
they	will have been	qualifying

Conditional

I	would	qualify
you	would	qualify
he/she/it	would	qualify
we	would	qualify
you	would	qualify
they	would	qualify

Conditional Past

I	would have	qualified
you	would have	qualified
he/she/it	would have	qualified
we	would have	qualified
you	would have	qualified
they	would have	qualified

question

befragen

Regelmäßiges Verb

Simple tenses

Present

I	question
you	question
he/she/it	questions
we	question
you	question
they	question

Past

I	questioned
you	questioned
he/she/it	questioned
we	questioned
you	questioned
they	questioned

Present Perfect

I	have	questioned
you	have	questioned
he/she/it	has	questioned
we	have	questioned
you	have	questioned
they	have	questioned

Past Perfect

I	had	questioned
you	had	questioned
he/she/it	had	questioned
we	had	questioned
you	had	questioned
they	had	questioned

Will-Future

I	will	question
you	will	question
he/she/it	will	question
we	will	question
you	will	question
they	will	question

Going to-Future

I	am	going to	question
you	are	going to	question
he/she/it	is	going to	question
we	are	going to	question
you	are	going to	question
they	are	going to	question

Future Perfect

I	will have	questioned
you	will have	questioned
he/she/it	will have	questioned
we	will have	questioned
you	will have	questioned
they	will have	questioned

Imperative

question

Impersonal

ing-Form

questioning

Past Participle

questioned

Continuous tenses

Present

I	am	questioning
you	are	questioning
he/she/it	is	questioning
we	are	questioning
you	are	questioning
they	are	questioning

Past

I	was	questioning
you	were	questioning
he/she/it	was	questioning
we	were	questioning
you	were	questioning
they	were	questioning

Present Perfect

I	have	been	questioning
you	have	been	questioning
he/she/it	has	been	questioning
we	have	been	questioning
you	have	been	questioning
they	have	been	questioning

Past Perfect

I	had been	questioning
you	had been	questioning
he/she/it	had been	questioning
we	had been	questioning
you	had been	questioning
they	had been	questioning

Will-Future

I	will be	questioning
you	will be	questioning
he/she/it	will be	questioning
we	will be	questioning
you	will be	questioning
they	will be	questioning

Going to-Future

I	am	going to be	questioning
you	are	going to be	questioning
he/she/it	is	going to be	questioning
we	are	going to be	questioning
you	are	going to be	questioning
they	are	going to be	questioning

Future Perfect

I	will have been questioning
you	will have been questioning
he/she/it	will have been questioning
we	will have been questioning
you	will have been questioning
they	will have been questioning

Conditional

I	would	question
you	would	question
he/she/it	would	question
we	would	question
you	would	question
they	would	question

Conditional Past

I	would have	questioned
you	would have	questioned
he/she/it	would have	questioned
we	would have	questioned
you	would have	questioned
they	would have	questioned

Konsonantenverdopplung
Unregelmäßiges Verb

aufhören

quit

- quit/quitted - quit/quitted

Simple tenses

Present

I	quit
you	quit
he/she/it	quits
we	quit
you	quit
they	quit

Past

I	quit | quitted
you	quit | quitted
he/she/it	quit | quitted
we	quit | quitted
you	quit | quitted
they	quit | quitted

Present Perfect

I	have	quit | quitted
you	have	quit | quitted
he/she/it	has	quit | quitted
we	have	quit | quitted
you	have	quit | quitted
they	have	quit | quitted

Past Perfect

I	had	quit | quitted
you	had	quit | quitted
he/she/it	had	quit | quitted
we	had	quit | quitted
you	had	quit | quitted
they	had	quit | quitted

Will-Future

I	will	quit
you	will	quit
he/she/it	will	quit
we	will	quit
you	will	quit
they	will	quit

Going to-Future

I	am	going to	quit
you	are	going to	quit
he/she/it	is	going to	quit
we	are	going to	quit
you	are	going to	quit
they	are	going to	quit

Future Perfect

I	will have	quit | quitted
you	will have	quit | quitted
he/she/it	will have	quit | quitted
we	will have	quit | quitted
you	will have	quit | quitted
they	will have	quit | quitted

Imperative

quit

Impersonal

ing-Form

quitting

Past Participle

quit | quitted

Continuous tenses

Present

I	am	quitting
you	are	quitting
he/she/it	is	quitting
we	are	quitting
you	are	quitting
they	are	quitting

Past

I	was	quitting
you	were	quitting
he/she/it	was	quitting
we	were	quitting
you	were	quitting
they	were	quitting

Present Perfect

I	have been	quitting
you	have been	quitting
he/she/it	has been	quitting
we	have been	quitting
you	have been	quitting
they	have been	quitting

Past Perfect

I	had been	quitting
you	had been	quitting
he/she/it	had been	quitting
we	had been	quitting
you	had been	quitting
they	had been	quitting

Will-Future

I	will be	quitting
you	will be	quitting
he/she/it	will be	quitting
we	will be	quitting
you	will be	quitting
they	will be	quitting

Going to-Future

I	am	going to be	quitting
you	are	going to be	quitting
he/she/it	is	going to be	quitting
we	are	going to be	quitting
you	are	going to be	quitting
they	are	going to be	quitting

Future Perfect

I	will have been	quitting
you	will have been	quitting
he/she/it	will have been	quitting
we	will have been	quitting
you	will have been	quitting
they	will have been	quitting

Conditional

I	would	quit
you	would	quit
he/she/it	would	quit
we	would	quit
you	would	quit
they	would	quit

Conditional Past

I	would have	quit | quitted
you	would have	quit | quitted
he/she/it	would have	quit | quitted
we	would have	quit | quitted
you	would have	quit | quitted
they	would have	quit | quitted

quote

zitieren

+ **-ing** → ~~e~~ / + **-d** nicht **-ed**
Regelmäßiges Verb

Simple tenses

Present

I quote
you quote
he/she/it quotes
we quote
you quote
they quote

Past

I quoted
you quoted
he/she/it quoted
we quoted
you quoted
they quoted

Present Perfect

I have quoted
you have quoted
he/she/it has quoted
we have quoted
you have quoted
they have quoted

Past Perfect

I had quoted
you had quoted
he/she/it had quoted
we had quoted
you had quoted
they had quoted

Will-Future

I will quote
you will quote
he/she/it will quote
we will quote
you will quote
they will quote

Going to-Future

I am going to quote
you are going to quote
he/she/it is going to quote
we are going to quote
you are going to quote
they are going to quote

Future Perfect

I will have quoted
you will have quoted
he/she/it will have quoted
we will have quoted
you will have quoted
they will have quoted

Imperative

quote

Impersonal

ing-Form

quoting

Past Participle

quoted

Continuous tenses

Present

I am quoting
you are quoting
he/she/it is quoting
we are quoting
you are quoting
they are quoting

Past

I was quoting
you were quoting
he/she/it was quoting
we were quoting
you were quoting
they were quoting

Present Perfect

I have been quoting
you have been quoting
he/she/it has been quoting
we have been quoting
you have been quoting
they have been quoting

Past Perfect

I had been quoting
you had been quoting
he/she/it had been quoting
we had been quoting
you had been quoting
they had been quoting

Will-Future

I will be quoting
you will be quoting
he/she/it will be quoting
we will be quoting
you will be quoting
they will be quoting

Going to-Future

I am going to be quoting
you are going to be quoting
he/she/it is going to be quoting
we are going to be quoting
you are going to be quoting
they are going to be quoting

Future Perfect

I will have been quoting
you will have been quoting
he/she/it will have been quoting
we will have been quoting
you will have been quoting
they will have been quoting

Conditional

I would quote
you would quote
he/she/it would quote
we would quote
you would quote
they would quote

Conditional Past

I would have quoted
you would have quoted
he/she/it would have quoted
we would have quoted
you would have quoted
they would have quoted

Simple tenses

Present

I	rain
you	rain
he/she/it	rains
we	rain
you	rain
they	rain

Past

I	rained
you	rained
he/she/it	rained
we	rained
you	rained
they	rained

Present Perfect

I	have	rained
you	have	rained
he/she/it	has	rained
we	have	rained
you	have	rained
they	have	rained

Past Perfect

I	had	rained
you	had	rained
he/she/it	had	rained
we	had	rained
you	had	rained
they	had	rained

Will-Future

I	will	rain
you	will	rain
he/she/it	will	rain
we	will	rain
you	will	rain
they	will	rain

Going to-Future

I	am	going to	rain
you	are	going to	rain
he/she/it	is	going to	rain
we	are	going to	rain
you	are	going to	rain
they	are	going to	rain

Future Perfect

I	will have	rained
you	will have	rained
he/she/it	will have	rained
we	will have	rained
you	will have	rained
they	will have	rained

Imperative

rain

Impersonal

ing-Form

raining

Past Participle

rained

Continuous tenses

Present

I	am	raining
you	are	raining
he/she/it	is	raining
we	are	raining
you	are	raining
they	are	raining

Past

I	was	raining
you	were	raining
he/she/it	was	raining
we	were	raining
you	were	raining
they	were	raining

Present Perfect

I	have been	raining
you	have been	raining
he/she/it	has been	raining
we	have been	raining
you	have been	raining
they	have been	raining

Past Perfect

I	had been	raining
you	had been	raining
he/she/it	had been	raining
we	had been	raining
you	had been	raining
they	had been	raining

Will-Future

I	will be	raining
you	will be	raining
he/she/it	will be	raining
we	will be	raining
you	will be	raining
they	will be	raining

Going to-Future

I	am	going to be	raining
you	are	going to be	raining
he/she/it	is	going to be	raining
we	are	going to be	raining
you	are	going to be	raining
they	are	going to be	raining

Future Perfect

I	will have been	raining
you	will have been	raining
he/she/it	will have been	raining
we	will have been	raining
you	will have been	raining
they	will have been	raining

Conditional

I	would	rain
you	would	rain
he/she/it	would	rain
we	would	rain
you	would	rain
they	would	rain

Conditional Past

I	would have	rained
you	would have	rained
he/she/it	would have	rained
we	would have	rained
you	would have	rained
they	would have	rained

raise

heben

+ **-ing** → ~~e~~ / + **-d** nicht **-ed**
Regelmäßiges Verb

Simple tenses

Present

I	raise
you	raise
he/she/it	raises
we	raise
you	raise
they	raise

Past

I	raised
you	raised
he/she/it	raised
we	raised
you	raised
they	raised

Present Perfect

I	have	raised
you	have	raised
he/she/it	has	raised
we	have	raised
you	have	raised
they	have	raised

Past Perfect

I	had	raised
you	had	raised
he/she/it	had	raised
we	had	raised
you	had	raised
they	had	raised

Will-Future

I	will	raise
you	will	raise
he/she/it	will	raise
we	will	raise
you	will	raise
they	will	raise

Going to-Future

I	am	going to	raise
you	are	going to	raise
he/she/it	is	going to	raise
we	are	going to	raise
you	are	going to	raise
they	are	going to	raise

Future Perfect

I	will have	raised
you	will have	raised
he/she/it	will have	raised
we	will have	raised
you	will have	raised
they	will have	raised

Imperative

raise

Impersonal

ing-Form

raising

Past Participle

raised

Continuous tenses

Present

I	am	raising
you	are	raising
he/she/it	is	raising
we	are	raising
you	are	raising
they	are	raising

Past

I	was	raising
you	were	raising
he/she/it	was	raising
we	were	raising
you	were	raising
they	were	raising

Present Perfect

I	have been	raising
you	have been	raising
he/she/it	has been	raising
we	have been	raising
you	have been	raising
they	have been	raising

Past Perfect

I	had been	raising
you	had been	raising
he/she/it	had been	raising
we	had been	raising
you	had been	raising
they	had been	raising

Will-Future

I	will be	raising
you	will be	raising
he/she/it	will be	raising
we	will be	raising
you	will be	raising
they	will be	raising

Going to-Future

I	am	going to be	raising
you	are	going to be	raising
he/she/it	is	going to be	raising
we	are	going to be	raising
you	are	going to be	raising
they	are	going to be	raising

Future Perfect

I	will have been	raising
you	will have been	raising
he/she/it	will have been	raising
we	will have been	raising
you	will have been	raising
they	will have been	raising

Conditional

I	would	raise
you	would	raise
he/she/it	would	raise
we	would	raise
you	would	raise
they	would	raise

Conditional Past

I	would have	raised
you	would have	raised
he/she/it	would have	raised
we	would have	raised
you	would have	raised
they	would have	raised

Simple tenses

Present

I	rate
you	rate
he/she/it	rates
we	rate
you	rate
they	rate

Past

I	rated
you	rated
he/she/it	rated
we	rated
you	rated
they	rated

Present Perfect

I	have	rated
you	have	rated
he/she/it	has	rated
we	have	rated
you	have	rated
they	have	rated

Past Perfect

I	had	rated
you	had	rated
he/she/it	had	rated
we	had	rated
you	had	rated
they	had	rated

Will-Future

I	will	rate
you	will	rate
he/she/it	will	rate
we	will	rate
you	will	rate
they	will	rate

Going to-Future

I	am	going to	rate
you	are	going to	rate
he/she/it	is	going to	rate
we	are	going to	rate
you	are	going to	rate
they	are	going to	rate

Future Perfect

I	will have	rated
you	will have	rated
he/she/it	will have	rated
we	will have	rated
you	will have	rated
they	will have	rated

Imperative

rate

Impersonal

ing-Form

rating

Past Participle

rated

Continuous tenses

Present

I	am	rating
you	are	rating
he/she/it	is	rating
we	are	rating
you	are	rating
they	are	rating

Past

I	was	rating
you	were	rating
he/she/it	was	rating
we	were	rating
you	were	rating
they	were	rating

Present Perfect

I	have been	rating
you	have been	rating
he/she/it	has been	rating
we	have been	rating
you	have been	rating
they	have been	rating

Past Perfect

I	had been	rating
you	had been	rating
he/she/it	had been	rating
we	had been	rating
you	had been	rating
they	had been	rating

Will-Future

I	will be	rating
you	will be	rating
he/she/it	will be	rating
we	will be	rating
you	will be	rating
they	will be	rating

Going to-Future

I	am	going to be	rating
you	are	going to be	rating
he/she/it	is	going to be	rating
we	are	going to be	rating
you	are	going to be	rating
they	are	going to be	rating

Future Perfect

I	will have been	rating
you	will have been	rating
he/she/it	will have been	rating
we	will have been	rating
you	will have been	rating
they	will have been	rating

Conditional

I	would	rate
you	would	rate
he/she/it	would	rate
we	would	rate
you	would	rate
they	would	rate

Conditional Past

I	would have	rated
you	would have	rated
he/she/it	would have	rated
we	would have	rated
you	would have	rated
they	would have	rated

reach

erreichen

\+ **-es** in 3. Person Singular
Regelmäßiges Verb

Simple tenses

Present

I	reach
you	reach
he/she/it	reaches
we	reach
you	reach
they	reach

Past

I	reached
you	reached
he/she/it	reached
we	reached
you	reached
they	reached

Present Perfect

I	have	reached
you	have	reached
he/she/it	has	reached
we	have	reached
you	have	reached
they	have	reached

Past Perfect

I	had	reached
you	had	reached
he/she/it	had	reached
we	had	reached
you	had	reached
they	had	reached

Will-Future

I	will	reach
you	will	reach
he/she/it	will	reach
we	will	reach
you	will	reach
they	will	reach

Going to-Future

I	am	going to	reach
you	are	going to	reach
he/she/it	is	going to	reach
we	are	going to	reach
you	are	going to	reach
they	are	going to	reach

Future Perfect

I	will have	reached
you	will have	reached
he/she/it	will have	reached
we	will have	reached
you	will have	reached
they	will have	reached

Imperative

reach

Impersonal

ing-Form

reaching

Past Participle

reached

Continuous tenses

Present

I	am	reaching
you	are	reaching
he/she/it	is	reaching
we	are	reaching
you	are	reaching
they	are	reaching

Past

I	was	reaching
you	were	reaching
he/she/it	was	reaching
we	were	reaching
you	were	reaching
they	were	reaching

Present Perfect

I	have been	reaching
you	have been	reaching
he/she/it	has been	reaching
we	have been	reaching
you	have been	reaching
they	have been	reaching

Past Perfect

I	had been	reaching
you	had been	reaching
he/she/it	had been	reaching
we	had been	reaching
you	had been	reaching
they	had been	reaching

Will-Future

I	will be	reaching
you	will be	reaching
he/she/it	will be	reaching
we	will be	reaching
you	will be	reaching
they	will be	reaching

Going to-Future

I	am	going to be	reaching
you	are	going to be	reaching
he/she/it	is	going to be	reaching
we	are	going to be	reaching
you	are	going to be	reaching
they	are	going to be	reaching

Future Perfect

I	will have been	reaching
you	will have been	reaching
he/she/it	will have been	reaching
we	will have been	reaching
you	will have been	reaching
they	will have been	reaching

Conditional

I	would	reach
you	would	reach
he/she/it	would	reach
we	would	reach
you	would	reach
they	would	reach

Conditional Past

I	would have	reached
you	would have	reached
he/she/it	would have	reached
we	would have	reached
you	would have	reached
they	would have	reached

Simple tenses

Present

I	react
you	react
he/she/it	reacts
we	react
you	react
they	react

Past

I	reacted
you	reacted
he/she/it	reacted
we	reacted
you	reacted
they	reacted

Present Perfect

I	have	reacted
you	have	reacted
he/she/it	has	reacted
we	have	reacted
you	have	reacted
they	have	reacted

Past Perfect

I	had	reacted
you	had	reacted
he/she/it	had	reacted
we	had	reacted
you	had	reacted
they	had	reacted

Will-Future

I	will	react
you	will	react
he/she/it	will	react
we	will	react
you	will	react
they	will	react

Going to-Future

I	am	going to	react
you	are	going to	react
he/she/it	is	going to	react
we	are	going to	react
you	are	going to	react
they	are	going to	react

Future Perfect

I	will have	reacted
you	will have	reacted
he/she/it	will have	reacted
we	will have	reacted
you	will have	reacted
they	will have	reacted

Imperative

react

Impersonal

ing-Form

reacting

Past Participle

reacted

Continuous tenses

Present

I	am	reacting
you	are	reacting
he/she/it	is	reacting
we	are	reacting
you	are	reacting
they	are	reacting

Past

I	was	reacting
you	were	reacting
he/she/it	was	reacting
we	were	reacting
you	were	reacting
they	were	reacting

Present Perfect

I	have been	reacting
you	have been	reacting
he/she/it	has been	reacting
we	have been	reacting
you	have been	reacting
they	have been	reacting

Past Perfect

I	had been	reacting
you	had been	reacting
he/she/it	had been	reacting
we	had been	reacting
you	had been	reacting
they	had been	reacting

Will-Future

I	will be	reacting
you	will be	reacting
he/she/it	will be	reacting
we	will be	reacting
you	will be	reacting
they	will be	reacting

Going to-Future

I	am	going to be	reacting
you	are	going to be	reacting
he/she/it	is	going to be	reacting
we	are	going to be	reacting
you	are	going to be	reacting
they	are	going to be	reacting

Future Perfect

I	will have been	reacting
you	will have been	reacting
he/she/it	will have been	reacting
we	will have been	reacting
you	will have been	reacting
they	will have been	reacting

Conditional

I	would	react
you	would	react
he/she/it	would	react
we	would	react
you	would	react
they	would	react

Conditional Past

I	would have	reacted
you	would have	reacted
he/she/it	would have	reacted
we	would have	reacted
you	would have	reacted
they	would have	reacted

read
- read - read

lesen

Die *Past Simple*-Form und das Partizip Perfekt werden wie die Farbe rot - *red* ausgesprochen [red]. Unregelmäßiges Verb

Simple tenses

Present

I	read
you	read
he/she/it	reads
we	read
you	read
they	read

Past

I	read
you	read
he/she/it	read
we	read
you	read
they	read

Present Perfect

I	have	read
you	have	read
he/she/it	has	read
we	have	read
you	have	read
they	have	read

Past Perfect

I	had	read
you	had	read
he/she/it	had	read
we	had	read
you	had	read
they	had	read

Will-Future

I	will	read
you	will	read
he/she/it	will	read
we	will	read
you	will	read
they	will	read

Going to-Future

I	am	going to	read
you	are	going to	read
he/she/it	is	going to	read
we	are	going to	read
you	are	going to	read
they	are	going to	read

Future Perfect

I	will have	read
you	will have	read
he/she/it	will have	read
we	will have	read
you	will have	read
they	will have	read

Imperative

read

Impersonal

ing-Form

reading

Past Participle

read

Continuous tenses

Present

I	am	reading
you	are	reading
he/she/it	is	reading
we	are	reading
you	are	reading
they	are	reading

Past

I	was	reading
you	were	reading
he/she/it	was	reading
we	were	reading
you	were	reading
they	were	reading

Present Perfect

I	have been	reading
you	have been	reading
he/she/it	has been	reading
we	have been	reading
you	have been	reading
they	have been	reading

Past Perfect

I	had been	reading
you	had been	reading
he/she/it	had been	reading
we	had been	reading
you	had been	reading
they	had been	reading

Will-Future

I	will be	reading
you	will be	reading
he/she/it	will be	reading
we	will be	reading
you	will be	reading
they	will be	reading

Going to-Future

I	am	going to be	reading
you	are	going to be	reading
he/she/it	is	going to be	reading
we	are	going to be	reading
you	are	going to be	reading
they	are	going to be	reading

Future Perfect

I	will have been	reading
you	will have been	reading
he/she/it	will have been	reading
we	will have been	reading
you	will have been	reading
they	will have been	reading

Conditional

I	would	read
you	would	read
he/she/it	would	read
we	would	read
you	would	read
they	would	read

Conditional Past

I	would have	read
you	would have	read
he/she/it	would have	read
we	would have	read
you	would have	read
they	would have	read

+ **-ing** → ~~e~~ / + **-d** nicht **-ed**
im BE auch **realise**
Regelmäßiges Verb

erkennen

realize

Simple tenses

Present

I	realize
you	realize
he/she/it	realizes
we	realize
you	realize
they	realize

Past

I	realized
you	realized
he/she/it	realized
we	realized
you	realized
they	realized

Present Perfect

I	have	realized
you	have	realized
he/she/it	has	realized
we	have	realized
you	have	realized
they	have	realized

Past Perfect

I	had	realized
you	had	realized
he/she/it	had	realized
we	had	realized
you	had	realized
they	had	realized

Will-Future

I	will	realize
you	will	realize
he/she/it	will	realize
we	will	realize
you	will	realize
they	will	realize

Going to-Future

I	am	going to	realize
you	are	going to	realize
he/she/it	is	going to	realize
we	are	going to	realize
you	are	going to	realize
they	are	going to	realize

Future Perfect

I	will have	realized
you	will have	realized
he/she/it	will have	realized
we	will have	realized
you	will have	realized
they	will have	realized

Imperative

realize

Impersonal

ing-Form

realizing

Past Participle

realized

Continuous tenses

Present

I	am	realizing
you	are	realizing
he/she/it	is	realizing
we	are	realizing
you	are	realizing
they	are	realizing

Past

I	was	realizing
you	were	realizing
he/she/it	was	realizing
we	were	realizing
you	were	realizing
they	were	realizing

Present Perfect

I	have been	realizing
you	have been	realizing
he/she/it	has been	realizing
we	have been	realizing
you	have been	realizing
they	have been	realizing

Past Perfect

I	had been	realizing
you	had been	realizing
he/she/it	had been	realizing
we	had been	realizing
you	had been	realizing
they	had been	realizing

Will-Future

I	will be	realizing
you	will be	realizing
he/she/it	will be	realizing
we	will be	realizing
you	will be	realizing
they	will be	realizing

Going to-Future

I	am	going to be	realizing
you	are	going to be	realizing
he/she/it	is	going to be	realizing
we	are	going to be	realizing
you	are	going to be	realizing
they	are	going to be	realizing

Future Perfect

I	will have been	realizing
you	will have been	realizing
he/she/it	will have been	realizing
we	will have been	realizing
you	will have been	realizing
they	will have been	realizing

Conditional

I	would	realize
you	would	realize
he/she/it	would	realize
we	would	realize
you	would	realize
they	would	realize

Conditional Past

I	would have	realized
you	would have	realized
he/she/it	would have	realized
we	would have	realized
you	would have	realized
they	would have	realized

recall

sich erinnern

Regelmäßiges Verb

Simple tenses

Present

I	recall
you	recall
he/she/it	recalls
we	recall
you	recall
they	recall

Past

I	recalled
you	recalled
he/she/it	recalled
we	recalled
you	recalled
they	recalled

Present Perfect

I	have	recalled
you	have	recalled
he/she/it	has	recalled
we	have	recalled
you	have	recalled
they	have	recalled

Past Perfect

I	had	recalled
you	had	recalled
he/she/it	had	recalled
we	had	recalled
you	had	recalled
they	had	recalled

Will-Future

I	will	recall
you	will	recall
he/she/it	will	recall
we	will	recall
you	will	recall
they	will	recall

Going to-Future

I	am	going to	recall
you	are	going to	recall
he/she/it	is	going to	recall
we	are	going to	recall
you	are	going to	recall
they	are	going to	recall

Future Perfect

I	will have	recalled
you	will have	recalled
he/she/it	will have	recalled
we	will have	recalled
you	will have	recalled
they	will have	recalled

Imperative

recall

Impersonal

ing-Form

recalling

Past Participle

recalled

Continuous tenses

Present

I	am	recalling
you	are	recalling
he/she/it	is	recalling
we	are	recalling
you	are	recalling
they	are	recalling

Past

I	was	recalling
you	were	recalling
he/she/it	was	recalling
we	were	recalling
you	were	recalling
they	were	recalling

Present Perfect

I	have been	recalling
you	have been	recalling
he/she/it	has been	recalling
we	have been	recalling
you	have been	recalling
they	have been	recalling

Past Perfect

I	had been	recalling
you	had been	recalling
he/she/it	had been	recalling
we	had been	recalling
you	had been	recalling
they	had been	recalling

Will-Future

I	will be	recalling
you	will be	recalling
he/she/it	will be	recalling
we	will be	recalling
you	will be	recalling
they	will be	recalling

Going to-Future

I	am	going to be	recalling
you	are	going to be	recalling
he/she/it	is	going to be	recalling
we	are	going to be	recalling
you	are	going to be	recalling
they	are	going to be	recalling

Future Perfect

I	will have been	recalling
you	will have been	recalling
he/she/it	will have been	recalling
we	will have been	recalling
you	will have been	recalling
they	will have been	recalling

Conditional

I	would	recall
you	would	recall
he/she/it	would	recall
we	would	recall
you	would	recall
they	would	recall

Conditional Past

I	would have	recalled
you	would have	recalled
he/she/it	would have	recalled
we	would have	recalled
you	would have	recalled
they	would have	recalled

Simple tenses

Present

I	receive
you	receive
he/she/it	receives
we	receive
you	receive
they	receive

Past

I	received
you	received
he/she/it	received
we	received
you	received
they	received

Present Perfect

I	have	received
you	have	received
he/she/it	has	received
we	have	received
you	have	received
they	have	received

Past Perfect

I	had	received
you	had	received
he/she/it	had	received
we	had	received
you	had	received
they	had	received

Will-Future

I	will	receive
you	will	receive
he/she/it	will	receive
we	will	receive
you	will	receive
they	will	receive

Going to-Future

I	am	going to	receive
you	are	going to	receive
he/she/it	is	going to	receive
we	are	going to	receive
you	are	going to	receive
they	are	going to	receive

Future Perfect

I	will have	received
you	will have	received
he/she/it	will have	received
we	will have	received
you	will have	received
they	will have	received

Imperative

receive

Impersonal

ing-Form

receiving

Past Participle

received

Continuous tenses

Present

I	am	receiving
you	are	receiving
he/she/it	is	receiving
we	are	receiving
you	are	receiving
they	are	receiving

Past

I	was	receiving
you	were	receiving
he/she/it	was	receiving
we	were	receiving
you	were	receiving
they	were	receiving

Present Perfect

I	have	been	receiving
you	have	been	receiving
he/she/it	has	been	receiving
we	have	been	receiving
you	have	been	receiving
they	have	been	receiving

Past Perfect

I	had been	receiving
you	had been	receiving
he/she/it	had been	receiving
we	had been	receiving
you	had been	receiving
they	had been	receiving

Will-Future

I	will be	receiving
you	will be	receiving
he/she/it	will be	receiving
we	will be	receiving
you	will be	receiving
they	will be	receiving

Going to-Future

I	am	going to be	receiving
you	are	going to be	receiving
he/she/it	is	going to be	receiving
we	are	going to be	receiving
you	are	going to be	receiving
they	are	going to be	receiving

Future Perfect

I	will have been	receiving
you	will have been	receiving
he/she/it	will have been	receiving
we	will have been	receiving
you	will have been	receiving
they	will have been	receiving

Conditional

I	would	receive
you	would	receive
he/she/it	would	receive
we	would	receive
you	would	receive
they	would	receive

Conditional Past

I	would have	received
you	would have	received
he/she/it	would have	received
we	would have	received
you	would have	received
they	would have	received

recognize

erkennen

+ **-ing** → ~~e~~ / + **-d** nicht **-ed**
im BE auch **recognise**
Regelmäßiges Verb

Simple tenses

Present

I	recognize
you	recognize
he/she/it	recognizes
we	recognize
you	recognize
they	recognize

Past

I	recognized
you	recognized
he/she/it	recognized
we	recognized
you	recognized
they	recognized

Present Perfect

I	have	recognized
you	have	recognized
he/she/it	has	recognized
we	have	recognized
you	have	recognized
they	have	recognized

Past Perfect

I	had	recognized
you	had	recognized
he/she/it	had	recognized
we	had	recognized
you	had	recognized
they	had	recognized

Will-Future

I	will	recognize
you	will	recognize
he/she/it	will	recognize
we	will	recognize
you	will	recognize
they	will	recognize

Going to-Future

I	am	going to	recognize
you	are	going to	recognize
he/she/it	is	going to	recognize
we	are	going to	recognize
you	are	going to	recognize
they	are	going to	recognize

Future Perfect

I	will have	recognized
you	will have	recognized
he/she/it	will have	recognized
we	will have	recognized
you	will have	recognized
they	will have	recognized

Imperative

recognize

Impersonal

ing-Form

recognizing

Past Participle

recognized

Continuous tenses

Present

I	am	recognizing
you	are	recognizing
he/she/it	is	recognizing
we	are	recognizing
you	are	recognizing
they	are	recognizing

Past

I	was	recognizing
you	were	recognizing
he/she/it	was	recognizing
we	were	recognizing
you	were	recognizing
they	were	recognizing

Present Perfect

I	have been	recognizing
you	have been	recognizing
he/she/it	has been	recognizing
we	have been	recognizing
you	have been	recognizing
they	have been	recognizing

Past Perfect

I	had been	recognizing
you	had been	recognizing
he/she/it	had been	recognizing
we	had been	recognizing
you	had been	recognizing
they	had been	recognizing

Will-Future

I	will be	recognizing
you	will be	recognizing
he/she/it	will be	recognizing
we	will be	recognizing
you	will be	recognizing
they	will be	recognizing

Going to-Future

I	am	going to be	recognizing
you	are	going to be	recognizing
he/she/it	is	going to be	recognizing
we	are	going to be	recognizing
you	are	going to be	recognizing
they	are	going to be	recognizing

Future Perfect

I	will have been recognizing
you	will have been recognizing
he/she/it	will have been recognizing
we	will have been recognizing
you	will have been recognizing
they	will have been recognizing

Conditional

I	would	recognize
you	would	recognize
he/she/it	would	recognize
we	would	recognize
you	would	recognize
they	would	recognize

Conditional Past

I	would have	recognized
you	would have	recognized
he/she/it	would have	recognized
we	would have	recognized
you	would have	recognized
they	would have	recognized

Simple tenses

Present

I	recommend
you	recommend
he/she/it	recommends
we	recommend
you	recommend
they	recommend

Past

I	recommended
you	recommended
he/she/it	recommended
we	recommended
you	recommended
they	recommended

Present Perfect

I	have	recommended
you	have	recommended
he/she/it	has	recommended
we	have	recommended
you	have	recommended
they	have	recommended

Past Perfect

I	had	recommended
you	had	recommended
he/she/it	had	recommended
we	had	recommended
you	had	recommended
they	had	recommended

Will-Future

I	will	recommend
you	will	recommend
he/she/it	will	recommend
we	will	recommend
you	will	recommend
they	will	recommend

Going to-Future

I	am	going to	recommend
you	are	going to	recommend
he/she/it	is	going to	recommend
we	are	going to	recommend
you	are	going to	recommend
they	are	going to	recommend

Future Perfect

I	will have	recommended
you	will have	recommended
he/she/it	will have	recommended
we	will have	recommended
you	will have	recommended
they	will have	recommended

Imperative

recommend

Impersonal

ing-Form

recommending

Past Participle

recommended

Continuous tenses

Present

I	am	recommending
you	are	recommending
he/she/it	is	recommending
we	are	recommending
you	are	recommending
they	are	recommending

Past

I	was	recommending
you	were	recommending
he/she/it	was	recommending
we	were	recommending
you	were	recommending
they	were	recommending

Present Perfect

I	have been	recommending
you	have been	recommending
he/she/it	has been	recommending
we	have been	recommending
you	have been	recommending
they	have been	recommending

Past Perfect

I	had been	recommending
you	had been	recommending
he/she/it	had been	recommending
we	had been	recommending
you	had been	recommending
they	had been	recommending

Will-Future

I	will be	recommending
you	will be	recommending
he/she/it	will be	recommending
we	will be	recommending
you	will be	recommending
they	will be	recommending

Going to-Future

I	am	going to be	recommending
you	are	going to be	recommending
he/she/it	is	going to be	recommending
we	are	going to be	recommending
you	are	going to be	recommending
they	are	going to be	recommending

Future Perfect

I	will have been	recommending
you	will have been	recommending
he/she/it	will have been	recommending
we	will have been	recommending
you	will have been	recommending
they	will have been	recommending

Conditional

I	would	recommend
you	would	recommend
he/she/it	would	recommend
we	would	recommend
you	would	recommend
they	would	recommend

Conditional Past

I	would have	recommended
you	would have	recommended
he/she/it	would have	recommended
we	would have	recommended
you	would have	recommended
they	would have	recommended

record

aufzeichnen

Regelmäßiges Verb

Simple tenses

Present

I	record
you	record
he/she/it	records
we	record
you	record
they	record

Past

I	recorded
you	recorded
he/she/it	recorded
we	recorded
you	recorded
they	recorded

Present Perfect

I	have	recorded
you	have	recorded
he/she/it	has	recorded
we	have	recorded
you	have	recorded
they	have	recorded

Past Perfect

I	had	recorded
you	had	recorded
he/she/it	had	recorded
we	had	recorded
you	had	recorded
they	had	recorded

Will-Future

I	will	record
you	will	record
he/she/it	will	record
we	will	record
you	will	record
they	will	record

Going to-Future

I	am	going to	record
you	are	going to	record
he/she/it	is	going to	record
we	are	going to	record
you	are	going to	record
they	are	going to	record

Future Perfect

I	will have	recorded
you	will have	recorded
he/she/it	will have	recorded
we	will have	recorded
you	will have	recorded
they	will have	recorded

Imperative

record

Impersonal

ing-Form

recording

Past Participle

recorded

Continuous tenses

Present

I	am	recording
you	are	recording
he/she/it	is	recording
we	are	recording
you	are	recording
they	are	recording

Past

I	was	recording
you	were	recording
he/she/it	was	recording
we	were	recording
you	were	recording
they	were	recording

Present Perfect

I	have been	recording
you	have been	recording
he/she/it	has been	recording
we	have been	recording
you	have been	recording
they	have been	recording

Past Perfect

I	had been	recording
you	had been	recording
he/she/it	had been	recording
we	had been	recording
you	had been	recording
they	had been	recording

Will-Future

I	will be	recording
you	will be	recording
he/she/it	will be	recording
we	will be	recording
you	will be	recording
they	will be	recording

Going to-Future

I	am	going to be	recording
you	are	going to be	recording
he/she/it	is	going to be	recording
we	are	going to be	recording
you	are	going to be	recording
they	are	going to be	recording

Future Perfect

I	will have been	recording
you	will have been	recording
he/she/it	will have been	recording
we	will have been	recording
you	will have been	recording
they	will have been	recording

Conditional

I	would	record
you	would	record
he/she/it	would	record
we	would	record
you	would	record
they	would	record

Conditional Past

I	would have	recorded
you	would have	recorded
he/she/it	would have	recorded
we	would have	recorded
you	would have	recorded
they	would have	recorded

Simple tenses

Present

I	recover
you	recover
he/she/it	recovers
we	recover
you	recover
they	recover

Past

I	recovered
you	recovered
he/she/it	recovered
we	recovered
you	recovered
they	recovered

Present Perfect

I	have	recovered
you	have	recovered
he/she/it	has	recovered
we	have	recovered
you	have	recovered
they	have	recovered

Past Perfect

I	had	recovered
you	had	recovered
he/she/it	had	recovered
we	had	recovered
you	had	recovered
they	had	recovered

Will-Future

I	will	recover
you	will	recover
he/she/it	will	recover
we	will	recover
you	will	recover
they	will	recover

Going to-Future

I	am	going to	recover
you	are	going to	recover
he/she/it	is	going to	recover
we	are	going to	recover
you	are	going to	recover
they	are	going to	recover

Future Perfect

I	will have	recovered
you	will have	recovered
he/she/it	will have	recovered
we	will have	recovered
you	will have	recovered
they	will have	recovered

Imperative

recover

Impersonal

ing-Form

recovering

Past Participle

recovered

Continuous tenses

Present

I	am	recovering
you	are	recovering
he/she/it	is	recovering
we	are	recovering
you	are	recovering
they	are	recovering

Past

I	was	recovering
you	were	recovering
he/she/it	was	recovering
we	were	recovering
you	were	recovering
they	were	recovering

Present Perfect

I	have been	recovering
you	have been	recovering
he/she/it	has been	recovering
we	have been	recovering
you	have been	recovering
they	have been	recovering

Past Perfect

I	had been	recovering
you	had been	recovering
he/she/it	had been	recovering
we	had been	recovering
you	had been	recovering
they	had been	recovering

Will-Future

I	will be	recovering
you	will be	recovering
he/she/it	will be	recovering
we	will be	recovering
you	will be	recovering
they	will be	recovering

Going to-Future

I	am	going to be	recovering
you	are	going to be	recovering
he/she/it	is	going to be	recovering
we	are	going to be	recovering
you	are	going to be	recovering
they	are	going to be	recovering

Future Perfect

I	will have been	recovering
you	will have been	recovering
he/she/it	will have been	recovering
we	will have been	recovering
you	will have been	recovering
they	will have been	recovering

Conditional

I	would	recover
you	would	recover
he/she/it	would	recover
we	would	recover
you	would	recover
they	would	recover

Conditional Past

I	would have	recovered
you	would have	recovered
he/she/it	would have	recovered
we	would have	recovered
you	would have	recovered
they	would have	recovered

reduce

verringern

+ **-ing** → ~~e~~ / + **-d** nicht **-ed**
Regelmäßiges Verb

Simple tenses

Present

I	reduce
you	reduce
he/she/it	reduces
we	reduce
you	reduce
they	reduce

Past

I	reduced
you	reduced
he/she/it	reduced
we	reduced
you	reduced
they	reduced

Present Perfect

I	have	reduced
you	have	reduced
he/she/it	has	reduced
we	have	reduced
you	have	reduced
they	have	reduced

Past Perfect

I	had	reduced
you	had	reduced
he/she/it	had	reduced
we	had	reduced
you	had	reduced
they	had	reduced

Will-Future

I	will	reduce
you	will	reduce
he/she/it	will	reduce
we	will	reduce
you	will	reduce
they	will	reduce

Going to-Future

I	am	going to	reduce
you	are	going to	reduce
he/she/it	is	going to	reduce
we	are	going to	reduce
you	are	going to	reduce
they	are	going to	reduce

Future Perfect

I	will have	reduced
you	will have	reduced
he/she/it	will have	reduced
we	will have	reduced
you	will have	reduced
they	will have	reduced

Imperative

reduce

Impersonal

ing-Form

reducing

Past Participle

reduced

Continuous tenses

Present

I	am	reducing
you	are	reducing
he/she/it	is	reducing
we	are	reducing
you	are	reducing
they	are	reducing

Past

I	was	reducing
you	were	reducing
he/she/it	was	reducing
we	were	reducing
you	were	reducing
they	were	reducing

Present Perfect

I	have been	reducing
you	have been	reducing
he/she/it	has been	reducing
we	have been	reducing
you	have been	reducing
they	have been	reducing

Past Perfect

I	had been	reducing
you	had been	reducing
he/she/it	had been	reducing
we	had been	reducing
you	had been	reducing
they	had been	reducing

Will-Future

I	will be	reducing
you	will be	reducing
he/she/it	will be	reducing
we	will be	reducing
you	will be	reducing
they	will be	reducing

Going to-Future

I	am	going to be	reducing
you	are	going to be	reducing
he/she/it	is	going to be	reducing
we	are	going to be	reducing
you	are	going to be	reducing
they	are	going to be	reducing

Future Perfect

I	will have been	reducing
you	will have been	reducing
he/she/it	will have been	reducing
we	will have been	reducing
you	will have been	reducing
they	will have been	reducing

Conditional

I	would	reduce
you	would	reduce
he/she/it	would	reduce
we	would	reduce
you	would	reduce
they	would	reduce

Conditional Past

I	would have	reduced
you	would have	reduced
he/she/it	would have	reduced
we	would have	reduced
you	would have	reduced
they	would have	reduced

Simple tenses

Present

I	reflect
you	reflect
he/she/it	reflects
we	reflect
you	reflect
they	reflect

Past

I	reflected
you	reflected
he/she/it	reflected
we	reflected
you	reflected
they	reflected

Present Perfect

I	have	reflected
you	have	reflected
he/she/it	has	reflected
we	have	reflected
you	have	reflected
they	have	reflected

Past Perfect

I	had	reflected
you	had	reflected
he/she/it	had	reflected
we	had	reflected
you	had	reflected
they	had	reflected

Will-Future

I	will	reflect
you	will	reflect
he/she/it	will	reflect
we	will	reflect
you	will	reflect
they	will	reflect

Going to-Future

I	am	going to	reflect
you	are	going to	reflect
he/she/it	is	going to	reflect
we	are	going to	reflect
you	are	going to	reflect
they	are	going to	reflect

Future Perfect

I	will have	reflected
you	will have	reflected
he/she/it	will have	reflected
we	will have	reflected
you	will have	reflected
they	will have	reflected

Imperative

reflect

Impersonal

ing-Form

reflecting

Past Participle

reflected

Continuous tenses

Present

I	am	reflecting
you	are	reflecting
he/she/it	is	reflecting
we	are	reflecting
you	are	reflecting
they	are	reflecting

Past

I	was	reflecting
you	were	reflecting
he/she/it	was	reflecting
we	were	reflecting
you	were	reflecting
they	were	reflecting

Present Perfect

I	have been	reflecting
you	have been	reflecting
he/she/it	has been	reflecting
we	have been	reflecting
you	have been	reflecting
they	have been	reflecting

Past Perfect

I	had been	reflecting
you	had been	reflecting
he/she/it	had been	reflecting
we	had been	reflecting
you	had been	reflecting
they	had been	reflecting

Will-Future

I	will be	reflecting
you	will be	reflecting
he/she/it	will be	reflecting
we	will be	reflecting
you	will be	reflecting
they	will be	reflecting

Going to-Future

I	am	going to be	reflecting
you	are	going to be	reflecting
he/she/it	is	going to be	reflecting
we	are	going to be	reflecting
you	are	going to be	reflecting
they	are	going to be	reflecting

Future Perfect

I	will have been	reflecting
you	will have been	reflecting
he/she/it	will have been	reflecting
we	will have been	reflecting
you	will have been	reflecting
they	will have been	reflecting

Conditional

I	would	reflect
you	would	reflect
he/she/it	would	reflect
we	would	reflect
you	would	reflect
they	would	reflect

Conditional Past

I	would have	reflected
you	would have	reflected
he/she/it	would have	reflected
we	would have	reflected
you	would have	reflected
they	would have	reflected

refuse

verweigern

Regelmäßiges Verb

Simple tenses

Present

I	refuse
you	refuse
he/she/it	refuses
we	refuse
you	refuse
they	refuse

Past

I	refused
you	refused
he/she/it	refused
we	refused
you	refused
they	refused

Present Perfect

I	have	refused
you	have	refused
he/she/it	has	refused
we	have	refused
you	have	refused
they	have	refused

Past Perfect

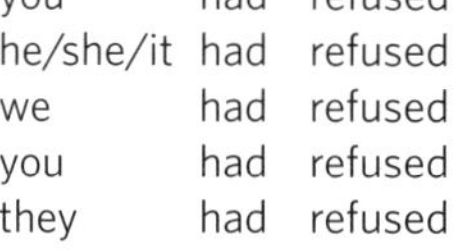

I	had	refused
you	had	refused
he/she/it	had	refused
we	had	refused
you	had	refused
they	had	refused

Will-Future

I	will	refuse
you	will	refuse
he/she/it	will	refuse
we	will	refuse
you	will	refuse
they	will	refuse

Going to-Future

I	am	going to	refuse
you	are	going to	refuse
he/she/it	is	going to	refuse
we	are	going to	refuse
you	are	going to	refuse
they	are	going to	refuse

Future Perfect

I	will have	refused
you	will have	refused
he/she/it	will have	refused
we	will have	refused
you	will have	refused
they	will have	refused

Imperative

refuse

Impersonal

ing-Form

refusing

Past Participle

refused

Continuous tenses

Present

I	am	refusing
you	are	refusing
he/she/it	is	refusing
we	are	refusing
you	are	refusing
they	are	refusing

Past

I	was	refusing
you	were	refusing
he/she/it	was	refusing
we	were	refusing
you	were	refusing
they	were	refusing

Present Perfect

I	have been	refusing
you	have been	refusing
he/she/it	has been	refusing
we	have been	refusing
you	have been	refusing
they	have been	refusing

Past Perfect

I	had been	refusing
you	had been	refusing
he/she/it	had been	refusing
we	had been	refusing
you	had been	refusing
they	had been	refusing

Will-Future

I	will be	refusing
you	will be	refusing
he/she/it	will be	refusing
we	will be	refusing
you	will be	refusing
they	will be	refusing

Going to-Future

I	am	going to be	refusing
you	are	going to be	refusing
he/she/it	is	going to be	refusing
we	are	going to be	refusing
you	are	going to be	refusing
they	are	going to be	refusing

Future Perfect

I	will have been	refusing
you	will have been	refusing
he/she/it	will have been	refusing
we	will have been	refusing
you	will have been	refusing
they	will have been	refusing

Conditional

I	would	refuse
you	would	refuse
he/she/it	would	refuse
we	would	refuse
you	would	refuse
they	would	refuse

Conditional Past

I	would have	refused
you	would have	refused
he/she/it	would have	refused
we	would have	refused
you	would have	refused
they	would have	refused

Simple tenses

Present

I	regard
you	regard
he/she/it	regards
we	regard
you	regard
they	regard

Past

I	regarded
you	regarded
he/she/it	regarded
we	regarded
you	regarded
they	regarded

Present Perfect

I	have	regarded
you	have	regarded
he/she/it	has	regarded
we	have	regarded
you	have	regarded
they	have	regarded

Past Perfect

I	had	regarded
you	had	regarded
he/she/it	had	regarded
we	had	regarded
you	had	regarded
they	had	regarded

Will-Future

I	will	regard
you	will	regard
he/she/it	will	regard
we	will	regard
you	will	regard
they	will	regard

Going to-Future

I	am	going to	regard
you	are	going to	regard
he/she/it	is	going to	regard
we	are	going to	regard
you	are	going to	regard
they	are	going to	regard

Future Perfect

I	will have	regarded
you	will have	regarded
he/she/it	will have	regarded
we	will have	regarded
you	will have	regarded
they	will have	regarded

Imperative

regard

Impersonal

ing-Form

regarding

Past Participle

regarded

Continuous tenses

Present

I	am	regarding
you	are	regarding
he/she/it	is	regarding
we	are	regarding
you	are	regarding
they	are	regarding

Past

I	was	regarding
you	were	regarding
he/she/it	was	regarding
we	were	regarding
you	were	regarding
they	were	regarding

Present Perfect

I	have been	regarding
you	have been	regarding
he/she/it	has been	regarding
we	have been	regarding
you	have been	regarding
they	have been	regarding

Past Perfect

I	had been	regarding
you	had been	regarding
he/she/it	had been	regarding
we	had been	regarding
you	had been	regarding
they	had been	regarding

Will-Future

I	will be	regarding
you	will be	regarding
he/she/it	will be	regarding
we	will be	regarding
you	will be	regarding
they	will be	regarding

Going to-Future

I	am	going to be	regarding
you	are	going to be	regarding
he/she/it	is	going to be	regarding
we	are	going to be	regarding
you	are	going to be	regarding
they	are	going to be	regarding

Future Perfect

I	will have been	regarding
you	will have been	regarding
he/she/it	will have been	regarding
we	will have been	regarding
you	will have been	regarding
they	will have been	regarding

Conditional

I	would	regard
you	would	regard
he/she/it	would	regard
we	would	regard
you	would	regard
they	would	regard

Conditional Past

I	would have	regarded
you	would have	regarded
he/she/it	would have	regarded
we	would have	regarded
you	would have	regarded
they	would have	regarded

register

registrieren

Regelmäßiges Verb

Simple tenses

Present

I	register
you	register
he/she/it	registers
we	register
you	register
they	register

Past

I	registered
you	registered
he/she/it	registered
we	registered
you	registered
they	registered

Present Perfect

I	have	registered
you	have	registered
he/she/it	has	registered
we	have	registered
you	have	registered
they	have	registered

Past Perfect

I	had	registered
you	had	registered
he/she/it	had	registered
we	had	registered
you	had	registered
they	had	registered

Will-Future

I	will	register
you	will	register
he/she/it	will	register
we	will	register
you	will	register
they	will	register

Going to-Future

I	am	going to	register
you	are	going to	register
he/she/it	is	going to	register
we	are	going to	register
you	are	going to	register
they	are	going to	register

Future Perfect

I	will have	registered
you	will have	registered
he/she/it	will have	registered
we	will have	registered
you	will have	registered
they	will have	registered

Imperative

register

Impersonal

ing-Form

registering

Past Participle

registered

Continuous tenses

Present

I	am	registering
you	are	registering
he/she/it	is	registering
we	are	registering
you	are	registering
they	are	registering

Past

I	was	registering
you	were	registering
he/she/it	was	registering
we	were	registering
you	were	registering
they	were	registering

Present Perfect

I	have been	registering
you	have been	registering
he/she/it	has been	registering
we	have been	registering
you	have been	registering
they	have been	registering

Past Perfect

I	had been	registering
you	had been	registering
he/she/it	had been	registering
we	had been	registering
you	had been	registering
they	had been	registering

Will-Future

I	will be	registering
you	will be	registering
he/she/it	will be	registering
we	will be	registering
you	will be	registering
they	will be	registering

Going to-Future

I	am	going to be	registering
you	are	going to be	registering
he/she/it	is	going to be	registering
we	are	going to be	registering
you	are	going to be	registering
they	are	going to be	registering

Future Perfect

I	will have been	registering
you	will have been	registering
he/she/it	will have been	registering
we	will have been	registering
you	will have been	registering
they	will have been	registering

Conditional

I	would	register
you	would	register
he/she/it	would	register
we	would	register
you	would	register
they	would	register

Conditional Past

I	would have	registered
you	would have	registered
he/she/it	would have	registered
we	would have	registered
you	would have	registered
they	would have	registered

Simple tenses

Present

I	regret
you	regret
he/she/it	regrets
we	regret
you	regret
they	regret

Past

I	regretted
you	regretted
he/she/it	regretted
we	regretted
you	regretted
they	regretted

Present Perfect

I	have	regretted
you	have	regretted
he/she/it	has	regretted
we	have	regretted
you	have	regretted
they	have	regretted

Past Perfect

I	had	regretted
you	had	regretted
he/she/it	had	regretted
we	had	regretted
you	had	regretted
they	had	regretted

Will-Future

I	will	regret
you	will	regret
he/she/it	will	regret
we	will	regret
you	will	regret
they	will	regret

Going to-Future

I	am	going to	regret
you	are	going to	regret
he/she/it	is	going to	regret
we	are	going to	regret
you	are	going to	regret
they	are	going to	regret

Future Perfect

I	will have	regretted
you	will have	regretted
he/she/it	will have	regretted
we	will have	regretted
you	will have	regretted
they	will have	regretted

Imperative

regret

Impersonal

ing-Form

regretting

Past Participle

regretted

Continuous tenses

Present

I	am	regretting
you	are	regretting
he/she/it	is	regretting
we	are	regretting
you	are	regretting
they	are	regretting

Past

I	was	regretting
you	were	regretting
he/she/it	was	regretting
we	were	regretting
you	were	regretting
they	were	regretting

Present Perfect

I	have been	regretting
you	have been	regretting
he/she/it	has been	regretting
we	have been	regretting
you	have been	regretting
they	have been	regretting

Past Perfect

I	had been	regretting
you	had been	regretting
he/she/it	had been	regretting
we	had been	regretting
you	had been	regretting
they	had been	regretting

Will-Future

I	will be	regretting
you	will be	regretting
he/she/it	will be	regretting
we	will be	regretting
you	will be	regretting
they	will be	regretting

Going to-Future

I	am	going to be	regretting
you	are	going to be	regretting
he/she/it	is	going to be	regretting
we	are	going to be	regretting
you	are	going to be	regretting
they	are	going to be	regretting

Future Perfect

I	will have been	regretting
you	will have been	regretting
he/she/it	will have been	regretting
we	will have been	regretting
you	will have been	regretting
they	will have been	regretting

Conditional

I	would	regret
you	would	regret
he/she/it	would	regret
we	would	regret
you	would	regret
they	would	regret

Conditional Past

I	would have	regretted
you	would have	regretted
he/she/it	would have	regretted
we	would have	regretted
you	would have	regretted
they	would have	regretted

regulate

regeln

+ **-ing** → ~~e~~ / + **-d** nicht **-ed**
Regelmäßiges Verb

Simple tenses

Present

I	regulate
you	regulate
he/she/it	regulates
we	regulate
you	regulate
they	regulate

Past

I	regulated
you	regulated
he/she/it	regulated
we	regulated
you	regulated
they	regulated

Present Perfect

I	have	regulated
you	have	regulated
he/she/it	has	regulated
we	have	regulated
you	have	regulated
they	have	regulated

Past Perfect

I	had	regulated
you	had	regulated
he/she/it	had	regulated
we	had	regulated
you	had	regulated
they	had	regulated

Will-Future

I	will	regulate
you	will	regulate
he/she/it	will	regulate
we	will	regulate
you	will	regulate
they	will	regulate

Going to-Future

I	am	going to	regulate
you	are	going to	regulate
he/she/it	is	going to	regulate
we	are	going to	regulate
you	are	going to	regulate
they	are	going to	regulate

Future Perfect

I	will have	regulated
you	will have	regulated
he/she/it	will have	regulated
we	will have	regulated
you	will have	regulated
they	will have	regulated

Imperative

regulate

Impersonal

ing-Form

regulating

Past Participle

regulated

Continuous tenses

Present

I	am	regulating
you	are	regulating
he/she/it	is	regulating
we	are	regulating
you	are	regulating
they	are	regulating

Past

I	was	regulating
you	were	regulating
he/she/it	was	regulating
we	were	regulating
you	were	regulating
they	were	regulating

Present Perfect

I	have been	regulating
you	have been	regulating
he/she/it	has been	regulating
we	have been	regulating
you	have been	regulating
they	have been	regulating

Past Perfect

I	had been	regulating
you	had been	regulating
he/she/it	had been	regulating
we	had been	regulating
you	had been	regulating
they	had been	regulating

Will-Future

I	will be	regulating
you	will be	regulating
he/she/it	will be	regulating
we	will be	regulating
you	will be	regulating
they	will be	regulating

Going to-Future

I	am	going to be	regulating
you	are	going to be	regulating
he/she/it	is	going to be	regulating
we	are	going to be	regulating
you	are	going to be	regulating
they	are	going to be	regulating

Future Perfect

I	will have been	regulating
you	will have been	regulating
he/she/it	will have been	regulating
we	will have been	regulating
you	will have been	regulating
they	will have been	regulating

Conditional

I	would	regulate
you	would	regulate
he/she/it	would	regulate
we	would	regulate
you	would	regulate
they	would	regulate

Conditional Past

I	would have	regulated
you	would have	regulated
he/she/it	would have	regulated
we	would have	regulated
you	would have	regulated
they	would have	regulated

+ **-ing** → ~~e~~ / + **-d** nicht **-ed**
Regelmäßiges Verb

in Verbindung bringen

relate

Simple tenses

Present

I	relate
you	relate
he/she/it	relates
we	relate
you	relate
they	relate

Past

I	related
you	related
he/she/it	related
we	related
you	related
they	related

Present Perfect

I	have	related
you	have	related
he/she/it	has	related
we	have	related
you	have	related
they	have	related

Past Perfect

I	had	related
you	had	related
he/she/it	had	related
we	had	related
you	had	related
they	had	related

Will-Future

I	will	relate
you	will	relate
he/she/it	will	relate
we	will	relate
you	will	relate
they	will	relate

Going to-Future

I	am	going to	relate
you	are	going to	relate
he/she/it	is	going to	relate
we	are	going to	relate
you	are	going to	relate
they	are	going to	relate

Future Perfect

I	will have	related
you	will have	related
he/she/it	will have	related
we	will have	related
you	will have	related
they	will have	related

Imperative

relate

Impersonal

ing-Form

relating

Past Participle

related

Continuous tenses

Present

I	am	relating
you	are	relating
he/she/it	is	relating
we	are	relating
you	are	relating
they	are	relating

Past

I	was	relating
you	were	relating
he/she/it	was	relating
we	were	relating
you	were	relating
they	were	relating

Present Perfect

I	have been	relating
you	have been	relating
he/she/it	has been	relating
we	have been	relating
you	have been	relating
they	have been	relating

Past Perfect

I	had been	relating
you	had been	relating
he/she/it	had been	relating
we	had been	relating
you	had been	relating
they	had been	relating

Will-Future

I	will be	relating
you	will be	relating
he/she/it	will be	relating
we	will be	relating
you	will be	relating
they	will be	relating

Going to-Future

I	am	going to be	relating
you	are	going to be	relating
he/she/it	is	going to be	relating
we	are	going to be	relating
you	are	going to be	relating
they	are	going to be	relating

Future Perfect

I	will have been	relating
you	will have been	relating
he/she/it	will have been	relating
we	will have been	relating
you	will have been	relating
they	will have been	relating

Conditional

I	would	relate
you	would	relate
he/she/it	would	relate
we	would	relate
you	would	relate
they	would	relate

Conditional Past

I	would have	related
you	would have	related
he/she/it	would have	related
we	would have	related
you	would have	related
they	would have	related

relax

sich entspannen

+ **-es** in 3. Person Singular
Regelmäßiges Verb

Simple tenses

Present

I	relax
you	relax
he/she/it	relaxes
we	relax
you	relax
they	relax

Past

I	relaxed
you	relaxed
he/she/it	relaxed
we	relaxed
you	relaxed
they	relaxed

Present Perfect

I	have	relaxed
you	have	relaxed
he/she/it	has	relaxed
we	have	relaxed
you	have	relaxed
they	have	relaxed

Past Perfect

I	had	relaxed
you	had	relaxed
he/she/it	had	relaxed
we	had	relaxed
you	had	relaxed
they	had	relaxed

Will-Future

I	will	relax
you	will	relax
he/she/it	will	relax
we	will	relax
you	will	relax
they	will	relax

Going to-Future

I	am	going to	relax
you	are	going to	relax
he/she/it	is	going to	relax
we	are	going to	relax
you	are	going to	relax
they	are	going to	relax

Future Perfect

I	will have	relaxed
you	will have	relaxed
he/she/it	will have	relaxed
we	will have	relaxed
you	will have	relaxed
they	will have	relaxed

Imperative

relax

Impersonal

ing-Form

relaxing

Past Participle

relaxed

Continuous tenses

Present

I	am	relaxing
you	are	relaxing
he/she/it	is	relaxing
we	are	relaxing
you	are	relaxing
they	are	relaxing

Past

I	was	relaxing
you	were	relaxing
he/she/it	was	relaxing
we	were	relaxing
you	were	relaxing
they	were	relaxing

Present Perfect

I	have been	relaxing
you	have been	relaxing
he/she/it	has been	relaxing
we	have been	relaxing
you	have been	relaxing
they	have been	relaxing

Past Perfect

I	had been	relaxing
you	had been	relaxing
he/she/it	had been	relaxing
we	had been	relaxing
you	had been	relaxing
they	had been	relaxing

Will-Future

I	will be	relaxing
you	will be	relaxing
he/she/it	will be	relaxing
we	will be	relaxing
you	will be	relaxing
they	will be	relaxing

Going to-Future

I	am	going to be	relaxing
you	are	going to be	relaxing
he/she/it	is	going to be	relaxing
we	are	going to be	relaxing
you	are	going to be	relaxing
they	are	going to be	relaxing

Future Perfect

I	will have been	relaxing
you	will have been	relaxing
he/she/it	will have been	relaxing
we	will have been	relaxing
you	will have been	relaxing
they	will have been	relaxing

Conditional

I	would	relax
you	would	relax
he/she/it	would	relax
we	would	relax
you	would	relax
they	would	relax

Conditional Past

I	would have	relaxed
you	would have	relaxed
he/she/it	would have	relaxed
we	would have	relaxed
you	would have	relaxed
they	would have	relaxed

+ **-ing** → ~~e~~ / + **-d** nicht **-ed**
Regelmäßiges Verb

freilassen

release

Simple tenses

Present

I	release
you	release
he/she/it	releases
we	release
you	release
they	release

Past

I	released
you	released
he/she/it	released
we	released
you	released
they	released

Present Perfect

I	have	released
you	have	released
he/she/it	has	released
we	have	released
you	have	released
they	have	released

Past Perfect

I	had	released
you	had	released
he/she/it	had	released
we	had	released
you	had	released
they	had	released

Will-Future

I	will	release
you	will	release
he/she/it	will	release
we	will	release
you	will	release
they	will	release

Going to-Future

I	am	going to	release
you	are	going to	release
he/she/it	is	going to	release
we	are	going to	release
you	are	going to	release
they	are	going to	release

Future Perfect

I	will have	released
you	will have	released
he/she/it	will have	released
we	will have	released
you	will have	released
they	will have	released

Imperative

release

Impersonal

ing-Form

releasing

Past Participle

released

Continuous tenses

Present

I	am	releasing
you	are	releasing
he/she/it	is	releasing
we	are	releasing
you	are	releasing
they	are	releasing

Past

I	was	releasing
you	were	releasing
he/she/it	was	releasing
we	were	releasing
you	were	releasing
they	were	releasing

Present Perfect

I	have been	releasing
you	have been	releasing
he/she/it	has been	releasing
we	have been	releasing
you	have been	releasing
they	have been	releasing

Past Perfect

I	had been	releasing
you	had been	releasing
he/she/it	had been	releasing
we	had been	releasing
you	had been	releasing
they	had been	releasing

Will-Future

I	will be	releasing
you	will be	releasing
he/she/it	will be	releasing
we	will be	releasing
you	will be	releasing
they	will be	releasing

Going to-Future

I	am	going to be	releasing
you	are	going to be	releasing
he/she/it	is	going to be	releasing
we	are	going to be	releasing
you	are	going to be	releasing
they	are	going to be	releasing

Future Perfect

I	will have been	releasing
you	will have been	releasing
he/she/it	will have been	releasing
we	will have been	releasing
you	will have been	releasing
they	will have been	releasing

Conditional

I	would	release
you	would	release
he/she/it	would	release
we	would	release
you	would	release
they	would	release

Conditional Past

I	would have	released
you	would have	released
he/she/it	would have	released
we	would have	released
you	would have	released
they	would have	released

rely

sich verlassen

-y → **-ie** vor **-s** / **-y** → **-i** vor **-ed**
Regelmäßiges Verb

Simple tenses

Present

I	rely
you	rely
he/she/it	relies
we	rely
you	rely
they	rely

Past

I	relied
you	relied
he/she/it	relied
we	relied
you	relied
they	relied

Present Perfect

I	have	relied
you	have	relied
he/she/it	has	relied
we	have	relied
you	have	relied
they	have	relied

Past Perfect

I	had	relied
you	had	relied
he/she/it	had	relied
we	had	relied
you	had	relied
they	had	relied

Will-Future

I	will	rely
you	will	rely
he/she/it	will	rely
we	will	rely
you	will	rely
they	will	rely

Going to-Future

I	am	going to	rely
you	are	going to	rely
he/she/it	is	going to	rely
we	are	going to	rely
you	are	going to	rely
they	are	going to	rely

Future Perfect

I	will have	relied
you	will have	relied
he/she/it	will have	relied
we	will have	relied
you	will have	relied
they	will have	relied

Imperative

rely

Impersonal

ing-Form

relying

Past Participle

relied

Continuous tenses

Present

I	am	relying
you	are	relying
he/she/it	is	relying
we	are	relying
you	are	relying
they	are	relying

Past

I	was	relying
you	were	relying
he/she/it	was	relying
we	were	relying
you	were	relying
they	were	relying

Present Perfect

I	have been	relying
you	have been	relying
he/she/it	has been	relying
we	have been	relying
you	have been	relying
they	have been	relying

Past Perfect

I	had been	relying
you	had been	relying
he/she/it	had been	relying
we	had been	relying
you	had been	relying
they	had been	relying

Will-Future

I	will be	relying
you	will be	relying
he/she/it	will be	relying
we	will be	relying
you	will be	relying
they	will be	relying

Going to-Future

I	am	going to be	relying
you	are	going to be	relying
he/she/it	is	going to be	relying
we	are	going to be	relying
you	are	going to be	relying
they	are	going to be	relying

Future Perfect

I	will have been	relying
you	will have been	relying
he/she/it	will have been	relying
we	will have been	relying
you	will have been	relying
they	will have been	relying

Conditional

I	would	rely
you	would	rely
he/she/it	would	rely
we	would	rely
you	would	rely
they	would	rely

Conditional Past

I	would have	relied
you	would have	relied
he/she/it	would have	relied
we	would have	relied
you	would have	relied
they	would have	relied

Simple tenses

Present

I	remain
you	remain
he/she/it	remains
we	remain
you	remain
they	remain

Past

I	remained
you	remained
he/she/it	remained
we	remained
you	remained
they	remained

Present Perfect

I	have	remained
you	have	remained
he/she/it	has	remained
we	have	remained
you	have	remained
they	have	remained

Past Perfect

I	had	remained
you	had	remained
he/she/it	had	remained
we	had	remained
you	had	remained
they	had	remained

Will-Future

I	will	remain
you	will	remain
he/she/it	will	remain
we	will	remain
you	will	remain
they	will	remain

Going to-Future

I	am	going to	remain
you	are	going to	remain
he/she/it	is	going to	remain
we	are	going to	remain
you	are	going to	remain
they	are	going to	remain

Future Perfect

I	will have	remained
you	will have	remained
he/she/it	will have	remained
we	will have	remained
you	will have	remained
they	will have	remained

Imperative

remain

Impersonal

ing-Form

remaining

Past Participle

remained

Continuous tenses

Present

I	am	remaining
you	are	remaining
he/she/it	is	remaining
we	are	remaining
you	are	remaining
they	are	remaining

Past

I	was	remaining
you	were	remaining
he/she/it	was	remaining
we	were	remaining
you	were	remaining
they	were	remaining

Present Perfect

I	have been	remaining
you	have been	remaining
he/she/it	has been	remaining
we	have been	remaining
you	have been	remaining
they	have been	remaining

Past Perfect

I	had been	remaining
you	had been	remaining
he/she/it	had been	remaining
we	had been	remaining
you	had been	remaining
they	had been	remaining

Will-Future

I	will be	remaining
you	will be	remaining
he/she/it	will be	remaining
we	will be	remaining
you	will be	remaining
they	will be	remaining

Going to-Future

I	am	going to be	remaining
you	are	going to be	remaining
he/she/it	is	going to be	remaining
we	are	going to be	remaining
you	are	going to be	remaining
they	are	going to be	remaining

Future Perfect

I	will have been	remaining
you	will have been	remaining
he/she/it	will have been	remaining
we	will have been	remaining
you	will have been	remaining
they	will have been	remaining

Conditional

I	would	remain
you	would	remain
he/she/it	would	remain
we	would	remain
you	would	remain
they	would	remain

Conditional Past

I	would have	remained
you	would have	remained
he/she/it	would have	remained
we	would have	remained
you	would have	remained
they	would have	remained

remark

bemerken

Regelmäßiges Verb

Simple tenses

Present

I	remark
you	remark
he/she/it	remarks
we	remark
you	remark
they	remark

Past

I	remarked
you	remarked
he/she/it	remarked
we	remarked
you	remarked
they	remarked

Present Perfect

I	have	remarked
you	have	remarked
he/she/it	has	remarked
we	have	remarked
you	have	remarked
they	have	remarked

Past Perfect

I	had	remarked
you	had	remarked
he/she/it	had	remarked
we	had	remarked
you	had	remarked
they	had	remarked

Will-Future

I	will	remark
you	will	remark
he/she/it	will	remark
we	will	remark
you	will	remark
they	will	remark

Going to-Future

I	am	going to	remark
you	are	going to	remark
he/she/it	is	going to	remark
we	are	going to	remark
you	are	going to	remark
they	are	going to	remark

Future Perfect

I	will have	remarked
you	will have	remarked
he/she/it	will have	remarked
we	will have	remarked
you	will have	remarked
they	will have	remarked

Imperative

remark

Impersonal

ing-Form

remarking

Past Participle

remarked

Continuous tenses

Present

I	am	remarking
you	are	remarking
he/she/it	is	remarking
we	are	remarking
you	are	remarking
they	are	remarking

Past

I	was	remarking
you	were	remarking
he/she/it	was	remarking
we	were	remarking
you	were	remarking
they	were	remarking

Present Perfect

I	have been	remarking
you	have been	remarking
he/she/it	has been	remarking
we	have been	remarking
you	have been	remarking
they	have been	remarking

Past Perfect

I	had been	remarking
you	had been	remarking
he/she/it	had been	remarking
we	had been	remarking
you	had been	remarking
they	had been	remarking

Will-Future

I	will be	remarking
you	will be	remarking
he/she/it	will be	remarking
we	will be	remarking
you	will be	remarking
they	will be	remarking

Going to-Future

I	am	going to be	remarking
you	are	going to be	remarking
he/she/it	is	going to be	remarking
we	are	going to be	remarking
you	are	going to be	remarking
they	are	going to be	remarking

Future Perfect

I	will have been	remarking
you	will have been	remarking
he/she/it	will have been	remarking
we	will have been	remarking
you	will have been	remarking
they	will have been	remarking

Conditional

I	would	remark
you	would	remark
he/she/it	would	remark
we	would	remark
you	would	remark
they	would	remark

Conditional Past

I	would have	remarked
you	would have	remarked
he/she/it	would have	remarked
we	would have	remarked
you	would have	remarked
they	would have	remarked

Simple tenses

Present

I	remember
you	remember
he/she/it	remembers
we	remember
you	remember
they	remember

Past

I	remembered
you	remembered
he/she/it	remembered
we	remembered
you	remembered
they	remembered

Present Perfect

I	have	remembered
you	have	remembered
he/she/it	has	remembered
we	have	remembered
you	have	remembered
they	have	remembered

Past Perfect

I	had	remembered
you	had	remembered
he/she/it	had	remembered
we	had	remembered
you	had	remembered
they	had	remembered

Will-Future

I	will	remember
you	will	remember
he/she/it	will	remember
we	will	remember
you	will	remember
they	will	remember

Going to-Future

I	am	going to	remember
you	are	going to	remember
he/she/it	is	going to	remember
we	are	going to	remember
you	are	going to	remember
they	are	going to	remember

Future Perfect

I	will have	remembered
you	will have	remembered
he/she/it	will have	remembered
we	will have	remembered
you	will have	remembered
they	will have	remembered

Imperative

remember

Impersonal

ing-Form

remembering

Past Participle

remembered

Continuous tenses

Present

I	am	remembering
you	are	remembering
he/she/it	is	remembering
we	are	remembering
you	are	remembering
they	are	remembering

Past

I	was	remembering
you	were	remembering
he/she/it	was	remembering
we	were	remembering
you	were	remembering
they	were	remembering

Present Perfect

I	have	been remembering
you	have	been remembering
he/she/it	has	been remembering
we	have	been remembering
you	have	been remembering
they	have	been remembering

Past Perfect

I	had been	remembering
you	had been	remembering
he/she/it	had been	remembering
we	had been	remembering
you	had been	remembering
they	had been	remembering

Will-Future

I	will be	remembering
you	will be	remembering
he/she/it	will be	remembering
we	will be	remembering
you	will be	remembering
they	will be	remembering

Going to-Future

I	am	going to be	remembering
you	are	going to be	remembering
he/she/it	is	going to be	remembering
we	are	going to be	remembering
you	are	going to be	remembering
they	are	going to be	remembering

Future Perfect

I	will have been remembering
you	will have been remembering
he/she/it	will have been remembering
we	will have been remembering
you	will have been remembering
they	will have been remembering

Conditional

I	would	remember
you	would	remember
he/she/it	would	remember
we	would	remember
you	would	remember
they	would	remember

Conditional Past

I	would have	remembered
you	would have	remembered
he/she/it	would have	remembered
we	would have	remembered
you	would have	remembered
they	would have	remembered

remind

erinnern

Regelmäßiges Verb

Simple tenses

Present

I	remind
you	remind
he/she/it	reminds
we	remind
you	remind
they	remind

Past

I	reminded
you	reminded
he/she/it	reminded
we	reminded
you	reminded
they	reminded

Present Perfect

I	have	reminded
you	have	reminded
he/she/it	has	reminded
we	have	reminded
you	have	reminded
they	have	reminded

Past Perfect

I	had	reminded
you	had	reminded
he/she/it	had	reminded
we	had	reminded
you	had	reminded
they	had	reminded

Will-Future

I	will	remind
you	will	remind
he/she/it	will	remind
we	will	remind
you	will	remind
they	will	remind

Going to-Future

I	am	going to	remind
you	are	going to	remind
he/she/it	is	going to	remind
we	are	going to	remind
you	are	going to	remind
they	are	going to	remind

Future Perfect

I	will have	reminded
you	will have	reminded
he/she/it	will have	reminded
we	will have	reminded
you	will have	reminded
they	will have	reminded

Imperative

remind

Impersonal

ing-Form

reminding

Past Participle

reminded

Continuous tenses

Present

I	am	reminding
you	are	reminding
he/she/it	is	reminding
we	are	reminding
you	are	reminding
they	are	reminding

Past

I	was	reminding
you	were	reminding
he/she/it	was	reminding
we	were	reminding
you	were	reminding
they	were	reminding

Present Perfect

I	have been	reminding
you	have been	reminding
he/she/it	has been	reminding
we	have been	reminding
you	have been	reminding
they	have been	reminding

Past Perfect

I	had been	reminding
you	had been	reminding
he/she/it	had been	reminding
we	had been	reminding
you	had been	reminding
they	had been	reminding

Will-Future

I	will be	reminding
you	will be	reminding
he/she/it	will be	reminding
we	will be	reminding
you	will be	reminding
they	will be	reminding

Going to-Future

I	am	going to be	reminding
you	are	going to be	reminding
he/she/it	is	going to be	reminding
we	are	going to be	reminding
you	are	going to be	reminding
they	are	going to be	reminding

Future Perfect

I	will have been	reminding
you	will have been	reminding
he/she/it	will have been	reminding
we	will have been	reminding
you	will have been	reminding
they	will have been	reminding

Conditional

I	would	remind
you	would	remind
he/she/it	would	remind
we	would	remind
you	would	remind
they	would	remind

Conditional Past

I	would have	reminded
you	would have	reminded
he/she/it	would have	reminded
we	would have	reminded
you	would have	reminded
they	would have	reminded

+ **-ing** → ~~e~~ / + **-d** nicht **-ed**
Regelmäßiges Verb

entfernen

remove

Simple tenses

Present

I	remove
you	remove
he/she/it	removes
we	remove
you	remove
they	remove

Past

I	removed
you	removed
he/she/it	removed
we	removed
you	removed
they	removed

Present Perfect

I	have	removed
you	have	removed
he/she/it	has	removed
we	have	removed
you	have	removed
they	have	removed

Past Perfect

I	had	removed
you	had	removed
he/she/it	had	removed
we	had	removed
you	had	removed
they	had	removed

Will-Future

I	will	remove
you	will	remove
he/she/it	will	remove
we	will	remove
you	will	remove
they	will	remove

Going to-Future

I	am	going to	remove
you	are	going to	remove
he/she/it	is	going to	remove
we	are	going to	remove
you	are	going to	remove
they	are	going to	remove

Future Perfect

I	will have	removed
you	will have	removed
he/she/it	will have	removed
we	will have	removed
you	will have	removed
they	will have	removed

Imperative

remove

Impersonal

ing-Form

removing

Past Participle

removed

Continuous tenses

Present

I	am	removing
you	are	removing
he/she/it	is	removing
we	are	removing
you	are	removing
they	are	removing

Past

I	was	removing
you	were	removing
he/she/it	was	removing
we	were	removing
you	were	removing
they	were	removing

Present Perfect

I	have been	removing
you	have been	removing
he/she/it	has been	removing
we	have been	removing
you	have been	removing
they	have been	removing

Past Perfect

I	had been	removing
you	had been	removing
he/she/it	had been	removing
we	had been	removing
you	had been	removing
they	had been	removing

Will-Future

I	will be	removing
you	will be	removing
he/she/it	will be	removing
we	will be	removing
you	will be	removing
they	will be	removing

Going to-Future

I	am	going to be	removing
you	are	going to be	removing
he/she/it	is	going to be	removing
we	are	going to be	removing
you	are	going to be	removing
they	are	going to be	removing

Future Perfect

I	will have been	removing
you	will have been	removing
he/she/it	will have been	removing
we	will have been	removing
you	will have been	removing
they	will have been	removing

Conditional

I	would	remove
you	would	remove
he/she/it	would	remove
we	would	remove
you	would	remove
they	would	remove

Conditional Past

I	would have	removed
you	would have	removed
he/she/it	would have	removed
we	would have	removed
you	would have	removed
they	would have	removed

rent

vermieten

Regelmäßiges Verb

Simple tenses

Present

I	rent
you	rent
he/she/it	rents
we	rent
you	rent
they	rent

Past

I	rented
you	rented
he/she/it	rented
we	rented
you	rented
they	rented

Present Perfect

I	have	rented
you	have	rented
he/she/it	has	rented
we	have	rented
you	have	rented
they	have	rented

Past Perfect

I	had	rented
you	had	rented
he/she/it	had	rented
we	had	rented
you	had	rented
they	had	rented

Will-Future

I	will	rent
you	will	rent
he/she/it	will	rent
we	will	rent
you	will	rent
they	will	rent

Going to-Future

I	am	going to	rent
you	are	going to	rent
he/she/it	is	going to	rent
we	are	going to	rent
you	are	going to	rent
they	are	going to	rent

Future Perfect

I	will have	rented
you	will have	rented
he/she/it	will have	rented
we	will have	rented
you	will have	rented
they	will have	rented

Imperative

rent

Impersonal

ing-Form

renting

Past Participle

rented

Continuous tenses

Present

I	am	renting
you	are	renting
he/she/it	is	renting
we	are	renting
you	are	renting
they	are	renting

Past

I	was	renting
you	were	renting
he/she/it	was	renting
we	were	renting
you	were	renting
they	were	renting

Present Perfect

I	have been	renting
you	have been	renting
he/she/it	has been	renting
we	have been	renting
you	have been	renting
they	have been	renting

Past Perfect

I	had been	renting
you	had been	renting
he/she/it	had been	renting
we	had been	renting
you	had been	renting
they	had been	renting

Will-Future

I	will be	renting
you	will be	renting
he/she/it	will be	renting
we	will be	renting
you	will be	renting
they	will be	renting

Going to-Future

I	am	going to be	renting
you	are	going to be	renting
he/she/it	is	going to be	renting
we	are	going to be	renting
you	are	going to be	renting
they	are	going to be	renting

Future Perfect

I	will have been	renting
you	will have been	renting
he/she/it	will have been	renting
we	will have been	renting
you	will have been	renting
they	will have been	renting

Conditional

I	would	rent
you	would	rent
he/she/it	would	rent
we	would	rent
you	would	rent
they	would	rent

Conditional Past

I	would have	rented
you	would have	rented
he/she/it	would have	rented
we	would have	rented
you	would have	rented
they	would have	rented

Simple tenses

Present

I	repair
you	repair
he/she/it	repairs
we	repair
you	repair
they	repair

Past

I	repaired
you	repaired
he/she/it	repaired
we	repaired
you	repaired
they	repaired

Present Perfect

I	have	repaired
you	have	repaired
he/she/it	has	repaired
we	have	repaired
you	have	repaired
they	have	repaired

Past Perfect

I	had	repaired
you	had	repaired
he/she/it	had	repaired
we	had	repaired
you	had	repaired
they	had	repaired

Will-Future

I	will	repair
you	will	repair
he/she/it	will	repair
we	will	repair
you	will	repair
they	will	repair

Going to-Future

I	am	going to	repair
you	are	going to	repair
he/she/it	is	going to	repair
we	are	going to	repair
you	are	going to	repair
they	are	going to	repair

Future Perfect

I	will have	repaired
you	will have	repaired
he/she/it	will have	repaired
we	will have	repaired
you	will have	repaired
they	will have	repaired

Imperative

repair

Impersonal

ing-Form

repairing

Past Participle

repaired

Continuous tenses

Present

I	am	repairing
you	are	repairing
he/she/it	is	repairing
we	are	repairing
you	are	repairing
they	are	repairing

Past

I	was	repairing
you	were	repairing
he/she/it	was	repairing
we	were	repairing
you	were	repairing
they	were	repairing

Present Perfect

I	have been	repairing
you	have been	repairing
he/she/it	has been	repairing
we	have been	repairing
you	have been	repairing
they	have been	repairing

Past Perfect

I	had been	repairing
you	had been	repairing
he/she/it	had been	repairing
we	had been	repairing
you	had been	repairing
they	had been	repairing

Will-Future

I	will be	repairing
you	will be	repairing
he/she/it	will be	repairing
we	will be	repairing
you	will be	repairing
they	will be	repairing

Going to-Future

I	am	going to be	repairing
you	are	going to be	repairing
he/she/it	is	going to be	repairing
we	are	going to be	repairing
you	are	going to be	repairing
they	are	going to be	repairing

Future Perfect

I	will have been	repairing
you	will have been	repairing
he/she/it	will have been	repairing
we	will have been	repairing
you	will have been	repairing
they	will have been	repairing

Conditional

I	would	repair
you	would	repair
he/she/it	would	repair
we	would	repair
you	would	repair
they	would	repair

Conditional Past

I	would have	repaired
you	would have	repaired
he/she/it	would have	repaired
we	would have	repaired
you	would have	repaired
they	would have	repaired

repeat

wiederholen

Regelmäßiges Verb

Simple tenses

Present

I	repeat
you	repeat
he/she/it	repeats
we	repeat
you	repeat
they	repeat

Past

I	repeated
you	repeated
he/she/it	repeated
we	repeated
you	repeated
they	repeated

Present Perfect

I	have	repeated
you	have	repeated
he/she/it	has	repeated
we	have	repeated
you	have	repeated
they	have	repeated

Past Perfect

I	had	repeated
you	had	repeated
he/she/it	had	repeated
we	had	repeated
you	had	repeated
they	had	repeated

Will-Future

I	will	repeat
you	will	repeat
he/she/it	will	repeat
we	will	repeat
you	will	repeat
they	will	repeat

Going to-Future

I	am	going to	repeat
you	are	going to	repeat
he/she/it	is	going to	repeat
we	are	going to	repeat
you	are	going to	repeat
they	are	going to	repeat

Future Perfect

I	will have	repeated
you	will have	repeated
he/she/it	will have	repeated
we	will have	repeated
you	will have	repeated
they	will have	repeated

Imperative

repeat

Impersonal

ing-Form

repeating

Past Participle

repeated

Continuous tenses

Present

I	am	repeating
you	are	repeating
he/she/it	is	repeating
we	are	repeating
you	are	repeating
they	are	repeating

Past

I	was	repeating
you	were	repeating
he/she/it	was	repeating
we	were	repeating
you	were	repeating
they	were	repeating

Present Perfect

I	have	been	repeating
you	have	been	repeating
he/she/it	has	been	repeating
we	have	been	repeating
you	have	been	repeating
they	have	been	repeating

Past Perfect

I	had been	repeating
you	had been	repeating
he/she/it	had been	repeating
we	had been	repeating
you	had been	repeating
they	had been	repeating

Will-Future

I	will be	repeating
you	will be	repeating
he/she/it	will be	repeating
we	will be	repeating
you	will be	repeating
they	will be	repeating

Going to-Future

I	am	going to be	repeating
you	are	going to be	repeating
he/she/it	is	going to be	repeating
we	are	going to be	repeating
you	are	going to be	repeating
they	are	going to be	repeating

Future Perfect

I	will have been	repeating
you	will have been	repeating
he/she/it	will have been	repeating
we	will have been	repeating
you	will have been	repeating
they	will have been	repeating

Conditional

I	would	repeat
you	would	repeat
he/she/it	would	repeat
we	would	repeat
you	would	repeat
they	would	repeat

Conditional Past

I	would have	repeated
you	would have	repeated
he/she/it	would have	repeated
we	would have	repeated
you	would have	repeated
they	would have	repeated

+ **-ing** → ~~e~~ / + **-d** nicht **-ed**
Regelmäßiges Verb

ersetzen

replace

Simple tenses

Present

I	replace
you	replace
he/she/it	replaces
we	replace
you	replace
they	replace

Past

I	replaced
you	replaced
he/she/it	replaced
we	replaced
you	replaced
they	replaced

Present Perfect

I	have	replaced
you	have	replaced
he/she/it	has	replaced
we	have	replaced
you	have	replaced
they	have	replaced

Past Perfect

I	had	replaced
you	had	replaced
he/she/it	had	replaced
we	had	replaced
you	had	replaced
they	had	replaced

Will-Future

I	will	replace
you	will	replace
he/she/it	will	replace
we	will	replace
you	will	replace
they	will	replace

Going to-Future

I	am	going to	replace
you	are	going to	replace
he/she/it	is	going to	replace
we	are	going to	replace
you	are	going to	replace
they	are	going to	replace

Future Perfect

I	will have	replaced
you	will have	replaced
he/she/it	will have	replaced
we	will have	replaced
you	will have	replaced
they	will have	replaced

Imperative

replace

Impersonal

ing-Form

replacing

Past Participle

replaced

Continuous tenses

Present

I	am	replacing
you	are	replacing
he/she/it	is	replacing
we	are	replacing
you	are	replacing
they	are	replacing

Past

I	was	replacing
you	were	replacing
he/she/it	was	replacing
we	were	replacing
you	were	replacing
they	were	replacing

Present Perfect

I	have been	replacing
you	have been	replacing
he/she/it	has been	replacing
we	have been	replacing
you	have been	replacing
they	have been	replacing

Past Perfect

I	had been	replacing
you	had been	replacing
he/she/it	had been	replacing
we	had been	replacing
you	had been	replacing
they	had been	replacing

Will-Future

I	will be	replacing
you	will be	replacing
he/she/it	will be	replacing
we	will be	replacing
you	will be	replacing
they	will be	replacing

Going to-Future

I	am	going to be	replacing
you	are	going to be	replacing
he/she/it	is	going to be	replacing
we	are	going to be	replacing
you	are	going to be	replacing
they	are	going to be	replacing

Future Perfect

I	will have been	replacing
you	will have been	replacing
he/she/it	will have been	replacing
we	will have been	replacing
you	will have been	replacing
they	will have been	replacing

Conditional

I	would	replace
you	would	replace
he/she/it	would	replace
we	would	replace
you	would	replace
they	would	replace

Conditional Past

I	would have	replaced
you	would have	replaced
he/she/it	would have	replaced
we	would have	replaced
you	would have	replaced
they	would have	replaced

reply

antwerten

-y → -ie vor **-s** / **-y → -i** vor **-ed**
Regelmäßiges Verb

Simple tenses

Present

I	reply
you	reply
he/she/it	replies
we	reply
you	reply
they	reply

Past

I	replied
you	replied
he/she/it	replied
we	replied
you	replied
they	replied

Present Perfect

I	have	replied
you	have	replied
he/she/it	has	replied
we	have	replied
you	have	replied
they	have	replied

Past Perfect

I	had	replied
you	had	replied
he/she/it	had	replied
we	had	replied
you	had	replied
they	had	replied

Will-Future

I	will	reply
you	will	reply
he/she/it	will	reply
we	will	reply
you	will	reply
they	will	reply

Going to-Future

I	am	going to	reply
you	are	going to	reply
he/she/it	is	going to	reply
we	are	going to	reply
you	are	going to	reply
they	are	going to	reply

Future Perfect

I	will have	replied
you	will have	replied
he/she/it	will have	replied
we	will have	replied
you	will have	replied
they	will have	replied

Imperative

reply

Impersonal

ing-Form

replying

Past Participle

replied

Continuous tenses

Present

I	am	replying
you	are	replying
he/she/it	is	replying
we	are	replying
you	are	replying
they	are	replying

Past

I	was	replying
you	were	replying
he/she/it	was	replying
we	were	replying
you	were	replying
they	were	replying

Present Perfect

I	have	been	replying
you	have	been	replying
he/she/it	has	been	replying
we	have	been	replying
you	have	been	replying
they	have	been	replying

Past Perfect

I	had been	replying
you	had been	replying
he/she/it	had been	replying
we	had been	replying
you	had been	replying
they	had been	replying

Will-Future

I	will be	replying
you	will be	replying
he/she/it	will be	replying
we	will be	replying
you	will be	replying
they	will be	replying

Going to-Future

I	am	going to be	replying
you	are	going to be	replying
he/she/it	is	going to be	replying
we	are	going to be	replying
you	are	going to be	replying
they	are	going to be	replying

Future Perfect

I	will have been	replying
you	will have been	replying
he/she/it	will have been	replying
we	will have been	replying
you	will have been	replying
they	will have been	replying

Conditional

I	would	reply
you	would	reply
he/she/it	would	reply
we	would	reply
you	would	reply
they	would	reply

Conditional Past

I	would have	replied
you	would have	replied
he/she/it	would have	replied
we	would have	replied
you	would have	replied
they	would have	replied

Simple tenses

Present

I	report
you	report
he/she/it	reports
we	report
you	report
they	report

Past

I	reported
you	reported
he/she/it	reported
we	reported
you	reported
they	reported

Present Perfect

I	have	reported
you	have	reported
he/she/it	has	reported
we	have	reported
you	have	reported
they	have	reported

Past Perfect

I	had	reported
you	had	reported
he/she/it	had	reported
we	had	reported
you	had	reported
they	had	reported

Will-Future

I	will	report
you	will	report
he/she/it	will	report
we	will	report
you	will	report
they	will	report

Going to-Future

I	am	going to	report
you	are	going to	report
he/she/it	is	going to	report
we	are	going to	report
you	are	going to	report
they	are	going to	report

Future Perfect

I	will have	reported
you	will have	reported
he/she/it	will have	reported
we	will have	reported
you	will have	reported
they	will have	reported

Imperative

report

Impersonal

ing-Form

reporting

Past Participle

reported

Continuous tenses

Present

I	am	reporting
you	are	reporting
he/she/it	is	reporting
we	are	reporting
you	are	reporting
they	are	reporting

Past

I	was	reporting
you	were	reporting
he/she/it	was	reporting
we	were	reporting
you	were	reporting
they	were	reporting

Present Perfect

I	have	been	reporting
you	have	been	reporting
he/she/it	has	been	reporting
we	have	been	reporting
you	have	been	reporting
they	have	been	reporting

Past Perfect

I	had been	reporting
you	had been	reporting
he/she/it	had been	reporting
we	had been	reporting
you	had been	reporting
they	had been	reporting

Will-Future

I	will be	reporting
you	will be	reporting
he/she/it	will be	reporting
we	will be	reporting
you	will be	reporting
they	will be	reporting

Going to-Future

I	am	going to be	reporting
you	are	going to be	reporting
he/she/it	is	going to be	reporting
we	are	going to be	reporting
you	are	going to be	reporting
they	are	going to be	reporting

Future Perfect

I	will have been	reporting
you	will have been	reporting
he/she/it	will have been	reporting
we	will have been	reporting
you	will have been	reporting
they	will have been	reporting

Conditional

I	would	report
you	would	report
he/she/it	would	report
we	would	report
you	would	report
they	would	report

Conditional Past

I	would have	reported
you	would have	reported
he/she/it	would have	reported
we	would have	reported
you	would have	reported
they	would have	reported

represent

repräsentieren

Regelmäßiges Verb

Simple tenses

Present

I	represent
you	represent
he/she/it	represents
we	represent
you	represent
they	represent

Past

I	represented
you	represented
he/she/it	represented
we	represented
you	represented
they	represented

Present Perfect

I	have	represented
you	have	represented
he/she/it	has	represented
we	have	represented
you	have	represented
they	have	represented

Past Perfect

I	had	represented
you	had	represented
he/she/it	had	represented
we	had	represented
you	had	represented
they	had	represented

Will-Future

I	will	represent
you	will	represent
he/she/it	will	represent
we	will	represent
you	will	represent
they	will	represent

Going to-Future

I	am	going to	represent
you	are	going to	represent
he/she/it	is	going to	represent
we	are	going to	represent
you	are	going to	represent
they	are	going to	represent

Future Perfect

I	will have	represented
you	will have	represented
he/she/it	will have	represented
we	will have	represented
you	will have	represented
they	will have	represented

Imperative

represent

Impersonal

ing-Form

representing

Past Participle

represented

Continuous tenses

Present

I	am	representing
you	are	representing
he/she/it	is	representing
we	are	representing
you	are	representing
they	are	representing

Past

I	was	representing
you	were	representing
he/she/it	was	representing
we	were	representing
you	were	representing
they	were	representing

Present Perfect

I	have been	representing
you	have been	representing
he/she/it	has been	representing
we	have been	representing
you	have been	representing
they	have been	representing

Past Perfect

I	had been	representing
you	had been	representing
he/she/it	had been	representing
we	had been	representing
you	had been	representing
they	had been	representing

Will-Future

I	will be	representing
you	will be	representing
he/she/it	will be	representing
we	will be	representing
you	will be	representing
they	will be	representing

Going to-Future

I	am	going to be	representing
you	are	going to be	representing
he/she/it	is	going to be	representing
we	are	going to be	representing
you	are	going to be	representing
they	are	going to be	representing

Future Perfect

I	will have been representing
you	will have been representing
he/she/it	will have been representing
we	will have been representing
you	will have been representing
they	will have been representing

Conditional

I	would	represent
you	would	represent
he/she/it	would	represent
we	would	represent
you	would	represent
they	would	represent

Conditional Past

I	would have	represented
you	would have	represented
he/she/it	would have	represented
we	would have	represented
you	would have	represented
they	would have	represented

Vorwürfe machen

reproach

Simple tenses

Present

I	reproach
you	reproach
he/she/it	reproaches
we	reproach
you	reproach
they	reproach

Past

I	reproached
you	reproached
he/she/it	reproached
we	reproached
you	reproached
they	reproached

Present Perfect

I	have	reproached
you	have	reproached
he/she/it	has	reproached
we	have	reproached
you	have	reproached
they	have	reproached

Past Perfect

I	had	reproached
you	had	reproached
he/she/it	had	reproached
we	had	reproached
you	had	reproached
they	had	reproached

Will-Future

I	will	reproach
you	will	reproach
he/she/it	will	reproach
we	will	reproach
you	will	reproach
they	will	reproach

Going to-Future

I	am	going to	reproach
you	are	going to	reproach
he/she/it	is	going to	reproach
we	are	going to	reproach
you	are	going to	reproach
they	are	going to	reproach

Future Perfect

I	will have	reproached
you	will have	reproached
he/she/it	will have	reproached
we	will have	reproached
you	will have	reproached
they	will have	reproached

Imperative

reproach

Impersonal

ing-Form

reproaching

Past Participle

reproached

Continuous tenses

Present

I	am	reproaching
you	are	reproaching
he/she/it	is	reproaching
we	are	reproaching
you	are	reproaching
they	are	reproaching

Past

I	was	reproaching
you	were	reproaching
he/she/it	was	reproaching
we	were	reproaching
you	were	reproaching
they	were	reproaching

Present Perfect

I	have been	reproaching
you	have been	reproaching
he/she/it	has been	reproaching
we	have been	reproaching
you	have been	reproaching
they	have been	reproaching

Past Perfect

I	had been	reproaching
you	had been	reproaching
he/she/it	had been	reproaching
we	had been	reproaching
you	had been	reproaching
they	had been	reproaching

Will-Future

I	will be	reproaching
you	will be	reproaching
he/she/it	will be	reproaching
we	will be	reproaching
you	will be	reproaching
they	will be	reproaching

Going to-Future

I	am going to be	reproaching
you	are going to be	reproaching
he/she/it	is going to be	reproaching
we	are going to be	reproaching
you	are going to be	reproaching
they	are going to be	reproaching

Future Perfect

I	will have been reproaching
you	will have been reproaching
he/she/it	will have been reproaching
we	will have been reproaching
you	will have been reproaching
they	will have been reproaching

Conditional

I	would	reproach
you	would	reproach
he/she/it	would	reproach
we	would	reproach
you	would	reproach
they	would	reproach

Conditional Past

I	would have	reproached
you	would have	reproached
he/she/it	would have	reproached
we	would have	reproached
you	would have	reproached
they	would have	reproached

request

bitten

Regelmäßiges Verb

Simple tenses

Present

I	request
you	request
he/she/it	requests
we	request
you	request
they	request

Past

I	requested
you	requested
he/she/it	requested
we	requested
you	requested
they	requested

Present Perfect

I	have	requested
you	have	requested
he/she/it	has	requested
we	have	requested
you	have	requested
they	have	requested

Past Perfect

I	had	requested
you	had	requested
he/she/it	had	requested
we	had	requested
you	had	requested
they	had	requested

Will-Future

I	will	request
you	will	request
he/she/it	will	request
we	will	request
you	will	request
they	will	request

Going to-Future

I	am	going to	request
you	are	going to	request
he/she/it	is	going to	request
we	are	going to	request
you	are	going to	request
they	are	going to	request

Future Perfect

I	will have	requested
you	will have	requested
he/she/it	will have	requested
we	will have	requested
you	will have	requested
they	will have	requested

Imperative

request

Impersonal

ing-Form

requesting

Past Participle

requested

Continuous tenses

Present

I	am	requesting
you	are	requesting
he/she/it	is	requesting
we	are	requesting
you	are	requesting
they	are	requesting

Past

I	was	requesting
you	were	requesting
he/she/it	was	requesting
we	were	requesting
you	were	requesting
they	were	requesting

Present Perfect

I	have been	requesting
you	have been	requesting
he/she/it	has been	requesting
we	have been	requesting
you	have been	requesting
they	have been	requesting

Past Perfect

I	had been	requesting
you	had been	requesting
he/she/it	had been	requesting
we	had been	requesting
you	had been	requesting
they	had been	requesting

Will-Future

I	will be	requesting
you	will be	requesting
he/she/it	will be	requesting
we	will be	requesting
you	will be	requesting
they	will be	requesting

Going to-Future

I	am	going to be	requesting
you	are	going to be	requesting
he/she/it	is	going to be	requesting
we	are	going to be	requesting
you	are	going to be	requesting
they	are	going to be	requesting

Future Perfect

I	will have been	requesting
you	will have been	requesting
he/she/it	will have been	requesting
we	will have been	requesting
you	will have been	requesting
they	will have been	requesting

Conditional

I	would	request
you	would	request
he/she/it	would	request
we	would	request
you	would	request
they	would	request

Conditional Past

I	would have	requested
you	would have	requested
he/she/it	would have	requested
we	would have	requested
you	would have	requested
they	would have	requested

+ **-ing** → ~~e~~ / + **-d** nicht **-ed**
Regelmäßiges Verb

brauchen

require

Simple tenses

Present

I	require
you	require
he/she/it	requires
we	require
you	require
they	require

Past

I	required
you	required
he/she/it	required
we	required
you	required
they	required

Present Perfect

I	have	required
you	have	required
he/she/it	has	required
we	have	required
you	have	required
they	have	required

Past Perfect

I	had	required
you	had	required
he/she/it	had	required
we	had	required
you	had	required
they	had	required

Will-Future

I	will	require
you	will	require
he/she/it	will	require
we	will	require
you	will	require
they	will	require

Going to-Future

I	am	going to	require
you	are	going to	require
he/she/it	is	going to	require
we	are	going to	require
you	are	going to	require
they	are	going to	require

Future Perfect

I	will have	required
you	will have	required
he/she/it	will have	required
we	will have	required
you	will have	required
they	will have	required

Imperative

require

Impersonal

ing-Form

requiring

Past Participle

required

Continuous tenses

Present

I	am	requiring
you	are	requiring
he/she/it	is	requiring
we	are	requiring
you	are	requiring
they	are	requiring

Past

I	was	requiring
you	were	requiring
he/she/it	was	requiring
we	were	requiring
you	were	requiring
they	were	requiring

Present Perfect

I	have	been	requiring
you	have	been	requiring
he/she/it	has	been	requiring
we	have	been	requiring
you	have	been	requiring
they	have	been	requiring

Past Perfect

I	had been	requiring
you	had been	requiring
he/she/it	had been	requiring
we	had been	requiring
you	had been	requiring
they	had been	requiring

Will-Future

I	will be	requiring
you	will be	requiring
he/she/it	will be	requiring
we	will be	requiring
you	will be	requiring
they	will be	requiring

Going to-Future

I	am	going to be	requiring
you	are	going to be	requiring
he/she/it	is	going to be	requiring
we	are	going to be	requiring
you	are	going to be	requiring
they	are	going to be	requiring

Future Perfect

I	will have been	requiring
you	will have been	requiring
he/she/it	will have been	requiring
we	will have been	requiring
you	will have been	requiring
they	will have been	requiring

Conditional

I	would	require
you	would	require
he/she/it	would	require
we	would	require
you	would	require
they	would	require

Conditional Past

I	would have	required
you	would have	required
he/she/it	would have	required
we	would have	required
you	would have	required
they	would have	required

rescue

retten

+ **-ing** → ~~e~~ / + **-d** nicht **-ed**
Regelmäßiges Verb

Simple tenses

Present

I	rescue
you	rescue
he/she/it	rescues
we	rescue
you	rescue
they	rescue

Past

I	rescued
you	rescued
he/she/it	rescued
we	rescued
you	rescued
they	rescued

Present Perfect

I	have	rescued
you	have	rescued
he/she/it	has	rescued
we	have	rescued
you	have	rescued
they	have	rescued

Past Perfect

I	had	rescued
you	had	rescued
he/she/it	had	rescued
we	had	rescued
you	had	rescued
they	had	rescued

Will-Future

I	will	rescue
you	will	rescue
he/she/it	will	rescue
we	will	rescue
you	will	rescue
they	will	rescue

Going to-Future

I	am	going to	rescue
you	are	going to	rescue
he/she/it	is	going to	rescue
we	are	going to	rescue
you	are	going to	rescue
they	are	going to	rescue

Future Perfect

I	will have	rescued
you	will have	rescued
he/she/it	will have	rescued
we	will have	rescued
you	will have	rescued
they	will have	rescued

Imperative

rescue

Impersonal

ing-Form

rescuing

Past Participle

rescued

Continuous tenses

Present

I	am	rescuing
you	are	rescuing
he/she/it	is	rescuing
we	are	rescuing
you	are	rescuing
they	are	rescuing

Past

I	was	rescuing
you	were	rescuing
he/she/it	was	rescuing
we	were	rescuing
you	were	rescuing
they	were	rescuing

Present Perfect

I	have been	rescuing
you	have been	rescuing
he/she/it	has been	rescuing
we	have been	rescuing
you	have been	rescuing
they	have been	rescuing

Past Perfect

I	had been	rescuing
you	had been	rescuing
he/she/it	had been	rescuing
we	had been	rescuing
you	had been	rescuing
they	had been	rescuing

Will-Future

I	will be	rescuing
you	will be	rescuing
he/she/it	will be	rescuing
we	will be	rescuing
you	will be	rescuing
they	will be	rescuing

Going to-Future

I	am	going to be	rescuing
you	are	going to be	rescuing
he/she/it	is	going to be	rescuing
we	are	going to be	rescuing
you	are	going to be	rescuing
they	are	going to be	rescuing

Future Perfect

I	will have been	rescuing
you	will have been	rescuing
he/she/it	will have been	rescuing
we	will have been	rescuing
you	will have been	rescuing
they	will have been	rescuing

Conditional

I	would	rescue
you	would	rescue
he/she/it	would	rescue
we	would	rescue
you	would	rescue
they	would	rescue

Conditional Past

I	would have	rescued
you	would have	rescued
he/she/it	would have	rescued
we	would have	rescued
you	would have	rescued
they	would have	rescued

Simple tenses

Present

I	research
you	research
he/she/it	researches
we	research
you	research
they	research

Past

I	researched
you	researched
he/she/it	researched
we	researched
you	researched
they	researched

Present Perfect

I	have	researched
you	have	researched
he/she/it	has	researched
we	have	researched
you	have	researched
they	have	researched

Past Perfect

I	had	researched
you	had	researched
he/she/it	had	researched
we	had	researched
you	had	researched
they	had	researched

Will-Future

I	will	research
you	will	research
he/she/it	will	research
we	will	research
you	will	research
they	will	research

Going to-Future

I	am	going to	research
you	are	going to	research
he/she/it	is	going to	research
we	are	going to	research
you	are	going to	research
they	are	going to	research

Future Perfect

I	will have	researched
you	will have	researched
he/she/it	will have	researched
we	will have	researched
you	will have	researched
they	will have	researched

Imperative

research

Impersonal

ing-Form

researching

Past Participle

researched

Continuous tenses

Present

I	am	researching
you	are	researching
he/she/it	is	researching
we	are	researching
you	are	researching
they	are	researching

Past

I	was	researching
you	were	researching
he/she/it	was	researching
we	were	researching
you	were	researching
they	were	researching

Present Perfect

I	have been	researching
you	have been	researching
he/she/it	has been	researching
we	have been	researching
you	have been	researching
they	have been	researching

Past Perfect

I	had been	researching
you	had been	researching
he/she/it	had been	researching
we	had been	researching
you	had been	researching
they	had been	researching

Will-Future

I	will be	researching
you	will be	researching
he/she/it	will be	researching
we	will be	researching
you	will be	researching
they	will be	researching

Going to-Future

I	am	going to be	researching
you	are	going to be	researching
he/she/it	is	going to be	researching
we	are	going to be	researching
you	are	going to be	researching
they	are	going to be	researching

Future Perfect

I	will have been researching
you	will have been researching
he/she/it	will have been researching
we	will have been researching
you	will have been researching
they	will have been researching

Conditional

I	would	research
you	would	research
he/she/it	would	research
we	would	research
you	would	research
they	would	research

Conditional Past

I	would have	researched
you	would have	researched
he/she/it	would have	researched
we	would have	researched
you	would have	researched
they	would have	researched

reserve

reservieren

+ **-ing** → ~~e~~ / + **-d** nicht **-ed**
Regelmäßiges Verb

Simple tenses

Present

I	reserve
you	reserve
he/she/it	reserves
we	reserve
you	reserve
they	reserve

Past

I	reserved
you	reserved
he/she/it	reserved
we	reserved
you	reserved
they	reserved

Present Perfect

I	have	reserved
you	have	reserved
he/she/it	has	reserved
we	have	reserved
you	have	reserved
they	have	reserved

Past Perfect

I	had	reserved
you	had	reserved
he/she/it	had	reserved
we	had	reserved
you	had	reserved
they	had	reserved

Will-Future

I	will	reserve
you	will	reserve
he/she/it	will	reserve
we	will	reserve
you	will	reserve
they	will	reserve

Going to-Future

I	am	going to	reserve
you	are	going to	reserve
he/she/it	is	going to	reserve
we	are	going to	reserve
you	are	going to	reserve
they	are	going to	reserve

Future Perfect

I	will have	reserved
you	will have	reserved
he/she/it	will have	reserved
we	will have	reserved
you	will have	reserved
they	will have	reserved

Imperative

reserve

Impersonal

ing-Form

reserving

Past Participle

reserved

Continuous tenses

Present

I	am	reserving
you	are	reserving
he/she/it	is	reserving
we	are	reserving
you	are	reserving
they	are	reserving

Past

I	was	reserving
you	were	reserving
he/she/it	was	reserving
we	were	reserving
you	were	reserving
they	were	reserving

Present Perfect

I	have been	reserving
you	have been	reserving
he/she/it	has been	reserving
we	have been	reserving
you	have been	reserving
they	have been	reserving

Past Perfect

I	had been	reserving
you	had been	reserving
he/she/it	had been	reserving
we	had been	reserving
you	had been	reserving
they	had been	reserving

Will-Future

I	will be	reserving
you	will be	reserving
he/she/it	will be	reserving
we	will be	reserving
you	will be	reserving
they	will be	reserving

Going to-Future

I	am	going to be	reserving
you	are	going to be	reserving
he/she/it	is	going to be	reserving
we	are	going to be	reserving
you	are	going to be	reserving
they	are	going to be	reserving

Future Perfect

I	will have been	reserving
you	will have been	reserving
he/she/it	will have been	reserving
we	will have been	reserving
you	will have been	reserving
they	will have been	reserving

Conditional

I	would	reserve
you	would	reserve
he/she/it	would	reserve
we	would	reserve
you	would	reserve
they	would	reserve

Conditional Past

I	would have	reserved
you	would have	reserved
he/she/it	would have	reserved
we	would have	reserved
you	would have	reserved
they	would have	reserved

Simple tenses

Present

I	resign
you	resign
he/she/it	resigns
we	resign
you	resign
they	resign

Past

I	resigned
you	resigned
he/she/it	resigned
we	resigned
you	resigned
they	resigned

Present Perfect

I	have	resigned
you	have	resigned
he/she/it	has	resigned
we	have	resigned
you	have	resigned
they	have	resigned

Past Perfect

I	had	resigned
you	had	resigned
he/she/it	had	resigned
we	had	resigned
you	had	resigned
they	had	resigned

Will-Future

I	will	resign
you	will	resign
he/she/it	will	resign
we	will	resign
you	will	resign
they	will	resign

Going to-Future

I	am	going to	resign
you	are	going to	resign
he/she/it	is	going to	resign
we	are	going to	resign
you	are	going to	resign
they	are	going to	resign

Future Perfect

I	will have	resigned
you	will have	resigned
he/she/it	will have	resigned
we	will have	resigned
you	will have	resigned
they	will have	resigned

Imperative

resign

Impersonal

ing-Form

resigning

Past Participle

resigned

Continuous tenses

Present

I	am	resigning
you	are	resigning
he/she/it	is	resigning
we	are	resigning
you	are	resigning
they	are	resigning

Past

I	was	resigning
you	were	resigning
he/she/it	was	resigning
we	were	resigning
you	were	resigning
they	were	resigning

Present Perfect

I	have been	resigning
you	have been	resigning
he/she/it	has been	resigning
we	have been	resigning
you	have been	resigning
they	have been	resigning

Past Perfect

I	had been	resigning
you	had been	resigning
he/she/it	had been	resigning
we	had been	resigning
you	had been	resigning
they	had been	resigning

Will-Future

I	will be	resigning
you	will be	resigning
he/she/it	will be	resigning
we	will be	resigning
you	will be	resigning
they	will be	resigning

Going to-Future

I	am	going to be	resigning
you	are	going to be	resigning
he/she/it	is	going to be	resigning
we	are	going to be	resigning
you	are	going to be	resigning
they	are	going to be	resigning

Future Perfect

I	will have been	resigning
you	will have been	resigning
he/she/it	will have been	resigning
we	will have been	resigning
you	will have been	resigning
they	will have been	resigning

Conditional

I	would	resign
you	would	resign
he/she/it	would	resign
we	would	resign
you	would	resign
they	would	resign

Conditional Past

I	would have	resigned
you	would have	resigned
he/she/it	would have	resigned
we	would have	resigned
you	would have	resigned
they	would have	resigned

resist

sich widersetzen

Regelmäßiges Verb

Simple tenses

Present

I	resist
you	resist
he/she/it	resists
we	resist
you	resist
they	resist

Past

I	resisted
you	resisted
he/she/it	resisted
we	resisted
you	resisted
they	resisted

Present Perfect

I	have	resisted
you	have	resisted
he/she/it	has	resisted
we	have	resisted
you	have	resisted
they	have	resisted

Past Perfect

I	had	resisted
you	had	resisted
he/she/it	had	resisted
we	had	resisted
you	had	resisted
they	had	resisted

Will-Future

I	will	resist
you	will	resist
he/she/it	will	resist
we	will	resist
you	will	resist
they	will	resist

Going to-Future

I	am	going to	resist
you	are	going to	resist
he/she/it	is	going to	resist
we	are	going to	resist
you	are	going to	resist
they	are	going to	resist

Future Perfect

I	will have	resisted
you	will have	resisted
he/she/it	will have	resisted
we	will have	resisted
you	will have	resisted
they	will have	resisted

Imperative

resist

Impersonal

ing-Form

resisting

Past Participle

resisted

Continuous tenses

Present

I	am	resisting
you	are	resisting
he/she/it	is	resisting
we	are	resisting
you	are	resisting
they	are	resisting

Past

I	was	resisting
you	were	resisting
he/she/it	was	resisting
we	were	resisting
you	were	resisting
they	were	resisting

Present Perfect

I	have been	resisting
you	have been	resisting
he/she/it	has been	resisting
we	have been	resisting
you	have been	resisting
they	have been	resisting

Past Perfect

I	had been	resisting
you	had been	resisting
he/she/it	had been	resisting
we	had been	resisting
you	had been	resisting
they	had been	resisting

Will-Future

I	will be	resisting
you	will be	resisting
he/she/it	will be	resisting
we	will be	resisting
you	will be	resisting
they	will be	resisting

Going to-Future

I	am	going to be	resisting
you	are	going to be	resisting
he/she/it	is	going to be	resisting
we	are	going to be	resisting
you	are	going to be	resisting
they	are	going to be	resisting

Future Perfect

I	will have been	resisting
you	will have been	resisting
he/she/it	will have been	resisting
we	will have been	resisting
you	will have been	resisting
they	will have been	resisting

Conditional

I	would	resist
you	would	resist
he/she/it	would	resist
we	would	resist
you	would	resist
they	would	resist

Conditional Past

I	would have	resisted
you	would have	resisted
he/she/it	would have	resisted
we	would have	resisted
you	would have	resisted
they	would have	resisted

Simple tenses

Present

I	respect
you	respect
he/she/it	respects
we	respect
you	respect
they	respect

Past

I	respected
you	respected
he/she/it	respected
we	respected
you	respected
they	respected

Present Perfect

I	have	respected
you	have	respected
he/she/it	has	respected
we	have	respected
you	have	respected
they	have	respected

Past Perfect

I	had	respected
you	had	respected
he/she/it	had	respected
we	had	respected
you	had	respected
they	had	respected

Will-Future

I	will	respect
you	will	respect
he/she/it	will	respect
we	will	respect
you	will	respect
they	will	respect

Going to-Future

I	am	going to	respect
you	are	going to	respect
he/she/it	is	going to	respect
we	are	going to	respect
you	are	going to	respect
they	are	going to	respect

Future Perfect

I	will have	respected
you	will have	respected
he/she/it	will have	respected
we	will have	respected
you	will have	respected
they	will have	respected

Imperative

respect

Impersonal

ing-Form

respecting

Past Participle

respected

Continuous tenses

Present

I	am	respecting
you	are	respecting
he/she/it	is	respecting
we	are	respecting
you	are	respecting
they	are	respecting

Past

I	was	respecting
you	were	respecting
he/she/it	was	respecting
we	were	respecting
you	were	respecting
they	were	respecting

Present Perfect

I	have been	respecting
you	have been	respecting
he/she/it	has been	respecting
we	have been	respecting
you	have been	respecting
they	have been	respecting

Past Perfect

I	had been	respecting
you	had been	respecting
he/she/it	had been	respecting
we	had been	respecting
you	had been	respecting
they	had been	respecting

Will-Future

I	will be	respecting
you	will be	respecting
he/she/it	will be	respecting
we	will be	respecting
you	will be	respecting
they	will be	respecting

Going to-Future

I	am	going to be	respecting
you	are	going to be	respecting
he/she/it	is	going to be	respecting
we	are	going to be	respecting
you	are	going to be	respecting
they	are	going to be	respecting

Future Perfect

I	will have been	respecting
you	will have been	respecting
he/she/it	will have been	respecting
we	will have been	respecting
you	will have been	respecting
they	will have been	respecting

Conditional

I	would	respect
you	would	respect
he/she/it	would	respect
we	would	respect
you	would	respect
they	would	respect

Conditional Past

I	would have	respected
you	would have	respected
he/she/it	would have	respected
we	would have	respected
you	would have	respected
they	would have	respected

retire

sich zurückziehen

\+ **-ing** → ~~e~~ / + **-d** nicht **-ed**
Regelmäßiges Verb

Simple tenses

Present

I	retire
you	retire
he/she/it	retires
we	retire
you	retire
they	retire

Past

I	retired
you	retired
he/she/it	retired
we	retired
you	retired
they	retired

Present Perfect

I	have	retired
you	have	retired
he/she/it	has	retired
we	have	retired
you	have	retired
they	have	retired

Past Perfect

I	had	retired
you	had	retired
he/she/it	had	retired
we	had	retired
you	had	retired
they	had	retired

Will-Future

I	will	retire
you	will	retire
he/she/it	will	retire
we	will	retire
you	will	retire
they	will	retire

Going to-Future

I	am	going to	retire
you	are	going to	retire
he/she/it	is	going to	retire
we	are	going to	retire
you	are	going to	retire
they	are	going to	retire

Future Perfect

I	will have	retired
you	will have	retired
he/she/it	will have	retired
we	will have	retired
you	will have	retired
they	will have	retired

Imperative

retire

Impersonal

ing-Form

retiring

Past Participle

retired

Continuous tenses

Present

I	am	retiring
you	are	retiring
he/she/it	is	retiring
we	are	retiring
you	are	retiring
they	are	retiring

Past

I	was	retiring
you	were	retiring
he/she/it	was	retiring
we	were	retiring
you	were	retiring
they	were	retiring

Present Perfect

I	have	been	retiring
you	have	been	retiring
he/she/it	has	been	retiring
we	have	been	retiring
you	have	been	retiring
they	have	been	retiring

Past Perfect

I	had been	retiring
you	had been	retiring
he/she/it	had been	retiring
we	had been	retiring
you	had been	retiring
they	had been	retiring

Will-Future

I	will be	retiring
you	will be	retiring
he/she/it	will be	retiring
we	will be	retiring
you	will be	retiring
they	will be	retiring

Going to-Future

I	am	going to be	retiring
you	are	going to be	retiring
he/she/it	is	going to be	retiring
we	are	going to be	retiring
you	are	going to be	retiring
they	are	going to be	retiring

Future Perfect

I	will have been	retiring
you	will have been	retiring
he/she/it	will have been	retiring
we	will have been	retiring
you	will have been	retiring
they	will have been	retiring

Conditional

I	would	retire
you	would	retire
he/she/it	would	retire
we	would	retire
you	would	retire
they	would	retire

Conditional Past

I	would have	retired
you	would have	retired
he/she/it	would have	retired
we	would have	retired
you	would have	retired
they	would have	retired

Simple tenses

Present

I	return
you	return
he/she/it	returns
we	return
you	return
they	return

Past

I	returned
you	returned
he/she/it	returned
we	returned
you	returned
they	returned

Present Perfect

I	have	returned
you	have	returned
he/she/it	has	returned
we	have	returned
you	have	returned
they	have	returned

Past Perfect

I	had	returned
you	had	returned
he/she/it	had	returned
we	had	returned
you	had	returned
they	had	returned

Will-Future

I	will	return
you	will	return
he/she/it	will	return
we	will	return
you	will	return
they	will	return

Going to-Future

I	am	going to	return
you	are	going to	return
he/she/it	is	going to	return
we	are	going to	return
you	are	going to	return
they	are	going to	return

Future Perfect

I	will have	returned
you	will have	returned
he/she/it	will have	returned
we	will have	returned
you	will have	returned
they	will have	returned

Imperative

return

Impersonal

ing-Form

returning

Past Participle

returned

Continuous tenses

Present

I	am	returning
you	are	returning
he/she/it	is	returning
we	are	returning
you	are	returning
they	are	returning

Past

I	was	returning
you	were	returning
he/she/it	was	returning
we	were	returning
you	were	returning
they	were	returning

Present Perfect

I	have been	returning
you	have been	returning
he/she/it	has been	returning
we	have been	returning
you	have been	returning
they	have been	returning

Past Perfect

I	had been	returning
you	had been	returning
he/she/it	had been	returning
we	had been	returning
you	had been	returning
they	had been	returning

Will-Future

I	will be	returning
you	will be	returning
he/she/it	will be	returning
we	will be	returning
you	will be	returning
they	will be	returning

Going to-Future

I	am	going to be	returning
you	are	going to be	returning
he/she/it	is	going to be	returning
we	are	going to be	returning
you	are	going to be	returning
they	are	going to be	returning

Future Perfect

I	will have been	returning
you	will have been	returning
he/she/it	will have been	returning
we	will have been	returning
you	will have been	returning
they	will have been	returning

Conditional

I	would	return
you	would	return
he/she/it	would	return
we	would	return
you	would	return
they	would	return

Conditional Past

I	would have	returned
you	would have	returned
he/she/it	would have	returned
we	would have	returned
you	would have	returned
they	would have	returned

reveal

enthüllen

Regelmäßiges Verb

Simple tenses

Present

I	reveal
you	reveal
he/she/it	reveals
we	reveal
you	reveal
they	reveal

Past

I	revealed
you	revealed
he/she/it	revealed
we	revealed
you	revealed
they	revealed

Present Perfect

I	have	revealed
you	have	revealed
he/she/it	has	revealed
we	have	revealed
you	have	revealed
they	have	revealed

Past Perfect

I	had	revealed
you	had	revealed
he/she/it	had	revealed
we	had	revealed
you	had	revealed
they	had	revealed

Will-Future

I	will	reveal
you	will	reveal
he/she/it	will	reveal
we	will	reveal
you	will	reveal
they	will	reveal

Going to-Future

I	am	going to	reveal
you	are	going to	reveal
he/she/it	is	going to	reveal
we	are	going to	reveal
you	are	going to	reveal
they	are	going to	reveal

Future Perfect

I	will have	revealed
you	will have	revealed
he/she/it	will have	revealed
we	will have	revealed
you	will have	revealed
they	will have	revealed

Imperative

reveal

Impersonal

ing-Form

revealing

Past Participle

revealed

Continuous tenses

Present

I	am	revealing
you	are	revealing
he/she/it	is	revealing
we	are	revealing
you	are	revealing
they	are	revealing

Past

I	was	revealing
you	were	revealing
he/she/it	was	revealing
we	were	revealing
you	were	revealing
they	were	revealing

Present Perfect

I	have	been	revealing
you	have	been	revealing
he/she/it	has	been	revealing
we	have	been	revealing
you	have	been	revealing
they	have	been	revealing

Past Perfect

I	had been	revealing
you	had been	revealing
he/she/it	had been	revealing
we	had been	revealing
you	had been	revealing
they	had been	revealing

Will-Future

I	will be	revealing
you	will be	revealing
he/she/it	will be	revealing
we	will be	revealing
you	will be	revealing
they	will be	revealing

Going to-Future

I	am	going to be	revealing
you	are	going to be	revealing
he/she/it	is	going to be	revealing
we	are	going to be	revealing
you	are	going to be	revealing
they	are	going to be	revealing

Future Perfect

I	will have been	revealing
you	will have been	revealing
he/she/it	will have been	revealing
we	will have been	revealing
you	will have been	revealing
they	will have been	revealing

Conditional

I	would	reveal
you	would	reveal
he/she/it	would	reveal
we	would	reveal
you	would	reveal
they	would	reveal

Conditional Past

I	would have	revealed
you	would have	revealed
he/she/it	would have	revealed
we	would have	revealed
you	would have	revealed
they	would have	revealed

Simple tenses

Present

I	reverse
you	reverse
he/she/it	reverses
we	reverse
you	reverse
they	reverse

Past

I	reversed
you	reversed
he/she/it	reversed
we	reversed
you	reversed
they	reversed

Present Perfect

I	have	reversed
you	have	reversed
he/she/it	has	reversed
we	have	reversed
you	have	reversed
they	have	reversed

Past Perfect

I	had	reversed
you	had	reversed
he/she/it	had	reversed
we	had	reversed
you	had	reversed
they	had	reversed

Will-Future

I	will	reverse
you	will	reverse
he/she/it	will	reverse
we	will	reverse
you	will	reverse
they	will	reverse

Going to-Future

I	am	going to	reverse
you	are	going to	reverse
he/she/it	is	going to	reverse
we	are	going to	reverse
you	are	going to	reverse
they	are	going to	reverse

Future Perfect

I	will have	reversed
you	will have	reversed
he/she/it	will have	reversed
we	will have	reversed
you	will have	reversed
they	will have	reversed

Imperative

reverse

Impersonal

ing-Form

reversing

Past Participle

reversed

Continuous tenses

Present

I	am	reversing
you	are	reversing
he/she/it	is	reversing
we	are	reversing
you	are	reversing
they	are	reversing

Past

I	was	reversing
you	were	reversing
he/she/it	was	reversing
we	were	reversing
you	were	reversing
they	were	reversing

Present Perfect

I	have been	reversing
you	have been	reversing
he/she/it	has been	reversing
we	have been	reversing
you	have been	reversing
they	have been	reversing

Past Perfect

I	had been	reversing
you	had been	reversing
he/she/it	had been	reversing
we	had been	reversing
you	had been	reversing
they	had been	reversing

Will-Future

I	will be	reversing
you	will be	reversing
he/she/it	will be	reversing
we	will be	reversing
you	will be	reversing
they	will be	reversing

Going to-Future

I	am	going to be	reversing
you	are	going to be	reversing
he/she/it	is	going to be	reversing
we	are	going to be	reversing
you	are	going to be	reversing
they	are	going to be	reversing

Future Perfect

I	will have been	reversing
you	will have been	reversing
he/she/it	will have been	reversing
we	will have been	reversing
you	will have been	reversing
they	will have been	reversing

Conditional

I	would	reverse
you	would	reverse
he/she/it	would	reverse
we	would	reverse
you	would	reverse
they	would	reverse

Conditional Past

I	would have	reversed
you	would have	reversed
he/she/it	would have	reversed
we	would have	reversed
you	would have	reversed
they	would have	reversed

review

überprüfen

Regelmäßiges Verb

Simple tenses

Present

I	review
you	review
he/she/it	reviews
we	review
you	review
they	review

Past

I	reviewed
you	reviewed
he/she/it	reviewed
we	reviewed
you	reviewed
they	reviewed

Present Perfect

I	have	reviewed
you	have	reviewed
he/she/it	has	reviewed
we	have	reviewed
you	have	reviewed
they	have	reviewed

Past Perfect

I	had	reviewed
you	had	reviewed
he/she/it	had	reviewed
we	had	reviewed
you	had	reviewed
they	had	reviewed

Will-Future

I	will	review
you	will	review
he/she/it	will	review
we	will	review
you	will	review
they	will	review

Going to-Future

I	am	going to	review
you	are	going to	review
he/she/it	is	going to	review
we	are	going to	review
you	are	going to	review
they	are	going to	review

Future Perfect

I	will have	reviewed
you	will have	reviewed
he/she/it	will have	reviewed
we	will have	reviewed
you	will have	reviewed
they	will have	reviewed

Imperative

review

Impersonal

ing-Form

reviewing

Past Participle

reviewed

Continuous tenses

Present

I	am	reviewing
you	are	reviewing
he/she/it	is	reviewing
we	are	reviewing
you	are	reviewing
they	are	reviewing

Past

I	was	reviewing
you	were	reviewing
he/she/it	was	reviewing
we	were	reviewing
you	were	reviewing
they	were	reviewing

Present Perfect

I	have been	reviewing
you	have been	reviewing
he/she/it	has been	reviewing
we	have been	reviewing
you	have been	reviewing
they	have been	reviewing

Past Perfect

I	had been	reviewing
you	had been	reviewing
he/she/it	had been	reviewing
we	had been	reviewing
you	had been	reviewing
they	had been	reviewing

Will-Future

I	will be	reviewing
you	will be	reviewing
he/she/it	will be	reviewing
we	will be	reviewing
you	will be	reviewing
they	will be	reviewing

Going to-Future

I	am	going to be	reviewing
you	are	going to be	reviewing
he/she/it	is	going to be	reviewing
we	are	going to be	reviewing
you	are	going to be	reviewing
they	are	going to be	reviewing

Future Perfect

I	will have been	reviewing
you	will have been	reviewing
he/she/it	will have been	reviewing
we	will have been	reviewing
you	will have been	reviewing
they	will have been	reviewing

Conditional

I	would	review
you	would	review
he/she/it	would	review
we	would	review
you	would	review
they	would	review

Conditional Past

I	would have	reviewed
you	would have	reviewed
he/she/it	would have	reviewed
we	would have	reviewed
you	would have	reviewed
they	would have	reviewed

Regelmäßiges Verb

Simple tenses

Present

I	reward
you	reward
he/she/it	rewards
we	reward
you	reward
they	reward

Past

I	rewarded
you	rewarded
he/she/it	rewarded
we	rewarded
you	rewarded
they	rewarded

Present Perfect

I	have	rewarded
you	have	rewarded
he/she/it	has	rewarded
we	have	rewarded
you	have	rewarded
they	have	rewarded

Past Perfect

I	had	rewarded
you	had	rewarded
he/she/it	had	rewarded
we	had	rewarded
you	had	rewarded
they	had	rewarded

Will-Future

I	will	reward
you	will	reward
he/she/it	will	reward
we	will	reward
you	will	reward
they	will	reward

Going to-Future

I	am	going to	reward
you	are	going to	reward
he/she/it	is	going to	reward
we	are	going to	reward
you	are	going to	reward
they	are	going to	reward

Future Perfect

I	will have	rewarded
you	will have	rewarded
he/she/it	will have	rewarded
we	will have	rewarded
you	will have	rewarded
they	will have	rewarded

Imperative

reward

Impersonal

ing-Form

rewarding

Past Participle

rewarded

Continuous tenses

Present

I	am	rewarding
you	are	rewarding
he/she/it	is	rewarding
we	are	rewarding
you	are	rewarding
they	are	rewarding

Past

I	was	rewarding
you	were	rewarding
he/she/it	was	rewarding
we	were	rewarding
you	were	rewarding
they	were	rewarding

Present Perfect

I	have been	rewarding
you	have been	rewarding
he/she/it	has been	rewarding
we	have been	rewarding
you	have been	rewarding
they	have been	rewarding

Past Perfect

I	had been	rewarding
you	had been	rewarding
he/she/it	had been	rewarding
we	had been	rewarding
you	had been	rewarding
they	had been	rewarding

Will-Future

I	will be	rewarding
you	will be	rewarding
he/she/it	will be	rewarding
we	will be	rewarding
you	will be	rewarding
they	will be	rewarding

Going to-Future

I	am	going to be	rewarding
you	are	going to be	rewarding
he/she/it	is	going to be	rewarding
we	are	going to be	rewarding
you	are	going to be	rewarding
they	are	going to be	rewarding

Future Perfect

I	will have been	rewarding
you	will have been	rewarding
he/she/it	will have been	rewarding
we	will have been	rewarding
you	will have been	rewarding
they	will have been	rewarding

Conditional

I	would	reward
you	would	reward
he/she/it	would	reward
we	would	reward
you	would	reward
they	would	reward

Conditional Past

I	would have	rewarded
you	would have	rewarded
he/she/it	would have	rewarded
we	would have	rewarded
you	would have	rewarded
they	would have	rewarded

ride
- rode - ridden

reiten

+ **-ing** → ~~e~~
Unregelmäßiges Verb

Simple tenses

Present

I	ride
you	ride
he/she/it	rides
we	ride
you	ride
they	ride

Past

I	rode
you	rode
he/she/it	rode
we	rode
you	rode
they	rode

Present Perfect

I	have	ridden
you	have	ridden
he/she/it	has	ridden
we	have	ridden
you	have	ridden
they	have	ridden

Past Perfect

I	had	ridden
you	had	ridden
he/she/it	had	ridden
we	had	ridden
you	had	ridden
they	had	ridden

Will-Future

I	will	ride
you	will	ride
he/she/it	will	ride
we	will	ride
you	will	ride
they	will	ride

Going to-Future

I	am	going to	ride
you	are	going to	ride
he/she/it	is	going to	ride
we	are	going to	ride
you	are	going to	ride
they	are	going to	ride

Future Perfect

I	will have	ridden
you	will have	ridden
he/she/it	will have	ridden
we	will have	ridden
you	will have	ridden
they	will have	ridden

Imperative

ride

Impersonal

ing-Form

riding

Past Participle

ridden

Continuous tenses

Present

I	am	riding
you	are	riding
he/she/it	is	riding
we	are	riding
you	are	riding
they	are	riding

Past

I	was	riding
you	were	riding
he/she/it	was	riding
we	were	riding
you	were	riding
they	were	riding

Present Perfect

I	have	been	riding
you	have	been	riding
he/she/it	has	been	riding
we	have	been	riding
you	have	been	riding
they	have	been	riding

Past Perfect

I	had been	riding
you	had been	riding
he/she/it	had been	riding
we	had been	riding
you	had been	riding
they	had been	riding

Will-Future

I	will be	riding
you	will be	riding
he/she/it	will be	riding
we	will be	riding
you	will be	riding
they	will be	riding

Going to-Future

I	am	going to be	riding
you	are	going to be	riding
he/she/it	is	going to be	riding
we	are	going to be	riding
you	are	going to be	riding
they	are	going to be	riding

Future Perfect

I	will have been	riding
you	will have been	riding
he/she/it	will have been	riding
we	will have been	riding
you	will have been	riding
they	will have been	riding

Conditional

I	would	ride
you	would	ride
he/she/it	would	ride
we	would	ride
you	would	ride
they	would	ride

Conditional Past

I	would have	ridden
you	would have	ridden
he/she/it	would have	ridden
we	would have	ridden
you	would have	ridden
they	would have	ridden

Simple tenses

Present

I	ring
you	ring
he/she/it	rings
we	ring
you	ring
they	ring

Past

I	rang
you	rang
he/she/it	rang
we	rang
you	rang
they	rang

Present Perfect

I	have	rung
you	have	rung
he/she/it	has	rung
we	have	rung
you	have	rung
they	have	rung

Past Perfect

I	had	rung
you	had	rung
he/she/it	had	rung
we	had	rung
you	had	rung
they	had	rung

Will-Future

I	will	ring
you	will	ring
he/she/it	will	ring
we	will	ring
you	will	ring
they	will	ring

Going to-Future

I	am	going to	ring
you	are	going to	ring
he/she/it	is	going to	ring
we	are	going to	ring
you	are	going to	ring
they	are	going to	ring

Future Perfect

I	will have	rung
you	will have	rung
he/she/it	will have	rung
we	will have	rung
you	will have	rung
they	will have	rung

Imperative

ring

Impersonal

ing-Form

ringing

Past Participle

rung

Continuous tenses

Present

I	am	ringing
you	are	ringing
he/she/it	is	ringing
we	are	ringing
you	are	ringing
they	are	ringing

Past

I	was	ringing
you	were	ringing
he/she/it	was	ringing
we	were	ringing
you	were	ringing
they	were	ringing

Present Perfect

I	have been	ringing
you	have been	ringing
he/she/it	has been	ringing
we	have been	ringing
you	have been	ringing
they	have been	ringing

Past Perfect

I	had been	ringing
you	had been	ringing
he/she/it	had been	ringing
we	had been	ringing
you	had been	ringing
they	had been	ringing

Will-Future

I	will be	ringing
you	will be	ringing
he/she/it	will be	ringing
we	will be	ringing
you	will be	ringing
they	will be	ringing

Going to-Future

I	am	going to be	ringing
you	are	going to be	ringing
he/she/it	is	going to be	ringing
we	are	going to be	ringing
you	are	going to be	ringing
they	are	going to be	ringing

Future Perfect

I	will have been	ringing
you	will have been	ringing
he/she/it	will have been	ringing
we	will have been	ringing
you	will have been	ringing
they	will have been	ringing

Conditional

I	would	ring
you	would	ring
he/she/it	would	ring
we	would	ring
you	would	ring
they	would	ring

Conditional Past

I	would have	rung
you	would have	rung
he/she/it	would have	rung
we	would have	rung
you	would have	rung
they	would have	rung

rise

- rose - risen

steigen

\+ -ing → e̶
Unregelmäßiges Verb

Simple tenses

Present

I	rise
you	rise
he/she/it	rises
we	rise
you	rise
they	rise

Past

I	rose
you	rose
he/she/it	rose
we	rose
you	rose
they	rose

Present Perfect

I	have	risen
you	have	risen
he/she/it	has	risen
we	have	risen
you	have	risen
they	have	risen

Past Perfect

I	had	risen
you	had	risen
he/she/it	had	risen
we	had	risen
you	had	risen
they	had	risen

***Will*-Future**

I	will	rise
you	will	rise
he/she/it	will	rise
we	will	rise
you	will	rise
they	will	rise

***Going to*-Future**

I	am	going to	rise
you	are	going to	rise
he/she/it	is	going to	rise
we	are	going to	rise
you	are	going to	rise
they	are	going to	rise

Future Perfect

I	will have	risen
you	will have	risen
he/she/it	will have	risen
we	will have	risen
you	will have	risen
they	will have	risen

Imperative

rise

Impersonal

***ing*-Form**

rising

Past Participle

risen

Continuous tenses

Present

I	am	rising
you	are	rising
he/she/it	is	rising
we	are	rising
you	are	rising
they	are	rising

Past

I	was	rising
you	were	rising
he/she/it	was	rising
we	were	rising
you	were	rising
they	were	rising

Present Perfect

I	have	been	rising
you	have	been	rising
he/she/it	has	been	rising
we	have	been	rising
you	have	been	rising
they	have	been	rising

Past Perfect

I	had been	rising
you	had been	rising
he/she/it	had been	rising
we	had been	rising
you	had been	rising
they	had been	rising

***Will*-Future**

I	will be	rising
you	will be	rising
he/she/it	will be	rising
we	will be	rising
you	will be	rising
they	will be	rising

***Going to*-Future**

I	am	going to be	rising
you	are	going to be	rising
he/she/it	is	going to be	rising
we	are	going to be	rising
you	are	going to be	rising
they	are	going to be	rising

Future Perfect

I	will have been	rising
you	will have been	rising
he/she/it	will have been	rising
we	will have been	rising
you	will have been	rising
they	will have been	rising

Conditional

I	would	rise
you	would	rise
he/she/it	would	rise
we	would	rise
you	would	rise
they	would	rise

Conditional Past

I	would have	risen
you	would have	risen
he/she/it	would have	risen
we	would have	risen
you	would have	risen
they	would have	risen

Simple tenses

Present

I	rock
you	rock
he/she/it	rocks
we	rock
you	rock
they	rock

Past

I	rocked
you	rocked
he/she/it	rocked
we	rocked
you	rocked
they	rocked

Present Perfect

I	have	rocked
you	have	rocked
he/she/it	has	rocked
we	have	rocked
you	have	rocked
they	have	rocked

Past Perfect

I	had	rocked
you	had	rocked
he/she/it	had	rocked
we	had	rocked
you	had	rocked
they	had	rocked

Will-Future

I	will	rock
you	will	rock
he/she/it	will	rock
we	will	rock
you	will	rock
they	will	rock

Going to-Future

I	am	going to	rock
you	are	going to	rock
he/she/it	is	going to	rock
we	are	going to	rock
you	are	going to	rock
they	are	going to	rock

Future Perfect

I	will have	rocked
you	will have	rocked
he/she/it	will have	rocked
we	will have	rocked
you	will have	rocked
they	will have	rocked

Imperative

rock

Impersonal

ing-Form

rocking

Past Participle

rocked

Continuous tenses

Present

I	am	rocking
you	are	rocking
he/she/it	is	rocking
we	are	rocking
you	are	rocking
they	are	rocking

Past

I	was	rocking
you	were	rocking
he/she/it	was	rocking
we	were	rocking
you	were	rocking
they	were	rocking

Present Perfect

I	have been	rocking
you	have been	rocking
he/she/it	has been	rocking
we	have been	rocking
you	have been	rocking
they	have been	rocking

Past Perfect

I	had been	rocking
you	had been	rocking
he/she/it	had been	rocking
we	had been	rocking
you	had been	rocking
they	had been	rocking

Will-Future

I	will be	rocking
you	will be	rocking
he/she/it	will be	rocking
we	will be	rocking
you	will be	rocking
they	will be	rocking

Going to-Future

I	am	going to be	rocking
you	are	going to be	rocking
he/she/it	is	going to be	rocking
we	are	going to be	rocking
you	are	going to be	rocking
they	are	going to be	rocking

Future Perfect

I	will have been	rocking
you	will have been	rocking
he/she/it	will have been	rocking
we	will have been	rocking
you	will have been	rocking
they	will have been	rocking

Conditional

I	would	rock
you	would	rock
he/she/it	would	rock
we	would	rock
you	would	rock
they	would	rock

Conditional Past

I	would have	rocked
you	would have	rocked
he/she/it	would have	rocked
we	would have	rocked
you	would have	rocked
they	would have	rocked

roll

rollen

Regelmäßiges Verb

Simple tenses

Present

I	roll
you	roll
he/she/it	rolls
we	roll
you	roll
they	roll

Past

I	rolled
you	rolled
he/she/it	rolled
we	rolled
you	rolled
they	rolled

Present Perfect

I	have	rolled
you	have	rolled
he/she/it	has	rolled
we	have	rolled
you	have	rolled
they	have	rolled

Past Perfect

I	had	rolled
you	had	rolled
he/she/it	had	rolled
we	had	rolled
you	had	rolled
they	had	rolled

Will-Future

I	will	roll
you	will	roll
he/she/it	will	roll
we	will	roll
you	will	roll
they	will	roll

Going to-Future

I	am	going to	roll
you	are	going to	roll
he/she/it	is	going to	roll
we	are	going to	roll
you	are	going to	roll
they	are	going to	roll

Future Perfect

I	will have	rolled
you	will have	rolled
he/she/it	will have	rolled
we	will have	rolled
you	will have	rolled
they	will have	rolled

Imperative

roll

Impersonal

ing-Form

rolling

Past Participle

rolled

Continuous tenses

Present

I	am	rolling
you	are	rolling
he/she/it	is	rolling
we	are	rolling
you	are	rolling
they	are	rolling

Past

I	was	rolling
you	were	rolling
he/she/it	was	rolling
we	were	rolling
you	were	rolling
they	were	rolling

Present Perfect

I	have been	rolling
you	have been	rolling
he/she/it	has been	rolling
we	have been	rolling
you	have been	rolling
they	have been	rolling

Past Perfect

I	had been	rolling
you	had been	rolling
he/she/it	had been	rolling
we	had been	rolling
you	had been	rolling
they	had been	rolling

Will-Future

I	will be	rolling
you	will be	rolling
he/she/it	will be	rolling
we	will be	rolling
you	will be	rolling
they	will be	rolling

Going to-Future

I	am	going to be	rolling
you	are	going to be	rolling
he/she/it	is	going to be	rolling
we	are	going to be	rolling
you	are	going to be	rolling
they	are	going to be	rolling

Future Perfect

I	will have been	rolling
you	will have been	rolling
he/she/it	will have been	rolling
we	will have been	rolling
you	will have been	rolling
they	will have been	rolling

Conditional

I	would	roll
you	would	roll
he/she/it	would	roll
we	would	roll
you	would	roll
they	would	roll

Conditional Past

I	would have	rolled
you	would have	rolled
he/she/it	would have	rolled
we	would have	rolled
you	would have	rolled
they	would have	rolled

Simple tenses

Present

I	row
you	row
he/she/it	rows
we	row
you	row
they	row

Past

I	rowed
you	rowed
he/she/it	rowed
we	rowed
you	rowed
they	rowed

Present Perfect

I	have	rowed
you	have	rowed
he/she/it	has	rowed
we	have	rowed
you	have	rowed
they	have	rowed

Past Perfect

I	had	rowed
you	had	rowed
he/she/it	had	rowed
we	had	rowed
you	had	rowed
they	had	rowed

Will-Future

I	will	row
you	will	row
he/she/it	will	row
we	will	row
you	will	row
they	will	row

Going to-Future

I	am	going to	row
you	are	going to	row
he/she/it	is	going to	row
we	are	going to	row
you	are	going to	row
they	are	going to	row

Future Perfect

I	will have	rowed
you	will have	rowed
he/she/it	will have	rowed
we	will have	rowed
you	will have	rowed
they	will have	rowed

Imperative

row

Impersonal

ing-Form

rowing

Past Participle

rowed

Continuous tenses

Present

I	am	rowing
you	are	rowing
he/she/it	is	rowing
we	are	rowing
you	are	rowing
they	are	rowing

Past

I	was	rowing
you	were	rowing
he/she/it	was	rowing
we	were	rowing
you	were	rowing
they	were	rowing

Present Perfect

I	have been	rowing
you	have been	rowing
he/she/it	has been	rowing
we	have been	rowing
you	have been	rowing
they	have been	rowing

Past Perfect

I	had been	rowing
you	had been	rowing
he/she/it	had been	rowing
we	had been	rowing
you	had been	rowing
they	had been	rowing

Will-Future

I	will be	rowing
you	will be	rowing
he/she/it	will be	rowing
we	will be	rowing
you	will be	rowing
they	will be	rowing

Going to-Future

I	am	going to be	rowing
you	are	going to be	rowing
he/she/it	is	going to be	rowing
we	are	going to be	rowing
you	are	going to be	rowing
they	are	going to be	rowing

Future Perfect

I	will have been	rowing
you	will have been	rowing
he/she/it	will have been	rowing
we	will have been	rowing
you	will have been	rowing
they	will have been	rowing

Conditional

I	would	row
you	would	row
he/she/it	would	row
we	would	row
you	would	row
they	would	row

Conditional Past

I	would have	rowed
you	would have	rowed
he/she/it	would have	rowed
we	would have	rowed
you	would have	rowed
they	would have	rowed

rub

einreiben

Konsonantenverdopplung
Regelmäßiges Verb

Simple tenses

Present

I	rub
you	rub
he/she/it	rubs
we	rub
you	rub
they	rub

Past

I	rubbed
you	rubbed
he/she/it	rubbed
we	rubbed
you	rubbed
they	rubbed

Present Perfect

I	have	rubbed
you	have	rubbed
he/she/it	has	rubbed
we	have	rubbed
you	have	rubbed
they	have	rubbed

Past Perfect

I	had	rubbed
you	had	rubbed
he/she/it	had	rubbed
we	had	rubbed
you	had	rubbed
they	had	rubbed

Will-Future

I	will	rub
you	will	rub
he/she/it	will	rub
we	will	rub
you	will	rub
they	will	rub

Going to-Future

I	am	going to	rub
you	are	going to	rub
he/she/it	is	going to	rub
we	are	going to	rub
you	are	going to	rub
they	are	going to	rub

Future Perfect

I	will have	rubbed
you	will have	rubbed
he/she/it	will have	rubbed
we	will have	rubbed
you	will have	rubbed
they	will have	rubbed

Imperative

rub

Impersonal

ing-Form

rubbing

Past Participle

rubbed

Continuous tenses

Present

I	am	rubbing
you	are	rubbing
he/she/it	is	rubbing
we	are	rubbing
you	are	rubbing
they	are	rubbing

Past

I	was	rubbing
you	were	rubbing
he/she/it	was	rubbing
we	were	rubbing
you	were	rubbing
they	were	rubbing

Present Perfect

I	have been	rubbing
you	have been	rubbing
he/she/it	has been	rubbing
we	have been	rubbing
you	have been	rubbing
they	have been	rubbing

Past Perfect

I	had been	rubbing
you	had been	rubbing
he/she/it	had been	rubbing
we	had been	rubbing
you	had been	rubbing
they	had been	rubbing

Will-Future

I	will be	rubbing
you	will be	rubbing
he/she/it	will be	rubbing
we	will be	rubbing
you	will be	rubbing
they	will be	rubbing

Going to-Future

I	am	going to be	rubbing
you	are	going to be	rubbing
he/she/it	is	going to be	rubbing
we	are	going to be	rubbing
you	are	going to be	rubbing
they	are	going to be	rubbing

Future Perfect

I	will have been	rubbing
you	will have been	rubbing
he/she/it	will have been	rubbing
we	will have been	rubbing
you	will have been	rubbing
they	will have been	rubbing

Conditional

I	would	rub
you	would	rub
he/she/it	would	rub
we	would	rub
you	would	rub
they	would	rub

Conditional Past

I	would have	rubbed
you	would have	rubbed
he/she/it	would have	rubbed
we	would have	rubbed
you	would have	rubbed
they	would have	rubbed

Simple tenses

Present

I	rule
you	rule
he/she/it	rules
we	rule
you	rule
they	rule

Past

I	ruled
you	ruled
he/she/it	ruled
we	ruled
you	ruled
they	ruled

Present Perfect

I	have	ruled
you	have	ruled
he/she/it	has	ruled
we	have	ruled
you	have	ruled
they	have	ruled

Past Perfect

I	had	ruled
you	had	ruled
he/she/it	had	ruled
we	had	ruled
you	had	ruled
they	had	ruled

Will-Future

I	will	rule
you	will	rule
he/she/it	will	rule
we	will	rule
you	will	rule
they	will	rule

Going to-Future

I	am	going to	rule
you	are	going to	rule
he/she/it	is	going to	rule
we	are	going to	rule
you	are	going to	rule
they	are	going to	rule

Future Perfect

I	will have	ruled
you	will have	ruled
he/she/it	will have	ruled
we	will have	ruled
you	will have	ruled
they	will have	ruled

Imperative

rule

Impersonal

ing-Form

ruling

Past Participle

ruled

Continuous tenses

Present

I	am	ruling
you	are	ruling
he/she/it	is	ruling
we	are	ruling
you	are	ruling
they	are	ruling

Past

I	was	ruling
you	were	ruling
he/she/it	was	ruling
we	were	ruling
you	were	ruling
they	were	ruling

Present Perfect

I	have been	ruling
you	have been	ruling
he/she/it	has been	ruling
we	have been	ruling
you	have been	ruling
they	have been	ruling

Past Perfect

I	had been	ruling
you	had been	ruling
he/she/it	had been	ruling
we	had been	ruling
you	had been	ruling
they	had been	ruling

Will-Future

I	will be	ruling
you	will be	ruling
he/she/it	will be	ruling
we	will be	ruling
you	will be	ruling
they	will be	ruling

Going to-Future

I	am	going to be	ruling
you	are	going to be	ruling
he/she/it	is	going to be	ruling
we	are	going to be	ruling
you	are	going to be	ruling
they	are	going to be	ruling

Future Perfect

I	will have been	ruling
you	will have been	ruling
he/she/it	will have been	ruling
we	will have been	ruling
you	will have been	ruling
they	will have been	ruling

Conditional

I	would	rule
you	would	rule
he/she/it	would	rule
we	would	rule
you	would	rule
they	would	rule

Conditional Past

I	would have	ruled
you	would have	ruled
he/she/it	would have	ruled
we	would have	ruled
you	would have	ruled
they	would have	ruled

run

- ran - run

rennen

Konsonantenverdopplung
Unregelmäßiges Verb

Simple tenses

Present

I	run
you	run
he/she/it	runs
we	run
you	run
they	run

Past

I	ran
you	ran
he/she/it	ran
we	ran
you	ran
they	ran

Present Perfect

I	have	run
you	have	run
he/she/it	has	run
we	have	run
you	have	run
they	have	run

Past Perfect

I	had	run
you	had	run
he/she/it	had	run
we	had	run
you	had	run
they	had	run

Will-Future

I	will	run
you	will	run
he/she/it	will	run
we	will	run
you	will	run
they	will	run

Going to-Future

I	am	going to	run
you	are	going to	run
he/she/it	is	going to	run
we	are	going to	run
you	are	going to	run
they	are	going to	run

Future Perfect

I	will have	run
you	will have	run
he/she/it	will have	run
we	will have	run
you	will have	run
they	will have	run

Imperative

run

Impersonal

ing-Form

running

Past Participle

run

Continuous tenses

Present

I	am	running
you	are	running
he/she/it	is	running
we	are	running
you	are	running
they	are	running

Past

I	was	running
you	were	running
he/she/it	was	running
we	were	running
you	were	running
they	were	running

Present Perfect

I	have been	running
you	have been	running
he/she/it	has been	running
we	have been	running
you	have been	running
they	have been	running

Past Perfect

I	had been	running
you	had been	running
he/she/it	had been	running
we	had been	running
you	had been	running
they	had been	running

Will-Future

I	will be	running
you	will be	running
he/she/it	will be	running
we	will be	running
you	will be	running
they	will be	running

Going to-Future

I	am	going to be	running
you	are	going to be	running
he/she/it	is	going to be	running
we	are	going to be	running
you	are	going to be	running
they	are	going to be	running

Future Perfect

I	will have been	running
you	will have been	running
he/she/it	will have been	running
we	will have been	running
you	will have been	running
they	will have been	running

Conditional

I	would	run
you	would	run
he/she/it	would	run
we	would	run
you	would	run
they	would	run

Conditional Past

I	would have	run
you	would have	run
he/she/it	would have	run
we	would have	run
you	would have	run
they	would have	run

-y → -ie vor -s / -y → -i vor -ed
Regelmäßiges Verb

zufriedenstellen

satisfy

Simple tenses

Present

I	satisfy
you	satisfy
he/she/it	satisfies
we	satisfy
you	satisfy
they	satisfy

Past

I	satisfied
you	satisfied
he/she/it	satisfied
we	satisfied
you	satisfied
they	satisfied

Present Perfect

I	have	satisfied
you	have	satisfied
he/she/it	has	satisfied
we	have	satisfied
you	have	satisfied
they	have	satisfied

Past Perfect

I	had	satisfied
you	had	satisfied
he/she/it	had	satisfied
we	had	satisfied
you	had	satisfied
they	had	satisfied

Will-Future

I	will	satisfy
you	will	satisfy
he/she/it	will	satisfy
we	will	satisfy
you	will	satisfy
they	will	satisfy

Going to-Future

I	am	going to	satisfy
you	are	going to	satisfy
he/she/it	is	going to	satisfy
we	are	going to	satisfy
you	are	going to	satisfy
they	are	going to	satisfy

Future Perfect

I	will have	satisfied
you	will have	satisfied
he/she/it	will have	satisfied
we	will have	satisfied
you	will have	satisfied
they	will have	satisfied

Imperative

satisfy

Impersonal

ing-Form

satisfying

Past Participle

satisfied

Continuous tenses

Present

I	am	satisfying
you	are	satisfying
he/she/it	is	satisfying
we	are	satisfying
you	are	satisfying
they	are	satisfying

Past

I	was	satisfying
you	were	satisfying
he/she/it	was	satisfying
we	were	satisfying
you	were	satisfying
they	were	satisfying

Present Perfect

I	have been	satisfying
you	have been	satisfying
he/she/it	has been	satisfying
we	have been	satisfying
you	have been	satisfying
they	have been	satisfying

Past Perfect

I	had been	satisfying
you	had been	satisfying
he/she/it	had been	satisfying
we	had been	satisfying
you	had been	satisfying
they	had been	satisfying

Will-Future

I	will be	satisfying
you	will be	satisfying
he/she/it	will be	satisfying
we	will be	satisfying
you	will be	satisfying
they	will be	satisfying

Going to-Future

I	am	going to be	satisfying
you	are	going to be	satisfying
he/she/it	is	going to be	satisfying
we	are	going to be	satisfying
you	are	going to be	satisfying
they	are	going to be	satisfying

Future Perfect

I	will have been	satisfying
you	will have been	satisfying
he/she/it	will have been	satisfying
we	will have been	satisfying
you	will have been	satisfying
they	will have been	satisfying

Conditional

I	would	satisfy
you	would	satisfy
he/she/it	would	satisfy
we	would	satisfy
you	would	satisfy
they	would	satisfy

Conditional Past

I	would have	satisfied
you	would have	satisfied
he/she/it	would have	satisfied
we	would have	satisfied
you	would have	satisfied
they	would have	satisfied

save

retten

+ **-ing** → ~~e~~ / + **-d** nicht **-ed**
Regelmäßiges Verb

Simple tenses

Present

I	save
you	save
he/she/it	saves
we	save
you	save
they	save

Past

I	saved
you	saved
he/she/it	saved
we	saved
you	saved
they	saved

Present Perfect

I	have	saved
you	have	saved
he/she/it	has	saved
we	have	saved
you	have	saved
they	have	saved

Past Perfect

I	had	saved
you	had	saved
he/she/it	had	saved
we	had	saved
you	had	saved
they	had	saved

Will-Future

I	will	save
you	will	save
he/she/it	will	save
we	will	save
you	will	save
they	will	save

Going to-Future

I	am	going to	save
you	are	going to	save
he/she/it	is	going to	save
we	are	going to	save
you	are	going to	save
they	are	going to	save

Future Perfect

I	will have	saved
you	will have	saved
he/she/it	will have	saved
we	will have	saved
you	will have	saved
they	will have	saved

Imperative

save

Impersonal

ing-Form

saving

Past Participle

saved

Continuous tenses

Present

I	am	saving
you	are	saving
he/she/it	is	saving
we	are	saving
you	are	saving
they	are	saving

Past

I	was	saving
you	were	saving
he/she/it	was	saving
we	were	saving
you	were	saving
they	were	saving

Present Perfect

I	have been	saving
you	have been	saving
he/she/it	has been	saving
we	have been	saving
you	have been	saving
they	have been	saving

Past Perfect

I	had been	saving
you	had been	saving
he/she/it	had been	saving
we	had been	saving
you	had been	saving
they	had been	saving

Will-Future

I	will be	saving
you	will be	saving
he/she/it	will be	saving
we	will be	saving
you	will be	saving
they	will be	saving

Going to-Future

I	am	going to be	saving
you	are	going to be	saving
he/she/it	is	going to be	saving
we	are	going to be	saving
you	are	going to be	saving
they	are	going to be	saving

Future Perfect

I	will have been	saving
you	will have been	saving
he/she/it	will have been	saving
we	will have been	saving
you	will have been	saving
they	will have been	saving

Conditional

I	would	save
you	would	save
he/she/it	would	save
we	would	save
you	would	save
they	would	save

Conditional Past

I	would have	saved
you	would have	saved
he/she/it	would have	saved
we	would have	saved
you	would have	saved
they	would have	saved

Die Aussprache von *says* weicht von den restlichen Formen ab. Es wird [sez] ausgesprochen.
Unregelmäßiges Verb

sagen

say
- said - said

Simple tenses

Present

I	say
you	say
he/she/it	says
we	say
you	say
they	say

Past

I	said
you	said
he/she/it	said
we	said
you	said
they	said

Present Perfect

I	have	said
you	have	said
he/she/it	has	said
we	have	said
you	have	said
they	have	said

Past Perfect

I	had	said
you	had	said
he/she/it	had	said
we	had	said
you	had	said
they	had	said

Will-Future

I	will	say
you	will	say
he/she/it	will	say
we	will	say
you	will	say
they	will	say

Going to-Future

I	am	going to	say
you	are	going to	say
he/she/it	is	going to	say
we	are	going to	say
you	are	going to	say
they	are	going to	say

Future Perfect

I	will have	said
you	will have	said
he/she/it	will have	said
we	will have	said
you	will have	said
they	will have	said

Imperative

say

Impersonal

ing-Form

saying

Past Participle

said

Continuous tenses

Present

I	am	saying
you	are	saying
he/she/it	is	saying
we	are	saying
you	are	saying
they	are	saying

Past

I	was	saying
you	were	saying
he/she/it	was	saying
we	were	saying
you	were	saying
they	were	saying

Present Perfect

I	have been	saying
you	have been	saying
he/she/it	has been	saying
we	have been	saying
you	have been	saying
they	have been	saying

Past Perfect

I	had been	saying
you	had been	saying
he/she/it	had been	saying
we	had been	saying
you	had been	saying
they	had been	saying

Will-Future

I	will be	saying
you	will be	saying
he/she/it	will be	saying
we	will be	saying
you	will be	saying
they	will be	saying

Going to-Future

I	am	going to be	saying
you	are	going to be	saying
he/she/it	is	going to be	saying
we	are	going to be	saying
you	are	going to be	saying
they	are	going to be	saying

Future Perfect

I	will have been	saying
you	will have been	saying
he/she/it	will have been	saying
we	will have been	saying
you	will have been	saying
they	will have been	saying

Conditional

I	would	say
you	would	say
he/she/it	would	say
we	would	say
you	would	say
they	would	say

Conditional Past

I	would have	said
you	would have	said
he/she/it	would have	said
we	would have	said
you	would have	said
they	would have	said

schedule

ansetzen

+ **-ing** → ~~e~~ / + **-d** nicht **-ed**
Regelmäßiges Verb

Simple tenses

Present

I	schedule
you	schedule
he/she/it	schedules
we	schedule
you	schedule
they	schedule

Past

I	scheduled
you	scheduled
he/she/it	scheduled
we	scheduled
you	scheduled
they	scheduled

Present Perfect

I	have	scheduled
you	have	scheduled
he/she/it	has	scheduled
we	have	scheduled
you	have	scheduled
they	have	scheduled

Past Perfect

I	had	scheduled
you	had	scheduled
he/she/it	had	scheduled
we	had	scheduled
you	had	scheduled
they	had	scheduled

Will-Future

I	will	schedule
you	will	schedule
he/she/it	will	schedule
we	will	schedule
you	will	schedule
they	will	schedule

Going to-Future

I	am	going to	schedule
you	are	going to	schedule
he/she/it	is	going to	schedule
we	are	going to	schedule
you	are	going to	schedule
they	are	going to	schedule

Future Perfect

I	will have	scheduled
you	will have	scheduled
he/she/it	will have	scheduled
we	will have	scheduled
you	will have	scheduled
they	will have	scheduled

Imperative

schedule

Impersonal

ing-Form

scheduling

Past Participle

scheduled

Continuous tenses

Present

I	am	scheduling
you	are	scheduling
he/she/it	is	scheduling
we	are	scheduling
you	are	scheduling
they	are	scheduling

Past

I	was	scheduling
you	were	scheduling
he/she/it	was	scheduling
we	were	scheduling
you	were	scheduling
they	were	scheduling

Present Perfect

I	have been	scheduling
you	have been	scheduling
he/she/it	has been	scheduling
we	have been	scheduling
you	have been	scheduling
they	have been	scheduling

Past Perfect

I	had been	scheduling
you	had been	scheduling
he/she/it	had been	scheduling
we	had been	scheduling
you	had been	scheduling
they	had been	scheduling

Will-Future

I	will be	scheduling
you	will be	scheduling
he/she/it	will be	scheduling
we	will be	scheduling
you	will be	scheduling
they	will be	scheduling

Going to-Future

I	am	going to be	scheduling
you	are	going to be	scheduling
he/she/it	is	going to be	scheduling
we	are	going to be	scheduling
you	are	going to be	scheduling
they	are	going to be	scheduling

Future Perfect

I	will have been	scheduling
you	will have been	scheduling
he/she/it	will have been	scheduling
we	will have been	scheduling
you	will have been	scheduling
they	will have been	scheduling

Conditional

I	would	schedule
you	would	schedule
he/she/it	would	schedule
we	would	schedule
you	would	schedule
they	would	schedule

Conditional Past

I	would have	scheduled
you	would have	scheduled
he/she/it	would have	scheduled
we	would have	scheduled
you	would have	scheduled
they	would have	scheduled

+ **-es** in 3. Person Singular
Regelmäßiges Verb

kratzen

scratch

Simple tenses

Present

I	scratch
you	scratch
he/she/it	scratches
we	scratch
you	scratch
they	scratch

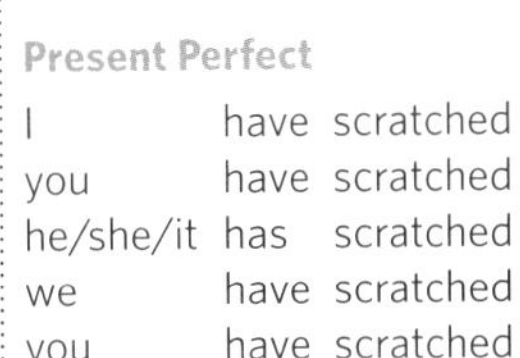

Past

I	scratched
you	scratched
he/she/it	scratched
we	scratched
you	scratched
they	scratched

Present Perfect

I	have	scratched
you	have	scratched
he/she/it	has	scratched
we	have	scratched
you	have	scratched
they	have	scratched

Past Perfect

I	had	scratched
you	had	scratched
he/she/it	had	scratched
we	had	scratched
you	had	scratched
they	had	scratched

Will-Future

I	will	scratch
you	will	scratch
he/she/it	will	scratch
we	will	scratch
you	will	scratch
they	will	scratch

Going to-Future

I	am	going to	scratch
you	are	going to	scratch
he/she/it	is	going to	scratch
we	are	going to	scratch
you	are	going to	scratch
they	are	going to	scratch

Future Perfect

I	will have	scratched
you	will have	scratched
he/she/it	will have	scratched
we	will have	scratched
you	will have	scratched
they	will have	scratched

Imperative

scratch

Impersonal

ing-Form

scratching

Past Participle

scratched

Continuous tenses

Present

I	am	scratching
you	are	scratching
he/she/it	is	scratching
we	are	scratching
you	are	scratching
they	are	scratching

Past

I	was	scratching
you	were	scratching
he/she/it	was	scratching
we	were	scratching
you	were	scratching
they	were	scratching

Present Perfect

I	have been	scratching
you	have been	scratching
he/she/it	has been	scratching
we	have been	scratching
you	have been	scratching
they	have been	scratching

Past Perfect

I	had been	scratching
you	had been	scratching
he/she/it	had been	scratching
we	had been	scratching
you	had been	scratching
they	had been	scratching

Will-Future

I	will be	scratching
you	will be	scratching
he/she/it	will be	scratching
we	will be	scratching
you	will be	scratching
they	will be	scratching

Going to-Future

I	am	going to be	scratching
you	are	going to be	scratching
he/she/it	is	going to be	scratching
we	are	going to be	scratching
you	are	going to be	scratching
they	are	going to be	scratching

Future Perfect

I	will have been scratching
you	will have been scratching
he/she/it	will have been scratching
we	will have been scratching
you	will have been scratching
they	will have been scratching

Conditional

I	would	scratch
you	would	scratch
he/she/it	would	scratch
we	would	scratch
you	would	scratch
they	would	scratch

Conditional Past

I	would have	scratched
you	would have	scratched
he/she/it	would have	scratched
we	would have	scratched
you	would have	scratched
they	would have	scratched

scream

schreien

Regelmäßiges Verb

Simple tenses

Present

I	scream
you	scream
he/she/it	screams
we	scream
you	scream
they	scream

Past

I	screamed
you	screamed
he/she/it	screamed
we	screamed
you	screamed
they	screamed

Present Perfect

I	have	screamed
you	have	screamed
he/she/it	has	screamed
we	have	screamed
you	have	screamed
they	have	screamed

Past Perfect

I	had	screamed
you	had	screamed
he/she/it	had	screamed
we	had	screamed
you	had	screamed
they	had	screamed

Will-Future

I	will	scream
you	will	scream
he/she/it	will	scream
we	will	scream
you	will	scream
they	will	scream

Going to-Future

I	am	going to	scream
you	are	going to	scream
he/she/it	is	going to	scream
we	are	going to	scream
you	are	going to	scream
they	are	going to	scream

Future Perfect

I	will have	screamed
you	will have	screamed
he/she/it	will have	screamed
we	will have	screamed
you	will have	screamed
they	will have	screamed

Imperative

scream

Impersonal

ing-Form

screaming

Past Participle

screamed

Continuous tenses

Present

I	am	screaming
you	are	screaming
he/she/it	is	screaming
we	are	screaming
you	are	screaming
they	are	screaming

Past

I	was	screaming
you	were	screaming
he/she/it	was	screaming
we	were	screaming
you	were	screaming
they	were	screaming

Present Perfect

I	have been	screaming
you	have been	screaming
he/she/it	has been	screaming
we	have been	screaming
you	have been	screaming
they	have been	screaming

Past Perfect

I	had been	screaming
you	had been	screaming
he/she/it	had been	screaming
we	had been	screaming
you	had been	screaming
they	had been	screaming

Will-Future

I	will be	screaming
you	will be	screaming
he/she/it	will be	screaming
we	will be	screaming
you	will be	screaming
they	will be	screaming

Going to-Future

I	am	going to be	screaming
you	are	going to be	screaming
he/she/it	is	going to be	screaming
we	are	going to be	screaming
you	are	going to be	screaming
they	are	going to be	screaming

Future Perfect

I	will have been	screaming
you	will have been	screaming
he/she/it	will have been	screaming
we	will have been	screaming
you	will have been	screaming
they	will have been	screaming

Conditional

I	would	scream
you	would	scream
he/she/it	would	scream
we	would	scream
you	would	scream
they	would	scream

Conditional Past

I	would have	screamed
you	would have	screamed
he/she/it	would have	screamed
we	would have	screamed
you	would have	screamed
they	would have	screamed

sehen

see

– saw – seen

Simple tenses

Present

I	see
you	see
he/she/it	sees
we	see
you	see
they	see

Past

I	saw
you	saw
he/she/it	saw
we	saw
you	saw
they	saw

Present Perfect

I	have	seen
you	have	seen
he/she/it	has	seen
we	have	seen
you	have	seen
they	have	seen

Past Perfect

I	had	seen
you	had	seen
he/she/it	had	seen
we	had	seen
you	had	seen
they	had	seen

Will-Future

I	will	see
you	will	see
he/she/it	will	see
we	will	see
you	will	see
they	will	see

Going to-Future

I	am	going to	see
you	are	going to	see
he/she/it	is	going to	see
we	are	going to	see
you	are	going to	see
they	are	going to	see

Future Perfect

I	will have	seen
you	will have	seen
he/she/it	will have	seen
we	will have	seen
you	will have	seen
they	will have	seen

Imperative

see

Impersonal

ing-Form

seeing

Past Participle

seen

Continuous tenses

Present

I	am	seeing
you	are	seeing
he/she/it	is	seeing
we	are	seeing
you	are	seeing
they	are	seeing

Past

I	was	seeing
you	were	seeing
he/she/it	was	seeing
we	were	seeing
you	were	seeing
they	were	seeing

Present Perfect

I	have	been	seeing
you	have	been	seeing
he/she/it	has	been	seeing
we	have	been	seeing
you	have	been	seeing
they	have	been	seeing

Past Perfect

I	had been	seeing
you	had been	seeing
he/she/it	had been	seeing
we	had been	seeing
you	had been	seeing
they	had been	seeing

Will-Future

I	will be	seeing
you	will be	seeing
he/she/it	will be	seeing
we	will be	seeing
you	will be	seeing
they	will be	seeing

Going to-Future

I	am	going to be	seeing
you	are	going to be	seeing
he/she/it	is	going to be	seeing
we	are	going to be	seeing
you	are	going to be	seeing
they	are	going to be	seeing

Future Perfect

I	will have been	seeing
you	will have been	seeing
he/she/it	will have been	seeing
we	will have been	seeing
you	will have been	seeing
they	will have been	seeing

Conditional

I	would	see
you	would	see
he/she/it	would	see
we	would	see
you	would	see
they	would	see

Conditional Past

I	would have	seen
you	would have	seen
he/she/it	would have	seen
we	would have	seen
you	would have	seen
they	would have	seen

seek
- sought - sought

suchen

Unregelmäßiges Verb

Simple tenses

Present

I	seek
you	seek
he/she/it	seeks
we	seek
you	seek
they	seek

Past

I	sought
you	sought
he/she/it	sought
we	sought
you	sought
they	sought

Present Perfect

I	have	sought
you	have	sought
he/she/it	has	sought
we	have	sought
you	have	sought
they	have	sought

Past Perfect

I	had	sought
you	had	sought
he/she/it	had	sought
we	had	sought
you	had	sought
they	had	sought

***Will*-Future**

I	will	seek
you	will	seek
he/she/it	will	seek
we	will	seek
you	will	seek
they	will	seek

***Going to*-Future**

I	am	going to	seek
you	are	going to	seek
he/she/it	is	going to	seek
we	are	going to	seek
you	are	going to	seek
they	are	going to	seek

Future Perfect

I	will have	sought
you	will have	sought
he/she/it	will have	sought
we	will have	sought
you	will have	sought
they	will have	sought

Imperative

seek

Impersonal

***ing*-Form**

seeking

Past Participle

sought

Continuous tenses

Present

I	am	seeking
you	are	seeking
he/she/it	is	seeking
we	are	seeking
you	are	seeking
they	are	seeking

Past

I	was	seeking
you	were	seeking
he/she/it	was	seeking
we	were	seeking
you	were	seeking
they	were	seeking

Present Perfect

I	have	been	seeking
you	have	been	seeking
he/she/it	has	been	seeking
we	have	been	seeking
you	have	been	seeking
they	have	been	seeking

Past Perfect

I	had been	seeking
you	had been	seeking
he/she/it	had been	seeking
we	had been	seeking
you	had been	seeking
they	had been	seeking

***Will*-Future**

I	will be	seeking
you	will be	seeking
he/she/it	will be	seeking
we	will be	seeking
you	will be	seeking
they	will be	seeking

***Going to*-Future**

I	am	going to be	seeking
you	are	going to be	seeking
he/she/it	is	going to be	seeking
we	are	going to be	seeking
you	are	going to be	seeking
they	are	going to be	seeking

Future Perfect

I	will have been	seeking
you	will have been	seeking
he/she/it	will have been	seeking
we	will have been	seeking
you	will have been	seeking
they	will have been	seeking

Conditional

I	would	seek
you	would	seek
he/she/it	would	seek
we	would	seek
you	would	seek
they	would	seek

Conditional Past

I	would have	sought
you	would have	sought
he/she/it	would have	sought
we	would have	sought
you	would have	sought
they	would have	sought

Simple tenses

Present

I	seem
you	seem
he/she/it	seems
we	seem
you	seem
they	seem

Past

I	seemed
you	seemed
he/she/it	seemed
we	seemed
you	seemed
they	seemed

Present Perfect

I	have	seemed
you	have	seemed
he/she/it	has	seemed
we	have	seemed
you	have	seemed
they	have	seemed

Past Perfect

I	had	seemed
you	had	seemed
he/she/it	had	seemed
we	had	seemed
you	had	seemed
they	had	seemed

Will-Future

I	will	seem
you	will	seem
he/she/it	will	seem
we	will	seem
you	will	seem
they	will	seem

Going to-Future

I	am	going to	seem
you	are	going to	seem
he/she/it	is	going to	seem
we	are	going to	seem
you	are	going to	seem
they	are	going to	seem

Future Perfect

I	will have	seemed
you	will have	seemed
he/she/it	will have	seemed
we	will have	seemed
you	will have	seemed
they	will have	seemed

Imperative

seem

Impersonal

ing-Form

seeming

Past Participle

seemed

Continuous tenses

Present

I	am	seeming
you	are	seeming
he/she/it	is	seeming
we	are	seeming
you	are	seeming
they	are	seeming

Past

I	was	seeming
you	were	seeming
he/she/it	was	seeming
we	were	seeming
you	were	seeming
they	were	seeming

Present Perfect

I	have been	seeming
you	have been	seeming
he/she/it	has been	seeming
we	have been	seeming
you	have been	seeming
they	have been	seeming

Past Perfect

I	had been	seeming
you	had been	seeming
he/she/it	had been	seeming
we	had been	seeming
you	had been	seeming
they	had been	seeming

Will-Future

I	will be	seeming
you	will be	seeming
he/she/it	will be	seeming
we	will be	seeming
you	will be	seeming
they	will be	seeming

Going to-Future

I	am	going to be	seeming
you	are	going to be	seeming
he/she/it	is	going to be	seeming
we	are	going to be	seeming
you	are	going to be	seeming
they	are	going to be	seeming

Future Perfect

I	will have been	seeming
you	will have been	seeming
he/she/it	will have been	seeming
we	will have been	seeming
you	will have been	seeming
they	will have been	seeming

Conditional

I	would	seem
you	would	seem
he/she/it	would	seem
we	would	seem
you	would	seem
they	would	seem

Conditional Past

I	would have	seemed
you	would have	seemed
he/she/it	would have	seemed
we	would have	seemed
you	would have	seemed
they	would have	seemed

select

aussuchen

Regelmäßiges Verb

Simple tenses

Present

I	select
you	select
he/she/it	selects
we	select
you	select
they	select

Past

I	selected
you	selected
he/she/it	selected
we	selected
you	selected
they	selected

Present Perfect

I	have	selected
you	have	selected
he/she/it	has	selected
we	have	selected
you	have	selected
they	have	selected

Past Perfect

I	had	selected
you	had	selected
he/she/it	had	selected
we	had	selected
you	had	selected
they	had	selected

Will-Future

I	will	select
you	will	select
he/she/it	will	select
we	will	select
you	will	select
they	will	select

Going to-Future

I	am	going to	select
you	are	going to	select
he/she/it	is	going to	select
we	are	going to	select
you	are	going to	select
they	are	going to	select

Future Perfect

I	will have	selected
you	will have	selected
he/she/it	will have	selected
we	will have	selected
you	will have	selected
they	will have	selected

Imperative

select

Impersonal

ing-Form

selecting

Past Participle

selected

Continuous tenses

Present

I	am	selecting
you	are	selecting
he/she/it	is	selecting
we	are	selecting
you	are	selecting
they	are	selecting

Past

I	was	selecting
you	were	selecting
he/she/it	was	selecting
we	were	selecting
you	were	selecting
they	were	selecting

Present Perfect

I	have been	selecting
you	have been	selecting
he/she/it	has been	selecting
we	have been	selecting
you	have been	selecting
they	have been	selecting

Past Perfect

I	had been	selecting
you	had been	selecting
he/she/it	had been	selecting
we	had been	selecting
you	had been	selecting
they	had been	selecting

Will-Future

I	will be	selecting
you	will be	selecting
he/she/it	will be	selecting
we	will be	selecting
you	will be	selecting
they	will be	selecting

Going to-Future

I	am	going to be	selecting
you	are	going to be	selecting
he/she/it	is	going to be	selecting
we	are	going to be	selecting
you	are	going to be	selecting
they	are	going to be	selecting

Future Perfect

I	will have been	selecting
you	will have been	selecting
he/she/it	will have been	selecting
we	will have been	selecting
you	will have been	selecting
they	will have been	selecting

Conditional

I	would	select
you	would	select
he/she/it	would	select
we	would	select
you	would	select
they	would	select

Conditional Past

I	would have	selected
you	would have	selected
he/she/it	would have	selected
we	would have	selected
you	would have	selected
they	would have	selected

Simple tenses

Present

I	sell
you	sell
he/she/it	sells
we	sell
you	sell
they	sell

Past

I	sold
you	sold
he/she/it	sold
we	sold
you	sold
they	sold

Present Perfect

I	have	sold
you	have	sold
he/she/it	has	sold
we	have	sold
you	have	sold
they	have	sold

Past Perfect

I	had	sold
you	had	sold
he/she/it	had	sold
we	had	sold
you	had	sold
they	had	sold

Will-Future

I	will	sell
you	will	sell
he/she/it	will	sell
we	will	sell
you	will	sell
they	will	sell

Going to-Future

I	am	going to	sell
you	are	going to	sell
he/she/it	is	going to	sell
we	are	going to	sell
you	are	going to	sell
they	are	going to	sell

Future Perfect

I	will have	sold
you	will have	sold
he/she/it	will have	sold
we	will have	sold
you	will have	sold
they	will have	sold

Imperative

sell

Impersonal

ing-Form

selling

Past Participle

sold

Continuous tenses

Present

I	am	selling
you	are	selling
he/she/it	is	selling
we	are	selling
you	are	selling
they	are	selling

Past

I	was	selling
you	were	selling
he/she/it	was	selling
we	were	selling
you	were	selling
they	were	selling

Present Perfect

I	have been	selling
you	have been	selling
he/she/it	has been	selling
we	have been	selling
you	have been	selling
they	have been	selling

Past Perfect

I	had been	selling
you	had been	selling
he/she/it	had been	selling
we	had been	selling
you	had been	selling
they	had been	selling

Will-Future

I	will be	selling
you	will be	selling
he/she/it	will be	selling
we	will be	selling
you	will be	selling
they	will be	selling

Going to-Future

I	am	going to be	selling
you	are	going to be	selling
he/she/it	is	going to be	selling
we	are	going to be	selling
you	are	going to be	selling
they	are	going to be	selling

Future Perfect

I	will have been	selling
you	will have been	selling
he/she/it	will have been	selling
we	will have been	selling
you	will have been	selling
they	will have been	selling

Conditional

I	would	sell
you	would	sell
he/she/it	would	sell
we	would	sell
you	would	sell
they	would	sell

Conditional Past

I	would have	sold
you	would have	sold
he/she/it	would have	sold
we	would have	sold
you	would have	sold
they	would have	sold

send

– sent – sent

schicken

Unregelmäßiges Verb

Simple tenses

Present

I	send
you	send
he/she/it	sends
we	send
you	send
they	send

Past

I	sent
you	sent
he/she/it	sent
we	sent
you	sent
they	sent

Present Perfect

I	have	sent
you	have	sent
he/she/it	has	sent
we	have	sent
you	have	sent
they	have	sent

Past Perfect

I	had	sent
you	had	sent
he/she/it	had	sent
we	had	sent
you	had	sent
they	had	sent

***Will*-Future**

I	will	send
you	will	send
he/she/it	will	send
we	will	send
you	will	send
they	will	send

***Going to*-Future**

I	am	going to	send
you	are	going to	send
he/she/it	is	going to	send
we	are	going to	send
you	are	going to	send
they	are	going to	send

Future Perfect

I	will have	sent
you	will have	sent
he/she/it	will have	sent
we	will have	sent
you	will have	sent
they	will have	sent

Imperative

send

Impersonal

***ing*-Form**

sending

Past Participle

sent

Continuous tenses

Present

I	am	sending
you	are	sending
he/she/it	is	sending
we	are	sending
you	are	sending
they	are	sending

Past

I	was	sending
you	were	sending
he/she/it	was	sending
we	were	sending
you	were	sending
they	were	sending

Present Perfect

I	have been	sending
you	have been	sending
he/she/it	has been	sending
we	have been	sending
you	have been	sending
they	have been	sending

Past Perfect

I	had been	sending
you	had been	sending
he/she/it	had been	sending
we	had been	sending
you	had been	sending
they	had been	sending

***Will*-Future**

I	will be	sending
you	will be	sending
he/she/it	will be	sending
we	will be	sending
you	will be	sending
they	will be	sending

***Going to*-Future**

I	am	going to be	sending
you	are	going to be	sending
he/she/it	is	going to be	sending
we	are	going to be	sending
you	are	going to be	sending
they	are	going to be	sending

Future Perfect

I	will have been sending
you	will have been sending
he/she/it	will have been sending
we	will have been sending
you	will have been sending
they	will have been sending

Conditional

I	would	send
you	would	send
he/she/it	would	send
we	would	send
you	would	send
they	would	send

Conditional Past

I	would have	sent
you	would have	sent
he/she/it	would have	sent
we	would have	sent
you	would have	sent
they	would have	sent

+ **-ing** → ~~e~~ / + **-d** nicht **-ed**
Regelmäßiges Verb

trennen

separate

Simple tenses

Present

I	separate
you	separate
he/she/it	separates
we	separate
you	separate
they	separate

Past

I	separated
you	separated
he/she/it	separated
we	separated
you	separated
they	separated

Present Perfect

I	have	separated
you	have	separated
he/she/it	has	separated
we	have	separated
you	have	separated
they	have	separated

Past Perfect

I	had	separated
you	had	separated
he/she/it	had	separated
we	had	separated
you	had	separated
they	had	separated

Will-Future

I	will	separate
you	will	separate
he/she/it	will	separate
we	will	separate
you	will	separate
they	will	separate

Going to-Future

I	am	going to	separate
you	are	going to	separate
he/she/it	is	going to	separate
we	are	going to	separate
you	are	going to	separate
they	are	going to	separate

Future Perfect

I	will have	separated
you	will have	separated
he/she/it	will have	separated
we	will have	separated
you	will have	separated
they	will have	separated

Imperative

separate

Impersonal

ing-Form

separating

Past Participle

separated

Continuous tenses

Present

I	am	separating
you	are	separating
he/she/it	is	separating
we	are	separating
you	are	separating
they	are	separating

Past

I	was	separating
you	were	separating
he/she/it	was	separating
we	were	separating
you	were	separating
they	were	separating

Present Perfect

I	have been	separating
you	have been	separating
he/she/it	has been	separating
we	have been	separating
you	have been	separating
they	have been	separating

Past Perfect

I	had been	separating
you	had been	separating
he/she/it	had been	separating
we	had been	separating
you	had been	separating
they	had been	separating

Will-Future

I	will be	separating
you	will be	separating
he/she/it	will be	separating
we	will be	separating
you	will be	separating
they	will be	separating

Going to-Future

I	am	going to be	separating
you	are	going to be	separating
he/she/it	is	going to be	separating
we	are	going to be	separating
you	are	going to be	separating
they	are	going to be	separating

Future Perfect

I	will have been	separating
you	will have been	separating
he/she/it	will have been	separating
we	will have been	separating
you	will have been	separating
they	will have been	separating

Conditional

I	would	separate
you	would	separate
he/she/it	would	separate
we	would	separate
you	would	separate
they	would	separate

Conditional Past

I	would have	separated
you	would have	separated
he/she/it	would have	separated
we	would have	separated
you	would have	separated
they	would have	separated

serve

bedienen

+ **-ing** → ~~e~~ / + **-d** nicht **-ed**
Regelmäßiges Verb

Simple tenses

Present

I serve
you serve
he/she/it serves
we serve
you serve
they serve

Past

I served
you served
he/she/it served
we served
you served
they served

Present Perfect

I have served
you have served
he/she/it has served
we have served
you have served
they have served

Past Perfect

I had served
you had served
he/she/it had served
we had served
you had served
they had served

Will-Future

I will serve
you will serve
he/she/it will serve
we will serve
you will serve
they will serve

Going to-Future

I am going to serve
you are going to serve
he/she/it is going to serve
we are going to serve
you are going to serve
they are going to serve

Future Perfect

I will have served
you will have served
he/she/it will have served
we will have served
you will have served
they will have served

Imperative

serve

Impersonal

ing-Form

serving

Past Participle

served

Continuous tenses

Present

I am serving
you are serving
he/she/it is serving
we are serving
you are serving
they are serving

Past

I was serving
you were serving
he/she/it was serving
we were serving
you were serving
they were serving

Present Perfect

I have been serving
you have been serving
he/she/it has been serving
we have been serving
you have been serving
they have been serving

Past Perfect

I had been serving
you had been serving
he/she/it had been serving
we had been serving
you had been serving
they had been serving

Will-Future

I will be serving
you will be serving
he/she/it will be serving
we will be serving
you will be serving
they will be serving

Going to-Future

I am going to be serving
you are going to be serving
he/she/it is going to be serving
we are going to be serving
you are going to be serving
they are going to be serving

Future Perfect

I will have been serving
you will have been serving
he/she/it will have been serving
we will have been serving
you will have been serving
they will have been serving

Conditional

I would serve
you would serve
he/she/it would serve
we would serve
you would serve
they would serve

Conditional Past

I would have served
you would have served
he/she/it would have served
we would have served
you would have served
they would have served

Simple tenses

Present

I	set
you	set
he/she/it	sets
we	set
you	set
they	set

Past

I	set
you	set
he/she/it	set
we	set
you	set
they	set

Present Perfect

I	have	set
you	have	set
he/she/it	has	set
we	have	set
you	have	set
they	have	set

Past Perfect

I	had	set
you	had	set
he/she/it	had	set
we	had	set
you	had	set
they	had	set

Will-Future

I	will	set
you	will	set
he/she/it	will	set
we	will	set
you	will	set
they	will	set

Going to-Future

I	am	going to	set
you	are	going to	set
he/she/it	is	going to	set
we	are	going to	set
you	are	going to	set
they	are	going to	set

Future Perfect

I	will have	set
you	will have	set
he/she/it	will have	set
we	will have	set
you	will have	set
they	will have	set

Imperative

set

Impersonal

ing-Form

setting

Past Participle

set

Continuous tenses

Present

I	am	setting
you	are	setting
he/she/it	is	setting
we	are	setting
you	are	setting
they	are	setting

Past

I	was	setting
you	were	setting
he/she/it	was	setting
we	were	setting
you	were	setting
they	were	setting

Present Perfect

I	have been	setting
you	have been	setting
he/she/it	has been	setting
we	have been	setting
you	have been	setting
they	have been	setting

Past Perfect

I	had been	setting
you	had been	setting
he/she/it	had been	setting
we	had been	setting
you	had been	setting
they	had been	setting

Will-Future

I	will be	setting
you	will be	setting
he/she/it	will be	setting
we	will be	setting
you	will be	setting
they	will be	setting

Going to-Future

I	am	going to be	setting
you	are	going to be	setting
he/she/it	is	going to be	setting
we	are	going to be	setting
you	are	going to be	setting
they	are	going to be	setting

Future Perfect

I	will have been	setting
you	will have been	setting
he/she/it	will have been	setting
we	will have been	setting
you	will have been	setting
they	will have been	setting

Conditional

I	would	set
you	would	set
he/she/it	would	set
we	would	set
you	would	set
they	would	set

Conditional Past

I	would have	set
you	would have	set
he/she/it	would have	set
we	would have	set
you	would have	set
they	would have	set

shake
- shook - shaken

schütteln

+ **-ing** → ~~e~~
Unregelmäßiges Verb

Simple tenses

Present

I	shake
you	shake
he/she/it	shakes
we	shake
you	shake
they	shake

Past

I	shook
you	shook
he/she/it	shook
we	shook
you	shook
they	shook

Present Perfect

I	have	shaken
you	have	shaken
he/she/it	has	shaken
we	have	shaken
you	have	shaken
they	have	shaken

Past Perfect

I	had	shaken
you	had	shaken
he/she/it	had	shaken
we	had	shaken
you	had	shaken
they	had	shaken

Will-Future

I	will	shake
you	will	shake
he/she/it	will	shake
we	will	shake
you	will	shake
they	will	shake

Going to-Future

I	am	going to	shake
you	are	going to	shake
he/she/it	is	going to	shake
we	are	going to	shake
you	are	going to	shake
they	are	going to	shake

Future Perfect

I	will have	shaken
you	will have	shaken
he/she/it	will have	shaken
we	will have	shaken
you	will have	shaken
they	will have	shaken

Imperative

shake

Impersonal

ing-Form

shaking

Past Participle

shaken

Continuous tenses

Present

I	am	shaking
you	are	shaking
he/she/it	is	shaking
we	are	shaking
you	are	shaking
they	are	shaking

Past

I	was	shaking
you	were	shaking
he/she/it	was	shaking
we	were	shaking
you	were	shaking
they	were	shaking

Present Perfect

I	have been	shaking
you	have been	shaking
he/she/it	has been	shaking
we	have been	shaking
you	have been	shaking
they	have been	shaking

Past Perfect

I	had been	shaking
you	had been	shaking
he/she/it	had been	shaking
we	had been	shaking
you	had been	shaking
they	had been	shaking

Will-Future

I	will be	shaking
you	will be	shaking
he/she/it	will be	shaking
we	will be	shaking
you	will be	shaking
they	will be	shaking

Going to-Future

I	am	going to be	shaking
you	are	going to be	shaking
he/she/it	is	going to be	shaking
we	are	going to be	shaking
you	are	going to be	shaking
they	are	going to be	shaking

Future Perfect

I	will have been	shaking
you	will have been	shaking
he/she/it	will have been	shaking
we	will have been	shaking
you	will have been	shaking
they	will have been	shaking

Conditional

I	would	shake
you	would	shake
he/she/it	would	shake
we	would	shake
you	would	shake
they	would	shake

Conditional Past

I	would have	shaken
you	would have	shaken
he/she/it	would have	shaken
we	would have	shaken
you	would have	shaken
they	would have	shaken

+ **-ing** → ~~e~~ / + **-d** nicht **-ed**
Regelmäßiges Verb

formen

shape

Simple tenses

Present

I	shape
you	shape
he/she/it	shapes
we	shape
you	shape
they	shape

Past

I	shaped
you	shaped
he/she/it	shaped
we	shaped
you	shaped
they	shaped

Present Perfect

I	have	shaped
you	have	shaped
he/she/it	has	shaped
we	have	shaped
you	have	shaped
they	have	shaped

Past Perfect

I	had	shaped
you	had	shaped
he/she/it	had	shaped
we	had	shaped
you	had	shaped
they	had	shaped

Will-Future

I	will	shape
you	will	shape
he/she/it	will	shape
we	will	shape
you	will	shape
they	will	shape

Going to-Future

I	am	going to	shape
you	are	going to	shape
he/she/it	is	going to	shape
we	are	going to	shape
you	are	going to	shape
they	are	going to	shape

Future Perfect

I	will have	shaped
you	will have	shaped
he/she/it	will have	shaped
we	will have	shaped
you	will have	shaped
they	will have	shaped

Imperative

shape

Impersonal

ing-Form

shaping

Past Participle

shaped

Continuous tenses

Present

I	am	shaping
you	are	shaping
he/she/it	is	shaping
we	are	shaping
you	are	shaping
they	are	shaping

Past

I	was	shaping
you	were	shaping
he/she/it	was	shaping
we	were	shaping
you	were	shaping
they	were	shaping

Present Perfect

I	have been	shaping
you	have been	shaping
he/she/it	has been	shaping
we	have been	shaping
you	have been	shaping
they	have been	shaping

Past Perfect

I	had been	shaping
you	had been	shaping
he/she/it	had been	shaping
we	had been	shaping
you	had been	shaping
they	had been	shaping

Will-Future

I	will be	shaping
you	will be	shaping
he/she/it	will be	shaping
we	will be	shaping
you	will be	shaping
they	will be	shaping

Going to-Future

I	am	going to be	shaping
you	are	going to be	shaping
he/she/it	is	going to be	shaping
we	are	going to be	shaping
you	are	going to be	shaping
they	are	going to be	shaping

Future Perfect

I	will have been	shaping
you	will have been	shaping
he/she/it	will have been	shaping
we	will have been	shaping
you	will have been	shaping
they	will have been	shaping

Conditional

I	would	shape
you	would	shape
he/she/it	would	shape
we	would	shape
you	would	shape
they	would	shape

Conditional Past

I	would have	shaped
you	would have	shaped
he/she/it	would have	shaped
we	would have	shaped
you	would have	shaped
they	would have	shaped

share

teilen

+ **-ing** → ~~e~~ / + **-d** nicht **-ed**
Regelmäßiges Verb

Simple tenses

Present

I	share
you	share
he/she/it	shares
we	share
you	share
they	share

Past

I	shared
you	shared
he/she/it	shared
we	shared
you	shared
they	shared

Present Perfect

I	have	shared
you	have	shared
he/she/it	has	shared
we	have	shared
you	have	shared
they	have	shared

Past Perfect

I	had	shared
you	had	shared
he/she/it	had	shared
we	had	shared
you	had	shared
they	had	shared

Will-Future

I	will	share
you	will	share
he/she/it	will	share
we	will	share
you	will	share
they	will	share

Going to-Future

I	am	going to	share
you	are	going to	share
he/she/it	is	going to	share
we	are	going to	share
you	are	going to	share
they	are	going to	share

Future Perfect

I	will have	shared
you	will have	shared
he/she/it	will have	shared
we	will have	shared
you	will have	shared
they	will have	shared

Imperative

share

Impersonal

ing-Form

sharing

Past Participle

shared

Continuous tenses

Present

I	am	sharing
you	are	sharing
he/she/it	is	sharing
we	are	sharing
you	are	sharing
they	are	sharing

Past

I	was	sharing
you	were	sharing
he/she/it	was	sharing
we	were	sharing
you	were	sharing
they	were	sharing

Present Perfect

I	have	been	sharing
you	have	been	sharing
he/she/it	has	been	sharing
we	have	been	sharing
you	have	been	sharing
they	have	been	sharing

Past Perfect

I	had been	sharing
you	had been	sharing
he/she/it	had been	sharing
we	had been	sharing
you	had been	sharing
they	had been	sharing

Will-Future

I	will be	sharing
you	will be	sharing
he/she/it	will be	sharing
we	will be	sharing
you	will be	sharing
they	will be	sharing

Going to-Future

I	am	going to be	sharing
you	are	going to be	sharing
he/she/it	is	going to be	sharing
we	are	going to be	sharing
you	are	going to be	sharing
they	are	going to be	sharing

Future Perfect

I	will have been	sharing
you	will have been	sharing
he/she/it	will have been	sharing
we	will have been	sharing
you	will have been	sharing
they	will have been	sharing

Conditional

I	would	share
you	would	share
he/she/it	would	share
we	would	share
you	would	share
they	would	share

Conditional Past

I	would have	shared
you	would have	shared
he/she/it	would have	shared
we	would have	shared
you	would have	shared
they	would have	shared

Simple tenses

Present

I	shift
you	shift
he/she/it	shifts
we	shift
you	shift
they	shift

Past

I	shifted
you	shifted
he/she/it	shifted
we	shifted
you	shifted
they	shifted

Present Perfect

I	have	shifted
you	have	shifted
he/she/it	has	shifted
we	have	shifted
you	have	shifted
they	have	shifted

Past Perfect

I	had	shifted
you	had	shifted
he/she/it	had	shifted
we	had	shifted
you	had	shifted
they	had	shifted

Will-Future

I	will	shift
you	will	shift
he/she/it	will	shift
we	will	shift
you	will	shift
they	will	shift

Going to-Future

I	am	going to	shift
you	are	going to	shift
he/she/it	is	going to	shift
we	are	going to	shift
you	are	going to	shift
they	are	going to	shift

Future Perfect

I	will have	shifted
you	will have	shifted
he/she/it	will have	shifted
we	will have	shifted
you	will have	shifted
they	will have	shifted

Imperative

shift

Impersonal

ing-Form

shifting

Past Participle

shifted

Continuous tenses

Present

I	am	shifting
you	are	shifting
he/she/it	is	shifting
we	are	shifting
you	are	shifting
they	are	shifting

Past

I	was	shifting
you	were	shifting
he/she/it	was	shifting
we	were	shifting
you	were	shifting
they	were	shifting

Present Perfect

I	have been	shifting
you	have been	shifting
he/she/it	has been	shifting
we	have been	shifting
you	have been	shifting
they	have been	shifting

Past Perfect

I	had been	shifting
you	had been	shifting
he/she/it	had been	shifting
we	had been	shifting
you	had been	shifting
they	had been	shifting

Will-Future

I	will be	shifting
you	will be	shifting
he/she/it	will be	shifting
we	will be	shifting
you	will be	shifting
they	will be	shifting

Going to-Future

I	am	going to be	shifting
you	are	going to be	shifting
he/she/it	is	going to be	shifting
we	are	going to be	shifting
you	are	going to be	shifting
they	are	going to be	shifting

Future Perfect

I	will have been	shifting
you	will have been	shifting
he/she/it	will have been	shifting
we	will have been	shifting
you	will have been	shifting
they	will have been	shifting

Conditional

I	would	shift
you	would	shift
he/she/it	would	shift
we	would	shift
you	would	shift
they	would	shift

Conditional Past

I	would have	shifted
you	would have	shifted
he/she/it	would have	shifted
we	would have	shifted
you	would have	shifted
they	would have	shifted

shine

- shone/shined - shone/shined

scheinen

+ **-ing** → ~~e~~ / + **-d** nicht **-ed**
Unregelmäßiges Verb

Simple tenses

Present

I shine
you shine
he/she/it shines
we shine
you shine
they shine

Past

I shone | shined
you shone | shined
he/she/it shone | shined
we shone | shined
you shone | shined
they shone | shined

Present Perfect

I have shone | shined
you have shone | shined
he/she/it has shone | shined
we have shone | shined
you have shone | shined
they have shone | shined

Past Perfect

I had shone | shined
you had shone | shined
he/she/it had shone | shined
we had shone | shined
you had shone | shined
they had shone | shined

Will-Future

I will shine
you will shine
he/she/it will shine
we will shine
you will shine
they will shine

Going to-Future

I am going to shine
you are going to shine
he/she/it is going to shine
we are going to shine
you are going to shine
they are going to shine

Future Perfect

I will have shone | shined
you will have shone | shined
he/she/it will have shone | shined
we will have shone | shined
you will have shone | shined
they will have shone | shined

Imperative

shine

Impersonal

ing-Form

shining

Past Participle

shone | shined

Continuous tenses

Present

I am shining
you are shining
he/she/it is shining
we are shining
you are shining
they are shining

Past

I was shining
you were shining
he/she/it was shining
we were shining
you were shining
they were shining

Present Perfect

I have been shining
you have been shining
he/she/it has been shining
we have been shining
you have been shining
they have been shining

Past Perfect

I had been shining
you had been shining
he/she/it had been shining
we had been shining
you had been shining
they had been shining

Will-Future

I will be shining
you will be shining
he/she/it will be shining
we will be shining
you will be shining
they will be shining

Going to-Future

I am going to be shining
you are going to be shining
he/she/it is going to be shining
we are going to be shining
you are going to be shining
they are going to be shining

Future Perfect

I will have been shining
you will have been shining
he/she/it will have been shining
we will have been shining
you will have been shining
they will have been shining

Conditional

I would shine
you would shine
he/she/it would shine
we would shine
you would shine
they would shine

Conditional Past

I would have shone | shined
you would have shone | shined
he/she/it would have shone | shined
we would have shone | shined
you would have shone | shined
they would have shone | shined

Simple tenses

Present

I	shock
you	shock
he/she/it	shocks
we	shock
you	shock
they	shock

Past

I	shocked
you	shocked
he/she/it	shocked
we	shocked
you	shocked
they	shocked

Present Perfect

I	have	shocked
you	have	shocked
he/she/it	has	shocked
we	have	shocked
you	have	shocked
they	have	shocked

Past Perfect

I	had	shocked
you	had	shocked
he/she/it	had	shocked
we	had	shocked
you	had	shocked
they	had	shocked

Will-Future

I	will	shock
you	will	shock
he/she/it	will	shock
we	will	shock
you	will	shock
they	will	shock

Going to-Future

I	am	going to	shock
you	are	going to	shock
he/she/it	is	going to	shock
we	are	going to	shock
you	are	going to	shock
they	are	going to	shock

Future Perfect

I	will have	shocked
you	will have	shocked
he/she/it	will have	shocked
we	will have	shocked
you	will have	shocked
they	will have	shocked

Imperative

shock

Impersonal

ing-Form

shocking

Past Participle

shocked

Continuous tenses

Present

I	am	shocking
you	are	shocking
he/she/it	is	shocking
we	are	shocking
you	are	shocking
they	are	shocking

Past

I	was	shocking
you	were	shocking
he/she/it	was	shocking
we	were	shocking
you	were	shocking
they	were	shocking

Present Perfect

I	have been	shocking
you	have been	shocking
he/she/it	has been	shocking
we	have been	shocking
you	have been	shocking
they	have been	shocking

Past Perfect

I	had been	shocking
you	had been	shocking
he/she/it	had been	shocking
we	had been	shocking
you	had been	shocking
they	had been	shocking

Will-Future

I	will be	shocking
you	will be	shocking
he/she/it	will be	shocking
we	will be	shocking
you	will be	shocking
they	will be	shocking

Going to-Future

I	am	going to be	shocking
you	are	going to be	shocking
he/she/it	is	going to be	shocking
we	are	going to be	shocking
you	are	going to be	shocking
they	are	going to be	shocking

Future Perfect

I	will have been	shocking
you	will have been	shocking
he/she/it	will have been	shocking
we	will have been	shocking
you	will have been	shocking
they	will have been	shocking

Conditional

I	would	shock
you	would	shock
he/she/it	would	shock
we	would	shock
you	would	shock
they	would	shock

Conditional Past

I	would have	shocked
you	would have	shocked
he/she/it	would have	shocked
we	would have	shocked
you	would have	shocked
they	would have	shocked

shoot

- shot - shot

schießen

Unregelmäßiges Verb

Simple tenses

Present

I	shoot
you	shoot
he/she/it	shoots
we	shoot
you	shoot
they	shoot

Past

I	shot
you	shot
he/she/it	shot
we	shot
you	shot
they	shot

Present Perfect

I	have	shot
you	have	shot
he/she/it	has	shot
we	have	shot
you	have	shot
they	have	shot

Past Perfect

I	had	shot
you	had	shot
he/she/it	had	shot
we	had	shot
you	had	shot
they	had	shot

Will-Future

I	will	shoot
you	will	shoot
he/she/it	will	shoot
we	will	shoot
you	will	shoot
they	will	shoot

Going to-Future

I	am	going to	shoot
you	are	going to	shoot
he/she/it	is	going to	shoot
we	are	going to	shoot
you	are	going to	shoot
they	are	going to	shoot

Future Perfect

I	will have	shot
you	will have	shot
he/she/it	will have	shot
we	will have	shot
you	will have	shot
they	will have	shot

Imperative

shoot

Impersonal

ing-Form

shooting

Past Participle

shot

Continuous tenses

Present

I	am	shooting
you	are	shooting
he/she/it	is	shooting
we	are	shooting
you	are	shooting
they	are	shooting

Past

I	was	shooting
you	were	shooting
he/she/it	was	shooting
we	were	shooting
you	were	shooting
they	were	shooting

Present Perfect

I	have been	shooting
you	have been	shooting
he/she/it	has been	shooting
we	have been	shooting
you	have been	shooting
they	have been	shooting

Past Perfect

I	had been	shooting
you	had been	shooting
he/she/it	had been	shooting
we	had been	shooting
you	had been	shooting
they	had been	shooting

Will-Future

I	will be	shooting
you	will be	shooting
he/she/it	will be	shooting
we	will be	shooting
you	will be	shooting
they	will be	shooting

Going to-Future

I	am	going to be	shooting
you	are	going to be	shooting
he/she/it	is	going to be	shooting
we	are	going to be	shooting
you	are	going to be	shooting
they	are	going to be	shooting

Future Perfect

I	will have been	shooting
you	will have been	shooting
he/she/it	will have been	shooting
we	will have been	shooting
you	will have been	shooting
they	will have been	shooting

Conditional

I	would	shoot
you	would	shoot
he/she/it	would	shoot
we	would	shoot
you	would	shoot
they	would	shoot

Conditional Past

I	would have	shot
you	would have	shot
he/she/it	would have	shot
we	would have	shot
you	would have	shot
they	would have	shot

Konsonantenverdopplung
Regelmäßiges Verb

einkaufen

Simple tenses

Present

I	shop
you	shop
he/she/it	shops
we	shop
you	shop
they	shop

Past

I	shopped
you	shopped
he/she/it	shopped
we	shopped
you	shopped
they	shopped

Present Perfect

I	have	shopped
you	have	shopped
he/she/it	has	shopped
we	have	shopped
you	have	shopped
they	have	shopped

Past Perfect

I	had	shopped
you	had	shopped
he/she/it	had	shopped
we	had	shopped
you	had	shopped
they	had	shopped

Will-Future

I	will	shop
you	will	shop
he/she/it	will	shop
we	will	shop
you	will	shop
they	will	shop

Going to-Future

I	am	going to	shop
you	are	going to	shop
he/she/it	is	going to	shop
we	are	going to	shop
you	are	going to	shop
they	are	going to	shop

Future Perfect

I	will have	shopped
you	will have	shopped
he/she/it	will have	shopped
we	will have	shopped
you	will have	shopped
they	will have	shopped

Imperative

shop

Impersonal

ing-Form

shopping

Past Participle

shopped

Continuous tenses

Present

I	am	shopping
you	are	shopping
he/she/it	is	shopping
we	are	shopping
you	are	shopping
they	are	shopping

Past

I	was	shopping
you	were	shopping
he/she/it	was	shopping
we	were	shopping
you	were	shopping
they	were	shopping

Present Perfect

I	have been	shopping
you	have been	shopping
he/she/it	has been	shopping
we	have been	shopping
you	have been	shopping
they	have been	shopping

Past Perfect

I	had been	shopping
you	had been	shopping
he/she/it	had been	shopping
we	had been	shopping
you	had been	shopping
they	had been	shopping

Will-Future

I	will be	shopping
you	will be	shopping
he/she/it	will be	shopping
we	will be	shopping
you	will be	shopping
they	will be	shopping

Going to-Future

I	am	going to be	shopping
you	are	going to be	shopping
he/she/it	is	going to be	shopping
we	are	going to be	shopping
you	are	going to be	shopping
they	are	going to be	shopping

Future Perfect

I	will have been	shopping
you	will have been	shopping
he/she/it	will have been	shopping
we	will have been	shopping
you	will have been	shopping
they	will have been	shopping

Conditional

I	would	shop
you	would	shop
he/she/it	would	shop
we	would	shop
you	would	shop
they	would	shop

Conditional Past

I	would have	shopped
you	would have	shopped
he/she/it	would have	shopped
we	would have	shopped
you	would have	shopped
they	would have	shopped

shout

rufen

Regelmäßiges Verb

Simple tenses

Present

I	shout
you	shout
he/she/it	shouts
we	shout
you	shout
they	shout

Past

I	shouted
you	shouted
he/she/it	shouted
we	shouted
you	shouted
they	shouted

Present Perfect

I	have	shouted
you	have	shouted
he/she/it	has	shouted
we	have	shouted
you	have	shouted
they	have	shouted

Past Perfect

I	had	shouted
you	had	shouted
he/she/it	had	shouted
we	had	shouted
you	had	shouted
they	had	shouted

Will-Future

I	will	shout
you	will	shout
he/she/it	will	shout
we	will	shout
you	will	shout
they	will	shout

Going to-Future

I	am	going to	shout
you	are	going to	shout
he/she/it	is	going to	shout
we	are	going to	shout
you	are	going to	shout
they	are	going to	shout

Future Perfect

I	will have	shouted
you	will have	shouted
he/she/it	will have	shouted
we	will have	shouted
you	will have	shouted
they	will have	shouted

Imperative

shout

Impersonal

ing-Form

shouting

Past Participle

shouted

Continuous tenses

Present

I	am	shouting
you	are	shouting
he/she/it	is	shouting
we	are	shouting
you	are	shouting
they	are	shouting

Past

I	was	shouting
you	were	shouting
he/she/it	was	shouting
we	were	shouting
you	were	shouting
they	were	shouting

Present Perfect

I	have been	shouting
you	have been	shouting
he/she/it	has been	shouting
we	have been	shouting
you	have been	shouting
they	have been	shouting

Past Perfect

I	had been	shouting
you	had been	shouting
he/she/it	had been	shouting
we	had been	shouting
you	had been	shouting
they	had been	shouting

Will-Future

I	will be	shouting
you	will be	shouting
he/she/it	will be	shouting
we	will be	shouting
you	will be	shouting
they	will be	shouting

Going to-Future

I	am	going to be	shouting
you	are	going to be	shouting
he/she/it	is	going to be	shouting
we	are	going to be	shouting
you	are	going to be	shouting
they	are	going to be	shouting

Future Perfect

I	will have been	shouting
you	will have been	shouting
he/she/it	will have been	shouting
we	will have been	shouting
you	will have been	shouting
they	will have been	shouting

Conditional

I	would	shout
you	would	shout
he/she/it	would	shout
we	would	shout
you	would	shout
they	would	shout

Conditional Past

I	would have	shouted
you	would have	shouted
he/she/it	would have	shouted
we	would have	shouted
you	would have	shouted
they	would have	shouted

Unregelmäßiges Verb

zeigen

show

- showed - shown/showed

Simple tenses

Present

I	show
you	show
he/she/it	show
we	show
you	show
they	show

Past

I	showed
you	showed
he/she/it	showed
we	showed
you	showed
they	showed

Present Perfect

I	have	shown | showed
you	have	shown | showed
he/she/it	has	shown | showed
we	have	shown | showed
you	have	shown | showed
they	have	shown | showed

Past Perfect

I	had	shown | showed
you	had	shown | showed
he/she/it	had	shown | showed
we	had	shown | showed
you	had	shown | showed
they	had	shown | showed

Will-Future

I	will	show
you	will	show
he/she/it	will	show
we	will	show
you	will	show
they	will	show

Going to-Future

I	am	going to	show
you	are	going to	show
he/she/it	is	going to	show
we	are	going to	show
you	are	going to	show
they	are	going to	show

Future Perfect

I	will have	shown | showed
you	will have	shown | showed
he/she/it	will have	shown | showed
we	will have	shown | showed
you	will have	shown | showed
they	will have	shown | showed

Imperative

show

Impersonal

ing-Form

showing

Past Participle

shown | showed

Continuous tenses

Present

I	am	showing
you	are	showing
he/she/it	is	showing
we	are	showing
you	are	showing
they	are	showing

Past

I	was	showing
you	were	showing
he/she/it	was	showing
we	were	showing
you	were	showing
they	were	showing

Present Perfect

I	have been	showing
you	have been	showing
he/she/it	has been	showing
we	have been	showing
you	have been	showing
they	have been	showing

Past Perfect

I	had been	showing
you	had been	showing
he/she/it	had been	showing
we	had been	showing
you	had been	showing
they	had been	showing

Will-Future

I	will be	showing
you	will be	showing
he/she/it	will be	showing
we	will be	showing
you	will be	showing
they	will be	showing

Going to-Future

I	am	going to be	showing
you	are	going to be	showing
he/she/it	is	going to be	showing
we	are	going to be	showing
you	are	going to be	showing
they	are	going to be	showing

Future Perfect

I	will have been	showing
you	will have been	showing
he/she/it	will have been	showing
we	will have been	showing
you	will have been	showing
they	will have been	showing

Conditional

I	would	show
you	would	show
he/she/it	would	show
we	would	show
you	would	show
they	would	show

Conditional Past

I	would have	shown | showed
you	would have	shown | showed
he/she/it	would have	shown | showed
we	would have	shown | showed
you	would have	shown | showed
they	would have	shown | showed

shut

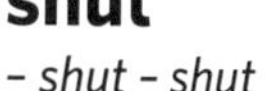

- shut - shut

schließen

Konsonantenverdopplung
Unregelmäßiges Verb

Simple tenses

Present

I	shut
you	shut
he/she/it	shuts
we	shut
you	shut
they	shut

Past

I	shut
you	shut
he/she/it	shut
we	shut
you	shut
they	shut

Present Perfect

I	have	shut
you	have	shut
he/she/it	has	shut
we	have	shut
you	have	shut
they	have	shut

Past Perfect

I	had	shut
you	had	shut
he/she/it	had	shut
we	had	shut
you	had	shut
they	had	shut

Will-Future

I	will	shut
you	will	shut
he/she/it	will	shut
we	will	shut
you	will	shut
they	will	shut

Going to-Future

I	am	going to	shut
you	are	going to	shut
he/she/it	is	going to	shut
we	are	going to	shut
you	are	going to	shut
they	are	going to	shut

Future Perfect

I	will have	shut
you	will have	shut
he/she/it	will have	shut
we	will have	shut
you	will have	shut
they	will have	shut

Imperative

shut

Impersonal

ing-Form

shutting

Past Participle

shut

Continuous tenses

Present

I	am	shutting
you	are	shutting
he/she/it	is	shutting
we	are	shutting
you	are	shutting
they	are	shutting

Past

I	was	shutting
you	were	shutting
he/she/it	was	shutting
we	were	shutting
you	were	shutting
they	were	shutting

Present Perfect

I	have been	shutting
you	have been	shutting
he/she/it	has been	shutting
we	have been	shutting
you	have been	shutting
they	have been	shutting

Past Perfect

I	had been	shutting
you	had been	shutting
he/she/it	had been	shutting
we	had been	shutting
you	had been	shutting
they	had been	shutting

Will-Future

I	will be	shutting
you	will be	shutting
he/she/it	will be	shutting
we	will be	shutting
you	will be	shutting
they	will be	shutting

Going to-Future

I	am	going to be	shutting
you	are	going to be	shutting
he/she/it	is	going to be	shutting
we	are	going to be	shutting
you	are	going to be	shutting
they	are	going to be	shutting

Future Perfect

I	will have been	shutting
you	will have been	shutting
he/she/it	will have been	shutting
we	will have been	shutting
you	will have been	shutting
they	will have been	shutting

Conditional

I	would	shut
you	would	shut
he/she/it	would	shut
we	would	shut
you	would	shut
they	would	shut

Conditional Past

I	would have	shut
you	would have	shut
he/she/it	would have	shut
we	would have	shut
you	would have	shut
they	would have	shut

Simple tenses

Present

I	sign
you	sign
he/she/it	signs
we	sign
you	sign
they	sign

Past

I	signed
you	signed
he/she/it	signed
we	signed
you	signed
they	signed

Present Perfect

I	have	signed
you	have	signed
he/she/it	has	signed
we	have	signed
you	have	signed
they	have	signed

Past Perfect

I	had	signed
you	had	signed
he/she/it	had	signed
we	had	signed
you	had	signed
they	had	signed

Will-Future

I	will	sign
you	will	sign
he/she/it	will	sign
we	will	sign
you	will	sign
they	will	sign

Going to-Future

I	am	going to	sign
you	are	going to	sign
he/she/it	is	going to	sign
we	are	going to	sign
you	are	going to	sign
they	are	going to	sign

Future Perfect

I	will have	signed
you	will have	signed
he/she/it	will have	signed
we	will have	signed
you	will have	signed
they	will have	signed

Imperative

sign

Impersonal

ing-Form

signing

Past Participle

signed

Continuous tenses

Present

I	am	signing
you	are	signing
he/she/it	is	signing
we	are	signing
you	are	signing
they	are	signing

Past

I	was	signing
you	were	signing
he/she/it	was	signing
we	were	signing
you	were	signing
they	were	signing

Present Perfect

I	have	been	signing
you	have	been	signing
he/she/it	has	been	signing
we	have	been	signing
you	have	been	signing
they	have	been	signing

Past Perfect

I	had been	signing
you	had been	signing
he/she/it	had been	signing
we	had been	signing
you	had been	signing
they	had been	signing

Will-Future

I	will be	signing
you	will be	signing
he/she/it	will be	signing
we	will be	signing
you	will be	signing
they	will be	signing

Going to-Future

I	am	going to be	signing
you	are	going to be	signing
he/she/it	is	going to be	signing
we	are	going to be	signing
you	are	going to be	signing
they	are	going to be	signing

Future Perfect

I	will have been	signing
you	will have been	signing
he/she/it	will have been	signing
we	will have been	signing
you	will have been	signing
they	will have been	signing

Conditional

I	would	sign
you	would	sign
he/she/it	would	sign
we	would	sign
you	would	sign
they	would	sign

Conditional Past

I	would have	signed
you	would have	signed
he/she/it	would have	signed
we	would have	signed
you	would have	signed
they	would have	signed

sing
– sang – sung

singen

Unregelmäßiges Verb

Simple tenses

Present

I	sing
you	sing
he/she/it	sings
we	sing
you	sing
they	sing

Past

I	sang
you	sang
he/she/it	sang
we	sang
you	sang
they	sang

Present Perfect

I	have	sung
you	have	sung
he/she/it	has	sung
we	have	sung
you	have	sung
they	have	sung

Past Perfect

I	had	sung
you	had	sung
he/she/it	had	sung
we	had	sung
you	had	sung
they	had	sung

***Will*-Future**

I	will	sing
you	will	sing
he/she/it	will	sing
we	will	sing
you	will	sing
they	will	sing

***Going to*-Future**

I	am	going to	sing
you	are	going to	sing
he/she/it	is	going to	sing
we	are	going to	sing
you	are	going to	sing
they	are	going to	sing

Future Perfect

I	will have	sung
you	will have	sung
he/she/it	will have	sung
we	will have	sung
you	will have	sung
they	will have	sung

Imperative

sing

Impersonal

***ing*-Form**

singing

Past Participle

sung

Continuous tenses

Present

I	am	singing
you	are	singing
he/she/it	is	singing
we	are	singing
you	are	singing
they	are	singing

Past

I	was	singing
you	were	singing
he/she/it	was	singing
we	were	singing
you	were	singing
they	were	singing

Present Perfect

I	have been	singing
you	have been	singing
he/she/it	has been	singing
we	have been	singing
you	have been	singing
they	have been	singing

Past Perfect

I	had been	singing
you	had been	singing
he/she/it	had been	singing
we	had been	singing
you	had been	singing
they	had been	singing

***Will*-Future**

I	will be	singing
you	will be	singing
he/she/it	will be	singing
we	will be	singing
you	will be	singing
they	will be	singing

***Going to*-Future**

I	am	going to be	singing
you	are	going to be	singing
he/she/it	is	going to be	singing
we	are	going to be	singing
you	are	going to be	singing
they	are	going to be	singing

Future Perfect

I	will have been	singing
you	will have been	singing
he/she/it	will have been	singing
we	will have been	singing
you	will have been	singing
they	will have been	singing

Conditional

I	would	sing
you	would	sing
he/she/it	would	sing
we	would	sing
you	would	sing
they	would	sing

Conditional Past

I	would have	sung
you	would have	sung
he/she/it	would have	sung
we	would have	sung
you	would have	sung
they	would have	sung

sink

- sank - sunk

Simple tenses

Present

I	sink
you	sink
he/she/it	sinks
we	sink
you	sink
they	sink

Past

I	sank
you	sank
he/she/it	sank
we	sank
you	sank
they	sank

Present Perfect

I	have	sunk
you	have	sunk
he/she/it	has	sunk
we	have	sunk
you	have	sunk
they	have	sunk

Past Perfect

I	had	sunk
you	had	sunk
he/she/it	had	sunk
we	had	sunk
you	had	sunk
they	had	sunk

Will-Future

I	will	sink
you	will	sink
he/she/it	will	sink
we	will	sink
you	will	sink
they	will	sink

Going to-Future

I	am	going to	sink
you	are	going to	sink
he/she/it	is	going to	sink
we	are	going to	sink
you	are	going to	sink
they	are	going to	sink

Future Perfect

I	will have	sunk
you	will have	sunk
he/she/it	will have	sunk
we	will have	sunk
you	will have	sunk
they	will have	sunk

Imperative

sink

Impersonal

ing-Form

sinking

Past Participle

sunk

Continuous tenses

Present

I	am	sinking
you	are	sinking
he/she/it	is	sinking
we	are	sinking
you	are	sinking
they	are	sinking

Past

I	was	sinking
you	were	sinking
he/she/it	was	sinking
we	were	sinking
you	were	sinking
they	were	sinking

Present Perfect

I	have been	sinking
you	have been	sinking
he/she/it	has been	sinking
we	have been	sinking
you	have been	sinking
they	have been	sinking

Past Perfect

I	had been	sinking
you	had been	sinking
he/she/it	had been	sinking
we	had been	sinking
you	had been	sinking
they	had been	sinking

Will-Future

I	will be	sinking
you	will be	sinking
he/she/it	will be	sinking
we	will be	sinking
you	will be	sinking
they	will be	sinking

Going to-Future

I	am	going to be	sinking
you	are	going to be	sinking
he/she/it	is	going to be	sinking
we	are	going to be	sinking
you	are	going to be	sinking
they	are	going to be	sinking

Future Perfect

I	will have been	sinking
you	will have been	sinking
he/she/it	will have been	sinking
we	will have been	sinking
you	will have been	sinking
they	will have been	sinking

Conditional

I	would	sink
you	would	sink
he/she/it	would	sink
we	would	sink
you	would	sink
they	would	sink

Conditional Past

I	would have	sunk
you	would have	sunk
he/she/it	would have	sunk
we	would have	sunk
you	would have	sunk
they	would have	sunk

sit

- sat - sat

sitzen

Konsonantenverdopplung
Unregelmäßiges Verb

Simple tenses

Present

I	sit
you	sit
he/she/it	sits
we	sit
you	sit
they	sit

Past

I	sat
you	sat
he/she/it	sat
we	sat
you	sat
they	sat

Present Perfect

I	have	sat
you	have	sat
he/she/it	has	sat
we	have	sat
you	have	sat
they	have	sat

Past Perfect

I	had	sat
you	had	sat
he/she/it	had	sat
we	had	sat
you	had	sat
they	had	sat

Will-Future

I	will	sit
you	will	sit
he/she/it	will	sit
we	will	sit
you	will	sit
they	will	sit

Going to-Future

I	am	going to	sit
you	are	going to	sit
he/she/it	is	going to	sit
we	are	going to	sit
you	are	going to	sit
they	are	going to	sit

Future Perfect

I	will have	sat
you	will have	sat
he/she/it	will have	sat
we	will have	sat
you	will have	sat
they	will have	sat

Imperative

sit

Impersonal

ing-Form

sitting

Past Participle

sat

Continuous tenses

Present

I	am	sitting
you	are	sitting
he/she/it	is	sitting
we	are	sitting
you	are	sitting
they	are	sitting

Past

I	was	sitting
you	were	sitting
he/she/it	was	sitting
we	were	sitting
you	were	sitting
they	were	sitting

Present Perfect

I	have been	sitting
you	have been	sitting
he/she/it	has been	sitting
we	have been	sitting
you	have been	sitting
they	have been	sitting

Past Perfect

I	had been	sitting
you	had been	sitting
he/she/it	had been	sitting
we	had been	sitting
you	had been	sitting
they	had been	sitting

Will-Future

I	will be	sitting
you	will be	sitting
he/she/it	will be	sitting
we	will be	sitting
you	will be	sitting
they	will be	sitting

Going to-Future

I	am	going to be	sitting
you	are	going to be	sitting
he/she/it	is	going to be	sitting
we	are	going to be	sitting
you	are	going to be	sitting
they	are	going to be	sitting

Future Perfect

I	will have been	sitting
you	will have been	sitting
he/she/it	will have been	sitting
we	will have been	sitting
you	will have been	sitting
they	will have been	sitting

Conditional

I	would	sit
you	would	sit
he/she/it	would	sit
we	would	sit
you	would	sit
they	would	sit

Conditional Past

I	would have	sat
you	would have	sat
he/she/it	would have	sat
we	would have	sat
you	would have	sat
they	would have	sat

Konsonantenverdopplung
Regelmäßiges Verb

überspringen

skip

Simple tenses

Present

I	skip
you	skip
he/she/it	skips
we	skip
you	skip
they	skip

Past

I	skipped
you	skipped
he/she/it	skipped
we	skipped
you	skipped
they	skipped

Present Perfect

I	have	skipped
you	have	skipped
he/she/it	has	skipped
we	have	skipped
you	have	skipped
they	have	skipped

Past Perfect

I	had	skipped
you	had	skipped
he/she/it	had	skipped
we	had	skipped
you	had	skipped
they	had	skipped

Will-Future

I	will	skip
you	will	skip
he/she/it	will	skip
we	will	skip
you	will	skip
they	will	skip

Going to-Future

I	am	going to	skip
you	are	going to	skip
he/she/it	is	going to	skip
we	are	going to	skip
you	are	going to	skip
they	are	going to	skip

Future Perfect

I	will have	skipped
you	will have	skipped
he/she/it	will have	skipped
we	will have	skipped
you	will have	skipped
they	will have	skipped

Imperative

skip

Impersonal

ing-Form

skipping

Past Participle

skipped

Continuous tenses

Present

I	am	skipping
you	are	skipping
he/she/it	is	skipping
we	are	skipping
you	are	skipping
they	are	skipping

Past

I	was	skipping
you	were	skipping
he/she/it	was	skipping
we	were	skipping
you	were	skipping
they	were	skipping

Present Perfect

I	have been	skipping
you	have been	skipping
he/she/it	has been	skipping
we	have been	skipping
you	have been	skipping
they	have been	skipping

Past Perfect

I	had been	skipping
you	had been	skipping
he/she/it	had been	skipping
we	had been	skipping
you	had been	skipping
they	had been	skipping

Will-Future

I	will be	skipping
you	will be	skipping
he/she/it	will be	skipping
we	will be	skipping
you	will be	skipping
they	will be	skipping

Going to-Future

I	am	going to be	skipping
you	are	going to be	skipping
he/she/it	is	going to be	skipping
we	are	going to be	skipping
you	are	going to be	skipping
they	are	going to be	skipping

Future Perfect

I	will have been	skipping
you	will have been	skipping
he/she/it	will have been	skipping
we	will have been	skipping
you	will have been	skipping
they	will have been	skipping

Conditional

I	would	skip
you	would	skip
he/she/it	would	skip
we	would	skip
you	would	skip
they	would	skip

Conditional Past

I	would have	skipped
you	would have	skipped
he/she/it	would have	skipped
we	would have	skipped
you	would have	skipped
they	would have	skipped

sleep
- slept - slept

schlafen

Unregelmäßiges Verb

Simple tenses

Present

I	sleep
you	sleep
he/she/it	sleeps
we	sleep
you	sleep
they	sleep

Past

I	slept
you	slept
he/she/it	slept
we	slept
you	slept
they	slept

Present Perfect

I	have	slept
you	have	slept
he/she/it	has	slept
we	have	slept
you	have	slept
they	have	slept

Past Perfect

I	had	slept
you	had	slept
he/she/it	had	slept
we	had	slept
you	had	slept
they	had	slept

***Will*-Future**

I	will	sleep
you	will	sleep
he/she/it	will	sleep
we	will	sleep
you	will	sleep
they	will	sleep

***Going to*-Future**

I	am	going to	sleep
you	are	going to	sleep
he/she/it	is	going to	sleep
we	are	going to	sleep
you	are	going to	sleep
they	are	going to	sleep

Future Perfect

I	will have	slept
you	will have	slept
he/she/it	will have	slept
we	will have	slept
you	will have	slept
they	will have	slept

Imperative

sleep

Impersonal

***ing*-Form**

sleeping

Past Participle

slept

Continuous tenses

Present

I	am	sleeping
you	are	sleeping
he/she/it	is	sleeping
we	are	sleeping
you	are	sleeping
they	are	sleeping

Past

I	was	sleeping
you	were	sleeping
he/she/it	was	sleeping
we	were	sleeping
you	were	sleeping
they	were	sleeping

Present Perfect

I	have	been	sleeping
you	have	been	sleeping
he/she/it	has	been	sleeping
we	have	been	sleeping
you	have	been	sleeping
they	have	been	sleeping

Past Perfect

I	had been	sleeping
you	had been	sleeping
he/she/it	had been	sleeping
we	had been	sleeping
you	had been	sleeping
they	had been	sleeping

***Will*-Future**

I	will be	sleeping
you	will be	sleeping
he/she/it	will be	sleeping
we	will be	sleeping
you	will be	sleeping
they	will be	sleeping

***Going to*-Future**

I	am	going to be	sleeping
you	are	going to be	sleeping
he/she/it	is	going to be	sleeping
we	are	going to be	sleeping
you	are	going to be	sleeping
they	are	going to be	sleeping

Future Perfect

I	will have been	sleeping
you	will have been	sleeping
he/she/it	will have been	sleeping
we	will have been	sleeping
you	will have been	sleeping
they	will have been	sleeping

Conditional

I	would	sleep
you	would	sleep
he/she/it	would	sleep
we	would	sleep
you	would	sleep
they	would	sleep

Conditional Past

I	would have	slept
you	would have	slept
he/she/it	would have	slept
we	would have	slept
you	would have	slept
they	would have	slept

rutschen

slide
- slid - slid

Simple tenses

Present
I	slide
you	slide
he/she/it	slides
we	slide
you	slide
they	slide

Past
I	slid
you	slid
he/she/it	slid
we	slid
you	slid
they	slid

Present Perfect
I	have	slid
you	have	slid
he/she/it	has	slid
we	have	slid
you	have	slid
they	have	slid

Past Perfect
I	had	slid
you	had	slid
he/she/it	had	slid
we	had	slid
you	had	slid
they	had	slid

Will-Future
I	will	slide
you	will	slide
he/she/it	will	slide
we	will	slide
you	will	slide
they	will	slide

Going to-Future
I	am	going to	slide
you	are	going to	slide
he/she/it	is	going to	slide
we	are	going to	slide
you	are	going to	slide
they	are	going to	slide

Future Perfect
I	will have	slid
you	will have	slid
he/she/it	will have	slid
we	will have	slid
you	will have	slid
they	will have	slid

Imperative
slide

Impersonal

ing-Form
sliding

Past Participle
slid

Continuous tenses

Present
I	am	sliding
you	are	sliding
he/she/it	is	sliding
we	are	sliding
you	are	sliding
they	are	sliding

Past
I	was	sliding
you	were	sliding
he/she/it	was	sliding
we	were	sliding
you	were	sliding
they	were	sliding

Present Perfect
I	have been	sliding
you	have been	sliding
he/she/it	has been	sliding
we	have been	sliding
you	have been	sliding
they	have been	sliding

Past Perfect
I	had been	sliding
you	had been	sliding
he/she/it	had been	sliding
we	had been	sliding
you	had been	sliding
they	had been	sliding

Will-Future
I	will be	sliding
you	will be	sliding
he/she/it	will be	sliding
we	will be	sliding
you	will be	sliding
they	will be	sliding

Going to-Future
I	am	going to be	sliding
you	are	going to be	sliding
he/she/it	is	going to be	sliding
we	are	going to be	sliding
you	are	going to be	sliding
they	are	going to be	sliding

Future Perfect
I	will have been	sliding
you	will have been	sliding
he/she/it	will have been	sliding
we	will have been	sliding
you	will have been	sliding
they	will have been	sliding

Conditional
I	would	slide
you	would	slide
he/she/it	would	slide
we	would	slide
you	would	slide
they	would	slide

Conditional Past
I	would have	slid
you	would have	slid
he/she/it	would have	slid
we	would have	slid
you	would have	slid
they	would have	slid

slip

ausrutschen

Konsonantenverdopplung
Regelmäßiges Verb

Simple tenses

Present

I	slip
you	slip
he/she/it	slips
we	slip
you	slip
they	slip

Past

I	slipped
you	slipped
he/she/it	slipped
we	slipped
you	slipped
they	slipped

Present Perfect

I	have	slipped
you	have	slipped
he/she/it	has	slipped
we	have	slipped
you	have	slipped
they	have	slipped

Past Perfect

I	had	slipped
you	had	slipped
he/she/it	had	slipped
we	had	slipped
you	had	slipped
they	had	slipped

Will-Future

I	will	slip
you	will	slip
he/she/it	will	slip
we	will	slip
you	will	slip
they	will	slip

Going to-Future

I	am	going to	slip
you	are	going to	slip
he/she/it	is	going to	slip
we	are	going to	slip
you	are	going to	slip
they	are	going to	slip

Future Perfect

I	will have	slipped
you	will have	slipped
he/she/it	will have	slipped
we	will have	slipped
you	will have	slipped
they	will have	slipped

Imperative

slip

Impersonal

ing-Form

slipping

Past Participle

slipped

Continuous tenses

Present

I	am	slipping
you	are	slipping
he/she/it	is	slipping
we	are	slipping
you	are	slipping
they	are	slipping

Past

I	was	slipping
you	were	slipping
he/she/it	was	slipping
we	were	slipping
you	were	slipping
they	were	slipping

Present Perfect

I	have been	slipping
you	have been	slipping
he/she/it	has been	slipping
we	have been	slipping
you	have been	slipping
they	have been	slipping

Past Perfect

I	had been	slipping
you	had been	slipping
he/she/it	had been	slipping
we	had been	slipping
you	had been	slipping
they	had been	slipping

Will-Future

I	will be	slipping
you	will be	slipping
he/she/it	will be	slipping
we	will be	slipping
you	will be	slipping
they	will be	slipping

Going to-Future

I	am	going to be	slipping
you	are	going to be	slipping
he/she/it	is	going to be	slipping
we	are	going to be	slipping
you	are	going to be	slipping
they	are	going to be	slipping

Future Perfect

I	will have been	slipping
you	will have been	slipping
he/she/it	will have been	slipping
we	will have been	slipping
you	will have been	slipping
they	will have been	slipping

Conditional

I	would	slip
you	would	slip
he/she/it	would	slip
we	would	slip
you	would	slip
they	would	slip

Conditional Past

I	would have	slipped
you	would have	slipped
he/she/it	would have	slipped
we	would have	slipped
you	would have	slipped
they	would have	slipped

Konsonantenverdopplung
Unregelmäßiges Verb

aufschlitzen

slit
- slit - slit

Simple tenses

Present

I	slit
you	slit
he/she/it	slits
we	slit
you	slit
they	slit

Past

I	slit
you	slit
he/she/it	slit
we	slit
you	slit
they	slit

Present Perfect

I	have	slit
you	have	slit
he/she/it	has	slit
we	have	slit
you	have	slit
they	have	slit

Past Perfect

I	had	slit
you	had	slit
he/she/it	had	slit
we	had	slit
you	had	slit
they	had	slit

Will-Future

I	will	slit
you	will	slit
he/she/it	will	slit
we	will	slit
you	will	slit
they	will	slit

Going to-Future

I	am	going to	slit
you	are	going to	slit
he/she/it	is	going to	slit
we	are	going to	slit
you	are	going to	slit
they	are	going to	slit

Future Perfect

I	will have	slit
you	will have	slit
he/she/it	will have	slit
we	will have	slit
you	will have	slit
they	will have	slit

Imperative

slit

Impersonal

ing-Form

slitting

Past Participle

slit

Continuous tenses

Present

I	am	slitting
you	are	slitting
he/she/it	is	slitting
we	are	slitting
you	are	slitting
they	are	slitting

Past

I	was	slitting
you	were	slitting
he/she/it	was	slitting
we	were	slitting
you	were	slitting
they	were	slitting

Present Perfect

I	have been	slitting
you	have been	slitting
he/she/it	has been	slitting
we	have been	slitting
you	have been	slitting
they	have been	slitting

Past Perfect

I	had been	slitting
you	had been	slitting
he/she/it	had been	slitting
we	had been	slitting
you	had been	slitting
they	had been	slitting

Will-Future

I	will be	slitting
you	will be	slitting
he/she/it	will be	slitting
we	will be	slitting
you	will be	slitting
they	will be	slitting

Going to-Future

I	am	going to be	slitting
you	are	going to be	slitting
he/she/it	is	going to be	slitting
we	are	going to be	slitting
you	are	going to be	slitting
they	are	going to be	slitting

Future Perfect

I	will have been	slitting
you	will have been	slitting
he/she/it	will have been	slitting
we	will have been	slitting
you	will have been	slitting
they	will have been	slitting

Conditional

I	would	slit
you	would	slit
he/she/it	would	slit
we	would	slit
you	would	slit
they	would	slit

Conditional Past

I	would have	slit
you	would have	slit
he/she/it	would have	slit
we	would have	slit
you	would have	slit
they	would have	slit

smell
- smelled/smelt - smelled/smelt

riechen

Unregelmäßiges Verb

Simple tenses

Present

I	smell
you	smell
he/she/it	smells
we	smell
you	smell
they	smell

Past

I	smelled | smelt
you	smelled | smelt
he/she/it	smelled | smelt
we	smelled | smelt
you	smelled | smelt
they	smelled | smelt

Present Perfect

I	have	smelled | smelt
you	have	smelled | smelt
he/she/it	has	smelled | smelt
we	have	smelled | smelt
you	have	smelled | smelt
they	have	smelled | smelt

Past Perfect

I	had	smelled | smelt
you	had	smelled | smelt
he/she/it	had	smelled | smelt
we	had	smelled | smelt
you	had	smelled | smelt
they	had	smelled | smelt

Will-Future

I	will	smell
you	will	smell
he/she/it	will	smell
we	will	smell
you	will	smell
they	will	smell

Going to-Future

I	am	going to	smell
you	are	going to	smell
he/she/it	is	going to	smell
we	are	going to	smell
you	are	going to	smell
they	are	going to	smell

Future Perfect

I	will have	smelled | smelt
you	will have	smelled | smelt
he/she/it	will have	smelled | smelt
we	will have	smelled | smelt
you	will have	smelled | smelt
they	will have	smelled | smelt

Imperative

smell

Impersonal

ing-Form

smelling

Past Participle

smelled | smelt

Continuous tenses

Present

I	am	smelling
you	are	smelling
he/she/it	is	smelling
we	are	smelling
you	are	smelling
they	are	smelling

Past

I	was	smelling
you	were	smelling
he/she/it	was	smelling
we	were	smelling
you	were	smelling
they	were	smelling

Present Perfect

I	have been	smelling
you	have been	smelling
he/she/it	has been	smelling
we	have been	smelling
you	have been	smelling
they	have been	smelling

Past Perfect

I	had been	smelling
you	had been	smelling
he/she/it	had been	smelling
we	had been	smelling
you	had been	smelling
they	had been	smelling

Will-Future

I	will be	smelling
you	will be	smelling
he/she/it	will be	smelling
we	will be	smelling
you	will be	smelling
they	will be	smelling

Going to-Future

I	am	going to be	smelling
you	are	going to be	smelling
he/she/it	is	going to be	smelling
we	are	going to be	smelling
you	are	going to be	smelling
they	are	going to be	smelling

Future Perfect

I	will have been	smelling
you	will have been	smelling
he/she/it	will have been	smelling
we	will have been	smelling
you	will have been	smelling
they	will have been	smelling

Conditional

I	would	smell
you	would	smell
he/she/it	would	smell
we	would	smell
you	would	smell
they	would	smell

Conditional Past

I	would have	smelled | smelt
you	would have	smelled | smelt
he/she/it	would have	smelled | smelt
we	would have	smelled | smelt
you	would have	smelled | smelt
they	would have	smelled | smelt

+ **-ing** → ~~e~~ / + **-d** nicht **-ed**
Regelmäßiges Verb

lächeln

smile

Simple tenses

Present

I	smile
you	smile
he/she/it	smiles
we	smile
you	smile
they	smile

Past

I	smiled
you	smiled
he/she/it	smiled
we	smiled
you	smiled
they	smiled

Present Perfect

I	have	smiled
you	have	smiled
he/she/it	has	smiled
we	have	smiled
you	have	smiled
they	have	smiled

Past Perfect

I	had	smiled
you	had	smiled
he/she/it	had	smiled
we	had	smiled
you	had	smiled
they	had	smiled

Will-Future

I	will	smile
you	will	smile
he/she/it	will	smile
we	will	smile
you	will	smile
they	will	smile

Going to-Future

I	am	going to	smile
you	are	going to	smile
he/she/it	is	going to	smile
we	are	going to	smile
you	are	going to	smile
they	are	going to	smile

Future Perfect

I	will have	smiled
you	will have	smiled
he/she/it	will have	smiled
we	will have	smiled
you	will have	smiled
they	will have	smiled

Imperative

smile

Impersonal

ing-Form

smiling

Past Participle

smiled

Continuous tenses

Present

I	am	smiling
you	are	smiling
he/she/it	is	smiling
we	are	smiling
you	are	smiling
they	are	smiling

Past

I	was	smiling
you	were	smiling
he/she/it	was	smiling
we	were	smiling
you	were	smiling
they	were	smiling

Present Perfect

I	have	been	smiling
you	have	been	smiling
he/she/it	has	been	smiling
we	have	been	smiling
you	have	been	smiling
they	have	been	smiling

Past Perfect

I	had been	smiling
you	had been	smiling
he/she/it	had been	smiling
we	had been	smiling
you	had been	smiling
they	had been	smiling

Will-Future

I	will be	smiling
you	will be	smiling
he/she/it	will be	smiling
we	will be	smiling
you	will be	smiling
they	will be	smiling

Going to-Future

I	am	going to be	smiling
you	are	going to be	smiling
he/she/it	is	going to be	smiling
we	are	going to be	smiling
you	are	going to be	smiling
they	are	going to be	smiling

Future Perfect

I	will have been	smiling
you	will have been	smiling
he/she/it	will have been	smiling
we	will have been	smiling
you	will have been	smiling
they	will have been	smiling

Conditional

I	would	smile
you	would	smile
he/she/it	would	smile
we	would	smile
you	would	smile
they	would	smile

Conditional Past

I	would have	smiled
you	would have	smiled
he/she/it	would have	smiled
we	would have	smiled
you	would have	smiled
they	would have	smiled

smoke

rauchen

\+ **-ing** → ~~**e**~~ / + **-d** nicht **-ed**
Regelmäßiges Verb

Simple tenses

Present

I	smoke
you	smoke
he/she/it	smokes
we	smoke
you	smoke
they	smoke

Past

I	smoked
you	smoked
he/she/it	smoked
we	smoked
you	smoked
they	smoked

Present Perfect

I	have	smoked
you	have	smoked
he/she/it	has	smoked
we	have	smoked
you	have	smoked
they	have	smoked

Past Perfect

I	had	smoked
you	had	smoked
he/she/it	had	smoked
we	had	smoked
you	had	smoked
they	had	smoked

Will-Future

I	will	smoke
you	will	smoke
he/she/it	will	smoke
we	will	smoke
you	will	smoke
they	will	smoke

Going to-Future

I	am	going to	smoke
you	are	going to	smoke
he/she/it	is	going to	smoke
we	are	going to	smoke
you	are	going to	smoke
they	are	going to	smoke

Future Perfect

I	will have	smoked
you	will have	smoked
he/she/it	will have	smoked
we	will have	smoked
you	will have	smoked
they	will have	smoked

Imperative

smoke

Impersonal

ing-Form

smoking

Past Participle

smoked

Continuous tenses

Present

I	am	smoking
you	are	smoking
he/she/it	is	smoking
we	are	smoking
you	are	smoking
they	are	smoking

Past

I	was	smoking
you	were	smoking
he/she/it	was	smoking
we	were	smoking
you	were	smoking
they	were	smoking

Present Perfect

I	have been	smoking
you	have been	smoking
he/she/it	has been	smoking
we	have been	smoking
you	have been	smoking
they	have been	smoking

Past Perfect

I	had been	smoking
you	had been	smoking
he/she/it	had been	smoking
we	had been	smoking
you	had been	smoking
they	had been	smoking

Will-Future

I	will be	smoking
you	will be	smoking
he/she/it	will be	smoking
we	will be	smoking
you	will be	smoking
they	will be	smoking

Going to-Future

I	am	going to be	smoking
you	are	going to be	smoking
he/she/it	is	going to be	smoking
we	are	going to be	smoking
you	are	going to be	smoking
they	are	going to be	smoking

Future Perfect

I	will have been	smoking
you	will have been	smoking
he/she/it	will have been	smoking
we	will have been	smoking
you	will have been	smoking
they	will have been	smoking

Conditional

I	would	smoke
you	would	smoke
he/she/it	would	smoke
we	would	smoke
you	would	smoke
they	would	smoke

Conditional Past

I	would have	smoked
you	would have	smoked
he/she/it	would have	smoked
we	would have	smoked
you	would have	smoked
they	would have	smoked

+ -ing → ~~e~~ / + -d nicht -ed
Regelmäßiges Verb

schnarchen

snore

Simple tenses

Present

I	snore
you	snore
he/she/it	snores
we	snore
you	snore
they	snore

Past

I	snored
you	snored
he/she/it	snored
we	snored
you	snored
they	snored

Present Perfect

I	have	snored
you	have	snored
he/she/it	has	snored
we	have	snored
you	have	snored
they	have	snored

Past Perfect

I	had	snored
you	had	snored
he/she/it	had	snored
we	had	snored
you	had	snored
they	had	snored

Will-Future

I	will	snore
you	will	snore
he/she/it	will	snore
we	will	snore
you	will	snore
they	will	snore

Going to-Future

I	am	going to	snore
you	are	going to	snore
he/she/it	is	going to	snore
we	are	going to	snore
you	are	going to	snore
they	are	going to	snore

Future Perfect

I	will have	snored
you	will have	snored
he/she/it	will have	snored
we	will have	snored
you	will have	snored
they	will have	snored

Imperative

snore

Impersonal

ing-Form

snoring

Past Participle

snored

Continuous tenses

Present

I	am	snoring
you	are	snoring
he/she/it	is	snoring
we	are	snoring
you	are	snoring
they	are	snoring

Past

I	was	snoring
you	were	snoring
he/she/it	was	snoring
we	were	snoring
you	were	snoring
they	were	snoring

Present Perfect

I	have been	snoring
you	have been	snoring
he/she/it	has been	snoring
we	have been	snoring
you	have been	snoring
they	have been	snoring

Past Perfect

I	had been	snoring
you	had been	snoring
he/she/it	had been	snoring
we	had been	snoring
you	had been	snoring
they	had been	snoring

Will-Future

I	will be	snoring
you	will be	snoring
he/she/it	will be	snoring
we	will be	snoring
you	will be	snoring
they	will be	snoring

Going to-Future

I	am	going to be	snoring
you	are	going to be	snoring
he/she/it	is	going to be	snoring
we	are	going to be	snoring
you	are	going to be	snoring
they	are	going to be	snoring

Future Perfect

I	will have been	snoring
you	will have been	snoring
he/she/it	will have been	snoring
we	will have been	snoring
you	will have been	snoring
they	will have been	snoring

Conditional

I	would	snore
you	would	snore
he/she/it	would	snore
we	would	snore
you	would	snore
they	would	snore

Conditional Past

I	would have	snored
you	would have	snored
he/she/it	would have	snored
we	would have	snored
you	would have	snored
they	would have	snored

snow

schneien

Regelmäßiges Verb

Simple tenses

Present

I	snow
you	snow
he/she/it	snows
we	snow
you	snow
they	snow

Past

I	snowed
you	snowed
he/she/it	snowed
we	snowed
you	snowed
they	snowed

Present Perfect

I	have	snowed
you	have	snowed
he/she/it	has	snowed
we	have	snowed
you	have	snowed
they	have	snowed

Past Perfect

I	had	snowed
you	had	snowed
he/she/it	had	snowed
we	had	snowed
you	had	snowed
they	had	snowed

Will-Future

I	will	snow
you	will	snow
he/she/it	will	snow
we	will	snow
you	will	snow
they	will	snow

Going to-Future

I	am	going to	snow
you	are	going to	snow
he/she/it	is	going to	snow
we	are	going to	snow
you	are	going to	snow
they	are	going to	snow

Future Perfect

I	will have	snowed
you	will have	snowed
he/she/it	will have	snowed
we	will have	snowed
you	will have	snowed
they	will have	snowed

Imperative

snow

Impersonal

ing-Form

snowing

Past Participle

snowed

Continuous tenses

Present

I	am	snowing
you	are	snowing
he/she/it	is	snowing
we	are	snowing
you	are	snowing
they	are	snowing

Past

I	was	snowing
you	were	snowing
he/she/it	was	snowing
we	were	snowing
you	were	snowing
they	were	snowing

Present Perfect

I	have	been	snowing
you	have	been	snowing
he/she/it	has	been	snowing
we	have	been	snowing
you	have	been	snowing
they	have	been	snowing

Past Perfect

I	had been	snowing
you	had been	snowing
he/she/it	had been	snowing
we	had been	snowing
you	had been	snowing
they	had been	snowing

Will-Future

I	will be	snowing
you	will be	snowing
he/she/it	will be	snowing
we	will be	snowing
you	will be	snowing
they	will be	snowing

Going to-Future

I	am	going to be	snowing
you	are	going to be	snowing
he/she/it	is	going to be	snowing
we	are	going to be	snowing
you	are	going to be	snowing
they	are	going to be	snowing

Future Perfect

I	will have been	snowing
you	will have been	snowing
he/she/it	will have been	snowing
we	will have been	snowing
you	will have been	snowing
they	will have been	snowing

Conditional

I	would	snow
you	would	snow
he/she/it	would	snow
we	would	snow
you	would	snow
they	would	snow

Conditional Past

I	would have	snowed
you	would have	snowed
he/she/it	would have	snowed
we	would have	snowed
you	would have	snowed
they	would have	snowed

+ **-ing** → ~~e~~ / + **-d** nicht **-ed**
Regelmäßiges Verb

aufklären

solve

Simple tenses

Present

I	solve
you	solve
he/she/it	solves
we	solve
you	solve
they	solve

Past

I	solved
you	solved
he/she/it	solved
we	solved
you	solved
they	solved

Present Perfect

I	have	solved
you	have	solved
he/she/it	has	solved
we	have	solved
you	have	solved
they	have	solved

Past Perfect

I	had	solved
you	had	solved
he/she/it	had	solved
we	had	solved
you	had	solved
they	had	solved

Will-Future

I	will	solve
you	will	solve
he/she/it	will	solve
we	will	solve
you	will	solve
they	will	solve

Going to-Future

I	am	going to	solve
you	are	going to	solve
he/she/it	is	going to	solve
we	are	going to	solve
you	are	going to	solve
they	are	going to	solve

Future Perfect

I	will have	solved
you	will have	solved
he/she/it	will have	solved
we	will have	solved
you	will have	solved
they	will have	solved

Imperative

solve

Impersonal

ing-Form

solving

Past Participle

solved

Continuous tenses

Present

I	am	solving
you	are	solving
he/she/it	is	solving
we	are	solving
you	are	solving
they	are	solving

Past

I	was	solving
you	were	solving
he/she/it	was	solving
we	were	solving
you	were	solving
they	were	solving

Present Perfect

I	have been	solving
you	have been	solving
he/she/it	has been	solving
we	have been	solving
you	have been	solving
they	have been	solving

Past Perfect

I	had been	solving
you	had been	solving
he/she/it	had been	solving
we	had been	solving
you	had been	solving
they	had been	solving

Will-Future

I	will be	solving
you	will be	solving
he/she/it	will be	solving
we	will be	solving
you	will be	solving
they	will be	solving

Going to-Future

I	am	going to be	solving
you	are	going to be	solving
he/she/it	is	going to be	solving
we	are	going to be	solving
you	are	going to be	solving
they	are	going to be	solving

Future Perfect

I	will have been	solving
you	will have been	solving
he/she/it	will have been	solving
we	will have been	solving
you	will have been	solving
they	will have been	solving

Conditional

I	would	solve
you	would	solve
he/she/it	would	solve
we	would	solve
you	would	solve
they	would	solve

Conditional Past

I	would have	solved
you	would have	solved
he/she/it	would have	solved
we	would have	solved
you	would have	solved
they	would have	solved

sort

sortieren

Regelmäßiges Verb

Simple tenses

Present

I	sort
you	sort
he/she/it	sorts
we	sort
you	sort
they	sort

Past

I	sorted
you	sorted
he/she/it	sorted
we	sorted
you	sorted
they	sorted

Present Perfect

I	have	sorted
you	have	sorted
he/she/it	has	sorted
we	have	sorted
you	have	sorted
they	have	sorted

Past Perfect

I	had	sorted
you	had	sorted
he/she/it	had	sorted
we	had	sorted
you	had	sorted
they	had	sorted

***Will*-Future**

I	will	sort
you	will	sort
he/she/it	will	sort
we	will	sort
you	will	sort
they	will	sort

***Going to*-Future**

I	am	going to	sort
you	are	going to	sort
he/she/it	is	going to	sort
we	are	going to	sort
you	are	going to	sort
they	are	going to	sort

Future Perfect

I	will have	sorted
you	will have	sorted
he/she/it	will have	sorted
we	will have	sorted
you	will have	sorted
they	will have	sorted

Imperative

sort

Impersonal

***ing*-Form**

sorting

Past Participle

sorted

Continuous tenses

Present

I	am	sorting
you	are	sorting
he/she/it	is	sorting
we	are	sorting
you	are	sorting
they	are	sorting

Past

I	was	sorting
you	were	sorting
he/she/it	was	sorting
we	were	sorting
you	were	sorting
they	were	sorting

Present Perfect

I	have	been	sorting
you	have	been	sorting
he/she/it	has	been	sorting
we	have	been	sorting
you	have	been	sorting
they	have	been	sorting

Past Perfect

I	had been	sorting
you	had been	sorting
he/she/it	had been	sorting
we	had been	sorting
you	had been	sorting
they	had been	sorting

***Will*-Future**

I	will be	sorting
you	will be	sorting
he/she/it	will be	sorting
we	will be	sorting
you	will be	sorting
they	will be	sorting

***Going to*-Future**

I	am	going to be	sorting
you	are	going to be	sorting
he/she/it	is	going to be	sorting
we	are	going to be	sorting
you	are	going to be	sorting
they	are	going to be	sorting

Future Perfect

I	will have been	sorting
you	will have been	sorting
he/she/it	will have been	sorting
we	will have been	sorting
you	will have been	sorting
they	will have been	sorting

Conditional

I	would	sort
you	would	sort
he/she/it	would	sort
we	would	sort
you	would	sort
they	would	sort

Conditional Past

I	would have	sorted
you	would have	sorted
he/she/it	would have	sorted
we	would have	sorted
you	would have	sorted
they	would have	sorted

Simple tenses

Present

I	sound
you	sound
he/she/it	sounds
we	sound
you	sound
they	sound

Past

I	sounded
you	sounded
he/she/it	sounded
we	sounded
you	sounded
they	sounded

Present Perfect

I	have	sounded
you	have	sounded
he/she/it	has	sounded
we	have	sounded
you	have	sounded
they	have	sounded

Past Perfect

I	had	sounded
you	had	sounded
he/she/it	had	sounded
we	had	sounded
you	had	sounded
they	had	sounded

Will-Future

I	will	sound
you	will	sound
he/she/it	will	sound
we	will	sound
you	will	sound
they	will	sound

Going to-Future

I	am	going to	sound
you	are	going to	sound
he/she/it	is	going to	sound
we	are	going to	sound
you	are	going to	sound
they	are	going to	sound

Future Perfect

I	will have	sounded
you	will have	sounded
he/she/it	will have	sounded
we	will have	sounded
you	will have	sounded
they	will have	sounded

Imperative

sound

Impersonal

ing-Form

sounding

Past Participle

sounded

Continuous tenses

Present

I	am	sounding
you	are	sounding
he/she/it	is	sounding
we	are	sounding
you	are	sounding
they	are	sounding

Past

I	was	sounding
you	were	sounding
he/she/it	was	sounding
we	were	sounding
you	were	sounding
they	were	sounding

Present Perfect

I	have been	sounding
you	have been	sounding
he/she/it	has been	sounding
we	have been	sounding
you	have been	sounding
they	have been	sounding

Past Perfect

I	had been	sounding
you	had been	sounding
he/she/it	had been	sounding
we	had been	sounding
you	had been	sounding
they	had been	sounding

Will-Future

I	will be	sounding
you	will be	sounding
he/she/it	will be	sounding
we	will be	sounding
you	will be	sounding
they	will be	sounding

Going to-Future

I	am	going to be	sounding
you	are	going to be	sounding
he/she/it	is	going to be	sounding
we	are	going to be	sounding
you	are	going to be	sounding
they	are	going to be	sounding

Future Perfect

I	will have been	sounding
you	will have been	sounding
he/she/it	will have been	sounding
we	will have been	sounding
you	will have been	sounding
they	will have been	sounding

Conditional

I	would	sound
you	would	sound
he/she/it	would	sound
we	would	sound
you	would	sound
they	would	sound

Conditional Past

I	would have	sounded
you	would have	sounded
he/she/it	would have	sounded
we	would have	sounded
you	would have	sounded
they	would have	sounded

spare

verschonen

\+ **-ing** → ~~e~~ / + **-d** nicht **-ed**
Regelmäßiges Verb

Simple tenses

Present

I	spare
you	spare
he/she/it	spares
we	spare
you	spare
they	spare

Past

I	spared
you	spared
he/she/it	spared
we	spared
you	spared
they	spared

Present Perfect

I	have	spared
you	have	spared
he/she/it	has	spared
we	have	spared
you	have	spared
they	have	spared

Past Perfect

I	had	spared
you	had	spared
he/she/it	had	spared
we	had	spared
you	had	spared
they	had	spared

***Will*-Future**

I	will	spare
you	will	spare
he/she/it	will	spare
we	will	spare
you	will	spare
they	will	spare

***Going to*-Future**

I	am	going to	spare
you	are	going to	spare
he/she/it	is	going to	spare
we	are	going to	spare
you	are	going to	spare
they	are	going to	spare

Future Perfect

I	will have	spared
you	will have	spared
he/she/it	will have	spared
we	will have	spared
you	will have	spared
they	will have	spared

Imperative

spare

Impersonal

***ing*-Form**

sparing

Past Participle

spared

Continuous tenses

Present

I	am	sparing
you	are	sparing
he/she/it	is	sparing
we	are	sparing
you	are	sparing
they	are	sparing

Past

I	was	sparing
you	were	sparing
he/she/it	was	sparing
we	were	sparing
you	were	sparing
they	were	sparing

Present Perfect

I	have been	sparing
you	have been	sparing
he/she/it	has been	sparing
we	have been	sparing
you	have been	sparing
they	have been	sparing

Past Perfect

I	had been	sparing
you	had been	sparing
he/she/it	had been	sparing
we	had been	sparing
you	had been	sparing
they	had been	sparing

***Will*-Future**

I	will be	sparing
you	will be	sparing
he/she/it	will be	sparing
we	will be	sparing
you	will be	sparing
they	will be	sparing

***Going to*-Future**

I	am	going to be	sparing
you	are	going to be	sparing
he/she/it	is	going to be	sparing
we	are	going to be	sparing
you	are	going to be	sparing
they	are	going to be	sparing

Future Perfect

I	will have been	sparing
you	will have been	sparing
he/she/it	will have been	sparing
we	will have been	sparing
you	will have been	sparing
they	will have been	sparing

Conditional

I	would	spare
you	would	spare
he/she/it	would	spare
we	would	spare
you	would	spare
they	would	spare

Conditional Past

I	would have	spared
you	would have	spared
he/she/it	would have	spared
we	would have	spared
you	would have	spared
they	would have	spared

+ **-ing** → ~~e~~ / + **-d** nicht **-ed**
Regelmäßiges Verb

funkeln

sparkle

Simple tenses

Present

I	sparkle
you	sparkle
he/she/it	sparkles
we	sparkle
you	sparkle
they	sparkle

Past

I	sparkled
you	sparkled
he/she/it	sparkled
we	sparkled
you	sparkled
they	sparkled

Present Perfect

I	have	sparkled
you	have	sparkled
he/she/it	has	sparkled
we	have	sparkled
you	have	sparkled
they	have	sparkled

Past Perfect

I	had	sparkled
you	had	sparkled
he/she/it	had	sparkled
we	had	sparkled
you	had	sparkled
they	had	sparkled

Will-Future

I	will	sparkle
you	will	sparkle
he/she/it	will	sparkle
we	will	sparkle
you	will	sparkle
they	will	sparkle

Going to-Future

I	am	going to	sparkle
you	are	going to	sparkle
he/she/it	is	going to	sparkle
we	are	going to	sparkle
you	are	going to	sparkle
they	are	going to	sparkle

Future Perfect

I	will have	sparkled
you	will have	sparkled
he/she/it	will have	sparkled
we	will have	sparkled
you	will have	sparkled
they	will have	sparkled

Imperative

sparkle

Impersonal

ing-Form

sparkling

Past Participle

sparkled

Continuous tenses

Present

I	am	sparkling
you	are	sparkling
he/she/it	is	sparkling
we	are	sparkling
you	are	sparkling
they	are	sparkling

Past

I	was	sparkling
you	were	sparkling
he/she/it	was	sparkling
we	were	sparkling
you	were	sparkling
they	were	sparkling

Present Perfect

I	have been	sparkling
you	have been	sparkling
he/she/it	has been	sparkling
we	have been	sparkling
you	have been	sparkling
they	have been	sparkling

Past Perfect

I	had been	sparkling
you	had been	sparkling
he/she/it	had been	sparkling
we	had been	sparkling
you	had been	sparkling
they	had been	sparkling

Will-Future

I	will be	sparkling
you	will be	sparkling
he/she/it	will be	sparkling
we	will be	sparkling
you	will be	sparkling
they	will be	sparkling

Going to-Future

I	am	going to be	sparkling
you	are	going to be	sparkling
he/she/it	is	going to be	sparkling
we	are	going to be	sparkling
you	are	going to be	sparkling
they	are	going to be	sparkling

Future Perfect

I	will have been	sparkling
you	will have been	sparkling
he/she/it	will have been	sparkling
we	will have been	sparkling
you	will have been	sparkling
they	will have been	sparkling

Conditional

I	would	sparkle
you	would	sparkle
he/she/it	would	sparkle
we	would	sparkle
you	would	sparkle
they	would	sparkle

Conditional Past

I	would have	sparkled
you	would have	sparkled
he/she/it	would have	sparkled
we	would have	sparkled
you	would have	sparkled
they	would have	sparkled

speak
- spoke - spoken

sprechen

Unregelmäßiges Verb

Simple tenses

Present

I	speak
you	speak
he/she/it	speaks
we	speak
you	speak
they	speak

Past

I	spoke
you	spoke
he/she/it	spoke
we	spoke
you	spoke
they	spoke

Present Perfect

I	have	spoken
you	have	spoken
he/she/it	has	spoken
we	have	spoken
you	have	spoken
they	have	spoken

Past Perfect

I	had	spoken
you	had	spoken
he/she/it	had	spoken
we	had	spoken
you	had	spoken
they	had	spoken

***Will*-Future**

I	will	speak
you	will	speak
he/she/it	will	speak
we	will	speak
you	will	speak
they	will	speak

***Going to*-Future**

I	am	going to	speak
you	are	going to	speak
he/she/it	is	going to	speak
we	are	going to	speak
you	are	going to	speak
they	are	going to	speak

Future Perfect

I	will have	spoken
you	will have	spoken
he/she/it	will have	spoken
we	will have	spoken
you	will have	spoken
they	will have	spoken

Imperative

speak

Impersonal

***ing*-Form**

speaking

Past Participle

spoken

Continuous tenses

Present

I	am	speaking
you	are	speaking
he/she/it	is	speaking
we	are	speaking
you	are	speaking
they	are	speaking

Past

I	was	speaking
you	were	speaking
he/she/it	was	speaking
we	were	speaking
you	were	speaking
they	were	speaking

Present Perfect

I	have	been	speaking
you	have	been	speaking
he/she/it	has	been	speaking
we	have	been	speaking
you	have	been	speaking
they	have	been	speaking

Past Perfect

I	had been	speaking
you	had been	speaking
he/she/it	had been	speaking
we	had been	speaking
you	had been	speaking
they	had been	speaking

***Will*-Future**

I	will be	speaking
you	will be	speaking
he/she/it	will be	speaking
we	will be	speaking
you	will be	speaking
they	will be	speaking

***Going to*-Future**

I	am	going to be	speaking
you	are	going to be	speaking
he/she/it	is	going to be	speaking
we	are	going to be	speaking
you	are	going to be	speaking
they	are	going to be	speaking

Future Perfect

I	will have been	speaking
you	will have been	speaking
he/she/it	will have been	speaking
we	will have been	speaking
you	will have been	speaking
they	will have been	speaking

Conditional

I	would	speak
you	would	speak
he/she/it	would	speak
we	would	speak
you	would	speak
they	would	speak

Conditional Past

I	would have	spoken
you	would have	spoken
he/she/it	would have	spoken
we	would have	spoken
you	would have	spoken
they	would have	spoken

spell

buchstabieren

- spelled/spelt - spelled/spelt

Simple tenses

Present

I	spell
you	spell
he/she/it	spells
we	spell
you	spell
they	spell

Past

I	spelled | spelt
you	spelled | spelt
he/she/it	spelled | spelt
we	spelled | spelt
you	spelled | spelt
they	spelled | spelt

Present Perfect

I	have	spelled | spelt
you	have	spelled | spelt
he/she/it	has	spelled | spelt
we	have	spelled | spelt
you	have	spelled | spelt
they	have	spelled | spelt

Past Perfect

I	had	spelled | spelt
you	had	spelled | spelt
he/she/it	had	spelled | spelt
we	had	spelled | spelt
you	had	spelled | spelt
they	had	spelled | spelt

Will-Future

I	will	spell
you	will	spell
he/she/it	will	spell
we	will	spell
you	will	spell
they	will	spell

Going to-Future

I	am	going to	spell
you	are	going to	spell
he/she/it	is	going to	spell
we	are	going to	spell
you	are	going to	spell
they	are	going to	spell

Future Perfect

I	will have	spelled | spelt
you	will have	spelled | spelt
he/she/it	will have	spelled | spelt
we	will have	spelled | spelt
you	will have	spelled | spelt
they	will have	spelled | spelt

Imperative

spell

Impersonal

ing-Form

spelling

Past Participle

spelled | spelt

Continuous tenses

Present

I	am	spelling
you	are	spelling
he/she/it	is	spelling
we	are	spelling
you	are	spelling
they	are	spelling

Past

I	was	spelling
you	were	spelling
he/she/it	was	spelling
we	were	spelling
you	were	spelling
they	were	spelling

Present Perfect

I	have	been	spelling
you	have	been	spelling
he/she/it	has	been	spelling
we	have	been	spelling
you	have	been	spelling
they	have	been	spelling

Past Perfect

I	had been	spelling
you	had been	spelling
he/she/it	had been	spelling
we	had been	spelling
you	had been	spelling
they	had been	spelling

Will-Future

I	will be	spelling
you	will be	spelling
he/she/it	will be	spelling
we	will be	spelling
you	will be	spelling
they	will be	spelling

Going to-Future

I	am	going to be	spelling
you	are	going to be	spelling
he/she/it	is	going to be	spelling
we	are	going to be	spelling
you	are	going to be	spelling
they	are	going to be	spelling

Future Perfect

I	will have been	spelling
you	will have been	spelling
he/she/it	will have been	spelling
we	will have been	spelling
you	will have been	spelling
they	will have been	spelling

Conditional

I	would	spell
you	would	spell
he/she/it	would	spell
we	would	spell
you	would	spell
they	would	spell

Conditional Past

I	would have	spelled | spelt
you	would have	spelled | spelt
he/she/it	would have	spelled | spelt
we	would have	spelled | spelt
you	would have	spelled | spelt
they	would have	spelled | spelt

spend

– *spent* – *spent*

ausgeben

Unregelmäßiges Verb

Simple tenses

Present

I	spend
you	spend
he/she/it	spends
we	spend
you	spend
they	spend

Past

I	spent
you	spent
he/she/it	spent
we	spent
you	spent
they	spent

Present Perfect

I	have	spent
you	have	spent
he/she/it	has	spent
we	have	spent
you	have	spent
they	have	spent

Past Perfect

I	had	spent
you	had	spent
he/she/it	had	spent
we	had	spent
you	had	spent
they	had	spent

***Will*-Future**

I	will	spend
you	will	spend
he/she/it	will	spend
we	will	spend
you	will	spend
they	will	spend

***Going to*-Future**

I	am	going to	spend
you	are	going to	spend
he/she/it	is	going to	spend
we	are	going to	spend
you	are	going to	spend
they	are	going to	spend

Future Perfect

I	will have	spent
you	will have	spent
he/she/it	will have	spent
we	will have	spent
you	will have	spent
they	will have	spent

Imperative

spend

Impersonal

***ing*-Form**

spending

Past Participle

spent

Continuous tenses

Present

I	am	spending
you	are	spending
he/she/it	is	spending
we	are	spending
you	are	spending
they	are	spending

Past

I	was	spending
you	were	spending
he/she/it	was	spending
we	were	spending
you	were	spending
they	were	spending

Present Perfect

I	have been	spending
you	have been	spending
he/she/it	has been	spending
we	have been	spending
you	have been	spending
they	have been	spending

Past Perfect

I	had been	spending
you	had been	spending
he/she/it	had been	spending
we	had been	spending
you	had been	spending
they	had been	spending

***Will*-Future**

I	will be	spending
you	will be	spending
he/she/it	will be	spending
we	will be	spending
you	will be	spending
they	will be	spending

***Going to*-Future**

I	am	going to be	spending
you	are	going to be	spending
he/she/it	is	going to be	spending
we	are	going to be	spending
you	are	going to be	spending
they	are	going to be	spending

Future Perfect

I	will have been	spending
you	will have been	spending
he/she/it	will have been	spending
we	will have been	spending
you	will have been	spending
they	will have been	spending

Conditional

I	would	spend
you	would	spend
he/she/it	would	spend
we	would	spend
you	would	spend
they	would	spend

Conditional Past

I	would have	spent
you	would have	spent
he/she/it	would have	spent
we	would have	spent
you	would have	spent
they	would have	spent

schleudern

spin
- spun - spun

Simple tenses

Present

I	spin
you	spin
he/she/it	spins
we	spin
you	spin
they	spin

Past

I	spun
you	spun
he/she/it	spun
we	spun
you	spun
they	spun

Present Perfect

I	have	spun
you	have	spun
he/she/it	has	spun
we	have	spun
you	have	spun
they	have	spun

Past Perfect

I	had	spun
you	had	spun
he/she/it	had	spun
we	had	spun
you	had	spun
they	had	spun

Will-Future

I	will	spin
you	will	spin
he/she/it	will	spin
we	will	spin
you	will	spin
they	will	spin

Going to-Future

I	am	going to	spin
you	are	going to	spin
he/she/it	is	going to	spin
we	are	going to	spin
you	are	going to	spin
they	are	going to	spin

Future Perfect

I	will have	spun
you	will have	spun
he/she/it	will have	spun
we	will have	spun
you	will have	spun
they	will have	spun

Imperative

spin

Impersonal

ing-Form

spinning

Past Participle

spun

Continuous tenses

Present

I	am	spinning
you	are	spinning
he/she/it	is	spinning
we	are	spinning
you	are	spinning
they	are	spinning

Past

I	was	spinning
you	were	spinning
he/she/it	was	spinning
we	were	spinning
you	were	spinning
they	were	spinning

Present Perfect

I	have been	spinning
you	have been	spinning
he/she/it	has been	spinning
we	have been	spinning
you	have been	spinning
they	have been	spinning

Past Perfect

I	had been	spinning
you	had been	spinning
he/she/it	had been	spinning
we	had been	spinning
you	had been	spinning
they	had been	spinning

Will-Future

I	will be	spinning
you	will be	spinning
he/she/it	will be	spinning
we	will be	spinning
you	will be	spinning
they	will be	spinning

Going to-Future

I	am	going to be	spinning
you	are	going to be	spinning
he/she/it	is	going to be	spinning
we	are	going to be	spinning
you	are	going to be	spinning
they	are	going to be	spinning

Future Perfect

I	will have been	spinning
you	will have been	spinning
he/she/it	will have been	spinning
we	will have been	spinning
you	will have been	spinning
they	will have been	spinning

Conditional

I	would	spin
you	would	spin
he/she/it	would	spin
we	would	spin
you	would	spin
they	would	spin

Conditional Past

I	would have	spun
you	would have	spun
he/she/it	would have	spun
we	would have	spun
you	would have	spun
they	would have	spun

spit
- spat - spat

spucken

Unregelmäßiges Verb

Simple tenses

Present

I	spit
you	spit
he/she/it	spits
we	spit
you	spit
they	spit

Past

I	spat
you	spat
he/she/it	spat
we	spat
you	spat
they	spat

Present Perfect

I	have	spat
you	have	spat
he/she/it	has	spat
we	have	spat
you	have	spat
they	have	spat

Past Perfect

I	had	spat
you	had	spat
he/she/it	had	spat
we	had	spat
you	had	spat
they	had	spat

***Will*-Future**

I	will	spit
you	will	spit
he/she/it	will	spit
we	will	spit
you	will	spit
they	will	spit

***Going to*-Future**

I	am	going to	spit
you	are	going to	spit
he/she/it	is	going to	spit
we	are	going to	spit
you	are	going to	spit
they	are	going to	spit

Future Perfect

I	will have	spat
you	will have	spat
he/she/it	will have	spat
we	will have	spat
you	will have	spat
they	will have	spat

Imperative

spit

Impersonal

***ing*-Form**

spitting

Past Participle

spat

Continuous tenses

Present

I	am	spitting
you	are	spitting
he/she/it	is	spitting
we	are	spitting
you	are	spitting
they	are	spitting

Past

I	was	spitting
you	were	spitting
he/she/it	was	spitting
we	were	spitting
you	were	spitting
they	were	spitting

Present Perfect

I	have been	spitting
you	have been	spitting
he/she/it	has been	spitting
we	have been	spitting
you	have been	spitting
they	have been	spitting

Past Perfect

I	had been	spitting
you	had been	spitting
he/she/it	had been	spitting
we	had been	spitting
you	had been	spitting
they	had been	spitting

***Will*-Future**

I	will be	spitting
you	will be	spitting
he/she/it	will be	spitting
we	will be	spitting
you	will be	spitting
they	will be	spitting

***Going to*-Future**

I	am	going to be	spitting
you	are	going to be	spitting
he/she/it	is	going to be	spitting
we	are	going to be	spitting
you	are	going to be	spitting
they	are	going to be	spitting

Future Perfect

I	will have been	spitting
you	will have been	spitting
he/she/it	will have been	spitting
we	will have been	spitting
you	will have been	spitting
they	will have been	spitting

Conditional

I	would	spit
you	would	spit
he/she/it	would	spit
we	would	spit
you	would	spit
they	would	spit

Conditional Past

I	would have	spat
you	would have	spat
he/she/it	would have	spat
we	would have	spat
you	would have	spat
they	would have	spat

spalten

split
- split - split

Simple tenses

Present

I	split
you	split
he/she/it	splits
we	split
you	split
they	split

Past

I	split
you	split
he/she/it	split
we	split
you	split
they	split

Present Perfect

I	have	split
you	have	split
he/she/it	has	split
we	have	split
you	have	split
they	have	split

Past Perfect

I	had	split
you	had	split
he/she/it	had	split
we	had	split
you	had	split
they	had	split

Will-Future

I	will	split
you	will	split
he/she/it	will	split
we	will	split
you	will	split
they	will	split

Going to-Future

I	am	going to	split
you	are	going to	split
he/she/it	is	going to	split
we	are	going to	split
you	are	going to	split
they	are	going to	split

Future Perfect

I	will have	split
you	will have	split
he/she/it	will have	split
we	will have	split
you	will have	split
they	will have	split

Imperative

split

Impersonal

ing-Form

splitting

Past Participle

split

Continuous tenses

Present

I	am	splitting
you	are	splitting
he/she/it	is	splitting
we	are	splitting
you	are	splitting
they	are	splitting

Past

I	was	splitting
you	were	splitting
he/she/it	was	splitting
we	were	splitting
you	were	splitting
they	were	splitting

Present Perfect

I	have been	splitting
you	have been	splitting
he/she/it	has been	splitting
we	have been	splitting
you	have been	splitting
they	have been	splitting

Past Perfect

I	had been	splitting
you	had been	splitting
he/she/it	had been	splitting
we	had been	splitting
you	had been	splitting
they	had been	splitting

Will-Future

I	will be	splitting
you	will be	splitting
he/she/it	will be	splitting
we	will be	splitting
you	will be	splitting
they	will be	splitting

Going to-Future

I	am	going to be	splitting
you	are	going to be	splitting
he/she/it	is	going to be	splitting
we	are	going to be	splitting
you	are	going to be	splitting
they	are	going to be	splitting

Future Perfect

I	will have been	splitting
you	will have been	splitting
he/she/it	will have been	splitting
we	will have been	splitting
you	will have been	splitting
they	will have been	splitting

Conditional

I	would	split
you	would	split
he/she/it	would	split
we	would	split
you	would	split
they	would	split

Conditional Past

I	would have	split
you	would have	split
he/she/it	would have	split
we	would have	split
you	would have	split
they	would have	split

spoil *verderben*
- spoiled/spoilt (BE) - spoiled/spoilt (BE) Unregelmäßiges Verb

Simple tenses

Present

I	spoil
you	spoil
he/she/it	spoils
we	spoil
you	spoil
they	spoil

Past

I	spoiled | spoilt
you	spoiled | spoilt
he/she/it	spoiled | spoilt
we	spoiled | spoilt
you	spoiled | spoilt
they	spoiled | spoilt

Present Perfect

I	have	spoiled | spoilt
you	have	spoiled | spoilt
he/she/it	has	spoiled | spoilt
we	have	spoiled | spoilt
you	have	spoiled | spoilt
they	have	spoiled | spoilt

Past Perfect

I	had	spoiled | spoilt
you	had	spoiled | spoilt
he/she/it	had	spoiled | spoilt
we	had	spoiled | spoilt
you	had	spoiled | spoilt
they	had	spoiled | spoilt

Will-Future

I	will	spoil
you	will	spoil
he/she/it	will	spoil
we	will	spoil
you	will	spoil
they	will	spoil

Going to-Future

I	am	going to	spoil
you	are	going to	spoil
he/she/it	is	going to	spoil
we	are	going to	spoil
you	are	going to	spoil
they	are	going to	spoil

Future Perfect

I	will have	spoiled | spoilt
you	will have	spoiled | spoilt
he/she/it	will have	spoiled | spoilt
we	will have	spoiled | spoilt
you	will have	spoiled | spoilt
they	will have	spoiled | spoilt

Imperative

spoil

Impersonal

ing-Form

spoiling

Past Participle

spoiled | spoilt

Continuous tenses

Present

I	am	spoiling
you	are	spoiling
he/she/it	is	spoiling
we	are	spoiling
you	are	spoiling
they	are	spoiling

Past

I	was	spoiling
you	were	spoiling
he/she/it	was	spoiling
we	were	spoiling
you	were	spoiling
they	were	spoiling

Present Perfect

I	have	been	spoiling
you	have	been	spoiling
he/she/it	has	been	spoiling
we	have	been	spoiling
you	have	been	spoiling
they	have	been	spoiling

Past Perfect

I	had been	spoiling
you	had been	spoiling
he/she/it	had been	spoiling
we	had been	spoiling
you	had been	spoiling
they	had been	spoiling

Will-Future

I	will be	spoiling
you	will be	spoiling
he/she/it	will be	spoiling
we	will be	spoiling
you	will be	spoiling
they	will be	spoiling

Going to-Future

I	am	going to be	spoiling
you	are	going to be	spoiling
he/she/it	is	going to be	spoiling
we	are	going to be	spoiling
you	are	going to be	spoiling
they	are	going to be	spoiling

Future Perfect

I	will have been spoiling
you	will have been spoiling
he/she/it	will have been spoiling
we	will have been spoiling
you	will have been spoiling
they	will have been spoiling

Conditional

I	would	spoil
you	would	spoil
he/she/it	would	spoil
we	would	spoil
you	would	spoil
they	would	spoil

Conditional Past

I	would have	spoiled | spoilt
you	would have	spoiled | spoilt
he/she/it	would have	spoiled | spoilt
we	would have	spoiled | spoilt
you	would have	spoiled | spoilt
they	would have	spoiled | spoilt

ausbreiten

spread

- spread - spread

Simple tenses

Present

I	spread
you	spread
he/she/it	spreads
we	spread
you	spread
they	spread

Past

I	spread
you	spread
he/she/it	spread
we	spread
you	spread
they	spread

Present Perfect

I	have	spread
you	have	spread
he/she/it	has	spread
we	have	spread
you	have	spread
they	have	spread

Past Perfect

I	had	spread
you	had	spread
he/she/it	had	spread
we	had	spread
you	had	spread
they	had	spread

Will-Future

I	will	spread
you	will	spread
he/she/it	will	spread
we	will	spread
you	will	spread
they	will	spread

Going to-Future

I	am	going to	spread
you	are	going to	spread
he/she/it	is	going to	spread
we	are	going to	spread
you	are	going to	spread
they	are	going to	spread

Future Perfect

I	will have	spread
you	will have	spread
he/she/it	will have	spread
we	will have	spread
you	will have	spread
they	will have	spread

Imperative

spread

Impersonal

ing-Form

spreading

Past Participle

spread

Continuous tenses

Present

I	am	spreading
you	are	spreading
he/she/it	is	spreading
we	are	spreading
you	are	spreading
they	are	spreading

Past

I	was	spreading
you	were	spreading
he/she/it	was	spreading
we	were	spreading
you	were	spreading
they	were	spreading

Present Perfect

I	have	been	spreading
you	have	been	spreading
he/she/it	has	been	spreading
we	have	been	spreading
you	have	been	spreading
they	have	been	spreading

Past Perfect

I	had been	spreading
you	had been	spreading
he/she/it	had been	spreading
we	had been	spreading
you	had been	spreading
they	had been	spreading

Will-Future

I	will be	spreading
you	will be	spreading
he/she/it	will be	spreading
we	will be	spreading
you	will be	spreading
they	will be	spreading

Going to-Future

I	am	going to be	spreading
you	are	going to be	spreading
he/she/it	is	going to be	spreading
we	are	going to be	spreading
you	are	going to be	spreading
they	are	going to be	spreading

Future Perfect

I	will have been	spreading
you	will have been	spreading
he/she/it	will have been	spreading
we	will have been	spreading
you	will have been	spreading
they	will have been	spreading

Conditional

I	would	spread
you	would	spread
he/she/it	would	spread
we	would	spread
you	would	spread
they	would	spread

Conditional Past

I	would have	spread
you	would have	spread
he/she/it	would have	spread
we	would have	spread
you	would have	spread
they	would have	spread

spring

springen

- sprang/sprung (AE) - sprung

Unregelmäßiges Verb

Simple tenses

Present

I	spring
you	spring
he/she/it	springs
we	spring
you	spring
they	spring

Past

I	sprang
you	sprang
he/she/it	sprang
we	sprang
you	sprang
they	sprang

Present Perfect

I	have	sprung
you	have	sprung
he/she/it	has	sprung
we	have	sprung
you	have	sprung
they	have	sprung

Past Perfect

I	had	sprung
you	had	sprung
he/she/it	had	sprung
we	had	sprung
you	had	sprung
they	had	sprung

Will-Future

I	will	spring
you	will	spring
he/she/it	will	spring
we	will	spring
you	will	spring
they	will	spring

Going to-Future

I	am	going to	spring
you	are	going to	spring
he/she/it	is	going to	spring
we	are	going to	spring
you	are	going to	spring
they	are	going to	spring

Future Perfect

I	will have	sprung
you	will have	sprung
he/she/it	will have	sprung
we	will have	sprung
you	will have	sprung
they	will have	sprung

Imperative

spring

Impersonal

ing-Form

springing

Past Participle

sprung

Continuous tenses

Present

I	am	springing
you	are	springing
he/she/it	is	springing
we	are	springing
you	are	springing
they	are	springing

Past

I	was	springing
you	were	springing
he/she/it	was	springing
we	were	springing
you	were	springing
they	were	springing

Present Perfect

I	have been	springing
you	have been	springing
he/she/it	has been	springing
we	have been	springing
you	have been	springing
they	have been	springing

Past Perfect

I	had been	springing
you	had been	springing
he/she/it	had been	springing
we	had been	springing
you	had been	springing
they	had been	springing

Will-Future

I	will be	springing
you	will be	springing
he/she/it	will be	springing
we	will be	springing
you	will be	springing
they	will be	springing

Going to-Future

I	am	going to be	springing
you	are	going to be	springing
he/she/it	is	going to be	springing
we	are	going to be	springing
you	are	going to be	springing
they	are	going to be	springing

Future Perfect

I	will have been	springing
you	will have been	springing
he/she/it	will have been	springing
we	will have been	springing
you	will have been	springing
they	will have been	springing

Conditional

I	would	spring
you	would	spring
he/she/it	would	spring
we	would	spring
you	would	spring
they	would	spring

Conditional Past

I	would have	sprung
you	would have	sprung
he/she/it	would have	sprung
we	would have	sprung
you	would have	sprung
they	would have	sprung

+ **-ing** → ~~e~~ / + **-d** nicht **-ed**
Regelmäßiges Verb

drücken

squeeze

Simple tenses

Present

I squeeze
you squeeze
he/she/it squeezes
we squeeze
you squeeze
they squeeze

Past

I squeezed
you squeezed
he/she/it squeezed
we squeezed
you squeezed
they squeezed

Present Perfect

I have squeezed
you have squeezed
he/she/it has squeezed
we have squeezed
you have squeezed
they have squeezed

Past Perfect

I had squeezed
you had squeezed
he/she/it had squeezed
we had squeezed
you had squeezed
they had squeezed

Will-Future

I will squeeze
you will squeeze
he/she/it will squeeze
we will squeeze
you will squeeze
they will squeeze

Going to-Future

I am going to squeeze
you are going to squeeze
he/she/it is going to squeeze
we are going to squeeze
you are going to squeeze
they are going to squeeze

Future Perfect

I will have squeezed
you will have squeezed
he/she/it will have squeezed
we will have squeezed
you will have squeezed
they will have squeezed

Imperative

squeeze

Impersonal

ing-Form

squeezing

Past Participle

squeezed

Continuous tenses

Present

I am squeezing
you are squeezing
he/she/it is squeezing
we are squeezing
you are squeezing
they are squeezing

Past

I was squeezing
you were squeezing
he/she/it was squeezing
we were squeezing
you were squeezing
they were squeezing

Present Perfect

I have been squeezing
you have been squeezing
he/she/it has been squeezing
we have been squeezing
you have been squeezing
they have been squeezing

Past Perfect

I had been squeezing
you had been squeezing
he/she/it had been squeezing
we had been squeezing
you had been squeezing
they had been squeezing

Will-Future

I will be squeezing
you will be squeezing
he/she/it will be squeezing
we will be squeezing
you will be squeezing
they will be squeezing

Going to-Future

I am going to be squeezing
you are going to be squeezing
he/she/it is going to be squeezing
we are going to be squeezing
you are going to be squeezing
they are going to be squeezing

Future Perfect

I will have been squeezing
you will have been squeezing
he/she/it will have been squeezing
we will have been squeezing
you will have been squeezing
they will have been squeezing

Conditional

I would squeeze
you would squeeze
he/she/it would squeeze
we would squeeze
you would squeeze
they would squeeze

Conditional Past

I would have squeezed
you would have squeezed
he/she/it would have squeezed
we would have squeezed
you would have squeezed
they would have squeezed

stamp

stampfen

Regelmäßiges Verb

Simple tenses

Present

I	stamp
you	stamp
he/she/it	stamps
we	stamp
you	stamp
they	stamp

Past

I	stamped
you	stamped
he/she/it	stamped
we	stamped
you	stamped
they	stamped

Present Perfect

I	have	stamped
you	have	stamped
he/she/it	has	stamped
we	have	stamped
you	have	stamped
they	have	stamped

Past Perfect

I	had	stamped
you	had	stamped
he/she/it	had	stamped
we	had	stamped
you	had	stamped
they	had	stamped

Will-Future

I	will	stamp
you	will	stamp
he/she/it	will	stamp
we	will	stamp
you	will	stamp
they	will	stamp

Going to-Future

I	am	going to	stamp
you	are	going to	stamp
he/she/it	is	going to	stamp
we	are	going to	stamp
you	are	going to	stamp
they	are	going to	stamp

Future Perfect

I	will have	stamped
you	will have	stamped
he/she/it	will have	stamped
we	will have	stamped
you	will have	stamped
they	will have	stamped

Imperative

stamp

Impersonal

ing-Form

stamping

Past Participle

stamped

Continuous tenses

Present

I	am	stamping
you	are	stamping
he/she/it	is	stamping
we	are	stamping
you	are	stamping
they	are	stamping

Past

I	was	stamping
you	were	stamping
he/she/it	was	stamping
we	were	stamping
you	were	stamping
they	were	stamping

Present Perfect

I	have been	stamping
you	have been	stamping
he/she/it	has been	stamping
we	have been	stamping
you	have been	stamping
they	have been	stamping

Past Perfect

I	had been	stamping
you	had been	stamping
he/she/it	had been	stamping
we	had been	stamping
you	had been	stamping
they	had been	stamping

Will-Future

I	will be	stamping
you	will be	stamping
he/she/it	will be	stamping
we	will be	stamping
you	will be	stamping
they	will be	stamping

Going to-Future

I	am	going to be	stamping
you	are	going to be	stamping
he/she/it	is	going to be	stamping
we	are	going to be	stamping
you	are	going to be	stamping
they	are	going to be	stamping

Future Perfect

I	will have been	stamping
you	will have been	stamping
he/she/it	will have been	stamping
we	will have been	stamping
you	will have been	stamping
they	will have been	stamping

Conditional

I	would	stamp
you	would	stamp
he/she/it	would	stamp
we	would	stamp
you	would	stamp
they	would	stamp

Conditional Past

I	would have	stamped
you	would have	stamped
he/she/it	would have	stamped
we	would have	stamped
you	would have	stamped
they	would have	stamped

stehen

stand

– stood – stood

Simple tenses

Present

I	stand
you	stand
he/she/it	stands
we	stand
you	stand
they	stand

Past

I	stood
you	stood
he/she/it	stood
we	stood
you	stood
they	stood

Present Perfect

I	have	stood
you	have	stood
he/she/it	has	stood
we	have	stood
you	have	stood
they	have	stood

Past Perfect

I	had	stood
you	had	stood
he/she/it	had	stood
we	had	stood
you	had	stood
they	had	stood

Will-Future

I	will	stand
you	will	stand
he/she/it	will	stand
we	will	stand
you	will	stand
they	will	stand

Going to-Future

I	am	going to	stand
you	are	going to	stand
he/she/it	is	going to	stand
we	are	going to	stand
you	are	going to	stand
they	are	going to	stand

Future Perfect

I	will have	stood
you	will have	stood
he/she/it	will have	stood
we	will have	stood
you	will have	stood
they	will have	stood

Imperative

stand

Impersonal

ing-Form

standing

Past Participle

stood

Continuous tenses

Present

I	am	standing
you	are	standing
he/she/it	is	standing
we	are	standing
you	are	standing
they	are	standing

Past

I	was	standing
you	were	standing
he/she/it	was	standing
we	were	standing
you	were	standing
they	were	standing

Present Perfect

I	have been	standing
you	have been	standing
he/she/it	has been	standing
we	have been	standing
you	have been	standing
they	have been	standing

Past Perfect

I	had been	standing
you	had been	standing
he/she/it	had been	standing
we	had been	standing
you	had been	standing
they	had been	standing

Will-Future

I	will be	standing
you	will be	standing
he/she/it	will be	standing
we	will be	standing
you	will be	standing
they	will be	standing

Going to-Future

I	am	going to be	standing
you	are	going to be	standing
he/she/it	is	going to be	standing
we	are	going to be	standing
you	are	going to be	standing
they	are	going to be	standing

Future Perfect

I	will have been	standing
you	will have been	standing
he/she/it	will have been	standing
we	will have been	standing
you	will have been	standing
they	will have been	standing

Conditional

I	would	stand
you	would	stand
he/she/it	would	stand
we	would	stand
you	would	stand
they	would	stand

Conditional Past

I	would have	stood
you	would have	stood
he/she/it	would have	stood
we	would have	stood
you	would have	stood
they	would have	stood

stare

starren

+ **-ing** → ~~e~~ / + **-d** nicht **-ed**
Regelmäßiges Verb

Simple tenses

Present

I	stare
you	stare
he/she/it	stares
we	stare
you	stare
they	stare

Past

I	stared
you	stared
he/she/it	stared
we	stared
you	stared
they	stared

Present Perfect

I	have	stared
you	have	stared
he/she/it	has	stared
we	have	stared
you	have	stared
they	have	stared

Past Perfect

I	had	stared
you	had	stared
he/she/it	had	stared
we	had	stared
you	had	stared
they	had	stared

Will-Future

I	will	stare
you	will	stare
he/she/it	will	stare
we	will	stare
you	will	stare
they	will	stare

Going to-Future

I	am	going to	stare
you	are	going to	stare
he/she/it	is	going to	stare
we	are	going to	stare
you	are	going to	stare
they	are	going to	stare

Future Perfect

I	will have	stared
you	will have	stared
he/she/it	will have	stared
we	will have	stared
you	will have	stared
they	will have	stared

Imperative

stare

Impersonal

ing-Form

staring

Past Participle

stared

Continuous tenses

Present

I	am	staring
you	are	staring
he/she/it	is	staring
we	are	staring
you	are	staring
they	are	staring

Past

I	was	staring
you	were	staring
he/she/it	was	staring
we	were	staring
you	were	staring
they	were	staring

Present Perfect

I	have	been	staring
you	have	been	staring
he/she/it	has	been	staring
we	have	been	staring
you	have	been	staring
they	have	been	staring

Past Perfect

I	had been	staring
you	had been	staring
he/she/it	had been	staring
we	had been	staring
you	had been	staring
they	had been	staring

Will-Future

I	will be	staring
you	will be	staring
he/she/it	will be	staring
we	will be	staring
you	will be	staring
they	will be	staring

Going to-Future

I	am	going to be	staring
you	are	going to be	staring
he/she/it	is	going to be	staring
we	are	going to be	staring
you	are	going to be	staring
they	are	going to be	staring

Future Perfect

I	will have been	staring
you	will have been	staring
he/she/it	will have been	staring
we	will have been	staring
you	will have been	staring
they	will have been	staring

Conditional

I	would	stare
you	would	stare
he/she/it	would	stare
we	would	stare
you	would	stare
they	would	stare

Conditional Past

I	would have	stared
you	would have	stared
he/she/it	would have	stared
we	would have	stared
you	would have	stared
they	would have	stared

Simple tenses

Present

I	start
you	start
he/she/it	starts
we	start
you	start
they	start

Past

I	started
you	started
he/she/it	started
we	started
you	started
they	started

Present Perfect

I	have	started
you	have	started
he/she/it	has	started
we	have	started
you	have	started
they	have	started

Past Perfect

I	had	started
you	had	started
he/she/it	had	started
we	had	started
you	had	started
they	had	started

Will-Future

I	will	start
you	will	start
he/she/it	will	start
we	will	start
you	will	start
they	will	start

Going to-Future

I	am	going to	start
you	are	going to	start
he/she/it	is	going to	start
we	are	going to	start
you	are	going to	start
they	are	going to	start

Future Perfect

I	will have	started
you	will have	started
he/she/it	will have	started
we	will have	started
you	will have	started
they	will have	started

Imperative

start

Impersonal

ing-Form

starting

Past Participle

started

Continuous tenses

Present

I	am	starting
you	are	starting
he/she/it	is	starting
we	are	starting
you	are	starting
they	are	starting

Past

I	was	starting
you	were	starting
he/she/it	was	starting
we	were	starting
you	were	starting
they	were	starting

Present Perfect

I	have	been	starting
you	have	been	starting
he/she/it	has	been	starting
we	have	been	starting
you	have	been	starting
they	have	been	starting

Past Perfect

I	had been	starting
you	had been	starting
he/she/it	had been	starting
we	had been	starting
you	had been	starting
they	had been	starting

Will-Future

I	will be	starting
you	will be	starting
he/she/it	will be	starting
we	will be	starting
you	will be	starting
they	will be	starting

Going to-Future

I	am	going to be	starting
you	are	going to be	starting
he/she/it	is	going to be	starting
we	are	going to be	starting
you	are	going to be	starting
they	are	going to be	starting

Future Perfect

I	will have been	starting
you	will have been	starting
he/she/it	will have been	starting
we	will have been	starting
you	will have been	starting
they	will have been	starting

Conditional

I	would	start
you	would	start
he/she/it	would	start
we	would	start
you	would	start
they	would	start

Conditional Past

I	would have	started
you	would have	started
he/she/it	would have	started
we	would have	started
you	would have	started
they	would have	started

state

darlegen

+ **-ing** → ~~e~~ / + **-d** nicht **-ed**
Regelmäßiges Verb

Simple tenses

Present

I	state
you	state
he/she/it	states
we	state
you	state
they	state

Past

I	stated
you	stated
he/she/it	stated
we	stated
you	stated
they	stated

Present Perfect

I	have	stated
you	have	stated
he/she/it	has	stated
we	have	stated
you	have	stated
they	have	stated

Past Perfect

I	had	stated
you	had	stated
he/she/it	had	stated
we	had	stated
you	had	stated
they	had	stated

Will-Future

I	will	state
you	will	state
he/she/it	will	state
we	will	state
you	will	state
they	will	state

Going to-Future

I	am	going to	state
you	are	going to	state
he/she/it	is	going to	state
we	are	going to	state
you	are	going to	state
they	are	going to	state

Future Perfect

I	will have	stated
you	will have	stated
he/she/it	will have	stated
we	will have	stated
you	will have	stated
they	will have	stated

Imperative

state

Impersonal

ing-Form

stating

Past Participle

stated

Continuous tenses

Present

I	am	stating
you	are	stating
he/she/it	is	stating
we	are	stating
you	are	stating
they	are	stating

Past

I	was	stating
you	were	stating
he/she/it	was	stating
we	were	stating
you	were	stating
they	were	stating

Present Perfect

I	have	been	stating
you	have	been	stating
he/she/it	has	been	stating
we	have	been	stating
you	have	been	stating
they	have	been	stating

Past Perfect

I	had been	stating
you	had been	stating
he/she/it	had been	stating
we	had been	stating
you	had been	stating
they	had been	stating

Will-Future

I	will be	stating
you	will be	stating
he/she/it	will be	stating
we	will be	stating
you	will be	stating
they	will be	stating

Going to-Future

I	am	going to be	stating
you	are	going to be	stating
he/she/it	is	going to be	stating
we	are	going to be	stating
you	are	going to be	stating
they	are	going to be	stating

Future Perfect

I	will have been	stating
you	will have been	stating
he/she/it	will have been	stating
we	will have been	stating
you	will have been	stating
they	will have been	stating

Conditional

I	would	state
you	would	state
he/she/it	would	state
we	would	state
you	would	state
they	would	state

Conditional Past

I	would have	stated
you	would have	stated
he/she/it	would have	stated
we	would have	stated
you	would have	stated
they	would have	stated

Simple tenses

Present

I	stay
you	stay
he/she/it	stays
we	stay
you	stay
they	stay

Past

I	stayed
you	stayed
he/she/it	stayed
we	stayed
you	stayed
they	stayed

Present Perfect

I	have	stayed
you	have	stayed
he/she/it	has	stayed
we	have	stayed
you	have	stayed
they	have	stayed

Past Perfect

I	had	stayed
you	had	stayed
he/she/it	had	stayed
we	had	stayed
you	had	stayed
they	had	stayed

Will-Future

I	will	stay
you	will	stay
he/she/it	will	stay
we	will	stay
you	will	stay
they	will	stay

Going to-Future

I	am	going to	stay
you	are	going to	stay
he/she/it	is	going to	stay
we	are	going to	stay
you	are	going to	stay
they	are	going to	stay

Future Perfect

I	will have	stayed
you	will have	stayed
he/she/it	will have	stayed
we	will have	stayed
you	will have	stayed
they	will have	stayed

Imperative

stay

Impersonal

ing-Form

staying

Past Participle

stayed

Continuous tenses

Present

I	am	staying
you	are	staying
he/she/it	is	staying
we	are	staying
you	are	staying
they	are	staying

Past

I	was	staying
you	were	staying
he/she/it	was	staying
we	were	staying
you	were	staying
they	were	staying

Present Perfect

I	have been	staying
you	have been	staying
he/she/it	has been	staying
we	have been	staying
you	have been	staying
they	have been	staying

Past Perfect

I	had been	staying
you	had been	staying
he/she/it	had been	staying
we	had been	staying
you	had been	staying
they	had been	staying

Will-Future

I	will be	staying
you	will be	staying
he/she/it	will be	staying
we	will be	staying
you	will be	staying
they	will be	staying

Going to-Future

I	am	going to be	staying
you	are	going to be	staying
he/she/it	is	going to be	staying
we	are	going to be	staying
you	are	going to be	staying
they	are	going to be	staying

Future Perfect

I	will have been	staying
you	will have been	staying
he/she/it	will have been	staying
we	will have been	staying
you	will have been	staying
they	will have been	staying

Conditional

I	would	stay
you	would	stay
he/she/it	would	stay
we	would	stay
you	would	stay
they	would	stay

Conditional Past

I	would have	stayed
you	would have	stayed
he/she/it	would have	stayed
we	would have	stayed
you	would have	stayed
they	would have	stayed

steal

- *stole* - *stolen*

stehlen

Unregelmäßiges Verb

Simple tenses

Present

I	steal
you	steal
he/she/it	steals
we	steal
you	steal
they	steal

Past

I	stole
you	stole
he/she/it	stole
we	stole
you	stole
they	stole

Present Perfect

I	have	stolen
you	have	stolen
he/she/it	has	stolen
we	have	stolen
you	have	stolen
they	have	stolen

Past Perfect

I	had	stolen
you	had	stolen
he/she/it	had	stolen
we	had	stolen
you	had	stolen
they	had	stolen

Will-Future

I	will	steal
you	will	steal
he/she/it	will	steal
we	will	steal
you	will	steal
they	will	steal

Going to-Future

I	am	going to	steal
you	are	going to	steal
he/she/it	is	going to	steal
we	are	going to	steal
you	are	going to	steal
they	are	going to	steal

Future Perfect

I	will have	stolen
you	will have	stolen
he/she/it	will have	stolen
we	will have	stolen
you	will have	stolen
they	will have	stolen

Imperative

steal

Impersonal

ing-Form

stealing

Past Participle

stolen

Continuous tenses

Present

I	am	stealing
you	are	stealing
he/she/it	is	stealing
we	are	stealing
you	are	stealing
they	are	stealing

Past

I	was	stealing
you	were	stealing
he/she/it	was	stealing
we	were	stealing
you	were	stealing
they	were	stealing

Present Perfect

I	have been	stealing
you	have been	stealing
he/she/it	has been	stealing
we	have been	stealing
you	have been	stealing
they	have been	stealing

Past Perfect

I	had been	stealing
you	had been	stealing
he/she/it	had been	stealing
we	had been	stealing
you	had been	stealing
they	had been	stealing

Will-Future

I	will be	stealing
you	will be	stealing
he/she/it	will be	stealing
we	will be	stealing
you	will be	stealing
they	will be	stealing

Going to-Future

I	am	going to be	stealing
you	are	going to be	stealing
he/she/it	is	going to be	stealing
we	are	going to be	stealing
you	are	going to be	stealing
they	are	going to be	stealing

Future Perfect

I	will have been	stealing
you	will have been	stealing
he/she/it	will have been	stealing
we	will have been	stealing
you	will have been	stealing
they	will have been	stealing

Conditional

I	would	steal
you	would	steal
he/she/it	would	steal
we	would	steal
you	would	steal
they	would	steal

Conditional Past

I	would have	stolen
you	would have	stolen
he/she/it	would have	stolen
we	would have	stolen
you	would have	stolen
they	would have	stolen

steam

Regelmäßiges Verb

Simple tenses

Present

I	steam
you	steam
he/she/it	steams
we	steam
you	steam
they	steam

Past

I	steamed
you	steamed
he/she/it	steamed
we	steamed
you	steamed
they	steamed

Present Perfect

I	have	steamed
you	have	steamed
he/she/it	has	steamed
we	have	steamed
you	have	steamed
they	have	steamed

Past Perfect

I	had	steamed
you	had	steamed
he/she/it	had	steamed
we	had	steamed
you	had	steamed
they	had	steamed

Will-Future

I	will	steam
you	will	steam
he/she/it	will	steam
we	will	steam
you	will	steam
they	will	steam

Going to-Future

I	am	going to	steam
you	are	going to	steam
he/she/it	is	going to	steam
we	are	going to	steam
you	are	going to	steam
they	are	going to	steam

Future Perfect

I	will have	steamed
you	will have	steamed
he/she/it	will have	steamed
we	will have	steamed
you	will have	steamed
they	will have	steamed

Imperative

steam

Impersonal

ing-Form

steaming

Past Participle

steamed

Continuous tenses

Present

I	am	steaming
you	are	steaming
he/she/it	is	steaming
we	are	steaming
you	are	steaming
they	are	steaming

Past

I	was	steaming
you	were	steaming
he/she/it	was	steaming
we	were	steaming
you	were	steaming
they	were	steaming

Present Perfect

I	have been	steaming
you	have been	steaming
he/she/it	has been	steaming
we	have been	steaming
you	have been	steaming
they	have been	steaming

Past Perfect

I	had been	steaming
you	had been	steaming
he/she/it	had been	steaming
we	had been	steaming
you	had been	steaming
they	had been	steaming

Will-Future

I	will be	steaming
you	will be	steaming
he/she/it	will be	steaming
we	will be	steaming
you	will be	steaming
they	will be	steaming

Going to-Future

I	am	going to be	steaming
you	are	going to be	steaming
he/she/it	is	going to be	steaming
we	are	going to be	steaming
you	are	going to be	steaming
they	are	going to be	steaming

Future Perfect

I	will have been	steaming
you	will have been	steaming
he/she/it	will have been	steaming
we	will have been	steaming
you	will have been	steaming
they	will have been	steaming

Conditional

I	would	steam
you	would	steam
he/she/it	would	steam
we	would	steam
you	would	steam
they	would	steam

Conditional Past

I	would have	steamed
you	would have	steamed
he/she/it	would have	steamed
we	would have	steamed
you	would have	steamed
they	would have	steamed

step

treten

Konsonantenverdopplung
Regelmäßiges Verb

Simple tenses

Present

I	step
you	step
he/she/it	steps
we	step
you	step
they	step

Past

I	stepped
you	stepped
he/she/it	stepped
we	stepped
you	stepped
they	stepped

Present Perfect

I	have	stepped
you	have	stepped
he/she/it	has	stepped
we	have	stepped
you	have	stepped
they	have	stepped

Past Perfect

I	had	stepped
you	had	stepped
he/she/it	had	stepped
we	had	stepped
you	had	stepped
they	had	stepped

Will-Future

I	will	step
you	will	step
he/she/it	will	step
we	will	step
you	will	step
they	will	step

Going to-Future

I	am	going to	step
you	are	going to	step
he/she/it	is	going to	step
we	are	going to	step
you	are	going to	step
they	are	going to	step

Future Perfect

I	will have	stepped
you	will have	stepped
he/she/it	will have	stepped
we	will have	stepped
you	will have	stepped
they	will have	stepped

Imperative

step

Impersonal

ing-Form

stepping

Past Participle

stepped

Continuous tenses

Present

I	am	stepping
you	are	stepping
he/she/it	is	stepping
we	are	stepping
you	are	stepping
they	are	stepping

Past

I	was	stepping
you	were	stepping
he/she/it	was	stepping
we	were	stepping
you	were	stepping
they	were	stepping

Present Perfect

I	have	been	stepping
you	have	been	stepping
he/she/it	has	been	stepping
we	have	been	stepping
you	have	been	stepping
they	have	been	stepping

Past Perfect

I	had been	stepping
you	had been	stepping
he/she/it	had been	stepping
we	had been	stepping
you	had been	stepping
they	had been	stepping

Will-Future

I	will be	stepping
you	will be	stepping
he/she/it	will be	stepping
we	will be	stepping
you	will be	stepping
they	will be	stepping

Going to-Future

I	am	going to be	stepping
you	are	going to be	stepping
he/she/it	is	going to be	stepping
we	are	going to be	stepping
you	are	going to be	stepping
they	are	going to be	stepping

Future Perfect

I	will have been	stepping
you	will have been	stepping
he/she/it	will have been	stepping
we	will have been	stepping
you	will have been	stepping
they	will have been	stepping

Conditional

I	would	step
you	would	step
he/she/it	would	step
we	would	step
you	would	step
they	would	step

Conditional Past

I	would have	stepped
you	would have	stepped
he/she/it	would have	stepped
we	would have	stepped
you	would have	stepped
they	would have	stepped

kleben

stick
- stuck - stuck

Simple tenses

Present

I	stick
you	stick
he/she/it	sticks
we	stick
you	stick
they	stick

Past

I	stuck
you	stuck
he/she/it	stuck
we	stuck
you	stuck
they	stuck

Present Perfect

I	have	stuck
you	have	stuck
he/she/it	has	stuck
we	have	stuck
you	have	stuck
they	have	stuck

Past Perfect

I	had	stuck
you	had	stuck
he/she/it	had	stuck
we	had	stuck
you	had	stuck
they	had	stuck

Will-Future

I	will	stick
you	will	stick
he/she/it	will	stick
we	will	stick
you	will	stick
they	will	stick

Going to-Future

I	am	going to	stick
you	are	going to	stick
he/she/it	is	going to	stick
we	are	going to	stick
you	are	going to	stick
they	are	going to	stick

Future Perfect

I	will have	stuck
you	will have	stuck
he/she/it	will have	stuck
we	will have	stuck
you	will have	stuck
they	will have	stuck

Imperative

stick

Impersonal

ing-Form

sticking

Past Participle

stuck

Continuous tenses

Present

I	am	sticking
you	are	sticking
he/she/it	is	sticking
we	are	sticking
you	are	sticking
they	are	sticking

Past

I	was	sticking
you	were	sticking
he/she/it	was	sticking
we	were	sticking
you	were	sticking
they	were	sticking

Present Perfect

I	have	been	sticking
you	have	been	sticking
he/she/it	has	been	sticking
we	have	been	sticking
you	have	been	sticking
they	have	been	sticking

Past Perfect

I	had been	sticking
you	had been	sticking
he/she/it	had been	sticking
we	had been	sticking
you	had been	sticking
they	had been	sticking

Will-Future

I	will be	sticking
you	will be	sticking
he/she/it	will be	sticking
we	will be	sticking
you	will be	sticking
they	will be	sticking

Going to-Future

I	am	going to be	sticking
you	are	going to be	sticking
he/she/it	is	going to be	sticking
we	are	going to be	sticking
you	are	going to be	sticking
they	are	going to be	sticking

Future Perfect

I	will have been	sticking
you	will have been	sticking
he/she/it	will have been	sticking
we	will have been	sticking
you	will have been	sticking
they	will have been	sticking

Conditional

I	would	stick
you	would	stick
he/she/it	would	stick
we	would	stick
you	would	stick
they	would	stick

Conditional Past

I	would have	stuck
you	would have	stuck
he/she/it	would have	stuck
we	would have	stuck
you	would have	stuck
they	would have	stuck

sting

– stung – stung

stechen

Unregelmäßiges Verb

Simple tenses

Present

I	sting
you	sting
he/she/it	stings
we	sting
you	sting
they	sting

Past

I	stung
you	stung
he/she/it	stung
we	stung
you	stung
they	stung

Present Perfect

I	have	stung
you	have	stung
he/she/it	has	stung
we	have	stung
you	have	stung
they	have	stung

Past Perfect

I	had	stung
you	had	stung
he/she/it	had	stung
we	had	stung
you	had	stung
they	had	stung

Will-Future

I	will	sting
you	will	sting
he/she/it	will	sting
we	will	sting
you	will	sting
they	will	sting

Going to-Future

I	am	going to	sting
you	are	going to	sting
he/she/it	is	going to	sting
we	are	going to	sting
you	are	going to	sting
they	are	going to	sting

Future Perfect

I	will have	stung
you	will have	stung
he/she/it	will have	stung
we	will have	stung
you	will have	stung
they	will have	stung

Imperative

sting

Impersonal

ing-Form

stinging

Past Participle

stung

Continuous tenses

Present

I	am	stinging
you	are	stinging
he/she/it	is	stinging
we	are	stinging
you	are	stinging
they	are	stinging

Past

I	was	stinging
you	were	stinging
he/she/it	was	stinging
we	were	stinging
you	were	stinging
they	were	stinging

Present Perfect

I	have been	stinging
you	have been	stinging
he/she/it	has been	stinging
we	have been	stinging
you	have been	stinging
they	have been	stinging

Past Perfect

I	had been	stinging
you	had been	stinging
he/she/it	had been	stinging
we	had been	stinging
you	had been	stinging
they	had been	stinging

Will-Future

I	will be	stinging
you	will be	stinging
he/she/it	will be	stinging
we	will be	stinging
you	will be	stinging
they	will be	stinging

Going to-Future

I	am	going to be	stinging
you	are	going to be	stinging
he/she/it	is	going to be	stinging
we	are	going to be	stinging
you	are	going to be	stinging
they	are	going to be	stinging

Future Perfect

I	will have been	stinging
you	will have been	stinging
he/she/it	will have been	stinging
we	will have been	stinging
you	will have been	stinging
they	will have been	stinging

Conditional

I	would	sting
you	would	sting
he/she/it	would	sting
we	would	sting
you	would	sting
they	would	sting

Conditional Past

I	would have	stung
you	would have	stung
he/she/it	would have	stung
we	would have	stung
you	would have	stung
they	would have	stung

Simple tenses

Present

I	stink
you	stink
he/she/it	stinks
we	stink
you	stink
they	stink

Past

I	stank | stunk
you	stank | stunk
he/she/it	stank | stunk
we	stank | stunk
you	stank | stunk
they	stank | stunk

Present Perfect

I	have	stunk
you	have	stunk
he/she/it	has	stunk
we	have	stunk
you	have	stunk
they	have	stunk

Past Perfect

I	had	stunk
you	had	stunk
he/she/it	had	stunk
we	had	stunk
you	had	stunk
they	had	stunk

Will-Future

I	will	stink
you	will	stink
he/she/it	will	stink
we	will	stink
you	will	stink
they	will	stink

Going to-Future

I	am	going to	stink
you	are	going to	stink
he/she/it	is	going to	stink
we	are	going to	stink
you	are	going to	stink
they	are	going to	stink

Future Perfect

I	will have	stunk
you	will have	stunk
he/she/it	will have	stunk
we	will have	stunk
you	will have	stunk
they	will have	stunk

Imperative

stink

Impersonal

ing-Form

stinking

Past Participle

stunk

Continuous tenses

Present

I	am	stinking
you	are	stinking
he/she/it	is	stinking
we	are	stinking
you	are	stinking
they	are	stinking

Past

I	was	stinking
you	were	stinking
he/she/it	was	stinking
we	were	stinking
you	were	stinking
they	were	stinking

Present Perfect

I	have been	stinking
you	have been	stinking
he/she/it	has been	stinking
we	have been	stinking
you	have been	stinking
they	have been	stinking

Past Perfect

I	had been	stinking
you	had been	stinking
he/she/it	had been	stinking
we	had been	stinking
you	had been	stinking
they	had been	stinking

Will-Future

I	will be	stinking
you	will be	stinking
he/she/it	will be	stinking
we	will be	stinking
you	will be	stinking
they	will be	stinking

Going to-Future

I	am	going to be	stinking
you	are	going to be	stinking
he/she/it	is	going to be	stinking
we	are	going to be	stinking
you	are	going to be	stinking
they	are	going to be	stinking

Future Perfect

I	will have been	stinking
you	will have been	stinking
he/she/it	will have been	stinking
we	will have been	stinking
you	will have been	stinking
they	will have been	stinking

Conditional

I	would	stink
you	would	stink
he/she/it	would	stink
we	would	stink
you	would	stink
they	would	stink

Conditional Past

I	would have	stunk
you	would have	stunk
he/she/it	would have	stunk
we	would have	stunk
you	would have	stunk
they	would have	stunk

stir

rühren

Konsonantenverdopplung
Regelmäßiges Verb

Simple tenses

Present

I	stir
you	stir
he/she/it	stirs
we	stir
you	stir
they	stir

Past

I	stirred
you	stirred
he/she/it	stirred
we	stirred
you	stirred
they	stirred

Present Perfect

I	have	stirred
you	have	stirred
he/she/it	has	stirred
we	have	stirred
you	have	stirred
they	have	stirred

Past Perfect

I	had	stirred
you	had	stirred
he/she/it	had	stirred
we	had	stirred
you	had	stirred
they	had	stirred

Will-Future

I	will	stir
you	will	stir
he/she/it	will	stir
we	will	stir
you	will	stir
they	will	stir

Going to-Future

I	am	going to	stir
you	are	going to	stir
he/she/it	is	going to	stir
we	are	going to	stir
you	are	going to	stir
they	are	going to	stir

Future Perfect

I	will have	stirred
you	will have	stirred
he/she/it	will have	stirred
we	will have	stirred
you	will have	stirred
they	will have	stirred

Imperative

stir

Impersonal

ing-Form

stirring

Past Participle

stirred

Continuous tenses

Present

I	am	stirring
you	are	stirring
he/she/it	is	stirring
we	are	stirring
you	are	stirring
they	are	stirring

Past

I	was	stirring
you	were	stirring
he/she/it	was	stirring
we	were	stirring
you	were	stirring
they	were	stirring

Present Perfect

I	have been	stirring
you	have been	stirring
he/she/it	has been	stirring
we	have been	stirring
you	have been	stirring
they	have been	stirring

Past Perfect

I	had been	stirring
you	had been	stirring
he/she/it	had been	stirring
we	had been	stirring
you	had been	stirring
they	had been	stirring

Will-Future

I	will be	stirring
you	will be	stirring
he/she/it	will be	stirring
we	will be	stirring
you	will be	stirring
they	will be	stirring

Going to-Future

I	am	going to be	stirring
you	are	going to be	stirring
he/she/it	is	going to be	stirring
we	are	going to be	stirring
you	are	going to be	stirring
they	are	going to be	stirring

Future Perfect

I	will have been	stirring
you	will have been	stirring
he/she/it	will have been	stirring
we	will have been	stirring
you	will have been	stirring
they	will have been	stirring

Conditional

I	would	stir
you	would	stir
he/she/it	would	stir
we	would	stir
you	would	stir
they	would	stir

Conditional Past

I	would have	stirred
you	would have	stirred
he/she/it	would have	stirred
we	would have	stirred
you	would have	stirred
they	would have	stirred

Simple tenses

Present

I	stop
you	stop
he/she/it	stops
we	stop
you	stop
they	stop

Past

I	stopped
you	stopped
he/she/it	stopped
we	stopped
you	stopped
they	stopped

Present Perfect

I	have	stopped
you	have	stopped
he/she/it	has	stopped
we	have	stopped
you	have	stopped
they	have	stopped

Past Perfect

I	had	stopped
you	had	stopped
he/she/it	had	stopped
we	had	stopped
you	had	stopped
they	had	stopped

Will-Future

I	will	stop
you	will	stop
he/she/it	will	stop
we	will	stop
you	will	stop
they	will	stop

Going to-Future

I	am	going to	stop
you	are	going to	stop
he/she/it	is	going to	stop
we	are	going to	stop
you	are	going to	stop
they	are	going to	stop

Future Perfect

I	will have	stopped
you	will have	stopped
he/she/it	will have	stopped
we	will have	stopped
you	will have	stopped
they	will have	stopped

Imperative

stop

Impersonal

ing-Form

stopping

Past Participle

stopped

Continuous tenses

Present

I	am	stopping
you	are	stopping
he/she/it	is	stopping
we	are	stopping
you	are	stopping
they	are	stopping

Past

I	was	stopping
you	were	stopping
he/she/it	was	stopping
we	were	stopping
you	were	stopping
they	were	stopping

Present Perfect

I	have been	stopping
you	have been	stopping
he/she/it	has been	stopping
we	have been	stopping
you	have been	stopping
they	have been	stopping

Past Perfect

I	had been	stopping
you	had been	stopping
he/she/it	had been	stopping
we	had been	stopping
you	had been	stopping
they	had been	stopping

Will-Future

I	will be	stopping
you	will be	stopping
he/she/it	will be	stopping
we	will be	stopping
you	will be	stopping
they	will be	stopping

Going to-Future

I	am	going to be	stopping
you	are	going to be	stopping
he/she/it	is	going to be	stopping
we	are	going to be	stopping
you	are	going to be	stopping
they	are	going to be	stopping

Future Perfect

I	will have been	stopping
you	will have been	stopping
he/she/it	will have been	stopping
we	will have been	stopping
you	will have been	stopping
they	will have been	stopping

Conditional

I	would	stop
you	would	stop
he/she/it	would	stop
we	would	stop
you	would	stop
they	would	stop

Conditional Past

I	would have	stopped
you	would have	stopped
he/she/it	would have	stopped
we	would have	stopped
you	would have	stopped
they	would have	stopped

stream

strömen

Regelmäßiges Verb

Simple tenses

Present

I	stream
you	stream
he/she/it	streams
we	stream
you	stream
they	stream

Past

I	streamed
you	streamed
he/she/it	streamed
we	streamed
you	streamed
they	streamed

Present Perfect

I	have	streamed
you	have	streamed
he/she/it	has	streamed
we	have	streamed
you	have	streamed
they	have	streamed

Past Perfect

I	had	streamed
you	had	streamed
he/she/it	had	streamed
we	had	streamed
you	had	streamed
they	had	streamed

Will-Future

I	will	stream
you	will	stream
he/she/it	will	stream
we	will	stream
you	will	stream
they	will	stream

Going to-Future

I	am	going to	stream
you	are	going to	stream
he/she/it	is	going to	stream
we	are	going to	stream
you	are	going to	stream
they	are	going to	stream

Future Perfect

I	will have	streamed
you	will have	streamed
he/she/it	will have	streamed
we	will have	streamed
you	will have	streamed
they	will have	streamed

Imperative

stream

Impersonal

ing-Form

streaming

Past Participle

streamed

Continuous tenses

Present

I	am	streaming
you	are	streaming
he/she/it	is	streaming
we	are	streaming
you	are	streaming
they	are	streaming

Past

I	was	streaming
you	were	streaming
he/she/it	was	streaming
we	were	streaming
you	were	streaming
they	were	streaming

Present Perfect

I	have	been	streaming
you	have	been	streaming
he/she/it	has	been	streaming
we	have	been	streaming
you	have	been	streaming
they	have	been	streaming

Past Perfect

I	had been	streaming
you	had been	streaming
he/she/it	had been	streaming
we	had been	streaming
you	had been	streaming
they	had been	streaming

Will-Future

I	will be	streaming
you	will be	streaming
he/she/it	will be	streaming
we	will be	streaming
you	will be	streaming
they	will be	streaming

Going to-Future

I	am	going to be	streaming
you	are	going to be	streaming
he/she/it	is	going to be	streaming
we	are	going to be	streaming
you	are	going to be	streaming
they	are	going to be	streaming

Future Perfect

I	will have been	streaming
you	will have been	streaming
he/she/it	will have been	streaming
we	will have been	streaming
you	will have been	streaming
they	will have been	streaming

Conditional

I	would	stream
you	would	stream
he/she/it	would	stream
we	would	stream
you	would	stream
they	would	stream

Conditional Past

I	would have	streamed
you	would have	streamed
he/she/it	would have	streamed
we	would have	streamed
you	would have	streamed
they	would have	streamed

Simple tenses

Present

I	stress
you	stress
he/she/it	stresses
we	stress
you	stress
they	stress

Past

I	stressed
you	stressed
he/she/it	stressed
we	stressed
you	stressed
they	stressed

Present Perfect

I	have	stressed
you	have	stressed
he/she/it	has	stressed
we	have	stressed
you	have	stressed
they	have	stressed

Past Perfect

I	had	stressed
you	had	stressed
he/she/it	had	stressed
we	had	stressed
you	had	stressed
they	had	stressed

Will-Future

I	will	stress
you	will	stress
he/she/it	will	stress
we	will	stress
you	will	stress
they	will	stress

Going to-Future

I	am	going to	stress
you	are	going to	stress
he/she/it	is	going to	stress
we	are	going to	stress
you	are	going to	stress
they	are	going to	stress

Future Perfect

I	will have	stressed
you	will have	stressed
he/she/it	will have	stressed
we	will have	stressed
you	will have	stressed
they	will have	stressed

Imperative

stress

Impersonal

ing-Form

stressing

Past Participle

stressed

Continuous tenses

Present

I	am	stressing
you	are	stressing
he/she/it	is	stressing
we	are	stressing
you	are	stressing
they	are	stressing

Past

I	was	stressing
you	were	stressing
he/she/it	was	stressing
we	were	stressing
you	were	stressing
they	were	stressing

Present Perfect

I	have been	stressing
you	have been	stressing
he/she/it	has been	stressing
we	have been	stressing
you	have been	stressing
they	have been	stressing

Past Perfect

I	had been	stressing
you	had been	stressing
he/she/it	had been	stressing
we	had been	stressing
you	had been	stressing
they	had been	stressing

Will-Future

I	will be	stressing
you	will be	stressing
he/she/it	will be	stressing
we	will be	stressing
you	will be	stressing
they	will be	stressing

Going to-Future

I	am	going to be	stressing
you	are	going to be	stressing
he/she/it	is	going to be	stressing
we	are	going to be	stressing
you	are	going to be	stressing
they	are	going to be	stressing

Future Perfect

I	will have been	stressing
you	will have been	stressing
he/she/it	will have been	stressing
we	will have been	stressing
you	will have been	stressing
they	will have been	stressing

Conditional

I	would	stress
you	would	stress
he/she/it	would	stress
we	would	stress
you	would	stress
they	would	stress

Conditional Past

I	would have	stressed
you	would have	stressed
he/she/it	would have	stressed
we	would have	stressed
you	would have	stressed
they	would have	stressed

stretch

dehnen

\+ **-es** in 3. Person Singular
Regelmäßiges Verb

Simple tenses

Present

I	stretch
you	stretch
he/she/it	stretches
we	stretch
you	stretch
they	stretch

Past

I	stretched
you	stretched
he/she/it	stretched
we	stretched
you	stretched
they	stretched

Present Perfect

I	have	stretched
you	have	stretched
he/she/it	has	stretched
we	have	stretched
you	have	stretched
they	have	stretched

Past Perfect

I	had	stretched
you	had	stretched
he/she/it	had	stretched
we	had	stretched
you	had	stretched
they	had	stretched

Will-Future

I	will	stretch
you	will	stretch
he/she/it	will	stretch
we	will	stretch
you	will	stretch
they	will	stretch

Going to-Future

I	am	going to	stretch
you	are	going to	stretch
he/she/it	is	going to	stretch
we	are	going to	stretch
you	are	going to	stretch
they	are	going to	stretch

Future Perfect

I	will have	stretched
you	will have	stretched
he/she/it	will have	stretched
we	will have	stretched
you	will have	stretched
they	will have	stretched

Imperative

stretch

Impersonal

ing-Form

stretching

Past Participle

stretched

Continuous tenses

Present

I	am	stretching
you	are	stretching
he/she/it	is	stretching
we	are	stretching
you	are	stretching
they	are	stretching

Past

I	was	stretching
you	were	stretching
he/she/it	was	stretching
we	were	stretching
you	were	stretching
they	were	stretching

Present Perfect

I	have been	stretching
you	have been	stretching
he/she/it	has been	stretching
we	have been	stretching
you	have been	stretching
they	have been	stretching

Past Perfect

I	had been	stretching
you	had been	stretching
he/she/it	had been	stretching
we	had been	stretching
you	had been	stretching
they	had been	stretching

Will-Future

I	will be	stretching
you	will be	stretching
he/she/it	will be	stretching
we	will be	stretching
you	will be	stretching
they	will be	stretching

Going to-Future

I	am	going to be	stretching
you	are	going to be	stretching
he/she/it	is	going to be	stretching
we	are	going to be	stretching
you	are	going to be	stretching
they	are	going to be	stretching

Future Perfect

I	will have been	stretching
you	will have been	stretching
he/she/it	will have been	stretching
we	will have been	stretching
you	will have been	stretching
they	will have been	stretching

Conditional

I	would	stretch
you	would	stretch
he/she/it	would	stretch
we	would	stretch
you	would	stretch
they	would	stretch

Conditional Past

I	would have	stretched
you	would have	stretched
he/she/it	would have	stretched
we	would have	stretched
you	would have	stretched
they	would have	stretched

schreiten

stride

– strode – stridden

Simple tenses

Present

I	stride
you	stride
he/she/it	strides
we	stride
you	stride
they	stride

Past

I	strode
you	strode
he/she/it	strode
we	strode
you	strode
they	strode

Present Perfect

I	have	stridden
you	have	stridden
he/she/it	has	stridden
we	have	stridden
you	have	stridden
they	have	stridden

Past Perfect

I	had	stridden
you	had	stridden
he/she/it	had	stridden
we	had	stridden
you	had	stridden
they	had	stridden

Will-Future

I	will	stride
you	will	stride
he/she/it	will	stride
we	will	stride
you	will	stride
they	will	stride

Going to-Future

I	am	going to	stride
you	are	going to	stride
he/she/it	is	going to	stride
we	are	going to	stride
you	are	going to	stride
they	are	going to	stride

Future Perfect

I	will have	stridden
you	will have	stridden
he/she/it	will have	stridden
we	will have	stridden
you	will have	stridden
they	will have	stridden

Imperative

stride

Impersonal

ing-Form

striding

Past Participle

stridden

Continuous tenses

Present

I	am	striding
you	are	striding
he/she/it	is	striding
we	are	striding
you	are	striding
they	are	striding

Past

I	was	striding
you	were	striding
he/she/it	was	striding
we	were	striding
you	were	striding
they	were	striding

Present Perfect

I	have	been	striding
you	have	been	striding
he/she/it	has	been	striding
we	have	been	striding
you	have	been	striding
they	have	been	striding

Past Perfect

I	had been	striding
you	had been	striding
he/she/it	had been	striding
we	had been	striding
you	had been	striding
they	had been	striding

Will-Future

I	will be	striding
you	will be	striding
he/she/it	will be	striding
we	will be	striding
you	will be	striding
they	will be	striding

Going to-Future

I	am	going to be	striding
you	are	going to be	striding
he/she/it	is	going to be	striding
we	are	going to be	striding
you	are	going to be	striding
they	are	going to be	striding

Future Perfect

I	will have been	striding
you	will have been	striding
he/she/it	will have been	striding
we	will have been	striding
you	will have been	striding
they	will have been	striding

Conditional

I	would	stride
you	would	stride
he/she/it	would	stride
we	would	stride
you	would	stride
they	would	stride

Conditional Past

I	would have	stridden
you	would have	stridden
he/she/it	would have	stridden
we	would have	stridden
you	would have	stridden
they	would have	stridden

strive

- strove/strived - stiven/strived

sich bemühen

Unregelmäßiges Verb

Simple tenses

Present

I	strive
you	strive
he/she/it	strives
we	strive
you	strive
they	strive

Past

I	strove | strived
you	strove | strived
he/she/it	strove | strived
we	strove | strived
you	strove | strived
they	strove | strived

Present Perfect

I	have	striven | strived
you	have	striven | strived
he/she/it	has	striven | strived
we	have	striven | strived
you	have	striven | strived
they	have	striven | strived

Past Perfect

I	had	striven | strived
you	had	striven | strived
he/she/it	had	striven | strived
we	had	striven | strived
you	had	striven | strived
they	had	striven | strived

Will-Future

I	will	strive
you	will	strive
he/she/it	will	strive
we	will	strive
you	will	strive
they	will	strive

Going to-Future

I	am	going to	strive
you	are	going to	strive
he/she/it	is	going to	strive
we	are	going to	strive
you	are	going to	strive
they	are	going to	strive

Future Perfect

I	will have	striven | strived
you	will have	striven | strived
he/she/it	will have	striven | strived
we	will have	striven | strived
you	will have	striven | strived
they	will have	striven | strived

Imperative

strive

Impersonal

ing-Form

striving

Past Participle

striven | strived

Continuous tenses

Present

I	am	striving
you	are	striving
he/she/it	is	striving
we	are	striving
you	are	striving
they	are	striving

Past

I	was	striving
you	were	striving
he/she/it	was	striving
we	were	striving
you	were	striving
they	were	striving

Present Perfect

I	have	been	striving
you	have	been	striving
he/she/it	has	been	striving
we	have	been	striving
you	have	been	striving
they	have	been	striving

Past Perfect

I	had been	striving
you	had been	striving
he/she/it	had been	striving
we	had been	striving
you	had been	striving
they	had been	striving

Will-Future

I	will be	striving
you	will be	striving
he/she/it	will be	striving
we	will be	striving
you	will be	striving
they	will be	striving

Going to-Future

I	am	going to be	striving
you	are	going to be	striving
he/she/it	is	going to be	striving
we	are	going to be	striving
you	are	going to be	striving
they	are	going to be	striving

Future Perfect

I	will have been	striving
you	will have been	striving
he/she/it	will have been	striving
we	will have been	striving
you	will have been	striving
they	will have been	striving

Conditional

I	would	strive
you	would	strive
he/she/it	would	strive
we	would	strive
you	would	strive
they	would	strive

Conditional Past

I	would have	striven | strived
you	would have	striven | strived
he/she/it	would have	striven | strived
we	would have	striven | strived
you	would have	striven | strived
they	would have	striven | strived

struggle

sich abmühen

+ **-ing** → ~~e~~ / + **-d** nicht **-ed**
Regelmäßiges Verb

Simple tenses

Present

I	struggle
you	struggle
he/she/it	struggles
we	struggle
you	struggle
they	struggle

Past

I	struggled
you	struggled
he/she/it	struggled
we	struggled
you	struggled
they	struggled

Present Perfect

I	have	struggled
you	have	struggled
he/she/it	has	struggled
we	have	struggled
you	have	struggled
they	have	struggled

Past Perfect

I	had	struggled
you	had	struggled
he/she/it	had	struggled
we	had	struggled
you	had	struggled
they	had	struggled

Will-Future

I	will	struggle
you	will	struggle
he/she/it	will	struggle
we	will	struggle
you	will	struggle
they	will	struggle

Going to-Future

I	am	going to	struggle
you	are	going to	struggle
he/she/it	is	going to	struggle
we	are	going to	struggle
you	are	going to	struggle
they	are	going to	struggle

Future Perfect

I	will have	struggled
you	will have	struggled
he/she/it	will have	struggled
we	will have	struggled
you	will have	struggled
they	will have	struggled

Imperative

struggle

Impersonal

ing-Form

struggling

Past Participle

struggled

Continuous tenses

Present

I	am	struggling
you	are	struggling
he/she/it	is	struggling
we	are	struggling
you	are	struggling
they	are	struggling

Past

I	was	struggling
you	were	struggling
he/she/it	was	struggling
we	were	struggling
you	were	struggling
they	were	struggling

Present Perfect

I	have been	struggling
you	have been	struggling
he/she/it	has been	struggling
we	have been	struggling
you	have been	struggling
they	have been	struggling

Past Perfect

I	had been	struggling
you	had been	struggling
he/she/it	had been	struggling
we	had been	struggling
you	had been	struggling
they	had been	struggling

Will-Future

I	will be	struggling
you	will be	struggling
he/she/it	will be	struggling
we	will be	struggling
you	will be	struggling
they	will be	struggling

Going to-Future

I	am	going to be	struggling
you	are	going to be	struggling
he/she/it	is	going to be	struggling
we	are	going to be	struggling
you	are	going to be	struggling
they	are	going to be	struggling

Future Perfect

I	will have been	struggling
you	will have been	struggling
he/she/it	will have been	struggling
we	will have been	struggling
you	will have been	struggling
they	will have been	struggling

Conditional

I	would	struggle
you	would	struggle
he/she/it	would	struggle
we	would	struggle
you	would	struggle
they	would	struggle

Conditional Past

I	would have	struggled
you	would have	struggled
he/she/it	would have	struggled
we	would have	struggled
you	would have	struggled
they	would have	struggled

study

studieren

-y → -ie vor **-s** / **-y → -i** vor **-ed**
Regelmäßiges Verb

Simple tenses

Present

I	study
you	study
he/she/it	studies
we	study
you	study
they	study

Past

I	studied
you	studied
he/she/it	studied
we	studied
you	studied
they	studied

Present Perfect

I	have	studied
you	have	studied
he/she/it	has	studied
we	have	studied
you	have	studied
they	have	studied

Past Perfect

I	had	studied
you	had	studied
he/she/it	had	studied
we	had	studied
you	had	studied
they	had	studied

Will-Future

I	will	study
you	will	study
he/she/it	will	study
we	will	study
you	will	study
they	will	study

Going to-Future

I	am	going to	study
you	are	going to	study
he/she/it	is	going to	study
we	are	going to	study
you	are	going to	study
they	are	going to	study

Future Perfect

I	will have	studied
you	will have	studied
he/she/it	will have	studied
we	will have	studied
you	will have	studied
they	will have	studied

Imperative

study

Impersonal

ing-Form

studying

Past Participle

studied

Continuous tenses

Present

I	am	studying
you	are	studying
he/she/it	is	studying
we	are	studying
you	are	studying
they	are	studying

Past

I	was	studying
you	were	studying
he/she/it	was	studying
we	were	studying
you	were	studying
they	were	studying

Present Perfect

I	have been	studying
you	have been	studying
he/she/it	has been	studying
we	have been	studying
you	have been	studying
they	have been	studying

Past Perfect

I	had been	studying
you	had been	studying
he/she/it	had been	studying
we	had been	studying
you	had been	studying
they	had been	studying

Will-Future

I	will be	studying
you	will be	studying
he/she/it	will be	studying
we	will be	studying
you	will be	studying
they	will be	studying

Going to-Future

I	am	going to be	studying
you	are	going to be	studying
he/she/it	is	going to be	studying
we	are	going to be	studying
you	are	going to be	studying
they	are	going to be	studying

Future Perfect

I	will have been	studying
you	will have been	studying
he/she/it	will have been	studying
we	will have been	studying
you	will have been	studying
they	will have been	studying

Conditional

I	would	study
you	would	study
he/she/it	would	study
we	would	study
you	would	study
they	would	study

Conditional Past

I	would have	studied
you	would have	studied
he/she/it	would have	studied
we	would have	studied
you	would have	studied
they	would have	studied

stolpern

stumble

Simple tenses

Present

I	stumble
you	stumble
he/she/it	stumbles
we	stumble
you	stumble
they	stumble

Past

I	stumbled
you	stumbled
he/she/it	stumbled
we	stumbled
you	stumbled
they	stumbled

Present Perfect

I	have	stumbled
you	have	stumbled
he/she/it	has	stumbled
we	have	stumbled
you	have	stumbled
they	have	stumbled

Past Perfect

I	had	stumbled
you	had	stumbled
he/she/it	had	stumbled
we	had	stumbled
you	had	stumbled
they	had	stumbled

Will-Future

I	will	stumble
you	will	stumble
he/she/it	will	stumble
we	will	stumble
you	will	stumble
they	will	stumble

Going to-Future

I	am	going to	stumble
you	are	going to	stumble
he/she/it	is	going to	stumble
we	are	going to	stumble
you	are	going to	stumble
they	are	going to	stumble

Future Perfect

I	will have	stumbled
you	will have	stumbled
he/she/it	will have	stumbled
we	will have	stumbled
you	will have	stumbled
they	will have	stumbled

Imperative

stumble

Impersonal

ing-Form

stumbling

Past Participle

stumbled

Continuous tenses

Present

I	am	stumbling
you	are	stumbling
he/she/it	is	stumbling
we	are	stumbling
you	are	stumbling
they	are	stumbling

Past

I	was	stumbling
you	were	stumbling
he/she/it	was	stumbling
we	were	stumbling
you	were	stumbling
they	were	stumbling

Present Perfect

I	have	been	stumbling
you	have	been	stumbling
he/she/it	has	been	stumbling
we	have	been	stumbling
you	have	been	stumbling
they	have	been	stumbling

Past Perfect

I	had been	stumbling
you	had been	stumbling
he/she/it	had been	stumbling
we	had been	stumbling
you	had been	stumbling
they	had been	stumbling

Will-Future

I	will be	stumbling
you	will be	stumbling
he/she/it	will be	stumbling
we	will be	stumbling
you	will be	stumbling
they	will be	stumbling

Going to-Future

I	am	going to be	stumbling
you	are	going to be	stumbling
he/she/it	is	going to be	stumbling
we	are	going to be	stumbling
you	are	going to be	stumbling
they	are	going to be	stumbling

Future Perfect

I	will have been	stumbling
you	will have been	stumbling
he/she/it	will have been	stumbling
we	will have been	stumbling
you	will have been	stumbling
they	will have been	stumbling

Conditional

I	would	stumble
you	would	stumble
he/she/it	would	stumble
we	would	stumble
you	would	stumble
they	would	stumble

Conditional Past

I	would have	stumbled
you	would have	stumbled
he/she/it	would have	stumbled
we	would have	stumbled
you	would have	stumbled
they	would have	stumbled

succeed

Erfolg haben

Regelmäßiges Verb

Simple tenses

Present

I	succeed
you	succeed
he/she/it	succeeds
we	succeed
you	succeed
they	succeed

Past

I	succeeded
you	succeeded
he/she/it	succeeded
we	succeeded
you	succeeded
they	succeeded

Present Perfect

I	have	succeeded
you	have	succeeded
he/she/it	has	succeeded
we	have	succeeded
you	have	succeeded
they	have	succeeded

Past Perfect

I	had	succeeded
you	had	succeeded
he/she/it	had	succeeded
we	had	succeeded
you	had	succeeded
they	had	succeeded

Will-Future

I	will	succeed
you	will	succeed
he/she/it	will	succeed
we	will	succeed
you	will	succeed
they	will	succeed

Going to-Future

I	am	going to	succeed
you	are	going to	succeed
he/she/it	is	going to	succeed
we	are	going to	succeed
you	are	going to	succeed
they	are	going to	succeed

Future Perfect

I	will have	succeeded
you	will have	succeeded
he/she/it	will have	succeeded
we	will have	succeeded
you	will have	succeeded
they	will have	succeeded

Imperative

succeed

Impersonal

ing-Form

succeeding

Past Participle

succeeded

Continuous tenses

Present

I	am	succeeding
you	are	succeeding
he/she/it	is	succeeding
we	are	succeeding
you	are	succeeding
they	are	succeeding

Past

I	was	succeeding
you	were	succeeding
he/she/it	was	succeeding
we	were	succeeding
you	were	succeeding
they	were	succeeding

Present Perfect

I	have been	succeeding
you	have been	succeeding
he/she/it	has been	succeeding
we	have been	succeeding
you	have been	succeeding
they	have been	succeeding

Past Perfect

I	had been	succeeding
you	had been	succeeding
he/she/it	had been	succeeding
we	had been	succeeding
you	had been	succeeding
they	had been	succeeding

Will-Future

I	will be	succeeding
you	will be	succeeding
he/she/it	will be	succeeding
we	will be	succeeding
you	will be	succeeding
they	will be	succeeding

Going to-Future

I	am	going to be	succeeding
you	are	going to be	succeeding
he/she/it	is	going to be	succeeding
we	are	going to be	succeeding
you	are	going to be	succeeding
they	are	going to be	succeeding

Future Perfect

I	will have been	succeeding
you	will have been	succeeding
he/she/it	will have been	succeeding
we	will have been	succeeding
you	will have been	succeeding
they	will have been	succeeding

Conditional

I	would	succeed
you	would	succeed
he/she/it	would	succeed
we	would	succeed
you	would	succeed
they	would	succeed

Conditional Past

I	would have	succeeded
you	would have	succeeded
he/she/it	would have	succeeded
we	would have	succeeded
you	would have	succeeded
they	would have	succeeded

Simple tenses

Present

I	suffer
you	suffer
he/she/it	suffers
we	suffer
you	suffer
they	suffer

Past

I	suffered
you	suffered
he/she/it	suffered
we	suffered
you	suffered
they	suffered

Present Perfect

I	have	suffered
you	have	suffered
he/she/it	has	suffered
we	have	suffered
you	have	suffered
they	have	suffered

Past Perfect

I	had	suffered
you	had	suffered
he/she/it	had	suffered
we	had	suffered
you	had	suffered
they	had	suffered

Will-Future

I	will	suffer
you	will	suffer
he/she/it	will	suffer
we	will	suffer
you	will	suffer
they	will	suffer

Going to-Future

I	am	going to	suffer
you	are	going to	suffer
he/she/it	is	going to	suffer
we	are	going to	suffer
you	are	going to	suffer
they	are	going to	suffer

Future Perfect

I	will have	suffered
you	will have	suffered
he/she/it	will have	suffered
we	will have	suffered
you	will have	suffered
they	will have	suffered

Imperative

suffer

Impersonal

ing-Form

suffering

Past Participle

suffered

Continuous tenses

Present

I	am	suffering
you	are	suffering
he/she/it	is	suffering
we	are	suffering
you	are	suffering
they	are	suffering

Past

I	was	suffering
you	were	suffering
he/she/it	was	suffering
we	were	suffering
you	were	suffering
they	were	suffering

Present Perfect

I	have been	suffering
you	have been	suffering
he/she/it	has been	suffering
we	have been	suffering
you	have been	suffering
they	have been	suffering

Past Perfect

I	had been	suffering
you	had been	suffering
he/she/it	had been	suffering
we	had been	suffering
you	had been	suffering
they	had been	suffering

Will-Future

I	will be	suffering
you	will be	suffering
he/she/it	will be	suffering
we	will be	suffering
you	will be	suffering
they	will be	suffering

Going to-Future

I	am	going to be	suffering
you	are	going to be	suffering
he/she/it	is	going to be	suffering
we	are	going to be	suffering
you	are	going to be	suffering
they	are	going to be	suffering

Future Perfect

I	will have been	suffering
you	will have been	suffering
he/she/it	will have been	suffering
we	will have been	suffering
you	will have been	suffering
they	will have been	suffering

Conditional

I	would	suffer
you	would	suffer
he/she/it	would	suffer
we	would	suffer
you	would	suffer
they	would	suffer

Conditional Past

I	would have	suffered
you	would have	suffered
he/she/it	would have	suffered
we	would have	suffered
you	would have	suffered
they	would have	suffered

suggest

vorschlagen

Regelmäßiges Verb

Simple tenses

Present

I	suggest
you	suggest
he/she/it	suggests
we	suggest
you	suggest
they	suggest

Past

I	suggested
you	suggested
he/she/it	suggested
we	suggested
you	suggested
they	suggested

Present Perfect

I	have	suggested
you	have	suggested
he/she/it	has	suggested
we	have	suggested
you	have	suggested
they	have	suggested

Past Perfect

I	had	suggested
you	had	suggested
he/she/it	had	suggested
we	had	suggested
you	had	suggested
they	had	suggested

Will-Future

I	will	suggest
you	will	suggest
he/she/it	will	suggest
we	will	suggest
you	will	suggest
they	will	suggest

Going to-Future

I	am	going to	suggest
you	are	going to	suggest
he/she/it	is	going to	suggest
we	are	going to	suggest
you	are	going to	suggest
they	are	going to	suggest

Future Perfect

I	will have	suggested
you	will have	suggested
he/she/it	will have	suggested
we	will have	suggested
you	will have	suggested
they	will have	suggested

Imperative

suggest

Impersonal

ing-Form

suggesting

Past Participle

suggested

Continuous tenses

Present

I	am	suggesting
you	are	suggesting
he/she/it	is	suggesting
we	are	suggesting
you	are	suggesting
they	are	suggesting

Past

I	was	suggesting
you	were	suggesting
he/she/it	was	suggesting
we	were	suggesting
you	were	suggesting
they	were	suggesting

Present Perfect

I	have been	suggesting
you	have been	suggesting
he/she/it	has been	suggesting
we	have been	suggesting
you	have been	suggesting
they	have been	suggesting

Past Perfect

I	had been	suggesting
you	had been	suggesting
he/she/it	had been	suggesting
we	had been	suggesting
you	had been	suggesting
they	had been	suggesting

Will-Future

I	will be	suggesting
you	will be	suggesting
he/she/it	will be	suggesting
we	will be	suggesting
you	will be	suggesting
they	will be	suggesting

Going to-Future

I	am	going to be	suggesting
you	are	going to be	suggesting
he/she/it	is	going to be	suggesting
we	are	going to be	suggesting
you	are	going to be	suggesting
they	are	going to be	suggesting

Future Perfect

I	will have been suggesting
you	will have been suggesting
he/she/it	will have been suggesting
we	will have been suggesting
you	will have been suggesting
they	will have been suggesting

Conditional

I	would	suggest
you	would	suggest
he/she/it	would	suggest
we	would	suggest
you	would	suggest
they	would	suggest

Conditional Past

I	would have	suggested
you	would have	suggested
he/she/it	would have	suggested
we	would have	suggested
you	would have	suggested
they	would have	suggested

Simple tenses

Present

I	suit
you	suit
he/she/it	suits
we	suit
you	suit
they	suit

Past

I	suited
you	suited
he/she/it	suited
we	suited
you	suited
they	suited

Present Perfect

I	have	suited
you	have	suited
he/she/it	has	suited
we	have	suited
you	have	suited
they	have	suited

Past Perfect

I	had	suited
you	had	suited
he/she/it	had	suited
we	had	suited
you	had	suited
they	had	suited

Will-Future

I	will	suit
you	will	suit
he/she/it	will	suit
we	will	suit
you	will	suit
they	will	suit

Going to-Future

I	am	going to	suit
you	are	going to	suit
he/she/it	is	going to	suit
we	are	going to	suit
you	are	going to	suit
they	are	going to	suit

Future Perfect

I	will have	suited
you	will have	suited
he/she/it	will have	suited
we	will have	suited
you	will have	suited
they	will have	suited

Imperative

suit

Impersonal

ing-Form

suiting

Past Participle

suited

Continuous tenses

Present

I	am	suiting
you	are	suiting
he/she/it	is	suiting
we	are	suiting
you	are	suiting
they	are	suiting

Past

I	was	suiting
you	were	suiting
he/she/it	was	suiting
we	were	suiting
you	were	suiting
they	were	suiting

Present Perfect

I	have been	suiting
you	have been	suiting
he/she/it	has been	suiting
we	have been	suiting
you	have been	suiting
they	have been	suiting

Past Perfect

I	had been	suiting
you	had been	suiting
he/she/it	had been	suiting
we	had been	suiting
you	had been	suiting
they	had been	suiting

Will-Future

I	will be	suiting
you	will be	suiting
he/she/it	will be	suiting
we	will be	suiting
you	will be	suiting
they	will be	suiting

Going to-Future

I	am	going to be	suiting
you	are	going to be	suiting
he/she/it	is	going to be	suiting
we	are	going to be	suiting
you	are	going to be	suiting
they	are	going to be	suiting

Future Perfect

I	will have been	suiting
you	will have been	suiting
he/she/it	will have been	suiting
we	will have been	suiting
you	will have been	suiting
they	will have been	suiting

Conditional

I	would	suit
you	would	suit
he/she/it	would	suit
we	would	suit
you	would	suit
they	would	suit

Conditional Past

I	would have	suited
you	would have	suited
he/she/it	would have	suited
we	would have	suited
you	would have	suited
they	would have	suited

supply

bereitstellen

-y → **-ie** vor **-s** / **-y** → **-i** vor **-ed**
Regelmäßiges Verb

Simple tenses

Present

I	supply
you	supply
he/she/it	supplies
we	supply
you	supply
they	supply

Past

I	supplied
you	supplied
he/she/it	supplied
we	supplied
you	supplied
they	supplied

Present Perfect

I	have	supplied
you	have	supplied
he/she/it	has	supplied
we	have	supplied
you	have	supplied
they	have	supplied

Past Perfect

I	had	supplied
you	had	supplied
he/she/it	had	supplied
we	had	supplied
you	had	supplied
they	had	supplied

Will-Future

I	will	supply
you	will	supply
he/she/it	will	supply
we	will	supply
you	will	supply
they	will	supply

Going to-Future

I	am	going to	supply
you	are	going to	supply
he/she/it	is	going to	supply
we	are	going to	supply
you	are	going to	supply
they	are	going to	supply

Future Perfect

I	will have	supplied
you	will have	supplied
he/she/it	will have	supplied
we	will have	supplied
you	will have	supplied
they	will have	supplied

Imperative

supply

Impersonal

ing-Form

supplying

Past Participle

supplied

Continuous tenses

Present

I	am	supplying
you	are	supplying
he/she/it	is	supplying
we	are	supplying
you	are	supplying
they	are	supplying

Past

I	was	supplying
you	were	supplying
he/she/it	was	supplying
we	were	supplying
you	were	supplying
they	were	supplying

Present Perfect

I	have been	supplying
you	have been	supplying
he/she/it	has been	supplying
we	have been	supplying
you	have been	supplying
they	have been	supplying

Past Perfect

I	had been	supplying
you	had been	supplying
he/she/it	had been	supplying
we	had been	supplying
you	had been	supplying
they	had been	supplying

Will-Future

I	will be	supplying
you	will be	supplying
he/she/it	will be	supplying
we	will be	supplying
you	will be	supplying
they	will be	supplying

Going to-Future

I	am	going to be	supplying
you	are	going to be	supplying
he/she/it	is	going to be	supplying
we	are	going to be	supplying
you	are	going to be	supplying
they	are	going to be	supplying

Future Perfect

I	will have been	supplying
you	will have been	supplying
he/she/it	will have been	supplying
we	will have been	supplying
you	will have been	supplying
they	will have been	supplying

Conditional

I	would	supply
you	would	supply
he/she/it	would	supply
we	would	supply
you	would	supply
they	would	supply

Conditional Past

I	would have	supplied
you	would have	supplied
he/she/it	would have	supplied
we	would have	supplied
you	would have	supplied
they	would have	supplied

Simple tenses

Present

I	support
you	support
he/she/it	supports
we	support
you	support
they	support

Past

I	supported
you	supported
he/she/it	supported
we	supported
you	supported
they	supported

Present Perfect

I	have	supported
you	have	supported
he/she/it	has	supported
we	have	supported
you	have	supported
they	have	supported

Past Perfect

I	had	supported
you	had	supported
he/she/it	had	supported
we	had	supported
you	had	supported
they	had	supported

Will-Future

I	will	support
you	will	support
he/she/it	will	support
we	will	support
you	will	support
they	will	support

Going to-Future

I	am	going to	support
you	are	going to	support
he/she/it	is	going to	support
we	are	going to	support
you	are	going to	support
they	are	going to	support

Future Perfect

I	will have	supported
you	will have	supported
he/she/it	will have	supported
we	will have	supported
you	will have	supported
they	will have	supported

Imperative

support

Impersonal

ing-Form

supporting

Past Participle

supported

Continuous tenses

Present

I	am	supporting
you	are	supporting
he/she/it	is	supporting
we	are	supporting
you	are	supporting
they	are	supporting

Past

I	was	supporting
you	were	supporting
he/she/it	was	supporting
we	were	supporting
you	were	supporting
they	were	supporting

Present Perfect

I	have	been	supporting
you	have	been	supporting
he/she/it	has	been	supporting
we	have	been	supporting
you	have	been	supporting
they	have	been	supporting

Past Perfect

I	had been	supporting
you	had been	supporting
he/she/it	had been	supporting
we	had been	supporting
you	had been	supporting
they	had been	supporting

Will-Future

I	will be	supporting
you	will be	supporting
he/she/it	will be	supporting
we	will be	supporting
you	will be	supporting
they	will be	supporting

Going to-Future

I	am	going to be	supporting
you	are	going to be	supporting
he/she/it	is	going to be	supporting
we	are	going to be	supporting
you	are	going to be	supporting
they	are	going to be	supporting

Future Perfect

I	will have been	supporting
you	will have been	supporting
he/she/it	will have been	supporting
we	will have been	supporting
you	will have been	supporting
they	will have been	supporting

Conditional

I	would	support
you	would	support
he/she/it	would	support
we	would	support
you	would	support
they	would	support

Conditional Past

I	would have	supported
you	would have	supported
he/she/it	would have	supported
we	would have	supported
you	would have	supported
they	would have	supported

suppose

vermuten

+ **-ing** → ~~e~~ / + **-d** nicht **-ed**
Regelmäßiges Verb

Simple tenses

Present

I	suppose
you	suppose
he/she/it	supposes
we	suppose
you	suppose
they	suppose

Past

I	supposed
you	supposed
he/she/it	supposed
we	supposed
you	supposed
they	supposed

Present Perfect

I	have	supposed
you	have	supposed
he/she/it	has	supposed
we	have	supposed
you	have	supposed
they	have	supposed

Past Perfect

I	had	supposed
you	had	supposed
he/she/it	had	supposed
we	had	supposed
you	had	supposed
they	had	supposed

Will-Future

I	will	suppose
you	will	suppose
he/she/it	will	suppose
we	will	suppose
you	will	suppose
they	will	suppose

Going to-Future

I	am	going to	suppose
you	are	going to	suppose
he/she/it	is	going to	suppose
we	are	going to	suppose
you	are	going to	suppose
they	are	going to	suppose

Future Perfect

I	will have	supposed
you	will have	supposed
he/she/it	will have	supposed
we	will have	supposed
you	will have	supposed
they	will have	supposed

Imperative

suppose

Impersonal

ing-Form

supposing

Past Participle

supposed

Continuous tenses

Present

I	am	supposing
you	are	supposing
he/she/it	is	supposing
we	are	supposing
you	are	supposing
they	are	supposing

Past

I	was	supposing
you	were	supposing
he/she/it	was	supposing
we	were	supposing
you	were	supposing
they	were	supposing

Present Perfect

I	have been	supposing
you	have been	supposing
he/she/it	has been	supposing
we	have been	supposing
you	have been	supposing
they	have been	supposing

Past Perfect

I	had been	supposing
you	had been	supposing
he/she/it	had been	supposing
we	had been	supposing
you	had been	supposing
they	had been	supposing

Will-Future

I	will be	supposing
you	will be	supposing
he/she/it	will be	supposing
we	will be	supposing
you	will be	supposing
they	will be	supposing

Going to-Future

I	am	going to be	supposing
you	are	going to be	supposing
he/she/it	is	going to be	supposing
we	are	going to be	supposing
you	are	going to be	supposing
they	are	going to be	supposing

Future Perfect

I	will have been	supposing
you	will have been	supposing
he/she/it	will have been	supposing
we	will have been	supposing
you	will have been	supposing
they	will have been	supposing

Conditional

I	would	suppose
you	would	suppose
he/she/it	would	suppose
we	would	suppose
you	would	suppose
they	would	suppose

Conditional Past

I	would have	supposed
you	would have	supposed
he/she/it	would have	supposed
we	would have	supposed
you	would have	supposed
they	would have	supposed

Simple tenses

Present

I	surprise
you	surprise
he/she/it	surprises
we	surprise
you	surprise
they	surprise

Past

I	surprised
you	surprised
he/she/it	surprised
we	surprised
you	surprised
they	surprised

Present Perfect

I	have	surprised
you	have	surprised
he/she/it	has	surprised
we	have	surprised
you	have	surprised
they	have	surprised

Past Perfect

I	had	surprised
you	had	surprised
he/she/it	had	surprised
we	had	surprised
you	had	surprised
they	had	surprised

Will-Future

I	will	surprise
you	will	surprise
he/she/it	will	surprise
we	will	surprise
you	will	surprise
they	will	surprise

Going to-Future

I	am	going to	surprise
you	are	going to	surprise
he/she/it	is	going to	surprise
we	are	going to	surprise
you	are	going to	surprise
they	are	going to	surprise

Future Perfect

I	will have	surprised
you	will have	surprised
he/she/it	will have	surprised
we	will have	surprised
you	will have	surprised
they	will have	surprised

Imperative

surprise

Impersonal

ing-Form

surprising

Past Participle

surprised

Continuous tenses

Present

I	am	surprising
you	are	surprising
he/she/it	is	surprising
we	are	surprising
you	are	surprising
they	are	surprising

Past

I	was	surprising
you	were	surprising
he/she/it	was	surprising
we	were	surprising
you	were	surprising
they	were	surprising

Present Perfect

I	have been	surprising
you	have been	surprising
he/she/it	has been	surprising
we	have been	surprising
you	have been	surprising
they	have been	surprising

Past Perfect

I	had been	surprising
you	had been	surprising
he/she/it	had been	surprising
we	had been	surprising
you	had been	surprising
they	had been	surprising

Will-Future

I	will be	surprising
you	will be	surprising
he/she/it	will be	surprising
we	will be	surprising
you	will be	surprising
they	will be	surprising

Going to-Future

I	am	going to be	surprising
you	are	going to be	surprising
he/she/it	is	going to be	surprising
we	are	going to be	surprising
you	are	going to be	surprising
they	are	going to be	surprising

Future Perfect

I	will have been	surprising
you	will have been	surprising
he/she/it	will have been	surprising
we	will have been	surprising
you	will have been	surprising
they	will have been	surprising

Conditional

I	would	surprise
you	would	surprise
he/she/it	would	surprise
we	would	surprise
you	would	surprise
they	would	surprise

Conditional Past

I	would have	surprised
you	would have	surprised
he/she/it	would have	surprised
we	would have	surprised
you	would have	surprised
they	would have	surprised

surround

umgeben

Regelmäßiges Verb

Simple tenses

Present

I	surround
you	surround
he/she/it	surrounds
we	surround
you	surround
they	surround

Past

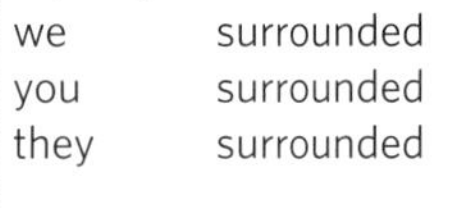

I	surrounded
you	surrounded
he/she/it	surrounded
we	surrounded
you	surrounded
they	surrounded

Present Perfect

I	have	surrounded
you	have	surrounded
he/she/it	has	surrounded
we	have	surrounded
you	have	surrounded
they	have	surrounded

Past Perfect

I	had	surrounded
you	had	surrounded
he/she/it	had	surrounded
we	had	surrounded
you	had	surrounded
they	had	surrounded

Will-Future

I	will	surround
you	will	surround
he/she/it	will	surround
we	will	surround
you	will	surround
they	will	surround

Going to-Future

I	am	going to	surround
you	are	going to	surround
he/she/it	is	going to	surround
we	are	going to	surround
you	are	going to	surround
they	are	going to	surround

Future Perfect

I	will have	surrounded
you	will have	surrounded
he/she/it	will have	surrounded
we	will have	surrounded
you	will have	surrounded
they	will have	surrounded

Imperative

surround

Impersonal

ing-Form

surrounding

Past Participle

surrounded

Continuous tenses

Present

I	am	surrounding
you	are	surrounding
he/she/it	is	surrounding
we	are	surrounding
you	are	surrounding
they	are	surrounding

Past

I	was	surrounding
you	were	surrounding
he/she/it	was	surrounding
we	were	surrounding
you	were	surrounding
they	were	surrounding

Present Perfect

I	have been	surrounding
you	have been	surrounding
he/she/it	has been	surrounding
we	have been	surrounding
you	have been	surrounding
they	have been	surrounding

Past Perfect

I	had been	surrounding
you	had been	surrounding
he/she/it	had been	surrounding
we	had been	surrounding
you	had been	surrounding
they	had been	surrounding

Will-Future

I	will be	surrounding
you	will be	surrounding
he/she/it	will be	surrounding
we	will be	surrounding
you	will be	surrounding
they	will be	surrounding

Going to-Future

I	am	going to be	surrounding
you	are	going to be	surrounding
he/she/it	is	going to be	surrounding
we	are	going to be	surrounding
you	are	going to be	surrounding
they	are	going to be	surrounding

Future Perfect

I	will have been	surrounding
you	will have been	surrounding
he/she/it	will have been	surrounding
we	will have been	surrounding
you	will have been	surrounding
they	will have been	surrounding

Conditional

I	would	surround
you	would	surround
he/she/it	would	surround
we	would	surround
you	would	surround
they	would	surround

Conditional Past

I	would have	surrounded
you	would have	surrounded
he/she/it	would have	surrounded
we	would have	surrounded
you	would have	surrounded
they	would have	surrounded

Simple tenses

Present
I	survey
you	survey
he/she/it	surveys
we	survey
you	survey
they	survey

Past
I	surveyed
you	surveyed
he/she/it	surveyed
we	surveyed
you	surveyed
they	surveyed

Present Perfect
I	have	surveyed
you	have	surveyed
he/she/it	has	surveyed
we	have	surveyed
you	have	surveyed
they	have	surveyed

Past Perfect
I	had	surveyed
you	had	surveyed
he/she/it	had	surveyed
we	had	surveyed
you	had	surveyed
they	had	surveyed

Will-Future
I	will	survey
you	will	survey
he/she/it	will	survey
we	will	survey
you	will	survey
they	will	survey

Going to-Future
I	am	going to	survey
you	are	going to	survey
he/she/it	is	going to	survey
we	are	going to	survey
you	are	going to	survey
they	are	going to	survey

Future Perfect
I	will have	surveyed
you	will have	surveyed
he/she/it	will have	surveyed
we	will have	surveyed
you	will have	surveyed
they	will have	surveyed

Imperative
survey

Impersonal

ing-Form
surveying

Past Participle
surveyed

Continuous tenses

Present
I	am	surveying
you	are	surveying
he/she/it	is	surveying
we	are	surveying
you	are	surveying
they	are	surveying

Past
I	was	surveying
you	were	surveying
he/she/it	was	surveying
we	were	surveying
you	were	surveying
they	were	surveying

Present Perfect
I	have been	surveying
you	have been	surveying
he/she/it	has been	surveying
we	have been	surveying
you	have been	surveying
they	have been	surveying

Past Perfect
I	had been	surveying
you	had been	surveying
he/she/it	had been	surveying
we	had been	surveying
you	had been	surveying
they	had been	surveying

Will-Future
I	will be	surveying
you	will be	surveying
he/she/it	will be	surveying
we	will be	surveying
you	will be	surveying
they	will be	surveying

Going to-Future
I	am	going to be	surveying
you	are	going to be	surveying
he/she/it	is	going to be	surveying
we	are	going to be	surveying
you	are	going to be	surveying
they	are	going to be	surveying

Future Perfect
I	will have been	surveying
you	will have been	surveying
he/she/it	will have been	surveying
we	will have been	surveying
you	will have been	surveying
they	will have been	surveying

Conditional
I	would	survey
you	would	survey
he/she/it	would	survey
we	would	survey
you	would	survey
they	would	survey

Conditional Past
I	would have	surveyed
you	would have	surveyed
he/she/it	would have	surveyed
we	would have	surveyed
you	would have	surveyed
they	would have	surveyed

survive

überleben

+ **-ing** → ~~e~~ / + **-d** nicht **-ed**
Regelmäßiges Verb

Simple tenses

Present

I	survive
you	survive
he/she/it	survives
we	survive
you	survive
they	survive

Past

I	survived
you	survived
he/she/it	survived
we	survived
you	survived
they	survived

Present Perfect

I	have	survived
you	have	survived
he/she/it	has	survived
we	have	survived
you	have	survived
they	have	survived

Past Perfect

I	had	survived
you	had	survived
he/she/it	had	survived
we	had	survived
you	had	survived
they	had	survived

Will-Future

I	will	survive
you	will	survive
he/she/it	will	survive
we	will	survive
you	will	survive
they	will	survive

Going to-Future

I	am	going to	survive
you	are	going to	survive
he/she/it	is	going to	survive
we	are	going to	survive
you	are	going to	survive
they	are	going to	survive

Future Perfect

I	will have	survived
you	will have	survived
he/she/it	will have	survived
we	will have	survived
you	will have	survived
they	will have	survived

Imperative

survive

Impersonal

ing-Form

surviving

Past Participle

survived

Continuous tenses

Present

I	am	surviving
you	are	surviving
he/she/it	is	surviving
we	are	surviving
you	are	surviving
they	are	surviving

Past

I	was	surviving
you	were	surviving
he/she/it	was	surviving
we	were	surviving
you	were	surviving
they	were	surviving

Present Perfect

I	have been	surviving
you	have been	surviving
he/she/it	has been	surviving
we	have been	surviving
you	have been	surviving
they	have been	surviving

Past Perfect

I	had been	surviving
you	had been	surviving
he/she/it	had been	surviving
we	had been	surviving
you	had been	surviving
they	had been	surviving

Will-Future

I	will be	surviving
you	will be	surviving
he/she/it	will be	surviving
we	will be	surviving
you	will be	surviving
they	will be	surviving

Going to-Future

I	am	going to be	surviving
you	are	going to be	surviving
he/she/it	is	going to be	surviving
we	are	going to be	surviving
you	are	going to be	surviving
they	are	going to be	surviving

Future Perfect

I	will have been	surviving
you	will have been	surviving
he/she/it	will have been	surviving
we	will have been	surviving
you	will have been	surviving
they	will have been	surviving

Conditional

I	would	survive
you	would	survive
he/she/it	would	survive
we	would	survive
you	would	survive
they	would	survive

Conditional Past

I	would have	survived
you	would have	survived
he/she/it	would have	survived
we	would have	survived
you	would have	survived
they	would have	survived

Simple tenses

Present

I	suspect
you	suspect
he/she/it	suspects
we	suspect
you	suspect
they	suspect

Past

I	suspected
you	suspected
he/she/it	suspected
we	suspected
you	suspected
they	suspected

Present Perfect

I	have	suspected
you	have	suspected
he/she/it	has	suspected
we	have	suspected
you	have	suspected
they	have	suspected

Past Perfect

I	had	suspected
you	had	suspected
he/she/it	had	suspected
we	had	suspected
you	had	suspected
they	had	suspected

Will-Future

I	will	suspect
you	will	suspect
he/she/it	will	suspect
we	will	suspect
you	will	suspect
they	will	suspect

Going to-Future

I	am	going to	suspect
you	are	going to	suspect
he/she/it	is	going to	suspect
we	are	going to	suspect
you	are	going to	suspect
they	are	going to	suspect

Future Perfect

I	will have	suspected
you	will have	suspected
he/she/it	will have	suspected
we	will have	suspected
you	will have	suspected
they	will have	suspected

Imperative

suspect

Impersonal

ing-Form

suspecting

Past Participle

suspected

Continuous tenses

Present

I	am	suspecting
you	are	suspecting
he/she/it	is	suspecting
we	are	suspecting
you	are	suspecting
they	are	suspecting

Past

I	was	suspecting
you	were	suspecting
he/she/it	was	suspecting
we	were	suspecting
you	were	suspecting
they	were	suspecting

Present Perfect

I	have been	suspecting
you	have been	suspecting
he/she/it	has been	suspecting
we	have been	suspecting
you	have been	suspecting
they	have been	suspecting

Past Perfect

I	had been	suspecting
you	had been	suspecting
he/she/it	had been	suspecting
we	had been	suspecting
you	had been	suspecting
they	had been	suspecting

Will-Future

I	will be	suspecting
you	will be	suspecting
he/she/it	will be	suspecting
we	will be	suspecting
you	will be	suspecting
they	will be	suspecting

Going to-Future

I	am	going to be	suspecting
you	are	going to be	suspecting
he/she/it	is	going to be	suspecting
we	are	going to be	suspecting
you	are	going to be	suspecting
they	are	going to be	suspecting

Future Perfect

I	will have been	suspecting
you	will have been	suspecting
he/she/it	will have been	suspecting
we	will have been	suspecting
you	will have been	suspecting
they	will have been	suspecting

Conditional

I	would	suspect
you	would	suspect
he/she/it	would	suspect
we	would	suspect
you	would	suspect
they	would	suspect

Conditional Past

I	would have	suspected
you	would have	suspected
he/she/it	would have	suspected
we	would have	suspected
you	would have	suspected
they	would have	suspected

swear

- swore - sworn

schwören

Unregelmäßiges Verb

Simple tenses

Present

I	swear
you	swear
he/she/it	swears
we	swear
you	swear
they	swear

Past

I	swore
you	swore
he/she/it	swore
we	swore
you	swore
they	swore

Present Perfect

I	have	sworn
you	have	sworn
he/she/it	has	sworn
we	have	sworn
you	have	sworn
they	have	sworn

Past Perfect

I	had	sworn
you	had	sworn
he/she/it	had	sworn
we	had	sworn
you	had	sworn
they	had	sworn

Will-Future

I	will	swear
you	will	swear
he/she/it	will	swear
we	will	swear
you	will	swear
they	will	swear

Going to-Future

I	am	going to	swear
you	are	going to	swear
he/she/it	is	going to	swear
we	are	going to	swear
you	are	going to	swear
they	are	going to	swear

Future Perfect

I	will have	sworn
you	will have	sworn
he/she/it	will have	sworn
we	will have	sworn
you	will have	sworn
they	will have	sworn

Imperative

swear

Impersonal

ing-Form

swearing

Past Participle

sworn

Continuous tenses

Present

I	am	swearing
you	are	swearing
he/she/it	is	swearing
we	are	swearing
you	are	swearing
they	are	swearing

Past

I	was	swearing
you	were	swearing
he/she/it	was	swearing
we	were	swearing
you	were	swearing
they	were	swearing

Present Perfect

I	have been	swearing
you	have been	swearing
he/she/it	has been	swearing
we	have been	swearing
you	have been	swearing
they	have been	swearing

Past Perfect

I	had been	swearing
you	had been	swearing
he/she/it	had been	swearing
we	had been	swearing
you	had been	swearing
they	had been	swearing

Will-Future

I	will be	swearing
you	will be	swearing
he/she/it	will be	swearing
we	will be	swearing
you	will be	swearing
they	will be	swearing

Going to-Future

I	am	going to be	swearing
you	are	going to be	swearing
he/she/it	is	going to be	swearing
we	are	going to be	swearing
you	are	going to be	swearing
they	are	going to be	swearing

Future Perfect

I	will have been	swearing
you	will have been	swearing
he/she/it	will have been	swearing
we	will have been	swearing
you	will have been	swearing
they	will have been	swearing

Conditional

I	would	swear
you	would	swear
he/she/it	would	swear
we	would	swear
you	would	swear
they	would	swear

Conditional Past

I	would have	sworn
you	would have	sworn
he/she/it	would have	sworn
we	would have	sworn
you	would have	sworn
they	would have	sworn

Simple tenses

Present

I	sweep
you	sweep
he/she/it	sweeps
we	sweep
you	sweep
they	sweep

Past

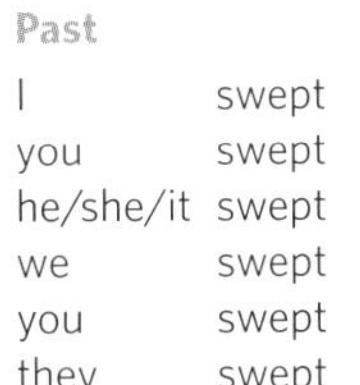

I	swept
you	swept
he/she/it	swept
we	swept
you	swept
they	swept

Present Perfect

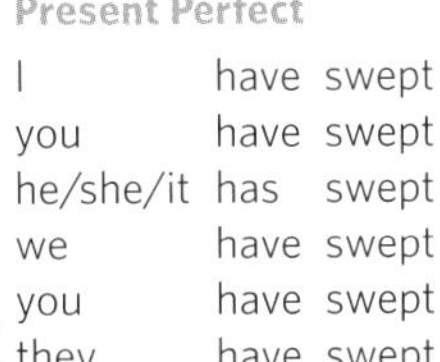

I	have	swept
you	have	swept
he/she/it	has	swept
we	have	swept
you	have	swept
they	have	swept

Past Perfect

I	had	swept
you	had	swept
he/she/it	had	swept
we	had	swept
you	had	swept
they	had	swept

Will-Future

I	will	sweep
you	will	sweep
he/she/it	will	sweep
we	will	sweep
you	will	sweep
they	will	sweep

Going to-Future

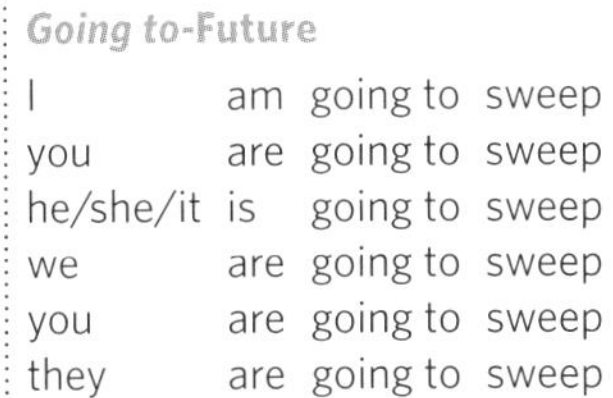

I	am	going to	sweep
you	are	going to	sweep
he/she/it	is	going to	sweep
we	are	going to	sweep
you	are	going to	sweep
they	are	going to	sweep

Future Perfect

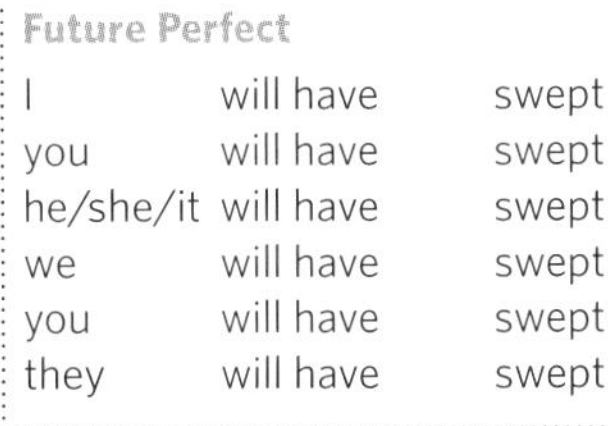

I	will have	swept
you	will have	swept
he/she/it	will have	swept
we	will have	swept
you	will have	swept
they	will have	swept

Imperative

sweep

Impersonal

ing-Form

sweeping

Past Participle

swept

Continuous tenses

Present

I	am	sweeping
you	are	sweeping
he/she/it	is	sweeping
we	are	sweeping
you	are	sweeping
they	are	sweeping

Past

I	was	sweeping
you	were	sweeping
he/she/it	was	sweeping
we	were	sweeping
you	were	sweeping
they	were	sweeping

Present Perfect

I	have been	sweeping
you	have been	sweeping
he/she/it	has been	sweeping
we	have been	sweeping
you	have been	sweeping
they	have been	sweeping

Past Perfect

I	had been	sweeping
you	had been	sweeping
he/she/it	had been	sweeping
we	had been	sweeping
you	had been	sweeping
they	had been	sweeping

Will-Future

I	will be	sweeping
you	will be	sweeping
he/she/it	will be	sweeping
we	will be	sweeping
you	will be	sweeping
they	will be	sweeping

Going to-Future

I	am	going to be	sweeping
you	are	going to be	sweeping
he/she/it	is	going to be	sweeping
we	are	going to be	sweeping
you	are	going to be	sweeping
they	are	going to be	sweeping

Future Perfect

I	will have been	sweeping
you	will have been	sweeping
he/she/it	will have been	sweeping
we	will have been	sweeping
you	will have been	sweeping
they	will have been	sweeping

Conditional

I	would	sweep
you	would	sweep
he/she/it	would	sweep
we	would	sweep
you	would	sweep
they	would	sweep

Conditional Past

I	would have	swept
you	would have	swept
he/she/it	would have	swept
we	would have	swept
you	would have	swept
they	would have	swept

swim
- swam - swum

schwimmen

Konsonantenverdopplung
Unregelmäßiges Verb

Simple tenses

Present

I	swim
you	swim
he/she/it	swims
we	swim
you	swim
they	swim

Past

I	swam
you	swam
he/she/it	swam
we	swam
you	swam
they	swam

Present Perfect

I	have	swum
you	have	swum
he/she/it	has	swum
we	have	swum
you	have	swum
they	have	swum

Past Perfect

I	had	swum
you	had	swum
he/she/it	had	swum
we	had	swum
you	had	swum
they	had	swum

Will-Future

I	will	swim
you	will	swim
he/she/it	will	swim
we	will	swim
you	will	swim
they	will	swim

Going to-Future

I	am	going to	swim
you	are	going to	swim
he/she/it	is	going to	swim
we	are	going to	swim
you	are	going to	swim
they	are	going to	swim

Future Perfect

I	will have	swum
you	will have	swum
he/she/it	will have	swum
we	will have	swum
you	will have	swum
they	will have	swum

Imperative

swim

Impersonal

ing-Form

swimming

Past Participle

swum

Continuous tenses

Present

I	am	swimming
you	are	swimming
he/she/it	is	swimming
we	are	swimming
you	are	swimming
they	are	swimming

Past

I	was	swimming
you	were	swimming
he/she/it	was	swimming
we	were	swimming
you	were	swimming
they	were	swimming

Present Perfect

I	have been	swimming
you	have been	swimming
he/she/it	has been	swimming
we	have been	swimming
you	have been	swimming
they	have been	swimming

Past Perfect

I	had been	swimming
you	had been	swimming
he/she/it	had been	swimming
we	had been	swimming
you	had been	swimming
they	had been	swimming

Will-Future

I	will be	swimming
you	will be	swimming
he/she/it	will be	swimming
we	will be	swimming
you	will be	swimming
they	will be	swimming

Going to-Future

I	am	going to be	swimming
you	are	going to be	swimming
he/she/it	is	going to be	swimming
we	are	going to be	swimming
you	are	going to be	swimming
they	are	going to be	swimming

Future Perfect

I	will have been	swimming
you	will have been	swimming
he/she/it	will have been	swimming
we	will have been	swimming
you	will have been	swimming
they	will have been	swimming

Conditional

I	would	swim
you	would	swim
he/she/it	would	swim
we	would	swim
you	would	swim
they	would	swim

Conditional Past

I	would have	swum
you	would have	swum
he/she/it	would have	swum
we	would have	swum
you	would have	swum
they	would have	swum

+ **-es** in 3. Person Singular
Regelmäßiges Verb

wechseln

switch

Simple tenses

Present

I	switch
you	switch
he/she/it	switches
we	switch
you	switch
they	switch

Past

I	switched
you	switched
he/she/it	switched
we	switched
you	switched
they	switched

Present Perfect

I	have	switched
you	have	switched
he/she/it	has	switched
we	have	switched
you	have	switched
they	have	switched

Past Perfect

I	had	switched
you	had	switched
he/she/it	had	switched
we	had	switched
you	had	switched
they	had	switched

Will-Future

I	will	switch
you	will	switch
he/she/it	will	switch
we	will	switch
you	will	switch
they	will	switch

Going to-Future

I	am	going to	switch
you	are	going to	switch
he/she/it	is	going to	switch
we	are	going to	switch
you	are	going to	switch
they	are	going to	switch

Future Perfect

I	will have	switched
you	will have	switched
he/she/it	will have	switched
we	will have	switched
you	will have	switched
they	will have	switched

Imperative

switch

Impersonal

ing-Form

switching

Past Participle

switched

Continuous tenses

Present

I	am	switching
you	are	switching
he/she/it	is	switching
we	are	switching
you	are	switching
they	are	switching

Past

I	was	switching
you	were	switching
he/she/it	was	switching
we	were	switching
you	were	switching
they	were	switching

Present Perfect

I	have been	switching
you	have been	switching
he/she/it	has been	switching
we	have been	switching
you	have been	switching
they	have been	switching

Past Perfect

I	had been	switching
you	had been	switching
he/she/it	had been	switching
we	had been	switching
you	had been	switching
they	had been	switching

Will-Future

I	will be	switching
you	will be	switching
he/she/it	will be	switching
we	will be	switching
you	will be	switching
they	will be	switching

Going to-Future

I	am	going to be	switching
you	are	going to be	switching
he/she/it	is	going to be	switching
we	are	going to be	switching
you	are	going to be	switching
they	are	going to be	switching

Future Perfect

I	will have been	switching
you	will have been	switching
he/she/it	will have been	switching
we	will have been	switching
you	will have been	switching
they	will have been	switching

Conditional

I	would	switch
you	would	switch
he/she/it	would	switch
we	would	switch
you	would	switch
they	would	switch

Conditional Past

I	would have	switched
you	would have	switched
he/she/it	would have	switched
we	would have	switched
you	would have	switched
they	would have	switched

take
- took - taken

nehmen

+ -ing → e̸
Unregelmäßiges Verb

Simple tenses

Present

I	take
you	take
he/she/it	takes
we	take
you	take
they	take

Past

I	took
you	took
he/she/it	took
we	took
you	took
they	took

Present Perfect

I	have	taken
you	have	taken
he/she/it	has	taken
we	have	taken
you	have	taken
they	have	taken

Past Perfect

I	had	taken
you	had	taken
he/she/it	had	taken
we	had	taken
you	had	taken
they	had	taken

Will-Future

I	will	take
you	will	take
he/she/it	will	take
we	will	take
you	will	take
they	will	take

Going to-Future

I	am	going to	take
you	are	going to	take
he/she/it	is	going to	take
we	are	going to	take
you	are	going to	take
they	are	going to	take

Future Perfect

I	will have	taken
you	will have	taken
he/she/it	will have	taken
we	will have	taken
you	will have	taken
they	will have	taken

Imperative

take

Impersonal

ing-Form

taking

Past Participle

taken

Continuous tenses

Present

I	am	taking
you	are	taking
he/she/it	is	taking
we	are	taking
you	are	taking
they	are	taking

Past

I	was	taking
you	were	taking
he/she/it	was	taking
we	were	taking
you	were	taking
they	were	taking

Present Perfect

I	have been	taking
you	have been	taking
he/she/it	has been	taking
we	have been	taking
you	have been	taking
they	have been	taking

Past Perfect

I	had been	taking
you	had been	taking
he/she/it	had been	taking
we	had been	taking
you	had been	taking
they	had been	taking

Will-Future

I	will be	taking
you	will be	taking
he/she/it	will be	taking
we	will be	taking
you	will be	taking
they	will be	taking

Going to-Future

I	am	going to be	taking
you	are	going to be	taking
he/she/it	is	going to be	taking
we	are	going to be	taking
you	are	going to be	taking
they	are	going to be	taking

Future Perfect

I	will have been	taking
you	will have been	taking
he/she/it	will have been	taking
we	will have been	taking
you	will have been	taking
they	will have been	taking

Conditional

I	would	take
you	would	take
he/she/it	would	take
we	would	take
you	would	take
they	would	take

Conditional Past

I	would have	taken
you	would have	taken
he/she/it	would have	taken
we	would have	taken
you	would have	taken
they	would have	taken

Simple tenses

Present

I	talk
you	talk
he/she/it	talks
we	talk
you	talk
they	talk

Past

I	talked
you	talked
he/she/it	talked
we	talked
you	talked
they	talked

Present Perfect

I	have	talked
you	have	talked
he/she/it	has	talked
we	have	talked
you	have	talked
they	have	talked

Past Perfect

I	had	talked
you	had	talked
he/she/it	had	talked
we	had	talked
you	had	talked
they	had	talked

Will-Future

I	will	talk
you	will	talk
he/she/it	will	talk
we	will	talk
you	will	talk
they	will	talk

Going to-Future

I	am	going to	talk
you	are	going to	talk
he/she/it	is	going to	talk
we	are	going to	talk
you	are	going to	talk
they	are	going to	talk

Future Perfect

I	will have	talked
you	will have	talked
he/she/it	will have	talked
we	will have	talked
you	will have	talked
they	will have	talked

Imperative

talk

Impersonal

ing-Form

talking

Past Participle

talked

Continuous tenses

Present

I	am	talking
you	are	talking
he/she/it	is	talking
we	are	talking
you	are	talking
they	are	talking

Past

I	was	talking
you	were	talking
he/she/it	was	talking
we	were	talking
you	were	talking
they	were	talking

Present Perfect

I	have	been	talking
you	have	been	talking
he/she/it	has	been	talking
we	have	been	talking
you	have	been	talking
they	have	been	talking

Past Perfect

I	had been	talking
you	had been	talking
he/she/it	had been	talking
we	had been	talking
you	had been	talking
they	had been	talking

Will-Future

I	will be	talking
you	will be	talking
he/she/it	will be	talking
we	will be	talking
you	will be	talking
they	will be	talking

Going to-Future

I	am	going to be	talking
you	are	going to be	talking
he/she/it	is	going to be	talking
we	are	going to be	talking
you	are	going to be	talking
they	are	going to be	talking

Future Perfect

I	will have been	talking
you	will have been	talking
he/she/it	will have been	talking
we	will have been	talking
you	will have been	talking
they	will have been	talking

Conditional

I	would	talk
you	would	talk
he/she/it	would	talk
we	would	talk
you	would	talk
they	would	talk

Conditional Past

I	would have	talked
you	would have	talked
he/she/it	would have	talked
we	would have	talked
you	would have	talked
they	would have	talked

tap

klopfen

Konsonantenverdopplung
Regelmäßiges Verb

Simple tenses

Present

I	tap
you	tap
he/she/it	taps
we	tap
you	tap
they	tap

Past

I	tapped
you	tapped
he/she/it	tapped
we	tapped
you	tapped
they	tapped

Present Perfect

I	have	tapped
you	have	tapped
he/she/it	has	tapped
we	have	tapped
you	have	tapped
they	have	tapped

Past Perfect

I	had	tapped
you	had	tapped
he/she/it	had	tapped
we	had	tapped
you	had	tapped
they	had	tapped

Will-Future

I	will	tap
you	will	tap
he/she/it	will	tap
we	will	tap
you	will	tap
they	will	tap

Going to-Future

I	am	going to	tap
you	are	going to	tap
he/she/it	is	going to	tap
we	are	going to	tap
you	are	going to	tap
they	are	going to	tap

Future Perfect

I	will have	tapped
you	will have	tapped
he/she/it	will have	tapped
we	will have	tapped
you	will have	tapped
they	will have	tapped

Imperative

tap

Impersonal

ing-Form

tapping

Past Participle

tapped

Continuous tenses

Present

I	am	tapping
you	are	tapping
he/she/it	is	tapping
we	are	tapping
you	are	tapping
they	are	tapping

Past

I	was	tapping
you	were	tapping
he/she/it	was	tapping
we	were	tapping
you	were	tapping
they	were	tapping

Present Perfect

I	have been	tapping
you	have been	tapping
he/she/it	has been	tapping
we	have been	tapping
you	have been	tapping
they	have been	tapping

Past Perfect

I	had been	tapping
you	had been	tapping
he/she/it	had been	tapping
we	had been	tapping
you	had been	tapping
they	had been	tapping

Will-Future

I	will be	tapping
you	will be	tapping
he/she/it	will be	tapping
we	will be	tapping
you	will be	tapping
they	will be	tapping

Going to-Future

I	am	going to be	tapping
you	are	going to be	tapping
he/she/it	is	going to be	tapping
we	are	going to be	tapping
you	are	going to be	tapping
they	are	going to be	tapping

Future Perfect

I	will have been	tapping
you	will have been	tapping
he/she/it	will have been	tapping
we	will have been	tapping
you	will have been	tapping
they	will have been	tapping

Conditional

I	would	tap
you	would	tap
he/she/it	would	tap
we	would	tap
you	would	tap
they	would	tap

Conditional Past

I	would have	tapped
you	would have	tapped
he/she/it	would have	tapped
we	would have	tapped
you	would have	tapped
they	would have	tapped

+ **-ing** → ~~e~~ / + **-d** nicht **-ed**
Regelmäßiges Verb

schmecken

taste

Simple tenses

Present

I	taste
you	taste
he/she/it	tastes
we	taste
you	taste
they	taste

Past

I	tasted
you	tasted
he/she/it	tasted
we	tasted
you	tasted
they	tasted

Present Perfect

I	have	tasted
you	have	tasted
he/she/it	has	tasted
we	have	tasted
you	have	tasted
they	have	tasted

Past Perfect

I	had	tasted
you	had	tasted
he/she/it	had	tasted
we	had	tasted
you	had	tasted
they	had	tasted

Will-Future

I	will	taste
you	will	taste
he/she/it	will	taste
we	will	taste
you	will	taste
they	will	taste

Going to-Future

I	am	going to	taste
you	are	going to	taste
he/she/it	is	going to	taste
we	are	going to	taste
you	are	going to	taste
they	are	going to	taste

Future Perfect

I	will have	tasted
you	will have	tasted
he/she/it	will have	tasted
we	will have	tasted
you	will have	tasted
they	will have	tasted

Imperative

taste

Impersonal

ing-Form

tasting

Past Participle

tasted

Continuous tenses

Present

I	am	tasting
you	are	tasting
he/she/it	is	tasting
we	are	tasting
you	are	tasting
they	are	tasting

Past

I	was	tasting
you	were	tasting
he/she/it	was	tasting
we	were	tasting
you	were	tasting
they	were	tasting

Present Perfect

I	have been	tasting
you	have been	tasting
he/she/it	has been	tasting
we	have been	tasting
you	have been	tasting
they	have been	tasting

Past Perfect

I	had been	tasting
you	had been	tasting
he/she/it	had been	tasting
we	had been	tasting
you	had been	tasting
they	had been	tasting

Will-Future

I	will be	tasting
you	will be	tasting
he/she/it	will be	tasting
we	will be	tasting
you	will be	tasting
they	will be	tasting

Going to-Future

I	am	going to be	tasting
you	are	going to be	tasting
he/she/it	is	going to be	tasting
we	are	going to be	tasting
you	are	going to be	tasting
they	are	going to be	tasting

Future Perfect

I	will have been	tasting
you	will have been	tasting
he/she/it	will have been	tasting
we	will have been	tasting
you	will have been	tasting
they	will have been	tasting

Conditional

I	would	taste
you	would	taste
he/she/it	would	taste
we	would	taste
you	would	taste
they	would	taste

Conditional Past

I	would have	tasted
you	would have	tasted
he/she/it	would have	tasted
we	would have	tasted
you	would have	tasted
they	would have	tasted

tax

besteuern

+ **-es** in 3. Person Singular
Regelmäßiges Verb

Simple tenses

Present

I	tax
you	tax
he/she/it	taxes
we	tax
you	tax
they	tax

Past

I	taxed
you	taxed
he/she/it	taxed
we	taxed
you	taxed
they	taxed

Present Perfect

I	have	taxed
you	have	taxed
he/she/it	has	taxed
we	have	taxed
you	have	taxed
they	have	taxed

Past Perfect

I	had	taxed
you	had	taxed
he/she/it	had	taxed
we	had	taxed
you	had	taxed
they	had	taxed

Will-Future

I	will	tax
you	will	tax
he/she/it	will	tax
we	will	tax
you	will	tax
they	will	tax

Going to-Future

I	am	going to	tax
you	are	going to	tax
he/she/it	is	going to	tax
we	are	going to	tax
you	are	going to	tax
they	are	going to	tax

Future Perfect

I	will have	taxed
you	will have	taxed
he/she/it	will have	taxed
we	will have	taxed
you	will have	taxed
they	will have	taxed

Imperative

tax

Impersonal

ing-Form

taxing

Past Participle

taxed

Continuous tenses

Present

I	am	taxing
you	are	taxing
he/she/it	is	taxing
we	are	taxing
you	are	taxing
they	are	taxing

Past

I	was	taxing
you	were	taxing
he/she/it	was	taxing
we	were	taxing
you	were	taxing
they	were	taxing

Present Perfect

I	have been	taxing
you	have been	taxing
he/she/it	has been	taxing
we	have been	taxing
you	have been	taxing
they	have been	taxing

Past Perfect

I	had been	taxing
you	had been	taxing
he/she/it	had been	taxing
we	had been	taxing
you	had been	taxing
they	had been	taxing

Will-Future

I	will be	taxing
you	will be	taxing
he/she/it	will be	taxing
we	will be	taxing
you	will be	taxing
they	will be	taxing

Going to-Future

I	am	going to be	taxing
you	are	going to be	taxing
he/she/it	is	going to be	taxing
we	are	going to be	taxing
you	are	going to be	taxing
they	are	going to be	taxing

Future Perfect

I	will have been	taxing
you	will have been	taxing
he/she/it	will have been	taxing
we	will have been	taxing
you	will have been	taxing
they	will have been	taxing

Conditional

I	would	tax
you	would	tax
he/she/it	would	tax
we	would	tax
you	would	tax
they	would	tax

Conditional Past

I	would have	taxed
you	would have	taxed
he/she/it	would have	taxed
we	would have	taxed
you	would have	taxed
they	would have	taxed

Unregelmäßiges Verb

lehren

teach
- taught - taught

Simple tenses

Present

I	teach
you	teach
he/she/it	teaches
we	teach
you	teach
they	teach

Past

I	taught
you	taught
he/she/it	taught
we	taught
you	taught
they	taught

Present Perfect

I	have	taught
you	have	taught
he/she/it	has	taught
we	have	taught
you	have	taught
they	have	taught

Past Perfect

I	had	taught
you	had	taught
he/she/it	had	taught
we	had	taught
you	had	taught
they	had	taught

Will-Future

I	will	teach
you	will	teach
he/she/it	will	teach
we	will	teach
you	will	teach
they	will	teach

Going to-Future

I	am	going to	teach
you	are	going to	teach
he/she/it	is	going to	teach
we	are	going to	teach
you	are	going to	teach
they	are	going to	teach

Future Perfect

I	will have	taught
you	will have	taught
he/she/it	will have	taught
we	will have	taught
you	will have	taught
they	will have	taught

Imperative

teach

Impersonal

ing-Form

teaching

Past Participle

taught

Continuous tenses

Present

I	am	teaching
you	are	teaching
he/she/it	is	teaching
we	are	teaching
you	are	teaching
they	are	teaching

Past

I	was	teaching
you	were	teaching
he/she/it	was	teaching
we	were	teaching
you	were	teaching
they	were	teaching

Present Perfect

I	have	been	teaching
you	have	been	teaching
he/she/it	has	been	teaching
we	have	been	teaching
you	have	been	teaching
they	have	been	teaching

Past Perfect

I	had been	teaching
you	had been	teaching
he/she/it	had been	teaching
we	had been	teaching
you	had been	teaching
they	had been	teaching

Will-Future

I	will be	teaching
you	will be	teaching
he/she/it	will be	teaching
we	will be	teaching
you	will be	teaching
they	will be	teaching

Going to-Future

I	am	going to be	teaching
you	are	going to be	teaching
he/she/it	is	going to be	teaching
we	are	going to be	teaching
you	are	going to be	teaching
they	are	going to be	teaching

Future Perfect

I	will have been	teaching
you	will have been	teaching
he/she/it	will have been	teaching
we	will have been	teaching
you	will have been	teaching
they	will have been	teaching

Conditional

I	would	teach
you	would	teach
he/she/it	would	teach
we	would	teach
you	would	teach
they	would	teach

Conditional Past

I	would have	taught
you	would have	taught
he/she/it	would have	taught
we	would have	taught
you	would have	taught
they	would have	taught

tear
- tore - torn

zerreißen

Unregelmäßiges Verb

Simple tenses

Present

I	tear
you	tear
he/she/it	tears
we	tear
you	tear
they	tear

Past

I	tore
you	tore
he/she/it	tore
we	tore
you	tore
they	tore

Present Perfect

I	have	torn
you	have	torn
he/she/it	has	torn
we	have	torn
you	have	torn
they	have	torn

Past Perfect

I	had	torn
you	had	torn
he/she/it	had	torn
we	had	torn
you	had	torn
they	had	torn

Will-Future

I	will	tear
you	will	tear
he/she/it	will	tear
we	will	tear
you	will	tear
they	will	tear

Going to-Future

I	am	going to	tear
you	are	going to	tear
he/she/it	is	going to	tear
we	are	going to	tear
you	are	going to	tear
they	are	going to	tear

Future Perfect

I	will have	torn
you	will have	torn
he/she/it	will have	torn
we	will have	torn
you	will have	torn
they	will have	torn

Imperative

tear

Impersonal

ing-Form

tearing

Past Participle

torn

Continuous tenses

Present

I	am	tearing
you	are	tearing
he/she/it	is	tearing
we	are	tearing
you	are	tearing
they	are	tearing

Past

I	was	tearing
you	were	tearing
he/she/it	was	tearing
we	were	tearing
you	were	tearing
they	were	tearing

Present Perfect

I	have been	tearing
you	have been	tearing
he/she/it	has been	tearing
we	have been	tearing
you	have been	tearing
they	have been	tearing

Past Perfect

I	had been	tearing
you	had been	tearing
he/she/it	had been	tearing
we	had been	tearing
you	had been	tearing
they	had been	tearing

Will-Future

I	will be	tearing
you	will be	tearing
he/she/it	will be	tearing
we	will be	tearing
you	will be	tearing
they	will be	tearing

Going to-Future

I	am	going to be	tearing
you	are	going to be	tearing
he/she/it	is	going to be	tearing
we	are	going to be	tearing
you	are	going to be	tearing
they	are	going to be	tearing

Future Perfect

I	will have been	tearing
you	will have been	tearing
he/she/it	will have been	tearing
we	will have been	tearing
you	will have been	tearing
they	will have been	tearing

Conditional

I	would	tear
you	would	tear
he/she/it	would	tear
we	would	tear
you	would	tear
they	would	tear

Conditional Past

I	would have	torn
you	would have	torn
he/she/it	would have	torn
we	would have	torn
you	would have	torn
they	would have	torn

Simple tenses

Present

I	tell
you	tell
he/she/it	tells
we	tell
you	tell
they	tell

Past

I	told
you	told
he/she/it	told
we	told
you	told
they	told

Present Perfect

I	have	told
you	have	told
he/she/it	has	told
we	have	told
you	have	told
they	have	told

Past Perfect

I	had	told
you	had	told
he/she/it	had	told
we	had	told
you	had	told
they	had	told

Will-Future

I	will	tell
you	will	tell
he/she/it	will	tell
we	will	tell
you	will	tell
they	will	tell

Going to-Future

I	am	going to	tell
you	are	going to	tell
he/she/it	is	going to	tell
we	are	going to	tell
you	are	going to	tell
they	are	going to	tell

Future Perfect

I	will have	told
you	will have	told
he/she/it	will have	told
we	will have	told
you	will have	told
they	will have	told

Imperative

tell

Impersonal

ing-Form

telling

Past Participle

told

Continuous tenses

Present

I	am	telling
you	are	telling
he/she/it	is	telling
we	are	telling
you	are	telling
they	are	telling

Past

I	was	telling
you	were	telling
he/she/it	was	telling
we	were	telling
you	were	telling
they	were	telling

Present Perfect

I	have been	telling
you	have been	telling
he/she/it	has been	telling
we	have been	telling
you	have been	telling
they	have been	telling

Past Perfect

I	had been	telling
you	had been	telling
he/she/it	had been	telling
we	had been	telling
you	had been	telling
they	had been	telling

Will-Future

I	will be	telling
you	will be	telling
he/she/it	will be	telling
we	will be	telling
you	will be	telling
they	will be	telling

Going to-Future

I	am	going to be	telling
you	are	going to be	telling
he/she/it	is	going to be	telling
we	are	going to be	telling
you	are	going to be	telling
they	are	going to be	telling

Future Perfect

I	will have been	telling
you	will have been	telling
he/she/it	will have been	telling
we	will have been	telling
you	will have been	telling
they	will have been	telling

Conditional

I	would	tell
you	would	tell
he/she/it	would	tell
we	would	tell
you	would	tell
they	would	tell

Conditional Past

I	would have	told
you	would have	told
he/she/it	would have	told
we	would have	told
you	would have	told
they	would have	told

test

prüfen

Regelmäßiges Verb

Simple tenses

Present

I	test
you	test
he/she/it	tests
we	test
you	test
they	test

Past

I	tested
you	tested
he/she/it	tested
we	tested
you	tested
they	tested

Present Perfect

I	have	tested
you	have	tested
he/she/it	has	tested
we	have	tested
you	have	tested
they	have	tested

Past Perfect

I	had	tested
you	had	tested
he/she/it	had	tested
we	had	tested
you	had	tested
they	had	tested

Will-Future

I	will	test
you	will	test
he/she/it	will	test
we	will	test
you	will	test
they	will	test

Going to-Future

I	am	going to	test
you	are	going to	test
he/she/it	is	going to	test
we	are	going to	test
you	are	going to	test
they	are	going to	test

Future Perfect

I	will have	tested
you	will have	tested
he/she/it	will have	tested
we	will have	tested
you	will have	tested
they	will have	tested

Imperative

test

Impersonal

ing-Form

testing

Past Participle

tested

Continuous tenses

Present

I	am	testing
you	are	testing
he/she/it	is	testing
we	are	testing
you	are	testing
they	are	testing

Past

I	was	testing
you	were	testing
he/she/it	was	testing
we	were	testing
you	were	testing
they	were	testing

Present Perfect

I	have	been	testing
you	have	been	testing
he/she/it	has	been	testing
we	have	been	testing
you	have	been	testing
they	have	been	testing

Past Perfect

I	had been	testing
you	had been	testing
he/she/it	had been	testing
we	had been	testing
you	had been	testing
they	had been	testing

Will-Future

I	will be	testing
you	will be	testing
he/she/it	will be	testing
we	will be	testing
you	will be	testing
they	will be	testing

Going to-Future

I	am	going to be	testing
you	are	going to be	testing
he/she/it	is	going to be	testing
we	are	going to be	testing
you	are	going to be	testing
they	are	going to be	testing

Future Perfect

I	will have been	testing
you	will have been	testing
he/she/it	will have been	testing
we	will have been	testing
you	will have been	testing
they	will have been	testing

Conditional

I	would	test
you	would	test
he/she/it	would	test
we	would	test
you	would	test
they	would	test

Conditional Past

I	would have	tested
you	would have	tested
he/she/it	would have	tested
we	would have	tested
you	would have	tested
they	would have	tested

Regelmäßiges Verb

Simple tenses

Present

I	thank
you	thank
he/she/it	thanks
we	thank
you	thank
they	thank

Past

I	thanked
you	thanked
he/she/it	thanked
we	thanked
you	thanked
they	thanked

Present Perfect

I	have	thanked
you	have	thanked
he/she/it	has	thanked
we	have	thanked
you	have	thanked
they	have	thanked

Past Perfect

I	had	thanked
you	had	thanked
he/she/it	had	thanked
we	had	thanked
you	had	thanked
they	had	thanked

Will-Future

I	will	thank
you	will	thank
he/she/it	will	thank
we	will	thank
you	will	thank
they	will	thank

Going to-Future

I	am	going to	thank
you	are	going to	thank
he/she/it	is	going to	thank
we	are	going to	thank
you	are	going to	thank
they	are	going to	thank

Future Perfect

I	will have	thanked
you	will have	thanked
he/she/it	will have	thanked
we	will have	thanked
you	will have	thanked
they	will have	thanked

Imperative

thank

Impersonal

ing-Form

thanking

Past Participle

thanked

Continuous tenses

Present

I	am	thanking
you	are	thanking
he/she/it	is	thanking
we	are	thanking
you	are	thanking
they	are	thanking

Past

I	was	thanking
you	were	thanking
he/she/it	was	thanking
we	were	thanking
you	were	thanking
they	were	thanking

Present Perfect

I	have been	thanking
you	have been	thanking
he/she/it	has been	thanking
we	have been	thanking
you	have been	thanking
they	have been	thanking

Past Perfect

I	had been	thanking
you	had been	thanking
he/she/it	had been	thanking
we	had been	thanking
you	had been	thanking
they	had been	thanking

Will-Future

I	will be	thanking
you	will be	thanking
he/she/it	will be	thanking
we	will be	thanking
you	will be	thanking
they	will be	thanking

Going to-Future

I	am	going to be	thanking
you	are	going to be	thanking
he/she/it	is	going to be	thanking
we	are	going to be	thanking
you	are	going to be	thanking
they	are	going to be	thanking

Future Perfect

I	will have been	thanking
you	will have been	thanking
he/she/it	will have been	thanking
we	will have been	thanking
you	will have been	thanking
they	will have been	thanking

Conditional

I	would	thank
you	would	thank
he/she/it	would	thank
we	would	thank
you	would	thank
they	would	thank

Conditional Past

I	would have	thanked
you	would have	thanked
he/she/it	would have	thanked
we	would have	thanked
you	would have	thanked
they	would have	thanked

think
– thought – thought

denken

Unregelmäßiges Verb

Simple tenses

Present

I	think
you	think
he/she/it	thinks
we	think
you	think
they	think

Past

I	thought
you	thought
he/she/it	thought
we	thought
you	thought
they	thought

Present Perfect

I	have	thought
you	have	thought
he/she/it	has	thought
we	have	thought
you	have	thought
they	have	thought

Past Perfect

I	had	thought
you	had	thought
he/she/it	had	thought
we	had	thought
you	had	thought
they	had	thought

Will-Future

I	will	think
you	will	think
he/she/it	will	think
we	will	think
you	will	think
they	will	think

Going to-Future

I	am	going to	think
you	are	going to	think
he/she/it	is	going to	think
we	are	going to	think
you	are	going to	think
they	are	going to	think

Future Perfect

I	will have	thought
you	will have	thought
he/she/it	will have	thought
we	will have	thought
you	will have	thought
they	will have	thought

Imperative

think

Impersonal

ing-Form

thinking

Past Participle

thought

Continuous tenses

Present

I	am	thinking
you	are	thinking
he/she/it	is	thinking
we	are	thinking
you	are	thinking
they	are	thinking

Past

I	was	thinking
you	were	thinking
he/she/it	was	thinking
we	were	thinking
you	were	thinking
they	were	thinking

Present Perfect

I	have been	thinking
you	have been	thinking
he/she/it	has been	thinking
we	have been	thinking
you	have been	thinking
they	have been	thinking

Past Perfect

I	had been	thinking
you	had been	thinking
he/she/it	had been	thinking
we	had been	thinking
you	had been	thinking
they	had been	thinking

Will-Future

I	will be	thinking
you	will be	thinking
he/she/it	will be	thinking
we	will be	thinking
you	will be	thinking
they	will be	thinking

Going to-Future

I	am	going to be	thinking
you	are	going to be	thinking
he/she/it	is	going to be	thinking
we	are	going to be	thinking
you	are	going to be	thinking
they	are	going to be	thinking

Future Perfect

I	will have been	thinking
you	will have been	thinking
he/she/it	will have been	thinking
we	will have been	thinking
you	will have been	thinking
they	will have been	thinking

Conditional

I	would	think
you	would	think
he/she/it	would	think
we	would	think
you	would	think
they	would	think

Conditional Past

I	would have	thought
you	would have	thought
he/she/it	would have	thought
we	would have	thought
you	would have	thought
they	would have	thought

Simple tenses

Present

I	threaten
you	threaten
he/she/it	threatens
we	threaten
you	threaten
they	threaten

Past

I	threatened
you	threatened
he/she/it	threatened
we	threatened
you	threatened
they	threatened

Present Perfect

I	have	threatened
you	have	threatened
he/she/it	has	threatened
we	have	threatened
you	have	threatened
they	have	threatened

Past Perfect

I	had	threatened
you	had	threatened
he/she/it	had	threatened
we	had	threatened
you	had	threatened
they	had	threatened

Will-Future

I	will	threaten
you	will	threaten
he/she/it	will	threaten
we	will	threaten
you	will	threaten
they	will	threaten

Going to-Future

I	am	going to	threaten
you	are	going to	threaten
he/she/it	is	going to	threaten
we	are	going to	threaten
you	are	going to	threaten
they	are	going to	threaten

Future Perfect

I	will have	threatened
you	will have	threatened
he/she/it	will have	threatened
we	will have	threatened
you	will have	threatened
they	will have	threatened

Imperative

threaten

Impersonal

ing-Form

threatening

Past Participle

threatened

Continuous tenses

Present

I	am	threatening
you	are	threatening
he/she/it	is	threatening
we	are	threatening
you	are	threatening
they	are	threatening

Past

I	was	threatening
you	were	threatening
he/she/it	was	threatening
we	were	threatening
you	were	threatening
they	were	threatening

Present Perfect

I	have been	threatening
you	have been	threatening
he/she/it	has been	threatening
we	have been	threatening
you	have been	threatening
they	have been	threatening

Past Perfect

I	had been	threatening
you	had been	threatening
he/she/it	had been	threatening
we	had been	threatening
you	had been	threatening
they	had been	threatening

Will-Future

I	will be	threatening
you	will be	threatening
he/she/it	will be	threatening
we	will be	threatening
you	will be	threatening
they	will be	threatening

Going to-Future

I	am	going to be	threatening
you	are	going to be	threatening
he/she/it	is	going to be	threatening
we	are	going to be	threatening
you	are	going to be	threatening
they	are	going to be	threatening

Future Perfect

I	will have been	threatening
you	will have been	threatening
he/she/it	will have been	threatening
we	will have been	threatening
you	will have been	threatening
they	will have been	threatening

Conditional

I	would	threaten
you	would	threaten
he/she/it	would	threaten
we	would	threaten
you	would	threaten
they	would	threaten

Conditional Past

I	would have	threatened
you	would have	threatened
he/she/it	would have	threatened
we	would have	threatened
you	would have	threatened
they	would have	threatened

throw

- threw - thrown

werfen

Unregelmäßiges Verb

Simple tenses

Present

I	throw
you	throw
he/she/it	throws
we	throw
you	throw
they	throw

Past

I	threw
you	threw
he/she/it	threw
we	threw
you	threw
they	threw

Present Perfect

I	have	thrown
you	have	thrown
he/she/it	has	thrown
we	have	thrown
you	have	thrown
they	have	thrown

Past Perfect

I	had	thrown
you	had	thrown
he/she/it	had	thrown
we	had	thrown
you	had	thrown
they	had	thrown

Will-Future

I	will	throw
you	will	throw
he/she/it	will	throw
we	will	throw
you	will	throw
they	will	throw

Going to-Future

I	am	going to	throw
you	are	going to	throw
he/she/it	is	going to	throw
we	are	going to	throw
you	are	going to	throw
they	are	going to	throw

Future Perfect

I	will have	thrown
you	will have	thrown
he/she/it	will have	thrown
we	will have	thrown
you	will have	thrown
they	will have	thrown

Imperative

throw

Impersonal

ing-Form

throwing

Past Participle

thrown

Continuous tenses

Present

I	am	throwing
you	are	throwing
he/she/it	is	throwing
we	are	throwing
you	are	throwing
they	are	throwing

Past

I	was	throwing
you	were	throwing
he/she/it	was	throwing
we	were	throwing
you	were	throwing
they	were	throwing

Present Perfect

I	have been	throwing
you	have been	throwing
he/she/it	has been	throwing
we	have been	throwing
you	have been	throwing
they	have been	throwing

Past Perfect

I	had been	throwing
you	had been	throwing
he/she/it	had been	throwing
we	had been	throwing
you	had been	throwing
they	had been	throwing

Will-Future

I	will be	throwing
you	will be	throwing
he/she/it	will be	throwing
we	will be	throwing
you	will be	throwing
they	will be	throwing

Going to-Future

I	am	going to be	throwing
you	are	going to be	throwing
he/she/it	is	going to be	throwing
we	are	going to be	throwing
you	are	going to be	throwing
they	are	going to be	throwing

Future Perfect

I	will have been	throwing
you	will have been	throwing
he/she/it	will have been	throwing
we	will have been	throwing
you	will have been	throwing
they	will have been	throwing

Conditional

I	would	throw
you	would	throw
he/she/it	would	throw
we	would	throw
you	would	throw
they	would	throw

Conditional Past

I	would have	thrown
you	would have	thrown
he/she/it	would have	thrown
we	would have	thrown
you	would have	thrown
they	would have	thrown

Simple tenses

Present

I	touch
you	touch
he/she/it	touches
we	touch
you	touch
they	touch

Past

I	touched
you	touched
he/she/it	touched
we	touched
you	touched
they	touched

Present Perfect

I	have	touched
you	have	touched
he/she/it	has	touched
we	have	touched
you	have	touched
they	have	touched

Past Perfect

I	had	touched
you	had	touched
he/she/it	had	touched
we	had	touched
you	had	touched
they	had	touched

Will-Future

I	will	touch
you	will	touch
he/she/it	will	touch
we	will	touch
you	will	touch
they	will	touch

Going to-Future

I	am	going to	touch
you	are	going to	touch
he/she/it	is	going to	touch
we	are	going to	touch
you	are	going to	touch
they	are	going to	touch

Future Perfect

I	will have	touched
you	will have	touched
he/she/it	will have	touched
we	will have	touched
you	will have	touched
they	will have	touched

Imperative

touch

Impersonal

ing-Form

touching

Past Participle

touched

Continuous tenses

Present

I	am	touching
you	are	touching
he/she/it	is	touching
we	are	touching
you	are	touching
they	are	touching

Past

I	was	touching
you	were	touching
he/she/it	was	touching
we	were	touching
you	were	touching
they	were	touching

Present Perfect

I	have	been	touching
you	have	been	touching
he/she/it	has	been	touching
we	have	been	touching
you	have	been	touching
they	have	been	touching

Past Perfect

I	had been	touching
you	had been	touching
he/she/it	had been	touching
we	had been	touching
you	had been	touching
they	had been	touching

Will-Future

I	will be	touching
you	will be	touching
he/she/it	will be	touching
we	will be	touching
you	will be	touching
they	will be	touching

Going to-Future

I	am	going to be	touching
you	are	going to be	touching
he/she/it	is	going to be	touching
we	are	going to be	touching
you	are	going to be	touching
they	are	going to be	touching

Future Perfect

I	will have been	touching
you	will have been	touching
he/she/it	will have been	touching
we	will have been	touching
you	will have been	touching
they	will have been	touching

Conditional

I	would	touch
you	would	touch
he/she/it	would	touch
we	would	touch
you	would	touch
they	would	touch

Conditional Past

I	would have	touched
you	would have	touched
he/she/it	would have	touched
we	would have	touched
you	would have	touched
they	would have	touched

track

verfolgen

Regelmäßiges Verb

Simple tenses

Present

I	track
you	track
he/she/it	tracks
we	track
you	track
they	track

Past

I	tracked
you	tracked
he/she/it	tracked
we	tracked
you	tracked
they	tracked

Present Perfect

I	have	tracked
you	have	tracked
he/she/it	has	tracked
we	have	tracked
you	have	tracked
they	have	tracked

Past Perfect

I	had	tracked
you	had	tracked
he/she/it	had	tracked
we	had	tracked
you	had	tracked
they	had	tracked

***Will*-Future**

I	will	track
you	will	track
he/she/it	will	track
we	will	track
you	will	track
they	will	track

***Going to*-Future**

I	am	going to	track
you	are	going to	track
he/she/it	is	going to	track
we	are	going to	track
you	are	going to	track
they	are	going to	track

Future Perfect

I	will have	tracked
you	will have	tracked
he/she/it	will have	tracked
we	will have	tracked
you	will have	tracked
they	will have	tracked

Imperative

track

Impersonal

***ing*-Form**

tracking

Past Participle

tracked

Continuous tenses

Present

I	am	tracking
you	are	tracking
he/she/it	is	tracking
we	are	tracking
you	are	tracking
they	are	tracking

Past

I	was	tracking
you	were	tracking
he/she/it	was	tracking
we	were	tracking
you	were	tracking
they	were	tracking

Present Perfect

I	have been	tracking
you	have been	tracking
he/she/it	has been	tracking
we	have been	tracking
you	have been	tracking
they	have been	tracking

Past Perfect

I	had been	tracking
you	had been	tracking
he/she/it	had been	tracking
we	had been	tracking
you	had been	tracking
they	had been	tracking

***Will*-Future**

I	will be	tracking
you	will be	tracking
he/she/it	will be	tracking
we	will be	tracking
you	will be	tracking
they	will be	tracking

***Going to*-Future**

I	am	going to be	tracking
you	are	going to be	tracking
he/she/it	is	going to be	tracking
we	are	going to be	tracking
you	are	going to be	tracking
they	are	going to be	tracking

Future Perfect

I	will have been	tracking
you	will have been	tracking
he/she/it	will have been	tracking
we	will have been	tracking
you	will have been	tracking
they	will have been	tracking

Conditional

I	would	track
you	would	track
he/she/it	would	track
we	would	track
you	would	track
they	would	track

Conditional Past

I	would have	tracked
you	would have	tracked
he/she/it	would have	tracked
we	would have	tracked
you	would have	tracked
they	would have	tracked

Simple tenses

Present

I	trade
you	trade
he/she/it	trades
we	trade
you	trade
they	trade

Past

I	traded
you	traded
he/she/it	traded
we	traded
you	traded
they	traded

Present Perfect

I	have	traded
you	have	traded
he/she/it	has	traded
we	have	traded
you	have	traded
they	have	traded

Past Perfect

I	had	traded
you	had	traded
he/she/it	had	traded
we	had	traded
you	had	traded
they	had	traded

Will-Future

I	will	trade
you	will	trade
he/she/it	will	trade
we	will	trade
you	will	trade
they	will	trade

Going to-Future

I	am	going to	trade
you	are	going to	trade
he/she/it	is	going to	trade
we	are	going to	trade
you	are	going to	trade
they	are	going to	trade

Future Perfect

I	will have	traded
you	will have	traded
he/she/it	will have	traded
we	will have	traded
you	will have	traded
they	will have	traded

Imperative

trade

Impersonal

ing-Form

trading

Past Participle

traded

Continuous tenses

Present

I	am	trading
you	are	trading
he/she/it	is	trading
we	are	trading
you	are	trading
they	are	trading

Past

I	was	trading
you	were	trading
he/she/it	was	trading
we	were	trading
you	were	trading
they	were	trading

Present Perfect

I	have been	trading
you	have been	trading
he/she/it	has been	trading
we	have been	trading
you	have been	trading
they	have been	trading

Past Perfect

I	had been	trading
you	had been	trading
he/she/it	had been	trading
we	had been	trading
you	had been	trading
they	had been	trading

Will-Future

I	will be	trading
you	will be	trading
he/she/it	will be	trading
we	will be	trading
you	will be	trading
they	will be	trading

Going to-Future

I	am	going to be	trading
you	are	going to be	trading
he/she/it	is	going to be	trading
we	are	going to be	trading
you	are	going to be	trading
they	are	going to be	trading

Future Perfect

I	will have been	trading
you	will have been	trading
he/she/it	will have been	trading
we	will have been	trading
you	will have been	trading
they	will have been	trading

Conditional

I	would	trade
you	would	trade
he/she/it	would	trade
we	would	trade
you	would	trade
they	would	trade

Conditional Past

I	would have	traded
you	would have	traded
he/she/it	would have	traded
we	would have	traded
you	would have	traded
they	would have	traded

transfer

überweisen

Konsonantenverdopplung
Regelmäßiges Verb

Simple tenses

Present

I	transfer
you	transfer
he/she/it	transfers
we	transfer
you	transfer
they	transfer

Past

I	transferred
you	transferred
he/she/it	transferred
we	transferred
you	transferred
they	transferred

Present Perfect

I	have	transferred
you	have	transferred
he/she/it	has	transferred
we	have	transferred
you	have	transferred
they	have	transferred

Past Perfect

I	had	transferred
you	had	transferred
he/she/it	had	transferred
we	had	transferred
you	had	transferred
they	had	transferred

Will-Future

I	will	transfer
you	will	transfer
he/she/it	will	transfer
we	will	transfer
you	will	transfer
they	will	transfer

Going to-Future

I	am	going to	transfer
you	are	going to	transfer
he/she/it	is	going to	transfer
we	are	going to	transfer
you	are	going to	transfer
they	are	going to	transfer

Future Perfect

I	will have	transferred
you	will have	transferred
he/she/it	will have	transferred
we	will have	transferred
you	will have	transferred
they	will have	transferred

Imperative

transfer

Impersonal

ing-Form

transferring

Past Participle

transferred

Continuous tenses

Present

I	am	transferring
you	are	transferring
he/she/it	is	transferring
we	are	transferring
you	are	transferring
they	are	transferring

Past

I	was	transferring
you	were	transferring
he/she/it	was	transferring
we	were	transferring
you	were	transferring
they	were	transferring

Present Perfect

I	have been	transferring
you	have been	transferring
he/she/it	has been	transferring
we	have been	transferring
you	have been	transferring
they	have been	transferring

Past Perfect

I	had been	transferring
you	had been	transferring
he/she/it	had been	transferring
we	had been	transferring
you	had been	transferring
they	had been	transferring

Will-Future

I	will be	transferring
you	will be	transferring
he/she/it	will be	transferring
we	will be	transferring
you	will be	transferring
they	will be	transferring

Going to-Future

I	am	going to be	transferring
you	are	going to be	transferring
he/she/it	is	going to be	transferring
we	are	going to be	transferring
you	are	going to be	transferring
they	are	going to be	transferring

Future Perfect

I	will have been	transferring
you	will have been	transferring
he/she/it	will have been	transferring
we	will have been	transferring
you	will have been	transferring
they	will have been	transferring

Conditional

I	would	transfer
you	would	transfer
he/she/it	would	transfer
we	would	transfer
you	would	transfer
they	would	transfer

Conditional Past

I	would have	transferred
you	would have	transferred
he/she/it	would have	transferred
we	would have	transferred
you	would have	transferred
they	would have	transferred

+ **-ing** → ~~e~~ / + **-d** nicht **-ed**
Regelmäßiges Verb

übersetzen

translate

Simple tenses

Present

I	translate
you	translate
he/she/it	translates
we	translate
you	translate
they	translate

Past

I	translated
you	translated
he/she/it	translated
we	translated
you	translated
they	translated

Present Perfect

I	have	translated
you	have	translated
he/she/it	has	translated
we	have	translated
you	have	translated
they	have	translated

Past Perfect

I	had	translated
you	had	translated
he/she/it	had	translated
we	had	translated
you	had	translated
they	had	translated

Will-Future

I	will	translate
you	will	translate
he/she/it	will	translate
we	will	translate
you	will	translate
they	will	translate

Going to-Future

I	am	going to	translate
you	are	going to	translate
he/she/it	is	going to	translate
we	are	going to	translate
you	are	going to	translate
they	are	going to	translate

Future Perfect

I	will have	translated
you	will have	translated
he/she/it	will have	translated
we	will have	translated
you	will have	translated
they	will have	translated

Imperative

translate

Impersonal

ing-Form

translating

Past Participle

translated

Continuous tenses

Present

I	am	translating
you	are	translating
he/she/it	is	translating
we	are	translating
you	are	translating
they	are	translating

Past

I	was	translating
you	were	translating
he/she/it	was	translating
we	were	translating
you	were	translating
they	were	translating

Present Perfect

I	have been	translating
you	have been	translating
he/she/it	has been	translating
we	have been	translating
you	have been	translating
they	have been	translating

Past Perfect

I	had been	translating
you	had been	translating
he/she/it	had been	translating
we	had been	translating
you	had been	translating
they	had been	translating

Will-Future

I	will be	translating
you	will be	translating
he/she/it	will be	translating
we	will be	translating
you	will be	translating
they	will be	translating

Going to-Future

I	am	going to be	translating
you	are	going to be	translating
he/she/it	is	going to be	translating
we	are	going to be	translating
you	are	going to be	translating
they	are	going to be	translating

Future Perfect

I	will have been	translating
you	will have been	translating
he/she/it	will have been	translating
we	will have been	translating
you	will have been	translating
they	will have been	translating

Conditional

I	would	translate
you	would	translate
he/she/it	would	translate
we	would	translate
you	would	translate
they	would	translate

Conditional Past

I	would have	translated
you	would have	translated
he/she/it	would have	translated
we	would have	translated
you	would have	translated
they	would have	translated

transport

transportieren

Regelmäßiges Verb

Simple tenses

Present

I	transport
you	transport
he/she/it	transports
we	transport
you	transport
they	transport

Past

I	transported
you	transported
he/she/it	transported
we	transported
you	transported
they	transported

Present Perfect

I	have	transported
you	have	transported
he/she/it	has	transported
we	have	transported
you	have	transported
they	have	transported

Past Perfect

I	had	transported
you	had	transported
he/she/it	had	transported
we	had	transported
you	had	transported
they	had	transported

Will-Future

I	will	transport
you	will	transport
he/she/it	will	transport
we	will	transport
you	will	transport
they	will	transport

Going to-Future

I	am	going to	transport
you	are	going to	transport
he/she/it	is	going to	transport
we	are	going to	transport
you	are	going to	transport
they	are	going to	transport

Future Perfect

I	will have	transported
you	will have	transported
he/she/it	will have	transported
we	will have	transported
you	will have	transported
they	will have	transported

Imperative

transport

Impersonal

ing-Form

transporting

Past Participle

transported

Continuous tenses

Present

I	am	transporting
you	are	transporting
he/she/it	is	transporting
we	are	transporting
you	are	transporting
they	are	transporting

Past

I	was	transporting
you	were	transporting
he/she/it	was	transporting
we	were	transporting
you	were	transporting
they	were	transporting

Present Perfect

I	have been	transporting
you	have been	transporting
he/she/it	has been	transporting
we	have been	transporting
you	have been	transporting
they	have been	transporting

Past Perfect

I	had been	transporting
you	had been	transporting
he/she/it	had been	transporting
we	had been	transporting
you	had been	transporting
they	had been	transporting

Will-Future

I	will be	transporting
you	will be	transporting
he/she/it	will be	transporting
we	will be	transporting
you	will be	transporting
they	will be	transporting

Going to-Future

I	am	going to be	transporting
you	are	going to be	transporting
he/she/it	is	going to be	transporting
we	are	going to be	transporting
you	are	going to be	transporting
they	are	going to be	transporting

Future Perfect

I	will have been transporting
you	will have been transporting
he/she/it	will have been transporting
we	will have been transporting
you	will have been transporting
they	will have been transporting

Conditional

I	would	transport
you	would	transport
he/she/it	would	transport
we	would	transport
you	would	transport
they	would	transport

Conditional Past

I	would have	transported
you	would have	transported
he/she/it	would have	transported
we	would have	transported
you	would have	transported
they	would have	transported

Konsonantenverdopplung im BE.
Im AE keine Verdopplung.
Regelmäßiges Verb

reisen

travel

Simple tenses

Present

I	travel
you	travel
he/she/it	travels
we	travel
you	travel
they	travel

Past

I	travelled
you	travelled
he/she/it	travelled
we	travelled
you	travelled
they	travelled

Present Perfect

I	have	travelled
you	have	travelled
he/she/it	has	travelled
we	have	travelled
you	have	travelled
they	have	travelled

Past Perfect

I	had	travelled
you	had	travelled
he/she/it	had	travelled
we	had	travelled
you	had	travelled
they	had	travelled

Will-Future

I	will	travel
you	will	travel
he/she/it	will	travel
we	will	travel
you	will	travel
they	will	travel

Going to-Future

I	am	going to	travel
you	are	going to	travel
he/she/it	is	going to	travel
we	are	going to	travel
you	are	going to	travel
they	are	going to	travel

Future Perfect

I	will have	travelled
you	will have	travelled
he/she/it	will have	travelled
we	will have	travelled
you	will have	travelled
they	will have	travelled

Imperative

travel

Impersonal

ing-Form

travelling

Past Participle

travelled

Continuous tenses

Present

I	am	travelling
you	are	travelling
he/she/it	is	travelling
we	are	travelling
you	are	travelling
they	are	travelling

Past

I	was	travelling
you	were	travelling
he/she/it	was	travelling
we	were	travelling
you	were	travelling
they	were	travelling

Present Perfect

I	have been	travelling
you	have been	travelling
he/she/it	has been	travelling
we	have been	travelling
you	have been	travelling
they	have been	travelling

Past Perfect

I	had been	travelling
you	had been	travelling
he/she/it	had been	travelling
we	had been	travelling
you	had been	travelling
they	had been	travelling

Will-Future

I	will be	travelling
you	will be	travelling
he/she/it	will be	travelling
we	will be	travelling
you	will be	travelling
they	will be	travelling

Going to-Future

I	am	going to be	travelling
you	are	going to be	travelling
he/she/it	is	going to be	travelling
we	are	going to be	travelling
you	are	going to be	travelling
they	are	going to be	travelling

Future Perfect

I	will have been	travelling
you	will have been	travelling
he/she/it	will have been	travelling
we	will have been	travelling
you	will have been	travelling
they	will have been	travelling

Conditional

I	would	travel
you	would	travel
he/she/it	would	travel
we	would	travel
you	would	travel
they	would	travel

Conditional Past

I	would have	travelled
you	would have	travelled
he/she/it	would have	travelled
we	would have	travelled
you	would have	travelled
they	would have	travelled

treat

behandeln

Regelmäßiges Verb

Simple tenses

Present

I	treat
you	treat
he/she/it	treats
we	treat
you	treat
they	treat

Past

I	treated
you	treated
he/she/it	treated
we	treated
you	treated
they	treated

Present Perfect

I	have	treated
you	have	treated
he/she/it	has	treated
we	have	treated
you	have	treated
they	have	treated

Past Perfect

I	had	treated
you	had	treated
he/she/it	had	treated
we	had	treated
you	had	treated
they	had	treated

Will-Future

I	will	treat
you	will	treat
he/she/it	will	treat
we	will	treat
you	will	treat
they	will	treat

Going to-Future

I	am	going to	treat
you	are	going to	treat
he/she/it	is	going to	treat
we	are	going to	treat
you	are	going to	treat
they	are	going to	treat

Future Perfect

I	will have	treated
you	will have	treated
he/she/it	will have	treated
we	will have	treated
you	will have	treated
they	will have	treated

Imperative

treat

Impersonal

ing-Form

treating

Past Participle

treated

Continuous tenses

Present

I	am	treating
you	are	treating
he/she/it	is	treating
we	are	treating
you	are	treating
they	are	treating

Past

I	was	treating
you	were	treating
he/she/it	was	treating
we	were	treating
you	were	treating
they	were	treating

Present Perfect

I	have been	treating
you	have been	treating
he/she/it	has been	treating
we	have been	treating
you	have been	treating
they	have been	treating

Past Perfect

I	had been	treating
you	had been	treating
he/she/it	had been	treating
we	had been	treating
you	had been	treating
they	had been	treating

Will-Future

I	will be	treating
you	will be	treating
he/she/it	will be	treating
we	will be	treating
you	will be	treating
they	will be	treating

Going to-Future

I	am	going to be	treating
you	are	going to be	treating
he/she/it	is	going to be	treating
we	are	going to be	treating
you	are	going to be	treating
they	are	going to be	treating

Future Perfect

I	will have been	treating
you	will have been	treating
he/she/it	will have been	treating
we	will have been	treating
you	will have been	treating
they	will have been	treating

Conditional

I	would	treat
you	would	treat
he/she/it	would	treat
we	would	treat
you	would	treat
they	would	treat

Conditional Past

I	would have	treated
you	would have	treated
he/she/it	would have	treated
we	would have	treated
you	would have	treated
they	would have	treated

trust

Regelmäßiges Verb

Simple tenses

Present

I	trust
you	trust
he/she/it	trusts
we	trust
you	trust
they	trust

Past

I	trusted
you	trusted
he/she/it	trusted
we	trusted
you	trusted
they	trusted

Present Perfect

I	have	trusted
you	have	trusted
he/she/it	has	trusted
we	have	trusted
you	have	trusted
they	have	trusted

Past Perfect

I	had	trusted
you	had	trusted
he/she/it	had	trusted
we	had	trusted
you	had	trusted
they	had	trusted

Will-Future

I	will	trust
you	will	trust
he/she/it	will	trust
we	will	trust
you	will	trust
they	will	trust

Going to-Future

I	am	going to	trust
you	are	going to	trust
he/she/it	is	going to	trust
we	are	going to	trust
you	are	going to	trust
they	are	going to	trust

Future Perfect

I	will have	trusted
you	will have	trusted
he/she/it	will have	trusted
we	will have	trusted
you	will have	trusted
they	will have	trusted

Imperative

trust

Impersonal

ing-Form

trusting

Past Participle

trusted

Continuous tenses

Present

I	am	trusting
you	are	trusting
he/she/it	is	trusting
we	are	trusting
you	are	trusting
they	are	trusting

Past

I	was	trusting
you	were	trusting
he/she/it	was	trusting
we	were	trusting
you	were	trusting
they	were	trusting

Present Perfect

I	have been	trusting
you	have been	trusting
he/she/it	has been	trusting
we	have been	trusting
you	have been	trusting
they	have been	trusting

Past Perfect

I	had been	trusting
you	had been	trusting
he/she/it	had been	trusting
we	had been	trusting
you	had been	trusting
they	had been	trusting

Will-Future

I	will be	trusting
you	will be	trusting
he/she/it	will be	trusting
we	will be	trusting
you	will be	trusting
they	will be	trusting

Going to-Future

I	am	going to be	trusting
you	are	going to be	trusting
he/she/it	is	going to be	trusting
we	are	going to be	trusting
you	are	going to be	trusting
they	are	going to be	trusting

Future Perfect

I	will have been	trusting
you	will have been	trusting
he/she/it	will have been	trusting
we	will have been	trusting
you	will have been	trusting
they	will have been	trusting

Conditional

I	would	trust
you	would	trust
he/she/it	would	trust
we	would	trust
you	would	trust
they	would	trust

Conditional Past

I	would have	trusted
you	would have	trusted
he/she/it	would have	trusted
we	would have	trusted
you	would have	trusted
they	would have	trusted

turn

drehen

Regelmäßiges Verb

Simple tenses

Present

I	turn
you	turn
he/she/it	turns
we	turn
you	turn
they	turn

Past

I	turned
you	turned
he/she/it	turned
we	turned
you	turned
they	turned

Present Perfect

I	have	turned
you	have	turned
he/she/it	has	turned
we	have	turned
you	have	turned
they	have	turned

Past Perfect

I	had	turned
you	had	turned
he/she/it	had	turned
we	had	turned
you	had	turned
they	had	turned

Will-Future

I	will	turn
you	will	turn
he/she/it	will	turn
we	will	turn
you	will	turn
they	will	turn

Going to-Future

I	am	going to	turn
you	are	going to	turn
he/she/it	is	going to	turn
we	are	going to	turn
you	are	going to	turn
they	are	going to	turn

Future Perfect

I	will have	turned
you	will have	turned
he/she/it	will have	turned
we	will have	turned
you	will have	turned
they	will have	turned

Imperative

turn

Impersonal

ing-Form

turning

Past Participle

turned

Continuous tenses

Present

I	am	turning
you	are	turning
he/she/it	is	turning
we	are	turning
you	are	turning
they	are	turning

Past

I	was	turning
you	were	turning
he/she/it	was	turning
we	were	turning
you	were	turning
they	were	turning

Present Perfect

I	have been	turning
you	have been	turning
he/she/it	has been	turning
we	have been	turning
you	have been	turning
they	have been	turning

Past Perfect

I	had been	turning
you	had been	turning
he/she/it	had been	turning
we	had been	turning
you	had been	turning
they	had been	turning

Will-Future

I	will be	turning
you	will be	turning
he/she/it	will be	turning
we	will be	turning
you	will be	turning
they	will be	turning

Going to-Future

I	am	going to be	turning
you	are	going to be	turning
he/she/it	is	going to be	turning
we	are	going to be	turning
you	are	going to be	turning
they	are	going to be	turning

Future Perfect

I	will have been	turning
you	will have been	turning
he/she/it	will have been	turning
we	will have been	turning
you	will have been	turning
they	will have been	turning

Conditional

I	would	turn
you	would	turn
he/she/it	would	turn
we	would	turn
you	would	turn
they	would	turn

Conditional Past

I	would have	turned
you	would have	turned
he/she/it	would have	turned
we	would have	turned
you	would have	turned
they	would have	turned

Simple tenses

Present

I	twist
you	twist
he/she/it	twists
we	twist
you	twist
they	twist

Past

I	twisted
you	twisted
he/she/it	twisted
we	twisted
you	twisted
they	twisted

Present Perfect

I	have	twisted
you	have	twisted
he/she/it	has	twisted
we	have	twisted
you	have	twisted
they	have	twisted

Past Perfect

I	had	twisted
you	had	twisted
he/she/it	had	twisted
we	had	twisted
you	had	twisted
they	had	twisted

Will-Future

I	will	twist
you	will	twist
he/she/it	will	twist
we	will	twist
you	will	twist
they	will	twist

Going to-Future

I	am	going to	twist
you	are	going to	twist
he/she/it	is	going to	twist
we	are	going to	twist
you	are	going to	twist
they	are	going to	twist

Future Perfect

I	will have	twisted
you	will have	twisted
he/she/it	will have	twisted
we	will have	twisted
you	will have	twisted
they	will have	twisted

Imperative

twist

Impersonal

ing-Form

twisting

Past Participle

twisted

Continuous tenses

Present

I	am	twisting
you	are	twisting
he/she/it	is	twisting
we	are	twisting
you	are	twisting
they	are	twisting

Past

I	was	twisting
you	were	twisting
he/she/it	was	twisting
we	were	twisting
you	were	twisting
they	were	twisting

Present Perfect

I	have been	twisting
you	have been	twisting
he/she/it	has been	twisting
we	have been	twisting
you	have been	twisting
they	have been	twisting

Past Perfect

I	had been	twisting
you	had been	twisting
he/she/it	had been	twisting
we	had been	twisting
you	had been	twisting
they	had been	twisting

Will-Future

I	will be	twisting
you	will be	twisting
he/she/it	will be	twisting
we	will be	twisting
you	will be	twisting
they	will be	twisting

Going to-Future

I	am	going to be	twisting
you	are	going to be	twisting
he/she/it	is	going to be	twisting
we	are	going to be	twisting
you	are	going to be	twisting
they	are	going to be	twisting

Future Perfect

I	will have been	twisting
you	will have been	twisting
he/she/it	will have been	twisting
we	will have been	twisting
you	will have been	twisting
they	will have been	twisting

Conditional

I	would	twist
you	would	twist
he/she/it	would	twist
we	would	twist
you	would	twist
they	would	twist

Conditional Past

I	would have	twisted
you	would have	twisted
he/she/it	would have	twisted
we	would have	twisted
you	would have	twisted
they	would have	twisted

understand

- understood - understood

verstehen

Unregelmäßiges Verb

Simple tenses

Present

I	understand
you	understand
he/she/it	understands
we	understand
you	understand
they	understand

Past

I	understood
you	understood
he/she/it	understood
we	understood
you	understood
they	understood

Present Perfect

I	have	understood
you	have	understood
he/she/it	has	understood
we	have	understood
you	have	understood
they	have	understood

Past Perfect

I	had	understood
you	had	understood
he/she/it	had	understood
we	had	understood
you	had	understood
they	had	understood

Will-Future

I	will	understand
you	will	understand
he/she/it	will	understand
we	will	understand
you	will	understand
they	will	understand

Going to-Future

I	am	going to	understand
you	are	going to	understand
he/she/it	is	going to	understand
we	are	going to	understand
you	are	going to	understand
they	are	going to	understand

Future Perfect

I	will have	understood
you	will have	understood
he/she/it	will have	understood
we	will have	understood
you	will have	understood
they	will have	understood

Imperative

understand

Impersonal

ing-Form

understanding

Past Participle

understood

Continuous tenses

Present

I	am	understanding
you	are	understanding
he/she/it	is	understanding
we	are	understanding
you	are	understanding
they	are	understanding

Past

I	was	understanding
you	were	understanding
he/she/it	was	understanding
we	were	understanding
you	were	understanding
they	were	understanding

Present Perfect

I	have been	understanding
you	have been	understanding
he/she/it	has been	understanding
we	have been	understanding
you	have been	understanding
they	have been	understanding

Past Perfect

I	had been	understanding
you	had been	understanding
he/she/it	had been	understanding
we	had been	understanding
you	had been	understanding
they	had been	understanding

Will-Future

I	will be	understanding
you	will be	understanding
he/she/it	will be	understanding
we	will be	understanding
you	will be	understanding
they	will be	understanding

Going to-Future

I	am	going to be	understanding
you	are	going to be	understanding
he/she/it	is	going to be	understanding
we	are	going to be	understanding
you	are	going to be	understanding
they	are	going to be	understanding

Future Perfect

I	will have been	understanding
you	will have been	understanding
he/she/it	will have been	understanding
we	will have been	understanding
you	will have been	understanding
they	will have been	understanding

Conditional

I	would	understand
you	would	understand
he/she/it	would	understand
we	would	understand
you	would	understand
they	would	understand

Conditional Past

I	would have	understood
you	would have	understood
he/she/it	would have	understood
we	would have	understood
you	would have	understood
they	would have	understood

benutzen

use

Simple tenses

Present

I	use
you	use
he/she/it	uses
we	use
you	use
they	use

Past

I	used
you	used
he/she/it	used
we	used
you	used
they	used

Present Perfect

I	have	used
you	have	used
he/she/it	has	used
we	have	used
you	have	used
they	have	used

Past Perfect

I	had	used
you	had	used
he/she/it	had	used
we	had	used
you	had	used
they	had	used

Will-Future

I	will	use
you	will	use
he/she/it	will	use
we	will	use
you	will	use
they	will	use

Going to-Future

I	am	going to	use
you	are	going to	use
he/she/it	is	going to	use
we	are	going to	use
you	are	going to	use
they	are	going to	use

Future Perfect

I	will have	used
you	will have	used
he/she/it	will have	used
we	will have	used
you	will have	used
they	will have	used

Imperative

use

Impersonal

ing-Form

using

Past Participle

used

Continuous tenses

Present

I	am	using
you	are	using
he/she/it	is	using
we	are	using
you	are	using
they	are	using

Past

I	was	using
you	were	using
he/she/it	was	using
we	were	using
you	were	using
they	were	using

Present Perfect

I	have been	using
you	have been	using
he/she/it	has been	using
we	have been	using
you	have been	using
they	have been	using

Past Perfect

I	had been	using
you	had been	using
he/she/it	had been	using
we	had been	using
you	had been	using
they	had been	using

Will-Future

I	will be	using
you	will be	using
he/she/it	will be	using
we	will be	using
you	will be	using
they	will be	using

Going to-Future

I	am	going to be	using
you	are	going to be	using
he/she/it	is	going to be	using
we	are	going to be	using
you	are	going to be	using
they	are	going to be	using

Future Perfect

I	will have been	using
you	will have been	using
he/she/it	will have been	using
we	will have been	using
you	will have been	using
they	will have been	using

Conditional

I	would	use
you	would	use
he/she/it	would	use
we	would	use
you	would	use
they	would	use

Conditional Past

I	would have	used
you	would have	used
he/she/it	would have	used
we	would have	used
you	would have	used
they	would have	used

vary

variieren

-y → **-ie** vor **-s** / **-y** → **-i** vor **-ed**
Regelmäßiges Verb

Simple tenses

Present

I	vary
you	vary
he/she/it	varies
we	vary
you	vary
they	vary

Past

I	varied
you	varied
he/she/it	varied
we	varied
you	varied
they	varied

Present Perfect

I	have	varied
you	have	varied
he/she/it	has	varied
we	have	varied
you	have	varied
they	have	varied

Past Perfect

I	had	varied
you	had	varied
he/she/it	had	varied
we	had	varied
you	had	varied
they	had	varied

Will-Future

I	will	vary
you	will	vary
he/she/it	will	vary
we	will	vary
you	will	vary
they	will	vary

Going to-Future

I	am	going to	vary
you	are	going to	vary
he/she/it	is	going to	vary
we	are	going to	vary
you	are	going to	vary
they	are	going to	vary

Future Perfect

I	will have	varied
you	will have	varied
he/she/it	will have	varied
we	will have	varied
you	will have	varied
they	will have	varied

Imperative

vary

Impersonal

ing-Form

varying

Past Participle

varied

Continuous tenses

Present

I	am	varying
you	are	varying
he/she/it	is	varying
we	are	varying
you	are	varying
they	are	varying

Past

I	was	varying
you	were	varying
he/she/it	was	varying
we	were	varying
you	were	varying
they	were	varying

Present Perfect

I	have been	varying
you	have been	varying
he/she/it	has been	varying
we	have been	varying
you	have been	varying
they	have been	varying

Past Perfect

I	had been	varying
you	had been	varying
he/she/it	had been	varying
we	had been	varying
you	had been	varying
they	had been	varying

Will-Future

I	will be	varying
you	will be	varying
he/she/it	will be	varying
we	will be	varying
you	will be	varying
they	will be	varying

Going to-Future

I	am	going to be	varying
you	are	going to be	varying
he/she/it	is	going to be	varying
we	are	going to be	varying
you	are	going to be	varying
they	are	going to be	varying

Future Perfect

I	will have been	varying
you	will have been	varying
he/she/it	will have been	varying
we	will have been	varying
you	will have been	varying
they	will have been	varying

Conditional

I	would	vary
you	would	vary
he/she/it	would	vary
we	would	vary
you	would	vary
they	would	vary

Conditional Past

I	would have	varied
you	would have	varied
he/she/it	would have	varied
we	would have	varied
you	would have	varied
they	would have	varied

Simple tenses

Present

I	visit
you	visit
he/she/it	visits
we	visit
you	visit
they	visit

Past

I	visited
you	visited
he/she/it	visited
we	visited
you	visited
they	visited

Present Perfect

I	have	visited
you	have	visited
he/she/it	has	visited
we	have	visited
you	have	visited
they	have	visited

Past Perfect

I	had	visited
you	had	visited
he/she/it	had	visited
we	had	visited
you	had	visited
they	had	visited

Will-Future

I	will	visit
you	will	visit
he/she/it	will	visit
we	will	visit
you	will	visit
they	will	visit

Going to-Future

I	am	going to	visit
you	are	going to	visit
he/she/it	is	going to	visit
we	are	going to	visit
you	are	going to	visit
they	are	going to	visit

Future Perfect

I	will have	visited
you	will have	visited
he/she/it	will have	visited
we	will have	visited
you	will have	visited
they	will have	visited

Imperative

visit

Impersonal

ing-Form

visiting

Past Participle

visited

Continuous tenses

Present

I	am	visiting
you	are	visiting
he/she/it	is	visiting
we	are	visiting
you	are	visiting
they	are	visiting

Past

I	was	visiting
you	were	visiting
he/she/it	was	visiting
we	were	visiting
you	were	visiting
they	were	visiting

Present Perfect

I	have been	visiting
you	have been	visiting
he/she/it	has been	visiting
we	have been	visiting
you	have been	visiting
they	have been	visiting

Past Perfect

I	had been	visiting
you	had been	visiting
he/she/it	had been	visiting
we	had been	visiting
you	had been	visiting
they	had been	visiting

Will-Future

I	will be	visiting
you	will be	visiting
he/she/it	will be	visiting
we	will be	visiting
you	will be	visiting
they	will be	visiting

Going to-Future

I	am	going to be	visiting
you	are	going to be	visiting
he/she/it	is	going to be	visiting
we	are	going to be	visiting
you	are	going to be	visiting
they	are	going to be	visiting

Future Perfect

I	will have been	visiting
you	will have been	visiting
he/she/it	will have been	visiting
we	will have been	visiting
you	will have been	visiting
they	will have been	visiting

Conditional

I	would	visit
you	would	visit
he/she/it	would	visit
we	would	visit
you	would	visit
they	would	visit

Conditional Past

I	would have	visited
you	would have	visited
he/she/it	would have	visited
we	would have	visited
you	would have	visited
they	would have	visited

vote

wählen

+ **-ing** → ~~e~~ / + **-d** nicht **-ed**
Regelmäßiges Verb

Simple tenses

Present

I	vote
you	vote
he/she/it	votes
we	vote
you	vote
they	vote

Past

I	voted
you	voted
he/she/it	voted
we	voted
you	voted
they	voted

Present Perfect

I	have	voted
you	have	voted
he/she/it	has	voted
we	have	voted
you	have	voted
they	have	voted

Past Perfect

I	had	voted
you	had	voted
he/she/it	had	voted
we	had	voted
you	had	voted
they	had	voted

Will-Future

I	will	vote
you	will	vote
he/she/it	will	vote
we	will	vote
you	will	vote
they	will	vote

Going to-Future

I	am	going to	vote
you	are	going to	vote
he/she/it	is	going to	vote
we	are	going to	vote
you	are	going to	vote
they	are	going to	vote

Future Perfect

I	will have	voted
you	will have	voted
he/she/it	will have	voted
we	will have	voted
you	will have	voted
they	will have	voted

Imperative

vote

Impersonal

ing-Form

voting

Past Participle

voted

Continuous tenses

Present

I	am	voting
you	are	voting
he/she/it	is	voting
we	are	voting
you	are	voting
they	are	voting

Past

I	was	voting
you	were	voting
he/she/it	was	voting
we	were	voting
you	were	voting
they	were	voting

Present Perfect

I	have been	voting
you	have been	voting
he/she/it	has been	voting
we	have been	voting
you	have been	voting
they	have been	voting

Past Perfect

I	had been	voting
you	had been	voting
he/she/it	had been	voting
we	had been	voting
you	had been	voting
they	had been	voting

Will-Future

I	will be	voting
you	will be	voting
he/she/it	will be	voting
we	will be	voting
you	will be	voting
they	will be	voting

Going to-Future

I	am	going to be	voting
you	are	going to be	voting
he/she/it	is	going to be	voting
we	are	going to be	voting
you	are	going to be	voting
they	are	going to be	voting

Future Perfect

I	will have been	voting
you	will have been	voting
he/she/it	will have been	voting
we	will have been	voting
you	will have been	voting
they	will have been	voting

Conditional

I	would	vote
you	would	vote
he/she/it	would	vote
we	would	vote
you	would	vote
they	would	vote

Conditional Past

I	would have	voted
you	would have	voted
he/she/it	would have	voted
we	would have	voted
you	would have	voted
they	would have	voted

Simple tenses

Present

I	wait
you	wait
he/she/it	waits
we	wait
you	wait
they	wait

Past

I	waited
you	waited
he/she/it	waited
we	waited
you	waited
they	waited

Present Perfect

I	have	waited
you	have	waited
he/she/it	has	waited
we	have	waited
you	have	waited
they	have	waited

Past Perfect

I	had	waited
you	had	waited
he/she/it	had	waited
we	had	waited
you	had	waited
they	had	waited

Will-Future

I	will	wait
you	will	wait
he/she/it	will	wait
we	will	wait
you	will	wait
they	will	wait

Going to-Future

I	am	going to	wait
you	are	going to	wait
he/she/it	is	going to	wait
we	are	going to	wait
you	are	going to	wait
they	are	going to	wait

Future Perfect

I	will have	waited
you	will have	waited
he/she/it	will have	waited
we	will have	waited
you	will have	waited
they	will have	waited

Imperative

wait

Impersonal

ing-Form

waiting

Past Participle

waited

Continuous tenses

Present

I	am	waiting
you	are	waiting
he/she/it	is	waiting
we	are	waiting
you	are	waiting
they	are	waiting

Past

I	was	waiting
you	were	waiting
he/she/it	was	waiting
we	were	waiting
you	were	waiting
they	were	waiting

Present Perfect

I	have been	waiting
you	have been	waiting
he/she/it	has been	waiting
we	have been	waiting
you	have been	waiting
they	have been	waiting

Past Perfect

I	had been	waiting
you	had been	waiting
he/she/it	had been	waiting
we	had been	waiting
you	had been	waiting
they	had been	waiting

Will-Future

I	will be	waiting
you	will be	waiting
he/she/it	will be	waiting
we	will be	waiting
you	will be	waiting
they	will be	waiting

Going to-Future

I	am	going to be	waiting
you	are	going to be	waiting
he/she/it	is	going to be	waiting
we	are	going to be	waiting
you	are	going to be	waiting
they	are	going to be	waiting

Future Perfect

I	will have been	waiting
you	will have been	waiting
he/she/it	will have been	waiting
we	will have been	waiting
you	will have been	waiting
they	will have been	waiting

Conditional

I	would	wait
you	would	wait
he/she/it	would	wait
we	would	wait
you	would	wait
they	would	wait

Conditional Past

I	would have	waited
you	would have	waited
he/she/it	would have	waited
we	would have	waited
you	would have	waited
they	would have	waited

wake

- woke/waked - woken/waked

aufwachen

+ **-ing** → ~~e~~ / + **-d** nicht **-ed**
Unregelmäßiges Verb

Simple tenses

Present

I	wake
you	wake
he/she/it	wakes
we	wake
you	wake
they	wake

Past

I	woke | waked
you	woke | waked
he/she/it	woke | waked
we	woke | waked
you	woke | waked
they	woke | waked

Present Perfect

I	have	woken | waked
you	have	woken | waked
he/she/it	has	woken | waked
we	have	woken | waked
you	have	woken | waked
they	have	woken | waked

Past Perfect

I	had	woken | waked
you	had	woken | waked
he/she/it	had	woken | waked
we	had	woken | waked
you	had	woken | waked
they	had	woken | waked

Will-Future

I	will	wake
you	will	wake
he/she/it	will	wake
we	will	wake
you	will	wake
they	will	wake

Going to-Future

I	am	going to	wake
you	are	going to	wake
he/she/it	is	going to	wake
we	are	going to	wake
you	are	going to	wake
they	are	going to	wake

Future Perfect

I	will have	woken | waked
you	will have	woken | waked
he/she/it	will have	woken | waked
we	will have	woken | waked
you	will have	woken | waked
they	will have	woken | waked

Imperative

wake

Impersonal

ing-Form

waking

Past Participle

woken | waked

Continuous tenses

Present

I	am	waking
you	are	waking
he/she/it	is	waking
we	are	waking
you	are	waking
they	are	waking

Past

I	was	waking
you	were	waking
he/she/it	was	waking
we	were	waking
you	were	waking
they	were	waking

Present Perfect

I	have	been	waking
you	have	been	waking
he/she/it	has	been	waking
we	have	been	waking
you	have	been	waking
they	have	been	waking

Past Perfect

I	had been	waking
you	had been	waking
he/she/it	had been	waking
we	had been	waking
you	had been	waking
they	had been	waking

Will-Future

I	will be	waking
you	will be	waking
he/she/it	will be	waking
we	will be	waking
you	will be	waking
they	will be	waking

Going to-Future

I	am	going to be	waking
you	are	going to be	waking
he/she/it	is	going to be	waking
we	are	going to be	waking
you	are	going to be	waking
they	are	going to be	waking

Future Perfect

I	will have been	waking
you	will have been	waking
he/she/it	will have been	waking
we	will have been	waking
you	will have been	waking
they	will have been	waking

Conditional

I	would	wake
you	would	wake
he/she/it	would	wake
we	would	wake
you	would	wake
they	would	wake

Conditional Past

I	would have	woken | waked
you	would have	woken | waked
he/she/it	would have	woken | waked
we	would have	woken | waked
you	would have	woken | waked
they	would have	woken | waked

walk

Regelmäßiges Verb

Simple tenses

Present

I	walk
you	walk
he/she/it	walks
we	walk
you	walk
they	walk

Past

I	walked
you	walked
he/she/it	walked
we	walked
you	walked
they	walked

Present Perfect

I	have	walked
you	have	walked
he/she/it	has	walked
we	have	walked
you	have	walked
they	have	walked

Past Perfect

I	had	walked
you	had	walked
he/she/it	had	walked
we	had	walked
you	had	walked
they	had	walked

Will-Future

I	will	walk
you	will	walk
he/she/it	will	walk
we	will	walk
you	will	walk
they	will	walk

Going to-Future

I	am	going to	walk
you	are	going to	walk
he/she/it	is	going to	walk
we	are	going to	walk
you	are	going to	walk
they	are	going to	walk

Future Perfect

I	will have	walked
you	will have	walked
he/she/it	will have	walked
we	will have	walked
you	will have	walked
they	will have	walked

Imperative

walk

Impersonal

ing-Form

walking

Past Participle

walked

Continuous tenses

Present

I	am	walking
you	are	walking
he/she/it	is	walking
we	are	walking
you	are	walking
they	are	walking

Past

I	was	walking
you	were	walking
he/she/it	was	walking
we	were	walking
you	were	walking
they	were	walking

Present Perfect

I	have been	walking
you	have been	walking
he/she/it	has been	walking
we	have been	walking
you	have been	walking
they	have been	walking

Past Perfect

I	had been	walking
you	had been	walking
he/she/it	had been	walking
we	had been	walking
you	had been	walking
they	had been	walking

Will-Future

I	will be	walking
you	will be	walking
he/she/it	will be	walking
we	will be	walking
you	will be	walking
they	will be	walking

Going to-Future

I	am	going to be	walking
you	are	going to be	walking
he/she/it	is	going to be	walking
we	are	going to be	walking
you	are	going to be	walking
they	are	going to be	walking

Future Perfect

I	will have been	walking
you	will have been	walking
he/she/it	will have been	walking
we	will have been	walking
you	will have been	walking
they	will have been	walking

Conditional

I	would	walk
you	would	walk
he/she/it	would	walk
we	would	walk
you	would	walk
they	would	walk

Conditional Past

I	would have	walked
you	would have	walked
he/she/it	would have	walked
we	would have	walked
you	would have	walked
they	would have	walked

want

wollen

Keine *Present Continuous*-Form möglich.
Regelmäßiges Verb, Modalverb

Simple tenses

Present

I	want
you	want
he/she/it	wants
we	want
you	want
they	want

Past

I	wanted
you	wanted
he/she/it	wanted
we	wanted
you	wanted
they	wanted

Present Perfect

I	have	wanted
you	have	wanted
he/she/it	has	wanted
we	have	wanted
you	have	wanted
they	have	wanted

Past Perfect

I	had	wanted
you	had	wanted
he/she/it	had	wanted
we	had	wanted
you	had	wanted
they	had	wanted

Will-Future

I	will	want
you	will	want
he/she/it	will	want
we	will	want
you	will	want
they	will	want

Going to-Future

I	am	going to	want
you	are	going to	want
he/she/it	is	going to	want
we	are	going to	want
you	are	going to	want
they	are	going to	want

Future Perfect

I	will have	wanted
you	will have	wanted
he/she/it	will have	wanted
we	will have	wanted
you	will have	wanted
they	will have	wanted

Imperative

want

Impersonal

ing-Form

wanting

Past Participle

wanted

Continuous tenses

Present

I	am	wanting
you	are	wanting
he/she/it	is	wanting
we	are	wanting
you	are	wanting
they	are	wanting

Past

I	was	wanting
you	were	wanting
he/she/it	was	wanting
we	were	wanting
you	were	wanting
they	were	wanting

Present Perfect

I	have been	wanting
you	have been	wanting
he/she/it	has been	wanting
we	have been	wanting
you	have been	wanting
they	have been	wanting

Past Perfect

I	had been	wanting
you	had been	wanting
he/she/it	had been	wanting
we	had been	wanting
you	had been	wanting
they	had been	wanting

Will-Future

I	will be	wanting
you	will be	wanting
he/she/it	will be	wanting
we	will be	wanting
you	will be	wanting
they	will be	wanting

Going to-Future

I	am	going to be	wanting
you	are	going to be	wanting
he/she/it	is	going to be	wanting
we	are	going to be	wanting
you	are	going to be	wanting
they	are	going to be	wanting

Future Perfect

I	will have been	wanting
you	will have been	wanting
he/she/it	will have been	wanting
we	will have been	wanting
you	will have been	wanting
they	will have been	wanting

Conditional

I	would	want
you	would	want
he/she/it	would	want
we	would	want
you	would	want
they	would	want

Conditional Past

I	would have	wanted
you	would have	wanted
he/she/it	would have	wanted
we	would have	wanted
you	would have	wanted
they	would have	wanted

Simple tenses

Present

I	warn
you	warn
he/she/it	warns
we	warn
you	warn
they	warn

Past

I	warned
you	warned
he/she/it	warned
we	warned
you	warned
they	warned

Present Perfect

I	have	warned
you	have	warned
he/she/it	has	warned
we	have	warned
you	have	warned
they	have	warned

Past Perfect

I	had	warned
you	had	warned
he/she/it	had	warned
we	had	warned
you	had	warned
they	had	warned

Will-Future

I	will	warn
you	will	warn
he/she/it	will	warn
we	will	warn
you	will	warn
they	will	warn

Going to-Future

I	am	going to	warn
you	are	going to	warn
he/she/it	is	going to	warn
we	are	going to	warn
you	are	going to	warn
they	are	going to	warn

Future Perfect

I	will have	warned
you	will have	warned
he/she/it	will have	warned
we	will have	warned
you	will have	warned
they	will have	warned

Imperative

warn

Impersonal

ing-Form

warning

Past Participle

warned

Continuous tenses

Present

I	am	warning
you	are	warning
he/she/it	is	warning
we	are	warning
you	are	warning
they	are	warning

Past

I	was	warning
you	were	warning
he/she/it	was	warning
we	were	warning
you	were	warning
they	were	warning

Present Perfect

I	have been	warning
you	have been	warning
he/she/it	has been	warning
we	have been	warning
you	have been	warning
they	have been	warning

Past Perfect

I	had been	warning
you	had been	warning
he/she/it	had been	warning
we	had been	warning
you	had been	warning
they	had been	warning

Will-Future

I	will be	warning
you	will be	warning
he/she/it	will be	warning
we	will be	warning
you	will be	warning
they	will be	warning

Going to-Future

I	am	going to be	warning
you	are	going to be	warning
he/she/it	is	going to be	warning
we	are	going to be	warning
you	are	going to be	warning
they	are	going to be	warning

Future Perfect

I	will have been	warning
you	will have been	warning
he/she/it	will have been	warning
we	will have been	warning
you	will have been	warning
they	will have been	warning

Conditional

I	would	warn
you	would	warn
he/she/it	would	warn
we	would	warn
you	would	warn
they	would	warn

Conditional Past

I	would have	warned
you	would have	warned
he/she/it	would have	warned
we	would have	warned
you	would have	warned
they	would have	warned

wash

waschen

\+ **-es** in 3. Person Singular
Regelmäßiges Verb

Simple tenses

Present

I	wash
you	wash
he/she/it	washes
we	wash
you	wash
they	wash

Past

I	washed
you	washed
he/she/it	washed
we	washed
you	washed
they	washed

Present Perfect

I	have	washed
you	have	washed
he/she/it	has	washed
we	have	washed
you	have	washed
they	have	washed

Past Perfect

I	had	washed
you	had	washed
he/she/it	had	washed
we	had	washed
you	had	washed
they	had	washed

Will-Future

I	will	wash
you	will	wash
he/she/it	will	wash
we	will	wash
you	will	wash
they	will	wash

Going to-Future

I	am	going to	wash
you	are	going to	wash
he/she/it	is	going to	wash
we	are	going to	wash
you	are	going to	wash
they	are	going to	wash

Future Perfect

I	will have	washed
you	will have	washed
he/she/it	will have	washed
we	will have	washed
you	will have	washed
they	will have	washed

Imperative

wash

Impersonal

ing-Form

washing

Past Participle

washed

Continuous tenses

Present

I	am	washing
you	are	washing
he/she/it	is	washing
we	are	washing
you	are	washing
they	are	washing

Past

I	was	washing
you	were	washing
he/she/it	was	washing
we	were	washing
you	were	washing
they	were	washing

Present Perfect

I	have been	washing
you	have been	washing
he/she/it	has been	washing
we	have been	washing
you	have been	washing
they	have been	washing

Past Perfect

I	had been	washing
you	had been	washing
he/she/it	had been	washing
we	had been	washing
you	had been	washing
they	had been	washing

Will-Future

I	will be	washing
you	will be	washing
he/she/it	will be	washing
we	will be	washing
you	will be	washing
they	will be	washing

Going to-Future

I	am	going to be	washing
you	are	going to be	washing
he/she/it	is	going to be	washing
we	are	going to be	washing
you	are	going to be	washing
they	are	going to be	washing

Future Perfect

I	will have been	washing
you	will have been	washing
he/she/it	will have been	washing
we	will have been	washing
you	will have been	washing
they	will have been	washing

Conditional

I	would	wash
you	would	wash
he/she/it	would	wash
we	would	wash
you	would	wash
they	would	wash

Conditional Past

I	would have	washed
you	would have	washed
he/she/it	would have	washed
we	would have	washed
you	would have	washed
they	would have	washed

+ -ing → ~~e~~ / + -d nicht -ed
Regelmäßiges Verb

verschwenden

waste

Simple tenses

Present

I	waste
you	waste
he/she/it	wastes
we	waste
you	waste
they	waste

Past

I	wasted
you	wasted
he/she/it	wasted
we	wasted
you	wasted
they	wasted

Present Perfect

I	have	wasted
you	have	wasted
he/she/it	has	wasted
we	have	wasted
you	have	wasted
they	have	wasted

Past Perfect

I	had	wasted
you	had	wasted
he/she/it	had	wasted
we	had	wasted
you	had	wasted
they	had	wasted

Will-Future

I	will	waste
you	will	waste
he/she/it	will	waste
we	will	waste
you	will	waste
they	will	waste

Going to-Future

I	am	going to	waste
you	are	going to	waste
he/she/it	is	going to	waste
we	are	going to	waste
you	are	going to	waste
they	are	going to	waste

Future Perfect

I	will have	wasted
you	will have	wasted
he/she/it	will have	wasted
we	will have	wasted
you	will have	wasted
they	will have	wasted

Imperative

waste

Impersonal

ing-Form

wasting

Past Participle

wasted

Continuous tenses

Present

I	am	wasting
you	are	wasting
he/she/it	is	wasting
we	are	wasting
you	are	wasting
they	are	wasting

Past

I	was	wasting
you	were	wasting
he/she/it	was	wasting
we	were	wasting
you	were	wasting
they	were	wasting

Present Perfect

I	have been	wasting
you	have been	wasting
he/she/it	has been	wasting
we	have been	wasting
you	have been	wasting
they	have been	wasting

Past Perfect

I	had been	wasting
you	had been	wasting
he/she/it	had been	wasting
we	had been	wasting
you	had been	wasting
they	had been	wasting

Will-Future

I	will be	wasting
you	will be	wasting
he/she/it	will be	wasting
we	will be	wasting
you	will be	wasting
they	will be	wasting

Going to-Future

I	am	going to be	wasting
you	are	going to be	wasting
he/she/it	is	going to be	wasting
we	are	going to be	wasting
you	are	going to be	wasting
they	are	going to be	wasting

Future Perfect

I	will have been	wasting
you	will have been	wasting
he/she/it	will have been	wasting
we	will have been	wasting
you	will have been	wasting
they	will have been	wasting

Conditional

I	would	waste
you	would	waste
he/she/it	would	waste
we	would	waste
you	would	waste
they	would	waste

Conditional Past

I	would have	wasted
you	would have	wasted
he/she/it	would have	wasted
we	would have	wasted
you	would have	wasted
they	would have	wasted

watch

beobachten

\+ **-es** in 3. Person Singular
Regelmäßiges Verb

Simple tenses

Present

I	watch
you	watch
he/she/it	watches
we	watch
you	watch
they	watch

Past

I	watched
you	watched
he/she/it	watched
we	watched
you	watched
they	watched

Present Perfect

I	have	watched
you	have	watched
he/she/it	has	watched
we	have	watched
you	have	watched
they	have	watched

Past Perfect

I	had	watched
you	had	watched
he/she/it	had	watched
we	had	watched
you	had	watched
they	had	watched

Will-Future

I	will	watch
you	will	watch
he/she/it	will	watch
we	will	watch
you	will	watch
they	will	watch

Going to-Future

I	am	going to	watch
you	are	going to	watch
he/she/it	is	going to	watch
we	are	going to	watch
you	are	going to	watch
they	are	going to	watch

Future Perfect

I	will have	watched
you	will have	watched
he/she/it	will have	watched
we	will have	watched
you	will have	watched
they	will have	watched

Imperative

watch

Impersonal

ing-Form

watching

Past Participle

watched

Continuous tenses

Present

I	am	watching
you	are	watching
he/she/it	is	watching
we	are	watching
you	are	watching
they	are	watching

Past

I	was	watching
you	were	watching
he/she/it	was	watching
we	were	watching
you	were	watching
they	were	watching

Present Perfect

I	have been	watching
you	have been	watching
he/she/it	has been	watching
we	have been	watching
you	have been	watching
they	have been	watching

Past Perfect

I	had been	watching
you	had been	watching
he/she/it	had been	watching
we	had been	watching
you	had been	watching
they	had been	watching

Will-Future

I	will be	watching
you	will be	watching
he/she/it	will be	watching
we	will be	watching
you	will be	watching
they	will be	watching

Going to-Future

I	am	going to be	watching
you	are	going to be	watching
he/she/it	is	going to be	watching
we	are	going to be	watching
you	are	going to be	watching
they	are	going to be	watching

Future Perfect

I	will have been	watching
you	will have been	watching
he/she/it	will have been	watching
we	will have been	watching
you	will have been	watching
they	will have been	watching

Conditional

I	would	watch
you	would	watch
he/she/it	would	watch
we	would	watch
you	would	watch
they	would	watch

Conditional Past

I	would have	watched
you	would have	watched
he/she/it	would have	watched
we	would have	watched
you	would have	watched
they	would have	watched

+ **-ing** → ~~e~~ / + **-d** nicht **-ed**
Regelmäßiges Verb

winken

wave

Simple tenses

Present

I wave
you wave
he/she/it waves
we wave
you wave
they wave

Past

I waved
you waved
he/she/it waved
we waved
you waved
they waved

Present Perfect

I have waved
you have waved
he/she/it has waved
we have waved
you have waved
they have waved

Past Perfect

I had waved
you had waved
he/she/it had waved
we had waved
you had waved
they had waved

Will-Future

I will wave
you will wave
he/she/it will wave
we will wave
you will wave
they will wave

Going to-Future

I am going to wave
you are going to wave
he/she/it is going to wave
we are going to wave
you are going to wave
they are going to wave

Future Perfect

I will have waved
you will have waved
he/she/it will have waved
we will have waved
you will have waved
they will have waved

Imperative

wave

Impersonal

ing-Form

waving

Past Participle

waved

Continuous tenses

Present

I am waving
you are waving
he/she/it is waving
we are waving
you are waving
they are waving

Past

I was waving
you were waving
he/she/it was waving
we were waving
you were waving
they were waving

Present Perfect

I have been waving
you have been waving
he/she/it has been waving
we have been waving
you have been waving
they have been waving

Past Perfect

I had been waving
you had been waving
he/she/it had been waving
we had been waving
you had been waving
they had been waving

Will-Future

I will be waving
you will be waving
he/she/it will be waving
we will be waving
you will be waving
they will be waving

Going to-Future

I am going to be waving
you are going to be waving
he/she/it is going to be waving
we are going to be waving
you are going to be waving
they are going to be waving

Future Perfect

I will have been waving
you will have been waving
he/she/it will have been waving
we will have been waving
you will have been waving
they will have been waving

Conditional

I would wave
you would wave
he/she/it would wave
we would wave
you would wave
they would wave

Conditional Past

I would have waved
you would have waved
he/she/it would have waved
we would have waved
you would have waved
they would have waved

wear

- wore - worn

tragen

Unregelmäßiges Verb

Simple tenses

Present

I	wear
you	wear
he/she/it	wears
we	wear
you	wear
they	wear

Past

I	wore
you	wore
he/she/it	wore
we	wore
you	wore
they	wore

Present Perfect

I	have	worn
you	have	worn
he/she/it	has	worn
we	have	worn
you	have	worn
they	have	worn

Past Perfect

I	had	worn
you	had	worn
he/she/it	had	worn
we	had	worn
you	had	worn
they	had	worn

Will-Future

I	will	wear
you	will	wear
he/she/it	will	wear
we	will	wear
you	will	wear
they	will	wear

Going to-Future

I	am	going to	wear
you	are	going to	wear
he/she/it	is	going to	wear
we	are	going to	wear
you	are	going to	wear
they	are	going to	wear

Future Perfect

I	will have	worn
you	will have	worn
he/she/it	will have	worn
we	will have	worn
you	will have	worn
they	will have	worn

Imperative

wear

Impersonal

ing-Form

wearing

Past Participle

worn

Continuous tenses

Present

I	am	wearing
you	are	wearing
he/she/it	is	wearing
we	are	wearing
you	are	wearing
they	are	wearing

Past

I	was	wearing
you	were	wearing
he/she/it	was	wearing
we	were	wearing
you	were	wearing
they	were	wearing

Present Perfect

I	have been	wearing
you	have been	wearing
he/she/it	has been	wearing
we	have been	wearing
you	have been	wearing
they	have been	wearing

Past Perfect

I	had been	wearing
you	had been	wearing
he/she/it	had been	wearing
we	had been	wearing
you	had been	wearing
they	had been	wearing

Will-Future

I	will be	wearing
you	will be	wearing
he/she/it	will be	wearing
we	will be	wearing
you	will be	wearing
they	will be	wearing

Going to-Future

I	am	going to be	wearing
you	are	going to be	wearing
he/she/it	is	going to be	wearing
we	are	going to be	wearing
you	are	going to be	wearing
they	are	going to be	wearing

Future Perfect

I	will have been	wearing
you	will have been	wearing
he/she/it	will have been	wearing
we	will have been	wearing
you	will have been	wearing
they	will have been	wearing

Conditional

I	would	wear
you	would	wear
he/she/it	would	wear
we	would	wear
you	would	wear
they	would	wear

Conditional Past

I	would have	worn
you	would have	worn
he/she/it	would have	worn
we	would have	worn
you	would have	worn
they	would have	worn

Simple tenses

Present

I	weep
you	weep
he/she/it	weeps
we	weep
you	weep
they	weep

Past

I	wept
you	wept
he/she/it	wept
we	wept
you	wept
they	wept

Present Perfect

I	have	wept
you	have	wept
he/she/it	has	wept
we	have	wept
you	have	wept
they	have	wept

Past Perfect

I	had	wept
you	had	wept
he/she/it	had	wept
we	had	wept
you	had	wept
they	had	wept

Will-Future

I	will	weep
you	will	weep
he/she/it	will	weep
we	will	weep
you	will	weep
they	will	weep

Going to-Future

I	am	going to	weep
you	are	going to	weep
he/she/it	is	going to	weep
we	are	going to	weep
you	are	going to	weep
they	are	going to	weep

Future Perfect

I	will have	wept
you	will have	wept
he/she/it	will have	wept
we	will have	wept
you	will have	wept
they	will have	wept

Imperative

weep

Impersonal

ing-Form

weeping

Past Participle

wept

Continuous tenses

Present

I	am	weeping
you	are	weeping
he/she/it	is	weeping
we	are	weeping
you	are	weeping
they	are	weeping

Past

I	was	weeping
you	were	weeping
he/she/it	was	weeping
we	were	weeping
you	were	weeping
they	were	weeping

Present Perfect

I	have been	weeping
you	have been	weeping
he/she/it	has been	weeping
we	have been	weeping
you	have been	weeping
they	have been	weeping

Past Perfect

I	had been	weeping
you	had been	weeping
he/she/it	had been	weeping
we	had been	weeping
you	had been	weeping
they	had been	weeping

Will-Future

I	will be	weeping
you	will be	weeping
he/she/it	will be	weeping
we	will be	weeping
you	will be	weeping
they	will be	weeping

Going to-Future

I	am	going to be	weeping
you	are	going to be	weeping
he/she/it	is	going to be	weeping
we	are	going to be	weeping
you	are	going to be	weeping
they	are	going to be	weeping

Future Perfect

I	will have been	weeping
you	will have been	weeping
he/she/it	will have been	weeping
we	will have been	weeping
you	will have been	weeping
they	will have been	weeping

Conditional

I	would	weep
you	would	weep
he/she/it	would	weep
we	would	weep
you	would	weep
they	would	weep

Conditional Past

I	would have	wept
you	would have	wept
he/she/it	would have	wept
we	would have	wept
you	would have	wept
they	would have	wept

whisper

flüstern

Regelmäßiges Verb

Simple tenses

Present

I	whisper
you	whisper
he/she/it	whispers
we	whisper
you	whisper
they	whisper

Past

I	whispered
you	whispered
he/she/it	whispered
we	whispered
you	whispered
they	whispered

Present Perfect

I	have	whispered
you	have	whispered
he/she/it	has	whispered
we	have	whispered
you	have	whispered
they	have	whispered

Past Perfect

I	had	whispered
you	had	whispered
he/she/it	had	whispered
we	had	whispered
you	had	whispered
they	had	whispered

Will-Future

I	will	whisper
you	will	whisper
he/she/it	will	whisper
we	will	whisper
you	will	whisper
they	will	whisper

Going to-Future

I	am	going to	whisper
you	are	going to	whisper
he/she/it	is	going to	whisper
we	are	going to	whisper
you	are	going to	whisper
they	are	going to	whisper

Future Perfect

I	will have	whispered
you	will have	whispered
he/she/it	will have	whispered
we	will have	whispered
you	will have	whispered
they	will have	whispered

Imperative

whisper

Impersonal

ing-Form

whispering

Past Participle

whispered

Continuous tenses

Present

I	am	whispering
you	are	whispering
he/she/it	is	whispering
we	are	whispering
you	are	whispering
they	are	whispering

Past

I	was	whispering
you	were	whispering
he/she/it	was	whispering
we	were	whispering
you	were	whispering
they	were	whispering

Present Perfect

I	have been	whispering
you	have been	whispering
he/she/it	has been	whispering
we	have been	whispering
you	have been	whispering
they	have been	whispering

Past Perfect

I	had been	whispering
you	had been	whispering
he/she/it	had been	whispering
we	had been	whispering
you	had been	whispering
they	had been	whispering

Will-Future

I	will be	whispering
you	will be	whispering
he/she/it	will be	whispering
we	will be	whispering
you	will be	whispering
they	will be	whispering

Going to-Future

I	am	going to be	whispering
you	are	going to be	whispering
he/she/it	is	going to be	whispering
we	are	going to be	whispering
you	are	going to be	whispering
they	are	going to be	whispering

Future Perfect

I	will have been	whispering
you	will have been	whispering
he/she/it	will have been	whispering
we	will have been	whispering
you	will have been	whispering
they	will have been	whispering

Conditional

I	would	whisper
you	would	whisper
he/she/it	would	whisper
we	would	whisper
you	would	whisper
they	would	whisper

Conditional Past

I	would have	whispered
you	would have	whispered
he/she/it	would have	whispered
we	would have	whispered
you	would have	whispered
they	would have	whispered

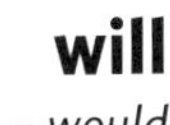

will

- would

wollen

Unregelmäßiges Verb, Modalverb

Simple tenses

Present

I	will | 'll
you	will | 'll
he/she/it	will | 'll
we	will | 'll
you	will | 'll
they	will | 'll

Past

I	would
you	would
he/she/it	would
we	would
you	would
they	would

Present Perfect

-
-
-
-
-
-

Past Perfect

-
-
-
-
-
-

Will-Future

I	will	will
you	will	will
he/she/it	will	will
we	will	will
you	will	will
they	will	will

Going to-Future

I	am	going to	will
you	are	going to	will
he/she/it	is	going to	will
we	are	going to	will
you	are	going to	will
they	are	going to	will

Future Perfect

-
-
-
-
-
-

Imperative

will

Impersonal

ing-Form

-

Past Participle

-

Continuous tenses

Present

-
-
-
-
-
-

Past

-
-
-
-
-
-

Present Perfect

-
-
-
-
-
-

Past Perfect

-
-
-
-
-
-

Will-Future

-
-
-
-
-
-

Going to-Future

-
-
-
-
-
-

Future Perfect

-
-
-
-
-
-

Conditional

I	would	will
you	would	will
he/she/it	would	will
we	would	will
you	would	will
they	would	will

Conditional Past

-
-
-
-
-
-

wind
- wound - wound

wickeln

Unregelmäßiges Verb

Simple tenses

Present

I	wind
you	wind
he/she/it	winds
we	wind
you	wind
they	wind

Past

I	wound
you	wound
he/she/it	wound
we	wound
you	wound
they	wound

Present Perfect

I	have	wound
you	have	wound
he/she/it	has	wound
we	have	wound
you	have	wound
they	have	wound

Past Perfect

I	had	wound
you	had	wound
he/she/it	had	wound
we	had	wound
you	had	wound
they	had	wound

Will-Future

I	will	wind
you	will	wind
he/she/it	will	wind
we	will	wind
you	will	wind
they	will	wind

Going to-Future

I	am	going to	wind
you	are	going to	wind
he/she/it	is	going to	wind
we	are	going to	wind
you	are	going to	wind
they	are	going to	wind

Future Perfect

I	will have	wound
you	will have	wound
he/she/it	will have	wound
we	will have	wound
you	will have	wound
they	will have	wound

Imperative

wind

Impersonal

ing-Form

winding

Past Participle

wound

Continuous tenses

Present

I	am	winding
you	are	winding
he/she/it	is	winding
we	are	winding
you	are	winding
they	are	winding

Past

I	was	winding
you	were	winding
he/she/it	was	winding
we	were	winding
you	were	winding
they	were	winding

Present Perfect

I	have	been	winding
you	have	been	winding
he/she/it	has	been	winding
we	have	been	winding
you	have	been	winding
they	have	been	winding

Past Perfect

I	had been	winding
you	had been	winding
he/she/it	had been	winding
we	had been	winding
you	had been	winding
they	had been	winding

Will-Future

I	will be	winding
you	will be	winding
he/she/it	will be	winding
we	will be	winding
you	will be	winding
they	will be	winding

Going to-Future

I	am	going to be	winding
you	are	going to be	winding
he/she/it	is	going to be	winding
we	are	going to be	winding
you	are	going to be	winding
they	are	going to be	winding

Future Perfect

I	will have been	winding
you	will have been	winding
he/she/it	will have been	winding
we	will have been	winding
you	will have been	winding
they	will have been	winding

Conditional

I	would	wind
you	would	wind
he/she/it	would	wind
we	would	wind
you	would	wind
they	would	wind

Conditional Past

I	would have	wound
you	would have	wound
he/she/it	would have	wound
we	would have	wound
you	would have	wound
they	would have	wound

Simple tenses

Present

I	wish
you	wish
he/she/it	wishes
we	wish
you	wish
they	wish

Past

I	wished
you	wished
he/she/it	wished
we	wished
you	wished
they	wished

Present Perfect

I	have	wished
you	have	wished
he/she/it	has	wished
we	have	wished
you	have	wished
they	have	wished

Past Perfect

I	had	wished
you	had	wished
he/she/it	had	wished
we	had	wished
you	had	wished
they	had	wished

Will-Future

I	will	wish
you	will	wish
he/she/it	will	wish
we	will	wish
you	will	wish
they	will	wish

Going to-Future

I	am	going to	wish
you	are	going to	wish
he/she/it	is	going to	wish
we	are	going to	wish
you	are	going to	wish
they	are	going to	wish

Future Perfect

I	will have	wished
you	will have	wished
he/she/it	will have	wished
we	will have	wished
you	will have	wished
they	will have	wished

Imperative

wish

Impersonal

ing-Form

wishing

Past Participle

wished

Continuous tenses

Present

I	am	wishing
you	are	wishing
he/she/it	is	wishing
we	are	wishing
you	are	wishing
they	are	wishing

Past

I	was	wishing
you	were	wishing
he/she/it	was	wishing
we	were	wishing
you	were	wishing
they	were	wishing

Present Perfect

I	have	been	wishing
you	have	been	wishing
he/she/it	has	been	wishing
we	have	been	wishing
you	have	been	wishing
they	have	been	wishing

Past Perfect

I	had been	wishing
you	had been	wishing
he/she/it	had been	wishing
we	had been	wishing
you	had been	wishing
they	had been	wishing

Will-Future

I	will be	wishing
you	will be	wishing
he/she/it	will be	wishing
we	will be	wishing
you	will be	wishing
they	will be	wishing

Going to-Future

I	am	going to be	wishing
you	are	going to be	wishing
he/she/it	is	going to be	wishing
we	are	going to be	wishing
you	are	going to be	wishing
they	are	going to be	wishing

Future Perfect

I	will have been	wishing
you	will have been	wishing
he/she/it	will have been	wishing
we	will have been	wishing
you	will have been	wishing
they	will have been	wishing

Conditional

I	would	wish
you	would	wish
he/she/it	would	wish
we	would	wish
you	would	wish
they	would	wish

Conditional Past

I	would have	wished
you	would have	wished
he/she/it	would have	wished
we	would have	wished
you	would have	wished
they	would have	wished

withdraw
- withdrew - withdrawn

zurückziehen

Unregelmäßiges Verb

Simple tenses

Present

I	withdraw
you	withdraw
he/she/it	withdraws
we	withdraw
you	withdraw
they	withdraw

Past

I	withdrew
you	withdrew
he/she/it	withdrew
we	withdrew
you	withdrew
they	withdrew

Present Perfect

I	have	withdrawn
you	have	withdrawn
he/she/it	has	withdrawn
we	have	withdrawn
you	have	withdrawn
they	have	withdrawn

Past Perfect

I	had	withdrawn
you	had	withdrawn
he/she/it	had	withdrawn
we	had	withdrawn
you	had	withdrawn
they	had	withdrawn

Will-Future

I	will	withdraw
you	will	withdraw
he/she/it	will	withdraw
we	will	withdraw
you	will	withdraw
they	will	withdraw

Going to-Future

I	am	going to	withdraw
you	are	going to	withdraw
he/she/it	is	going to	withdraw
we	are	going to	withdraw
you	are	going to	withdraw
they	are	going to	withdraw

Future Perfect

I	will have	withdrawn
you	will have	withdrawn
he/she/it	will have	withdrawn
we	will have	withdrawn
you	will have	withdrawn
they	will have	withdrawn

Imperative

withdraw

Impersonal

ing-Form

withdrawing

Past Participle

withdrawn

Continuous tenses

Present

I	am	withdrawing
you	are	withdrawing
he/she/it	is	withdrawing
we	are	withdrawing
you	are	withdrawing
they	are	withdrawing

Past

I	was	withdrawing
you	were	withdrawing
he/she/it	was	withdrawing
we	were	withdrawing
you	were	withdrawing
they	were	withdrawing

Present Perfect

I	have been	withdrawing
you	have been	withdrawing
he/she/it	has been	withdrawing
we	have been	withdrawing
you	have been	withdrawing
they	have been	withdrawing

Past Perfect

I	had been	withdrawing
you	had been	withdrawing
he/she/it	had been	withdrawing
we	had been	withdrawing
you	had been	withdrawing
they	had been	withdrawing

Will-Future

I	will be	withdrawing
you	will be	withdrawing
he/she/it	will be	withdrawing
we	will be	withdrawing
you	will be	withdrawing
they	will be	withdrawing

Going to-Future

I	am	going to be	withdrawing
you	are	going to be	withdrawing
he/she/it	is	going to be	withdrawing
we	are	going to be	withdrawing
you	are	going to be	withdrawing
they	are	going to be	withdrawing

Future Perfect

I	will have been withdrawing
you	will have been withdrawing
he/she/it	will have been withdrawing
we	will have been withdrawing
you	will have been withdrawing
they	will have been withdrawing

Conditional

I	would	withdraw
you	would	withdraw
he/she/it	would	withdraw
we	would	withdraw
you	would	withdraw
they	would	withdraw

Conditional Past

I	would have	withdrawn
you	would have	withdrawn
he/she/it	would have	withdrawn
we	would have	withdrawn
you	would have	withdrawn
they	would have	withdrawn

Simple tenses

Present

I	wonder
you	wonder
he/she/it	wonders
we	wonder
you	wonder
they	wonder

Past

I	wondered
you	wondered
he/she/it	wondered
we	wondered
you	wondered
they	wondered

Present Perfect

I	have	wondered
you	have	wondered
he/she/it	has	wondered
we	have	wondered
you	have	wondered
they	have	wondered

Past Perfect

I	had	wondered
you	had	wondered
he/she/it	had	wondered
we	had	wondered
you	had	wondered
they	had	wondered

Will-Future

I	will	wonder
you	will	wonder
he/she/it	will	wonder
we	will	wonder
you	will	wonder
they	will	wonder

Going to-Future

I	am	going to	wonder
you	are	going to	wonder
he/she/it	is	going to	wonder
we	are	going to	wonder
you	are	going to	wonder
they	are	going to	wonder

Future Perfect

I	will have	wondered
you	will have	wondered
he/she/it	will have	wondered
we	will have	wondered
you	will have	wondered
they	will have	wondered

Imperative

wonder

Impersonal

ing-Form

wondering

Past Participle

wondered

Continuous tenses

Present

I	am	wondering
you	are	wondering
he/she/it	is	wondering
we	are	wondering
you	are	wondering
they	are	wondering

Past

I	was	wondering
you	were	wondering
he/she/it	was	wondering
we	were	wondering
you	were	wondering
they	were	wondering

Present Perfect

I	have	been	wondering
you	have	been	wondering
he/she/it	has	been	wondering
we	have	been	wondering
you	have	been	wondering
they	have	been	wondering

Past Perfect

I	had been	wondering
you	had been	wondering
he/she/it	had been	wondering
we	had been	wondering
you	had been	wondering
they	had been	wondering

Will-Future

I	will be	wondering
you	will be	wondering
he/she/it	will be	wondering
we	will be	wondering
you	will be	wondering
they	will be	wondering

Going to-Future

I	am	going to be	wondering
you	are	going to be	wondering
he/she/it	is	going to be	wondering
we	are	going to be	wondering
you	are	going to be	wondering
they	are	going to be	wondering

Future Perfect

I	will have been	wondering
you	will have been	wondering
he/she/it	will have been	wondering
we	will have been	wondering
you	will have been	wondering
they	will have been	wondering

Conditional

I	would	wonder
you	would	wonder
he/she/it	would	wonder
we	would	wonder
you	would	wonder
they	would	wonder

Conditional Past

I	would have	wondered
you	would have	wondered
he/she/it	would have	wondered
we	would have	wondered
you	would have	wondered
they	would have	wondered

arbeiten

Regelmäßiges Verb

Simple tenses

Present

I	work
you	work
he/she/it	works
we	work
you	work
they	work

Past

I	worked
you	worked
he/she/it	worked
we	worked
you	worked
they	worked

Present Perfect

I	have	worked
you	have	worked
he/she/it	has	worked
we	have	worked
you	have	worked
they	have	worked

Past Perfect

I	had	worked
you	had	worked
he/she/it	had	worked
we	had	worked
you	had	worked
they	had	worked

Will-Future

I	will	work
you	will	work
he/she/it	will	work
we	will	work
you	will	work
they	will	work

Going to-Future

I	am	going to	work
you	are	going to	work
he/she/it	is	going to	work
we	are	going to	work
you	are	going to	work
they	are	going to	work

Future Perfect

I	will have	worked
you	will have	worked
he/she/it	will have	worked
we	will have	worked
you	will have	worked
they	will have	worked

Imperative

work

Impersonal

ing-Form

working

Past Participle

worked

Continuous tenses

Present

I	am	working
you	are	working
he/she/it	is	working
we	are	working
you	are	working
they	are	working

Past

I	was	working
you	were	working
he/she/it	was	working
we	were	working
you	were	working
they	were	working

Present Perfect

I	have been	working
you	have been	working
he/she/it	has been	working
we	have been	working
you	have been	working
they	have been	working

Past Perfect

I	had been	working
you	had been	working
he/she/it	had been	working
we	had been	working
you	had been	working
they	had been	working

Will-Future

I	will be	working
you	will be	working
he/she/it	will be	working
we	will be	working
you	will be	working
they	will be	working

Going to-Future

I	am	going to be	working
you	are	going to be	working
he/she/it	is	going to be	working
we	are	going to be	working
you	are	going to be	working
they	are	going to be	working

Future Perfect

I	will have been	working
you	will have been	working
he/she/it	will have been	working
we	will have been	working
you	will have been	working
they	will have been	working

Conditional

I	would	work
you	would	work
he/she/it	would	work
we	would	work
you	would	work
they	would	work

Conditional Past

I	would have	worked
you	would have	worked
he/she/it	would have	worked
we	would have	worked
you	would have	worked
they	would have	worked

Simple tenses

Present

I	worry
you	worry
he/she/it	worries
we	worry
you	worry
they	worry

Past

I	worried
you	worried
he/she/it	worried
we	worried
you	worried
they	worried

Present Perfect

I	have	worried
you	have	worried
he/she/it	has	worried
we	have	worried
you	have	worried
they	have	worried

Past Perfect

I	had	worried
you	had	worried
he/she/it	had	worried
we	had	worried
you	had	worried
they	had	worried

Will-Future

I	will	worry
you	will	worry
he/she/it	will	worry
we	will	worry
you	will	worry
they	will	worry

Going to-Future

I	am	going to	worry
you	are	going to	worry
he/she/it	is	going to	worry
we	are	going to	worry
you	are	going to	worry
they	are	going to	worry

Future Perfect

I	will have	worried
you	will have	worried
he/she/it	will have	worried
we	will have	worried
you	will have	worried
they	will have	worried

Imperative

worry

Impersonal

ing-Form

worrying

Past Participle

worried

Continuous tenses

Present

I	am	worrying
you	are	worrying
he/she/it	is	worrying
we	are	worrying
you	are	worrying
they	are	worrying

Past

I	was	worrying
you	were	worrying
he/she/it	was	worrying
we	were	worrying
you	were	worrying
they	were	worrying

Present Perfect

I	have	been	worrying
you	have	been	worrying
he/she/it	has	been	worrying
we	have	been	worrying
you	have	been	worrying
they	have	been	worrying

Past Perfect

I	had been	worrying
you	had been	worrying
he/she/it	had been	worrying
we	had been	worrying
you	had been	worrying
they	had been	worrying

Will-Future

I	will be	worrying
you	will be	worrying
he/she/it	will be	worrying
we	will be	worrying
you	will be	worrying
they	will be	worrying

Going to-Future

I	am	going to be	worrying
you	are	going to be	worrying
he/she/it	is	going to be	worrying
we	are	going to be	worrying
you	are	going to be	worrying
they	are	going to be	worrying

Future Perfect

I	will have been	worrying
you	will have been	worrying
he/she/it	will have been	worrying
we	will have been	worrying
you	will have been	worrying
they	will have been	worrying

Conditional

I	would	worry
you	would	worry
he/she/it	would	worry
we	would	worry
you	would	worry
they	would	worry

Conditional Past

I	would have	worried
you	would have	worried
he/she/it	would have	worried
we	would have	worried
you	would have	worried
they	would have	worried

wrap

einpacken

Konsonantenverdopplung
Regelmäßiges Verb

Simple tenses

Present

I	wrap
you	wrap
he/she/it	wraps
we	wrap
you	wrap
they	wrap

Past

I	wrapped
you	wrapped
he/she/it	wrapped
we	wrapped
you	wrapped
they	wrapped

Present Perfect

I	have	wrapped
you	have	wrapped
he/she/it	has	wrapped
we	have	wrapped
you	have	wrapped
they	have	wrapped

Past Perfect

I	had	wrapped
you	had	wrapped
he/she/it	had	wrapped
we	had	wrapped
you	had	wrapped
they	had	wrapped

Will-Future

I	will	wrap
you	will	wrap
he/she/it	will	wrap
we	will	wrap
you	will	wrap
they	will	wrap

Going to-Future

I	am	going to	wrap
you	are	going to	wrap
he/she/it	is	going to	wrap
we	are	going to	wrap
you	are	going to	wrap
they	are	going to	wrap

Future Perfect

I	will have	wrapped
you	will have	wrapped
he/she/it	will have	wrapped
we	will have	wrapped
you	will have	wrapped
they	will have	wrapped

Imperative

wrap

Impersonal

ing-Form

wrapping

Past Participle

wrapped

Continuous tenses

Present

I	am	wrapping
you	are	wrapping
he/she/it	is	wrapping
we	are	wrapping
you	are	wrapping
they	are	wrapping

Past

I	was	wrapping
you	were	wrapping
he/she/it	was	wrapping
we	were	wrapping
you	were	wrapping
they	were	wrapping

Present Perfect

I	have been	wrapping
you	have been	wrapping
he/she/it	has been	wrapping
we	have been	wrapping
you	have been	wrapping
they	have been	wrapping

Past Perfect

I	had been	wrapping
you	had been	wrapping
he/she/it	had been	wrapping
we	had been	wrapping
you	had been	wrapping
they	had been	wrapping

Will-Future

I	will be	wrapping
you	will be	wrapping
he/she/it	will be	wrapping
we	will be	wrapping
you	will be	wrapping
they	will be	wrapping

Going to-Future

I	am	going to be	wrapping
you	are	going to be	wrapping
he/she/it	is	going to be	wrapping
we	are	going to be	wrapping
you	are	going to be	wrapping
they	are	going to be	wrapping

Future Perfect

I	will have been	wrapping
you	will have been	wrapping
he/she/it	will have been	wrapping
we	will have been	wrapping
you	will have been	wrapping
they	will have been	wrapping

Conditional

I	would	wrap
you	would	wrap
he/she/it	would	wrap
we	would	wrap
you	would	wrap
they	would	wrap

Conditional Past

I	would have	wrapped
you	would have	wrapped
he/she/it	would have	wrapped
we	would have	wrapped
you	would have	wrapped
they	would have	wrapped

Simple tenses

Present

I	write
you	write
he/she/it	writes
we	write
you	write
they	write

Past

I	wrote
you	wrote
he/she/it	wrote
we	wrote
you	wrote
they	wrote

Present Perfect

I	have	written
you	have	written
he/she/it	has	written
we	have	written
you	have	written
they	have	written

Past Perfect

I	had	written
you	had	written
he/she/it	had	written
we	had	written
you	had	written
they	had	written

Will-Future

I	will	write
you	will	write
he/she/it	will	write
we	will	write
you	will	write
they	will	write

Going to-Future

I	am	going to	write
you	are	going to	write
he/she/it	is	going to	write
we	are	going to	write
you	are	going to	write
they	are	going to	write

Future Perfect

I	will have	written
you	will have	written
he/she/it	will have	written
we	will have	written
you	will have	written
they	will have	written

Imperative

write

Impersonal

ing-Form

writing

Past Participle

written

Continuous tenses

Present

I	am	writing
you	are	writing
he/she/it	is	writing
we	are	writing
you	are	writing
they	are	writing

Past

I	was	writing
you	were	writing
he/she/it	was	writing
we	were	writing
you	were	writing
they	were	writing

Present Perfect

I	have been	writing
you	have been	writing
he/she/it	has been	writing
we	have been	writing
you	have been	writing
they	have been	writing

Past Perfect

I	had been	writing
you	had been	writing
he/she/it	had been	writing
we	had been	writing
you	had been	writing
they	had been	writing

Will-Future

I	will be	writing
you	will be	writing
he/she/it	will be	writing
we	will be	writing
you	will be	writing
they	will be	writing

Going to-Future

I	am	going to be	writing
you	are	going to be	writing
he/she/it	is	going to be	writing
we	are	going to be	writing
you	are	going to be	writing
they	are	going to be	writing

Future Perfect

I	will have been	writing
you	will have been	writing
he/she/it	will have been	writing
we	will have been	writing
you	will have been	writing
they	will have been	writing

Conditional

I	would	write
you	would	write
he/she/it	would	write
we	would	write
you	would	write
they	would	write

Conditional Past

I	would have	written
you	would have	written
he/she/it	would have	written
we	would have	written
you	would have	written
they	would have	written

yield

hervorbringen

Regelmäßiges Verb

Simple tenses

Present

I	yield
you	yield
he/she/it	yields
we	yield
you	yield
they	yield

Past

I	yielded
you	yielded
he/she/it	yielded
we	yielded
you	yielded
they	yielded

Present Perfect

I	have	yielded
you	have	yielded
he/she/it	has	yielded
we	have	yielded
you	have	yielded
they	have	yielded

Past Perfect

I	had	yielded
you	had	yielded
he/she/it	had	yielded
we	had	yielded
you	had	yielded
they	had	yielded

Will-Future

I	will	yield
you	will	yield
he/she/it	will	yield
we	will	yield
you	will	yield
they	will	yield

Going to-Future

I	am	going to	yield
you	are	going to	yield
he/she/it	is	going to	yield
we	are	going to	yield
you	are	going to	yield
they	are	going to	yield

Future Perfect

I	will have	yielded
you	will have	yielded
he/she/it	will have	yielded
we	will have	yielded
you	will have	yielded
they	will have	yielded

Imperative

yield

Impersonal

ing-Form

yielding

Past Participle

yielded

Continuous tenses

Present

I	am	yielding
you	are	yielding
he/she/it	is	yielding
we	are	yielding
you	are	yielding
they	are	yielding

Past

I	was	yielding
you	were	yielding
he/she/it	was	yielding
we	were	yielding
you	were	yielding
they	were	yielding

Present Perfect

I	have been	yielding
you	have been	yielding
he/she/it	has been	yielding
we	have been	yielding
you	have been	yielding
they	have been	yielding

Past Perfect

I	had been	yielding
you	had been	yielding
he/she/it	had been	yielding
we	had been	yielding
you	had been	yielding
they	had been	yielding

Will-Future

I	will be	yielding
you	will be	yielding
he/she/it	will be	yielding
we	will be	yielding
you	will be	yielding
they	will be	yielding

Going to-Future

I	am	going to be	yielding
you	are	going to be	yielding
he/she/it	is	going to be	yielding
we	are	going to be	yielding
you	are	going to be	yielding
they	are	going to be	yielding

Future Perfect

I	will have been	yielding
you	will have been	yielding
he/she/it	will have been	yielding
we	will have been	yielding
you	will have been	yielding
they	will have been	yielding

Conditional

I	would	yield
you	would	yield
he/she/it	would	yield
we	would	yield
you	would	yield
they	would	yield

Conditional Past

I	would have	yielded
you	would have	yielded
he/she/it	would have	yielded
we	would have	yielded
you	would have	yielded
they	would have	yielded